# THE BOOK OF RUTH

# THE NEW INTERNATIONAL COMMENTARY ON THE OLD TESTAMENT

*General Editors*

E. J. YOUNG
(1965–1968)

R. K. HARRISON
(1968–1993)

ROBERT L. HUBBARD JR.
(1994–      )

BILL T. ARNOLD
(2020–      )

# The Book of RUTH

PETER H. W. LAU

WILLIAM B. EERDMANS PUBLISHING COMPANY
GRAND RAPIDS, MICHIGAN

Wm. B. Eerdmans Publishing Co.
4035 Park East Court SE, Grand Rapids, Michigan 49546
www.eerdmans.com

© 2023 Peter H. W. Lau
All rights reserved
Published 2023
Printed in the United States of America

29  28  27  26  25  24  23      1  2  3  4  5  6  7

ISBN 978-0-8028-7726-0

**Library of Congress Cataloging-in-Publication Data**

A catalog record for this book is available from the Library of Congress.

*For Kathryn*

# Contents

| | |
|---|---|
| *Series Editor's Preface* | ix |
| *Author's Preface* | xi |
| *List of Abbreviations* | xiii |
| *Bibliography* | xvii |

| | |
|---|---|
| **INTRODUCTION** | 1 |
| I. STRUCTURE AND MESSAGE | 2 |
| II. GENRE | 8 |
| III. AUTHORSHIP AND DATE | 12 |
|     A. Authorship | 12 |
|     B. Date of Composition | 12 |
|     C. Conclusions regarding the Dating of the Book of Ruth | 19 |
| IV. PURPOSE | 20 |
| V. CANONICITY | 29 |
| VI. THE HEBREW TEXT | 33 |
| VII. THEOLOGICAL MESSAGES | 35 |
|     A. Names of God | 35 |
|     B. God's Providence | 36 |
|     C. Human Action | 39 |
|     D. The Cycle of Divine-Human Kindness | 42 |
|     E. God's Blessing | 44 |
| VIII. THEMES | 45 |
|     A. Applying the Law | 45 |
|     B. Ruth's Ethnicity and Israelite Identity | 48 |

CONTENTS

| IX. RUTH AND THE NEW TESTAMENT | 52 |
| A. Matthean Genealogy | 52 |
| B. Mission | 53 |
| C. Redemption | 57 |

**TEXT AND COMMENTARY** 61

ACT 1: DEATH AND EMPTINESS (1:1–22) 61

A. The End of a Family Line in Moab (1:1–6) 62

B. En route: Naomi, Orpah, and Ruth Dialogue (1:7–19a) 79

C. Town Gate: Naomi Laments before the Townswomen (1:19b–22) 108

ACT 2: SEEKING SHORT-TERM SECURITY (2:1–23) 123

D. Home: Naomi Accepts Ruth's Plan (2:1–3) 123

E. Boaz's Field: Encounter between Ruth and Boaz (2:4–17) 133

F. Home: Naomi and Ruth Debrief (2:18–23) 168

ACT 3: SEEKING PERMANENT SECURITY (3:1–18) 184

F'. Home: Ruth Accepts Naomi's Plan (3:1–5) 184

E'. Threshing Floor: Encounter between Ruth and Boaz (3:6–15) 197

D'. Home: Naomi and Ruth Debrief (3:16–18) 219

ACT 4: REDEMPTION AND FULLNESS (4:1–22) 231

C'. Town Gate: Boaz Redeems before the Elders (4:1–12) 233

B'. Home: Naomi and the Women Dialogue (4:13–17) 277

A'. The Beginning of a Royal Line in Israel (4:18–22) 298

| *Index of Authors* | 309 |
| *Index of Subjects* | 315 |
| *Index of Scripture and Other Ancient Texts* | 320 |

viii

# Series Editor's Preface

"Do you *understand* what you're *reading*?"

What a question!

With this opening line, Philip, one of Christianity's first evangelists, approached a seeker from Africa, who had been in Jerusalem to worship. Somewhere along the Gaza Road, on his return trip to Ethiopia, the stranger was reading a portion of the Old Testament. Philip asked the question when he heard him "reading" the ancient text, an activity that almost certainly involved verbalizing the text by reciting it aloud (*anaginōskō*; Acts 8:30). An "angel of the Lord" had sent Philip to meet the Ethiopian for this very opportunity (8:26–29).

Realizing that the seeker was reading a difficult text, and yet also realizing how vitally important it was to the stranger's faith, Philip distinguished between reading and comprehending. "Understanding" is different from simply pronouncing the text aloud; comprehension involves grasping the significance of what is read (*ginōskō*).

Such a deep-level understanding of ancient Israel's Scriptures has always been the goal of The New International Commentary on the Old Testament. Since 1965, the editors of this series—Edward J. Young, Roland K. Harrison, and Robert L. Hubbard Jr.—have guided the series and its authors with the sole purpose of aiding the reader to gain understanding of the text. They have left us a treasured gift. Today a wide readership of scholars, priests, pastors, rabbis, and other serious students of the Bible turn to NICOT volumes for assistance in reading the ancient text.

The aim of the series has always been "to publish biblical scholarship of the highest quality" (to quote the preface of my predecessor, Professor Hubbard) and to do so respectfully from a position of faith seeking understanding. The series appeals to readers across the entire spectrum of theological or philosophical perspectives, and always with the conviction that the Old Testament is more than great literature from the past. Its authors engage the

## SERIES EDITOR'S PREFACE

range of traditional methodologies, always sensitive to newer innovations in recent scholarship, and always remembering that the books of the Old Testament constituted the first Bible for the earliest Christians.

Specifically, the NICOT authors believe the books they are writing about—ancient Israel's Scriptures—are God-breathed (*theopneustos*) or "inspired" and therefore "useful for teaching, for reproof, for correction, and for training in righteousness" (2 Timothy 3:16). This high regard of and respect for the authority of Scripture characterizes what has come to be known as "evangelicalism," together with conversionism, activism, and crucicentrism (according to noted historian David W. Bebbington). While the term "evangelical" today requires considerable qualification, the movement it denotes is of God and is still much needed in the Church universal. The authors of the NICOT come from diverse theological branches of the Church, and yet they hold firmly to this conviction that the Old Testament continues as God's means of grace for the Church today. In its pages, and by means of its message, God calls readers into an ever-deepening relational intimacy, inviting all who read (*anaginōskō*) to understand (*ginōskō*).

In response to Philip's question, the Ethiopian seeker admitted that he could not possibly read the ancient text with understanding "unless someone guides me" (Acts 8:31). He was aware of his need to have someone come alongside him to help him acquire the knowledge he desired. He invited Philip to join him in his chariot (and thus in his reading experience), and once he finally understood the Old Testament text, he immediately asked to be baptized (Acts 8:31–38).

This exchange illustrates the difficulty of reading for true understanding, the need for a faithful guide in one's reading, and the power of the ancient text to lead one into saving faith. The goal of each NICOT volume is to be such a guide. Readers around the world have invited the volumes of this series into their reading experience. The ancient text may seem obscure and distant. But God is still at work in its power, and reading it for understanding still makes a life-changing difference for the reader, as it did for Philip's new Ethiopian friend.

BILL T. ARNOLD

# Author's Preface

Bob Hubbard's original Ruth commentary in this series is one of my favorites, so it was with much hesitation and trepidation that I accepted his invitation to write this commentary. I am grateful for his confidence in my ability and the wonderful journey he launched me on.

My commentary journey has crystallized in my mind that reading the Bible does not happen acontextually. In reading and interpreting biblical texts, scholars have long been aware of the contexts of the author and original audience, but not so much the contemporary reader. So, in the interests of (self-)disclosure, here are the social contexts that have influenced and continue to influence my reading of the book of Ruth.

Ethnically Chinese, I was born in Hong Kong but grew up in Sydney, Australia. As a member of a minority ethnic group, I had a sense of belonging but not fully belonging. I grew up in a nondenominational church with Reformed overtones. I completed my undergraduate theological education at Sydney Missionary and Bible College. I completed my doctorate on social identity and ethics in the book of Ruth at Sydney University under two Jewish supervisors. My wife and I served in a Southeast Asian country for eight years, where I taught at a seminary. I was exposed to a variety of postures toward the authority of the Bible and the place of the reader in interpretation. The ethnic tensions in the country sensitized me to political interpretations of the Bible. Reading the Bible with my students, teaching and preaching in churches, and attending local Southeast Asian conferences sensitized me to Asian and postcolonial readings of the Bible as well as to honor-shame and fear-power cultural values. And reading Scripture with those in Southeast Asia, I realized that they tend not to make a distinction between theory and praxis; interaction with Scripture must have practical application. Now, as a member of the "sandwich generation" (attending to the needs of both my children and my parents), my family experiences help me be more empathetic in my reading of biblical texts. Working as a medical doctor once a

## Author's Preface

week teaches me to listen better and be more attuned to crises and problems people face in this world. Serving with a cross-cultural agency keeps me aware of the missional elements of the Bible. All these contexts affect my reading and interpretation of the Bible. Perhaps you will detect some of these influences in this commentary.

I am grateful to all those who have helped me along the way. The students and seminar participants and sermon listeners whose comments and questions enriched my thinking on Ruth. Those who read sections of the manuscript and gave feedback: Paul Barker and Jackson Wu. Bill Walton and Kathy Noftsinger, who reviewed and copyedited the manuscript, respectively. Their suggestions and corrections have enhanced the final product. I also thank Ruth Wong, my "in-house" proofreader, and Edwin Poh for preparing the indexes.

My wife, Kathryn, has been my partner on the journey even before I was interested in the book of Ruth. I thank her for her patience and many acts of kindness. This book is dedicated to her.

Finally, I am most thankful to God, who has placed me in the locations and times and communities and relationships mentioned above. Seemingly incidental, they are all providential. All praise and glory to him whose greatest act of kindness was in giving us his Son, the ultimate son of David, the ultimate redeemer of all.

Peter H. W. Lau
Easter 2022

# Abbreviations

| | |
|---|---|
| AB | Anchor Bible |
| *ABD* | *Anchor Bible Dictionary*. Edited by David N. Freedman. 6 vols. New York: Doubleday, 1992 |
| *AJT* | *American Journal of Theology* |
| Akk. | Akkadian |
| ANEM | Ancient Near East Monographs |
| *ANET* | *Ancient Near Eastern Texts Relating to the Old Testament*. Edited by James B. Pritchard. 3rd ed. Princeton: Princeton University Press, 1969 |
| *Ant.* | *Jewish Antiquities* |
| ApOTC | Apollos Old Testament Commentary |
| *BA* | *Biblical Archaeologist* |
| *BASOR* | *Bulletin of the American Schools of Oriental Research* |
| B. Bat. | Baba Batra |
| *BBR* | *Bulletin for Biblical Research* |
| BBRSup | Bulletin for Biblical Research, Supplements |
| BDB | Brown, Francis, S. R. Driver, and Charles A. Briggs. *A Hebrew and English Lexicon of the Old Testament*. Oxford: Clarendon Press, 1907 |
| BETL | Bibliotheca Ephemeridum Theologicarum Lovaniensium |
| *BHQ* | *Biblia Hebraica Quinta* |
| *BHS* | *Biblia Hebraica Stuttgartensia* |
| *Bib* | *Biblica* |
| *BibInt* | *Biblical Interpretation: A Journal of Contemporary Approaches* |
| BKAT | Biblischer Kommentar, Altes Testament |
| *BSac* | *Bibliotheca Sacra* |
| *BT* | *The Bible Translator* |
| *BTB* | *Biblical Theology Bulletin* |
| *BZ* | *Biblische Zeitschrift* |

## Abbreviations

| | |
|---|---|
| BZAW | Beihefte zur Zeitschrift für die Alttestamentliche Wissenschaft |
| CahRB | Cahiers de la Revue biblique |
| *CBQ* | *Catholic Biblical Quarterly* |
| CC | Continental Commentaries |
| CEV | Contemporary English Version |
| ConBOT | Coniectanea Biblica: Old Testament Series |
| *COS* | *The Context of Scripture.* Edited by William H. Hallo. 3 vols. Leiden: Brill, 1997–2002 |
| CSB | Christian Standard Bible |
| *CurBS* | *Currents in Research: Biblical Studies* |
| DCH | *Dictionary of Classical Hebrew.* Edited by D. J. A. Clines. 9 vols. Vols. 1–5, Sheffield: Sheffield Academic, 1993–2001; vols. 6–9, Sheffield: Sheffield Phoenix, 2007–2016 |
| DDD | *Dictionary of Deities and Demons in the Bible.* Edited by Karel van der Toorn, Bob Becking, and Pieter W. van der Horst. Leiden: Brill, 1995. 2nd rev. ed. Grand Rapids: Eerdmans, 1999 |
| EBTC | Evangelical Biblical Theology Commentary |
| ESV | English Standard Version |
| EVV | English versions |
| *ExpTim* | *Expository Times* |
| FAT | Forschungen zum Alten Testament |
| *FO* | *Folia Orientalia* |
| FOTL | Forms of the Old Testament Literature |
| GKC | *Gesenius' Hebrew Grammar.* Edited by E. Kautzsch. Translated by A. E. Cowley. 2nd ed. Oxford: Clarendon Press, 1910 |
| *HALOT* | Koehler, Ludwig, Walter Baumgartner, and Johann J. Stamm. *The Hebrew and Aramaic Lexicon of the Old Testament.* Translated and edited under the supervision of M. E. J. Richardson. 4 vols. Leiden, 1994–1999 |
| HAT | Handbuch zum Alten Testament |
| HCSB | Holman Christian Standard Bible |
| HSM | Harvard Semitic Monographs |
| HTKAT | Herder Theologischer Kommentar zum Alten Testament |
| *HTR* | *Harvard Theological Review* |
| *HUCA* | *Hebrew Union College Annual* |
| *IBHS* | *An Introduction to Biblical Hebrew Syntax.* Bruce K. Waltke and M. O'Connor. Winona Lake, IN: Eisenbrauns, 1990 |
| *IDB* | *The Interpreter's Dictionary of the Bible.* Edited by George A. Buttrick. 4 vols. Nashville: Abingdon, 1962 |
| IVBS | International Voices in Biblical Studies |
| *JAOS* | *Journal of the American Oriental Society* |
| *JBL* | *Journal of Biblical Literature* |

xiv

# ABBREVIATIONS

| | |
|---|---|
| *JETS* | *Journal of the Evangelical Theological Society* |
| *JHebS* | *Journal of Hebrew Scriptures* |
| JM | Joüon, Paul. *A Grammar of Biblical Hebrew*. Translated and revised by Takamitsu Muraoka. 2 vols. Rome: Pontifical Biblical Institute, 1991 |
| *JNSL* | *Journal of Northwest Semitic Languages* |
| JPS | Jewish Publication Society |
| *JSOT* | *Journal for the Study of the Old Testament* |
| JSOTSup | Journal for the Study of the Old Testament, Supplement Series |
| *JSS* | *Journal of Semitic Studies* |
| *JTI* | *Journal for Theological Interpretation* |
| KAT | Kommentar zum Alten Testament |
| LCL | Loeb Classical Library |
| LEB | Lexham English Bible |
| LHBOTS | Library of Hebrew Bible/Old Testament Studies |
| LXX | Septuagint |
| LXX$^A$ | Codex Alexandrinus |
| LXX$^B$ | Codex Vaticanus |
| LXX$^L$ | Major Lucianic manuscripts |
| Meg. | Megillah |
| *Midr. Ruth Rab.* | *Midrash Rabbah: Ruth*. Translated by Louis I. Rabinowitz. London: Sonsino, 1939 |
| MSS | Manuscripts |
| MT | Masoretic Text |
| MT$^A$ | Aleppo Codex |
| MT$^L$ | Leningrad Codex |
| MT$^Y$ | Cambridge University Add. Ms. 1753 |
| NAB | New American Bible |
| NAC | New American Commentary |
| NASB | New American Standard Bible |
| NCBC | New Century Bible Commentary |
| NET | New English Translation |
| NIBCOT | New International Biblical Commentary on the Old Testament |
| NICNT | New International Commentary on the New Testament |
| NICOT | New International Commentary on the Old Testament |
| *NIDOTTE* | *New International Dictionary of Old Testament Theology and Exegesis*. Edited by Willem A. VanGemeren. 5 vols. Grand Rapids: Zondervan, 1997 |
| NIGTC | New International Greek Testament Commentary |
| NIV | New International Version |
| NJPS | *Tanakh: The Holy Scriptures: The New JPS Translation according to the Traditional Hebrew Text* |

# Abbreviations

| | |
|---|---|
| NKJV | New King James Version |
| NLT | New Living Translation |
| NRSV | New Revised Standard Version |
| NSBT | New Studies in Biblical Theology |
| OBO | Orbis biblicus et orientalis |
| OL | Old Latin |
| *OTE* | *Old Testament Essays* |
| OTL | Old Testament Library |
| *OtSt* | *Oudtestamentische Studiën* |
| *RB* | *Revue Biblique* |
| *RTP* | *Revue de théologie et de philosophie* |
| *RTR* | *Reformed Theological Review* |
| SBL | Society of Biblical Literature |
| SBLDS | Society of Biblical Literature Dissertation Series |
| SBS | Stuttgarter Bibelstudien |
| *SJOT* | *Scandinavian Journal of the Old Testament* |
| Syr. | Syriac |
| *TDOT* | *Theological Dictionary of the Old Testament.* Edited by G. Johannes Botterweck, Helmer Ringgren, and Heinz-Josef Fabry. Translated by John T. Willis, Geoffrey W. Bromiley, David E. Green, and Douglas W. Stott. 15 vols. Grand Rapids: Eerdmans, 1974–2006 |
| Tg. | Targum |
| *TLOT* | *Theological Lexicon of the Old Testament.* Edited by E. Jenni with assistance from C. Westermann. Translated by Mark E. Biddle. 3 vols. Peabody, MA: Hendrickson, 1997 |
| TOTC | Tyndale Old Testament Commentaries |
| *Transeu* | *Transeuphratène* |
| *TWOT* | *Theological Wordbook of the Old Testament.* Edited by R. Laird Harris, Gleason L. Archer Jr., and Bruce K. Waltke. 2 vols. Chicago: Moody Press, 1980 |
| *TynBul* | *Tyndale Bulletin* |
| *TZ* | *Theologische Zeitschrift* |
| UBS | United Bible Societies |
| *USQR* | *Union Seminary Quarterly Review* |
| *VT* | *Vetus Testamentum* |
| VTSup | Supplements to Vetus Testamentum |
| Vulg. | Vulgate |
| WBC | Word Biblical Commentary |
| YNER | Yale Near Eastern Researches |
| *ZAW* | *Zeitschrift für die Alttestamentliche Wissenschaft* |
| ZBK | Zürcher Bibelkommentare |

# Bibliography

Alba, Richard, and Victor Nee. "Assimilation." Pages 400–417 in *The SAGE Handbook of International Migration*. Edited by Inglis Christine, Li Wei, and Khadria Binod. London: SAGE, 2019.

———. *Remaking the American Mainstream: Assimilation and Contemporary Immigration*. Cambridge: Harvard University Press, 2003.

Alexander, T. Desmond. "Seed." Pages 769–73 in *New Dictionary of Biblical Theology*. Edited by Brian S. Rosner, Donald A. Carson, and Graeme Goldsworthy. Leicester: Inter-Varsity, 2000.

Alter, Robert. *The Art of Biblical Narrative*. New York: Basic Books, 1981.

———. *Strong as Death Is Love: The Song of Songs, Ruth, Esther, Jonah, and Daniel; A Translation with Commentary*. New York: W. W. Norton & Company, 2015.

American Psychiatric Association. *Diagnostic and Statistical Manual of Mental Disorders*. 5th ed. Arlington: American Psychiatric Publishing, 2013.

Andersen, Francis I. *Job: An Introduction and Commentary*. Leicester: Inter-Varsity, 1976.

———. "Yahweh, the Kind and Sensitive God." Pages 41–88 in *God Who Is Rich in Mercy: Essays Presented to Dr. D. B. Knox*. Edited by Peter T. O'Brien and David G. Peterson. Sydney: Lancer, 1986.

Ap-Thomas, D. R. "The Book of Ruth." *ExpTim* 79 (1968): 369–73.

Arnold, Bill T. "The Love-Fear Antinomy in Deuteronomy 5–11." *VT* 61 (2011): 552–69.

Artus, Olivier J. "Les frontières de la communauté judéenne à la lumière du livre de Ruth." *Transeu* 37 (2009): 11–20.

Aschkenasy, Nehama. "Language as Female Empowerment in Ruth." Pages 111–24 in *Reading Ruth: Contemporary Women Reclaim a Sacred Story*. Edited by Judith A. Kates and Gail T. Reimer. New York: Ballantine Books, 1994.

Ashley, Timothy R. *The Book of Numbers*. NICOT. Grand Rapids: Eerdmans, 1993.

# BIBLIOGRAPHY

Baker, David L. "To Glean or Not to Glean . . ." *ExpTim* 117 (2006): 406–10.

Baker, David W. "Explicative Waw." In *Encyclopedia of Hebrew Language and Linguistics*. Edited by G. Khan, S. Bolokzy, S. E. Fassberg, Gary A. Rendsburg, A. D. Rubin, O. R. Schwartzwald, and T. Zewi. Leiden: Brill, 2013.

Barclay, John M. G. *Paul and the Gift*. Grand Rapids: Eerdmans, 2015.

Bar-Efrat, Shimon. *Narrative Art in the Bible*. JSOTSup 70. Sheffield: Almond Press, 1989.

———. "Some Observations on the Analysis of Structure in Biblical Narrative." *VT* 30 (1980): 154–73.

Barker, Paul A. *The Triumph of Grace in Deuteronomy: Faithless Israel, Faithful Yahweh in Deuteronomy*. Carlisle: Paternoster, 2004.

Bartholomew, Craig G., and Michael W. Goheen. *The Drama of Scripture: Finding Our Place in the Biblical Story*. Grand Rapids: Baker Academic, 2004.

Bauckham, Richard. "The Book of Ruth and the Possibility of a Feminist Canonical Hermeneutic." *BibInt* 5 (1997): 29–45.

Baylis, Charles P. "Naomi in the Book of Ruth in Light of the Mosaic Covenant." *BSac* 161 (2004): 413–31.

Beattie, D. R. G. "Ruth III." *JSOT* 5 (1978): 39–48.

Beckwith, Roger T. *The Old Testament Canon of the New Testament Church*. Grand Rapids: Eerdmans, 1985.

Beekman, John, John Callow, and Michael F. Kopesec. *The Semantic Structure of Written Communication*. Dallas: Summer Institute of Linguistics, 1981.

Beeston, A. F. L. "One Flesh." *VT* 36 (1986): 115–17.

Berger, Yitzhak. "Ruth and Inner-Biblical Allusion: The Case of 1 Samuel 25." *JBL* 128 (2009): 253–72.

———. "Ruth and the David-Bathsheba Story: Allusions and Contrasts." *JSOT* 33 (2009): 433–52.

Berlin, Adele. "Legal Fiction: Levirate cum Land Redemption in Ruth." *Journal of Ancient Judaism* 1 (2010): 3–18.

———. *Poetics and Interpretation of Biblical Narrative*. Sheffield: Almond Press, 1983.

Bernstein, Moshe J. "Two Multivalent Readings in the Ruth Narrative." *JSOT* 50 (1991): 15–26.

Berquist, Jon L. "Role Differentiation in the Book of Ruth." *JSOT* 57 (1993): 23–37.

Bertman, Stephen. "Symmetrical Design in the Book of Ruth." *JBL* 84 (1965): 165–68.

Black, James. "Ruth in the Dark: Folktale, Law and Creative Ambiguity in the Old Testament." *Literature and Theology* 5 (1991): 20–36.

Blackburn, W. Ross. *The God Who Makes Himself Known: The Missionary Heart of the Book of Exodus*. NSBT. Downers Grove, IL: InterVarsity, 2012.

Block, Daniel I. *Judges, Ruth*. NAC 6. Nashville: Broadman & Holman, 1999.

# BIBLIOGRAPHY

———. *Ruth: A Discourse Analysis of the Hebrew Bible*. Grand Rapids: Zondervan, 2015.

Bons, Eberhard. "Die Septuaginta-Version des Buches Rut." *BZ* 42 (1998): 46–68.

Borowski, Oded. *Agriculture in Iron Age Israel*. Winona Lake, IN: Eisenbrauns, 2002.

Bos, Johanna W. H. "Out of the Shadows: Genesis 38; Judges 4:17–22; Ruth 3." *Semeia* 42 (1988): 37–67.

Botte, P., and P.-M. Bogaert. "Septante et versions grecques." Pages 535–691 in *Septante au Dictionnaire de la Bible*. Edited by Pirot L. and A. Robert. Paris: Letouzey & Ané, 1996.

Brady, Christian M. M. "The Conversion of Ruth in Targum Ruth." *Review of Rabbinic Judaism* 16 (2013): 133–46.

Brichto, Herbert C. "Kin, Cult, Land, and Afterlife—A Biblical Complex." *HUCA* 44 (1973): 1–54.

Bridge, Edward J. "Female Slave vs Female Slave:*'āmâ* and *šipḥâ* in the HB." *JHebS* 12 (2012): 1–21.

———. "Self-Abasement as an Expression of Thanks in the Hebrew Bible." *Bib* 92 (2011): 255–73.

Brown, Raymond E. "*Rachab* in Mt 1,5 Probably Is Rahab of Jericho." *Bib* 63 (1982): 79–80.

Buhl, Frants. "Some Observations on the Social Institutions of the Israelites." *AJT* 1 (1897): 728–40.

Burrows, Millar. "The Marriage of Boaz and Ruth." *JBL* 59 (1940): 445–54.

Bush, Frederic W. *Ruth, Esther*. WBC 9. Dallas: Word Books, 1996.

Callaham, Scott N. "But Ruth Clung to Her: Textual Constraints on Ambiguity in Ruth 1:14." *TynBul* 63 (2012): 179–98.

Campbell, Edward F. *Ruth*. AB 7. Garden City: Doubleday, 1975.

Carroll R., M. Daniel. *The Bible and Borders: Hearing God's Word on Immigration*. Grand Rapids: Brazos, 2020.

———. "Once a Stranger, Always a Stranger? Immigration, Assimilation, and the Book of Ruth." *International Bulletin of Missionary Research* 39 (2015): 185–88.

Carson, D. A. *A Call to Spiritual Reformation: Priorities from Paul and His Prayers*. Grand Rapids: Baker Academic, 1992.

Cassuto, Umberto. *A Commentary on the Book of Genesis: Part II, From Noah to Abraham, Genesis VI 9–XI 32, with an Appendix: A Fragment of Part III*. Jerusalem: Magnes Press, 1974.

Chase, Elaine, and Grace Bantebya-Kyomuhendo. *Poverty and Shame: Global Experiences*. Oxford: Oxford University Press, 2014.

Cheung, Simon Chi-chung. "'Forget Your People and Your Father's House': The Core Theological Message of Psalm 45 and Its Canonical Position in the Hebrew Psalter." *BBR* 26 (2016): 325–40.

## BIBLIOGRAPHY

Chisholm, Robert B., Jr. *A Commentary on Judges and Ruth*. Grand Rapids: Kregel Academic, 2013.

Christiansen, Bent. "A Linguistic Analysis of the Biblical Hebrew Particle *nā'*: A Test Case." *VT* 59 (2009): 379–93.

Clark, Gordon R. *The Word Hesed in the Hebrew Bible*. JSOTSup 157. Sheffield: Sheffield Academic Press, 1993.

Clines, David J. A. *The Esther Scroll: The Story of the Story*. Sheffield: JSOT Press, 1984.

———. *Job 1–20*. WBC 17. Grand Rapids: Zondervan, 1989.

Craigie, Peter C. *The Book of Deuteronomy*. NICOT. Grand Rapids: Eerdmans, 1976.

Creach, Jerome F. D. *Yahweh as Refuge and the Editing of the Hebrew Psalter*. JSOTSup 217. Sheffield: Sheffield Academic, 1996.

Crook, Zeba. "Honor, Shame, and Social Status Revisited." *JBL* 128 (2009): 591–611.

Cuddon, J. A. *A Dictionary of Literary Terms and Literary Theory*. 5th ed. Oxford: Wiley-Blackwell, 2013.

Culp, A. J. "Of Wedding Songs and Prophecies: Canonical Reading as the Clue to Understanding Psalm 45 as Prophecy." *Crucible* 8 (2017).

Dagley, Kelly D. "Women's Experience of Migration and the Book of Ruth." PhD dissertation, Fuller Theological Seminary, Center for Advanced Theological Study, 2019.

Darr, Katheryn P. *Far More Precious Than Jewels: Perspectives on Biblical Women*. Louisville: Westminster John Knox, 1991.

Daube, David. *Ancient Jewish Law: Three Inaugural Lectures*. Leiden: Brill, 1981.

David, M. "The Date of the Book of Ruth." *OtSt* 1 (1942): 55–63.

Davies, Eryl W. "Inheritance Rights and the Hebrew Levirate Marriage: Part 2." *VT* 31 (1981): 257–68.

———. "Ruth IV 5 and the Duties of the *Go'el*." *VT* 33 (1983): 231–34.

Davies, John A. *Lift Up Your Heads: Nonverbal Communication and Related Body Imagery in the Bible*. Eugene, OR: Pickwick Publications, 2018.

———. *A Royal Priesthood: Literary and Intertextual Perspectives on an Image of Israel in Exodus 19:6*. JSOTSup 395. London: T&T Clark, 2004.

Davis, Ellen F. "'All That You Say I Will Do': A Sermon on the Book of Ruth." Pages 3–8 in *Scrolls of Love: Reading Ruth and the Song of Songs*. Edited by Peter S. Hawkins and Lesleigh Cushing Stahlberg. New York: Fordham University Press, 2006.

Davis, Ellen F., and Margaret Adams Parker. *Who Are You, My Daughter? Reading Ruth through Image and Text*. Louisville: Westminster John Knox, 2003.

Dearman, J. Andrew, ed. *Studies in the Mesha Inscription and Moab*. Atlanta: Scholars Press, 1989.

DeRouchie, Jason S. "The Heart of YHWH and His Chosen One in 1 Samuel 13:14." *BBR* 24 (2014): 467–89.

# BIBLIOGRAPHY

De-Whyte, Janice Pearl Ewurama. *Wom(b)an: A Cultural-Narrative Reading of the Hebrew Bible Barrenness Narratives.* Leiden: Brill, 2018.

Dobbs-Allsopp, F. W., J. J. M. Roberts, C. L. Seow, and R. E. Whitaker. *Hebrew Inscriptions: Texts from the Biblical Period of the Monarchy with Concordance.* New Haven: Yale University Press, 2005.

Dommershausen, Werner. "Leitwortstil in der Ruthrolle." Pages 394–407 in *Theologie im Wandel.* Edited by Johannes Neumann and Joseph Ratzinger. Munich-Freiberg: Wewel, 1967.

Donaldson, Laura E. "The Sign of Orpah: Reading Ruth through Native Eyes." Pages 138–51 in *Hope Abundant.* Maryknoll, NY: Orbis, 2010.

Driesbach, Jason. *Ruth.* Cornerstone Biblical Commentary. Carol Stream, IL: Tyndale House, 2016.

Durham, John I. *Exodus.* WBC 3. Waco, TX: Word Books, 1987.

Duvall, J. Scott, and J. Daniel Hays. *God's Relational Presence: The Cohesive Center of Biblical Theology.* Grand Rapids: Baker Academic, 2019.

Dyck, Jonathan E. *The Theocratic Ideology of the Chronicler.* Leiden: Brill, 1998.

Elliott, John H. "Deuteronomy—Shameful Encroachment on Shameful Parts: Deuteronomy 25:11–12 and Biblical Euphemism." Pages 161–76 in *Ancient Israel: The Old Testament in Its Social Context.* Edited by Philip F. Esler. Minneapolis: Fortress, 2006.

Elliott, Mark W. *Providence: A Biblical, Historical, and Theological Account.* Grand Rapids: Baker Academic, 2020.

Embry, Brad. "Legalities in the Book of Ruth: A Renewed Look." *JSOT* 41 (2016): 31–44.

———. "'Redemption-Acquisition': The Marriage of Ruth as a Theological Commentary on Yahweh and Yahweh's People." *JTI* 7 (2013): 257–73.

Epstein, Isidore, ed. *Baba Bathra: Hebrew-English Edition of the Babylonian Talmud.* London: Soncino Press, 1976.

Eskenazi, Tamara Cohn, and Tikva Frymer-Kensky. *Ruth.* JPS Bible Commentary. Philadelphia: Jewish Publication Society, 2011.

Esler, Philip F. "'All That You Have Done . . . Has Been Fully Told to Me': The Power of Gossip and the Story of Ruth." *JBL* 137 (2018): 645–66.

Evans, Mary J. *Judges and Ruth.* TOTC. Downers Grove, IL: InterVarsity, 2017.

Exum, J. Cheryl. *Plotted, Shot, and Painted: Cultural Representations of Biblical Women.* 2nd ed. Sheffield: Sheffield Phoenix, 2012.

Fentress-Williams, Judy. *Ruth.* Nashville: Abingdon, 2012.

Fewell, Danna N., and David M. Gunn. *Compromising Redemption: Relating Characters in the Book of Ruth.* Louisville: Westminster John Knox, 1990.

Finlay, Timothy D. *The Birth Report Genre in the Hebrew Bible.* FAT 2.12. Tübingen: Mohr Siebeck, 2005.

Firth, David G. *Including the Stranger: Foreigners in the Former Prophets.* NSBT. Downers Grove, IL: InterVarsity, 2019.

———. *Joshua.* EBTC. Bellingham: Lexham Academic, 2021.

# Bibliography

Fisch, Harold. "Ruth and the Structure of Covenant History." *VT* 32 (1982): 425–37.

Fischer, Irmtraud. "The Book of Ruth: A 'Feminist' Commentary on the Torah?" Pages 24–49 in *Ruth and Esther: A Feminist Companion to the Bible*. Second Series. Edited by Athalya Brenner. Sheffield: Sheffield Academic Press, 1999.

———. "The Book of Ruth as Exegetical Literature." *European Judaism* 40 (2007): 140–49.

———. *Rut*. HTKAT. Freiburg: Herder, 2001.

France, R. T. *The Gospel of Matthew*. NICNT. Grand Rapids: Eerdmans, 2007.

Frese, Daniel A. "Chambered Gatehouses in the Iron II Southern Levant: Their Architecture and Function." *Levant* 47 (2015): 75–92.

———. *The City Gate in Ancient Israel and Her Neighbors: The Form, Function, and Symbolism of the Civic Forum in the Southern Levant*. Leiden: Brill, 2020.

Frevel, Christian. *Das Buch Rut*. Neuer Stuttgarter Kommentar: Altes Testament 6. Stuttgart: Verlag Katholisches Bibelwerk, 1992.

Frymer-Kensky, Tikva. *Studies in Bible and Feminist Criticism*. Philadelphia: Jewish Publication Society, 2005.

Garsiel, Moshe. *Biblical Names: A Literary Study of Midrashic Derivations and Puns*. Translated by Phyllis Hackett. Ramat Gan: Bar-Ilan University Press, 1991.

Gerleman, Gillis. *Ruth. Das Hohelied*. BKAT 18. Neukirchen-Vluyn: Neukirchener Verlag, 1965.

Ginzberg, Louis. *The Legends of the Jews*. Vol. 4. Translated by Henrietta Szold, Paul Radin, and Boaz Cohen. Philadelphia: Jewish Publication Society of America, 1928.

Glanville, Mark R., and Luke Glanville. *Refuge Reimagined: Biblical Kinship in Global Politics*. Downers Grove, IL: IVP Academic, 2020.

Glanzman, George S. "The Origin and Date of the Book of Ruth." *CBQ* 21 (1959): 201–7.

Glover, Neil. "Your People, My People: An Exploration of Ethnicity in Ruth." *JSOT* 33 (2009): 293–313.

Glueck, Nelson. *Hesed in the Bible*. Translated by Alfred Gottschalk. Cincinnati: Hebrew Union College Press, 1967.

Goh, Samuel T. S. "Ruth as a Superior Woman of חיל? A Comparison between Ruth and the 'Capable' Woman in Proverbs 31.10–31." *JSOT* 38 (2014): 487–500.

Gordis, Robert. "Love, Marriage, and Business in the Book of Ruth: A Chapter in Hebrew Customary Law." Pages 241–64 in *A Light unto My Path*. Edited by Howard N. Bream, Ralph D. Heim, and Carey A. Moore. Philadelphia: Temple University Press, 1974.

Goslinga, C. J. *Joshua, Judges, Ruth*. Translated by Ray Togtman. Grand Rapids: Zondervan, 1986.

# BIBLIOGRAPHY

Gow, Murray D. *The Book of Ruth: Its Structure, Theme and Purpose*. Leicester: Apollos, 1992.

Gray, John. *Joshua, Judges, Ruth*. NCBC. Grand Rapids: Eerdmans, 1986.

Green, Barbara. "The Plot of the Biblical Story of Ruth." *JSOT* 23 (1982): 55–68.

Greenberg, Moshe. "The Hebrew Oath Particle *ḥay/ḥē*." *JBL* 76 (1957): 34–39.

Grossman, Jonathan. *Ruth: Bridges and Boundaries*. Bern: Peter Lang, 2015.

Gunkel, Hermann. "Ruth." Pages 2180–82 in vol. 4 of *Religion in Geschichte und Gegenwart*. Tübingen: J. C. B. Mohr, 1930.

———. "Ruth." Pages 65–92 in *Reden und Aufsätze*. Göttingen: Vandenhoeck und Ruprecht, 1913.

Guttmann, Michael. "The Term 'Foreigner' (נכרי) Historically Considered." *HUCA* 3 (1926): 1–20.

Habel, Norman C. "The Form and Significance of the Call Narratives." *ZAW* 77 (1965): 297–323.

Hallo, William W., ed. *Monumental Inscriptions from the Biblical World*. Vol. 2 of *The Context of Scripture*. Leiden: Brill, 1997.

Hals, Ronald M. "Ruth." Pages 758–59 in *Interpreter's Dictionary of the Bible: Supplementary Volume*. Edited by Keith Crim. Nashville: Abingdon, 1976.

———. *The Theology of the Book of Ruth*. Philadelphia: Fortress, 1969.

Halton, Charles. "An Indecent Proposal: The Theological Core of the Book of Ruth." *SJOT* 26 (2012): 30–43.

Harris, J. Gordon, Cheryl A. Brown, and Michael S. Moore. *Joshua, Judges, Ruth*. NIBCOT 5. Peabody, MA: Hendrickson, 2000.

Hawk, L. Daniel. *Ruth*. ApOTC. Nottingham: Apollos, 2015.

Hertig, Paul. "Jesus' Migrations and Liminal Withdrawals in Matthew." Pages 46–61 in *God's People on the Move: Biblical and Global Perspectives on Migration and Mission*. Edited by vanThanh Nguyen and John M. Prior. Eugene, OR: Wipf and Stock, 2014.

Hirsch, E. D. *Validity in Interpretation*. New Haven: Yale University Press, 1967.

Holmstedt, Robert D. *The Relative Clause in Biblical Hebrew*. Linguistic Studies in Ancient West Semitic 10. Winona Lake, IN: Eisenbrauns, 2016.

———. *Ruth: A Handbook on the Hebrew Text*. Waco, TX: Baylor University Press, 2010.

Honig, Bonnie. "Ruth, the Model Emigrée: Mourning and the Symbolic Politics of Immigration." Pages 50–74 in *Ruth and Esther: A Feminist Companion to the Bible*. Second Series. Edited by Athalya Brenner. Sheffield: Sheffield Academic, 1999.

Hubbard, Robert L. *The Book of Ruth*. NICOT. Grand Rapids: Eerdmans, 1988.

Hubbard, Robert L., and J. Andrew Dearman. *Introducing the Old Testament*. Grand Rapids: Eerdmans, 2018.

Humbert, Paul. "Art et leçon de l'historie de Ruth." *RTP* 26 (1938): 257–86.

Humphreys, W. "Novella." Pages 82–96 in *Saga, Legend, Tale, Novella, Fable:*

# BIBLIOGRAPHY

*Narrative Forms in Old Testament Literature*. Edited by George W. Coats. JSOTSup 35. Sheffield: JSOT Press, 1985.

Hurvitz, Avi. "Can Biblical Texts Be Dated Linguistically? Chronological Perspectives in the Historical Study of Biblical Hebrew." Pages 143–60 in *Congress Volume: Oslo 1998*. Edited by André Lemaire and Magne Sæbø. VTSup 80. Leiden: Brill, 2000.

———. *A Linguistic Study of the Relationship between the Priestly Source and the Book of Ezekiel*. CahRB 20. Paris: Gabalda, 1982.

———. "Ruth 2:7–'A Midrashic Gloss'?" *ZAW* 95 (1983): 121–23.

Hwang, Jerry. "'How Long Will My Glory Be Reproach?' Honour and Shame in Old Testament Lament Traditions." *OTE* 30 (2017): 684–706.

Hyman, Ronald T. "Questions and Changing Identity in the Book of Ruth." *USQR* 39 (1984): 189–201.

Irwin, Brian P. "Removing Ruth: *Tiqqune Sopherim* in Ruth 3.3–4?" *JSOT* 32 (2008): 331–38.

Jackson, Bernard S. "Ideas of Law and Legal Administration: A Semiotic Approach." Pages 185–202 in *The World of Ancient Israel: Sociological, Anthropological and Political Perspectives*. Edited by Ronald E. Clements. Cambridge: Cambridge University Press, 1989.

Jackson, Justin. "The One Who Returned: A Retrospective and Prospective Reading of Ruth." *JETS* 63 (2020): 435–54.

Jastrow, Marcus. *A Dictionary of the Targumim, the Talmud Babli and Yerushalmi, and the Midrashic Literature*. Peabody, MA: Hendrickson, 1926.

Jenni, Ernst. *Die hebräischen Präpositionen*. 3 vols. Stuttgart: Kohlhammer, 1992–2000.

Jobling, David. "Ruth Finds a Home: Canon, Politics, Method." Pages 125–39 in *The New Literary Criticism and the Hebrew Bible*. Edited by J. C. Exum and D. J. A. Clines. JSOTSup 143. Sheffield: JSOT Press, 1993.

Jones, Edward Allen, III. *Reading Ruth in the Restoration Period*. LHBOTS 604. New York: Bloomsbury T&T Clark, 2016.

———. "'Who Are You, My Daughter [מי את בתי]?' A Reassessment of Ruth and Naomi in Ruth 3." *CBQ* 76 (2014): 653–64.

Jongeling, B. "*hz't n'my* (Ruth I 19)." *VT* 28 (1978): 474–77.

Josephus, Flavius. *Jewish Antiquities*. Translated by William Whiston. Cambridge: Harvard University Press, 1966.

Joüon, Paul. *Ruth: Commentaire philologique et exégétique*. Rome: Pontifical Biblical Institute, 1924.

Juhás, Peter. *Die biblisch-hebräische Partikel נָה im Lichte der antiken Bibelübersetzungen*. Leiden: Brill, 2017.

Kawashima, Robert S. *Biblical Narrative and the Death of the Rhapsode*. Bloomington: Indiana University Press, 2004.

Keita, Schadrac, and Janet W. Dyk. "The Scene at the Threshing Floor: Suggestive Readings and Intercultural Considerations on Ruth 3." *BT* 57 (2006): 17–32.

Kennedy, James M. "The Root *G'R* in the Light of Semantic Analysis." *JBL* 106 (1987): 47–64.

Knoppers, Gary N. "Intermarriage, Social Complexity, and Ethnic Diversity in the Genealogy of Judah." *JBL* 120 (2001): 15–30.

Korpel, Marjo C. A. *The Structure of the Book of Ruth.* Pericope 2. Assen: Van Gorcum, 2001.

Köstenberger, Andreas J., and T. Desmond Alexander. *Salvation to the Ends of the Earth: A Biblical Theology of Mission.* 2nd ed. NSBT. Downers Grove, IL: InterVarsity, 2020.

Kruger, Paul A. "The Hem of Garment in Marriage: The Meaning of the Symbolic Gesture in Ruth 3:9 and Ezek 16:8." *JNSL* 12 (1984): 79–86.

Kwakkel, G. "Under Yahweh's Wings." Pages 141–65 in *Metaphors in the Psalms.* Edited by Pierre van Hecke and Antje Labahn. BETL. Leuven: Peeters, 2010.

Kwok, Pui-lan. *Postcolonial Imagination and Feminist Theology.* Louisville: Westminster John Knox, 2005.

LaCocque, André. *Ruth.* Translated by K. C. Hanson. CC. Minneapolis: Fortress, 2004.

Laniak, Timothy S. *Shame and Honor in the Book of Esther.* SBLDS 165. Atlanta: Scholars Press, 1998.

Lau, Peter H. W. "Back under Authority: Towards an Evangelical Postcolonial Hermeneutic." *TynBul* 63 (2012): 131–44.

———. "Gentile Incorporation into Israel in Ezra–Nehemiah?" *Bib* 90 (2009): 356–73.

———. *Identity and Ethics in the Book of Ruth: A Social Identity Approach.* BZAW 416. Berlin: de Gruyter, 2011.

Lau, Peter H. W., and Gregory Goswell. *Unceasing Kindness: A Biblical Theology of Ruth.* NSBT. Downers Grove, IL: InterVarsity, 2016.

Leach, Edmund R. *Culture and Communication.* Cambridge: Cambridge University Press, 1976.

Leggett, Donald A. *The Levirate and* Goel *Institutions in the Old Testament.* Cherry Hill, NJ: Mack, 1974.

Lehmann, Manfred R. "Biblical Oaths." *ZAW* 81 (1969): 74–92.

LeMon, Joel M. *Yahweh's Winged Form in the Psalms: Exploring Congruent Iconography and Texts.* OBO 242. Göttingen: Vandenhoeck & Ruprecht, 2010.

Levenson, Jon D. *Esther.* OTL. Louisville: Westminster John Knox, 1997.

Levin, Yigal. "Understanding Biblical Genealogies." *CurBS* 9 (2001): 11–46.

Levine, Amy-Jill. "Ruth." Pages 78–84 in *The Women's Bible Commentary.* Edited by Carol A. Newsom and Sharon H. Ringe. London: SPCK, 1992.

# BIBLIOGRAPHY

Lim, Timothy H. *The Formation of the Jewish Canon.* New Haven: Yale University Press, 2013.

———. "How Good Was Ruth's Hebrew? Ethnic and Linguistic Otherness in the Book of Ruth." Pages 101–15 in *The "Other" in Second Temple Judaism: Essays in Honor of John J. Collins.* Grand Rapids: Eerdmans, 2011.

Lin, Yan. "'Who Is More to You Than Seven Sons': A Cross-Textual Reading between the Book of Ruth and *A Pair of Peacocks to the Southeast Fly.*" Pages 47–55 in *Reading Ruth in Asia.* Edited by Jione Havea and Peter H. W. Lau. IVBS. Atlanta: SBL, 2015.

Linafelt, Tod. *Ruth.* Berit Olam. Collegeville, MN: Liturgical Press, 1999.

Linafelt, Tod, and Timothy K. Beal. *Ruth & Esther.* Berit Olam. Collegeville, MN: Liturgical Press, 1999.

Lipiński, E. "Le mariage de Ruth." *VT* 26 (1976): 124–27.

Long, V. Philips. *The Art of Biblical History.* Leicester: Apollos, 1994.

Longman, Tremper. *Song of Songs.* NICOT. Grand Rapids: Eerdmans, 2001.

Longman, Tremper, III, and Daniel G. Reid. *God Is a Warrior.* Grand Rapids: Zondervan, 1995.

Luter, A. Boyd, and Barry C. Davis. *Ruth and Esther: God Behind the Seen.* Fearn: Christian Focus, 1995.

Lys, Daniel. "Résidence ou repos? Notule sur Ruth ii 7." *VT* 21 (1971): 497–501.

MacDonald, Nathan. *What Did the Ancient Israelites Eat? Diet in Biblical Times.* Grand Rapids: Eerdmans, 2008.

Mace, D. R. *Hebrew Marriage: A Sociological Study.* London: Epworth, 1953.

Malamat, Abraham. "King Lists of the Old Babylonian Period and Biblical Genealogies." *JAOS* 88 (1968): 163–73.

Mathias, Steffan. *Paternity, Progeny, and Perpetuation: Creating Lives after Death in the Hebrew Bible.* LHBOTS 696. London: T&T Clark, 2020.

Matthews, Victor H. "The Determination of Social Identity in the Story of Ruth." *BTB* 36 (2006): 49–54.

———. *Judges/Ruth.* NCBC. Cambridge: Cambridge University Press, 2004.

Matthews, Victor H., and Don C. Benjamin. *Social World of Ancient Israel 1250–587 BCE.* Peabody, MA: Hendrickson, 1993.

May, Natalie N. "Gates and Their Functions in Mesopotamia and Ancient Israel." Pages 77–121 in *The Fabric of Cities: Aspects of Urbanism, Urban Topography and Society in Mesopotamia, Greece and Rome.* Edited by Natalie N. May and Ulrike Steinert. Leiden: Brill, 2014.

McKeown, James. *Ruth.* The Two Horizons Old Testament Commentary. Grand Rapids: Eerdmans, 2015.

Meinhold, Arndt. "Theologische Schwerpunkte im Buch Ruth und ihr Gewicht für Datierung." *TZ* 32 (1976): 129–37.

Meyers, Carol L. "The Family in Early Israel." Pages 1–47 in *Families in Ancient*

# BIBLIOGRAPHY

*Israel*. Edited by Leo G. Perdue, Joseph Blenkinsopp, John J. Collins, and Carol Meyers. Louisville: Westminster John Knox, 1997.

———. "'To Her Mother's House': Considering a Counterpart to the Israelite *bêt'ab*." Pages 39–51 in *The Bible and the Politics of Exegesis: Essays in Honor of Norman K. Gottwald on His Sixty-Fifth Birthday*. Edited by David Jobling, Peggy L. Day, and Gerald T. Shepherd. Cleveland: Pilgrim Press, 1991.

———. "'Women of the Neighbourhood' (Ruth 4.17): Informal Female Networks in Ancient Israel." Pages 110–27 in *Ruth and Esther: A Feminist Companion to the Bible*. Edited by Athalya Brenner. Sheffield: Sheffield Academic Press, 1999.

Milgrom, Jacob. *Leviticus 1–16*. AB 3. New York: Doubleday, 1991.

———. *Leviticus 23–27*. AB 3B. New York: Doubleday, 2000.

Miller, Robert D., II. "The Judges and the Early Iron Age." Pages 165–89 in *Ancient Israel's History: An Introduction to Issues and Sources*. Edited by Bill T. Arnold and Richard S. Hess. Grand Rapids: Baker Academic, 2014.

Miller-Naudé, Cynthia L., and Jacobus A. Naudé. "The Translation of Quotative Frames in the Hebrew Bible." *FO* 52 (2015): 249–69.

Moore, Michael S. "Two Textual Anomalies in Ruth." *CBQ* 59 (1997): 234–43.

Morris, Leon. *The Gospel According to Matthew*. Grand Rapids: Eerdmans, 1992.

———. *Ruth: An Introduction and Commentary*. TOTC. Downers Grove, IL: InterVarsity, 1968.

Murphy, Roland E. *Wisdom Literature: Job, Proverbs, Ruth, Canticles, Ecclesiastes, and Esther*. FOTL. Grand Rapids: Eerdmans, 1981.

Myers, Jacob M. *The Linguistic and Literary Form of the Book of Ruth*. Leiden: Brill, 1955.

Nash, Peter T. "Ruth: An Exercise in Israelite Political Correctness or a Call to Proper Conversion?" Pages 347–54 in *The Pitcher Is Broken: Memorial Essays for Gösta W. Ahlström*. Edited by Steven W. Holloway and Lowell K. Handy. JSOTSup 190. Sheffield: Sheffield Academic Press, 1995.

Nathanson, Donald L. *Shame and Pride: Affect, Sex, and the Birth of the Self*. New York: Norton, 1992.

Nazarov, Konstantin. *Focalization in the Old Testament Narratives with Specific Examples from the Book of Ruth*. Carlisle: Langham, 2021.

Niditch, Susan. "Legends of Wise Heroes and Heroines." Pages 445–63 in *The Hebrew Bible and Its Modern Interpreters*. Edited by Douglas A. Knight and Gene M. Tucker. Philadelphia: Fortress, 1985.

Nielsen, Kirsten. *Ruth: A Commentary*. Translated by Edward Broadbridge. OTL. Louisville: Westminster John Knox, 1997.

Niggemann, Andrew J. "Matriarch of Israel or Misnomer? Israelite Self-Identification in Ancient Israelite Law Code and the Implications for Ruth." *JSOT* 41 (2017): 355–77.

Nolland, John. *The Gospel of Matthew*. NIGTC. Grand Rapids: Eerdmans, 2005.

xxvii

# BIBLIOGRAPHY

Nu, Roi. "A Reinterpretation of Levirate Marriage in Ruth 4:1–12 for Kachin Society." Pages 57–72 in *Reading Ruth in Asia*. Edited by Jione Havea and Peter H. W. Lau. IVBS. Atlanta: SBL, 2015.

Oduyoye, Mercy A. *Beads and Strands: Reflections of an African Woman on Christianity in Africa*. Carlisle: Paternoster, 2002.

Oeste, Gordon. "Butchered Brothers and Betrayed Families: Degenerating Kinship Structures in the Book of Judges." *JSOT* 35 (2011): 295–316.

Olyan, Saul M. "Some Neglected Aspects of Israelite Interment Ideology." *JBL* 124 (2005): 601–16.

Ott, Craig, Stephen J. Strauss, and Timothy C. Tennent. *Encountering Theology of Mission: Biblical Foundations, Historical Developments, and Contemporary Issues*. Grand Rapids: Baker Academic, 2010.

Ovadia, Ben-Zion. "The Scene of Ruth's Encounter at the Threshing-Floor, in Light of the Story of Jacob's Deception of Isaac (Genesis 27)." *Beit Mikra* 65 (2020): 88–106.

Pa, Anna May Say. "Reading Ruth 3:1–5 from an Asian Woman's Perspective." Pages 47–59 in *Engaging the Bible in a Gendered World: An Introduction to Feminist Biblical Interpretations in Honor of Katherine Doob Sakenfeld*. Edited by Linda Day and Carolyn Pressler. Louisville: Westminster John Knox, 2006.

Payne, Jervis David. *Strangers Next Door: Immigration, Migration, and Mission*. Downers Grove, IL: InterVarsity, 2012.

Peters, George W. *A Biblical Theology of Missions.* Chicago: Moody Press, 1972.

Pfeiffer, Robert H. *Introduction to the Old Testament*. London: Adam and Charles Black, 1948.

Phinney, D. Nathan. "Call/Commission Narratives." Pages 65–71 in *Dictionary of Old Testament: Prophets*. Edited by Mark J. Boda and J. Gordon McConville. Downers Grove, IL: IVP, 2011.

Plevnik, Joseph, and John J. Pilch. "Honor and Shame." Pages 89–96 in *Handbook of Biblical Social Values*. Edited by John J. Pilch and Bruce J. Malina. Eugene, OR: Cascade, 2016.

Polzin, Robert. *Late Biblical Hebrew: Toward an Historical Typology of Biblical Hebrew Prose*. HSM 12. Missoula: Scholars Press, 1976.

Porten, Bezalel. "The Scroll of Ruth: A Rhetorical Study." *Gratz College Annual* 7 (1978): 23–49.

Powell, Stephanie Day. *Narrative Desire and the Book of Ruth*. LHBOTS 662. New York: Bloomsbury T&T Clark, 2018.

Pressler, Carolyn. *Joshua, Judges, Ruth*. Westminster Bible Companion. Louisville: Westminster John Knox, 2002.

Prill, Thorsten. *Global Mission on Our Doorstep: Forced Migration and the Future of the Church*. Münster: MV Wissenschaft, 2008.

Prinsloo, W. S. "The Theology of the Book of Ruth." *VT* 30 (1980): 330–41.

Queen-Sutherland, Kandy. *Ruth and Esther*. Macon, GA: Smyth & Helwys, 2016.

# BIBLIOGRAPHY

Quick, Laura. "The Book of Ruth and the Limits of Proverbial Wisdom." *JBL* 139 (2020): 47–66.

———. *Dress, Adornment and the Body in the Hebrew Bible*. Oxford: Oxford University Press, 2021.

Rebera, Basil. "Translating Ruth 3.16." *BT* 38 (1987): 234–37.

———. "Yahweh or Boaz? Ruth 2.20 Reconsidered." *BT* 36 (1985): 317–27.

Rendsburg, Gary A. "Confused Language as a Deliberate Literary Device in Biblical Hebrew Narrative." *JHebS* 2 (1999): 1–8.

———. "Eblaite *U-MA* and Hebrew *WM-*." Pages 33–41 in *Eblaitica: Essays on the Ebla Archives and Eblaite Language*. Edited by Cyrus H. Gordon, Gary A. Rendsburg, and Nathan H. Winter. Winona Lake, IN: Eisenbrauns, 1987.

———. *How the Bible Is Written*. Peabody, MA: Hendrickson, 2019.

———. "Notes on Genesis XV." *VT* 42 (1992): 266–72.

Revell, E. J. "The Two Forms of First Person Singular Pronouns in Biblical Hebrew: Redundancy or Expressive Contrast?" *JSS* 40 (1995): 199–217.

Rooker, Mark F. *Biblical Hebrew in Transition: The Language of the Book of Ezekiel*. JSOTSup 90. Sheffield: JSOT Press, 1990.

Roop, Eugene F. *Ruth, Jonah, Esther*. Believers Church Bible Commentary. Scottdale, PA: Herald, 2002.

Routledge, Bruce. *Moab in the Iron Age: Hegemony, Polity, Archaeology*. Philadelphia: University of Pennsylvania Press, 2004.

Rowley, H. H. "The Marriage of Ruth." Pages 169–94 in *The Servant of the Lord and Other Essays on the Old Testament*. Oxford: Blackwell, 1965.

Rudolph, Wilhelm. *Das Buch Ruth, das Hohe Lied, die Klagelieder*. KAT 17. Gütersloh: Mohn, 1962.

Rust, Eric C. *Judges, Ruth, 1 & 2 Samuel*. London: SCM, 1961.

Sakenfeld, Katharine D. *The Meaning of Hesed in the Hebrew Bible: A New Inquiry*. HSM 17. Missoula: Scholars Press, 1978.

———. "Naomi's Cry: Reflections on Ruth 1:20–21." Pages 129–43 in *A God So Near: Essays on Old Testament Theology in Honour of Patrick D. Miller*. Edited by Brent A. Strawn and Nancy R. Bowen. Winona Lake, IN: Eisenbrauns, 2003.

———. *Ruth*. Interpretation. Louisville: John Knox Press, 1999.

Sarna, Nahum M. *Genesis*. JPS Torah Commentary. Philadelphia: JPS, 1989.

Sasson, Jack M. *Ruth: A New Translation with a Philological Commentary and a Formalist-Folklorist Interpretation*. 2nd ed. Sheffield: JSOT Press, 1989.

Saxegaard, Kristin M. *Character Complexity in the Book of Ruth*. FAT II. Tübingen: Mohr Siebeck, 2010.

Schipper, Jeremy. *Ruth: A New Translation with Introduction and Commentary*. AB 7D. New Haven: Yale University Press, 2016.

———. "The Syntax and Rhetoric of Ruth 1:9a." *VT* 62 (2012): 642–45.

———. "Translating the Preposition *'m* in the Book of Ruth." *VT* 63 (2013): 663–69.

## BIBLIOGRAPHY

Shepherd, David. "Violence in the Fields? Translating, Reading, and Revising in Ruth 2." *CBQ* 63 (2001): 444–63.

Smalley, Beryl. *The Study of the Bible in the Middle Ages*. Oxford: Basil Blackwell, 1952.

Smith, Mark S. "'Your People Shall Be My People': Family and Covenant in Ruth 1:16–17." *CBQ* 69 (2007): 242–58.

Smith, W. Robertson. *Kinship and Marriage in Early Arabia*. Repr. ed. Boston: Beacon Press, 1903.

Southwood, Katherine E. "Will Naomi's Nation Be Ruth's Nation? Ethnic Translation as a Metaphor for Ruth's Assimilation within Judah." *Humanities* 3 (2014): 102–31.

Sparks, Kenton L. *Ethnicity and Identity in Ancient Israel: Prolegomena to the Study of Ethnic Sentiments and Their Expression in the Hebrew Bible*. Winona Lake, IN: Eisenbrauns, 1998.

Stager, Lawrence E. "The Archaeology of the Family in Ancient Israel." *BASOR* 260 (1985): 1–35.

Stansell, Gary. "The Gift in Ancient Israel." *Semeia* 87 (1999): 65–90.

Sternberg, Meir. *The Poetics of Biblical Narrative*. Bloomington: Indiana University Press, 1985.

Stone, Timothy J. *The Compilational History of the Megilloth: Canon, Contoured Intertextuality and Meaning in the Writings*. FAT. Tübingen: Mohr Siebeck, 2013.

———. "Six Measures of Barley: Seed Symbolism in Ruth." *JSOT* 38 (2013): 189–99.

Sun, Chloe. "Ruth and Esther: Negotiable Space in Christopher Wright's *The Mission of God*?" *Missiology* 46 (2018): 150–61.

Suriano, Matthew J. "Death, Disinheritance, and Job's Kinsman-Redeemer." *JBL* 129 (2010): 49–66.

Swete, Henry B. *An Introduction to the Old Testament in Greek, Appendix Containing the Letter of Aristeas*. Edited by Henry St. J. Thackeray. New York: Ktav, 1968.

Thambyrajah, Jonathan A. "When Is a Moabite Not a Moabite? Ethnicity in the Book of Ruth." *JSOT* 46 (2021): 44–63.

Thomas, Nancy J. "Weaving the Words: The Book of Ruth as Missiologically Effective Communication." *Missiology* 30 (2002): 155–70.

Thompson, Thomas, and Dorothy Thompson. "Some Legal Problems in the Book of Ruth." *VT* 18 (1968): 79–99.

Tigay, Jeffrey H. *Deuteronomy*. JPS Torah Commentary. Philadelphia: Jewish Publication Society, 1996.

Tov, Emanuel. "The Aramaic, Syriac, and Latin Translations of Hebrew Scripture vis-à-vis the Masoretic Text." Pages 82–94 in *Textual Criticism of the Hebrew Bible, Qumran, Septuagint: Collected Essays*. Leiden: Brill, 2015.

# BIBLIOGRAPHY

———. *Textual Criticism of the Hebrew Bible*. 3rd ed. Minneapolis: Fortress, 2012.

Triandis, Harry C. "Individualism and Collectivism." Pages 35–50 in *The Handbook of Culture and Psychology*. Edited by David R. Matsumoto. Oxford: Oxford University Press, 2001.

Trible, Phyllis. *God and the Rhetoric of Sexuality*. Philadelphia: Fortress, 1978.

———. "A Human Comedy: The Book of Ruth." Pages 161–90 in vol. 2 of *Literary Interpretations of Biblical Narratives*. Edited by Kenneth R. R. Gros Louis and James S. Ackerman. Nashville: Abingdon, 1982.

Tucker, Gene M. "Witnesses and 'Dates' in Israelite Contracts." *CBQ* 28 (1966): 42–45.

Tully, Eric J. "The Character of the Peshitta Version of Ruth." *BT* 70 (2019): 184–206.

Ulrich, Eugene. *The Biblical Qumran Scrolls: Transcriptions and Textual Variants*. VTSup 134. Leiden: Brill, 2010.

Van der Merwe, Christo H. J., Jackie A. Naudé, and Jan H. Kroeze. *A Biblical Hebrew Reference Grammar*. 2nd ed. London: Bloomsbury T&T Clark, 2017.

Vanhoozer, Kevin J. *The Drama of Doctrine: A Canonical-Linguistic Approach to Christian Theology*. Louisville: Westminster John Knox, 2005.

Vesco, Jean-Luc. "La date du livre de Ruth." *RB* 74 (1967): 235–47.

Viberg, Åke. *Symbols of Law: A Contextual Analysis of Legal Symbolic Acts in the Old Testament*. ConBOT 34. Stockholm: Almquist & Wiksell International, 1992.

Waard, J. de. "Translation Techniques Used by the Greek Translators of Ruth." *Bib* 54 (1973): 499–515.

Waard, Jan de, and Eugene A. Nida. *A Handbook on the Book of Ruth*. 2nd ed., UBS Handbook Series. New York: United Bible Societies, 1992.

Walker, Robert, and Grace Bantebya-Kyomuhendo. *The Shame of Poverty*. Oxford: Oxford University Press, 2014.

Wallace, Constance. "*WM-* in Nehemiah 5:11." Page 31 in *Eblaitica: Essays on the Ebla Archives and Eblaite Language*. Edited by Cyrus H. Gordon, Gary A. Rendsburg, and Nathan H. Winter. Winona Lake, IN: Eisenbrauns, 1987.

Wardlaw, Terrance R., Jr. "Shaddai, Providence, and the Narrative Structure of Ruth." *JETS* 58 (2015): 31–41.

Webb, Barry G. *The Book of Judges*. NICOT. Grand Rapids: Eerdmans, 2012.

———. *Five Festal Garments: Christian Reflections on the Song of Songs, Ruth, Lamentations, Ecclesiastes, Esther*. NSBT. Leicester: Apollos, 2000.

———. *Judges and Ruth: God in Chaos*. Wheaton, IL: Crossway, 2015.

Wechsler, Michael G. "Peshitta: Ruth." Pages 409–13 in *The Hebrew Bible*. Edited by Armin Lange and Emanuel Tov. Leiden: Brill, 2017.

Weinfeld, Moshe. "Ruth, Book of." Pages 518–22 in *Encyclopaedia Judaica*. Jerusalem: Keter Publishing House, 1996.

Weis, Richard D. "Biblia Hebraica Quinta and the Making of Critical Editions

xxxi

of the Hebrew Bible." *TC: A Journal of Biblical Textual Criticism* 7 (2002), http://www.jbtc.org/v07/Weis2002.html.

Weiss, David H. "The Use of *qnh* in Connection with Marriage." *HTR* 57 (1964): 244–48.

Wenham, Gordon J. *Genesis 1–15*. WBC 1. Waco, TX: Word Books, 1987.

———. *Story as Torah: Reading the Old Testament Ethically*. Edinburgh: T&T Clark, 2000.

West, Mona. "Ruth." Pages 190–94 in *The Queer Bible Commentary*. Edited by Deryn Guest. London: SCM, 2006.

Westbrook, Raymond. *Property and Family in Biblical Laws*. JSOTSup 113. Sheffield: Sheffield Academic, 1991.

Wetter, Anne-Mareike. *"On Her Account": Reconfiguring Israel in Ruth, Esther, and Judith*. LHBOTS 623. New York: Bloomsbury T&T Clark, 2015.

Whedbee, J. William. *The Bible and the Comic Vision*. Cambridge: Cambridge University Press, 1998.

Wilch, John R. *Ruth: A Theological Exposition of Sacred Scripture*. Concordia Commentary. St. Louis: Concordia Publishing House, 2006.

Williamson, Paul R. *Sealed with an Oath: Covenant in God's Unfolding Purpose*. NSBT. Downers Grove, IL: InterVarsity, 2007.

Willis, Timothy M. *The Elders of the City: A Study of the Elders-Laws in Deuteronomy*. Atlanta: SBL, 2001.

Wilson, Lindsay. "Job." Pages 148–56 in *Theological Interpretation of the Old Testament: A Book-by-Book Survey*. Edited by Kevin J. Vanhoozer, Craig G. Bartholomew, and Daniel J. Treier. Grand Rapids: Baker, 2008.

Wilson, Robert R. *Genealogy and History in the Biblical World*. YNER 7. New Haven: Yale University Press, 1977.

Witzenrath, H. H. *Das Buch Rut: Eine literaturwissenschaftliche Untersuchung*. Munich: Kösel, 1975.

Wright, Christopher J. H. *Deuteronomy*. NIBCOT 4. Peabody, MA: Hendrickson, 1996.

———. "Implications of Conversion in the Old Testament and the New." *International Bulletin of Missionary Research* 28 (2004): 14–19.

———. *The Mission of God: Unlocking the Bible's Grand Narrative*. Downers Grove, IL: InterVarsity, 2006.

Wright, N. T. "How Can the Bible Be Authoritative?" *Vox Evangelica* 21 (1991): 7–29.

Wu, Daniel. *Honor, Shame, and Guilt: Social-Scientific Approaches to the Book of Ezekiel*. BBRSup 14. Winona Lake, IN: Eisenbrauns, 2016.

Würthwein, Ernst. *Die Fünf Megilloth*. 2nd ed., HAT 18. Tübingen: Mohr, 1969.

Yamasaki, Gary. *Perspective Criticism: Point of View and Evaluative Guidance in Biblical Narrative*. Eugene, OR: Cascade, 2012.

## BIBLIOGRAPHY

Young, Ian, and Robert Rezetko. *Historical Linguistics and Biblical Hebrew.* ANEM 9. Atlanta: SBL Press, 2014.

Young, Ian, Robert Rezetko, and Martin Ehrensvärd. *Linguistic Dating of Biblical Texts.* Vol. 1, *An Introduction to Approaches and Problems.* London: Equinox, 2008.

Younger, K. Lawson. *Judges and Ruth.* NIV Application Commentary. Grand Rapids: Zondervan, 2002.

Zakovitch, Yair. *Das Buch Rut: Ein jüdischer Kommentar.* Translated by Andreas Lehnardt. SBS 177. Stuttgart: Katholisches Bibelwerk, 1999.

Zenger, Erich. *Das Buch Ruth.* ZBK 8. Zürich: Theologischer Verlag, 1986.

Zevit, Ziony. "Dating Ruth: Legal, Linguistic and Historical Observations." *ZAW* 117 (2005): 574–600.

Ziegert, Carsten. "Das Buch Ruth in der Septuaginta als Modell für eine integrative Übersetzungstechnik." *Bib* 89 (2008): 221–51.

Ziegler, Yael. *Promises to Keep: The Oath in Biblical Narrative.* Leiden: Brill, 2008.

———. "'So Shall God Do . . .': Variations of an Oath Formula and Its Literary Meaning." *JBL* 126 (2007): 59–81.

Zimmerli, Walther. *I Am Yahweh.* Translated by Douglas W. Stott. Atlanta: John Knox, 1982.

# Introduction

The book of Ruth is a remarkable book, aptly named after its remarkable main character. The book has the same title in both the Greek and Hebrew canonical traditions and may be further described as remarkable in at least three ways. First, the central character is actually Naomi, not Ruth.[1] The book depicts Naomi's crisis, moving from emptiness (1:21) to fullness (4:17), and all other characters are described in relation to her.[2] But it is Ruth who captures the audience's[3] interest. She features in every scene except that at the city gate (4:1–12), where she is the subject of conversation. The narrative traces the reversal of Naomi's hopeless situation, but the reversal takes place through the extraordinary loyalty and initiative of Ruth. Although the narrative presents Naomi's perspective, the audience is always aware of Ruth and more interested in what happens to her. This makes Ruth the main character in the narrative and Naomi the central character (the main character need not always be the central character). Second, the book is one of only two in the Old Testament named after a woman. This alerts us to the possibility that

---

1. Adele Berlin, *Poetics and Interpretation of Biblical Narrative* (Sheffield: Almond Press, 1983), 83–84; cf. André LaCocque, *Ruth*, trans. K. C. Hanson, CC (Minneapolis: Fortress, 2004), 6.

2. Naomi is named in reference to Elimelech in 1:2, but this is reversed in 1:3. Similarly, the sons are described as Elimelech's sons in 1:2, but then as Naomi's sons/children in 1:3, 5. Orpah and Ruth are described as Naomi's daughters-in-law (1:6–8), Boaz is described in reference to Naomi (2:1), and the son of Boaz and Ruth is "born for Naomi" (4:17).

3. In this commentary, I will use the broader term "audience" rather than "readers" because: (1) for ancient people, reading was an aural experience, with texts read orally rather than silently, even in private; (2) in the ancient world, many were not literate and most did not have their own copies of texts; and (3) Ruth was read orally at the Festival of Weeks (Shavuoth). Cf. Gary A. Rendsburg, *How the Bible Is Written* (Peabody, MA: Hendrickson, 2019), 25–29; Daniel I. Block, *Ruth: A Discourse Analysis of the Hebrew Bible* (Grand Rapids: Zondervan, 2015), 29n1.

# INTRODUCTION

it depicts a woman's story from a woman's perspective. Third, not only is the book named after a woman, but she is also a non-Israelite woman. As it is the only Old Testament book named after a non-Israelite, we are sensitized to how she will act and how the Bethlehemite community will respond.

## I. STRUCTURE AND MESSAGE

In the Ruth narrative, time, location, and the introduction of new characters are the structural indicators. Events are presented in a chronologically linear fashion. There are a few flashbacks, e.g., Naomi's summary of her life (1:20–21), Ruth's review of her day and night (2:19–21; 3:16–17), and Boaz's highlighting of Ruth's loyal actions (2:11–12; 3:10). These short flashbacks serve to advance the linear development of the plot. The location of events is also presented linearly. The audience focuses on one event with one set of characters; another event does not occur concurrently in a different location.[4] Even God's breaking of the famine in Bethlehem, which occurs while Naomi is in Moab, is introduced by a report of her present action in the narrative (1:6).

Although the plot is chronologically linear, the book of Ruth evidences a chiastic structure:[5]

Act 1: Death and emptiness (1:1–22)

    A  The end of a family line in Moab (1:1–6)
        B  En route: Naomi, Orpah, and Ruth dialogue (1:7–19a)
            C  Town gate: Naomi laments before the townswomen (1:19b–22)

---

4. The exception is when Boaz goes to the town gate while the narrative focuses on the widows (3:18–4:1).

5. See especially Stephen Bertman, "Symmetrical Design in the Book of Ruth," *JBL* 84 (1965): 167; Shimon Bar-Efrat, "Some Observations on the Analysis of Structure in Biblical Narrative," *VT* 30 (1980): 156–57; Bezalel Porten, "The Scroll of Ruth: A Rhetorical Study," *Gratz College Annual* 7 (1978): 23–49. With slight variations, a chiastic structure is accepted by, inter alios, Tod Linafelt and Timothy K. Beal, *Ruth & Esther*, Berit Olam (Collegeville, MN: Liturgical Press, 1999), xxi; Kirsten Nielsen, *Ruth: A Commentary*, trans. Edward Broadbridge, OTL (Louisville: Westminster John Knox, 1997), 1–2; Murray D. Gow, *The Book of Ruth: Its Structure, Theme and Purpose* (Leicester: Apollos, 1992), 91–93; A. Boyd Luter and Barry C. Davis, *Ruth and Esther: God Behind the Seen* (Fearn: Christian Focus, 1995), 21; Jonathan Grossman, *Ruth: Bridges and Boundaries* (Bern: Peter Lang, 2015), 26–27; Robert L. Hubbard and J. Andrew Dearman, *Introducing the Old Testament* (Grand Rapids: Eerdmans, 2018), 152. For a survey of proposed structures of the book of Ruth, see Marjo C. A. Korpel, *The Structure of the Book of Ruth*, Pericope 2 (Assen: Van Gorcum, 2001), 1–30.

## STRUCTURE AND MESSAGE

Act 2: Seeking short-term security (2:1–23)

> D  Home: Naomi accepts Ruth's plan (2:1–3)
>> E  Boaz's field: Encounter between Ruth and Boaz (2:4–17)
>>> F  Home: Naomi and Ruth debrief (2:18–23)

Act 3: Seeking permanent security (3:1–18)

>>> F'  Home: Ruth accepts Naomi's plan (3:1–5)
>> E'  Threshing floor: Encounter between Ruth and Boaz (3:6–15)
> D'  Home: Naomi and Ruth debrief (3:16–18)[6]

Act 4: Redemption and fullness (4:1–22)

> C'  Town gate: Boaz redeems before the elders (4:1–12)
B'  Home: Naomi and the women dialogue (4:13–17)
A'  The beginning of a royal line in Israel (4:18–22)

The narrative is artfully structured.[7] The four chapters correspond to the four acts of the plot, with each act composed of three scenes.[8] Each of the four acts has a sense of completion and forward momentum. By the end of the third scene of each act, there is some resolution to the issues raised in the first scene, yet there is also an anticipation of the action in the next act. This structure gives the audience the impression that there is order amid the tragedy, that things are not spiraling out of control. Perhaps we can detect a divine hand at work to send both famine and redemption.[9]

The narrative has a symmetrical structure: acts 2 and 3 are in parallel and are enveloped by acts 1 and 4. Act 1 begins and ends in Bethlehem (vv. 1, 19), but most of the act describes events taking place outside the promised land. Three deaths occur in Elimelech's line in approximately ten years in Moab (1:1–5) and are balanced by the ten-generation genealogy that begins

---

6. Act 3 could be structured as D'-E'-F' but the current structure also takes into account plot progression.

7. The specific structural details of each scene are presented at the beginning of the relevant sections in the commentary.

8. The present-day chapter divisions are those provided by Stephen Langton (1150–1228), who annotated the Latin Vulgate; see Beryl Smalley, *The Study of the Bible in the Middle Ages* (Oxford: Basil Blackwell, 1952), 221–24.

9. Cf. Nielsen, *Ruth*, 5.

3

# INTRODUCTION

with Perez and continues Elimelech's line down to King David (4:18–22).[10] Act 1 mentions the direct intervention of God in breaking the famine (1:6), which is balanced by his causing Ruth to conceive in act 4 (4:13), the only other mention of his direct intervention. The deceased Mahlon and Chilion did not fulfill their responsibilities as husbands and sons (1:4–5, 11–13), but Boaz steps in to resurrect their name and their family line, and to become the husband of Mahlon's widow (4:9–10, 13–17). The departure of one of the minor characters in the first act, Orpah (1:14), parallels the departure of another minor character, the nearer kinsman, in the last act (4:8). In both instances, the minor characters function as foils, illuminating the virtue of the main characters. In act 1, Orpah initially continues with Naomi and Ruth but finally desists and departs; in act 4, the nearer kinsman-redeemer is initially willing to redeem but then reneges and withdraws. In both acts there is a chorus of townswomen: they express their astonishment when Naomi enters Bethlehem (1:19), and in act 4 they utter words of blessing and consolation (4:14–15). The first and last acts are also enveloped by historical markers: the narrative begins with reference to the time of the judges (1:1)[11] and ends with a reference to the time of the kings (4:17, 22). Naomi becomes the central character after the death of her husband (1:3), and she is present throughout act 1. Most of the events of act 4 focus on Boaz, although he was nudged into action by Naomi and Ruth, and he acts on behalf of them. They are absent at the town gate, but Boaz and the nearer kinsman-redeemer negotiate a solution for them. Since Naomi is the central character of the narrative, the women of Bethlehem proclaim the significance of the newborn son for her (4:14–17).

The two central panes of the chiasm (acts 2 and 3) comprise parallel scenes based on location and conversation partners. Both start with Naomi and Ruth conversing at home (2:1–3; 3:1–5), then Ruth interacts with Boaz outside the town, in his domains (2:4–17; 3:6–15), and finish with Naomi and Ruth conversing at home again (2:18–23; 3:16–18). Although Naomi is the central character of the narrative, the central acts focus on Ruth and what happens to her. The parallel scenes highlight some contrasts. At the beginning of act 2, Ruth takes the initiative by making a request and Naomi consents, while in act 3, the roles are reversed (2:2; 3:1–5). The central scene of act 2 occurs during the day, with the interaction between Boaz and Ruth witnessed by others. The corresponding scene of act 3 takes place at night,

---

10. The unity of composition of the book of Ruth has not been seriously under question; for a discussion of two proposals for composite origin from earlier stories, see Frederic W. Bush, *Ruth, Esther*, WBC 9 (Dallas: Word Books, 1996), 10–12. The only debate about unity is whether the closing genealogy (4:18–22) is original or a secondary addition. For discussion and references, see the introductory comments for 4:18–22.

11. For a discussion of the historical background of this period, see Barry G. Webb, *The Book of Judges*, NICOT (Grand Rapids: Eerdmans, 2012), 10–15.

4

STRUCTURE AND MESSAGE

with no other witnesses. The field is buzzing with gleaners; the floor is quiet and intimate. In both acts, Boaz initiates the conversation by asking about the woman's identity (2:5; 3:9). In both, Ruth takes the posture of a client or supplicant, bowing down before Boaz (2:10) or lying down at his feet (3:7–8). In act 2, her request of this patron is made indirectly through the harvest overseer (2:7), while in act 3, she makes it directly (3:9). In both acts, Boaz attends to the well-being of Ruth. In act 2, he protects her from the male field workers (2:15–16) and provides her with abundant grain. In act 3, he is concerned that no one sees her with him at the threshing floor (3:14). He responds to her requests with acts of kindness, which bring her physical and emotional relief. In act 2, his acts of generosity go beyond the requirements of the law, yet in act 3, he is careful not to transgress the legal requirements by planning to offer redemption to the nearer kinsman-redeemer first (3:12–13). And in both acts, Ruth returns to Naomi with grain from Boaz (2:18; 3:15–17). In act 3, however, the grain is accompanied by a message from Boaz: the gift of barley is a symbol guaranteeing that Boaz will keep his word. The focus on Ruth in these acts highlights the indispensable role she plays in reversing Naomi's emptiness.

The narrative plot pivots on the pair of scenes at the center of the narrative (F-F'), both of which focus on the words of the narrative's central character, Naomi. In the first, Ruth debriefs with Naomi at home after Ruth's first day of gleaning (2:18–23). Ruth shares what she had brought back from the field, and when she reveals that she gleaned in Boaz's field, Naomi is rejuvenated. In Naomi's speech in the center of the scene, she prays a benediction on him and details his significance for her and Ruth—"he is one of our kinsman-redeemers" (2:20). Naomi's recognition of God's hand now extended for her good, instead of against her for her ill, forms the major turning point of the Ruth narrative. With this renewed hope, Naomi is transformed from bitter and withdrawn to revived and resourceful. And it is her threshing floor scheme that forms the second half of the double pivot (3:1–5). This scene, the secondary turning point, also occurs at Naomi and Ruth's home, as Naomi seeks to maximize the potential of the relationship formed between Ruth and Boaz during the harvest season. She devises a risky scheme for Ruth to "find rest" in Boaz's household.

This structure highlights human initiative at the core of the narrative, but two mentions of God's activity bookend the narrative action (1:6; 4:13). The reversals for Naomi (and also Ruth, Boaz, and the nation of Israel) are ultimately guided by God's hand, although his hand is mostly hidden. However, the characters' chatter about God and prayers to him throughout the narrative ensure that the audience does not forget his role in the proceedings.

The chiastic structure also highlights the reversals in the Ruth narrative. The reversals include death to life, childless widowhood to marriage and family, threatened extinction to the kingdom, exclusion to belonging, and shame to honor. This last reversal plot is a theme common to many narratives in the Bible. As a U-shaped pattern of status reversal, it is found in biblical narratives from Adam and Eve to Joseph, Moses, Saul and David, Daniel, Esther, Job, and the life and parables of Jesus, to name a few.[12] We can graph the U-shaped plot pattern in the Ruth narrative following Naomi as the central character:[13]

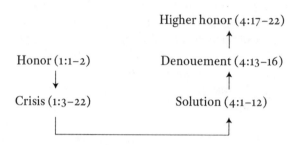

*Honor* (1:1–2). Despite the famine in the land of Israel, Naomi begins in a state of honor as a married woman with two sons. When viewed in the context of other narratives with a similar plot pattern, we can understand Naomi's state as a sign of God's favor.

*Crisis* (1:3–22). Naomi's family leaving the promised land triggers a crisis, with her husband then her two sons dying while in Moab. She is plunged into suffering the double shame of widowhood and poverty. Her life itself is

---

12. Adapted from Timothy S. Laniak, *Shame and Honor in the Book of Esther*, SBLDS 165 (Atlanta: Scholars Press, 1998), 7–15. His analysis focuses on the plot pattern of "challenge and honor," with an innocent victim of injustice through insult or attack, in contrast to the plot pattern of "guilt and reconciliation." But he notes that in the "challenge and honor" plot pattern, the victim is not always innocent (p. 9 n. 18). Examples include the book of Lamentations, which despairs over the punishment for Israel's sin. Daniel, Nehemiah, and Judith repent over national sin, although their personal stories also follow the same plot pattern. In biblical texts and reality, guilt and shame are not so easily separated; see Daniel Wu, *Honor, Shame, and Guilt: Social-Scientific Approaches to the Book of Ezekiel*, BBRSup 14 (Winona Lake, IN: Eisenbrauns, 2016). This allows for the possibility of guilt at the beginning of the Ruth narrative.

13. Such a U-shaped plot has similarities with the classic definition of "comedy," which typically focuses on ordinary people and moves from harmony to tragedy to celebration and reintegration. For an examination of how comedy is used in the Old Testament, see J. William Whedbee, *The Bible and the Comic Vision* (Cambridge: Cambridge University Press, 1998). Works viewing the book of Ruth as comedy include Phyllis Trible, "A Human Comedy: The Book of Ruth," in *Literary Interpretations of Biblical Narratives*, ed. Kenneth R. R. Gros Louis and James S. Ackerman (Nashville: Abingdon, 1982), 2:161–90; Judy Fentress-Williams, *Ruth* (Nashville: Abingdon, 2012).

at risk, but so is the line of her deceased husband. Upon her return to Bethlehem, she is "empty" and laments that she has lost God's favor. Indeed, she views him as her adversary.

*Reversal* (2:1–3:18). Naomi's return to her homeland triggers a reversal of her fortunes. The narrative hints that God is orchestrating his redemption of Naomi through "chance" events and the kindness of human actors. Ruth and Boaz—an unlikely pair of a lowly foreigner and an esteemed landowner— are instrumental in moving Naomi from poverty and shame to the brink of security and honor.

*Solution* (4:1–12). The nearer kinsman-redeemer gives up his right to redeem the land and marry Ruth, opening the way for Boaz to do so. He declares his determination to continue Elimelech's family line.

*Denouement* (4:13–16). Boaz marries Ruth, and God blesses them with a son. The initial crises are resolved. Elimelech's line is continued through Obed, and Naomi's emptiness is filled—she has a "son" and ongoing provision and protection as part of a new family. She basks in the respect of the women of the town, who praise the roles of God and Ruth in Naomi's regained fulfillment and status.

*Higher honor* (4:17–22). The "son" who continues Elimelech's line is not just known in Bethlehem but becomes famous in all Israel. For he is the forebear of Israel's greatest king. From the humble mother of Mahlon and Chilion, Naomi is exalted as an ancestor of King David. A family line on life support ends up producing the greatest Israelite king. Naomi's shame has been reversed to honor—but not only hers, also that of the nation of Israel.[14] This dual reversal has important implications for the purpose of the book (see section below, "Purpose").

This plot pattern—prevalent in many biblical narratives—reveals a concern for honor and shame in ancient Israelite society. These core values relate to a person's social standing within a community.[15] Honor is publicly acknowledged worth, while shame is a claim to worth that is publicly denied. Honor is primarily a group value, whereby an individual shares in the group's honor. Kinship groups inherit honor from honorable ancestors, which is maintained and defended in the current generation. Males achieve honor in public contests, while females maintain honor through privacy and integrity (personal and sexual). Parents command respect and obedience (Exod 20:12; Deut 21:18–21; Prov 30:17). Threats to family honor are taken seriously, leading to strong disapproval (e.g., the curse against Ham/Canaan; Gen 9:20–27)

---

14. In this sense, the U-shaped plot pattern can be viewed here as J-shaped.

15. For a summary, see Joseph Plevnik and John J. Pilch, "Honor and Shame," in *Handbook of Biblical Social Values*, ed. John J. Pilch and Bruce J. Malina (Eugene, OR: Cascade, 2016), 89–96.

INTRODUCTION

and sometimes to acts of vengeance (e.g., against Shechem; Gen 34). Ancient Near Eastern culture was collectivist, in which the social standing and well-being of the group (rather than the individual) were of the greatest impor-tance.[16] This commentary will use honor-shame dynamics to throw light on how the ancient audience would have understood elements of the narrative, such as widowhood, patronage, the nature of Naomi's threshing floor plan, and the significance of the closing genealogy.

## II. GENRE

The significance of identifying the genre of a literary work is in providing the audience guidelines for understanding the work. Different genres provoke interpretive expectations in an audience, including the nature of the reality that is conveyed and the meaning of the narrative (overall and particular elements of it).[17] The book of Ruth is a narrative, although scholars have suggested various classifications for the type of narrative. Gunkel has been influential in his description of Ruth as a "novella," developed out of folktales and saga.[18] He also described it as an "idyll," a term followed by Würthwein, which he defined as a "striving for an ideal and innocent state,"[19] with the implication of fictionality. Similarly, Sasson describes Ruth as "folkloristic," originating as a written composition modeled after oral "folk-tales."[20] Based on this genre, he argues that the book of Ruth need not be "burdened . . . by a historical background" and minimizes the religious importance of the work.[21] However, identification of genre finds a firmer grounding in form and content rather than origin and atmosphere.

---

16. For an overview of collectivism and individualism, see Harry C. Triandis, "Individual-ism and Collectivism," in *The Handbook of Culture and Psychology*, ed. David R. Matsumoto (Oxford: Oxford University Press, 2001), 35–50.

17. The genre-bound nature of understanding is a version of the hermeneutical circle: the whole is understood through its parts, the parts are understood through the whole; E. D. Hirsch, *Validity in Interpretation* (New Haven: Yale University Press, 1967), 68–77.

18. Hermann Gunkel, "Ruth," in *Reden und Aufsätze* (Göttingen: Vandenhoeck und Ruprecht, 1913), 85.

19. Hermann Gunkel, "Ruth," in *Religion in Geschichte und Gegenwart* (Tübingen: J. C. B. Mohr, 1930), 4:2181; Ernst Würthwein, *Die Fünf Megilloth*, 2nd ed., HAT 18 (Tübingen: Mohr, 1969), 4. Also Yair Zakovitch, *Das Buch Rut: Ein jüdischer Kommentar*, trans. Andreas Lehnardt, SBS 177 (Stuttgart: Katholisches Bibelwerk, 1999), 11–12.

20. Jack M. Sasson, *Ruth: A New Translation with a Philological Commentary and a Formalist-Folklorist Interpretation*, 2nd ed. (Sheffield: JSOT Press, 1989), 214–15.

21. Sasson, *Ruth*, 217, 221, 249.

# GENRE

Genre involves a grouping of literary works based on form (structure), mode, and content.[22] Yet genre is fluid because, although based on literary traditions, each author writes in a new context for a new audience, and thus genres can develop. For the sake of clarity, we can use definitions from modern literary studies to identify the genre of the book of Ruth. A "tale" is a written or spoken narrative in prose or verse. If written, it may be in the tone of voice of someone speaking.[23] It is short, moving quickly from problem to resolution. It lacks complications or subplots and focuses on an event rather than characterization. A "novella" is a fictional narrative usually restricted to a single event or situation or conflict, which produces suspense and leads to an unexpected turning point and surprising conclusion.[24] It is longer and more complex than a tale and develops the nature of situations or characters. A short story is similar to a novella in that it focuses on a single situation, but it is shorter and generally has fewer characters.[25] And, according to W. Humphreys, a short story *reveals* rather than *develops* the quality of characters or situations. In a short story, characters do not evolve with changing situations, but different situations reveal the quality of each character.[26]

Based on these definitions from modern literary studies together with the above analysis of the structure and content of the book of Ruth, it is best categorized as a short story. It is more complex than a tale since it contains complications. It is similar to a novella in that it focuses on one main situation or conflict (emptiness and shame of Naomi), and it contains unexpected turning points (2:20; 3:1–4) and a surprising conclusion (Obed is a forefather of King David; 4:17–22). Although there is some development in the characters of Naomi, Boaz, and Ruth,[27] the narrative primarily *reveals* their character and presents them as models of kindness.[28] On balance, the brevity of the Ruth narrative and its relative simplicity tip its classification toward short story rather than novella.

---

22. J. A. Cuddon, *A Dictionary of Literary Terms and Literary Theory*, 5th ed. (Oxford: Wiley-Blackwell, 2013), 298–99. Generic classifications are organized in different ways. Mode is associated with method, manner, and style; Cuddon, *Dictionary*, 441.

23. Cuddon, *Dictionary*, 710.

24. Cuddon, *Dictionary*, 480.

25. Cuddon, *Dictionary*, 653.

26. W. Humphreys, "Novella," in *Saga, Legend, Tale, Novella, Fable: Narrative Forms in Old Testament Literature*, ed. George W. Coats, JSOTSup 35 (Sheffield: JSOT Press, 1985), 84–85.

27. See Berlin, *Poetics*, 83–86; Kristin M. Saxegaard, *Character Complexity in the Book of Ruth*, FAT II (Tübingen: Mohr Siebeck, 2010), 16–18.

28. For an extended discussion of the main characters as exemplary figures, see Bush, *Ruth, Esther*, 42–46.

INTRODUCTION

While modern genre definitions provide a general classification, it is methodologically preferable to determine the genre of the book of Ruth by comparing it to ancient rather than modern texts. Campbell finds broad similarities in language, literary structure, and theme among the narratives of the Pentateuch, the books of Joshua, Judges, Samuel, Kings, and Ruth.[29] More specifically, he finds other "short stories" similar to the Ruth narrative: the story of Isaac and Rebekah (Gen 24), the account of Judah and Tamar (Gen 38), the Joseph cycle (Gen 37–50), episodes in Judges (e.g., Ehud-Eglon, 3:15–29), scenes in the court history of David (2 Sam 9–20), and the prose frame of Job (1–2; 42:7–17).[30] Campbell calls these "Hebrew historical short stories," a new literary category originating in the judges period. He outlines their four characteristics: (1) a distinct literary style with elevated prose and semi-poetic elements; (2) an interest in typical people and mundane affairs; (3) an entertaining and instructive purpose; and (4) a creative and artistic flair.[31]

As an Old Testament short story, the Ruth narrative has at least two distinctive features. First, although dialogue is common in biblical narratives, Ruth has an unusually high proportion compared to narration. Direct speech is found in fifty-nine of eighty-five verses, which gives the narrative a sense of immediacy and ambiguity. Speech and events reported in the third person by the reliable narrator carries authority, but direct speech allows for the questioning of the motivations of the speaker.[32] To take one example, does Naomi tell her daughters-in-law to return to Moab (1:8–9) because she is concerned for their well-being or because she is concerned for her reputation if she returned to Judah with a foreigner in tow? Second, unlike other narratives (e.g., Gen 11:27–32; 25:19–26), the genealogy concludes rather than introduces the narrative.[33] From a literary perspective, this location maintains suspense, allows the audience to suspend judgment on the book's purpose, fills in narrative gaps, and highlights the wider significance of the narrative.[34] The author has adapted the genealogy for his purposes.

Unlike the tale or novella, the short story allows for the historicity of the narrative. Short stories do not depend on historicity, and most short stories are fictional. Yet, the book of Ruth can be considered historical because it

---

29. Edward F. Campbell, *Ruth*, AB 7 (Garden City: Doubleday, 1975), 5, following Jacob M. Myers, *The Linguistic and Literary Form of the Book of Ruth* (Leiden: Brill, 1955), 4.

30. Campbell, *Ruth*, 5. From these examples, we see a range in what constitutes "short."

31. Campbell, *Ruth*, 5–6.

32. For further information on dialogue and narrative, see Robert Alter, *The Art of Biblical Narrative* (New York: Basic Books, 1981), 63–87.

33. On the originality of the genealogy to the narrative, see the section "Structure and Message" and commentary at 4:18–22.

34. For details, see comment on 4:22.

# GENRE

attempts to represent the past. It is intentionally referential. The narrative begins and ends with indications of its historical setting—the time of the judges (1:1) and the time of David (4:17–22). Within these bookends, there are no literary features that suggest the book of Ruth should be classified as poetry or drama or prophecy or parable. The events described have a historiographic quality. Its description of events is consistent with what is known of life in ancient Israel: a famine driving a family from Judah to Moab (1:1), the levirate customs and the responsibilities of a kinsman-redeemer, the burial customs of the Israelites (1:17), the layout of the Bethlehem town gate and the legal process there (4:1–12), the location of the threshing floor, the harvest times, and the specification of weights and measures.[35] The names of the characters are consistent with contemporaneous names in the second millennium BC (1:2, 4). The social relationships (mother- and daughter-in-law, landowner and workers, husband and wife, grandmother and grandson) and interactions (e.g., Naomi with townswomen, natives with a foreigner) are also consistent with those expected in ancient Israel.[36] The narratorial aside of 4:7 reinforces the historical character of the narrative. And it seems unlikely that the writer would have invented the idea that David descended from a Moabite.[37] Thus, we can consider the book of Ruth as a work of history.[38]

The book of Ruth should be interpreted as a historiographical document, crafted with literary artistry and weighted with ethical and theological implications. It is "historiographic" because it is selective writing about "history"—events from the past. Historiography allows for an artistic representation of the past,[39] such as we find in the Ruth narrative. It is weighted with implications because the author has selected particular events and shaped them into a narrative to communicate a message to a later audience. That is, he is not simply recording history, but has a purpose for doing so—to challenge the views of his audience. In short, the book of Ruth is a historical narrative or narrated history,[40] and, as part of Scripture, continues to challenge us ethically and theologically.

---

35. Campbell, *Ruth*, 10.

36. Block, *Discourse*, 37.

37. Campbell, *Ruth*, 169. Matthew's inclusion of Ruth in the genealogy of Jesus (Matt 1:1–17) supports her historicity.

38. For more on the historical period, see Robert D. Miller II, "The Judges and the Early Iron Age," in *Ancient Israel's History: An Introduction to Issues and Sources*, ed. Bill T. Arnold and Richard S. Hess (Grand Rapids: Baker Academic, 2014), 165–89.

39. V. Philips Long, *The Art of Biblical History* (Leicester: Apollos, 1994), 63.

40. David G. Firth, *Joshua*, EBTC (Bellingham: Lexham Academic, 2021), 23, argues for "narrated history" because of the priority of the narrated element.

Introduction

# III. AUTHORSHIP AND DATE

## A. AUTHORSHIP

The book of Ruth does not identify the author. The Talmud attributed it to Samuel, but this is unlikely since he was dead by the time David became king. The prophet Nathan has been suggested, and his membership of the royal court makes this suggestion more likely, but still uncertain. Based on the female perspective in the book, some have argued that it was written by a female, such as Tamar, the daughter of David. However, a female perspective does not necessitate a female author, and female authorship was rare in the ancient Near East. Other scholars assign the book of Ruth's composition to a general historical period without positing a specific author. In short, there is not enough evidence to name an author.

## B. DATE OF COMPOSITION

Since authorship cannot be determined, when it was written is a matter for exploration based on the text.[41] The historical setting of the narrative is the time of the judges, but internal evidence reveals that the book was written, or at least edited, at a later time. The mention of "the days when the judges ruled" (1:1) implies that the era of the judges already lay in the past. The narrator's explanation of the sandal custom (4:7) indicates that the custom had changed or was no longer current, so a considerable amount of time had passed since the institution of the custom found in Deuteronomy 25. The mention of David (4:17, 22) provides the earliest time for the composition of Ruth. The lack of explanation of who David is suggests that the book was composed after he was well known, but how much longer is unknown. The following two historical periods are the most likely.[42]

### A Postexilic Date

The main reasons scholars date the book of Ruth to the postexilic period include:

---

41. Material from this section has been adapted and expanded from Peter H. W. Lau, *Identity and Ethics in the Book of Ruth: A Social Identity Approach*, BZAW 416 (Berlin: de Gruyter, 2011), 44–52.

42. An exilic date of composition is possible, but this period has rightly only gained a few proponents.

## AUTHORSHIP AND DATE

(1)     the alleged Aramaisms and Late Biblical Hebrew (LBH) forms,

(2)     the legal customs reflecting a time when the customs were obsolete or required explanation,[43]

(3)     the similarity between the genealogy (4:18–22) and the "priestly" genealogies of the Pentateuch and Chronicles (e.g., 1 Chr 2:3–15),

(4)     the favorable portrayal of the Moabite Ruth, which is thought to balance the ethnocentrism of postexilic texts, especially Ezra and Nehemiah,[44]

(5)     the allusion to a postexilic "Deuteronomic" edition of the book of Judges (1:1),[45]

(6)     the canonical placement of Ruth among the Writings, based on the assumption that these were collected after the prophetic collection had been completed,[46] and

(7)     the suitability of the theme of outward/homeward journey with the experience of the exile.[47]

Within the postexilic period of dating, there are differences of opinion. Although most argue for an early postexilic date (fifth to fourth century BC) for the aforementioned reasons,[48] others argue for a later postexilic date. For example, Robert Gordis argues that the peaceful, idyllic tone presumes a period of relative tranquility and proposes a period between the "strife-ridden reforms" of Ezra/Nehemiah and the campaign of Alexander the Great.[49] The latest dating belongs to Erich Zenger, who views the final version of the book

---

43. For example, the explanation of the sandal custom (4:7) presupposes a time when the custom was no longer understood, and the difference in application of the levirate custom reflects either a reinterpretation or misunderstanding of the original custom. See Jean-Luc Vesco, "La date du livre de Ruth," *RB* 74 (1967): 242–43; LaCocque, *Ruth*, 18–21.

44. So, inter alios, Korpel, *Structure*, 230–33; Zakovitch, *Rut*, 38–41, 62–64; L. Daniel Hawk, *Ruth*, ApOTC (Nottingham: Apollos, 2015), 33–36.

45. Cf. Robert H. Pfeiffer, *Introduction to the Old Testament* (London: Adam and Charles Black, 1948), 718.

46. Cf. Peter T. Nash, "Ruth: An Exercise in Israelite Political Correctness or a Call to Proper Conversion?," in *The Pitcher Is Broken: Memorial Essays for Gösta W. Ahlström*, ed. Steven W. Holloway and Lowell K. Handy, JSOTSup 190 (Sheffield: Sheffield Academic Press, 1995), 350–51.

47. Christian Frevel, *Das Buch Rut*, Neuer Stuttgarter Kommentar: Altes Testament 6 (Stuttgart: Verlag Katholisches Bibelwerk, 1992), 34.

48. Ziony Zevit, "Dating Ruth: Legal, Linguistic and Historical Observations," *ZAW* 117 (2005): 576–94, tentatively suggests a postexilic date (525–500 BC) based on a combination of social, legal, and linguistic factors. Similarly, Tamara Cohn Eskenazi and Tikva Frymer-Kensky, *Ruth*, JPS Bible Commentary (Philadelphia: Jewish Publication Society, 2011), xvi–xix.

49. Robert Gordis, "Love, Marriage, and Business in the Book of Ruth: A Chapter in

INTRODUCTION

as belonging in the second century BC due to its alleged messianic aspect. He then proposes that the book promotes the Hasmoneans' political and religious ambitions.[50]

### A Monarchic Date

Influential among those who date the book of Ruth to the monarchic period is Edward Campbell, who proposes a date from about 950 to 700 BC.[51] His grounds for an earlier dating include similarities in genre and theological perspective to earlier stories such as the Joseph story in Genesis, the court history of David (2 Samuel), the book of Judges, and the account of Ahab (1 Kgs 22:1–36).[52] Campbell proposes that it was produced orally in the time of Solomon and written down in the ninth century BC, perhaps during the reign of Jehoshaphat.

Similar to the postexilic dating, there has been a wide range of proposals within the monarchic period. The earliest is a Davidic dating, based on the view that the book is a dynastic "apology" supporting David.[53] Robert Hubbard leans toward a Solomonic dating,[54] while Moshe Weinfeld suggests a Northern provenance during the time of Elisha.[55] Daniel Block accepts Weinfeld's Northern provenance but asserts a Josianic dating.[56] Jack Sasson, in looking for an appropriate setting for the glorification of David, also suggests a setting during the reign of Josiah.[57]

There is no consensus about Ruth's date of composition. Recent scholarship favors a postexilic date,[58] with a sizable minority holding a monarchic

---

Hebrew Customary Law," in *A Light unto My Path*, ed. Howard N. Bream, Ralph D. Heim and Carey A. Moore (Philadelphia: Temple University Press, 1974), 245–46.

50. Erich Zenger, *Das Buch Ruth*, ZBK 8 (Zürich: Theologischer Verlag, 1986), 28.

51. Campbell, *Ruth*, 24.

52. Campbell, *Ruth*, 23.

53. E.g., Gow, *Ruth*, 205–6. A defense of Davidic rule, however, does not necessarily have to be written during his reign; see Nielsen, *Ruth*, 28.

54. Robert L. Hubbard, *The Book of Ruth*, NICOT (Grand Rapids: Eerdmans, 1988), 34.

55. Moshe Weinfeld, "Ruth, Book of," in *Encyclopaedia Judaica* (Jerusalem: Keter Publishing House, 1996), 14:521–22.

56. Block, *Discourse*, 30–34.

57. Sasson, *Ruth*, 251.

58. In addition to those mentioned above, also, inter alios, Irmtraud Fischer, *Rut*, HTKAT (Freiburg: Herder, 2001), 86–91; Jeremy Schipper, *Ruth: A New Translation with Introduction and Commentary*, AB 7D (New Haven: Yale University Press, 2016), 20–22; Edward Allen Jones III, *Reading Ruth in the Restoration Period*, LHBOTS 604 (New York: Bloomsbury T&T Clark, 2016), 3–8; Kandy Queen-Sutherland, *Ruth and Esther* (Macon, GA: Smyth & Helwys, 2016), 33–35; Saxegaard, *Character*, 35–53.

AUTHORSHIP AND DATE

date.[59] Some commentators prefer either a late monarchic or early postexilic date,[60] while others leave the dating question open.[61] Complicating the dating is the possibility that the Ruth narrative could have circulated in oral form earlier (e.g., during the time of David) and was then written later.[62] The lack of consensus about dating mainly derives from the subjectivity of the arguments upon which dating is determined, and how much weight an interpreter places on each argument. Five main sets of arguments are usually adduced: (1) historical-chronological; (2) theological-ideological; (3) literary-stylistic; (4) social-scientific; and (5) linguistic-philological.

### *Historical-Chronological*

There are a few chronological hints in Ruth, but these can be interpreted differently. For example, the narrative is set "in the days when the judges ruled" (Ruth 1:1) and ends with a genealogy terminating with King David (Ruth 4:18–22). There is debate surrounding the significance of the concluding genealogy for the date of the book's composition, depending on whether it is viewed as original or a later gloss. Even among those who accept the genealogy as original, there is disagreement about which exact period it might point to.[63] It points to a time at least from the Davidic dynasty onward, but how far into the future? Murray Gow argues for a date during David's reign, while Marjo Korpel uses the setting in the time of the judges to argue for a

59. In addition to those mentioned above, also, inter alios, John R. Wilch, *Ruth: A Theological Exposition of Sacred Scripture*, Concordia Commentary (St. Louis: Concordia Publishing House, 2006), 15–16; Luter and Davis, *Ruth and Esther*, 14–16; Justin Jackson, "The One Who Returned: A Retrospective and Prospective Reading of Ruth," *JETS* 63 (2020): 436–38; Mary J. Evans, *Judges and Ruth*, TOTC (Downers Grove, IL: InterVarsity, 2017), 231–32.

60. K. Lawson Younger, *Judges and Ruth*, NIV Application Commentary (Grand Rapids: Zondervan, 2002); Carolyn Pressler, *Joshua, Judges, Ruth*, Westminster Bible Companion (Louisville: Westminster John Knox, 2002); Katharine D. Sakenfeld, *Ruth*, Interpretation (Louisville: John Knox Press, 1999), 1–5.

61. Eugene F. Roop, *Ruth, Jonah, Esther*, Believers Church Bible Commentary (Scottdale, PA: Herald, 2002); J. Gordon Harris, Cheryl A. Brown and Michael S. Moore, *Joshua, Judges, Ruth*, NIBCOT 5 (Peabody, MA: Hendrickson, 2000); Fentress-Williams, *Ruth*, 21–23; Jason Driesbach, *Ruth*, Cornerstone Biblical Commentary (Carol Stream, IL: Tyndale House, 2016), 497–500.

62. So, e.g., George S. Glanzman, "The Origin and Date of the Book of Ruth," *CBQ* 21 (1959): 201–7.

63. For a discussion regarding the originality of the genealogy, see, inter alios, LaCocque, *Ruth*, 8–14; Nielsen, *Ruth*, 21–28. Even if the genealogy is not original, the narrative would still end by mentioning King David (Ruth 4:17).

INTRODUCTION

postexilic date.[64] Or as Eric Rust argues, does the reference to judges mean that the author was familiar with the book of Judges in its final form?[65]

## Theological-Ideological

It is frequently argued that the ideology of Ruth is a strong indicator of its dating. In particular, its alleged universalist agenda points to a late date: although Ruth is a foreigner, she is nonetheless accepted into Israelite society and subsequently marries Boaz, an Israelite. This is most commonly viewed as propaganda against the Ezra-Nehemiah reforms banning exogamy.[66] However, this openness toward outsiders is used by Arndt Meinhold to argue for a pre-exilic date, and M. David for an exilic date.[67] Ronald Hals considers the theology of God's "hidden all-causality" as an outgrowth of the "Solomonic enlightenment."[68] At that time, there was a new humanism, and God appears more in the background of events. Yet this theology is also often attributed to the book of Esther, so this motif could support a Persian date.[69]

## Literary-Stylistic

The third methodological criterion, the literary characteristics of *Ruth*, is also open to interpretation. The peaceful, almost idyllic tone of the story prompts Leon Morris to assign an early monarchic date.[70] Yet this same feature prompts C. Goslinga to assign a Solomonic date, and Robert Gordis a postexilic date.[71] Dating has also been based on the similarities between Ruth

---

64. Gow, *Ruth*, 205–6; Korpel, *Structure*, 224–26.

65. Eric C. Rust, *Judges, Ruth, 1 & 2 Samuel* (London: SCM, 1961), 69. Rust seems to miss the point that the time of the judges may have been familiar to the implied reader without reference to a *book of* Judges. Other Old Testament books point to it being a well-known historical period (2 Sam 7:11; 2 Kgs 23:22; 1 Chr 17:6, 10).

66. See, inter alios, Zakovitch, *Rut*; LaCocque, *Ruth*.

67. Arndt Meinhold, "Theologische Schwerpunkte im Buch Ruth und ihr Gewicht für Datierung," *TZ* 32 (1976): 129–37; M. David, "The Date of the Book of Ruth," *OtSt* 1 (1942): 63.

68. Ronald M. Hals, *The Theology of the Book of Ruth* (Philadelphia: Fortress, 1969).

69. Cf. Susan Niditch, "Legends of Wise Heroes and Heroines," in *The Hebrew Bible and Its Modern Interpreters*, ed. Douglas A. Knight and Gene M. Tucker (Philadelphia: Fortress, 1985), 454.

70. Leon Morris, *Ruth: An Introduction and Commentary*, TOTC (Downers Grove, IL: InterVarsity, 1968), 239.

71. C. J. Goslinga, *Joshua, Judges, Ruth*, trans. Ray Togtman (Grand Rapids: Zondervan, 1986); Gordis, "Love," 246.

## AUTHORSHIP AND DATE

and other Old Testament "novellas" or "short stories." Edward Campbell compares Ruth to other novellas and suggests a monarchical date.[72] Kirsten Nielsen also proposes a date during the monarchy, but based on intertextuality, with allusions to the "patriarchal narratives."[73] In contrast, part of André LaCocque's argument for a postexilic date is based on his thesis that the main point of the book of Ruth is "ultimately a commentary on the Law."[74] So his dating for the book, in the same way as the other scholars mentioned, rests upon the dating of other texts. He assumes an exilic or postexilic dating for the prior texts, just as Campbell and Nielsen work from a premise of a monarchical dating for other "novellas."

### Social-Scientific

Viewing the book of Ruth through a social-scientific lens brings out certain emphases that can be used for dating. For instance, an application of social identity theory reveals that Ruth would have presented a message amid the social change due to external threat and the development of the monarchy.[75] Ruth would promote closer identification with kinship groups and present a message against gender stratification, a message especially pertinent during the time of Josiah's reforms. Ruth's message concerning foreigners, however, also resonates in the postexilic period, when the identity of God's people was placed under threat by the presence of non-Israelites.

### Linguistic-Philological

It is argued that the dating of Biblical Hebrew provides the most objective criterion to date the book. According to this approach, language must take precedence over historical and theological arguments.[76] Standard Biblical Hebrew (SBH) is understood to be pre-exilic, while LBH is postexilic, with the exile as a transitional period.[77] Frederic Bush has been influential among

72. Campbell, *Ruth*, 24.

73. Nielsen, *Ruth*, 12–17 *et passim*. These include women's stories dealing with infertility and triumph over it: Sarai and Hagar (Gen 16), Lot's daughters (Gen 19), Tamar (Gen 38).

74. LaCocque, *Ruth*, 19.

75. For the details of this paragraph, see Lau, *Identity and Ethics*, 145–90.

76. E.g., Avi Hurvitz, "Can Biblical Texts Be Dated Linguistically? Chronological Perspectives in the Historical Study of Biblical Hebrew," in *Congress Volume: Oslo 1998*, ed. André Lemaire and Magne Sæbø, VTSup 80 (Leiden: Brill, 2000), 144.

77. Major studies include Avi Hurvitz, *A Linguistic Study of the Relationship between the Priestly Source and the Book of Ezekiel*, CahRB 20 (Paris: Gabalda, 1982); Robert Polzin, *Late*

# INTRODUCTION

Ruth scholars in his analysis of the SBH and LBH features found in Ruth.[78] According to Bush, ten features are characteristic of SBH, and eight features are characteristic of LBH.[79] Based on these findings, he concludes the author lived no earlier than the transitional period between SBH and LBH, that is, the late pre-exilic to postexilic era. In his judgment, a date in the early postexilic period seems more likely.[80] Recent research, however, casts doubt on the assumptions behind this. Almost all the distinctive features of "Late" Biblical Hebrew are also attested in "Early" SBH texts.[81] Evidence both from parallel passages in the Masoretic Text and non-Masoretic biblical texts (e.g., from Qumran) demonstrates that individual linguistic peculiarities like those listed by Bush are highly unstable in textual transmission.[82] It is therefore methodologically unsound to argue that a few linguistic peculiarities in much later manuscripts allow us to establish the date of primary composition of the book of Ruth.

There are other possible explanations for the Aramaisms and other "late" features. They may reflect a regional dialect. Or the author used these linguistic features for literary effect. Unusual linguistic features of a character's speech can present the character as "foreign sounding." Also, unusual linguistic forms ("style shifting") can be used to present a character as from an older or younger generation or a higher or lower social class. In the book of Ruth, the majority of cases of style shifting are found in the speeches of Naomi and Boaz, with only one in the speech of Ruth.[83] Ruth is a foreigner but even on a linguistic level, the audience is encouraged to identify with her. Linguistic

---

*Biblical Hebrew: Toward an Historical Typology of Biblical Hebrew Prose*, HSM 12 (Missoula: Scholars Press, 1976); Mark F. Rooker, *Biblical Hebrew in Transition: The Language of the Book of Ezekiel*, JSOTSup 90 (Sheffield: JSOT Press, 1990).

78. Those who accept his findings in whole or in part, and its significance for dating include: Linafelt and Beal, *Ruth & Esther*; Victor H. Matthews, *Judges/Ruth*, NCBC (Cambridge: Cambridge University Press, 2004); Pressler, *Ruth*; Younger, *Judges and Ruth*; Sakenfeld, *Ruth*.

79. For details, see Bush, *Ruth, Esther*, 22–30.

80. Bush, *Ruth, Esther*, 30. Based on the same understanding of the linguistic development of Biblical Hebrew, Zevit also dates the book of Ruth to the early postexilic period; Zevit, "Dating Ruth," 592–93.

81. Ian Young, Robert Rezetko and Martin Ehrensvärd, *Linguistic Dating of Biblical Texts*, vol. 1, *An Introduction to Approaches and Problems* (London: Equinox, 2008), 111–19.

82. See, e.g., Ian Young and Robert Rezetko, *Historical Linguistics and Biblical Hebrew*, ANEM 9 (Atlanta: SBL Press, 2014), 145–210.

83. For ideas in the rest of this paragraph, I am indebted to Robert D. Holmstedt, *Ruth: A Handbook on the Hebrew Text* (Waco, TX: Baylor University Press, 2010), 46–49. On the use of less common language features for characterization in Ruth, see also Young, Rezetko and Ehrensvärd, *Linguistic Dating*, 190–93.

AUTHORSHIP AND DATE

features in the book of Ruth may be more useful for distinguishing characters than for determining the date of the book's composition.

## C. CONCLUSIONS REGARDING THE DATING OF THE BOOK OF RUTH

It is impossible to date the book of Ruth with absolute certainty due to the many variables and the required interpretation of the available evidence. Nonetheless, an evaluation of the evidence marginally favors a monarchic date.

An argument based on historical-chronological evidence requires a dating beyond the birth of David, but close enough to allow the readers to have familiarity with the circumstances and milieu of the period of the judges. It also requires enough time to pass for an explanation of the custom involving the sandal to be necessary.[84] Familiarity with the time of the judges suggests a monarchic provenance, with the explanation for the sandal custom suggesting a time from at least the early monarchy onward.

Ideological-theological and social-scientific evidence slightly favor a Persian date. The acceptance of Ruth as a foreigner into the people of God is significant because it is both a prominent theme in the book and one that is found relatively infrequently in Old Testament narrative. It thus suggests a concern during the time of the composition of Ruth. Although interaction with non-Israelites is present in accounts of both the monarchic and Persian periods, the closer interaction with foreigners in the Persian period (as found in Ezra-Nehemiah) is slightly in favor of a Persian origin for Ruth. Ruth's vow of allegiance to Yahweh (1:16), however, tempers the book of Ruth's relevance in the restoration period, since the issue was intermarriage with *non-believing* foreign women (Ezra 10; Neh 13:23–31).

Literary-stylistic evidence points to a monarchic date. Structurally, the closing genealogy is integral to the overall chiastic structure of Ruth, balancing the pseudo-genealogy that opens the book (1:1–5).[85] Narratologically, the final resolution of a plot is an important indicator of a narrative's theme. As such, the connection to David—in both the end of the plotline (4:17a) and the genealogy (4:18–22)—intimates a monarchic concern in general or a Davidic concern in particular. Within the monarchic period, some have suggested that the book of Ruth legitimized David's ancestry. This is possible, but against this understanding is the lack of specific evidence in the Old Tes-

---

84. Of course, this assumes that the explanation is part of the "original text." But if the note on the sandal is a later gloss, it tells us nothing about the date of the text.

85. See section above, "Structure and Message."

INTRODUCTION

tament that his Moabite strain was a concern. The only Moabite connections are when David left his parents in the care of the king of Moab (1 Sam 22:3–4) and when he executed two-thirds of the defeated Moabite army (2 Sam 8:2). Support for the Davidic line would be especially relevant during the turmoil following Solomon's death and the struggle to establish the legitimacy of the southern kingdom throughout the time of the divided monarchy. The promotion of David is also consistent with a nationalistic aim, as might be found, especially, in the time of Josiah.[86] Such reinforcement of the Davidic line is not as relevant in the Persian period, where the Davidic connection would represent a broader royalist hope.

It is impossible to determine a precise date for the composition of Ruth. The narrative's connection to David better fits a monarchic date, while the theme of acceptance of foreigners better fits a postexilic date. On balance, however, a date during the monarchy is more likely. The elevation of David aligns best with this era and is consistent with the book's primary purpose.

## IV. PURPOSE

The author and date of composition of the book of Ruth are not stated within the book, and neither is the purpose for which it was written. Nonetheless, how the Ruth narrative is written (structure, language, and literary features)[87] points to what it is trying to say (message; see "Structure and Message," above); here we consider the message and other factors to propose a purpose. As seen in the section above ("Date of Composition"), potential purposes are often intertwined with discussions about origin.[88] There can be an inherent circularity to this endeavor since the evidence is internal to the text: the book's alleged purpose is derived from assumptions about its dating and vice versa.[89] But dating does not need to be linked to purpose,

---

86. See Lau, *Identity and Ethics*, 157.

87. Language (e.g., sound, word play, imagery, and metaphor) and literary features (e.g., characterization, location, point of view, type-scenes) will be discussed throughout the commentary. For the application of this approach to Old Testament studies, see Alter, *Biblical Narrative*; Berlin, *Poetics*; Meir Sternberg, *The Poetics of Biblical Narrative* (Bloomington: Indiana University Press, 1985); Shimon Bar-Efrat, *Narrative Art in the Bible*, JSOTSup 70 (Sheffield: Almond Press, 1989).

88. Purpose and origin are not necessarily interdependent. For instance, dating the book to the postexilic period does not necessitate the conclusion that it was written to address the issue of foreign intermarriage; returnees faced other challenges, including the issue of the reinstitution of Davidic kingship.

89. Language and legal customs have been posited as "external" factors. The former was

PURPOSE

so a proposed purpose can be determined from the text even if the question of dating is left open.

Indeed, such a rich, multilayered narrative contains several themes and is likely to have multiple purposes, as evidenced by the range of suggestions identified by scholars:

(1) *To promote kindness.* Rabbi Zeira (*Midrash Ruth Rabbah* 2:14) comments that Ruth was written to teach about kindness and its great reward, a view adopted by several more recent scholars.[90] Bush, for instance, states that the "primary intention of the author is to present Ruth, Boaz, and Naomi as models . . . to emulate. They portray . . . what *ḥesed* looks like. . . ."[91] Kindness is a key theme in Ruth, but the structure of the narrative suggests that it is not the primary purpose. Instead, the theme of kindness seems to reinforce another purpose found in the narrative.

(2) *To encourage observance of the law, especially levirate marriage and redemption.*[92] Scholars debate whether the Ruth narrative deals with a genuine case of levirate marriage, but even if we accept its presence, the narrative assumes its presence rather than argue the case for its performance. Donald Leggett suggests that the role of the kinsman-redeemer is of "paramount importance within the book."[93] While the application of the law is a theme in the Ruth narrative, it is best to view it as supporting the book's purpose instead of motivation for writing it.

(3) *To provide a justification for the Davidic right to rule.* In this view, the narrative presents Ruth as a worthy forebear of David despite her Moabite ancestry[94] or, more generally, as a glorification of David through his ancestors.[95] Yet, there is no evidence in Old Testament texts that suggests that David's non-Israelite blood was a concern,

---

shown to be unreliable for the origin of the book of Ruth, and the latter is itself based on assumptions about the dating of Pentateuchal legal texts.

90. E.g., Paul Humbert, "Art et leçon de l'historie de Ruth," *RTP* 26 (1938): 285–86 (faithfulness, loyalty); Ellen F. Davis, "'All That You Say I Will Do': A Sermon on the Book of Ruth," in *Scrolls of Love: Reading Ruth and the Song of Songs*, ed. Peter S. Hawkins and Lesleigh Cushing Stahlberg (New York: Fordham University Press, 2006), 6–8.

91. Bush, *Ruth, Esther*, 52.

92. See John Gray, *Joshua, Judges, Ruth*, NCBC (Grand Rapids: Eerdmans, 1986), 370–71.

93. Donald A. Leggett, *The Levirate and* Goel *Institutions in the Old Testament* (Cherry Hill, NJ: Mack, 1974), 172.

94. See esp. Gow, *Ruth*, 120–39.

95. E.g., Werner Dommershausen, "Leitwortstil in der Ruthrolle," in *Theologie im Wandel*, ed. Johannes Neumann and Joseph Ratzinger (Munich-Freiberg: Wewel, 1967), 394;

INTRODUCTION

and there are other texts that reinforce David's divine election (esp.
1 Sam 16). The story does elevate David, but it seems unlikely this
was the primary purpose.

(4)   *To present a polemic against opposition to ethnic inter-marriages in
the time of Ezra-Nehemiah (Ezra 9–10; Neh 13).* This is the current
view of the majority of scholars, based on the emphasis on Ruth's
Moabite status, and the tracing of her acceptance into the Israelite
community and final acceptance as a forebear of King David. Four
factors, however, weaken this view. First, the ban on intermarriage
in Ezra-Nehemiah was against non-believing foreign women. Ruth
is an exceptional foreign woman because she commits to Israel's
God (1:16–17; alluded to by Boaz in 2:12). Ruth's foreignness remains an element in the narrative, but her commitment to Yahweh
takes the sting out of the anti-marriage polemic. Second, the Ruth
narrative can be read to reflect a critical stance of intermarriage.
The deaths of Mahlon and Chilion are unexplained, but might their
deaths (and their childless marriages) be correlated to their marriage to Moabite women? Such a reading is by no means certain, but
it seems unlikely that the author would juxtapose their marriage and
death if the aim was to legitimize such marriages.[96] Third, the character of Naomi drives the plot, not Ruth, and the structure of the
narrative points to other, more prominent concerns and purposes
(see sections "Structure and Message" and "Themes"). Fourth,
the gentle tone of the story lacks a disputatious edge which, while
not ruling out a polemical purpose, reduces its likelihood. If this
were the purpose, the author does not reinforce his point at the
most opportune point in the narrative—when the nearer kinsman-
redeemer declines to marry Ruth (4:6).[97] His reason was to avoid
impairing his inheritance, not because of Ruth's ethnicity. Nonetheless, Ruth's acceptance into Israelite society despite her ethnicity
is an important theme in the narrative, which explores the basis
of her acceptance and its impact on Israelite identity (see section
below, "Themes").

These four main proposed purposes focus on specific themes but do not
encapsulate the message and themes in the book of Ruth. In what follows,
I will present an alternative reading of the book of Ruth. I will propose a

---

Paul Joüon, *Ruth: Commentaire philologique et exégétique* (Rome: Pontifical Biblical Institute, 1924), 2.

96. Grossman, *Ruth*, 17.

97. Hubbard, *Ruth*, 36.

# PURPOSE

primary purpose and tie it to a secondary purpose, with the aim of unifying the multiple themes of the narrative. The Ruth narrative can be read in relation to the house of David, and its primary purpose was to present the providential preservation of the family that produced King David. There are three bases to this position.[98]

The first basis is the message of the Ruth narrative. Although narratives are subtle and open to different interpretations, it is possible to determine the message through an analysis of how the narrative is shaped. The end of a narrative transforms how an audience understands it as a whole, for a narrative's content and action lead up to its finale.[99] The uncovering of the link to David at the end of the Ruth narrative (4:17–22) requires the audience to reconsider the narrative and to discover what might have been missed on first hearing. And we can derive primary and secondary meanings from the prominence given to features of a narrative.[100] As discussed above (in "Structure and Message"), the plot focuses on Naomi as the central character and the filling of her emptiness (1:21). Yet the denouement directs our attention beyond Naomi, to Obed and ultimately King David (4:17). The resolution and denouement of a narrative are important indicators of the theme, in this case pointing to the Davidic connections of the narrative.[101] Sakenfeld acknowledges David's foregrounding in the narrative but views it as "the storyteller's means of legitimizing an inclusive attitude towards foreigners."[102] Similarly, Hawk views the Davidic connection as a historical reminder, "a powerful vehicle for countering the reformers' exclusivist hermeneutic and ideology."[103] Yet this underplays the Davidic connection. As Adele Berlin comments, the link "tends to elevate the status of the story as much as the story tends to elevate David."[104] It connects the Ruth narrative to the wider Israelite narrative story line.

The second basis is the genealogical material in 4:17b–22, which forges an explicit link between the family history of the book of Ruth and David. Scholars often reject the originality of the genealogy, with the verses seen

---

98. The following has been adapted from Peter H. W. Lau and Gregory Goswell, *Unceasing Kindness: A Biblical Theology of Ruth*, NSBT (Downers Grove, IL: InterVarsity, 2016), 22–35.

99. Jonathan E. Dyck, *The Theocratic Ideology of the Chronicler* (Leiden: Brill, 1998), 77–78.

100. Bush, *Ruth, Esther*, 48, who follows John Beekman, John Callow and Michael F. Kopesec, *The Semantic Structure of Written Communication* (Dallas: Summer Institute of Linguistics, 1981), 135–37.

101. For a discussion of acceptance of foreigners, see "Themes."

102. Sakenfeld, *Ruth*, 4.

103. Hawk, *Ruth*, 39.

104. Berlin, *Poetics*, 110.

INTRODUCTION

as an appendix to the narrative.[105] But the chiastic structure of the book requires a "family history" to balance what is found at the beginning (1:1–5).[106] All the other genealogies in the Bible introduce a story rather than conclude it, so its placement at the end of the narrative suggests that it is not complete.[107] Rather, it points forward to the life of David (in the books of Samuel). Moreover, Perez, the ancestral head, is common to both 4:12 and the genealogy (4:18), which implies the genealogy sits naturally in the context and was presumably tailored to fit the narrative. The genealogy thus links the Ruth narrative with the main narrative of the Old Testament (Primary History, Genesis–Kings). Kingship is a major theme of this larger narrative and is mentioned in the refrain found in chapters before the Ruth narrative, "In those days there was no king in Israel" ( Judg 17:6; 18:1; 19:1; 21:25 ESV). The name Perez connects back to the patriarchal narratives (esp. Gen 38) and forward to David (whose last years are recorded in 1 Kgs 1–2). Thus, the genealogical material in Ruth 4:17b–22 shows the wider significance of the narrative.[108]

The third basis is the literary connections between the opening of the Ruth narrative and the later history of David. The beginning of the Ruth narrative hints at the connection with the family of David since Elimelech and his family are "Ephrathites from Bethlehem" (Ruth 1:2), and David is the son of "an Ephrathite of Bethlehem" (1 Sam 17:12 ESV). The audience's suspicion of this link is confirmed at the end of the book (4:17–22). Similarly, the refuge sought by Elimelech and his family in Moab (1:1–5) is replicated when David leaves his parents in the safekeeping of the king of Moab (1 Sam 22:1–4). An earlier episode in the family's history foreshadows another in its most famous descendant. This is consistent with Israelite storytelling, in which typological parallels support a belief in the providential ordering of history (e.g., the description of Abram's Egyptian sojourn and exodus; Gen 12:10–13:1).[109] Each of these inner-biblical links in isolation might not be convincing, but the cumulative effect of these links in the opening of the book of Ruth invites the audience to seek other connections with the later history of David.[110]

---

105. For further discussion and references, see commentary on 4:18–22.

106. See section above, "Structure and Message."

107. Tod Linafelt, *Ruth*, Berit Olam (Collegeville, MN: Liturgical Press, 1999), xx.

108. See also the comments on 4:11–12, 14–15, 17b–22.

109. See Umberto Cassuto, *A Commentary on the Book of Genesis: Part II, From Noah to Abraham, Genesis VI 9–XI 32, with an Appendix: A Fragment of Part III* ( Jerusalem: Magnes Press, 1974), 334–37.

110. Linafelt, *Ruth*, xxi–xxiv, identifies a parallel between the chiastic structure of the book of Ruth and the central section of the story of David (2 Sam 5:13–8:18). See also Yitzhak Berger, "Ruth and the David-Bathsheba Story: Allusions and Contrasts," *JSOT* 33 (2009):

## PURPOSE

God's direct involvement is stated by the narrator only once (4:13), but God's name is repeatedly on the lips of the characters,[111] which creates an expectation that God will act to remedy problems or reward right behavior. One feature of the Ruth narrative is how the main characters act as God's agents in fulfilling his purposes. Naomi asks God to provide "rest" for her daughters-in-law (1:9), but later she seeks "rest" for Ruth (3:1). Boaz calls on God to recompense Ruth as one who has taken refuge under God's "wings" (2:12), but later Ruth calls on Boaz to act as God's agent by spreading his "wings" over her (3:9). God's kindness toward the family (2:20) is shown partly by Ruth's kindness in thinking of the family's needs by seeking marriage with Boaz (3:10). Significantly, these instances of human characters as divine agents (3:1, 9, 10) are found in the lead-up to the climactic scene of the book: the encounter between Ruth and Boaz on the threshing floor (3:6–15). Similarly, the rise of David to the throne in the books of Samuel is presented as providential (e.g., 1 Sam 16:13, 18; 18:12, 28). And the term "wing" is used in two important episodes concerning David's rise. Samuel turns Saul's tearing of the prophet's robe (15:27) into a prophetic sign: "Yahweh has torn the kingdom of Israel from you this day and has given it to a neighbor of yours" (15:28 ESV, adapted). When David cuts off the "corner" of Saul's robe, Saul acknowledges David's restraint as proof that David is more righteous than him and will inherit the kingdom (1 Sam 24). There are further connections between Ruth 3 and events in David's life. Ruth's self-reference as a "servant" is used by Abigail in her meeting with David (1 Sam 25:24–31), which also leads to marriage (25:42). And just as Boaz invokes a blessing on Ruth, so David blesses Abigail, whom he views as God's agent, since her initiative saves him from bloodguilt (25:32–34). Thus, both Ruth and Abigail play a vital role in securing the welfare of the Davidic house. The book of Ruth shows that divine providence (through human agents) was working on behalf of David through the lives of his ancestors.

Yet, the Ruth narrative's literary links with the patriarchal narratives show that divine providence was working even before David's immediate ancestors.[112] The explicit mention of Rachel, Leah, Perez, Judah, and Tamar (4:11–12) foreshadows Ruth's role in building up the house of Israel, like the matriarchs who gave birth to the twelve tribes of Israel. Boaz's house is compared to that of Perez, the son of Judah, whose birth is recalled with the mention of Tamar and Judah. The genealogy again recalls the descendants of Judah

---

433–52; Yitzhak Berger, "Ruth and Inner-Biblical Allusion: The Case of 1 Samuel 25," *JBL* 128 (2009): 253–72.

111. For further discussion of divine providence, see below, "Theological Messages."

112. I presume that the author of the book of Ruth narrative was aware of the patriarchal narratives, whether or not they were in a written form.

INTRODUCTION

between Perez and David (4:18–22), and the use of the *toledoth* formula ("these are the generations"), the only time it is found outside the Pentateuch, suggests that the Ruth narrative continues the story line from Genesis (Ruth 4:18; Gen 6:9; 10:1; 11:10, 27; 25:12, 19; 36:1, 9; 37:2; also Gen 2:4; Num 3:1), especially concerning the line of Judah.[113] There is also a host of allusions and parallels that recall the patriarchal narratives, including:[114]

(1) famine leading to a sojourn outside the promised land (Ruth 1:1; Gen 12:10; 26:1);

(2) childlessness threatening a family's survival (1:5; Gen 16–17; 25:21; 29:31; 30);

(3) a foreigner leaving their birthplace and ancestors to come to a place and people they did not know (1:16–17; 2:11; Gen 12:1–5);

(4) protection of the woman chosen to bear the son of destiny (2:8, 9, 22; Gen 12:17; 20:3, 6; 26:7–11);

(5) the betrothal type-scene (2:20; Gen 24);[115]

(6) female initiative overcoming male inaction to produce an heir (3:7–15; Gen 38);

(7) the buying of land as a result of death (4:3, 9; Gen 23; 33:19);

(8) the assimilation of foreign immigrants into their new homeland (2:10–12; 3:11; 4:10–13; Gen 14; 20; 21:22–34; 23; 26; 34);

(9) marriage to a foreigner leading to a ruling family (4:13, 17b–22; Gen 38; 41:45, 50–52; 48); and

(10) God's gift of conception providing the son of destiny (4:12, 13; Gen 21:1–2; 25:21; 29:31; 30:17, 22, 23; cf. 1 Sam 1:19–20; Judg 13).

These allusions and explicit mentions connect the Ruth narrative to the narratives of Abraham, Isaac, and Jacob, along with their wives and concubines. A historical and theological link is thereby drawn between the characters in Ruth and Israel's patriarchs and matriarchs. The same divine providence working in the lives of Israel's early ancestors is working in the family that leads to King David.[116]

Kindness is an important theme in the book of Ruth; for our present purposes, we focus on two aspects—the interaction between divine and human

113. For further discussion on the offspring/seed theme, see T. Desmond Alexander, "Seed," in *New Dictionary of Biblical Theology*, ed. Brian S. Rosner, Donald A. Carson, and Graeme Goldsworthy (Leicester: Inter-Varsity, 2000), 769–73; James McKeown, *Ruth*, The Two Horizons Old Testament Commentary (Grand Rapids: Eerdmans, 2015), 72–77.

114. Hubbard, *Ruth*, 40.

115. The mention of the mother's house also links Ruth with Rebekah (Ruth 1:8; Gen 24:28). The phrase "mother's house" only occurs elsewhere in Song 3:4 and 8:2.

116. Cf. Harold Fisch, "Ruth and the Structure of Covenant History," *VT* 32 (1982): 435.

# PURPOSE

kindness, and the theme's parallels with the life of David.[117] God is the ultimate source of kindness, not ceasing to bless the living and the dead (1:8; 2:20). He shows kindness through Orpah, Ruth, and Boaz, who imitate and live out God's kindness (1:8, 16–17; 2:11–12, 20; 3:10). The intertwining of divine and human kindness in Ruth 1:8–18 is similar to an episode in David's life. When he was leaving Jerusalem, he attempted to discourage a foreigner, Ittai the Gittite, from going with him (2 Sam 15:19–23).[118] David concludes his exhortation with "may Yahweh show kindness and faithfulness to you"[119] (v. 20), which recalls Naomi's words to her foreign daughters-in-law, "may Yahweh show kindness to you" (Ruth 1:8). And Ittai's response recalls Ruth's: both swear upon Yahweh; both pledge their allegiance to an Israelite in life or death (1:16–17; 2 Sam 15:21).[120] In the context of attempted leave-taking, David and Naomi both ask God to give what they cannot, but a foreigner affirms their commitment. There is also a close relationship between God's kindness and the Davidic covenant tradition. God promises he will not take away his kindness from David's son (2 Sam 7:15; cf. 22:51). Solomon said that God showed great kindness to David in giving him an heir to sit on his throne (1 Kgs 3:6; 2 Chr 1:8). Thus, the Ruth narrative can be understood as giving hope for the future of the Davidic house. David's ancestors experienced tragedies and dangers, yet God's kindness did not fail them. God's kindness will not fail the dynasty of David.

My proposed purpose of the book of Ruth finds support in the location of the book in the canonical orders. None of the canonical positions of the book of Ruth suggest *ancient readers* understood it as a critique of the restrictive views of intermarriage, whereas three of them assume a connection between the book and David.[121] In two of the Hebrew canonical orders, Ruth is placed before Psalms or between Proverbs and Song of Songs.[122] In these locations, the book functions as a biography of the psalmist David or presents Ruth as an embodiment of "a worthy woman" (Prov 31:10–31). The association of Proverbs and Song of Songs with Solomon also invites a reading of the Ruth narrative with an eye to its royal theme. In Greek canonical orders, Ruth is placed after Judges and before 1 Samuel. This placement links the book to its historical context, "in the days when the judges ruled" (Ruth 1:1). The town of Bethlehem links the book of Ruth to the end of Judges (17:8–9; 19:1–2) and 1 Samuel since it was the home of David (1 Sam 16:1–4). God's providence can

---

117. See below for further exploration of this theme, "Theological Messages."

118. Sakenfeld, *Ruth*, 24–25.

119. LXX; MT "May kindness and faithfulness be with you."

120. Eskenazi and Frymer-Kensky, *Ruth*, 18–19.

121. For further discussion on canonical placement, see section below, "Canonicity."

122. In the third, the book of Ruth is placed between Song of Songs and Lamentations. This arrangement follows the chronology of the liturgical year.

INTRODUCTION

be seen in his preservation of the Benjaminites (Judg 21), a family of Bethlehemites that eventually produces David (Ruth 4:5, 10, 18–22). Despite the variety in ordering in Greek lists of Old Testament books,[123] Genesis–Ruth is a group of eight books (Octateuch) and Ruth is always placed after (or joined to) Judges.[124] There are also connections between the Ruth narrative and the books of Samuel. In the Greek canon, the similar expressions about being better than seven/ten sons are only a dozen verses apart (Ruth 4:15 and 1 Sam 1:8).[125] The book of Ruth and the beginning of 1 Samuel cover the same transitional period between the judges and the monarchy.[126] In this canonical location, the Davidic house is presented as the answer to the turmoil in the time of the judges.

For these reasons, I propose that the primary purpose of the book of Ruth was *to present God's providence and kindness in preserving the family that produced King David.* As a narrative link between the judges and David and the monarchy,[127] the Ruth narrative shows how God acted to bring forth David even amid the religious, moral, and national degeneration of the time of the judges. This theological reading[128] of the book interprets it within the wider narrative of God's purposes for Israel, with divine providence and kindness upholding the Davidic dynasty for the benefit of wider Israel. Such a reading finds support in the Ruth narrative's message, the closing genealogy, and its literary links with the later history of David, especially key scenes in the Ruth narrative. Ancient readers, as reflected in the canonical placements of the book of Ruth, invite us to read the book in relation to David or the monarchy (esp. Solomon). And the connections of the Ruth narrative with the Genesis narratives extend the historical and theological continuity from the patriarchs to David's ancestors to David. The later history of the Davidic house is anticipated by the Ruth narrative's depiction of God's providence

123. P. Botte and P.-M. Bogaert, "Septante et versions grecques," in *Septante au Dictionnaire de la Bible*, ed. Pirot L. and A. Robert (Paris: Letouzey & Ané, 1996), 541–43.

124. Henry B. Swete, *An Introduction to the Old Testament in Greek, Appendix Containing the Letter of Aristeas*, ed. Henry St. J. Thackeray (New York: Ktav, 1968), 226–27.

125. David Jobling, "Ruth Finds a Home: Canon, Politics, Method," in *The New Literary Criticism and the Hebrew Bible*, ed. J. C. Exum and D. J. A. Clines, JSOTSup 143 (Sheffield: JSOT Press, 1993), 133–34.

126. Samuel is the last judge (1 Sam 7:15). For the transitional character of the book of Ruth, see Timothy J. Stone, *The Compilational History of the Megilloth: Canon, Contoured Intertextuality and Meaning in the Writings*, FAT (Tübingen: Mohr Siebeck, 2013), 119–30; Linafelt, *Ruth*, xviii–xxv.

127. See also Linafelt, *Ruth*, xvii–xxv; Block, *Discourse*, 38–40.

128. Cf. Alter, *Biblical Narrative*, 33: "The ancient Hebrew writers . . . seek through the process of narrative realization to reveal the enactment of God's purposes in historical events."

on behalf of the family that produced David and by its exploration of human and divine kindness in the lives of his ancestors.

This proposal of the Ruth narrative's primary purpose does not exclude other purposes. The prominence of the theme of kindness in the narrative serves to remind the audience of the importance of this virtue in the lives of God's people. For it is only as God's people (including their king) live such lives—as embodied by Ruth and Boaz—that Israel would find and continue to experience rest in the land. A concise purpose statement combining the primary purpose and the promotion of kindness would be: *God's unceasing providence and kindness encourage his people to follow a lifestyle of kindness.* This overall purpose statement incorporates and unifies the four proposed purpose statements mentioned above. A lifestyle of kindness involves loyalty, initiative, risk, generosity, and a liberal application of the law (esp. gleaning, levirate, redemption) for the sake of the needy and marginalized, including providing for widows and accepting (worthy) foreigners. Kindness in God's people reflects his character, and acts of kindness are one way God fulfills his purposes in the world. Theological and ethical purposes are inextricably intertwined.[129]

## V. CANONICITY

Both Jewish and Christian sources attest to the book of Ruth's secure canonical status. In the first century AD, Josephus (*Jewish Antiquities* 5.9.1–4) and New Testament authors (Matt 1:5; Luke 3:32) drew on its contents. A discussion in the Babylonian Talmud implies there was a question about the book's canonicity, where Rabbi Simeon ben Yohai (second century AD) is quoted to have said, "Ecclesiastes is among the matters on which the school of Shammai was more lenient and the School of Hillel more stringent, but [all agreed that] Ruth, Song of Songs, and Esther make the hands unclean [i.e., are canonical]" (b. Megillah 7a). Simeon appears to be affirming the book of Ruth's canonical status while acknowledging debate over Ecclesiastes.[130] And the fragments of the four manuscripts of Ruth found at Qumran attest to its importance within this community.

While the book's canonicity is widely accepted, its location in the canon has varied.

---

129. For an extended discussion, see below, "Theological Messages" and "Themes."

130. See Roger T. Beckwith, *The Old Testament Canon of the New Testament Church* (Grand Rapids: Eerdmans, 1985), 304–6.

## INTRODUCTION

| LXX | Babylonian Talmud (Baba Batra 14b) | MTᴬ and MTᴸ (Megilloth) | Medieval Manuscripts (Megilloth) |
|---|---|---|---|
| Judges | Ruth | Ruth | Song of Songs |
| Ruth | Psalms | Song of Songs | Ruth |
| 1 Samuel | Job | Ecclesiastes | Lamentations |
| | Proverbs | Lamentations | Ecclesiastes |
| | Ecclesiastes | Esther | Esther |
| | Song of Songs | | |
| | Lamentations | | |
| | Daniel | | |
| | Esther | | |
| | Ezra | | |
| | Chronicles | | |

These locations follow two traditions: the LXX, and Hebrew manuscripts. Despite much debate, there is no consensus about which tradition is original. It seems they arose from different elements of the Jewish community and probably coexisted.[131] The positioning of biblical books is a paratextual phenomenon that reflects varying perceptions and evaluations of *later generations of readers* (rather than the biblical authors). Hence, no one canonical position needs to be privileged above the others. Differing canonical positions make a difference to how we view and read the book of Ruth. The ordering of biblical books can highlight patterns and themes from which one can discern a central narrative story-line. Indeed, different canons of Scripture, Greek as well as Hebrew, can provide distinctive insights into the meaning of particular biblical books and Scripture as a whole.

In Hebrew canonical orders, Ruth is placed in the Writings, although in different locations. Some consider the Babylonian Talmud (B. Bat. 14b; sixth century AD) to be the earliest Hebrew Bible arrangement, although this cannot be proven.[132] It does not contain a Megilloth collection but instead places Ruth at the beginning of the Writings, immediately before the Psalms.[133] This is a fitting location, with David's genealogy leading directly to the Psalter, with which he is closely associated, especially Psalms 1 and 2, and Book One of the Psalter.[134] The book of Ruth thus functions as a prehistory of David. Two key words in Boaz's climactic statement of act 2 (Ruth 2:12)

131. For a recent discussion, see Timothy H. Lim, *The Formation of the Jewish Canon* (New Haven: Yale University Press, 2013).

132. E.g., Beckwith, *Canon*, 122–27, 154–66. See the discussion in Lau and Goswell, *Unceasing Kindness*, 55–58.

133. For the text, see Isidore Epstein, ed., *Baba Bathra: Hebrew-English Edition of the Babylonian Talmud* (London: Soncino Press, 1976).

134. Only two of the forty-one psalms (if Psalms 1 and 2 are considered one) in Book

# CANONICITY

find fuller elaboration in the Psalter.[135] First, Boaz's commendation of Ruth for "taking refuge" (*ḥāsâ*) in Yahweh parallels the portrayal of God helping her descendant David in his troubles (e.g., Pss 2:12; 5:12 [Eng. 11];[136] 17:7; 18:31[30]; 31:20[19]; 142:5–6[4–5]). Second, the metaphor of the protecting "wings" (*kanāpayim*) of Yahweh is found several times in the Psalter (17:8; 36:8[7]; 57:2[1]; 61:5[4]; 63:8[7]; 91:4). These two thematic links (finding refuge and protection in Yahweh) present Ruth as a model of piety of the Psalter. And the book of Ruth also anticipates the theology of divine "kindness" on display in the Psalter (esp. 18:51[50]; 21:8[7]; 100:5; 118:1–4; 136), as well as the movement from lament to praise.[137] Finally, the book's location at the beginning of the Writings also allows for it to be viewed as a prologue to Proverbs, Ecclesiastes, and Song of Songs, which are associated with David's son, Solomon.

The earliest extant Masoretic manuscripts, in the Ben Asher textual tradition (MT[A] [tenth century AD] and MT[L] [eleventh century AD], the latter the base text for *BHQ*), place Ruth first in the Megilloth, based on rabbinic understandings of authorship: Ruth (by Samuel), Song of Songs (young Solomon), Ecclesiastes (elderly Solomon), Lamentations (Jeremiah/exilic), and Esther (Persian period). In this canonical order, the Megilloth follow Proverbs, so Ruth follows immediately after the acrostic poem celebrating the "worthy woman" (Prov 31:10–31). Since Ruth is described as "a worthy woman" (Ruth 3:11), she can be viewed as an example of the ideal woman in Proverbs. Her husband is respected at the town gate (Prov 31:23; cf. Ruth 4:1–12), where she is praised (Prov 31:31; Ruth 3:11; cf. 4:11, 15). And although Ruth is compared to the matriarchs of Israel, unlike them, she is not described as "beautiful" (Sarai, Gen 12:11, 14; Rachel, 29:17). Her beauty is consistent with the proverbial ideal—industrious (e.g., Prov 31:15, 27; Ruth 2:2, 7, 17) to supply the needs of her household (Prov 31:15, 21; Ruth 2:18), taking initiative, and fearing Yahweh (Prov 31:30; cf. Ruth 1:16–17; 2:12).[138] The canonical location of the book of Ruth, immediately preceding

---

One are not associated with/attributed to David. Seventy-three psalmic titles directly link to David by the phrase "of David."

135. For elaboration on and references for ideas in the rest of this paragraph, see Lau and Goswell, *Unceasing Kindness*, 60–70.

136. Where English and Hebrew versification differ, the Hebrew will be given first with the English following in parentheses.

137. Just as the Psalter moves from individual lament to community praise, so does the Ruth narrative: a lamenting individual (Naomi; 1:20–21) to the rejoicing Bethlehemite community (those at the town gate, elders, women; 4:11–12, 14–15).

138. For further discussion of similarities and differences between Prov 31 and Ruth, and the themes highlighted by reading them as canonical conversation partners, see Lau and Goswell, *Unceasing Kindness*, 42–46.

# INTRODUCTION

the Song of Songs, brings to prominence certain motifs and themes.[139] Like Ruth, the woman in the Song is not passive; she actively seeks him out and is the first and main speaker in the Song. Also highlighted is the secretive nocturnal meeting of the man and the woman, and their wedding and consummation of their marriage (Ruth 4:10–13; Song 3:6–5:1). Both Ruth and the Song develop the picture of the virtuous and assertive woman pictured in Proverbs 31.[140] This canonical location brings out the romantic elements in the Ruth narrative and places more emphasis on the relationship between Ruth and Boaz than between Ruth and Naomi.

Medieval manuscripts, based on the Ben Hayyim textual tradition (sixteenth century AD) and used in modern Hebrew Bibles, place Ruth second in the Megilloth according to the chronology of the liturgical year: Song of Songs (Passover), Ruth (Shavuot/Feast of Weeks), Lamentations (Ninth of Ab), Ecclesiastes (Tabernacles), and Esther (Purim). The most likely reason for linking the book of Ruth to the Feast of Weeks is the thematic reference to the harvest. Naomi and Ruth return to Bethlehem at the beginning of the barley harvest (1:22), and Ruth gleans until the end of the barley and wheat harvests (2:23). The Feast of Weeks is a harvest festival (Exod 34:22), indicating the end of the harvest (Exod 23:16; Deut 16:9–12, 16), and celebrated fifty days after Passover (Lev 23:15–16). The book of Ruth also connects to the Feast of Weeks by the command to allow people to collect gleanings (Lev 23:22), which is placed directly after the regulations about the Feast of Weeks (23:15–21).[141] In another rabbinical tradition, the book of Ruth is also linked to the timing of the giving of the Torah (on the "third month"; Exod 19:1).[142] And just as Ruth sought protection under Yahweh's wings (Ruth 2:12), so did Israel when they accepted the Torah. The book can be viewed as celebrating the gift of the Torah by showing how to apply Yahweh's instructions in a life-promoting way.[143] Another rabbinic source links the book of Ruth with the death of David, who was thought to have died in the Feast of Weeks, on a Sabbath (*Midr. Ruth Rab.* 3:3).

In the LXX (ca. second century BC), Ruth is placed in the Former Prophets, between Judges and 1 Samuel. Josephus mentions twenty-two books for the Hebrew Bible (*Against Apion* 1.7–8), which suggests that Ruth was attached to Judges, just as Lamentations was to Jeremiah. The first clause of the Ruth narrative invites us to read it within the historical context of the judges.

---

139. Other links between the two books include the phrase "mother's house" (Ruth 1:8; Song 3:4; 8:2) and the dangers for a woman walking the streets at night (Ruth 3:2–3; cf. 3:13–14; Song 5:7).

140. Tremper Longman, *Song of Songs*, NICOT (Grand Rapids: Eerdmans, 2001), 2.

141. Zakovitch, *Rut*, 69.

142. Zakovitch, *Rut*, 70.

143. Fischer, *Rut*, 101.

## THE HEBREW TEXT

The book of Judges describes Israel's downward spiral, with the epilogue of the book ( Judg 17–21) representing a national nadir. Following directly after this despairing time, the book of Ruth is a welcome contrast. Although not without unrest and death, the Ruth narrative plays out in a gentler tone with a more peaceful mood. In place of spiritual disloyalty and anarchy, we find commitment and generosity, a heartfelt covenant loyalty. Mistreatment and violence against women are replaced with consideration and honor. The lack of a king ( Judg 17:6; 18:1; 19:1; 21:25) finds its solution by the end of the Ruth narrative (4:17–22). In short, Judges serves as a foil for the book of Ruth. In the Greek canonical order, the Ruth narrative also anticipates events in 1 Samuel. Ruth is connected to Hannah as the latter, through her offspring Samuel (the anointer of the first two kings), is also related to the coming monarchy (1 Sam 1–2). The marriage of Boaz and Ruth and the birth of a son thematically prepare for Elkanah and Hannah and their (at first) childless relationship. And in Hannah's prayer early in 1 Samuel, she predicts the coming king (2:10). Thus, in the LXX, the book of Ruth functions as a narrative and historical link between the books of Judges and Samuel.

The different canonical locations provide different insights into the book of Ruth. Three of the four locations predispose to readings in connection with David, each distinctive. All locations cast a different light on the book (just as it does to the books surrounding it), highlighting various elements and motifs, and producing a multilayered picture of the narrative.

## VI. THE HEBREW TEXT

This commentary translates Ruth from EBP I B 19a, the Leningrad Codex (MT[L]), as it appears in *BHQ*.[144] Dated to AD 1008, the MT[L] is the earliest known manuscript of the entire Hebrew Bible and is from the Ben Asher Masoretic scribal tradition.[145] The text of Ruth MT[L] is well preserved. There

---

144. I consulted the commentary on the critical apparatus in *BHQ* as well as *BHS*. For a comparison of the three scholarly editions of the Hebrew Bible in progress (*BHQ*, the Hebrew University Bible Project, and the Hebrew Bible: A Critical Edition [formerly the Oxford Hebrew Bible]), see Richard D. Weis, "Biblia Hebraica Quinta and the Making of Critical Editions of the Hebrew Bible," *TC: A Journal of Biblical Textual Criticism* 7 (2002), http://www.jbtc.org/v07/Weis2002.html. Weis describes the *BHQ* as a prescriptive critical edition of the collative type. Another Hebrew Bible project is in progress, *Mikra'ot Gedolot Haketer* (ed. Menachem Cohen). For more discussion on textual criticism, see Emanuel Tov, *Textual Criticism of the Hebrew Bible*, 3rd ed. (Minneapolis: Fortress, 2012).

145. For *BHQ*, two other Tiberian manuscripts have been collated, the Aleppo Codex (MT[A]), and Cambridge University Add. Ms. 1753 (MT[Y]). The Aleppo Codex (AD 930) is also in the Ben Asher stream but does not contain the complete Hebrew Bible.

# INTRODUCTION

are only a few spelling errors (e.g., 2:2, 10, 11; 3:9, 14). On the whole, I read with MT[L] *ketiv* and only occasionally with MT[L] *qere* (3:5, 9, 14, 17; 4:5). The only times I follow other versions against the MT[L] are 4:4 (*tigʾal* instead of *yigʾal*) and 4:20 (*śalmôn* for *śalmâ*; cf. v. 21). Although my translation is based on the MT[L], I also compare it with other versions, especially at points where the MT[L] was difficult to understand or translate. The versions were used to assist in determining the sense of the MT[L].

The Ruth material from Qumran is incomplete. The fragments of four Hebrew manuscripts include: 2QRuth[a] (ca. AD first century; 2:13–3:8; 4:3–4); 2QRuth[b] (ca. first century BC; 3:13–18); 4QRuth[a] (ca. 1st century BC; 1:1–12); and 4QRuth[b] (ca. AD first century; 1:1–6, 12–15).[146] They are without the vowels and accents of MT[L]. The MT[L] and Qumran material only differ at a few points, with only minor variations. For example, *margəlōtāw* for *margəlôtāô* (3:14; cf. *qere*) and *mâ* for *mî* (3:16). In my translation, I adopted the former but not the latter. Very rarely, there is an addition not found in other versions, e.g., *šm* in 3:15.

The Septuagint of Ruth (LXX; ca. second century BC) appears to be a literal Greek translation of the Hebrew antecedent to the MT.[147] The translation follows the Hebrew original, mostly verbatim, with even the style of the Hebrew replicated (2:7 is a possible exception).[148] Most differences seem to reflect the desire of the translator to produce a text easily understood by his audience. At some points, the LXX adds the name of the person in place of the pronoun, and it uses the name Abimelech instead of Elimelech. The short additions in the LXX, however, provide an insight into early interpretation of the Hebrew text. In this commentary, the LXX provides support for interpretations such as 4:7, which adds "and gave it to him," clarifying who takes off the shoe and who receives it. The LXX also commends the emendations listed above (4:4, 20).

Among the other versions, the Peshitta (Syr.; ca. AD second century), the Syrian translation, is a generally faithful rendering of the Hebrew text attested by MT[L].[149] Twice the length of MT[L], most adjustments simplify or clarify the text, although other changes present the translator's interpretation

---

146. See Eugene Ulrich, *The Biblical Qumran Scrolls: Transcriptions and Textual Variants*, VTSup 134 (Leiden: Brill, 2010), 735–38.

147. The Hebrew source text of LXX Ruth seems to be a form of the MT or a version very similar to it. See J. de Waard, "Translation Techniques Used by the Greek Translators of Ruth," *Bib* 54 (1973): 499–515; Eberhard Bons, "Die Septuaginta-Version des Buches Rut," *BZ* 42 (1998): 46–68.

148. Carsten Ziegert, "Das Buch Ruth in der Septuaginta als Modell für eine integrative Übersetzungstechnik," *Bib* 89 (2008): 221–51.

149. Michael G. Wechsler, "Peshitta: Ruth," in *The Hebrew Bible*, ed. Armin Lange and Emanuel Tov (Leiden: Brill, 2017), 411. The readings are sporadically consistent with LXX; e.g., it renders *šaʿar*, "gate," with "tribe" in 3:11 and 4:10 but not in 4:1, 11.

of the text.[150] For instance, it adds that the nearer kinsman-redeemer refuses to marry Ruth because of a lack of faith (4:5), and there appear to be attempts to avoid hints of impropriety between the characters (1:12; 3:4, 7, 8). The Old Latin (OL; originally ca. AD third century) is a translation from a late manuscript (ca. AD ninth century). Jerome's Latin translation of the Old Testament, the Vulgate (Vulg.; ca. AD fourth century), is a generally reliable witness of MT[L], and deviation from MT[L] is often consistent with LXX and Syr. (e.g., 1:6, 8, 21; 2:21). The Ruth Targum (Tg.; based on a manuscript dated to ca. AD twelfth century) is an Aramaic translation seemingly based on a version of the MT, with additions in a midrashic style.[151]

## VII. THEOLOGICAL MESSAGES

### A. NAMES OF GOD

God is mentioned by name twenty-three times in the Ruth narrative. In her bitter lament, Naomi twice refers to him as "Shaddai" (1:20–21). This name evokes ideas of God's power and justice and draws associations with Job's experience of God.[152] It is also the name used for God in the patriarchal narratives, and its use in the context of a threat to God's covenant promises to Abraham in those narratives is pertinent to the Ruth narrative. Ruth refers to him twice as *'ĕlōhîm*, "God," in her vow of allegiance (1:16). This generic name for God is appropriate for a foreigner, but in the next verse she uses *yhwh*, "Yahweh" (invoking the deity's proper name), in her self-imprecatory oath, thus indicating her personal acceptance of Israel's God. The only other time *'ĕlōhîm* is used of God is when Boaz calls him "the God of Israel" (2:12), but this is in apposition to "Yahweh," as he prays that God would bless this "foreigner" (see 2:10).[153] Indeed, in the rest of the narrative, the characters only refer to God as Yahweh, eighteen times spread throughout each of the acts of the Ruth narrative (1:6, 8–9, 13, 17, 21 [2×]; 2:4 [2×], 12–13, 20; 3:10, 13; 4:11–14). This is the personal, covenantal name of God, and its usage hints at a consciousness of his presence and activity in this community of faith, albeit in the background.

---

150. Eric J. Tully, "The Character of the Peshitta Version of Ruth," *BT* 70 (2019): 203.

151. Syr., Vulg., and Tg. reflect the MT[L]; Emanuel Tov, "The Aramaic, Syriac, and Latin Translations of Hebrew Scripture vis-à-vis the Masoretic Text," in *Textual Criticism of the Hebrew Bible, Qumran, Septuagint: Collected Essays* (Leiden: Brill, 2015), 82–94.

152. See comment on 1:20.

153. Ruth self-identifies as a "foreigner," but see the comments for 2:10.

INTRODUCTION

## B. GOD'S PROVIDENCE

Our analysis of the structure of the book of Ruth revealed that God's providence and human action (acts of kindness especially) are two of the central themes. Yet, unlike most Old Testament narratives, God's providence is mostly hidden: his actions are "in the shadows,"[154] he works "behind the seen"[155] or "scenes,"[156] his face is hidden.[157] He does not speak directly; he does not communicate through a messenger; he does not intervene in spectacular ways. Elimelech's name is ironic, but it portends a truth in the narrative: God is king. God's actions in the Ruth narrative are mostly implicit, but evidence for his presence can be found in at least two sources: the narrator and the main characters.[158]

The narrator only mentions God twice. In the first instance, God breaks the famine in Bethlehem. Strictly speaking, this is hearsay because the narrator reports that Naomi "heard in the territory of Moab that Yahweh had attended to his people by giving them food" (1:6). The narrator does not say explicitly that God broke the famine. That may be what we, as the audience, are led to understand, and probably what took place in reality. Yet, we are told that it is what Naomi *heard*. In contrast, the second mention of God's action is unequivocal: "And Yahweh *gave* [*wayyittēn*] her [Ruth] conception, and she bore a son" (4:13). There is an especially marked emphasis on God's direct intervention in this verse because the usual phrasing for a pregnancy is, "She conceived . . . and bore" (e.g., Gen 29:34–35; 30:19; 38:4) or "[God] opened her womb" (e.g., Gen 29:31; 30:22). There is a hint of the miraculous because she did not become pregnant in her ten-year marriage to Mahlon.[159] The throng at the town gate had wished that God would make (*yittēn*) Ruth fertile like the matriarchs (4:11), and here God responds to their prayer. If God's first stated action places him in the background, his second action in granting Ruth conception is emphasized to make sure it is not missed. God's two acts of giving fertility (1:6; 4:13) function as bookends, pointing to God's providential care over all activities in the narrative.

In addition to these two explicit actions of God are four implicit interventions dotted through the last three acts of the narrative. The clearest is

---

154. Campbell, *Ruth*, 28.

155. Luter and Davis, *Ruth and Esther*.

156. Katheryn P. Darr, *Far More Precious Than Jewels: Perspectives on Biblical Women* (Louisville: Westminster John Knox, 1991), 59. Cf. Bush, *Ruth, Esther*, 47: God's control over events in the world is "behind the scenes and in the shadows."

157. Eskenazi and Frymer-Kensky, *Ruth*, lii–liii. For God's hiddenness in Ruth, see, seminally, Hals, *Ruth*.

158. For a recent treatment of this theme, see Mark W. Elliott, *Providence: A Biblical, Historical, and Theological Account* (Grand Rapids: Baker Academic, 2020).

159. Cf. Block, *Discourse*, 232.

36

THEOLOGICAL MESSAGES

at the beginning of act 2, which sets up Boaz as a potential benefactor, and then Ruth "by chance came upon [*wayyiqer miqrehā*] the portion of the field belonging to Boaz" (2:3). From Ruth's perspective, this event might have seemed coincidental, and this is the surface idea portrayed to a reader. However, the event's juxtaposition with the earlier narratorial introduction of Boaz (2:1) points to God's hand in this apparent serendipity.[160] Two further interventions are signaled implicitly by the use of the particle *hinnēh*, "look," which draws attention to the arrival of the right person, at the right place, at the right time: Boaz (2:4) and the nearer kinsman-redeemer (4:1). The narrative sequence suggests divine appointment: Boaz was introduced just prior (2:1); and the nearer kinsman-redeemer was previously mentioned, along with an invocation of Yahweh's name (3:12–13). A single "coincidence" might not be significant, but it is harder to deny God's implicit intervention with three such events in the narrative. The final implicit divine intervention is Naomi's counsel to Ruth: "Sit tight . . . until you know how the matter falls out" (*yippōl dābār*; 3:18). The collocation of the words *nāpal* ("fall") and *dābār* ("matter, word, thing") elsewhere in the Old Testament in relation to God's superintending is suggestive of his intervention here.[161] God's actions might be unexpressed, but they are visible nonetheless.

While explicit mention of God's providence is scarce in the narrative, the audience is constantly reminded of him through the spoken words of the characters. Sometimes his providence is described as a bitter experience. In act 1, Naomi laments that the hand of Yahweh has gone out against her (1:13). She knows God's providence can bring blessing because she had just prayed for God to show kindness to her daughters-in-law by giving them security in the home of new husbands (1:8–9). Now she states that God's hand can also bring suffering.[162] That her complaint is addressed to her daughters-in-law rather than to God might reflect her sense of abandonment by God. When she arrives in Bethlehem, she again raises the issue of God's bitter providence: she says to the townswomen that God has brought her back "empty" and brought calamity upon her (1:21). Primarily, her sense of emptiness is because she has lost her husband and two sons, but this emptiness is most likely accentuated because she feels it is evidence that God has abandoned her. If blessing is associated with God's relational presence,[163] her deduction is sound. Upon hearing about God's visitation of his people by giving them food (1:6), she decided to return to the land of Israel, which signaled

---

160. Other biblical texts reinforce this understanding of *qārâ*; see comment on 2:3.

161. For biblical references and discussion, see comment on 3:18.

162. Cf. Job 2:10, "Shall we receive the good from God, and not the trouble?"

163. See J. Scott Duvall and J. Daniel Hays, *God's Relational Presence: The Cohesive Center of Biblical Theology* (Grand Rapids: Baker Academic, 2019), esp. 59–66.

INTRODUCTION

a turning back to Yahweh. Now that she has returned to Bethlehem, she has also returned to the sphere of God's blessing. Yet, her bitterness has led to blindness: she has not returned "empty" because her loyal daughter-in-law is standing beside her. And God is with her. As the narrator points out, Naomi and Ruth return "at the beginning of the barley harvest" (1:22). God has not abandoned her. He is not only with her people but also with Naomi—the provision of food is one tangible sign. In the Ruth narrative, God's providence is all-encompassing; it is found in both suffering and blessing.

It is the latter that predominates in the prayers of the characters, which are heard in each chapter of the Ruth narrative. These are not conventional prayers since they are not addressed to God directly in the second person. Instead, they are primarily addressed to other characters and refer to God in the third person. These expressions of thanksgiving and blessing can still be understood as prayers, not least because God—whose actions frame the narrative—can be presumed to have heard them.[164] In act 1, Naomi prays for her daughters-in-law in the first speech of the narrative (vv. 8–9). On the way to Bethlehem, she prays that God would grant husbands for these widows. In act 2, as Boaz arrives in his field, he says to his harvesters, "May Yahweh be with you," to which they reply, "May Yahweh bless you" (v. 4). The unique wording of his greeting draws attention to it, giving the audience pause to ponder its theological significance. Boaz prays that God will reward Ruth for her loyalty to Naomi (vv. 11–12), and at the end of the chapter Naomi blesses Boaz for his largesse (vv. 19, 20). In act 3, Boaz asks for God's blessing on Ruth for selecting him as a redeemer (v. 10). In act 4, the townspeople pray for fertility and prosperity for Ruth and Boaz (vv. 11–12). The women bless God for providing a redeemer and pray that his name be perpetuated and that he will sustain Naomi in her senescence (vv. 14–15). All these prayers are answered by the end of the Ruth narrative, which indicates God's activity. Adorning the narrative from beginning to end, on the lips of both main and secondary characters, the cumulative effect of these prayers is to point to God's behind-the-scenes providence throughout the whole narrative.

God's actions in the Ruth narrative are minimal and understated. Although the narrator only directly mentions God's actions twice, the four indirect mentions, along with the prayers of the characters, paint a picture of God's constant providence. Other Old Testament narratives depict him occasionally working the spectacular and supernatural; the Ruth narrative reveals that he also continuously works in the humdrum and mundane. He explicitly preserves and provides for peoples (1:6) and couples (4:13). He

---

164. Katharine D. Sakenfeld, "Naomi's Cry: Reflections on Ruth 1:20–21," in *A God So Near: Essays on Old Testament Theology in Honour of Patrick D. Miller*, ed. Brent A. Strawn and Nancy R. Bowen (Winona Lake, IN: Eisenbrauns, 2003), 141.

implicitly works in the day-to-day "chance" events of life and through the everyday prayers of his people. And he works through the agency of people to achieve his purposes.

## C.  HUMAN ACTION

The double pivot in the structure of the Ruth narrative (2:18–23; 3:1–5) indicates that human action is integral to producing the plot outcome. This is an aspect of theology because God works through human actions in his providential management of his world. In the first pivotal scene, Ruth returns from her first day of gleaning to show Naomi what she had brought back. Naomi's speech is highlighted by its central placement in the scene. In response to Ruth's revelation of Boaz's identity, Naomi points out that he is "one of [their] kinsman-redeemers" (2:20). This is a turning point for Naomi and the narrative because she begins to realize the implications of Boaz as their benefactor, and her passive acquiescence (2:2) gives way to active directiveness (2:22; 3:1–5). The intertwining of God's providence and human action is evidenced in Naomi's benediction: "May he be blessed by Yahweh, who has not abandoned his kindness to the living and the dead" (2:20). Scholars debate whether "who" refers to Yahweh or Boaz, but it is probably best to view this as a case of deliberate ambiguity by the author: it refers to both Yahweh and Boaz. The phrase "the living and the dead" closely links Yahweh's action with human action (1:8; 2:11). The narrative thus portrays the interworking of God's providence and human action: God is the ultimate source of kindness, not ceasing to act in blessing toward the living and the dead; yet he shows kindness through Orpah, Ruth, and Boaz, who imitate and live out God's kindness. And it will be through Boaz's acts of kindness that Ruth will eventually find "rest," which is God's provision (1:9).

The second of the pair of pivotal scenes showcases human initiative. Naomi had seen the generosity of Boaz the kinsman-redeemer to Ruth, but the harvests ended and with it the end of their contact in his field. Naomi does not want to miss such an opportunity to secure a long-term relationship between her daughter-in-law and Boaz, so she devises a scheme to send Ruth to the threshing floor (3:1–5). The scheme is riddled with risk, but in light of the realization of God's renewed blessing in her life, perhaps it is a step of faith. In response to Yahweh's blessing of breaking the famine in Israel, she makes the crucial decision to return to Bethlehem (1:6). She then saw the blessing of grain first-hand through Boaz (2:18). She had stated that God's hand was extended against her in suffering (1:13; 20–21) but perhaps now she sees Yahweh's hand opening in blessing. Providence, detected in retrospect, has implications for action in the present. If she realized that

# Introduction

God had directed Ruth to him, she is now taking the next logical step. She sends Ruth to force Boaz's hand to greater commitment (3:1–5). The Ruth narrative presents Naomi's actions, buoyed by faith, as a response to God's providential actions.

The actions of the other two main characters are also marked by initiative. On the way to Bethlehem, Ruth commits herself to Naomi, against convention, expectation, and her mother-in-law's pleading (Ruth 1). In Bethlehem, her resourcefulness drives her to request permission to go gleaning. In her interaction with Boaz, she grasps the opportunities presented to her to establish a relationship with him as her patron. She works hard in the field, making the most of Boaz's generosity (Ruth 2). At the threshing floor, she seizes the opportunity presented by Boaz's open question to direct the conversation (Ruth 3).

Boaz's actions also manifest initiative. In his field, Boaz asks after Ruth's identity, he allows her to glean in his field, he gives her food and drink at mealtime, he grants her special gleaning rights in his field, and he protects her from the untoward attentions of the male harvesters (Ruth 2). At the threshing floor, Boaz immediately accepts Ruth's proposal but points out that he must follow the legal procedures (Ruth 3). He takes on the responsibility to protect Ruth by allowing her to stay on the threshing floor and sending her back to Naomi with grain. At the town gate, Boaz's initiative is especially on view (Ruth 4). His strategy in his negotiations with the nearer kinsman-redeemer is well prepared and executed. Ruth becomes his wife, he goes into her and, providentially, God grants conception (v. 13). The actions of Ruth and Boaz show that God's providence does not limit the freedom of humans to choose or the value of their choices.

Humans are responsible for their actions, which have significant consequences. Ruth and Boaz are rewarded by God for their acts of kindness; Orpah and the nearer kinsman-redeemer are not rewarded in the same way. The latter two are character foils who choose the expedient, expected path, but they not only miss out on greater personal blessing, they miss out on partaking in God's greater purposes (4:17–22). Of course, they were not to know that at their point of decision, but such is the mystery of providence.

Human initiative cannot be separated from divine providence. This is particularly seen in the Ruth narrative in two ways. The first occurs through the wordplay with *kānāp*, "wing." At their initial meeting, Boaz prays: "May Yahweh repay your deed, and may your wages be complete from Yahweh . . . under whose wings you came to seek refuge" (2:12).[165] Ruth uses the word in her marriage proposal to Boaz at the threshing floor: "Spread the wing of your garment [*kənāpekā*] over your handmaid" (3:9). By reusing the same

---

165. Heb. "whom you came to seek refuge under his wings [*kənāpāyw*]."

40

# THEOLOGICAL MESSAGES

word, Ruth is effectively asking Boaz to be the human agent through whom Yahweh will answer his prayer. The Ruth narrative shows that God works through human actions in his providential management of his world.

Second, the prayers in the Ruth narrative show the effectiveness of the interaction between God's providence and human action. As noted above, all the prayers are answered by the end of the narrative, which points to God's activity. Concurrently, these prayers are human words, a human action. This divine-human interaction is particularly seen in the benedictions (e.g., 3:10), which invoke God's blessing but are spoken by one person to another. The blesser wants God to act in response to their blessing, but even in the act of blessing they become part of the means through which the other person is blessed. God also answers prayer through the actions of people. Naomi prays that God grant her daughters-in-law "rest," but she is the one who schemes to achieve that "rest" (1:9; 3:1). God hears and sees to Naomi's complaint of emptiness through Boaz, who ensures that Ruth does not return to her mother-in-law "empty-handed" (1:21; 3:17). The prayers thus express the characters' dependency on God as the source of life and sustenance and blessing. Blessed outcomes occur because the characters asked for them; perhaps they would not have if the characters had not.[166] In the Ruth narrative, God uses prayer as a means to bring about change in the world.

The Ruth narrative shows that although God's providence is often unexpressed, he works consistently and effectively *through* the godly actions of his people. God accomplishes his purposes through all the actions of all people, both good and bad.[167] But in the Ruth narrative, God accomplishes his purposes with a handful of faithful people within a predominantly anarchic nation.[168] He even effects his plan through the ordinary motivations and actions of his people.[169] However, from the Ruth narrative we can conclude that God works most effectively through the agency of a faithful people, instead of or despite a disobedient people. For it is through the initiative—motivated by and as expressions of kindness—of these seemingly insignificant characters that God would bring forth the most feted king of Israel, who himself would become an ancestor of the greatest king of all.

---

166. Jesus says, "Until now you have asked nothing in my name. Ask, and you will receive, that your joy may be full" (John 16:24 ESV); and James says, "You do not have, because you do not ask" (Jas 4:2 ESV).

167. Cf. Gen 50:20.

168. Hints of the anarchy described in Judg 17–21 can be found in the book of Ruth, especially in the danger for Ruth as she gleans in the field (Ruth 2:9, 22).

169. These ordinary hopes, intentions, and actions include "a young girl's accidental steps and an old woman's risky plan"; see Ronald M. Hals, "Ruth," in *Interpreter's Dictionary of the Bible: Supplementary Volume*, ed. Keith Crim (Nashville: Abingdon, 1976), 759.

INTRODUCTION

## D. THE CYCLE OF DIVINE-HUMAN KINDNESS

The word *ḥesed*, "kindness," only occurs three times in the Ruth narrative, but its influence encompasses the entire narrative. The first time is in Naomi's first speech (1:8). She asks Yahweh to "deal kindly" with her daughters-in-law because of the kindness they had shown to her and her family while they were in Moab. Naomi's words reveal that actions performed within a relationship, even acts of kindness, came with an expectation of reciprocation. The concept of reciprocity is prevalent in communal societies, including ancient Israel: favor begets favor. Since she was now ceasing their kinship bond and releasing them from their obligations to her, she could not reciprocate their benevolence. She therefore calls on Yahweh to pay back her foreign daughters-in-law for their kindness. Naomi's following words specify the nature of the kindness she desires: "May Yahweh give you . . . Find rest, each in the house of her husband" (1:9). She wants Yahweh to give them "rest" through remarriage; she wants them to find security in a new household. Notice in these words the interweaving of God's providence and human action—she asks God to "grant" rest but also commands her daughters-in-law to "find" it.[170] This description of their lack highlights a need that requires fulfilling by the end of the narrative, but also foreshadows the importance of divine-human interaction in effecting that resolution. When Ruth finds rest through marriage to Boaz, it can be viewed not only as the outcome of human initiative but also of divine kindness: acts of kindness led to a blessing and Naomi asking for further kindness, which eventuates. In the Ruth narrative, acts of kindness trigger a perpetuating feedback loop.

The second use of *ḥesed* is also on the lips of Naomi (2:20). She calls for Yahweh to bless Boaz for his kindness, as manifest in the abundant provision of grain for Ruth. He had granted her gleaning privileges and protection against assault. But there was only grain in Boaz's field to glean because Yahweh had given his people food (1:6). In 2:20 there is probably a double referent for the doer of kindness—God and Boaz—and the former answers Naomi's prayer by granting the latter a wife, a son, and a name of national renown. God's providence and human initiative can thus also be viewed through the lens of kindness. Boaz's acts of kindness induce a blessing from Naomi, which leads to greater acts of kindness from Yahweh. Ultimately, God blesses not just one family or clan or town but an entire nation and beyond. Again, we can detect a virtuous cycle: Boaz responds in kind to Ruth's first act of kindness.

The third use of *ḥesed* is on the lips of Boaz (3:10). He blesses Ruth for two acts of kindness. The first is her loyalty to Naomi, which required her to turn

---

170. See the comments on 1:8–9, which detail the interweaving of divine and human action in the structure and content of Naomi's speech.

42

# THEOLOGICAL MESSAGES

her back on her family and homeland. This kindness led to his generosity to her in his field (2:8–9, 11; cf. 1:16–17). Her loyalty to her mother-in-law also led to another request for God to reciprocate: "May Yahweh repay your deed, and may your wages be complete from Yahweh" (2:12). This reinforces the narrative's presentation of a positive feedback loop for acts of kindness and God as the rewarder of good deeds. The second act of kindness Boaz identifies is Ruth's selection of him as a husband, despite the presence of more eligible candidates (3:10). Blessing again follows kindness as Boaz blesses Ruth, setting up the expectation that God will grant her request—a husband to secure her "rest." Boaz, however, is the human agent who ensures her redemption. Viewed in this light, his guarantee to her at the threshing floor and his legal maneuvering at the town gate can be understood as acts of *ḥesed*. Yet, since her selection of Boaz, as a member of Elimelech's clan, allows for the possibility of an heir to inherit Elimelech's land and to continue his name, there is an anticipation that God will bless them with a son as well. When God does so by granting them Obed, we can view it as an act of *ḥesed*, and, as is consistent with the pattern in the rest of the Ruth narrative, the women proclaim a blessing on Yahweh.

Although the word only occurs three times in the narrative, its importance is magnified by its appearance at key points in the narrative and its presence in the narrative's virtuous feedback loop. Its first use is in the first speech of the narrative, in which Naomi sets up the expectation that God will reward Orpah and Ruth for their acts of kindness. The second and third instances of *ḥesed* are also at points of emphasis in the narrative. Naomi's speech to Ruth is the turning point of act 2 and the major turning point of the narrative overall. Boaz's speech to Ruth forms the climax to act 3. These peaks of the narrative naturally highlight *ḥesed*. Moreover, acts of kindness as catalysts for blessing and greater acts of kindness traverse the whole narrative, from beginning to end. The feedback loop connects human with divine acts of kindness, and although the first kindness is attributed to the Moabite daughters-in-law (1:8), tracing the feedback loop back, we find that the initiator is Yahweh (1:6). And as we follow the loop to its conclusion, we also find Yahweh—the giver of life (4:13) and the sustainer of the nation (4:17–22). God's providence is unveiled as acts of kindness. Viewed canonically, this is not surprising since he proclaimed that *ḥesed* is one of his core characteristics (esp. Exod 34:6–7), as shown in his repeated actions throughout Israel's history (see, e.g., Ps 136).

Reading the Ruth narrative in its historical context reveals that God's providence is broad enough to encompass both acts of sin and acts of *ḥesed*. The period of the judges lacked a king and was marked by anarchy and unrest (Judg 17:6; 21:25). In contrast to the virtuous cycle in the Ruth narrative, the book of Judges can be plotted as a downward spiral of disobedience. Yet

# INTRODUCTION

God still worked through the judges with their imperfect motivations; for instance, God gave Samson the victory, although his motivation was revenge (16:28–30). From the Ruth narrative, however, we might deduce that God prefers to achieve his will through acts of *ḥesed*. That such actions please him can be seen in the outcome of the narrative, for it is through such actions that God raises a king who would unite the tribes of Israel and bring to them the blessings of rest and peace.

That is not to say that the motives and actions of the characters in the Ruth narrative were perfect. Elimelech's decision to leave the promised land was questionable, Naomi's faith was so shaken that she expressed bitterness toward God, the nearer kinsman-redeemer declined to act as a levirate, and Boaz's choice to do more for the widows was nudged by Ruth's further act of kindness. The characters go about their lives seeking mundane ends, including their own survival and that of a family line. Yet, seemingly insignificant decisions and actions can be powerfully transformative. It is not as though the characters set out to perform acts of kindness. Instead, as the opportunity arose, they were driven by kindness in response to kindness to perform acts of loyalty and generosity, breaking the bounds of obligation to help those who could not help themselves. That these actions are marked by initiative and risk again hints at the functioning of faith. If God, in his providence, can reward acts of kindness, such acts can be undertaken in trust. He rewards acts of kindness with blessing, acting through humans to bring kindness and blessing to the world, often in ways beyond a person's deserving, expectation, or understanding. Such are the ways of a God whose heart is *ḥesed*.

## E.  GOD'S BLESSING

In the book of Ruth, God is the source of blessing, which is a consequence of being in relationship with him. In committing to Naomi, Ruth turns her back on her Moabite background and pledges her allegiance to God (1:16–17). Boaz highlights the remarkable nature of her decision and calls on Yahweh to repay her: ". . . and may your wages be complete from Yahweh, the God of Israel, under whose wings you came to seek refuge" (2:12). Her journey to Judah parallels Abraham's journey (Gen 12:1), although hers was even more remarkable because she did not depart with a word of promise from God. In this light, Ruth's decision to turn to Yahweh, his people, and land contrasts with that of Elimelech and his family. They journeyed in the opposite direction: away from God's people and land, and presumably away from relationship with God and his sphere of blessing. Patriarchs had left the promised land because of famine previously, but they had left under the direct guidance from God. In a covenantal context, the famine in the land can be understood as a consequence of Israel's disobedience (Lev 26:19–20; Deut 28:23–24). Although there is no narratorial evaluation of the action of Elimelech and his family, the disasters that befell them might be viewed as God's further punishment for their decisions. Naomi, at least, recognizes God's hand behind her suffering (1:13, 20–21). Whatever the case may be, as Naomi returns to Yahweh's land among Yahweh's people, the narrator points out that she is already surrounded by God's blessing (1:22). As we trace her journey back, we see that the turning point is her decision to return to Israel in response to God's blessing his people with food (1:6). Hers is a response to God's initial grace, and despite the seemingly tenuous nature of her faith, she becomes an instrument of blessing not just for her two foreign daughters-in-law but also for her husband's line, clan, tribe, and nation. The Ruth narrative reveals that to live in covenant relationship with God is to be blessed, and blessing flows from remaining in relationship with him.

Being in relationship with God also brings physical blessing. God blesses his people with fullness of life in his presence. In the Ruth narrative, this is primarily expressed in fertility—of field (1:6) and womb (4:13). The prayers of the characters attest to God as the provider of security, especially through marriage (1:8–9, 11–13), and the pursuant outcomes of perpetuity and legacy (4:11–12). And the benedictions of the characters (2:4, 12, 20; 3:10) attest to Yahweh as the ultimate source of *šālôm*, or wholeness (Num 6:24–26). When Boaz acts as the kinsman-redeemer to restore wholeness, God is praised for the outcome—a son, called a "redeemer" (4:14) because Obed will sustain Naomi's fullness of life into her old age. This is a picture of the blessed state: a person in right relationship with God experiencing the physical realities of *šālôm*.

Yet God's blessing is not realized in a mechanistic way. Just as the Ruth narrative resists a definite conclusion of a direct correspondence between disobedience and curse, so individual blessings are not automatically realized. Not every wicked person suffers disaster, and not every righteous person enjoys prosperity. God is sovereign and free in his providence; he shows kindness when and to whom he chooses. The benedictions in Ruth are thus not demands but petitions for blessing from God. God's answering of each petition portrays his grace, generosity, and willingness to use people—especially those in right relationship with him—to bring blessing to the world.

## VIII. THEMES

### A. APPLYING THE LAW

Whether the book of Ruth was written in the monarchic or postexilic period, it is likely that the legal texts, or at least their contents, were already well

# INTRODUCTION

known. Old Testament law exhibits Yahweh's character, which his people are called to reflect.[171] The law guides how life in covenant relationship with God should be worked out, although it does not cover every possible situation. If Old Testament law prescribes the baseline ethical requirements, then Old Testament narratives help us understand the ideal behavior.[172] In the Ruth narrative, this can be demonstrated in relation to five laws—gleaning, redemption and levirate, exclusion from the assembly, and intermarriage.[173]

The gleaning law (Lev 19:9–10; Deut 24:19–22) was one aspect of social security in ancient Israel. Landowners were not allowed to harvest to the edge of their fields, nor to return to harvest a sheaf that had been missed. They were to leave it for a group of people who did not have access to the produce of the land: the resident alien, the fatherless, and the widow. Two reasons are given: God is the landowner, and all Israelites are tenants on his land; and the Israelites were to remember that they were slaves in Egypt, with the implication that they were not to enslave others in their poverty. In the book of Ruth, Boaz goes beyond the requirements of the gleaning law. He not only allows her access to his field, he also offers her protection, and food and water to drink while she gleans in the field. He even instructs his workers to deliberately pull out stalks for her to glean so that she gleans enough on the first day to feed herself and Naomi for at least a week.

Based on the law, a kinsman-redeemer was a relative who restored to wholeness that which has been lost, usually at his own personal cost. The relative who needed redemption could not help themselves, and the redeemer acts because of family solidarity—every Israelite is linked by a series of widening networks: father's house, clan, tribe, and nation. If a relative was in need, there was an obligation to help: the closer the kinship relation, the stronger the obligation. The law outlined five main roles for a kinsman-redeemer: (1) buying back property that was lost outside the clan for an indebted relative (Lev 25:25–30); (2) buying back a relative who had sold themselves into slavery (Lev 25:47–55); (3) executing murderers of relatives as an "avenger of blood" (Num 35:12, 19–27; Deut 19:6, 11–13); (4) receiving restitution money on behalf of a deceased relative (Num 5:8); and (5) mediating for a relative in lawsuits (Job 19:25; Ps 119:154; Prov 23:11; Jer 50:34). Only the first of these applies to the book of Ruth. Naomi was probably selling the right to redeem the property of Elimelech (4:3–4). Boaz first offers the land to the nearer kinsman-redeemer, since he had the first right of refusal under the law (cf. Lev 25:48b–49). He accepts. However, when Boaz informs the

---

171. E.g., "Be holy, for I am holy" (Lev 11:44–45).

172. Gordon J. Wenham, *Story as Torah: Reading the Old Testament Ethically* (Edinburgh: T&T Clark, 2000), 4.

173. See also Lau and Goswell, *Unceasing Kindness*, 146–51.

# THEMES

nearer kinsman-redeemer that Ruth is part of the package, he reneges. On the one hand, his response is understandable since marriage to a widow is not a stated legal requirement of a kinsman-redeemer. On the other hand, the elders who form the legal quorum at the town gate do not object to Boaz's application of the law under the particular circumstances; in fact, the whole throng at the town gate gives their blessing (4:11–12). Boaz could have applied the redemption law according to the "moral logic" underlying the law: if the role of a kinsman was to restore wholeness, in this case, that role required marrying the widow (cf. Isa 54:4–5). Or he could have expanded the application of the redemption and levirate laws. Since, in this case, there was no heir to continue the name of the dead on his landed inheritance, the application of the redemption law could have triggered the levirate law (Deut 25:5–10). The allusions to the levirate custom in the book of Ruth (1:11–13; 2:20; 3:9–13; 4:7–8, 9–10, 11–12, 16–17) suggest that this is more likely, although not conclusively. If so, since Naomi was past childbearing age, Ruth was substituted for her to produce an heir to continue Elimelech's name on his inheritance. Some scholars accuse Boaz of underhanded tactics, but his application of the two laws was consistent with the principles underlying those laws.

On first reading, it seems Ruth's ethnicity should have excluded her from the assembly of Yahweh. Old Testament law prohibits Moabites from entering "the assembly of Yahweh . . . even to the *tenth generation*" (Deut 23:3 NASB, adapted).[174] The exclusion from corporate worship before Yahweh is "forever" (vv. 4, 7[3, 6]).[175] The rationale for the prohibition is that, in contrast to the Egyptians (v. 7), the Moabites did not bless the Israelites by showing them hospitality,[176] but tried to curse them through Balaam (vv. 4–6). A surface reading of this law would lead to Ruth's exclusion (and perhaps King David, since Ruth was his great-grandmother), but an examination of the principle underlying the law leads to another application. When an Israelite family sought hospitality outside the promised land, Ruth the Moabite obliged, even marrying an Israelite son, and so can be seen to "bless" instead of "curse" God's people (cf. Gen 12:3). Thus, an examination of the principle underlying the law leads to the understanding that this law does not apply to Ruth.

Boaz's marriage to Ruth the Moabite appears to contravene the law prohibiting intermarriage (Deut 7:3–4). Strictly speaking, this law prohibits an

---

174. Rabbinic sages suggested that Deut. 23:4–7[3–6] only applies to males (*Midr. Ruth Rab.* 2:10). Yet the gentilic "Moabite" functions as a collective noun for both males and females. Moreover, the law is applied to Moabite women in Neh 13:1, 23.

175. That is, the exclusion is permanent; cf. Jeffrey H. Tigay, *Deuteronomy*, JPS Torah Commentary (Philadelphia: Jewish Publication Society, 1996), 211.

176. Hospitality here signifies those who promote God's purposes for his people.

INTRODUCTION

Israelite from marrying any Canaanite—those incumbent in the promised land. The reason for the prohibition is crucial: to prevent the hearts of God's people from being turned aside to follow foreign gods (v. 4). Yet the door to Yahweh's kindness is left ajar since the recipients are described in general terms: "those who love him and keep his commandments" (v. 9 ESV). Moabites are not included in the seven nations in the promised land (v. 1), but this law would apply to them also if they "served other gods."[177] Thus, the underlying reason for prohibiting intermarriage is not ethnic but religious. Ruth, however, had turned from her foreign gods to commit herself exclusively to Yahweh (1:16–17; cf. 2:12). Her self-imprecatory oath in Yahweh's name reinforced the authenticity of her pledge (1:17). And her acts of kindness are exemplary of this foundational aspect of Israelite identity. In short, her ethnicity plus worship of a forbidden foreign deity would have rendered her off-limits to marriage with Boaz, but her ethnicity plus worship of Yahweh does not.

The application of these antecedent laws in the Ruth narrative encourages an expansive, rather than a restrictive application, based on the principles underlying the laws rather than strict adherence to the specifics of the laws. In New Testament terms, the spirit of the law was followed rather than the letter. The Ruth narrative promotes the virtue of kindness, and concerning the law, this is expressed in its generous application toward those in need—especially the widow and the resident alien. Since the law exhibits God's character, those in the Ruth narrative who live out the law in its fullness act as God's mediators to those in need. And those who follow God's law maintain their covenant relationship and are not only blessed but are also agents of blessing to others.

## B. RUTH'S ETHNICITY AND ISRAELITE IDENTITY

The redundant repetition of "the Moabite" spotlights Ruth's foreign origin. By the end of the narrative, she is accepted into Israelite society, but is she still viewed as a foreigner? I will argue that her ethnic distinction reduces but remains, which functions both to reinforce and challenge Israelite identity.

After her proper name, pronouns, and kinship terms, "the Moabite" is the most frequent description of Ruth, occurring seven times. The audience knows her origin (1:3–4), but the narrator emphasizes this when she arrives

---

177. Cf. 1 Kings 11:1–8; Neh 13:23–27; Ezra 9:1; 10:10. Conversely, intermarriage with foreigners outside the land of Canaan is allowed (Deut 21:10–14), presumably if they commit themselves to Yahweh; see Peter C. Craigie, *The Book of Deuteronomy*, NICOT (Grand Rapids: Eerdmans, 1976), 282.

in Bethlehem: "So Naomi returned, and Ruth the Moabite her daughter-in-law with her, who returned from the territory of Moab" (1:22). When she asks permission to glean from Naomi, she is called "Ruth the Moabite" (2:2). In the field, the overseer says Ruth is "a young Moabite woman, who returned with Naomi from the territory of Moab" (2:6). The overseer's description is understandable since it is his perspective of Ruth, but the narrator again attaches the designation to Ruth in her discussion with Naomi (2:21). Evidently, the narrator still views Ruth as "the Moabite" at this point in the narrative—after her vow of commitment to Naomi, her people, and her God, and after she has taken residence in the land of Israel.[178] By the end of the narrative, the narrator simply calls her "Ruth" or Boaz's "wife" (4:13). If the narrator here represents the view of the community of Bethlehem, the lack of the designation "the Moabite" suggests either that they no longer view her as a foreigner, or her ethnic status has become less relevant. Further evidence might be drawn from the words of the throng at the town gate, who refer to Ruth as "the woman" and "this young woman" (4:11, 12),[179] and from the words of the townswomen, who refer to her as "your daughter-in-law," one "who loves [Naomi]," and one who is "better . . . than seven sons" (4:15). I would suggest that Ruth has achieved a degree of acceptance and assimilation without necessarily losing her ethnic identity.

Religious and social factors are crucial to Ruth's assimilation, whereby assimilation is the decline of an ethnic distinction and its corollary cultural and social differences.[180] Ruth's ethnic differences are not erased or removed;

178. Neil Glover, "Your People, My People: An Exploration of Ethnicity in Ruth," *JSOT* 33 (2009): 302, suggests that this switch represents Naomi's change of opinion on Ruth, from "the Moabite" to "her daughter-in-law." But this is not consistent with Naomi's address to Ruth as "daughter" throughout the narrative.

179. Their wish for Ruth to become like Rachel and Leah will be discussed below.

180. Richard Alba and Victor Nee, *Remaking the American Mainstream: Assimilation and Contemporary Immigration* (Cambridge: Harvard University Press, 2003). Earlier assimilation theories were critiqued for their reflecting attitudes of superiority, expectations of conformity to the majority culture, and loss of identity. Alba and Nee's "neo–assimilation theory" tries to avoid such attitudes; see Richard Alba and Victor Nee, "Assimilation," in *The SAGE Handbook of International Migration*, ed. Inglis Christine, Li Wei, and Khadria Binod (London: SAGE, 2019), 400–417. Although it is an etic approach, I find that it fits well with the evidence of the Ruth narrative, prompts helpful questions of the text, and provides helpful insights. For a discussion of the tension in emic and etic approaches to Ruth's ethnicity, see Jonathan A. Thambyrajah, "When Is a Moabite Not a Moabite? Ethnicity in the Book of Ruth," *JSOT* 46 (2021): 44–63. For applications of Alba and Nee's theory to Ruth, see Katherine E. Southwood, "Will Naomi's Nation Be Ruth's Nation? Ethnic Translation as a Metaphor for Ruth's Assimilation within Judah," *Humanities* 3 (2014): 102–31; M. Daniel Carroll R., "Once a Stranger, Always a Stranger? Immigration, Assimilation, and the Book of Ruth," *International Bulletin of Missionary Research* 39 (2015): 185–88.

INTRODUCTION

instead, they become less relevant in the interactions between Ruth and the members of the Israelite community.[181] While in Moab, Ruth had married into a family with a background of worshipping Yahweh, but we do not know if she became a devotee of Yahweh. It is clear on the road to Bethlehem, however, that she commits herself to Naomi's God, with her self-imprecatory oath confirming the veracity of her religious commitment (1:16–17). Religion was a core aspect of ancient Near Eastern ethnic identity. To be an Israelite was to worship Yahweh. Not all members of Bethlehemite society might have fully followed Yahweh's instructions, but his presence permeated their life: he is often on the lips of the characters, and his laws guide their actions and decisions. Indeed, the transferring of her allegiance from Moab and its god(s) is a crucial factor that not only grants her access to gleaning privileges as a "resident alien" but also opens the way for her marriage to an Israelite.

Besides religion, social factors are important to Ruth's assimilation. Although they are "in-laws" (as repeatedly described by the narrator: 1:6, 7, 8, 14, 15, 22: 2:11, 18, 19, 20, 22, 23; 3:1, 6, 16, 17; 4:15), Naomi and Ruth interact at a closer kinship level, as biological family.[182] Even when Naomi implores Ruth to return to Moab, thereby releasing her from her "in-law" obligations, Ruth remains loyal to her. The extraordinary devotion of Ruth is signaled in verses where the narrator calls them "in-laws," but Naomi calls Ruth "my daughter" (2:22; 3:1, 16, 18; also "my daughters," including Orpah, 1:11, 12, 13). Her vow of commitment to Naomi not only marks her out as a "resident alien," it also forges a closer kinship bond between her and Naomi. Naomi's access to family networks in Bethlehem is crucial to her re-assimilation. She returned without her immediate family, but she was still connected to her husband's clan. Ruth's access to these networks through Naomi plays an important part in her assimilation, especially through her relationship to Boaz.

Boaz is introduced as "a relative of [Naomi's] husband's" (2:1), yet the narrative reveals his central importance not only for Naomi's re-assimilation, but also for Ruth's assimilation. When Ruth ventured out to glean, Boaz's harvest overseer primarily viewed her as a Moabite (v. 6). In her first conversation with Boaz, she self-consciously called herself a "foreigner" (v. 10), although Boaz "recognized" that she is not just a foreigner. In fact, he does not refer to her ethnic origin at all but views her as an individual, a person who has been tenaciously loyal to her Israelite mother-in-law and has come

181. For a reading of the book of Ruth in conversation with an experience of modern immigrant women (mostly Mexican), see Kelly D. Dagley, "Women's Experience of Migration and the Book of Ruth" (PhD dissertation, Fuller Theological Seminary, Center for Advanced Theological Study, 2019).

182. Naomi consistently calls Ruth "my daughter" (2:2, 22; 3:1, 16, 18). She describes Orpah as Ruth's "sister-in-law" (1:15) but she does not refer to Ruth as an "in-law" in the narrative.

50

to take refuge in the Israelite God (2:11–12). As the narrator reminds us, she is still a Moabite, but, for Boaz, her ethnic identity is not relevant. Instead, his response hints that he views her as kin, as a member of his clan, although Ruth does not know this at the time. His address to her as "my daughter" (2:8; 3:10, 11) not only indicates his benevolence and elder status (cf. Naomi's usage) but also suggests that he views her as kin.[183] Boaz's perception of Ruth is a turning point in Ruth's assimilation. She immediately switches her self-designation from "foreigner" to "your maidservant" (2:13) and thus begins her ascent in social status: she will call herself Boaz's "servant" (3:9) and eventually become Boaz's "wife" (4:10). Her intermarriage publicly and concretely binds her to Israelite society, and the birth of a son signals her successful assimilation: from a foreign outsider, she is honored as a wife and mother blessed by Yahweh, one who builds up the house of Israel (4:11, 13). And Naomi is re-assimilated into Israelite society: through Ruth she has a "son" (4:17). Her family is re-established; her name is restored; her shameful status as a childless widow is discarded. The townswomen, who first ignored Ruth, refer to her with kinship terms: "daughter-in-law," "who loves [Naomi]," "better . . . than seven sons" (4:15). Theirs is the last word on Ruth and, if indicative of wider Bethlehemite society, reveals that Ruth's ethnic origin has faded in salience.

Although Ruth is accepted and included in the Israelite community, and her ethnicity becomes less relevant, she cannot remove all vestiges of her "foreignness." The difficulties facing an immigrant are implicit in Naomi's speech to her daughters-in-law on the road to Bethlehem, not least of which was remarriage (1:8–9). Ruth's acceptance points to the "kindness" of the Bethlehemite community, but there are hints that they still see her as an "other." By the last chapter, she is still twice referred to as "the Moabite" (4:5, 10). Ironically, it is used by Boaz, the character who especially overlooks their ethnic differences. His usage of this designation might have been for legal precision or to point out the unusual nature of his redemption and marriage—to a "Moabite." But it probably also indicated the community's perception of Ruth or even the way they referred to her. As such, she is among them, counted as a member of Yahweh's people, but she is not an Israelite.[184]

The persistence of Ruth's Moabite ethnicity both reinforces and challenges the core aspects of Israelite identity. Although she is accepted and

---

183. Cf. Naomi's description of Boaz as "*our* close relative, . . . one of *our* kinsman-redeemers" (2:20).

184. Cf. Andrew J. Niggemann, "Matriarch of Israel or Misnomer? Israelite Self-Identification in Ancient Israelite Law Code and the Implications for Ruth," *JSOT* 41 (2017): 357, "Ruth cannot be considered a *bona fide* Israelite; she remained a partial foreigner even after her marriage to Boaz."

INTRODUCTION

included in the Israelite community, and her ethnicity becomes less relevant, she is still "Ruth the Moabite." The transformation of her identity included religious and social aspects, but her Moabite ethnicity is not expunged as a result of her assimilation. Thus, as a Moabite, she paradoxically reinforces the ideal Israelite virtue of "kindness" and embodies the ideal Israelite "worthy woman/wife" (3:11; Prov 31:10–31). She is a worthy member of Israel. And she counters negative Moabite stereotypes—not all are incestuous, inhospitable, and idolatrous. Yet, by maintaining elements of her "foreignness," she also challenges Israelite identity. Foreigners can be included within God's people; ethnicity does not preclude assimilation. Membership of and acceptance into Israelite society is not solely based on ethnicity or descent. The book of Ruth indicates that religious allegiance and personal character are even more important.

## IX. RUTH AND THE NEW TESTAMENT

### A. MATTHEAN GENEALOGY

The book of Ruth is not quoted in the New Testament, but some of its characters are mentioned in the genealogies of Jesus Christ (Matt 1:1–6; Luke 3:31–34). The Matthean genealogy in particular not only completes the messianic line from David to Jesus but also expands on and completes interlocking themes from Ruth. In Ruth, Perez begins the ten-generation genealogy, which is typical of ancient Near Eastern king lists, and places Boaz and David at prominent positions—seventh and tenth. The effect of the genealogy is to link the Ruth narrative with the grand narrative of the Old Testament, from Genesis to Kings, in which kingship is a major theme. Perez transports the audience back to the patriarchal stories of Genesis (esp. Gen 38), then we move forward to David, whose last days are recorded in 1 Kgs 1–2. The Ruth genealogy thus establishes a continuity between earlier biblical history and the beginning of the Davidic monarchy. The Matthean genealogy continues and completes this grand messianic narrative, pointing to its fulfillment in "Jesus Christ, the son of David, the son of Abraham" (Matt 1:1 ESV).

The Matthean genealogy also continues the trajectory of foreign females building the messianic line. Among Old Testament books, Ruth is noted for its uniquely female focus. Elimelech and his sons die early in the narrative, leaving Naomi and Ruth as the main characters (1:3–5). As the audience, we are concerned about the plight of Naomi—will her emptiness be filled? We side with Ruth as she gleans and as she proposes marriage. Boaz is the center of attention in the legal case, where he speaks of the male issues of property and progeny. However, he also acts for the sake and on behalf of the women.

RUTH AND THE NEW TESTAMENT

Soon, attention returns to women, and we again hear their perspective (4:13–17). Ruth, of course, is a foreign woman, a reality that she is sorely conscious of (2:10), and we are often reminded of by the narrator (Ruth's designation as "the Moabite" is found in 1:22; 2:2, 6, 21; 4:5, 10). Yet, remarkably, by the end of the Ruth narrative, a foreign woman not only belongs as a full member of God's people, she even contributes to the building of the Davidic dynasty.

In the New Testament, the foreign women who contributed to dynasty-building are listed in the genealogy of Jesus Christ, the greatest son of David: Tamar, Rahab, and Ruth (Matt 1:1–17). All these women have questionable backgrounds or behaviors: Tamar positioned herself to be viewed as a prostitute,[185] Rahab was a prostitute (Josh 2:1; 6:25), and Ruth snuck onto the threshing floor at night (if prostitutes frequented threshing floors [cf. Hos 9:1], she could have been mistaken as one). In addition, Bathsheba, although not mentioned by name and not a foreigner herself, is listed in the genealogy as "Uriah's [the Hittite's] wife."[186] Canonically, these women paved the way for Mary's scandalous conception of Jesus (Matt 1:19). Moreover, their inclusion is in fulfillment of God's promise of blessing to "all peoples" through Abraham (Gen 12:3). And the acceptance of these foreigners into Israel in the Old Testament anticipates the acceptance of Gentiles into the church in the New Testament (e.g., Acts 10:34–48; Rom 1:16). The kingdom of David's son will accept all who seek refuge under the Lord Jesus; all peoples from everywhere are one in him (Gal 3:28).

## B. MISSION

A motif from Ruth taken up in the New Testament is mission. Many Jews and Christians consider Ruth the prototypical convert in the Hebrew Bible /Old Testament.[187] She is a Moabite who accepts Yahweh as her exclusive deity and is incorporated into Israel. As noted above, she becomes not only an ancestor of David but also of Jesus (Matt 1:1–6). The term "mission" is not found in the Bible, but the concept of God's mission can be found when we read from Genesis to Revelation. From such a canonical reading can be derived this definition of mission: "the sending activity of God with the purpose of reconciling to himself and bringing into his kingdom fallen men and

185. Her veiled identity and her lone presence by the roadside contributed to Judah thinking she was a prostitute (Gen 38:13–16).

186. Second Samuel 11:3.

187. While a fully developed notion of "conversion" is only established centuries after the Ruth narrative, Ruth's turning away from a foreign god to serve Yahweh exclusively is akin to the same process. See comment on Ruth 1:17.

INTRODUCTION

women from every people, nation, and tongue."[188] However, restricting our attention to the Old Testament, we find that the "sending" element is not in view. Rather than God's people going out to other peoples, it is the other peoples coming to Israel (e.g., Ps 86:9; Isa 2:2–3; Zech 8:22–23; 14:16). Ruth comes from Moab to Israel and is incorporated into Israel, just as Rahab and the Gibeonites come to be incorporated into Israel (although they do not travel beyond the borders of the land allotted to Israel). The book of Ruth contributes to our understanding of God's mission in at least three ways.[189]

First, the book of Ruth is a witness to God's mission. The broad sweep of the Bible traces the story of God's mission in and for creation.[190] The story line can be described as acts in a drama: creation, fall, Israel, Jesus the Messiah, church, and new creation.[191] Within this story line, the book of Ruth shows how God was faithfully working to bring blessing to Israel, and through Israel to the whole world. Ruth, as a foreigner, links to the promise of blessing to "all peoples" through Israel, as found in God's promise to Abraham (Gen 12:1–3). In these verses, God promises to make Abraham into a great nation, and through Abraham's seed to bring blessing to all peoples of the earth.[192] God will bless whoever blesses Abraham, but the one who

---

188. Craig Ott, Stephen J. Strauss, and Timothy C. Tennent, *Encountering Theology of Mission: Biblical Foundations, Historical Developments, and Contemporary Issues* (Grand Rapids: Baker Academic, 2010), xv, xvii. Cf. Andreas J. Köstenberger and T. Desmond Alexander, *Salvation to the Ends of the Earth: A Biblical Theology of Mission*, 2nd ed., NSBT (Downers Grove, IL: InterVarsity, 2020), 260, who understand "mission" as bound up with God's saving plan from creation to new creation, reaching the ends of the earth. They argue that the notion of "sending" is central to any treatment of mission, but focus on the concept rather than the terminology of sending.

189. Material in this section has been adapted from Lau and Goswell, *Unceasing Kindness*, 141–56. For an exploration of Ruth as a wise woman who brings blessing to the nations, see Chloe Sun, "Ruth and Esther: Negotiable Space in Christopher Wright's *The Mission of God*?," *Missiology* 46 (2018): 156–58.

190. For more detail, see Köstenberger and Alexander, *Salvation*; Christopher J. H. Wright, *The Mission of God: Unlocking the Bible's Grand Narrative* (Downers Grove, IL: InterVarsity, 2006).

191. Cf. the six acts in Craig G. Bartholomew and Michael W. Goheen, *The Drama of Scripture: Finding Our Place in the Biblical Story* (Grand Rapids: Baker Academic, 2004): (1) God establishes his kingdom: creation; (2) rebellion in the kingdom: fall; (3) the king chooses Israel: redemption initiated; (4) the coming of the king: redemption accomplished; (5) spreading the news of the king: the mission of the church; (6) the return of the king: redemption completed. Others outline a five-act drama, although with slightly different acts; e.g., N. T. Wright, "How Can the Bible Be Authoritative?," *Vox Evangelica* 21 (1991): 7–29; Kevin J. Vanhoozer, *The Drama of Doctrine: A Canonical-Linguistic Approach to Christian Theology* (Louisville: Westminster John Knox, 2005).

192. In this passage Abraham is still called Abram, but I refer to him by his later name for the sake of simplicity.

RUTH AND THE NEW TESTAMENT

dishonors Abraham God will curse. This virtuous cycle of blessing in relation to Ruth was described above (see "Theological Messages").[193] By the end of the narrative, Ruth builds up the house of Israel, raising the name of the dead on his inheritance, thus keeping alive the Abrahamic promise. Without offspring, there is no continuation of the line of Perez and ultimately no blessing to the nations (through Obed, David, and Jesus). Exodus 19:4–6 details *how* God will bless the nations through Israel. As a "kingdom of priests," Israel was to represent God before the nations and mediate his presence.[194] Being a "holy nation" implied a different lifestyle, which would display to the world what it would look like to be in covenant relationship with Yahweh.[195] As Israel fulfilled this missional role, other nations would be drawn to Yahweh. The law provided Israel guidance for living out their calling as a priestly nation,[196] which we find demonstrated in the Ruth narrative.

Second, the book of Ruth functioned as an instrument of God's mission.[197] This element considers how the book of Ruth shaped Israel for their involvement in God's mission. Boaz primarily fulfills this missional calling by keeping the law. As noted above, one purpose of the book of Ruth was to promote a lifestyle of kindness. As such, the Ruth narrative shapes God's people as a missional community. How God's people were to treat Ruth as a foreigner is outlined in the law, but how the law should be applied—according to the principle of kindness—is a rhetorical aim of the Ruth narrative. As noted above (see section, "Applying the Law"), Boaz is generous beyond the requirements of three specific laws: gleaning, redemption, and levirate. Indeed, the Ruth narrative shows that Israel fulfilling its missional calling may require more than just obeying the law's strict requirements. Applying the

193. This reciprocal blessing is similar to Rahab's situation: she showed kindness by concealing the Israelite spies; Yahweh shows kindness to Rahab through the Israelites (Josh 2:12–14).

194. John A. Davies, *A Royal Priesthood: Literary and Intertextual Perspectives on an Image of Israel in Exodus 19:6*, JSOTSup 395 (London: T&T Clark, 2004), 238, points out that God's declaration (Exod 19:6) primarily describes how Israel is related to God, rather than how the nation is to relate to the nations, "though it is not denied that there may be implications for human relationships of what it means to be the chosen and treasured people of God."

195. John I. Durham, *Exodus*, WBC 3 (Waco, TX: Word Books, 1987), 263, comments that Israel was "a display-people, a showcase to the world of how being in covenant with Yahweh changes a people."

196. W. Ross Blackburn, *The God Who Makes Himself Known: The Missionary Heart of the Book of Exodus*, NSBT (Downers Grove, IL: InterVarsity, 2012), 210: "The means by which Israel carried out her missionary calling as a priestly nation was through keeping the law."

197. For a different approach to the same issue, see Nancy J Thomas, "Weaving the Words: The Book of Ruth as Missiologically Effective Communication," *Missiology* 30 (2002): 155–70.

INTRODUCTION

law according to the principle of kindness may be required to bring blessing to all peoples of the earth.

Third, the book of Ruth shapes God's people for participation in God's mission. This third element considers how the Ruth narrative equips readers for their witness as God's people in the world today. In the New Testament, we find that the church continues the identity and role of God's chosen people, royal priesthood, and holy nation (1 Pet 2:9; cf. Rev 1:6). Parallel to kindness as the guiding principle for applying the law, in the New Testament, love is the fulfillment of the law (Rom 13:8–10; Gal 5:14).[198] Since Christ fulfilled the law (Matt 5:17), Christians are not required specifically to follow each of the laws in the Old Testament. Nonetheless, since God does not change, the principles underlying the laws are still valid for God's people today. Three laws applied in the Ruth narrative continue to have implications. The gleaning law might not be literally applicable in developed countries but the underlying principle, to provide for the poor and marginalized in society, still holds. Assisting the marginalized in society, such as refugees,[199] is one way God's people can be conduits of God's kindness. The redemption and levirate laws can also guide the church in caring for those in need. Just as the redemption law promoted assistance within the kinship group, the New Testament promotes doing good to all but especially to those in the family of God (Gal 6:10). The specifics of the levirate law might not be relevant in most countries today,[200] but the principle of caring for widows is reinforced in the New Testament (e.g., Jas 1:27). The trajectory for the law regarding acceptance of foreigners into the assembly is traced through Christ, who has broken down the dividing wall of hostility. Now all have access to the Father in one Spirit (Eph 2:11–18).

In the Old Testament, the people of God were to live out their priestly role and thus attract people to God. This so-called centripetal movement is seen in Ruth, who comes to Israel. In the New Testament, the attractional dimension of the church's witness remains (e.g., Matt 5:14–16; 1 Pet 2:9–12), but there is an added dimension: Jesus sends his people out to make disciples of all nations (Matt 28:18–20). Some of God's people still need to cross sea and land, but with global migration, the new mantra in some missions circles

198. Jesus proclaims that the two greatest commandments are based on love: for God and neighbor (Matt 22:37–40; Mark 12:29–31).

199. For an exploration of this topic, see Mark R. Glanville and Luke Glanville, *Refuge Reimagined: Biblical Kinship in Global Politics* (Downers Grove, IL: IVP Academic, 2020).

200. Some societies still practice a custom similar to this law, e.g., parts of Africa and Southeast Asia. See, e.g., Roi Nu, "A Reinterpretation of Levirate Marriage in Ruth 4:1–12 for Kachin Society," in *Reading Ruth in Asia*, ed. Jione Havea and Peter H. W. Lau, IVBS (Atlanta: SBL, 2015), 57–72.

56

is "mission on our doorsteps"—a focus on God's mission to those in our local communities.[201] The Ruth narrative contributes to our thinking about this missions strategy.[202] Since Ruth arrived as a foreign outsider, the ways God's people interact with her are instructive. The words and actions of Boaz and Naomi testify to God's character. Naomi affirms God's sovereignty and providence in all things (1:8–9, 13; 2:20). Boaz's words reinforce Naomi's theology (2:12; 3:10), as do the sentiments of the throng at the town gate (4:11–12). Boaz's lifestyle reflects God's character, especially his generous application of the law. Other minor characters testify to the truth of God in their everyday speech. Similarly, the words and actions of God's people today are important in incorporating others into the people of God. In particular, we can extol the riches of God's grace "in his kindness to us in Christ Jesus" (Eph 2:4–9; cf. Titus 3:4). As God's people respond to his kindness by clothing themselves in kindness (Col 3:12), a fruit of the Spirit (Gal 5:22), others will be drawn to God (including those "on our doorsteps").

## C. REDEMPTION

A further important motif of the Ruth narrative taken up in the New Testament is redemption. Forms of the Hebrew root *g'l*, "to redeem," appear twenty-three times in the four chapters of Ruth, proportionately more than any other book in the Old Testament.[203] The first occurrence is at a turning point of the narrative, where Naomi explains that Boaz is "one of our kinsman-redeemers" (2:20). The next occurrence of the root clusters in Boaz's conversation with Ruth on the threshing floor, when Ruth asks Boaz to marry her because he is a "kinsman-redeemer" (3:9). Using the root six times, Boaz explains that he is a redeemer but there is a nearer redeemer with the first option of redemption (3:9–13). The largest cluster of the root is found in the scene that includes the conversation between Boaz and the nearer redeemer at the town gate, where it is used twelve times (4:1–6). Boaz first offers Naomi's land for redemption, but then marriage to Ruth is attached as part of a package deal, ostensibly an extension of the redemption responsi-

201. See, e.g., Jervis David Payne, *Strangers Next Door: Immigration, Migration, and Mission* (Downers Grove, IL: InterVarsity, 2012); Thorsten Prill, *Global Mission on Our Doorstep: Forced Migration and the Future of the Church* (Münster: MV Wissenschaft, 2008).

202. In contrast to "mission" (defined above), "missions" refers to the specific work of the church and agencies in reaching people for Christ by crossing cultural boundaries. Cf. George W. Peters, *A Biblical Theology of Missions* (Chicago: Moody Press, 1972), 11.

203. This compares with thirty-one times in the twenty-seven chapters of Leviticus and twenty-six times in the sixty-six chapters of Isaiah.

INTRODUCTION

bility.[204] In the last occurrence of the root, the townswomen praise Yahweh for not leaving Naomi without a "redeemer," referring to Obed (4:14).

The book of Ruth reveals four aspects of redemption that can be traced through to the New Testament.[205] First, the redeemed are in desperate straits. Naomi and Ruth were in material poverty, but Elimelech's family line was also under threat of extinction. Second, it was costly for the redeemer, an issue raised by the nearer kinsman-redeemer. He was willing to pay the initial cost of redeeming the property (Ruth 4:4). But he was not willing to pay the ongoing cost of feeding Naomi and Ruth, and any children through Ruth, especially since the redeemed property would be transferred to a son produced with Ruth. His refusal highlights the cost Boaz was willing to bear.

Third, the redeemer's actions are characterized by generosity and self-sacrifice; in other words, traits closely aligned with kindness. Boaz was willing to risk his immediate and future security to provide for Naomi and Ruth, and to raise up Mahlon's name and ongoing existence (4:10). In the Old Testament, God is the great Redeemer, with kindness one of his core characteristics (see esp. Exod 34:6, 7). He not only redeemed his people from physical bondage (esp. the exodus from Egypt) but also spiritual bondage (e.g., Ps 130:7–8; Isa 52:13–53:12). In the New Testament, such spiritual bondage is fatal for all humanity. All people are slaves to sin, which leads to death (e.g., Rom 5:12; 6:16–20, 23). Because of sin, all people fall short of God's glory (Rom 3:23). Like the widows in Ruth, we cannot save ourselves (cf. Eph 2:5; Col 2:13). Yet, in kindness, God has paid the redemption price—the precious blood of Christ (e.g., Rom 3:24–25; Eph 1:7; 1 Pet 1:18–19). Those who trust in Christ will no longer face guilt, shame (Rom 10:11; 1 Pet 2:6–7), and the eternal consequences of sin (Rom 6:23). In this sense, the kind actions of Boaz foreshadow God's greatest kindness in providing Jesus Christ. Boaz can be considered a type of Christ. His redemption was primarily material and temporary; Christ's redemption is primarily spiritual and eternal.

Fourth, there is a kinship connection between the redeemer and the redeemed. Boaz and the nearer kinsman-redeemer had an obligation to redeem because they were relatives of Elimelech. God redeemed Israel to be his covenant people, related to him as his own family by the covenant (Exod 6:6–7; 15:13). They were God's "firstborn son" (Exod 4:22–23). Isaiah described God as Israel's "father" and "redeemer" (63:16), "maker," "husband," and "re-

---

204. Since there was no male heir for Elimelech's land, the redemption of property probably triggered the levirate responsibility (Deut 25:5–10) so that the name of Elimelech could be raised up on his property (Ruth 4:5, 10). Redemption is thus understood in its broader sense of restoration to wholeness—restoring Elimelech's name on the family property and Ruth and Naomi's well-being.

205. Summarized from Lau and Goswell, *Unceasing Kindness*, 117–39.

58

## RUTH AND THE NEW TESTAMENT

deemer" (54:5). Just as the marriage covenant followed Ruth's redemption, so the Sinai covenant followed Israel's redemption.[206] The New Testament explains that Jesus had to be incarnated as a human to redeem humanity (e.g., John 1:14; Rom 8:3; Phil 2:7), and so could redeem us as our kinsman (cf. Heb 2:10–17). Those who are now "in Christ" are adopted into God's family as Jesus's brothers and sisters (e.g., Rom 8:29; Gal 4:3–7; Heb 2:11–13). It is a great honor to be a member of God's family (Rom 8:15–17). Jesus is thus the kinsman-redeemer par excellence, bringing all peoples into God's "household" (cf. Gal 6:10). The New Testament ends with a vision of the marriage of Christ and his bride (his people, the church), celebrating a wedding feast, where there is no bitterness or emptiness, only contentedness and fullness (Rev 19–22).

206. McKeown, *Ruth*, 215.

# Text and Commentary

## ACT 1: DEATH AND EMPTINESS (1:1–22)

Act 1 of the Ruth narrative comprises three scenes:

|  | Characters | Location | Action |
|---|---|---|---|
| 1:1–6 | Elimelech's family | Bethlehem then Moab | The end of a family line in Moab |
| 1:7–19a | Naomi, Orpah, and Ruth | En route: Moab to Bethlehem | Naomi, Orpah, and Ruth dialogue |
| 1:19b–22 | Naomi and Ruth | Town gate | Naomi laments before the townswomen |

This first act introduces the main characters and the problems that need resolution. It begins and ends in Bethlehem (vv. 1, 19), but the main events take place outside Israel—either in Moab or on the way to Bethlehem. In response to famine, Elimelech and his family leave the promised land for the fraught fields of Moab. Instead of survival, they experience death and sterility. As a result, Naomi and her sons' Moabite wives set out for the land of Judah. At the crossroads between Moab and Judah, Orpah turns back, while Ruth commits herself to Naomi. Yet upon their return to Bethlehem, the older widow feels empty and bitter. This brings out an ironic contrast with the beginning of the act: Naomi leaves the bread-free town with a "full" family; she returns to the bread-filled town "empty" of her family.[1] Bankrupt in social status, she lays the blame at Yahweh's feet. The rejection of her name signals the repudiation of her identity and former life. Will her return to Bethlehem restore her name and honor?

---

1. Fischer, *Rut*, 26.

# The Book of Ruth

## A. THE END OF A FAMILY LINE IN MOAB (1:1-6)

[1]*In the days when[a] the judges ruled,[b] there was[c] a famine in the land.[d] So a man from Bethlehem of Judah went[e] to sojourn in the territory of Moab[f]—he and his wife and two sons.[g]*

[2]*The name[h] of the man was Elimelech,[i] the name of his wife was Naomi,[j] and the names[k] of his two sons were Mahlon and Chilion—Ephrathites from Bethlehem of Judah.[l] They entered[m] the territory of Moab and stayed[n] there.*

[3]*Then Elimelech, the husband of Naomi, died. And she was left, she and her two sons.[o]*

[4]*They took[p] for themselves Moabite wives; the name of the first was Orpah, and the name of the second was Ruth. They lived there about ten years.*

[5]*Then the two of them[q] also died—Mahlon and Chilion. And the woman was left without[r] her two children[s] and without her husband.*

[6]*Then she arose, she and her daughters-in-law,[t] and she returned from the territory of Moab, because she heard[u] in the territory of Moab that Yahweh had attended to[v] his people by giving them food.[w]*

a. Since *wayəhî* functions in Ruth 1:1 as a temporal marker (cf. *IBHS* §33.2.4b), it can be left untranslated (e.g., Syr., ESV, NIV), instead of, e.g., "Now it came to pass" (e.g., LXX, NASB, NKJV).

b. The early versions either maintain (LXX: "When the judges were judging") or change (Syr.: "In the days of the judges") the syntax of this phrase. The phrase *šəpōṭ haššōpəṭîm* ("the judging of the judges") is an infinitive followed by the participle of the same root, *špṭ*. This root can be glossed as "to arbitrate, administer justice, govern" (*HALOT* 4:1622–25; BDB, 1048). Since the main role of the judges in the book of Judges is to lead in battle and to govern (e.g., Judg 2:16), rather than to act judicially (but cf. Deborah; Judg 4:4–5), "rule" is most appropriate. The "ruling" of the judges also anticipates the "ruling" by the next line of national leaders mentioned at the end of the Ruth narrative (4:17, 22).

c. This second *wayəhî* ("there was") begins the main narrative after the temporal reference.

d. Although not explicit in this clause, the next clause clarifies that "the land" included Judah and often refers to the Cisjordan or the land of Israel (e.g., Deut 4:14; 6:1; 12:10; Josh 1:2, 14). "The land" (*'ereṣ*) is contrasted with "the territory" (*śādeh*) of Moab. See comment on v. 1.

e. The syntax of *wayyēlek 'îš mibbêt leḥem yəhûdâ* allows for two possible translations: "A man went from Bethlehem of Judah" (e.g., LXX, HCSB) or "A man from Bethlehem of Judah went" (ESV, NIV). Both are true in the Ruth narrative: the man was from Bethlehem, and he left Bethlehem. The parallelism with "to sojourn in the territory of Moab" lends weight to the former translation. However, the latter is marginally preferred because in the Old Testament, people are usually introduced in reference to their place of origin (e.g., Judg 17:1; 1 Sam 1:1; Job 1:1). The description of Elimelech's family as "Ephrathites from Bethlehem of Judah" (1:2) also lends some support to the latter translation.

f. With LXX (*agros*) and 4QRuth[a] I take *śādê* as the singular construct form of *śāday*, which also occurs in 1:2, 6a, and 22. *Śədēh*, the singular construct form of *śādeh*, occurs in

62

# 1:1–6 The End of a Family Line in Moab

1:6b; 2:6; and 4:3 (see JM §96Bf). I translate "territory" of Moab for both, in contradistinction to the "land" (*'ereṣ*) of Judah.

g. Some MSS omit "two" (4QRuth^a, 4QRuth^b, LXX, Vulg., Tg.), but this does not significantly affect the meaning because the sons are subsequently named (1:2).

h. The lack of a past narrative *wayyiqtol* signals the beginning of an offline clause. Here the null–copula clause provides background information about Elimelech and his family.

i. LXX *Abimelech* instead of Elimelech, which may be an attempt to link him with the disgraced son of Gideon (Judg 8:31–9:57) or the foreign kings in Genesis (20:1–18; 21:22–34; 26:6–16).

j. *No'ŏmî* is the transliteration since the first vowel is a *qamets khatuf*, but I will use the conventional English spelling.

k. Heb. singular *šēm*, "name."

l. While it is possible to take the clause "Ephrathites from Bethlehem of Judah" as only referring to the last two referents (Mahlon and Chilion), it is more likely to refer to the whole family. "They were" is lacking in the Hebrew and has been supplied in most EVV.

m. The past narrative *wayyiqtol* (*wayyābō'û*) resumes the foreground narrative from v. 1—they departed (*hālak*; cf. 1:7, 18) Bethlehem, now they "entered" (*bô'*; cf. 1:19, 22) Moab.

n. The verb *hyh* and its translations in MT^L, LXX, and 4QRuth^b is preferable to *yšb* ("lived") in 4QRuth^a, which may be an attempt to maintain consistency with v. 4.

o. My translation is wooden, but reflects the emphasis on Naomi from the Hebrew syntax; so also LXX: *kai kateleiphthē hautē kai hoi dyo huioi autēs*. Some EVV bring out the fact that they were all left as a group (e.g., NET "she and her two sons were left alone"), while others place more emphasis on Naomi ("She was left with her two sons"; e.g., ESV, NIV). Tg. "And she was left a widow and her two sons orphans."

p. The verb *nāśā'*, here *take as wife*," is usually found in postexilic texts: Ezra 9:2, 12; 10:44; Neh 13:25; 2 Chr 11:21; 13:21; 24:3 (BDB, 671).

q. Although "both" is more elegant (almost all EVV), I translate *šənêhem* as "two of them" (cf. NET, NJPS) because it brings out the use of "two" in the rest of this chapter (1:1, 2, 3, 5, 7, 8, 19).

r. *Niphal* of *šā'ar* + *min* is privative, "without" (*DCH* 8:219; cf. *IBHS* §11.2.11e[2]).

s. *Yəlādêhā*, "her children," in MT^L, 4QRuth^a, and 4QRuth^b, is preferred to "her sons" in LXX, Syr, and Tg. EVV translate both "children" (HCSB, NASB1995) and "sons" (ESV, NJPS, NIV).

t. MT^L and Tg.: "daughters-in-law." LXX, Vulg., Syr. read "two daughters-in-law," perhaps to maintain consistency with vv. 7, 8.

u. LXX reads "they returned" and "they heard," and Syr. reads the third verb as plural. Major EVV translate both Naomi and her daughters-in-law returning, e.g., "she and her daughters-in-law prepared to return" (ESV, NIV; contrast NJPS, NKJV "she might return").

v. The *qal* verb *pāqad* when describing an action of God has a base meaning of "to look at, to see" but also with the sense of acting upon what is seen, hence, "see to something" (*HALOT* 3:956). With the accusative, the nuance is God visiting to examine the plight of a people or a person: (1) graciously (1:6; so also, e.g., Gen 21:1; 50:24, 25; Isa 23:17; Jer 15:15; Ps 65:10); (2) to punish (e.g., Exod 32:34; Jer 6:15; Ps 59:6[5]); or (3) to test (e.g., Job 7:18; Ps 17:3). See BDB, 823; *DCH* 6:738.

w. The noun *leḥem* means "bread" or "food" in general (BDB, 537). In this verse, it is the latter. *Leḥem* has already been mentioned twice, as part of "Beth*lehem*" (vv. 1, 2). In relation to the main verb *pāqad*, the infinitive construct *lātēt lāhem lāḥem* functions in two similar

# THE BOOK OF RUTH

ways. First, to express purpose: "to give them food" (e.g., LXX, LEB). Second, to provide explanation: "by giving them food" (e.g., HCSB, NIV). Cf. ESV: "and given them food." Whichever the case, the threefold combination of alliteration and vocalic assonance in *lātēt lāḥem lāḥem* gives it a rhythmic feel; Porten, "Scroll," 25.

Structurally, this scene comprises two parallel cycles bracketed by migrations.[2]

> A A man, his wife, and <u>two sons</u> journey to *Moab* because of famine.
>> B The man's *name* was Elimelech, his <u>wife's</u> Naomi, and his two sons Mahlon and Chilion—Ephrathites from Bethlehem, Judah.
>>> C They *stayed* in the territory of Moab.
>>>> D Elimelech, husband of Naomi, *died*. She <u>was left</u> with her two sons.
>> B' They took Moabite <u>wives</u>, the first *named* Orpah, the second Ruth.
>>> C' They *lived* there about ten years.
>>>> D' Mahlon and Chilion *died*. The woman <u>was left</u> without her two children and her husband.
> A' She arose with her <u>two daughters-in-law</u> to return from *Moab* because she heard that God had given his people food.

The first migration to Moab was because of famine, the second is a migration from Moab because God breaks the famine in Israel (A-A'). The first cycle begins with a wife and two sons from Ephrathah, then a stay in Moab, then the death of the husband, leaving Naomi with her two sons (B-C-D). The second cycle begins with the sons taking wives from Moab, then settling there, then the deaths of the two sons leave Naomi without her two children and husbands (B'-C'-D'). This cyclical structure (B-C-D // B'-C'-D') shifts the focus from the center to the periphery (A-A'). The outcome of the parallel cycles is Naomi's tragic loss of family and social status. Leaving Judah as a wife and mother (A), she prepares to return from Moab as a childless widow (A'). The momentous decision that triggered the cycles was Elimelech's decision to leave Judah for Moab. The second cycle begins with the sons taking Moabite wives (B), but this is a consequence of the first decision to journey to Moab (A). The orderly repetitive cycles hint at a sense of inevitability, the tight methodical reporting at a correspondence between sin and punishment. The structure and style at least raise the possibility of divine retribution, which would be consistent with the milieu of the judges era.

2. Similarly, Grossman, *Ruth*, 79–80.

64

## 1:1–6 The End of a Family Line in Moab

The repeated summaries of who died and who remains read like an account that has been settled.[3] If so, perhaps Naomi's decision to return due to God's renewed blessing is the first step in her restoration (A').

**1** The narrator begins in a way both familiar and unfamiliar. *In the days when* (*wayəhî bîmê*, "in the days of") is used four times in the Old Testament but is always followed by the personal name of a ruler (Gen 14:1; Esth 1:1; Isa 7:1; Jer 1:3).[4] Only here is it followed by an Old Testament era, *when the judges ruled*. The narrator refers to an era known to his audience but from which they are separated by time. The opening phrase raises expectations for a specific ruler but instead an era containing numerous "rulers" is inserted. The lack of specificity blurs the historical focus to the period generally and the end of the book of Judges in particular.[5] In the time of the judges, tribal chieftains only intermittently unified Israel. The end of the book of Judges is at pains to assert that "in those days there was no king in Israel" (Judg 17:6; 18:1; 19:1; 21:25). The narrator has not only provided a time stamp for the narrative, he has also made us, the audience, anticipate a specific type of ruler—a king—just as they had in the setting of the narrative. We are put on the alert for a king to fill this void.

The hope for a king was acute in the time of the judges because it was a time marked by chaos and anarchy. According to the book of Judges, the period after Joshua's leadership starts on a bad foot, with the tribes not completely driving out the inhabitants of Canaan (Judg 1). They do not break down the false worship sites, they worship Canaanite gods, and they do not pass on faith in Yahweh to the next generation (2:1–15). In his mercy, God raises up judges to save the people from their enemies (2:16–23), but the quality of the judges' leadership spirals downward throughout the book so that it is hard to recognize the last judge in the book—Samson—as a judge

---

3. Cf. Grossman, *Ruth*, 85: "Justice has been done, sins have been accounted for."

4. However, *wayəhî* begins several Old Testament books and is most frequently followed by a temporal indicator (e.g., Josh 1:1; Judg 1:1; 2 Sam 1:1; Ezek 1:1), the name of a person (1 Sam 1:1) or Yahweh's word (Jonah 1:1). Books that begin with *wayyiqtol* forms can be a continuation of a composition (e.g., Leviticus, Numbers, Joshua, 2 Samuel, 2 Kings, 2 Chronicles), but the *wayyiqtol* followed by a temporal indicator is also found at the beginning of stand-alone books (e.g., Ezekiel, Esther); that is, it can also have a scene-setting function. See Christo H. J. Van der Merwe, Jackie A. Naudé, and Jan H. Kroeze, *A Biblical Hebrew Reference Grammar*, 2nd ed. (London: Bloomsbury T&T Clark, 2017), 190; Holmstedt, *Handbook*, 53–54. Even if the book of Ruth was not written as a continuation of the book of Judges (as a literary extension), this initial clause invites the audience to understand the Ruth narrative within the context of the time of the judges.

5. Jewish commentators place Ruth in the period described in Judg 17–21 or the time of Ibzan (Judg 12:8–10); so Malbim and Babylonian Talmud *Baba Batra*, respectively. Hubbard, *Ruth*, 84, suggests the time between Ehud and Jephthah since Moab dominated then.

65

# The Book of Ruth

at all (3:7–16:31). Then follow two cycles of narratives describing the religious and political anarchy of the era (17–21). Levites use idols and their concubines to their own ends, a Benjaminite town is more like Sodom and Gomorrah than the original town, and the loose Israelite tribal confederate is only unified in civil war. Women are victims of intentional and collateral damage. It is within this morass that the Ruth narrative is set.

Immediately there is a crisis, for *there was a famine in the land*. Famine is an extreme scarcity of food affecting a large number of people, here most likely the entire land of Israel, since Elimelech and his family departed for Moab, not another part of Israel. Famine is usually caused by drought; other biblical causes include hailstorms (Exod 9:22–25), insects (e.g., Joel 1:4), enemy invasion (Deut 28:49–51), and siege (e.g., 2 Kgs 6:24–25; 25:1–3). Along with pestilence and warfare, famine was one of the classical triad of catastrophes (e.g., 2 Chr 20:9; Jer 14:12; Ezek 6:11; Rev 6:8). Drought was the most likely cause in the Ruth narrative (cf. 1:6), although the judges setting raises the possibility of enemy invasion (cf. Judg 6:3–5).

In response to the famine, *a man from Bethlehem of Judah went to sojourn in the territory of Moab*. The rare phrase "Bethlehem of Judah"[6] recalls the sojourns of the unnamed Levite (Judg 17:7, 9; 19:1, 18) and Jesse, David's father (1 Sam 17:12), and forms another link between the time of the judges and the start of the monarchy. The harrowing experience of the Levite and his concubine on their sojourn illustrates the worst outcome for those seeking refuge during that time (Judg 19:10–30). That such disgraceful behavior happened in an Israelite town makes matters worse, but surely a foreign country would commit such depravity (cf. vv. 10–12)? In any case, we are warned that to seek refuge in a strange place is a fraught decision.

It is ironic that a man from Bethlehem (*bêt leḥem*, "house of bread") had to leave with his family because they were starving. *He and his wife and two sons* presents him as the central character—his family is described in relation to him. This also hints that he is responsible for the decision to leave the promised land. It was meant to be a temporary stay (*gûr*, "sojourn") in Moab to avoid the famine, but they end up settling (v. 2) and then living there for at least ten years (v. 4).[7] Although another descriptor for Moab could have been chosen,[8] here it is "the fields of Moab" (*śədê mô'āb*; also 1:2, 6 [twice], 22),

---

6. As opposed to its counterpart in Zebulun (Josh 19:15–16), the possible hometown of the judge Ibzan (Judg 12:8, 10).

7. Although the verb *gûr* can mean dwelling temporarily or permanently (BDB, 157), the progression in vv. 1–4 suggests the former. EVV reflect both meanings: "live for a while" (NIV) and "to sojourn" (ESV); and "to dwell" (NJPS) and "to live" (HCSB).

8. Elsewhere in the Old Testament, several words are used to describe Moab, including field (*śādeh*), plains (*'ărābâ*), boundary/territory (*biḡbûl*), but also land (*'ereṣ*).

## 1:1–6 The End of a Family Line in Moab

whereas Judah is described as "the land of Judah" (*'ereṣ yəhûdâ*; 1:7).[9] The variation may simply be stylistic, or it may signal that Judah is a region while Moab is a land or country.[10] Yet the use of *śādeh* is evocative, and every time in this chapter it is used in relation to the family or a family member (vv. 1, 6, 22).[11] In this verse, the family sojourns in the fields of Moab, perhaps reflecting their hope that these fields will be full of grain to satiate their hunger.[12] Since the "house of bread" has no bread, a family seeks food in the "fields of Moab."

A famine triggering a sojourn to a foreign country evokes the patriarchal narratives (Gen 12:10–20; 26:1, 7–17; 46:2–4; cf. 47:4).[13] Each time, however, they journeyed to Egypt under God's direction. Here, an Israelite family journeys to Moab of their own accord. Seeking hospitality from the Moabites would have been frowned upon by the audience of Ruth. Although Moabites were distant relatives, Israelites held them with disdain because of their incestuous origins (Gen 19:30–38). They were to be excluded from the assembly of Yahweh (Deut 23:3–6)[14] because they refused to show hospitality toward Israel, a disgraceful act in an honor-shame society. And they even hired Balaam to curse Israel (Num 22–24). At Shittim, the Israelite men joined the Moabite women in worshipping the Baal Peor, which probably involved sexual immorality (Num 25:1–3).[15] Closer to the setting of the Ruth narrative, there were intermittently hostile relations between the two countries (Judg 3:12–30).[16] During the time of the judge Jephthah, Israel worshiped the gods of Moab along with the gods of the nations (10:6). There was a short period during which Israel probably enjoyed cordial relations with Moab, but the overall depiction of Moab was negative—they were considered outsiders.[17] Thus, for an Israelite man to uproot his family to sojourn in Moab was

---

9. Or, in relation to Bethlehem, "Bethlehem of Judah" (1:1, 2). Similar to *śādeh*, *'ereṣ* is an evocative term, the same word used for the land that God promised to Abram and his descendants (Gen 12:1, 7; 15:7; 17:8; 26:3–4; 28:13–15).

10. "Country" or "territory" of a nation is another gloss for *śādeh*; BDB, 961.

11. The noun *śādeh* refers to cultivated ground later in the Ruth narrative, where the two meanings ("field" and "territory") are juxtaposed (2:2, 3, 6).

12. In terms of climate, Moab could have received more rain than Israel because the Transjordan plateau is higher than the Cisjordan in some sections. Hence, rain would fall on the western margins of Moab.

13. For further discussion, see Lau and Goswell, *Unceasing Kindness*, 71–74.

14. Although Moab ceased to exist as a nation by the postexilic period, their exclusion from the assembly is mentioned in Neh 13:1; cf. Ezra 9:1.

15. Both the cultic center Beth Peor and the worship of the Baal of Peor became symbols of religious apostasy (Deut 4:3–4; cf. Josh 22:17; Ps 106:28; Hos 9:10).

16. Ten thousand Moabite men died when Yahweh raised up Ehud to deliver Israel (Judg 3:29).

17. The Moabite stone provides extrabiblical evidence of the hostility between Israel and

67

THE BOOK OF RUTH

both risky and shameful. The proximity of Moab may have been attractive since it was located east of the Dead Sea.[18] Nonetheless, the negative associations with the Moabites must have made it a last resort.

The words "honor" and "shame" are not found in this verse, but honor-shame dynamics are not far below the surface. The period of the judges (v. 1) was a time when the social fabric of the Israelite collectivist society was ripped apart.[19] The outcome of generation after generation not knowing Yahweh and what he had done for Israel was relational disharmony. Without a "king," everyone did what was right in their own eyes (17:6; 18:1; 19:1; 21:25), with the resultant chaos and anarchy bringing God and his people into disrepute. The hunger of famine is shameful in itself[20] but is heightened if it is understood as a punishment for covenantal disobedience. From God's perspective, he might have needed to punish his people, but in the eyes of the surrounding peoples this lack of provision causes God to "lose face." The problem is compounded when God's people leave the promised land because of famine, for the land was the sphere of God's blessing. In response to the Babylonian exile, the nations would say, "These are the people of Yahweh, and yet they had to go out of his land" (Ezek 36:20 ESV, adapted). Just as God's name would be profaned among the nations in the Babylonian exile, so it would have been when this Israelite chose a voluntary exile.

And it would have been shameful for Elimelech to uproot his family and leave Israel. In a collectivist culture, the group has precedence over the individual. A "famine in the land" affected the nation, so for a man and his family to abandon his nation in a time of disaster would have been frowned upon. If the famine was God's punishment, the response should have been to repent and call others to do the same. If the famine was not punishment, God's people are enjoined to trust in him and to plead for him to break the

---

Moab. It celebrates a number of military victories by Mesha, king of Moab, during the time of Omri. See J. Andrew Dearman, ed., *Studies in the Mesha Inscription and Moab* (Atlanta: Scholars Press, 1989), 93–95.

18. Moab was between the Zered and Arnon Rivers, with the Dead Sea marking its western border. We are not told where in Moab they settled and whether they took the route to the north or south of the Dead Sea. The journey could have ranged from 80 to 160 km (50 to 100 miles). A journey of 120 km (75 miles) would take about three days by foot. For a discussion of the routes and roadways in Moab, see Bruce Routledge, *Moab in the Iron Age: Hegemony, Polity, Archaeology* (Philadelphia: University of Pennsylvania Press, 2004), 44–45.

19. From a kinship perspective, see Gordon Oeste, "Butchered Brothers and Betrayed Families: Degenerating Kinship Structures in the Book of Judges," *JSOT* 35 (2011): 295–316.

20. The prophet Ezekiel speaks of "the disgrace of famine" (36:30). Humiliation is suffered by those who cannot provide for themselves. In the Old Testament, victims of the sword are more fortunate than victims of hunger (Lam 4:9).

## 1:1–6 The End of a Family Line in Moab

famine. Moreover, disgrace would have been attached to the chosen destination because Moabites were viewed as a despised outgroup. There is no narratorial evaluation, but the circumstances and actions of this family are loaded with shame elements.

It is difficult to assess Elimelech's decision to take his family out of the promised land because there is no explicit evaluation by the narrator. Do his actions spring from a lack of trust in God, and are the subsequent tragedies God's punishment?[21] Or should we understand the tragic events as incidental details that function to set the scene for the following plot?[22]

**2** Departing from Old Testament narrative convention, the characters are named after their action is described.[23] This withholding of their names not only piques audience curiosity, it also emphasizes the action of the characters. Moreover, it introduces *šēm*, "name," as an important motif in the book (also 1:4; 2:1, 19; 4:5, 10, 11, 14, 17; cf. 4:18–22).[24] We can see this in the three parallel clauses:

> The name [*wəšēm*] of the man was Elimelech,
> the name [*wəšēm*] of his wife was Naomi,
> and the names [*wəšēm*] of his two sons were Mahlon and Chilion.

Elimelech means "my God is king," which strikes both an orthodox and dissonant chord. The era of the judges lacked a human king, but this was not meant to be a problem. As Gideon states after the men of Israel tried to install his family as a dynasty, starting with him as king: "I will not rule over you, and my son will not rule over you; Yahweh will rule over you" (Judg 8:22–23 ESV). Yet the one given a theologically orthodox name, "my God is king," does not live up to his name because he leaves the promised land, the divine king's chosen earthly land. Perhaps his action betrays a lack of trust in God so that the physical departure reflects the spiritual.[25] When placed next to the patriarchal narratives, the dissonance is more jarring because Elimelech does not wait for a word from his king before he leaves. At the same time, although God is not mentioned explicitly in the narrative, this indirect mention gently reminds us he is sovereign. And so we watch for his subtle guidance of subsequent events.

---

21. E.g., Charles P. Baylis, "Naomi in the Book of Ruth in Light of the Mosaic Covenant," *BSac* 161 (2004): 420–22; Block, *Discourse*, 72–77; Younger, *Judges and Ruth*, 429.

22. E.g., Bush, *Ruth, Esther*, 67; Eskenazi and Frymer-Kensky, *Ruth*, 6, 8; Sakenfeld, *Ruth*, 21; and for an extended defense of this position, Robert B. Chisholm Jr., *A Commentary on Judges and Ruth* (Grand Rapids: Kregel Academic, 2013), 592–600.

23. Cf. Gen 2:10–14; 4:20–22; Grossman, *Ruth*, 75–76.

24. Cf. Saxegaard, *Character*, 57–61.

25. For a discussion of the irony of Elimelech's name, see Saxegaard, *Character*, 61–65.

# THE BOOK OF RUTH

His wife's name is Naomi, which means "pleasant" or "pleasant one." This is derived from the root *n'm*,[26] as confirmed by her speech upon her return to Bethlehem (vv. 20–21). Elimelech's sons are introduced with a clause that begins with *wəšēm* (singular, "the name"), although two names follow. The singular is consistent with the way the sons were first introduced as a single unit (*two sons*)—they together departed with their father—and prepares us for subsequent events that will happen to both of them. The meaning of the rhyming names Mahlon and Chilion[27] is uncertain, but probably mean "sickness" and "destruction," respectively.[28] Such tragic names could have been chosen by the narrator to anticipate their fate. Yet, they may be their given names. In the Old Testament, names derived from the circumstances surrounding the birth of a child and/or were predictive. For instance, Isaac ("he laughs") reflects the laughter of both Abram and Sarah in response to God's declaring that they would have a son (Gen 17:17, 19; 18:12). God changes Abram's name (meaning "exalted father") to Abraham because he would be the "father of a multitude nations" (Gen 17:5). The giving of shameful names for children is not unknown in the Old Testament. For instance, Jabez's mother said she named him as such "because I bore him with pain" (1 Chr 4:9 NASB1995).[29] If the names Mahlon and Chilion were given at birth, we might speculate that it was because they appeared "sickly" and

---

26. "To be pleasant, delightful, lovely" (cf. 1:20–21); cf. BDB, 653. The name may be shortened, missing the theophoric element, such as in *'abdî*, "servant of Yahweh" (e.g., 1 Kgs 18:3) or perhaps "servant of God" (1 Chr 5:15); contrast Elimelech and the masculine name Elnaam, "God is pleasant" (1 Chr 11:46). The name may also contain the first-person singular suffix, in which case the name means "my pleasant one, my delight," similar to the name Hephzibah, "my delight is in her" (2 Kgs 21:1; cf. Isa 62:4). In light of this uncertainty, "pleasant" or "pleasant one" is best. Names based on the root *n'm*, such as the female Ugaritic names *Nu-ú-ma-ya* and *Nu-ú-ma-ya-nu*, were prevalent by at least 1400 BCE; for references, see Campbell, *Ruth*, 53; Hubbard, *Ruth*, 88–89.

27. Other biblical brothers have rhyming names (e.g., Gen 4:20–21; 22:21; 36:26; 46:21).

28. Both names have an *-ôn* suffix, which indicates an adjective, abstract substantive, or diminutive (*IBHS* §5.7b). Mahlon apparently derives from the root *mḥl*, "to be sick" (cf. *HALOT* 2:569; *DCH* 5:218), although it may be related to the Arabic *maḥala*, "to be sterile." Chilion apparently derives from the root *klh*, "to be finished, to annihilate" (*HALOT* 2:479; BDB, 563). The personal name *klyn* is found in Ugaritic texts. For further discussion and other possible meanings of the sons' names, see Sasson, *Ruth*, 18–19.

29. For Jabez, as for Elimelech's sons, the ghastly association with his name is a heavy burden to carry for a lifetime. The first part of Jabez's prayer is well known, but the second part is relevant to our discussion here. He asks for blessing from God, and then he continues: "May your hand be with me, and you would keep me from harm, so that I would not be in pain." And God answered his prayer (1 Chr 4:10). Jabez was aware that his name was a grave portent of his future, but he did not resign himself to that fact. He actively sought the one who could change his destiny. In the Old Testament, given names are not absolutely predictive but changing one's destiny requires pleading with God for his active intervention.

## 1:1–6 The End of a Family Line in Moab

"deathly," perhaps because of the famine in Bethlehem. In any case, their similar names suggest a common fate.

The family is described as *Ephrathites from Bethlehem of Judah*. This unusual collocation of Ephrath and Bethlehem evokes an earlier Old Testament event—the death of the matriarch Rachel (Gen 35:18–20). Jacob buries her "on the way to Ephrath (that is, Bethlehem)" (Gen 35:19; cf. 48:7). "Ephrath" and "Bethlehem" evoke a more significant association closer to the historical period of the Ruth narrative. King David was an Ephrathite and is described similarly to Elimelech's family:

[They were] Ephrathites from Bethlehem of Judah (*'eprātîm mibbêt leḥem yəhûdâ*; Ruth 1:2)

David was the son of a certain Ephrathite from Bethlehem of Judah (*wədāwid ben-'îš 'eprātî hazzê mibbêt leḥem yəhûdâ*; 1 Sam 17:12)

The ears of the original audience would have pricked up at the mention of Ephrath, a clan resident in or around Bethlehem.[30] How might this family be linked to the greatest Israelite king?[31] And since this family's humiliating situation is jarring compared to its final esteemed position, how will honor be restored? The narrator reminds us of the difficulty facing this family: they departed Bethlehem (v. 1), then *entered the territory of Moab and stayed[32] there*. The lack of a time reference commonly found with the phrase "they stayed there" (*wayyihyû-šām*) might indicate the experience of many immigrants: the migration is a temporary sojourn without a definite return date.

**3** Given the introduction to the characters, and their safe emigration to Moab (v. 2), the narrator seems to be preparing us, the audience, for a long acquaintance with them. So we are surprised when Elimelech suddenly dies. Typical of Old Testament narrative, the fact is stated laconically—the narrator provides no explanation or contributing factors. We are left wondering: Did Elimelech die of "natural causes"? Or should we understand his death as punishment from God? In any case, we must not miss the undertone of shame in death and burial in a foreign unclean land (cf. Amos 7:17). Burial outside the promised land was undesirable, as indicated by the patriarch

---

30. The clan might be named after Ephrath, the wife of Caleb, the eponymous ancestor of Bethlehem (1 Chr 4:4; cf. 2:50–51). Elimelech and Boaz were from the same Ephrathite clan and probably inhabited the same region of Bethlehem (2:1, 3).

31. Later in biblical history, the prophet Micah would look forward to another messianic ruler from "Bethlehem Ephrathah" (5:1–4 [2–5]).

32. The verb *hyh* usually means "to be, become, occur, exist," but another gloss is "to remain, live" (Exod 34:28; 2 Sam 4:3; 13:38; 1 Chr 12:40 [39]); *HALOT* 1:244.

71

# THE BOOK OF RUTH

Jacob's instructions for his burial "with [his] fathers" (Gen 47:29–31; 49:29–33).[33] Sadly, Elimelech was not granted this option.

Previously introduced as Elimelech's wife, Naomi is now the central character, with her family described in relation to her: Elimelech is *the husband of Naomi* and *she was left, she and her two sons*. The rarity of this naming of a man in relation to a woman[34] highlights the poignancy of Naomi's situation and signals the family responsibilities passing to her as the remaining parent. The *niphal* verb *šā'ēr*, "to remain, to be left over," is often used in the context of bereavement, God's judgment (e.g., Gen 7:23; Lev 26:36, 39; Deut 4:27; Ezek 6:12), and his grace for those who remain (e.g., Gen 7:23; Joel 2:14).[35] Thankfully, all is not lost for Naomi because she still has two sons to care and provide for her. The first cycle of events ends with an ember of hope.

**4** Hope flares for the continuation of the family and their lineage as Naomi's sons take *for themselves Moabite wives*. The choice of the verb *nāśā'*, "lift," colors the sons' marriages since it has negative connotations in texts related to the Ruth narrative. In Judges, the phrase describes the Benjaminites' abduction of the dancers at Shiloh for their wives (21:23), and in Ezra-Nehemiah, the ethnic intermarriages (Ezra 9:2, 12; 10:44; Neh 13:25). The narrator later uses the verb *lāqaḥ*, "take" (Ruth 4:13), regularly used for marriage elsewhere in the Old Testament,[36] so the choice of *nāśā'* here is at least suggestive.

Just as the sons were named in the corresponding element in the first cycle, the wives are named here—*the first was Orpah, and the name of the second was Ruth*. While the sons were described as a single unit, their wives are described separately: "the first was . . . the second was. . . ." At this point, we do not know which son took which wife,[37] but the wives' separate naming anticipates their individual agency. The meaning of the name Orpah is uncertain, with suggestions including "back of the neck," "cloud," and "perfume."[38] The first suggestion is the most common and is usually interpreted negatively: Orpah will "turn her neck" on her mother-in-law.[39] However, there is no nar-

---

33. Joseph gave similar burial instructions (Gen 50:24–26), based on God's land promise (Gen 12:1–3, 7).

34. Exceptions include Judg 20:4 and Matt 1:16.

35. Cf. H. Wildberger, "*š'r*," *TLOT* 3:1286–87; Clements, "*šā'ar*," *TDOT* 14:275–76.

36. Cf. Seebass, "*lāqaḥ*," *TDOT* 8:19.

37. Mahlon is named before Chilion, so convention elsewhere in the Old Testament would suggest that he is the elder son (e.g., Gen 10:25; 41:50–52; Exod 18:3–4; 1 Chr 1:19). Since Orpah is named before Ruth (v. 4), the reader might conclude that Mahlon married Orpah while Chilion married Ruth. It will be revealed that Mahlon was Ruth's husband (4:10).

38. Ugaritic *'rpt* means "clouds" (cf. Akkadian *erpu* and Heb. *'ārîp*; BDB, 791). Arabic *'arf* means "perfume, scent." For further possibilities, see Hubbard, *Ruth*, 94n14.

39. Heb. *'ōrep* means "back of the neck." Figuratively, with the verb *qāšâ* it means "stiff

## 1:1–6 THE END OF A FAMILY LINE IN MOAB

ratorial censure, and Naomi even commends her (1:15). The meaning of the name Ruth is also uncertain, with suggestions including "friend, companion," and "refreshment, satiation."[40] Based on tentative biblical and extrabiblical evidence, the latter is the most likely.[41] If so, in the context of the famine in Judah, her name can be viewed ironically or portentously.[42] In any case, the opaque meanings of Orpah and Ruth's names are consistent with the obscurity of their characterizations and destinies at this point in the narrative.

The first cycle described how "they entered the territory of Moab and stayed there," and now the second cycle describes how *They lived there about ten years*. What began as a sojourn (v. 1) turned into a migration. Reflecting the experience of immigrants the world over, a temporary stay (in this case to ensure survival) turned into a permanent residence. If not for the deaths of Naomi's husband and two sons, presumably this family would have stayed even longer. This raises questions about their degree of assimilation into Moabite society. Had they taken on the local customs and way of life? Did they worship the local Moabite deity, either solely or syncretistically?

If Naomi's family maintained their allegiance to Yahweh, the marriages of Mahlon and Chilion to non-Israelites can be understood as the inevitable outcome of questionable prior decisions. Living in Moab, their range of marriage partners was restricted—Moabite or make the long journey back to find an Israelite. As the family matriarch, Naomi would have had a strong influence on their choice of partners, including the authority to forbid them from marrying foreigners.[43] It would have been more convenient to marry local women, and if they had taken up the local customs and way of living, it would have felt most natural to them. It is thus hard for us to cast harsh judgment on Mahlon and Chilion for their marriage to non-Israelites. But if we trace the events back, we will realize that this decision is the outcome of

---

necked" or "obstinate" (e.g., Exod 32:8; Deut 9:6, 13; Jer 7:26; Neh 9:16, 17; 2 Chr 30:8). Additionally, *'ōrep* in the phrase *pānâ 'el 'ōrep* ("turned to me their back") refers to apostasy (Jer 2:27; 32:33; cf. 2 Chr 29:6; BDB, 791).

40. Syr. reads *rə'ût* (cf. Heb. *rə'ût*, "companion"; Exod 11:2; Esth 1:19), although this reading is not supported by the other versions. However, the loss of the *'ayin* from the name is unlikely, which also militates against deriving the name from *r'h*, "to see."

41. The Moabite Mesha inscription (line 12) uses the word *ryt*, "satiation." A possible Hebrew root for the name is *rwh/rwy*, "saturate, satiate" (e.g., Isa 58:11); BDB, 924. For references, see Hubbard, *Ruth*, 94n15.

42. Eskenazi and Frymer-Kensky, *Ruth*, 7, observes a water connection: Orpah is a cloud that passes above without bringing rain; Ruth is the moisture from below that will bring life.

43. This would be consistent with how marriages were arranged in ancient Israelite society, e.g., Hagar for Ishmael (Gen 21:21); Abraham for Isaac (Gen 24); Laban for his daughters (Gen 29); Manoah and his wife for Samson (Judg 14:1–3). Naomi clearly directs Ruth later in the narrative (3:1–4).

73

## The Book of Ruth

a string of questionable decisions. Should Naomi have taken her sons back to Bethlehem after Elimelech died? Should they have returned to Bethlehem sooner, since their stay in Moab was only supposed to be temporary? Should they have left the promised land in the first place? A questionable decision can be the final consequence of a string of questionable decisions.

*Ten years* could refer to the length of time the sons lived in Moab after their marriage or the time elapsed since the family departed Bethlehem. The former is the better interpretation based on the cyclical structure of vv. 2–5, whereby the *wayyiqtol wayyēšəbû*, "and they lived," presents the next event after the marriage of the sons.[44] Ten years recalls the Abraham narrative, for "after Abram had lived ten years in the land of Canaan," his wife Sarah gave Hagar to Abram as a surrogate because she was frustrated with her barrenness (Gen 16:1–3 ESV). There are differences between the narratives,[45] but the allusion brings out an unstated fact in the Ruth narrative—the sons' marriages were childless. It was not just one marriage but two. The lack of an heir to continue the family line raises a major narrative tension. And at this point of the narrative, we wonder if Ruth and Orpah were barren or if the sons were sterile.

**5** An appreciation of the sequence of the first cycle (B-C-D) would leave the audience with a feeling of dread. A description of staying in Moab was followed by the death of Elimelech (vv. 2–3). Now, a description of staying (v. 4) is followed by *then the two of them also died—Mahlon and Chilion.* Not only did Elimelech die, so *also* did Mahlon and Chilion.[46] Their deaths are presented together, although we are not told whether they died at the same time. The effect is a double blow for Naomi—not just one, but both sons died. One significance of their death is that it signals the end of the family line since neither has produced a child. No future generations also means no ongoing existence for Elimelech. Only Naomi is left behind, stripped of her social roles. She is described barely, as *the woman,* one *left without her two children and without her husband.* A wife no more, a mother no more. Our empathy is aroused by the phrase *yəlādêhā,* "her children." Previously described as *bānêhā,* "her sons" (v. 3; cf. "his two sons" in vv. 1, 2), although they were married men, as a mother she still saw them as her precious "children."[47] The use of *yeled,* "child," raises the idea of giving birth, of new children, to which the

---

44. *Pace* Bush, *Ruth, Esther,* 65.

45. Sarah gives Hagar to Abraham after ten years of living in Canaan, while Naomi's sons marry Moabites and live in Moab for ten years.

46. Heb. *gam,* "also," refers back to the death of Elimelech (v. 3). Most EVV include "also" (e.g., HCSB, NJPS, NIV) but not all (e.g., ESV "and both Mahlon and Chilion died").

47. She will use *bānîm,* "sons," again in vv. 11, 12. Only here does *yeled* refer to married men. Usually the term means "child" (Ezra 10:1); "boy" (e.g., Joel 4:3; Zech 8:5), or "youth" (in contrast to "elders"; 1 Kgs 12:8, 10, 14 = 2 Chr 10:8, 10, 14); see BDB, 409.

## 1:1–6 The End of a Family Line in Moab

narrative will return (4:16, 18–22). For now, we feel for this woman who was left behind, exposed: she must fend for herself in a foreign country without family, without social support, and seemingly without hope.

Not only was Naomi materially destitute, she was also socially destitute. Widowhood was shameful in ancient Israel, as reflected in Isaiah. "And seven women will grab hold of one man in that day, saying, 'We will eat our own bread and wear our own clothes; only let us be called by your name. Take away our disgrace'" (4:1). "Fear not, for you will not be ashamed; be not confounded, for you will not be disgraced; for you will forget the shame of your youth, and the reproach of your widowhood you will remember no more" (54:4 ESV). In ancient Israel, a woman's primary roles were as a wife and a mother, yet Naomi was left without a husband and children. As we will find out, Ruth and Orpah had the option to return to their mother's houses (v. 8) and were young enough to remarry (v. 9) and bear children, but this option was not open to Naomi. Not surprisingly, the widow ('almānâ) is often grouped with the orphan (e.g., Job 22:9; 24:3; Isa 10:2; Ps 94:6; Mal 3:5), the sojourner (e.g., Ps 94:6; Mal 3:5; Zec 7:10), the hired worker (Mal 3:5), the poor (e.g., Isa 10:2; Job 24:3–4; 31:16), and the Levites (Deut 14:29).[48] There was no law prohibiting the remarriage of widows, but in a culture where virginity was prized (cf. Deut 22:20–21), she would not have been viewed as attractive. Naomi's loss of economic and social support is often mentioned but not what this leads to—social disgrace. By the end of the chapter, it will become clear that shame is one of Naomi's major problems that needs resolution.

The lack of narratorial evaluation throws the spotlight on Naomi's situation and shame, but leaves open the question of guilt before God. Why did the sons die? Like Elimelech, their deaths follow a description of their stay in Moab. But again, the narrator does not draw a causal link between these two events. On the one hand, reading these tragedies within the context of the Pentateuch/Torah allows us to understand them as God's punishment. Famine, the triggering event, is often God's judgment against covenant disobedience (Lev 26:18–20; Deut 28:20–24; cf. 2 Sam 21:1; 1 Kgs 8:35–40). It is a corporate punishment—all Israel suffers together—irrespective of the degree of individual culpability. Patriarchs migrated when there was a famine in the land, but a closer examination of these migrations indicates that migration was a valid response if directly commanded by God.[49] Otherwise,

---

48. Although the word is not used in the book of Ruth, 'almānâ denotes a woman without a male provider and protector (husband, sons, and often also brothers) and has completely negative connotations; Hoffner, "'almānâ," *TDOT* 1:288; J. Kühlewein, "'almānâ," *TLOT* 1:128.

49. See Lau and Goswell, *Unceasing Kindness*, 71–74.

THE BOOK OF RUTH

the appropriate response would have been to repent of any sin and remain in the promised land. Elimelech took his family out of the promised land, then died. Given the shorter life spans of the time, his death might not be surprising. But then both his sons also die, and we might suspect that their deaths are not just unfortunate. Our suspicions would be heightened when they take foreign wives, which is legally questionable (Deut 7:3–4). Indeed, foreign wives can be a curse for covenant disobedience (28:32), as can barrenness of the womb (28:18). Because of the Ruth narrative's close links with pentateuchal texts, I lean toward this understanding of events.

On the other hand, reading these family tragedies within the context of the Old Testament, especially the wisdom literature, loosens a strict correlation between sin and suffering. Indeed, there is a lack of an explicit mention of sin and divine punishment in these verses (vv. 1–5).[50] The famines in the time of the patriarchs are not tied to the sins of God's people, and famine drives God's people to Egypt, where God's promise of offspring and nation is fulfilled (Gen 46:3; cf. 12:1–3). Books such as Job, Proverbs, and Ecclesiastes militate against a mechanistic view of retributive justice, whereby God can only reward righteousness and punish wickedness.[51]

The famine and tragedy in the Ruth narrative spur us to ask why they happen. As in the narrative, God will not always reveal the cause of or the purpose for suffering. Sometimes the cause is obvious, sometimes we can discern God's purposes in retrospect, and sometimes we will never know either (see the book of Job). Often suffering is part of the general effect of sin in the world (Gen 3). Suffering cannot always be attributed to a specific sin, ours or that of others, and tragedies cannot automatically be attributed to God's judgment. This was Jesus's teaching after the collapse of the tower of Siloam (Luke 13:1–5). The right response to tragedy is to examine our own lives and to repent, to turn back to God. Whatever the cause, we trust God amid suffering, knowing that he is both sovereign and gracious. In all things, he is working for good (Gen 50:20; Rom 8:28–30) and for his glory, and his comforting presence is with us (Ps 23:4, 6; 2 Cor 1:3–4).

The description of Naomi's destitution ends the second parallel cycle of events (B'-C'-D'; vv. 4–5). Within this literary structure, we find the repetition of: "two"; the naming of characters; the duration of stays; and those who died and those who were left. This orderly presentation seems to clash with the disorderly nature of the events described. Or does it? Perhaps it is meant

---

50. Compare, e.g., Gen 38:10, "And what he did was wicked in the sight of Yahweh, and he put him to death also" (ESV).

51. Lindsay Wilson, "Job," in *Theological Interpretation of the Old Testament: A Book-by-Book Survey*, ed. Kevin J. Vanhoozer, Craig G. Bartholomew, and Daniel J. Treier (Grand Rapids: Baker, 2008), 154.

## 1:1–6 The End of a Family Line in Moab

to portray justice being served, the settling of an account.[52] Or perhaps it points to a hidden hand behind the events, so some hope amid the ruins. Echoes of the patriarchal narratives can already be heard, so we wonder if God will reverse Naomi's loss and barrenness.

**6** This verse functions as a hinge, closing the first scene and previewing the events of the next. Reading it as the narrative conclusion corresponding to the narrative opening (A-A'; vv. 1, 6) provides the following insights. Elimelech was established as the central character, but this role has shifted to Naomi. She is the subject of the verbs, beginning with *Then she arose . . . and she returned.* The Hebrew syntax highlights Naomi as the protagonist: *she and her daughters-in-law,* which is understated with translations such as "she arose with her daughters-in-law."[53] As the female head of an all-female household, a rare, although not unknown, role in the Old Testament (e.g., Gen 21:21; 1 Kgs 17:7–11), she now makes her first critical decision. If Elimelech was responsible for the decision to sojourn in a foreign land, then Naomi is responsible for the decision to depart and return. The use of *wattāqām,* "and she arose," primarily anticipates the main action: she arose to return to Bethlehem. But if *wayyēšəbû,* "and they stayed" (v. 4) implied assimilation into Moabite culture and religion, Naomi's decision hints at getting up and turning her back on it. At the very least, we are introduced to the concept of *šûb,* "to return," which will become a strong motif by the end of the chapter (1:6, 7, 8, 10, 11, 12, 15 [2×], 16, 21, 22 [2×]).[54] But since *wattāšāb,* "she returned," is singular, will her daughters-in-law also return? If so, in what sense? For they did not originate from Bethlehem.

Naomi decided to return *because she heard in the territory of Moab that Yahweh had attended to his people.* God was not mentioned when Elimelech departed, but his action is the trigger for Naomi's return. Strictly speaking, this is hearsay; Naomi heard it, the narrator did not describe God's action. Nonetheless, we have no reason to doubt the veracity of the statement. Most likely, we are to take it at face value—that Naomi heard the news from someone who had traveled from Judah. However, *šāmʿâ,* "she heard," might also imply "understanding."[55] Whether or not it includes this latter meaning, the description hints that Naomi is more spiritually attuned than Elimelech.

The first mention of Yahweh in the Ruth narrative is positive. He shows grace: *he attended to his people by giving them food.* The basic meaning of the

---

52. Grossman, *Ruth,* 84–85.

53. E.g., ESV and NJPS, but cf. NIV. The three verbs "to arise," "to return," and "to hear" are third-person feminine singular, despite Naomi's daughters-in-law accompanying her on her journey.

54. The verb is only used three times in the rest of the book (2:6; 4:3, 15).

55. The verb is used to refer to understanding a language (Gen 11:7; Deut 28:49; Ezek 3:6), and to "spiritual hearing" (e.g., Num 24:4; Ezek 3:12); *HALOT* 4:1572.

# The Book of Ruth

verb *pāqad* is "to attend to, to visit," but the specific meaning depends on the context. Used with Yahweh as the subject, he visits to examine the plight of his people: (1) graciously (e.g., Gen 21:1; 50:24, 25; Isa 23:17; Jer 15:15; Ps 65:10); (2) to punish (e.g., Exod 32:34; Jer 6:15; Ps 59:6[5]); or (3) to test (e.g., Job 7:18; Ps 17:3).[56] The first is the case here: God intervenes to bless his people with food. The basis upon which God will respond to his people is their covenant relationship. God redeemed his people in the exodus and formed them into the nation of Israel. Their grateful response was to remain loyal to him, and one main way this was expressed was through obedience to the law. If God's people obeyed him and hence maintained the covenant relationship, God would continue to bless them. But if they disobeyed the law, God would visit them in punishment. The lack of a cause for the famine becomes conspicuous now that God intervenes to break it.

Attention is drawn to God's provision by the alliteration and assonance in Hebrew, *lātēt lāhem lāḥem*, "to give them food," giving it a lovely rhythmic feel.[57] And the irony of Beth*lehem*—a house without bread (vv. 1, 2)—is now reversed. The reversal of the famine in Bethlehem triggers Naomi's locational reversal, as she begins to return from her exile in a foreign land. The repetition of *territory of Moab* in this verse is redundant and serves to draw attention to the spread of the news of God's intervention beyond the border of Israel. If the departure of an Israelite family caused dishonor to his name, the news of his provision begins its restoration. The actions of Yahweh, in both judgment and blessing, are known even in the land of Chemosh, the Moabite deity. The name of Yahweh was always meant to be great among the nations (cf. Mal 1:5, 11). When God's people were restored after the exile, the people of the nations said, "Yahweh has done great things for them" (Ps 126:1–2 ESV). Elimelech and his family had fled beyond the borders of Israel, cut themselves off from God's people, and brought dishonor to God's name. But now it is time for Naomi to swallow her pride and return—to Yahweh's people, Yahweh's land, and perhaps Yahweh himself.

Even amid chaos, suffering, and death, God is quietly working to restore lives and reputations. His actions might not be clearly manifest; spiritual discernment is required. But we keep in mind that our creator is also our sustainer. Even in famine, God remains faithful to those who fear him (Pss 33:18–19, 37:19; 1 Kgs 17:1–6). Although God might bring discipline through hardship, including famine, he will redeem his people from death (Job 5:17–27). In the New Testament, Jesus taught us to depend on our Heavenly Father as we pray, "Give us today our daily bread" (Matt 6:11 NIV; cf. Luke 11:3). We can pray this for ourselves and, if we are not suffering from hunger, for those in the world who are.

56. BDB, 823; *DCH* 6:738.
57. Porten, "Scroll," 25.

## B. EN ROUTE: NAOMI, ORPAH, AND RUTH DIALOGUE (1:7–19A)

The scene was set and the crisis outlined (vv. 1–5). Having heard that God broke the famine in Israel, Naomi prepared to return (v. 6). In the first scene, over ten years were compressed into six verses. In this scene, Naomi and her daughters-in-law are en route to Bethlehem (v. 7), and it details a conversation with three dialogues between Naomi and her two daughters-in-law. Naomi convinces Orpah to go back to Moab, while Ruth commits herself to Naomi (vv. 8–18). The narrator then telescopes the action to their arrival in Bethlehem (v. 19a).

[7] *So she set out from the place where she had stayed,[a] and her two daughters-in-law with her,[b] and they went on the way[c] to return[d] to the land of Judah.*

[8] *And Naomi said to her two[e] daughters-in-law, "Go, return, each[f] to the house of her mother![g] May Yahweh deal[h] kindly with you, just as you[i] have dealt with those who died[j] and with me.[k]*

[9] *May Yahweh give[l] you[m] . . .[n] Find rest, each[o] in the house[p] of her husband." Then she kissed them, and they raised their voice and wept.[q]*

[10] *But they said to her, "Surely[r] with you[s] we will return[t] to your people."*

[11] *And Naomi said, "Return, my daughters. Why would you go[u] with me? Do I still have[v] sons in my belly[w] that they might become[x] husbands[y] for you[z]?*

[12] *Return, my daughters. Go![aa] Because I am too old[ab] to belong to a husband.[ac] Even if I should say[ad] I have hope—if[ae] I belonged to a husband tonight,[af] and if I bore sons[ag]—*

[13] *for them[ah] would you wait[ai] until they were grown up? For them would you restrain yourselves[aj] by not belonging to a husband? No, my daughters! For my bitterness is much greater than yours,[ak] for[al] the hand of Yahweh has gone out against me."*

[14] *And they raised[am] their voice and wept again.[an] Then Orpah kissed her mother-in-law,[ao] but Ruth clung to her.[ap]*

[15] *And she said,[aq] "Look, your sister-in-law has returned to her people and to her god.[ar] Return after your sister-in-law."[as]*

[16] *But Ruth said, "Do not urge me to abandon you, to turn back from following after you.[at] For[au] wherever you go, I will go, and wherever you lodge, I will lodge. Your people are my people, and your God is my God.*

[17] *Wherever you die, I will die[av] and there I will be buried. Thus may Yahweh do to me and thus may he add even more, if even death separates[aw] me from you."*

[18] *When Naomi saw[ax] that she was determined to go with her, she ceased speaking to her.[ay]*

[19a] *The two of them[az] went on until they came to[ba] Bethlehem.*

a. I have left *šāmmâ* (*šam* with directional *he*) untranslated since it does not seem to add further information to the narrative. Cf. *wayyihyû-šām* (v. 2), which lacks the directional

# THE BOOK OF RUTH

*he.* Syriac specifies "the land of their sojourning" for "the place where she had stayed." *Hyh* most commonly means "to be, become, occur, exist," but another gloss is "to remain, live" (*HALOT* 1:244).

b. I have separated the non-*wayyiqtol* null-copula clause ("and her two daughters-in-law with her") from the main plot action because it provides circumstantial information. This is smoothed out in most EVV, e.g., NIV "With her two daughters-in-law she left."

c. The clause "on the way to return to the land of Judah" is omitted in some Tg. MSS, most likely due to homoioteleuton, the scribe's eye moving from the final *h* in *wattēlaknâ* and *yəhûdâ*. This reading is not supported in the versions.

d. The *le* + infinitive of *šûb* here provides the purpose of the main verb (*telaknâ*). See *IBHS* §36.2.3d.

e. Syr. and some LXX manuscripts lack "two," but Tg. and other LXX manuscripts support MT[L].

f. Heb. *'iššâ* here functions distributively (*IBHS* §15.6a–b).

g. Some LXX manuscripts and Syr. read "father's house." Other LXX manuscripts and Tg. support MT[L] reading, "mother's house." See comment on v. 8.

h. The *ketiv ya'aśeh* is modal, while the *qere ya'aś* is jussive (so LXX, Vulg.). Nonetheless, the *ketiv* can be translated as a jussive in this verse, "May Yahweh deal" (cf. Gen 41:34; Ruth 1:17; 1 Sam 3:18; 1 Kgs 2:23).

i. Both occurrences of "you" in this verse translate masculine plural suffixes, although Naomi is addressing her daughters-in-law. 4QRuth[a] and Tg. read second-person masculine plural suffixes, while Syr. has second-person feminine plural suffixes. Gender mismatches of the pronominal suffix (masculine for feminine) are occasionally found elsewhere in the Old Testament, with the preposition (e.g., Gen 31:9; Exod 2:17) and with the verb (e.g., Joel 2:22; Amos 4:1); see JM §149–50. There are eight masculine-for-feminine mismatches in the book of Ruth: (1) a pronominal suffix (1:8, 9, 11, 13, 19; 4:11); (2) a verbal suffix (1:8); and (3) an independent pronoun (1:22). A feminine-for-masculine mismatch of a pronominal suffix is also found (1:13 [2×]). Seven of the ten instances of gender mismatch are spoken by Naomi (1:8 [2×], 9, 11, 13 [3×]). None are spoken by Ruth or Boaz. The other instances are by the narrator (1:19, 22) and the people of Bethlehem (4:11). Scholars have suggested different reasons for these anomalies. The masculine plurals have often been viewed as archaic feminine dual forms; e.g., Bush, *Ruth, Esther*, 75–76; Campbell, *Ruth*, 65. This explanation, however, does not account for the feminine-masculine mismatch in 1:13, nor the regular feminine dual forms elsewhere (1:9, 19 [3×]). Holmstedt, *Handbook*, 24, 47–48, 73, suggests that the author used these cases of "gender confusion" (along with six other features) to give a foreign or archaic flavor to the narrative. Timothy H. Lim, "How Good Was Ruth's Hebrew? Ethnic and Linguistic Otherness in the Book of Ruth," in *The "Other" in Second Temple Judaism: Essays in Honor of John J. Collins* (Grand Rapids: Eerdmans, 2011), 109–12, similarly argues that it is a literary technique, to mark out the speech of the aged. This might account for Naomi's speech and those in Bethlehem, which include elders (4:11). Although Boaz is presumably of the older generation, he does not speak with a gender mismatch because the situation does not arise in the Ruth narrative. Yet this explanation does not account for the narrator's gender mismatches (1:19, 22), the former of which Lim explains away as "a scribal error of assimilation to 4:11." Nonetheless, I lean toward a stylistic explanation for the mismatches to mark out Naomi as from the older generation. Interestingly, Ruth the Moabite speaks in regular Hebrew. Perhaps this functions to render her more attractive to original hearers; at least it lowers one barrier for her acceptance.

## 1:7–19A En route: Naomi, Orpah, and Ruth Dialogue

j. Heb. *hammēṯîm* is comprised of a *ha* prefix and a masculine plural participle. Instead of a definite article, the *ha* can function as a relative marker with a participle; see JM §138c, 145d; Robert D. Holmstedt, *The Relative Clause in Biblical Hebrew*, Linguistic Studies in Ancient West Semitic 10 (Winona Lake, IN: Eisenbrauns, 2016), 69–76. For the relative *ha* with a verb, see 1:22; 2:6; 4:3. In this verse, "those who died" refers to Naomi's sons; cf. Syr., "with my two sons who died."

k. The preposition *'immādî* (with first-person common singular suffix) is an alternate form of *'im* ("with"); BDB, 767.

l. In MT^L and 4QRuth^a there is no object for the *qal* third-person masculine singular jussive verb *yittēn* ("may he give"). The versions add various objects for the verb, e.g., "mercy" (LXX^L), "a full reward" (Tg.), and "kindness" (Syr.; *rḥm'*). Campbell, *Ruth*, 65–66, also suggests adding an object, "recompense." Others read the following imperative clause as the object, "May Yahweh enable you to find rest," e.g., JM §177h; Hubbard, *Ruth*, 98n11. Others still read the imperative clause as expressing a consequence, "May Yahweh give you so that you will find rest" (e.g., GKC §110i). My reading is that it is interrupted syntax, following Holmstedt, *Handbook*, 75; Jeremy Schipper, "The Syntax and Rhetoric of Ruth 1:9a," *VT* 62 (2012): 642–45. Anacolutha are usually found after long parentheses (see GKC §167b for examples), but also in moments of high stress or emotion, such as in 2:7 and elsewhere in the Old Testament (e.g., Exod 32:32). Such a reading does not require emending the text, and maintaining the imperative is consistent with the structure of Naomi's speech in vv. 8–9; see comments.

m. Heb. *lākem* ("you") is another instance of gender mismatch; see note on 1:8.

n. The ellipsis denotes the anacoluthon described in note l.

o. Heb. *'iššâ* here functions distributively (*IBHS* §15.6a–b).

p. The noun *bêt* ("house") can be read either as an adverbial accusative of location (*IBHS* §10.2.2; JM §126h) or as a shortened form of *bəbêt* ("in [the] house"; JM §133c).

q. The noun is singular, "their voice." 4QRuth^a has a *-m* suffix, which Campbell, *Ruth*, 66, suggests is an old feminine dual ending; thus, "their voices" refers to only Orpah and Ruth. However, since evidence for a feminine dual is questionable, and based on MT^L, Tg., Syr., and LXX, the feminine plural form (*qôlān*) is preferred. Moreover, since it is common for the person kissing to weep also (Gen 29:11; 45:15; 50:1), it is likely that all three women raised their voices and wept.

r. The *kî* is read as part of the young women's speech, rather than introducing the speech.

s. *'ittāk*, "with you," is placed before the verb, emphasizing Orpah and Ruth's intention.

t. The use of the imperfect verb *nāšûb* ("we will return"), instead of the cohortative verb *nāšûbâ* ("let us return") adds to the sense of their resolve.

u. After *lāmmâ* ("why") the *yiqtol* verb *tēlaknâ* is modal, "why *would* you go" (e.g., NIV).

v. The *l-* in *lî* here indicates possession, so with the interrogative *h* and the temporal adverb *'ôd*, the translation is "Do I still have . . ."

w. The precise anatomical reference for *mē'îm* is often uncertain (BDB, 588; *DCH* 5:382), unlike the usual words for "womb" (e.g., *beṭen*). To reflect this imprecision, I have translated "belly."

x. The modal *qatal*, *hāyû*, indicates the consequences of the previous nominal clause (*IBHS* §32.2.4a), so the translation is "that they might become."

y. The *l-* in *la'ănāšîm* marks goal or purpose (*IBHS* §11.2.10d, ##38–45). The hypothetical "sons" in Naomi's womb would become "husbands" (*'ănāšîm*).

z. *Lākem* "for you" is another instance of gender mismatch; see note on 1:8. The *l-* here

81

# The Book of Ruth

in *lākem* indicates the person(s) for whom an action is directed (*IBHS* §11.2.10d, ##28–33), in this case, Orpah and Ruth.

aa. Some LXX manuscripts read *lāken* (Gk. *dioti*, "therefore") because *leknā* lacks a final *he-* for a feminine imperative. Syriac lacks the word altogether. However, *leknā* ("go") in MT[L], and supported by Vulg. and Tg., fits well in the literary context (note the full spelling, *leknâ*, in 1:8).

ab. The *min* and stative verb in *mihyôt* produces a "comparison of capability," which expresses the idea that a quality is "too much/too little for" an event or action (*IBHS* §14.4f). Here Naomi is "too old" to belong to a husband.

ac. The phrase *lə'îš*, "belong to a man/husband" occurs twice in this verse, and is a Hebrew idiom for marriage (e.g., Lev 22:12; Deut 24:2; Jer 3:1), which reflects the idea that a woman is under the authority, protection, and provision of a man. Although this is the usual meaning, there is sometimes a rarer meaning of "to have sexual intercourse" (Hos 3:3; so Sasson, *Ruth*, 24–25). This would be consistent with its second use in this verse, which results in pregnancy. If so, Naomi is not just saying that she is too old to get married, but also too old to bear children.

ad. The *kî* either provides a reason and the conditionality is unmarked (JM §167a), or it functions conditionally (for the latter, see *IBHS* §38.2). The modal *qatal* verb *'āmartî* indicates an irreal condition, so I read the phrase as the former option. It introduces a hypothetical situation which supports Naomi's argument that Orpah and Ruth should return to their mothers' houses.

ae. The two clauses marked with *gam* ("even if") are conditional, which build on the first unlikely situation (the presence of hope), and present increasingly unlikely events. The verbs in the three clauses are modal *qatal* first-person singular verbs (*'āmartî, hāyîtî, yāladtî*).

af. *Hallaylâ*, "tonight," in MT[L] is supported by Vulg. and Tg., and is most likely original. Old Latin reads "today." It is omitted in Syr. and some LXX manuscripts. Other LXX manuscripts read "profaned," which probably derives from a misreading of *hallaylâ* as *ḥălîlâ*.

ag. 4QRuth[b] reads "two sons," but the versions do not support this reading.

ah. The word *hălāhēn* occurs twice in this verse and could be read as an interrogative *h* with "therefore," from Aramaic (*lāhēn*; e.g., Dan 2:6, 9; 4:24; *HALOT* 2:521; BDB, 530; *DCH* 4:521). However, it is better to read it as an interrogative *h* with the preposition *lə*, and the third-person feminine plural suffix ("for them"), as also found in 4QRuth[b]. LXX, Syr., Tg., OL, and Vulg. support the reading, "for them," referring to Naomi's "sons" mentioned in the protasis (1:12). The *-n* suffix in MT[L] is thus probably another instance of gender mismatch; see note on v. 8. The fronting of "for them," in this question and the next, emphasizes the choice before the young widows: either they wait in vain for Naomi to produce husbands, or they marry other men.

ai. The *piel* of *śbr* ("to wait, hope") occurs rarely in the Old Testament (Isa 38:18; Pss 104:27; 119:166; 145:15; Esth 9:1), the *qal* ("to test, investigate, inspect") only twice (Neh 2:13, 15); cf. *śēber* ("hope"; Ps 119:116; 146:5). Some view this word as an Aramaism (e.g., *HALOT* 3:1304), thus as evidence for a late composition of Ruth (e.g., Bush, *Ruth, Esther*, 29). However, Zevit, "Dating Ruth," 575, argues that the Aramaisms in Ruth are not concentrated, and even if they are words borrowed from Aramaic, it could instead reflect a particular Hebrew dialect or casual speech with the occasional "chic 'foreign' element." From a literary-stylistic perspective, her speech might sound foreign to reflect the over ten years she spent outside Israel.

aj. The *niphal* of *'gn* (or perhaps *'gh*) is a hapax legomenon, although it does not correspond to the usual second-person feminine plural *niphal* form. In rabbinic Hebrew and

## 1:7–19A EN ROUTE: NAOMI, ORPAH, AND RUTH DIALOGUE

Aramaic, *'gn* means "to bind, tie, imprison," referring to wives bound to absent husbands (Jastrow, 1042; *HALOT* 2:785). Hence, "restrain oneself" is probably the best translation, considering the reflexive sense of *niphal* (so Hubbard, *Ruth*, 112). The two unusual words (*taśabbērnâ* and *tēʿāgēnâ*) in successive sentences, whether or not borrowed from Aramaic, add to the foreign flavor of Naomi's speech.

ak. There are three ways to understand the preposition *min* in *mar-lî mǝʾōd mikkem* (BDB, 580–81; *HALOT* 2:597–98). First, causal: "my bitterness is on account of you" (e.g., LXX, ESV). Second, comparison of suffering: "my bitterness is more than yours" (e.g., NIV, NJPS). Third, comparison of capability (*IBHS* §14.4f): "my bitterness is too much for you (to share)" (e.g., HCSB, NAB). Syriac attests a doublet, including both the first two options. This doublet may "reflect scribal interpolation of alternative renderings"; Michael G. Wechsler, "Peshitta: Ruth," in *The Hebrew Bible*, ed. Armin Lange and Emanuel Tov (Leiden: Brill, 2017), 412. Within the flow of Naomi's argument, the second and third options make the most sense because they provide reasons for her daughters-in-law not to follow her. The second option makes the best sense of the following clause ("because the hand of Yahweh has gone out against me"). However, based on the warm relationship between the women (vv. 9, 10, 14), the third option is a possible secondary double meaning.

al. Although reading the *kî* as causative ("because") rather than emphatic ("indeed, surely") produces a somewhat awkward sentence (Hubbard, *Ruth*, 107n13), the *kî* introduces a clause that provides a reason for Naomi's previous statement about her extreme bitterness. As in life, speech in narrative does not need to be grammatically perfect.

am. The verb *tiśśenâ*, "they raised," lacks the quiescent *aleph* which is found in 1:9 (*tiśśeʾnâ*). Consult GKC §74k for further examples of the omitted quiescent *aleph* (see also 2:9). Although the omitted *aleph* is found in greater frequency in Hebrew of the late first millennium (e.g., Dead Sea Scrolls), it is also present in earlier Hebrew, e.g., the Siloam Tunnel inscription (late eighth century BC); Holmstedt, *Handbook*, 19, 22. It is thus not a reliable indicator of the book's date of composition.

an. For a discussion of this phrase, see the note and comment on v. 9.

ao. Some versions make explicit the meaning of this gesture, e.g., "and returned to her people" (LXX; cf. 1:15), "and went on her way" (Tg.), and "and returned" (Vulg.); cf. *BHQ*, 52*. That it is a farewell gesture can be deduced from the immediate context, especially in Naomi's following speech (1:15). MT^L is thus most likely original, with some support from 4QRuth^b (although the text is obscured).

ap. LXX reads *ēkolouthēsen* ("she followed"), which may have resulted from a scribal mishearing of *kollaō* ("to adhere"; 2:8, 21, 23); so Campbell, *Ruth*, 72.

aq. In MT^L the subject of the verb *ʾmr* ("to speak") is not specified, as also in 4QRuth^b and Tg. The Vulg. specifies Naomi, while LXX specifies both Naomi as the speaker and Ruth as the hearer.

ar. LXX and Vulg. read "her gods," and Syr. "house of her parents." Schipper, *Ruth*, 99, translates *ʾĕlōhêhā* "her ancestors." The semantic range of *ʾĕlōhîm* includes household or ancestral gods (Gen 31:30; Judg 18:24), and spirits of the dead (1 Sam 28:13; possibly Isa 8:19); see W. H. Schmidt, "*ʾĕlōhîm*," *TLOT* 1:118. In some cases, *ʾĕlōhîm* might refer to deified family ancestors (2 Sam 14:16; possibly Exod 21:6); see K. van der Toorn, "God (I)," *DDD*, 364. But the semantic range does not extend to "ancestors." If, for the sake of argument, we accept the translation "ancestors," it might fit contextually with Ruth's declaration to be buried with Naomi and her ancestors upon her death (1:16–17); see also the discussion in Anne-Mareike Wetter, *"On Her Account": Reconfiguring Israel in Ruth, Esther, and Judith*, LHBOTS 623 (New York: Bloomsbury T&T Clark, 2015), 67n79. But "her ancestors" is

83

## The Book of Ruth

incongruous with Naomi's previous statement, that Orpah has returned to "her people and her ancestors." The translation of *'ĕlōhêhā* as "her god" remains the best. A chiastic structure for Ruth's speech supports this translation; see the comment on v. 16.

as. LXX and Syr. read "return also you after your sister-in-law," while Tg. adds, "to your people and to your gods," to the end of the verse.

at. The combination of two prepositions in *me'aḥărê*, "from after," with the verb *šûb* ("to turn back, return") has the meaning of "from following after" (e.g., 1 Sam 24:2; 2 Sam 2:26, 30); BDB, 30.

au. The *kî*, "for," introduces an explanatory clause.

av. The phrase *ba'ăšer tāmûtî*, "wherever you die," is fronted before the verb *'āmût*, "I will die," which produces the same focus as the two clauses in 1:16.

aw. The *hiphil* of *pārad* ("to separate") with *bên* ("between") is also found in 2 Kgs 2:11 and Prov 18:18.

ax. *wattēre'*, "when she saw." As in 1:15, the subject for the verb is not explicit. "Naomi" has been added in my translation, as also in LXX, Syr., and Vulg.

ay. Heb. *watteḥdal lədabbēr*, "she ceased to speak." The verb *ḥdl* with an infinitive and *lə* means "to cease to" (Gen 11:8; 18:11; 41:49; 1 Sam 12:23; Jer 44:18; 51:30; Ps 36:4[3]; Prov 19:27); *HALOT* 1:292.

az. Heb. *šətêhem*, "two of them," has a masculine plural suffix, which is probably another instance of gender mismatch; see note on 1:8.

ba. The unusual feminine plural suffix on *bō'ānâ*, "they came to" (cf. *kəbō'ānâ*; 1:19b), is probably for assonance with the preceding *wattēlaknâ*; consult JM §94h.

This section can be structured as:

> A  Narrative introduction (v. 7): Naomi, Orpah, and Ruth *went* on their way to Bethlehem.
> > B  <u>Dialogue 1</u> (8–9a): Naomi urges her daughters-in-law to return to Moab.
> > > C  Narrative transition (9b): Naomi kisses them farewell, they all weep.
> > > > D  <u>Dialogue 2</u> (10–13): Her daughters-in-law refuse, she presents an impassioned argument to convince them to return home.
> > > C'  Narrative transition (14): Orpah kisses Naomi farewell, Ruth clings to Naomi.
> > B'  <u>Dialogue 3</u> (15–18): Naomi urges Ruth to return after Orpah; Ruth commits herself to Naomi; Naomi stops urging her.
> A'  Narrative conclusion (19a): Naomi and Ruth *went on* until they came to Bethlehem.[58]

This scene is framed by descriptions of Naomi and her daughters-in-law setting forth to return to Judah, and Naomi and Ruth arriving in Bethlehem

---

58. Modified from Bush, *Ruth, Esther*, 72.

84

1:7–19A EN ROUTE: NAOMI, ORPAH, AND RUTH DIALOGUE

(A-A'). Three departed Moab, two returned to Judah. This resulted from Naomi urging both young widows to return to Moab, to their mothers' houses, asking Yahweh to bless them (B). In the parallel dialogue, Naomi urges Ruth to return, but Ruth vows her loyalty to Naomi, ending with a self-imprecatory oath using the name Yahweh (B'). Kissing, wailing, and weeping feature after the first and second dialogues, but the parallel narrative transitions contrast Orpah's leaving with Ruth's clinging (C-C').

Dialogue plays an important role in this section. The elements of the chiastic structure alternate between narrative and dialogue. Dialogue plays a leading role in the book of Ruth: it advances the narrative, reveals character traits, and involves the audience in the evaluation of the characters.[59] Dialogue puts us on the scene and makes the action feel immediate. It is thus appropriate that the turning point (D) is comprised of dialogue. In this element, "return," the *Leitwort* of this act, is used three times, which foregrounds the question: who is returning to where? In Naomi's speech, she not only urges her "daughters" to return, she also expresses her response to her loss, raises the core problems the narrative needs to resolve, and, from a literary perspective, foreshadows future solutions. She feels hopeless and bitter, and she is convinced she cannot provide husbands for her daughters-in-law. She feels that Yahweh's hand has struck out against her (v. 13), but will her fortunes change with her return to his land where he has opened his hand in blessing (v. 6)? And if her speech alludes to the levirate custom, might a solution be hiding in it despite its improbability?

7 This verse presents slightly different information than the previous verse. Whereas v. 6 previewed Naomi's return, this verse begins the actual journey: *So she set out from the place where she had stayed.*[60] Naomi finally heads for "home" after more than ten years in a foreign country. No doubt she would have had mixed feelings about going back, but the sparse narrative only focuses on her actions ("she set out . . . they went"), which perhaps signals a rushed departure.[61] Hers was a decisive response to hearing of God's action. Whereas v. 6 specified the origin, this verse specifies the destination. The narrator uses a plural, *wattēlaknâ*, "they went on the way," *to return to the land of Judah.*[62] In reality, it is only Naomi who is returning to her homeland. Perhaps this simply reflects their unity in purpose and destination, but the dissonance allows for the possibility that "return" means more than just a physical return.

59. On the primacy of dialogue in biblical narrative, see Alter, *Biblical Narrative*, 63–87.

60. The phrase *'ăšer hāyətāh-šāmmâ*, "where she had stayed," recalls *wayyihyû-šām*, "and they stayed there," in v. 2.

61. Morris, *Ruth*, 253, suggests that the hasty departure hints at the poverty of the women's household.

62. Here *'ereṣ yəhûdâ*, "land of Judah" denotes the tribal area (e.g., 1 Sam 22:5; 30:16), not the southern kingdom (e.g., 2 Kgs 23:24; 25:22).

In any case, they share the journey together, probably a few days' walk,[63] but hazardous for three women without the protection of a male.

**8** The road between Moab and Judah is a liminal space, an in-between zone, which is consonant with what Naomi is about to say. The narrative does not state why Naomi initiates the conversation at this point in the journey. Perhaps she had already discussed the departure with her daughters-in-law, but now she is having second thoughts. Alternatively, if there is a sense of a rushed departure from v. 7, it would be reinforced by Naomi's speech. In this scenario, Naomi had not discussed their departure and only urges her daughters-in-law to return after she realizes they intend to accompany her for the entire journey, not just part of it.[64]

Her speech can be structured as:

> A Go, return [two imperatives]
> each to the house of her mother!
> B May Yahweh deal kindly with you
> C just as you have dealt with those who died and with me.
> (v. 8)
> B' May Yahweh give you . . .
> A' Find rest [imperative]
> each in the house of her husband. (v. 9)

Naomi's speech begins and ends with imperatives followed by a location (A-A'). The action Naomi first urges for *her two daughters-in-law—Go, return—*is expressed as a strong instruction or command.[65] She wants each woman to return to her mother's house (A). If a woman is widowed without sons, she is usually sent back to her father's house (*bêt 'āb*; e.g., Gen 38:11; Lev 22:13). In the rest of the Old Testament, the Israelite household is described as a "father's house." This is understandable within a patriarchal culture, where males hold much of the power within society, especially in the public realm. It is thus remarkable that Naomi instructs her daughters-in-law to return to their "mother's house." Two suggested reasons for this are less likely. First, their fathers had died, so Naomi sent them back to the mother, who was now the head of the household. It seems unlikely that both fathers had died. Second, mother's houses were Moabite custom, rather than father's

---

63. A journey of approximately 120 km (75 mi) would take about three days. See note on v. 1.

64. If it is a hasty departure, it would recall the first biblical exodus (Exod 12:11; Deut 16:3), which also included non-Israelites heading for the land of Israel (Exod 12:38).

65. Heb. *lēknâ* and *šōbnâ* ("Go, return") are imperatives, used here (rather than jussives) to reflect Naomi's sense of urgency.

houses. However, since Israel and Moab were neighbors, their cultures were most likely similar in this regard.

Most likely, then, Naomi's mention of the "mother's house" provides an insight into her perspective as the head of her household. She encourages her widowed daughters-in-law to return to their mothers, instead of remaining with her, their mother-in-law. Moreover, the narrative thus far has focused on her relationship with her daughters-in-law. Naomi's instruction is thus balanced: one mother sending daughters back to another mother.[66] This is one instance in which a woman's perspective is seen in the Old Testament.[67] Nonetheless, Naomi's use of "mother's house" also provides a glimpse into the influence of women in the household sphere.[68] And the canonical associations of the "mother's house" with marriage and love (Gen 24:28; Song 3:4; 8:2)[69] anticipates the end of her speech (v. 9).

Two requests follow Naomi's two commands. First, she prays, *May Yahweh deal kindly with you* (Heb. "may Yahweh do *ḥesed* with you"). The term *ḥesed*, "kindness, steadfast love," is rich in meaning and is difficult to capture with a single English word.[70] Performed within the context of a covenant/kinship relationship, *ḥesed* has at its heart loyalty, generosity, and beneficence. But kind actions often go beyond obligation or duty. In this verse *ḥesed* describes the quality of an action, hence *deal kindly*. Repeated, habitual acts of kindness are characteristic of God (e.g., Exod 34:6–7; Ps 136). "Kindness" is a central theme in the Ruth narrative, appearing at crucial junctures (also 2:20; 3:10).

Here, Naomi prays that God would demonstrate the same kindness to her Moabite daughters-in-law that they had shown to *those who died and with me*. In Naomi's collectivist understanding, family includes not just the living members, so "those who died" refers to Naomi's sons, and, by extension, her

---

66. Cf. Porten, "Scroll," 36.

67. See Richard Bauckham, "The Book of Ruth and the Possibility of a Feminist Canonical Hermeneutic," *BibInt* 5 (1997): 29–45.

68. See Carol L. Meyers, "'To Her Mother's House': Considering a Counterpart to the Israelite *bêt'ab*," in *The Bible and the Politics of Exegesis: Essays in Honor of Norman K. Gottwald on His Sixty-Fifth Birthday*, ed. David Jobling, Peggy L. Day, and Gerald T. Shepherd (Cleveland: Pilgrim Press, 1991), 39–51; Amy-Jill Levine, "Ruth," in *The Women's Bible Commentary*, ed. Carol A. Newsom and Sharon H. Ringe (London: SPCK, 1992), 80.

69. See Hubbard, *Ruth*, 102–3.

70. See the studies by Francis I. Andersen, "Yahweh, the Kind and Sensitive God," in *God Who Is Rich in Mercy: Essays Presented to Dr. D. B. Knox*, ed. Peter T. O'Brien and David G. Peterson (Sydney: Lancer, 1986), 41–88; Gordon R. Clark, *The Word Hesed in the Hebrew Bible*, JSOTSup 157 (Sheffield: Sheffield Academic Press, 1993); Nelson Glueck, *Hesed in the Bible*, trans. Alfred Gottschalk (Cincinnati: Hebrew Union College Press, 1967); Katharine D. Sakenfeld, *The Meaning of Hesed in the Hebrew Bible: A New Inquiry*, HSM 17 (Missoula: Scholars Press, 1978).

husband. She prays on the basis of the kind hospitality her daughters-in-law had shown to her family while they were alive. Hospitality was important in ancient Israel as it still is today, especially in cultures with a strong honor-shame element. This Israelite family was in a foreign land and they had lost their father. Ruth and Orpah were willing to marry Naomi's sons, which would have meant turning their backs on their own families and pledging themselves to Israelite husbands. Naomi includes herself as a recipient of their kindness because she would have been cared for as a family member. She may also allude to the loyalty they showed in following her on the road to Judah.

In one sentence, Naomi reveals three aspects of her theology. (1) God is intimately involved with human activities (cf. v. 6). Here she mentions his benevolence, but his involvement in her pain will be raised soon. (2) God's sphere of influence spreads beyond the land of Israel to the land of Chemosh. This is significant because the idea of regional gods (cf. 1 Kgs 11:7, 33; 2 Kgs 23:13) would have been impressed upon her during her stay in Moab. Yet, she nevertheless expressed an orthodox view of Yahweh's sovereignty and universality. (3) God acts on the basis of retribution—a good deed deserves a reward. As the center of her speech, this forms the focus and fulcrum. Their actions are the trigger for Naomi to pray kindness from God upon them.[71]

From an honor-shame perspective, Naomi expresses her gratitude for their kindness to her family, but she would have also felt obliged to reciprocate. Presuming her daughters-in-law would leave her, she could not. The most she could do was to call on someone who could—God.[72] David uses similar language in response to the men of Jabesh-Gilead burying Saul. He asks Yahweh to bless them because of their *ḥesed*, "kindness, loyalty," and prays that Yahweh would show *ḥesed*, "kindness," and faithfulness to them. He then says he will do good to them because of what they did (2 Sam 2:5–6). One good deed toward another deserves a response, but such deeds also draw people closer together.

**9** The second of Naomi's requests in the prayer is left unfinished. She begins to pray, *May Yahweh give you . . .* but her request to God is interrupted, leaving it without an object. We wonder what she was going to request— security or peace? Instead, there is an abrupt change in her thinking as she addresses her daughters-in-law, urging them to *find rest*. So the object was probably going to be "rest," but instead of requesting it from God, Naomi asks Ruth and Orpah to seek it themselves. "Rest" (*mənûḥâ*; cf. 3:1) denotes a con-

---

71. Phyllis Trible, *God and the Rhetoric of Sexuality* (Philadelphia: Fortress, 1978), 170, views Ruth and Orpah's acts of kindness as a "model" for Yahweh to act toward them in kindness.

72. Cf. Sasson, *Ruth*, 23.

## 1:7–19A EN ROUTE: NAOMI, ORPAH, AND RUTH DIALOGUE

dition and its attendant experience.[73] It means to settle down after a period of wandering or of threat from enemies (e.g., 1 Kgs 8:56; cf. Esth 9:22), when there was uncertainty or distress (e.g., Ps 116:3, 7). Often it is used to describe the Israelites enjoying rest in the land (e.g., Deut 12:9; Ps 95:11), dwelling securely and at peace. Rest is often viewed as a gift from God (e.g., Ps 23:2), so Naomi rightly prays that *Yahweh give* her daughters-in-law rest.

Naomi's ultimate desire is for her daughters-in-law to find the blessing of rest *each in the house of her husband*. Naomi's desire, first, was for her daughters-in-law to return to their mothers (v. 6). Yet their mothers' households are not where she wants them to end up. Instead, the house of a husband is the ultimate destination. Her desire is that they find rest—security and well-being—in a husband and home. Naomi envisages uncertainty and anxiety if they returned with her to Judah, so she tries to persuade them to return to their mothers' houses in Moab (v. 8), then to settle down with a Moabite husband on his landed inheritance. She releases them from further obligation to her, for she knows that a man can reverse the shame of their widowhood.

But why the abrupt change in Naomi's speech, starting with a request to God, then, in mid-sentence, urging her daughters-in-law to seek rest? Perhaps she was struck by the thought that God would not give them rest. After all that she and her daughters-in-law had gone through, she might have lost confidence in God's providing a new husband and home. Her faith held firm as she made her first request to God (v. 8), but now it is slipping. A more sympathetic reading of Naomi's faith is perhaps preferable. Her setting out to return to Bethlehem in response to hearsay is a manifestation of her faith. She already made one request to God (v. 8), and now she feels a sudden urge to spur her daughters-in-law into action. Her abrupt change in thought mid-sentence is arresting and accentuates what she wants Ruth and Orpah to do.

The first speech of a character often reveals key aspects of their character.[74] What does this speech reveal about Naomi? Her double invocation of Yahweh might simply be a stylized or habitual way of speaking, which does not reveal her underlying beliefs. Yet, if speech can reflect what is in a person's heart (e.g., Prov 16:23; Matt 12:33–34; 15:18–19), then we can say that Naomi maintains a degree of faith in God. The chiastic structure of her speech interweaves God's providence with human action (vv. 8–9). Naomi urges Orpah and Ruth to act, yet at the same time, she prays that God would bless the outcome of their actions. The structure of her speech perhaps indicates that human action is more important in Naomi's mind. It begins and ends

---

73. See Preuss, "*nûaḥ*," *TDOT* 9:283–85; F. Stolz, "*nwḥ*," *TLOT* 2:722–23.

74. Cf. Alter, *Biblical Narrative*, 182. E.g., Moses's first words reveal his concern for justice (Exod 2:13).

## THE BOOK OF RUTH

with a call to action (go, return, find), and the central component highlights the prior actions of Orpah and Ruth. Because Orpah and Ruth have acted in kindness to her household, Naomi prays that God would respond in kind by blessing them with "rest" in their own households. Subsequent words and actions of Naomi will build a complete picture of her character.

As Naomi kissed Ruth and Orpah goodbye,[75] *they raised their voice and wept.*[76] This idiom describes loud wailing and mourning, often in response to tragedy and loss (e.g., Judg 21:2; 2 Sam 13:36; Job 2:12; see also v. 14). The singular *qôlān*, "their voice," indicates that they cry out as if in one voice, or their voices mingled as one. This response to Naomi's farewell kisses is a touching display of the deep emotional bond that had formed between the women over the years.

**10** But Orpah and Ruth are not so easily persuaded. They say, *Surely with you we will return to your people*. It may be, as we find in some cultures today, that they felt they could not accept Naomi's offer straight away.[77] From an honor-shame perspective, Orpah and Ruth would want to save Naomi's "face." Eagerness to abandon their mother-in-law would be to show a lack of respect. The journey to Bethlehem was not without its dangers, and upon her arrival, she would need someone to provide for and take care of her. The reluctance of her daughters-in-law to return to Moab probably stems from their loyalty to and responsibility they felt toward their mother-in-law.

Sometimes there is animosity between a mother-in-law and a daughter-in-law,[78] but this is not apparent in the Ruth narrative. Orpah and Ruth's sorrow at the thought of leaving their mother-in-law is backed up by their words. Although it is not a "return" for them, they acknowledge Naomi's authority and want to follow their mother-in-law as she returns to her people. In Hebrew, the strength of their assertion is indicated in three ways: (1) the

---

75. Here kissing is a gesture of family intimacy, often found in greetings (e.g., Gen 33:4), farewells (e.g., 1 Kgs 19:20), and blessings (e.g., Gen 48:10). For other connotations of kissing in the Old Testament, see Beyse, *"nāšaq," TDOT* 10:72–76; John A. Davies, *Lift Up Your Heads: Nonverbal Communication and Related Body Imagery in the Bible* (Eugene, OR: Pickwick Publications, 2018), 47–48.

76. This phrase can be read as a hendiadys: "they wept loudly."

77. Cf. Esther, who only accepts King Ahasuerus's offer the third time (Esth 5:3–4, 6–8; 7:2–4). Initial refusal arising from a feeling of inadequacy is also found in those whom God calls to take on a role, e.g., Moses, Gideon, Isaiah, and Jeremiah. For a discussion of Old Testament call narratives, see Norman C. Habel, "The Form and Significance of the Call Narratives," *ZAW* 77 (1965): 297–323; D. Nathan Phinney, "Call/Commission Narratives," in *Dictionary of Old Testament: Prophets*, ed. Mark J. Boda and J. Gordon McConville (Downers Grove, IL: IVP, 2011), 65–71.

78. See, e.g., Yan Lin, "'Who Is More to You Than Seven Sons': A Cross-Textual Reading between the Book of Ruth and *A Pair of Peacocks to the Southeast Fly*," in *Reading Ruth in Asia*, ed. Jione Havea and Peter H. W. Lau, IVBS (Atlanta: SBL, 2015), 47–55.

emphatic *kî*, "surely";[79] (2) the placement of *'ittāk*, "with you," at the beginning of their response, which asserts their intention against Naomi's; and (3) the use of the *yiqtol nāšûb*, "we will return," rather than the cohortative *nāšûbâ*, "let us return."[80] Their primary loyalty lies with their mother-in-law, yet, within a collectivist society, they know Naomi is integrally related to her *people*. It thus takes no little courage for these young women to commit themselves to Naomi, and to return with her. Leaving with Naomi to return to her people not only means heading out to a new country and a new people, it also means turning their backs on their own country and own people.[81] Orpah and Ruth's determination to return with Naomi to a strange land again shows the strong bond that had formed between them.

**11** Naomi's semi-poetic response is well structured, with repeated words highlighting her main concerns. It can be divided into three parts, with each part marked by a direct address—"my daughters." In the first two parts, she responds directly to their desire to return with her to her people. The third part of her speech forms her conclusion.

Part 1 (v. 11)

> Return [*šōbnâ*] my daughters [*bənōtay*].
> > Why would you go with me?
> > Do I still have sons in my belly
> > that they might become *husbands* [*la'ănāšîm*] for you?

Part 2 (vv. 12–13a)

> Return [*šōbnâ*] my daughters [*bənōtay*]. Go!
> > Because [*kî*] I am too old to belong to a *husband* [*lə'îš*].
> > Even if [*kî*] I should say I have hope—
> > > if [*gam*] I belonged to a *husband* [*lə'îš*] tonight,
> > > and if [*gam*] I bore sons—

---

79. The particle *kî* as emphatic ("surely") rather than adversative ("no") fits better within an honor–shame culture where speech is usually more indirect. Most EVV translate "no" (e.g., ESV, NJPS), and some "surely" (e.g., NKJV). For different functions of *kî*, see *HALOT* 2:470, and cf. 1:13; 3:12.

80. Holmstedt, *Handbook*, 77.

81. For studies of Ps 45, in which a foreigner woman is encouraged to forget her people and her father's house for the sake of marriage with an Israelite, see Simon Chi-chung Cheung, "'Forget Your People and Your Father's House': The Core Theological Message of Psalm 45 and Its Canonical Position in the Hebrew Psalter," *BBR* 26 (2016): 325–40; A. J. Culp, "Of Wedding Songs and Prophecies: Canonical Reading as the Clue to Understanding Psalm 45 as Prophecy," *Crucible* 8 (2017), www.crucibleonline.net.

# THE BOOK OF RUTH

> For them [*hălāhēn*] would you wait until they were grown up?
> For them [*hălāhēn*] would you restrain yourselves by not *belonging to a husband* (*ləʾîš*)?

Part 3 (v. 13b)

> No, <u>my daughters</u> [*bənōtay*].
> For [*kî*] my bitterness is much greater than yours.
> For [*kî*] the hand of Yahweh has gone out against me.

Naomi attempts to persuade her daughters-in-law to return to Moab by focusing on her inability to produce husbands for them. Naomi's fourfold repetition of *ʾîš* or its plural form in her speech reveals that the lack of husbands lies at the core of the widows' problem. The first and fourth uses of *ʾîš* are about husbands for her daughters-in-law, which enclose the two uses of *ʾîš* which are about a husband for herself. Parts 1 and 2 of her speech begin with an imperative—"return" (*šōbnâ*). They said they want to "return" with her (v. 10); she says they need to "return" to where they belong—Moab. Naomi addresses her daughters-in-law as "daughters," which reveals their close emotional bond. Three times the narrator reminds us they are her "daughters-in-law" (*kallōtêhā*; vv. 6, 7, 8), but three times Naomi calls them "my daughters" (*bənōtay*; vv. 11, 12, 13). Practically, they had left their mothers, so Naomi shows her concern for them as her "daughters."

After imploring them to return, Naomi continues with a rhetorical question, *Why would you go with me?* She is not asking them to detail the reasons they want to follow her; rather, she is stating that it would be foolish to do so. What she says next sounds strange to many readers, *Do I still have sons in my belly that they might become your husbands?* Naomi stated her desire for her daughters-in-law to return to their mothers' houses and then to find security with another husband (vv. 8–9). Now that they insist on returning with her, she argues that she does not have any sons *bəmēʿay*, "in my belly." The use of the poetic *mēʿîm*, "belly, internal organs, inward parts (intestines, bowels)"[82] instead of the more specific *beṭen*, "womb," brings associations with "gut feelings,"[83] deeply felt emotions such as sexual yearning (Song 5:4), pity (Isa 16:11),[84] compassion (Jer 31:20), or distress (Jer 4:19). Often used in laments (e.g., Lam 1:20; 2:11; Job 30:27), for Naomi the feeling is sorrow or despair.

What is the basis for her line of reasoning? First, she assumes their only source for another husband would be her because they will not be able to find

---

82. BDB, 588; *HALOT* 2:609.
83. Figuratively, *mēʿîm* is the seat of the emotions.
84. Cf. Campbell, *Ruth*, 66–67; Sasson, *Ruth*, 24.

## 1:7–19A EN ROUTE: NAOMI, ORPAH, AND RUTH DIALOGUE

another husband in Bethlehem. The implication is that no one in Bethlehem would marry Moabite widows. Second, she could be alluding to the levirate custom, as found in the narrative of Judah and Tamar (Gen 38) and codified in Old Testament Law (Deut 25:5–10).[85] If a man died without an heir, his nearest relative would marry his widow and produce a child to preserve the family line. Only a suggestion of this custom is found at this stage in the Ruth narrative, for its application seems impossible.[86]

**12** Naomi begins the second part of her speech (vv. 12–13a) by repeating, *Return, my daughters*. A sense of urgency is conveyed by the imperative, *Go!* Then follows her reason for wanting them to return: she is too old to have a husband. To emphasize her point further and remove any doubt in their minds whether she might still bear sons, Naomi presents a hypothetical situation:

> Even if I should say I have hope—
> if I belonged to a husband tonight
> and if I bore sons— (v. 12)

> for them would you
>     wait until they were grown up?
>          . . . restrain yourselves by not belonging to a husband?
>     (v. 13)

In the first part of her speech, Naomi argues that she *does not* have sons in her womb that could marry her daughters-in-law. Now she says she *cannot* have sons in the future because she is too old to remarry, with the implication that she is past child-bearing age. If she married at fifteen years old, then bore children at seventeen, and if her sons married around the same age then stayed for another ten years in Moab, she almost certainly would be postmenopausal.[87] But she raises a hypothetically hopeful[88] situation. First, she would need to find a husband tonight and consummate the marriage;

---

85. Levirate derives from *levir* in Latin, which means "brother-in-law." It is thus the brother-in-law law. For most readers, this sounds like a strange practice, perhaps even repugnant. Yet, in parts of the world, this practice, or some form of it, continues. Some societies derive their justification from the Old Testament levirate law; see, e.g., Nu, "Reinterpretation of Levirate Marriage," 57–72.

86. The law lists brothers-in-law as potentially taking on the duty (Deut 25:5), while Judah (inadvertently) performed it as a father-in-law (Gen 38:24–26). In the Ruth narrative, all these relatives have died.

87. In the ancient world and developing countries today, the age of menopause is lower.

88. *Tiqwâ*, "hope," can be expectant or futile. It is the latter here (also Job 3:9; 7:2; Isa 5:2, 4); see Daniel Schibler, "*qāwâ*," *NIDOTTE* 3:892–96.

## The Book of Ruth

second, she would need to conceive immediately; third, she would need to bear not just one, but two sons for her daughters-in-law. Naomi's point is that this situation is impossible, it is hopeless.

**13** Based on this hypothetical situation, she asks her daughters-in-law two rhetorical questions. First, *would you wait until they were grown up?* This would be at least fifteen years, which is not only a long time but would push them close to an age when they cannot bear children. Second, *would you restrain yourselves* by not marrying in the meantime? In setting up a hypothetical situation, followed by two rhetorical questions, we can imagine Naomi anticipating objections from Orpah and Ruth. If Naomi was alluding to the levirate custom in the first part of her speech, in the second she releases them from the responsibility, even as she details its impossibility. There is absolutely no reason for them to remain with her because, as she strongly argues, there is no hope of her producing husbands for them. In her mind, finding a husband is the prime need for these widows.

Part 3 of Naomi's speech (v. 13b) is the conclusion and, similar to the first two parts, contains the address, "my daughters." Just as the first two clauses in part 2 began with *kî*, so also the two clauses in part 3. The same word (*kî*) begins each clause, words that rhyme (*lî/bî*) fill the middle, and alliteration (*mə'ōd mikkem/yad-yhwh*) ends each clause. The presence of alliteration and rhyming, along with the invocation of Yahweh lend Naomi's words a sense of finality and gravity.

> *kî-mar-lî mə'ōd mikkem*
> *kî-yāṣ'â bî yad-yhwh*

> For my bitterness is much greater than yours
> for the hand of Yahweh has gone out against me.

Naomi begins part 3 of her speech with an emphatic negative, *No, my daughters!*[89] She does not wait for her daughters-in-law to reply but implores them to stop following her. The first two parts of her speech contained a pattern of imperative ("return") and address ("my daughters") followed by reasons for them to return to Moab. Following this pattern, *No* here has the same implication, "No, do not return with me." And the reason she provides for their return is her own experience: *For my bitterness is much greater than yours.* In effect, she is saying, "My life has become bitter and without hope. Avoid becoming like me." Most likely, she views her situation as more bitter

---

89. The negative *'al* usually negates a modal verb, but here the verb is absent, indicating an emphatic negation (e.g., Gen 19:18; 33:10; Judg 19:23; 2 Sam 13:16, 25; 2 Kgs 3:13; 4:16; see GKC §152g; *HALOT* 1:48).

## 1:7–19A EN ROUTE: NAOMI, ORPAH, AND RUTH DIALOGUE

than theirs because she is beyond the age for (re-)marriage and she also cannot have further children (v. 12). Her daughters-in-law are still young enough to remarry and produce children, so although they also have lost husbands, there is still hope for them.

Naomi then provides the ultimate reason, in her mind, for her bitterness: *For the hand of Yahweh has gone out against me.* In the Old Testament, *yad-yhwh*, the "hand of Yahweh," denotes the irresistible might of God (Deut 32:39), as displayed in his creation (Isa 45:12; 48:13; Ps 8:7[6]; Job 26:13) and maintenance of the world (Job 12:9–10), salvation (esp. "with a strong hand," Exod 13:9; "with a strong hand and outstretched arm," e.g., Deut 4:34; Ps 136:12), and judgment or punishment (Pss 32:4; 39:11[10]; Job 12:4–9).[90] The "hand of Yahweh" can also exercise grace (Ezra 7:6, 9; Neh 2:8, 18). The phrase *yad-yhwh* with the verb *yāṣā'* ("go out") and the preposition *bə* ("against" in this phrase; BDB, 89) does not occur elsewhere in the Old Testament. The usual phrase is *yad-yhwh* with a form of the verb *hāyâ* and *bə*, "the hand of Yahweh was against X," whereby X is most often an enemy of Israel (e.g., Exod 9:1–3; 1 Sam 5:9; 7:13), but sometimes God's people (e.g., Deut 2:13–15; Judg 2:15). The *qal* verb *yāṣā'* with God as the subject often refers to his departure to fight against his enemies (Judg 5:4; Isa 26:21; 42:13; Mic 1:3; Hab 3:13; Zech 14:3; Ps 68:8[7]; cf. Judg 4:14; 2 Sam 5:24).[91] Naomi feels that, as the divine warrior, God has come out (*yāṣā'*) against her.[92]

In her understanding, Yahweh is the source of both weal and woe. In her previous speech (vv. 8–9), she prayed that Yahweh would show kindness by providing husbands for them. Her current situation is one of woe because Yahweh has attacked her, but this need not be the case for her daughters-in-law. In her mind, the only way for them to experience blessing from God's hand is to not return to Bethlehem with her. Naomi uses her bitter experience to motivate her daughters-in-law to return to Moab. She emphatically releases them from any obligation to her and absolves them of any sense of guilt they may have felt about her misery.

Naomi urges her daughters-in-law to return to Moab, but what is her motivation? While not questioning Naomi's affection for them, some suggest self-interest: they would remind Naomi and the people of Bethlehem of her mistakes; it would be harder for her to find food for them and herself; there would be stigma attached to foreign daughters-in-law; they would remind Naomi of what she has lost; it would be harder for her to reintegrate into

---

90. A. S. van der Woude, "*yad*," *TLOT* 2:501–2.

91. E. Jenni, "*yāṣā'*," *TLOT* 2:564.

92. For an exploration of the divine warrior theme, see Tremper Longman III and Daniel G. Reid, *God Is a Warrior* (Grand Rapids: Zondervan, 1995).

THE BOOK OF RUTH

Bethlehem society; and Naomi would be the subject of gossip.[93] These motivations are certainly possible, and perhaps Naomi's motivations were mixed. But since her repeated focus in her speeches has been on the long-term well-being of her daughters-in-law (vv. 8–9, 11–13), it is best to read concern for them as her primary motivation.

**14** The actions of the women in response to Naomi's speech are now described in reverse order to verse 9. Previously Naomi kissed her daughters-in-law, which was followed by their loud weeping. Now *they raised their voice and wept again*, probably all three women, followed by Orpah kissing her mother-in-law. Similar to many societies throughout history, kissing in the ancient Near East expressed affection at the point of departure. It was a nonverbal way of saying farewell (e.g., Gen 31:28; 2 Sam 19:40[39]; 1 Kgs 19:20), and kissing is also associated with tears (e.g., Gen 33:4). Naomi has finally persuaded Orpah, and she signals her departure with a kiss, with the literary closure (kiss-weep-weep-kiss; vv. 9, 14) underlining the closure of the in-law relationship. Orpah turns around, showing the nape of her neck,[94] and heads for home.

At the same time,[95] Ruth signals her determination to stay with Naomi—she *clung to her*. Whereas their husbands were described as a single unit (vv. 4–5), Orpah and Ruth act individually. The subject-verb order in Hebrew strongly contrasts their actions: Orpah leaves, but Ruth clings.[96] The verb *dbq* means "to stick, cling, cleave, to be close by," such as the tongue clinging to the roof of the mouth (e.g., Job 29:10; Ezek 3:26), and a hand clinging to a sword (2 Sam 23:10).[97] The word is also used in interpersonal contexts with the preposition *bə* to express loyalty and affection (Gen 2:24; 2 Sam 20:2),[98] especially marriage (Gen 2:24), and ethnic intermarriage (Gen 34:3; Josh 23:12; 1 Kgs 11:2). In the Old Testament, *dbq* with *bə* is often used to express loyalty to God (Deut 10:20; 11:22; 30:20; Josh 22:5; 2 Kgs 18:6), and sometimes this unwavering loyalty to Yahweh is contrasted with those who follow after other gods, such as the Baal of Peor (Deut 4:3–4).[99] Between two peo-

93. Danna N. Fewell and David M. Gunn, *Compromising Redemption: Relating Characters in the Book of Ruth* (Louisville: Westminster John Knox, 1990), 28; Hawk, *Ruth*, 59.

94. "Back of the neck" is one possible meaning of the name Orpah; see comment on v. 4.

95. The *waw* with subject and *qatal* verb ("but Ruth clung") breaks a string of three *wayyiqtol* clauses and indicates that Ruth's action is simultaneous to Orpah's; JM §118f.

96. Holmstedt, *Handbook*, 86–87.

97. Consult E. Jenni, "*dbq*," *TLOT* 1:324–25; Wallis, "*dābaq*," *TDOT* 3:79–84. The verb is used four times in the book of Ruth, twice with the preposition *bə* (1:14; 2:23), and twice with the preposition *'im* (2:8, 21).

98. BDB, 179.

99. This contrast in loyalties is also seen in 2 Sam 20:2, where the men of Judah remained steadfast to King David, while the people of Israel deserted him to follow Sheba son of Bikri.

## 1:7–19A EN ROUTE: NAOMI, ORPAH, AND RUTH DIALOGUE

ple, the word is also used with forms of the verb *'hb* ("to love"), and in these instances, the words are almost synonymous (e.g., Gen 34:3; 1 Kgs 11:2; cf. Prov 18:24).[100]

Recently, based on the intertextual connection between Gen 2:24 and Ruth 1:14 (among other reasons), scholars have argued that Ruth "clinging" to her mother-in-law has erotic connotations.[101] There are similarities between Gen 2:24 and Ruth 1:14. Both describe individuals abandoning (*'zb*) a kinship group to cling to another individual: a man abandons (*'zb*) his family to cling (*dbq*) to his wife (Gen 2:24); Ruth abandons (*'zb*) her family, land, and people to cling (*dbq*) to Naomi (1:14, 16; 2:11). However, becoming "one flesh" in its immediate literary context (Gen 2:23–24) focuses on kinship rather than sexual relations.[102] Moreover, based on semantic and syntactic grounds, there is no reason to ascribe sexual undertones to *dbq* in Ruth 1:14.[103] Viewing the in-law relationship from an ancient Near Eastern and Asian cultural context also renders a homosexual relationship highly unlikely.[104] Ruth's clinging to Naomi indicates her loyalty to the kinship relationship formed when she married Mahlon, despite Naomi releasing her from that kinship bond because she cannot provide another husband for her (vv. 8–9, 11–13).

We will consider Ruth's commitment to her mother-in-law below (see comments on v. 17); for now, we will consider Orpah. There is no shame attached to her leaving her mother-in-law to return to Moab. In her two speeches, Naomi had implored her to do so. By obeying, Orpah showed respect to her mother-in-law. Even if Orpah wanted to depart after Naomi's first speech (and there is no indication that she did), it would have been

100. Later in the Ruth narrative, the women of the town will say that Ruth "loves" (from *'hb*) Naomi (4:15).

101. E.g., Mona West, "Ruth," in *The Queer Bible Commentary*, ed. Deryn Guest (London: SCM, 2006), 190–94; J. Cheryl Exum, *Plotted, Shot, and Painted: Cultural Representations of Biblical Women*, 2nd ed. (Sheffield: Sheffield Phoenix, 2012), 166–75, and most recently, Stephanie Day Powell, *Narrative Desire and the Book of Ruth*, LHBOTS 662 (New York: Bloomsbury T&T Clark, 2018), esp. 5, 24–31.

102. Cf. A. F. L. Beeston, "One Flesh," *VT* 36 (1986): 117. Adam calls Eve "bone of my bones, and flesh of my flesh" (Gen 2:23), which refers to kinship relations elsewhere in the Old Testament (Gen 29:14; Judg 9:2; 2 Sam 5:1; 19:13–14[12–13]); see Gordon J. Wenham, *Genesis 1–15*, WBC 1 (Waco, TX: Word Books, 1987), 70–71.

103. See Scott N. Callaham, "But Ruth Clung to Her: Textual Constraints on Ambiguity in Ruth 1:14," *TynBul* 63 (2012): 179–98. Thus, a man abandoning his parents to cling to his wife to become one flesh (Gen 2:24) describes the formation of a new kinship relationship.

104. As Pui-lan Kwok, *Postcolonial Imagination and Feminist Theology* (Louisville: Westminster John Knox, 2005), 111, states: "Coming from an Asian society where the mother-in-law has historically wielded so much power over the life of the daughter-in-law, it is difficult for me to imagine an egalitarian and even passionate friendship between [Naomi and Ruth]."

## The Book of Ruth

showing disrespect to do so. From an honor-shame perspective, it is not surprising for her to initially refuse. But having "shown face" already, it was acceptable for Orpah to take her leave now. After at least ten years of marriage and living as a family unit with Naomi and Ruth, the emotional turmoil of severing the relationship is evident in their wailing and tears. Yet Orpah's decision to depart is the rational and expected choice under the circumstances, which highlights all the more the extraordinary decision of Ruth.[105]

**15** Naomi's third speech is introduced briefly: *And she said*. Based on the pattern of Naomi taking the initiative in speaking after a narrative transition, we anticipate her words. Nonetheless, the lack of an explicit subject makes us, the audience, listen more intently to determine the speaker,[106] and prepares us for Naomi's stepping back from the spotlight.[107] She first draws attention to Orpah with the interjection *hinnēh, Look!* With Ruth, we, in our mind's eye, follow the line of Naomi's gesture and see Orpah trudging back to Moab. Naomi adds, *your sister-in-law has returned*. Naomi makes a separation between her and her daughters-in-law: no longer "my daughters" (vv. 11, 12, 13), she now says *yəbimtēk*, "your sister-in-law." Although probably not a solely technical legal term, the noun form of *ybm* here is evocative since the noun and verb forms are only used in passages dealing with the levirate custom (Gen 38:8; Deut 25:7, 9).[108] Ironically, Naomi tells Ruth to follow her sister-in-law because she hints that the application of the levirate custom is not possible if she follows her mother-in-law (vv. 11–13).[109]

Naomi says that Orpah has returned *to her people and to her god*.[110] For

---

105. Some view Orpah even more positively. For instance, Laura E. Donaldson, "The Sign of Orpah: Reading Ruth through Native Eyes," in *Hope Abundant* (Maryknoll, NY: Orbis, 2010), 138–51, views Orpah as a model for indigenous women to resist cultural assimilation. For my critique of this approach, see Peter H. W. Lau, "Back under Authority: Towards an Evangelical Postcolonial Hermeneutic," *TynBul* 63 (2012): 131–44.

106. Campbell, *Ruth*, 72.

107. Her first speech is introduced with "And Naomi said to her two daughters-in-law" (v. 8) and the second with "And Naomi said" (v. 11).

108. The *piel* of the verb *yābam* means "to do the duty of a brother-in-law" (Gen 38:8; Deut 25:7). In Gen 38:8, *'ešet 'āḥ*, "brother's wife," is used when *yəbāmâ* seems more appropriate. A text from Tell Al-Rimah (ca. 1775 BC) uses the Akk. cognate *yabamum*, "brother-in-law," in a general context; see Sasson, *Ruth*, 28–29.

109. Cf. Campbell, *Ruth*, 72–73.

110. The plural noun *'ĕlōhîm* can denote a plurality of deities (e.g., "the gods of Egypt"; Exod 12:12) or household gods (e.g., Gen 31:30; Judg 18:24). It can also denote a plural of excellence or majesty for a deity (JM §136d; GKC §124g), most often in reference to Yahweh, the God of Israel (e.g., Ps 42:3), but also in reference to a foreign god, such as Chemosh, the Moabite deity (1 Kgs 11:33; for a discussion of Judg 11:24, in which Jephthah seems to refer to Chemosh as the patron deity of the Ammonites, see Daniel I. Block, *Judges, Ruth*, NAC 6 [Nashville: Broadman & Holman, 1999], 361–62). Since, like ancient Israel's neigh-

## 1:7–19A EN ROUTE: NAOMI, ORPAH, AND RUTH DIALOGUE

Naomi, a "people"[111] and their "god" are inseparable; Ruth must return to both. Yahweh had visited "his people," and now Naomi urges Ruth to return to the people of Chemosh (cf. Num 21:29; Jer 48:46). The Old Testament generally does not recognize the reality of gods apart from Yahweh (e.g., Deut 4:35, 39; 32:39) and views idols as "no gods" (e.g., Deut 29:17; 32:16–17, 21), but theological orthodoxy is not Naomi's main concern.[112] She wants to persuade Ruth to *return* (cf. vv. 8, 11, 12), following her fellow Moabite's example (*after your sister-in-law*). In doing so, Naomi repeats a similar motif to her first speech, in which she urged her daughters-in-law to return to their families (v. 8). This time, however, she adopts the perspective of these Moabite women, who believe in the reality of Chemosh, the prime Moabite deity.[113] By highlighting their national and theological disparity, Naomi points out another implication of following her: not only does Ruth abandon her family and her people, she also abandons her god. Naomi did not know how Ruth would respond to her assertion about nation and deity, but we wonder if Naomi's mention of "her people" and "her god" rather than "your people" and "your god" triggered a reaction in Ruth.

We can imagine the pressure Ruth would have felt as she stood on the road between Moab and Judah. She must choose between her familiar homeland and the strange land beyond the Dead Sea. Migrants move for different reasons, including to escape suffering or to make a better life for themselves. The narrator does not tell us why Ruth clung to her mother-in-law. But Naomi told Ruth emphatically that her prospects would be negligible if she followed her. So, the spotlight shifts to Ruth. Seeing her sister-in-law turn around and go back to the safety of Moab, will she do the same?

**16** Ruth is resolute in the face of Naomi's direct urging. Her semi-poetic vow of commitment to Naomi is the first time she speaks as an individual character. It is the best-known speech in the Ruth narrative and can be structured as a chiasm:[114]

---

bors, Moab probably practiced functional monolatry, in which Chemosh was their national deity without denying the existence (or worship) of other gods, the translation "her god" is best here. Ruth's reference to Yahweh using the same noun (with a different suffix; v. 16) supports this reading.

111. In contrast to *gôy*, "nation," *'am*, "people," is a relational term deriving from the root *'amm*, "paternal uncle." See A. R. Hulst, "*'am/gôy*," *TLOT* 2:896–919.

112. Naomi can view Chemosh as an object of worship for the Moabites without accepting the reality of Chemosh as a god. Cf. Morris, *Ruth*, 260.

113. See Num 21:29; 1 Kgs 11:7; 2 Kgs 23:13; Jer 48:7, 13, 46; the Mesha Inscription from the ninth century BC, in *ANET*, 320–21; see also G. L. Mattingly, "Chemosh," *ABD* 1:895–97; H. -P. Müller, "Chemosh," *DDD*, 186–89.

114. Modified from Bush, *Ruth, Esther*, 74.

# The Book of Ruth

> A  Do not urge me to abandon you,
>   to turn back from following after you.
>   B  For <u>wherever</u> you go, I will go,
>     and wherever you lodge, I will lodge.
>       C  Your people, my people,
>         And your God, my God. (v. 16)
>   B′ <u>Wherever</u> you die, I will die
>     and there I will be buried.
> A′ Thus may Yahweh do to me and thus may he add even more
>   if even death separates me from you. (v. 17)

Ruth's strong command to Naomi (A) and her strong vow to God (A′) bracket her speech. Taken together, her promises to go and lodge wherever Naomi goes and lodges (B), and to die wherever Naomi dies (B′) signal Ruth's commitment to her mother-in-law in all of life—and perhaps beyond. Her declaration of allegiance (C) is the core and foundation of her speech, marked off by verbless couplets. The key words of each of Ruth's promises (go, lodge, people, God, die) are repeated within each clause (B-C-B′), but the pattern is broken in the last promise to reflect the subject matter (death)[115] and to mark the closure of Ruth's promises to Naomi.

Naomi's compelling threefold argument triggers a vigorous response from Ruth. Orpah and Ruth rebuffed Naomi's first speech by asserting what they would do, "Surely with you we will return" (v. 10). This polite, indirect way of speaking is now replaced by Ruth's command: *Do not urge me to abandon you*. The verb *pāgaʿ*, "to urge, entreat," shows the extreme pressure Ruth feels from Naomi, but now reflected back in her command to Naomi.[116] Ruth previously clung to Naomi, and here states that not to do so would be to "abandon" (*ʿāzab*) her mother-in-law.[117] In an honor-shame context, such strong direct words to a mother-in-law are startling and show the firmness of Ruth's conviction.

Nonetheless, the way she responds by using Naomi's words shows that she is not overcome by emotion. Naomi told Ruth to "return after" (*šûbî ʾaḥărê*)

---

115. Rendsburg, *How the Bible Is Written*, 297.

116. The verb *pāgaʿ*, usually with the preposition *bǝ*, basically means "to meet, encounter" (BDB, 803; *DCH* 6:648). The meeting often has a hostile sense—"to fall upon, attack, kill" (e.g., Exod 5:3; Josh 2:16; Judg 8:21; 15:12; 1 Sam 22:17; cf. 2:22). The sense of "to put pressure on, entreat, urge" is found in Gen 23:8; Jer 7:16; 27:18; Job 21:15.

117. The verb *ʿāzab* can mean "to leave," especially with reference to objects (e.g., stalks in 2:16), but usually has the stronger, more dramatic sense of "to forsake, abandon, desert" with reference to people (e.g., Gen 2:24; 44:22; Num 10:31; Josh 22:3; 2 Kgs 2:2, 4; Jer 9:1[2]; Ps 27:10; Prov 2:17; Ruth 2:11; cf. 2:20). In the context of Yahweh's covenant with Israel, people often abandon Yahweh to worship other gods (e.g., Deut 29:25; Josh 24:20; Judg 10:6), while Yahweh will not forsake his people (e.g., Deut 31:6; 1 Kgs 6:13; cf. Ruth 2:20).

## 1:7–19A En route: Naomi, Orpah, and Ruth Dialogue

her sister-in-law; Ruth says, do not urge me *to turn back from following after you* (*lāšûb mēʾaḥărāyik*). Ruth uses Naomi's words but with a different nuance. Naomi urged Ruth to follow Orpah's example, but Ruth says to do so is to "turn back from," to show disloyalty to her. She cannot abandon her mother-in-law; she feels a deep obligation to her. So far, "return" (*šûb*) has been to a place, but now it is with a person—Naomi. Ruth expands on this line of thinking: *For wherever you go, I will go*. Naomi told her daughters-in-law to "go" (*hālak*) back to Moab (vv. 8, 12), and not to "go" with her (v. 11); Ruth says she will "go" wherever Naomi "goes." Hers is an open-ended commitment to her mother-in-law,[118] including wherever she lodges. The verb *lîn* usually means "to lodge, stay overnight" (3:13; also, e.g., Gen 19:2; 28:11; Judg 18:2; 19:13, 15), but it sometimes means "to dwell, remain" longer (e.g., Josh 3:1; Judg 19:4), usually with a more figurative nuance (e.g., Job 17:2; Ps 25:13; Prov 19:23; Isa 1:21; Zech 5:4).[119] The former is more likely here but either makes sense and forms a merism: "wherever you *go*, wherever you *lodge*."[120] Ruth is willing to cast her lot with Naomi, even though her life might be unstable and itinerant—the opposite of finding rest (cf. v. 9).

Ruth's decision to go forth from her native land is reminiscent of Abraham's journey. They both ventured into the unknown, although Ruth's decision is all the more remarkable because she did not depart after a direct command from God. Moreover, she did not leave with her immediate family and many possessions, nor a promise of blessing and a great name from God (Gen 12:1–3). Ruth has not been presented with a vision of better life; rather, she expects hardship in following her mother-in-law.

Ruth's declaration is foundational, and she again reuses Naomi's words. Naomi said that Orpah has "returned to her people and to her god," Ruth says, *your people are my people, and your God is my God*. Surrounded by the verbs of going and lodging, dying and being buried, this declaration is immediately set apart. And they are subject-predicate null-copula clauses, *ʿammēk ʿammî* and *wēʾlōhayik ʾĕlōhāy*, are null-copula clauses, i.e., a form of the verb *be* is omitted ("your people, my people," and "your God, my God"). Based on the imperfect/future aspect of the two preceding and two following verbs, most EVV translate these clauses in the same way: "your people *will be* my people, and your God *will be* my God" (e.g., ESV, NIV, CSB, NJPS). However, this is not required by the syntax, which allows for a

---

118. The phrase *ʾel-ʾăšer telǝkî* ("to which you go" or "wherever you go") is fronted before *ʾēlēk* ("I will go"), just as in the next clause *ûbaʾăšer tālînî* ("in which you lodge" or "wherever you lodge") is fronted before *ʾālîn* ("I will lodge"). This syntax places particular focus on "*wherever*."

119. BDB, 533.

120. Cf. Bush, *Ruth, Esther*, 82.

## The Book of Ruth

present temporal reference: "your people *are* my people, and your God *is* my God." In fact, this is the best reading, viz., Ruth is committing or has already committed herself to Naomi's people and God. In an ancient Near Eastern context where people and deity cannot be separated (cf. v. 15), the former is more likely. It is unlikely Ruth would have made this commitment while in her homeland, despite living in Mahlon's and Naomi's household.[121] Ruth's change in membership to Naomi's people and allegiance to Naomi's God is crucial, for now there is no point in Naomi asking her to return to Moab. Again, Ruth's primary devotion is to Naomi, "*your* people are my people, *your* God is my God."

**17** Ruth promised to stick with Naomi in life and even in death: *Wherever you die, I will die and there I will be buried*. In this last promise, there is a break in the pattern. We expect "and wherever you are buried, I will be buried," but she only says, "and there I will be buried." This breakdown reflects and emphasizes the subject matter (death), and marks the closure of Ruth's promises to Naomi.[122] Ruth says that wherever Naomi lies buried, there in Judah, not in Moab, will she be buried.[123] Ruth's is not a fickle commitment, for she envisages that after Naomi dies, she will continue to live with her people and her God. Elimelech and his sons died and were involuntarily buried in a foreign land. Ruth's promise is that she will die and be voluntarily buried in a "foreign" land. This signals that Ruth sees herself as irreversibly part of Naomi's family, so much so that she wants to be buried side-by-side in her family plot. The importance of burial in ancestral ground is evidenced in the patriarchal narratives (e.g., Gen 50:13, 24–26; cf. Josh 24:32). Ruth's words also reflect the understanding that continuity with family does not cease at death, as reflected in phrases such as "gathered to/lie down with his people/fathers" (e.g., Gen 15:15; 25:8; 2 Kgs 20:21; 22:20). Indeed, burial in the family tomb was the most desirable and honorable form of entombment.[124] Probably located on or near the family's landholding,[125] Ruth would be brought into proximity with Naomi in death—perhaps not just physical but also spiritual or social proximity.

We must not underplay the significance of Ruth's decision to return with Naomi. Returning with Naomi meant permanently turning her back on her family, her people, her land, and her gods—in life and death. In group-

---

121. *Pace* Eskenazi and Frymer-Kensky, *Ruth*, 22.

122. Rendsburg, *How the Bible Is Written*, 297.

123. The fronting of *šām*, "there," before the verb is emphatic.

124. For a discussion and references, see Saul M. Olyan, "Some Neglected Aspects of Israelite Interment Ideology," *JBL* 124 (2005): esp. 607–8.

125. See Herbert C. Brichto, "Kin, Cult, Land, and Afterlife—A Biblical Complex," *HUCA* 44 (1973): 1–54; Lawrence E. Stager, "The Archaeology of the Family in Ancient Israel," *BASOR* 260 (1985): 23.

oriented cultures, loyalty is highly prized, while disloyalty is frowned upon. Harmonious relationships are based on loyalty, while disloyalty can tear apart a society. Ruth and Orpah might have already been seen as traitors by their people, and perhaps Ruth knew she had no future in Moab.[126] Nonetheless, in contrast to Orpah, Ruth's decision would be permanent. She was willing to be disloyal to her people to remain loyal to Naomi. In turning her back on her relationships in Moab, Ruth forfeits any hope of future benefit from her former society. And since loyalty is closely linked with honor, breaking from one's people and traditions is often considered shameful. Moreover, she was willing to live with the shame of perpetual widowhood (see comments on v. 5). Naomi made it clear that security and rest for her widowed daughters-in-law were to be found in a new husband and family—back in Moab. She could not produce any more sons for them, and the implication was that they would not be able to find husbands in Israel. Yet Ruth was willing to forgo personal security and restored social status for the sake of her mother-in-law. Ruth's is an all-in loyalty and commitment to Naomi at an exceptional personal cost.

Ruth underlines the seriousness of her promises of allegiance with a self-imprecatory oath. In narratives, oaths highlight a character's intentions and traits.[127] Ruth uses a formula found elsewhere in the Old Testament,[128] which typically comprises two parts. The first describes the punishment for breaching the oath and consists of two clauses, each beginning with *kô*, "thus": *thus may Yahweh do . . . and thus may he add*. God is usually invoked in these oath formulas, but here and in 1 Sam 20:13, Jonathan's oath to David, it is Yahweh. This inner-biblical allusion highlights the similarities: both Ruth and Jonathan vow their loyalty to non-kin to their own disadvantage. Since in pledging they undermine their futures, they use the most persuasive means available—Yahweh, the personal God of Israel.[129] In keeping with other uses of this oath formula, the use here does not specify what curse Yahweh will "do" or "add."[130] This may be because the oath taker believed there was danger in pronouncing the curse itself or because the oath formulae were abbreviated

---

126. It might have been difficult for her to find a husband in Moab if there was stigma attached to her marriage to a foreigner and questions about her fertility; so Carroll R., "Once a Stranger," 186.

127. Yael Ziegler, *Promises to Keep: The Oath in Biblical Narrative* (Leiden: Brill, 2008), 269.

128. For a recent discussion of this oath formula, see Ziegler, *Promises*, 55–70.

129. Yael Ziegler, "'So Shall God Do . . .': Variations of an Oath Formula and Its Literary Meaning," *JBL* 126 (2007): 79–80.

130. First Samuel 3:17; 14:44; 20:13; 25:22; 2 Sam 3:9, 35; 19:14(13); 1 Kgs 2:23; 19:2; 20:10; 2 Kgs 6:31.

## THE BOOK OF RUTH

over time.[131] On a national level, breaking the covenant would incur God's punishments, including infertility, famine, sword, plague, and death (Lev 26:14–39; Deut 28:15–68). An individual may invoke curses such as loss of property, family, or sickness (e.g., Job 31:7–10, 16–22).[132] The declaration of the self-imprecatory oath may have been accompanied by a gesture, such as passing an index finger across the throat.[133] This would be akin to covenant ratifications (Gen 15:7–17; Jer 34:18–20; cf. 1 Sam 11:7) in which the slaughtered animal symbolized the speaker's fate if they breached the oath. Ruth's was not a hollow oath, for she had heard about Yahweh stretching his hand out against Naomi (v. 13; cf. vv. 20–21).

The second part of the oath describes the condition of the vow. Here the particle *kî* could mean "if" or "for" or "indeed."[134] Ruth could be saying only death will separate them (e.g., ESV, NJPS, NKJV, NLT, CSB), or not even death will do so (e.g., NIV). Following Ruth's promise to die and be buried with Naomi, the better translation is *if even death separates me from you*. A self-imprecatory oath ("May God/Yahweh/the gods do to me and may he add") followed by a condition introduced by *kî*, "if," is also found in 1 Sam 20:13; 2 Sam 3:9; 1 Kgs 2:23; 19:2. The verb *pārad* is used for separation of people or individuals, including the separation of family, as when Abram and Lot part company (Gen 13:9, 11, 14).[135] It is only used of death here and in 2 Sam 1:23, where David says of Saul and Jonathan, "and in death they were not separated" (*niprādû*; 2 Sam 1:23). Just like Saul and Jonathan, Ruth says her kinship bond with Naomi will be so close that not even death will separate them.

In vv. 16–17, Ruth thus creates a covenant with Naomi.[136] Although the term itself (*bərît*) does not occur in the Ruth narrative, Naomi's words are reminiscent of covenantal language in the Old Testament and the ancient Near East. God says, "they will be my people, and I will be their God" (Jer 32:38; 31:33 NIV). Ruth's words also recall those of King Jehoshaphat of Judah in forming a royal covenant with the Israelite kings (1 Kgs 22:4; 2 Kgs 3:7; cf. 2 Chr 18:3).[137] By contrast, Ruth forms a personal covenant with

---

131. Cf. Manfred R. Lehmann, "Biblical Oaths," *ZAW* 81 (1969): 80–82.

132. Consult JM §165a n. 1.

133. Cf. Morris, *Ruth*, 261.

134. For discussions, see Campbell, *Ruth*, 74–75; Schipper, *Ruth*, 101.

135. See Hausmann, *"pārad," TDOT* 12:77–78.

136. A covenant can be defined as "a solemn commitment, guaranteeing promises or obligations undertaken by one or both parties, sealed with an oath"; Paul R. Williamson, *Sealed with an Oath: Covenant in God's Unfolding Purpose*, NSBT (Downers Grove, IL: InterVarsity, 2007), 11.

137. For a comparison with Ruth 1:16–17, see Mark S. Smith, "'Your People Shall Be My People': Family and Covenant in Ruth 1:16–17," *CBQ* 69 (2007): 255–58.

## 1:7–19A EN ROUTE: NAOMI, ORPAH, AND RUTH DIALOGUE

Naomi, as Jonathan did with David (1 Sam 20:13–17). Both instances contain promises and conditions, sealed with an oath in the name of Yahweh. David and Jonathan became like brothers; Ruth and Naomi like mother and daughter.[138] Some have suggested that since such vows are usually found on the lips of royalty or leaders, Ruth's oath anticipates her future royal role. Yet, the wide variety of nonroyal examples of covenants does not support this view. Instead, covenants expressed relations between persons or parties who were unrelated to each other, a formation of kinship "based on friendship rather than blood."[139] This is the case in the Ruth narrative, as Ruth devotes herself to Naomi. She establishes a kinship tie that transcends the death of the man who had connected them; it is a family tie closer than that of in-laws.[140] Her repetition of "you/your . . . I/my" emphasizes the sharing of person, people, and God. Ruth changes her personal and social identity to conform to the major aspects of Naomi's. Nonetheless, the use of "Yahweh" in both oath formulas (Ruth's and Jonathan's) forms an inner-biblical link that points to the importance of Ruth and Jonathan's covenants in the lead-up to the formation of the Davidic dynasty—an institution established by Yahweh.

Ruth's use of "Yahweh" instead of "God" (*'ĕlōhîm*) points to the authenticity of her faith. While Ruth's pledge centers on her loyalty to Naomi, it is inseparable from her pledge of allegiance to Naomi's people and God. Her use of the covenantal name, "Yahweh," highlights her acceptance of the personal God of Israel. Ruth's turning away from her Moabite gods can be inferred from Naomi's statement that Orpah has returned "to her people and her god" (v. 15). From the narrator's perspective, Ruth's commitment to Yahweh is not syncretistic; rather, she entrusts herself solely to Yahweh.[141] If she used "God" (*'ĕlōhîm*) in her self-imprecatory oath, we might think she was invoking Chemosh.[142] But as a reflection of her identification with her newly adopted God, she invokes Yahweh. Her use of "Yahweh" might also be an attempt to explain her decision.[143] Following Naomi for no personal gain makes no sense but invoking "Yahweh" suggests that her decision results from her understanding of what the personal God of Israel wants her to do. If so, Ruth's pledge of allegiance to Yahweh is not hollow, for she is already trying to live out his will. Echoing his own covenantal words, she is willing to fall under his punishment should she break her covenant with Naomi. Nonetheless, true faith is manifest in a life consistent with the requirements

---

138. Tikva Frymer-Kensky, *Studies in Bible and Feminist Criticism* (Philadelphia: Jewish Publication Society, 2005), 150–51.

139. Frymer-Kensky, *Studies*, 150.

140. Smith, "Family," 247.

141. Cf. Sakenfeld, *Ruth*, 33.

142. LaCocque, *Ruth*, 54.

143. After Ziegler, "Variations," 80.

## The Book of Ruth

of God's covenant law, so the genuineness of Ruth's faith will require the evidence of her subsequent actions.[144]

Ruth's vow recalls that of another foreigner to a Judahite from Bethlehem. When David fled from Absalom, Ittai the Gittite followed, but David urges Ittai using words reminiscent of Naomi, "Why do you also go [*tēlēk*] with us? Go back [*šûb*] and stay [*wašēb*] with the king for you are a foreigner [*nokrî*; cf. Ruth 2:10] and also an exile from your home. . . . Go back and take your brothers with you, and may Yahweh show kindness [*ḥesed*] and faithfulness to you" (2 Sam 15:19–20 ESV). Ittai responds similarly to Ruth, "As Yahweh lives, and as my lord the king lives, wherever my lord the king shall be, whether for death or for life, there also will your servant be" (15:21 ESV). Both foreigners remain loyal to a Judahite, choosing voluntary exile over the comfort and security of home. The differences highlight the remarkable decision of Ruth. She throws in her lot with a destitute widow, while Ittai is joined by his brothers and, presumably, their possessions. There is no immediate reward for Ittai or Ruth; there is the prospect of a reward for Ittai once David's situation improves, but there is no hope on the horizon for Naomi. Ittai swears an oath on Yahweh, while Ruth goes further and pledges allegiance to Yahweh. How might Yahweh reward such absolute devotion?[145]

**18** After three attempts to dissuade Ruth from following her, Naomi gives up. She saw that Ruth was *mit'ammeṣet*, "determined" *to go with her*. This participle expresses duration and persistence, a firm resolve in the face of Naomi's arguments, as manifest in her clinging and her vow.[146] Realizing that Ruth had made up her mind, Naomi knew that further attempts at persuasion would be futile. So *she ceased speaking to her*, that is, she gave up trying to persuade her to turn back to Moab. Naomi's silence contrasts with

---

144. While a fully developed notion of "conversion" is only established centuries after the Ruth narrative, Ruth's vow offers a great deal of insight calling for theological reflection among both Christians and Jews, so much so that she has sometimes been considered the prototypical convert. From a Christian perspective, see Christopher J. H. Wright, "Implications of Conversion in the Old Testament and the New," *International Bulletin of Missionary Research* 28 (2004): 18; Hubbard, *Ruth*, 41. From a Jewish perspective, see *Midr. Ruth Rab.* 2:10 and Rashi's comment to Ruth 1:1, 3. For a discussion of Ruth's conversion in Targum Ruth, see Christian M. M. Brady, "The Conversion of Ruth in Targum Ruth," *Review of Rabbinic Judaism* 16 (2013): 133–46. For further discussion and references, see Lau, *Identity and Ethics*, 92–95.

145. Cf. Ziegler, *Promises*, 269: Oaths reveal a narrative's "internal dynamics, the tensions and solutions at its core."

146. The *hithpael* of *'mṣ* ("to be strong") may carry the nuance of "to strengthen oneself," as may be detected in 1 Kgs 12:18 = 2 Chr 10:18 ("to exert oneself") and 2 Chr 13:7 ("to defy"; ESV). Cf. A. S. van der Woude, "*'mṣ*," *TLOT* 1:157–58; *DCH* 1:320. The participle is fronted before the pronominal subject *hi'*, which places focus on Ruth's determination; see Holmstedt, *Handbook*, 93.

## 1:7–19A EN ROUTE: NAOMI, ORPAH, AND RUTH DIALOGUE

David's verbal acceptance of Ittai's oath (2 Sam 15:22). Naomi's silence has been interpreted as resignation, resentment, preoccupation, and giving Ruth the "silent treatment," among others.[147] Since I read the clause as Naomi's response to Ruth's resolve, I take this as Naomi's reluctant acceptance. In an honor-shame culture, the younger generation should show respect by following the instructions of the older. But Ruth paradoxically showed respect by disobeying her mother-in-law and committing herself to her. Naomi had been concerned only for her daughters-in-law's futures; Ruth was only concerned for her mother-in-law. Now that Naomi saw Ruth could not be dissuaded, perhaps she saw the benefit of Ruth accompanying her on her journey. In any case, Naomi stopped speaking on the subject of Ruth's return to Moab, rather than she stopped speaking to her altogether on the journey to Bethlehem.

As we marvel at Ruth's extraordinary loyalty, we need to be careful not to apply her actions to every situation. The relationship between mother- and daughter-in-law can be fraught, and, in some cultures, there is much pressure on a daughter-in-law.[148] In such situations, we can imagine a misuse of Scripture whereby Ruth's commitment is held up as exemplary. The Bible upholds the principle of honoring parents and elders (e.g., Exod 20:12 = Deut 5:16; Lev 19:3, 32; cf. Eph 6:1–4), but how this is manifest in specific circumstances is a matter of wisdom. Ruth chose to cling to Naomi, Orpah did not. But Orpah is not castigated for her decision; rather, Naomi urges Ruth to follow her. And although genuine, Ruth's allegiance to Yahweh was secondary to her commitment to Naomi. In the New Testament, however, Jesus tells his followers to follow him before all and that all other allegiances—including family—are at a distant second (e.g., Matt 10:37; Luke 14:26).

**19a** *The two of them went on* closes the scene just as it began, "and they went on the way to return to the land of Judah" (v. 7). Three women had set out, two continue the journey. If Naomi had her way, it would have been one, but Ruth is still with her. Just as the two sons (vv. 1, 3, 5) and two daughters-in-law (vv. 7, 8) were described as a single entity, Naomi and Ruth walked in solidarity *until they came to Bethlehem*. Similar to other Old Testament narratives, the journey to Bethlehem is not described.[149] The two of them travel as one to one destination and one destiny.

---

147. See, e.g., Fewell and Gunn, *Compromising*, 74; Saxegaard, *Character*, 103; Hawk, *Ruth*, 61–62.

148. For expectations on a daughter-in-law in China, see Lin, "Cross-Textual Reading," 47–48.

149. E.g., Abram's journey from Haran to Canaan (Gen 12:4–5).

## THE BOOK OF RUTH

## C. TOWN GATE: NAOMI LAMENTS BEFORE
## THE TOWNSWOMEN (1:19B–22)

Naomi has returned to Bethlehem with her Moabite daughter-in-law in tow. The threefold use of forms of *šwb* in this scene continues the motif of "return" (vv. 21, 22 [2×]).[150] But it is not a happy homecoming for Naomi. Comparing her station in life now with when she departed Bethlehem, she is overwhelmed with feelings of emptiness and bitterness. She cannot even think of herself as the same person, so much so that she rejects her name and the social status it held. But she not only vents to the townswomen but also complains about, not to, God. She keeps her former social group at arm's length, but we wonder what her words show about her relationship with God, especially since her return from Moab was predicated on hearing of God's restored blessing of Israel (v. 6). In what sense is Naomi returning, and why does the narrator describe Ruth as also returning (v. 22)?

[19b]*As soon as they entered*[a] *Bethlehem, the whole town was abuzz*[b] *over them.*[c] *And the women said,*[d] *"Is this Naomi?"*

[20]*She said to them, "Do not call me 'Naomi' ['Pleasant'].*[e] *Call me 'Mara' ['Bitter'] because Shaddai*[f] *has made me very bitter.*[g]

[21]*I*[h] *went away full,*[i] *but empty Yahweh has returned me.*[j] *Why should you call me Naomi? Yahweh has testified against me. Shaddai has brought disaster upon me."*

[22]*So Naomi returned, and Ruth the Moabite her daughter-in-law with her, who returned*[k] *from the territory of Moab.*[l] *They*[m] *came to*[n] *Bethlehem at the beginning of the barley harvest.*

a. The phrase *wayǝhî kǝbōʾānâ* ("And it was as soon as they entered") is absent in some LXX manuscripts, which is most likely because of haplography, whereby the scribe saw "Bethlehem" in the preceding clause and the second "Bethlehem," then omitted the enclosed phrase. The prepositions *bǝ* and *kǝ* are both used with infinitives to create a temporal clause: *bǝ* denotes general temporal proximity, while *kǝ* denotes immediate temporal proximity ("as soon as"; e.g., Gen 24:30; 1 Kgs 15:29); see *IBHS* §36.2.2b. I translate the verb *bôʾ* here "entered" (cf. 1:2; 2:18) and elsewhere "came to" (1:19a, 22); cf. Hubbard, *Ruth*, 121n4. Contexts indicate different nuances of the verb. It can mean "to approach, arrive," as opposed to "to go, go away" (*hālak*; 1:19a; so also, e.g., Gen 16:8; 1 Sam 20:21, 22), and the arrival of the two women concludes their journey from Moab (*hālak*; 1:7, 18). The verb can also mean "to enter, come in," as opposed to "to go out, depart" (*yāṣāʾ*; e.g., Josh 6:1; 1 Kgs 15:17), as the three women had done from Moab (1:7).

b. The versions have various readings: "resound" (LXX); "rejoice" (Syr.); "the report was quickly spread" (Vulg.).

150. The motif appears in each scene of act 1 (1:6, 7, 8, 10, 11, 12, 15 [2×], 16), then in 2:6; 4:3, 15.

# 1:19B–22 TOWN GATE: NAOMI LAMENTS BEFORE THE TOWNSWOMEN

c. Some LXX manuscripts have a singular object, referring to Naomi alone. Supported by Tg., MT^L is most likely original.

d. Heb. *wattō'marnâ*, "and they said" (cf. 4:14), is feminine plural, which is specified in my translation.

e. *No'ŏmî* (the first vowel is a *qamets khatuf*), "Naomi," most likely derives from the root *n'm*, "to be pleasant, delightful, lovely." See note and comments on 1:2.

f. LXX reads *ho hikanós*, "the sufficient one," from an ancient Jewish understanding of the Hebrew, *še* ("who") plus *day* ("sufficiency"). The parallelism with Yahweh in v. 21 indicates that *šadday* is a divine epithet for God.

g. Heb. *hēmar . . . lî ma'ōd*, "has made me very bitter," cf. "has quite filled me with bitterness" (Vulg.), "has dealt very bitterly with me" (ESV), "has made my life very bitter" (NIV).

h. Naomi uses *'ănî* rather than *'ānōkî*. For a discussion of these two forms of the first person-singular pronoun, see the note on 2:10.

i. Heb. *'ănî malē'â hālaktî* contains an unnecessary pronoun ("I full I went away"), since Hebrew verbs are fully inflected. The use of the pronoun in *'ănî malē'â hālaktî* ("*I* went away full") signals the topic since there is a change from God in the preceding clause (v. 21) to Naomi. For a discussion of topic and focus, see Holmstedt, *Handbook*, 9–16. For a discussion of the fronting of *malē'â* see next note.

j. Heb. *'ănî malē'â hālaktî warêqām hĕšîbanî yhwh*, the adjectives *malē'â*, "full," and *rêqām*, "empty" (both used adverbially) are fronted to highlight the contrast between Naomi's status when she left and when Yahweh returned her to Bethlehem. My translation attempts to capture this emphasis, but in speech there can be added emphasis, "I went away *full*, but *empty* Yahweh has returned me."

k. In MT^L *haššābâ* is accented as a *qatal* instead of a participle, "who returned." As in v. 8, the *ha-* functions as a relative marker, here with a finite verb instead of with a participle (also in 2:6; 4:3); *IBHS* §19.7c. The *qatal* brings out the past time of the action, views the event as a whole, and is consistent with the clause as a summary; thus, there is no need to move the accent in MT^L, from the penultimate to the ultimate syllable to produce a participle (*pace* JM §145e; *IBHS* §19.7d). The narrator previously used a similar progression: singular subject, then the inclusion of others, ending with plural subjects (1:1b–2, 7).

l. Vulg. is the only version that reads "from the land of her sojournment" (also v. 7).

m. The pronoun *hēmmâ* is masculine, although it has two feminine referents, Naomi and Ruth (see note on 1:8 about gender mismatch).

n. Heb. *bā'û*, "they came to," here translating *bô'* the same as in 1:19a. See note on 1:19b.

This scene evidences a chiastic structure:

> A  Narrative introduction (v. 19b)
> > B  Dialogue (vv. 19c–21)
>
> A' Narrative conclusion (v. 22)

The beginning of this last scene of act 1 is marked by "and it was" (*wayahî*) followed by an expression of time, "as soon as they entered" (cf. v. 1).[151] It is

---

151. Heb. *wayahî* is left untranslated because it functions as a temporal marker; see v. 1.

## THE BOOK OF RUTH

framed by the phrases "as soon as they entered Bethlehem" (*wayəhî kəbō'ānâ bêt leḥem*; A) and "they came to Bethlehem" (*wəhēmmâ bā'û bêt leḥem*; A'), which provide transitions between the previous and the present scenes (v. 19b), and the present and the next scenes (v. 22). The focus of this scene is the dialogue between Naomi and the townswomen (B). The dialogue is prompted by a question from the townswomen, to which Naomi gives a two-part response.

**19b-c** *As soon as they entered Bethlehem*, presumably through the town gates (cf. 4:1), *the whole town was abuzz over them.* "The whole town" (*kol-hā'îr*) indicates a mixed crowd,[152] although during the day the able-bodied men would be working in the fields. The word *wattēhōm* probably derives from the root *hm*, "hum, murmur, roar, buzz,"[153] with the figurative meanings "to bring into unrest or confusion" (e.g., Isa 22:3; Prov 1:21), and "resound with excitement" (1 Sam 4:5; 1 Kgs 1:45).[154] It is an onomatopoeia, like the English word "murmur," "buzz," or "hum." Was the whole town abuzz with rumors in a positive (happy, excited) or negative (shocked, concerned, critical) way? Likely a mixture of both. Upon their arrival, people would have wondered who these strange women were. They would be intrigued to see a new face, yet the older one was vaguely familiar to some of them. Naomi's appearance would have changed markedly. Her Moabite style of clothing hinted at a foreign sojourn. The years of grief over the death of her husband and sons, along with the subsequent deprivation, probably left her looking worn out.[155] She had aged more than the ten years she was away.

Among the mixed crowd, there is a glint of recognition from the women of the town (cf. 4:14), as they say to each other: *Is this Naomi?*[156] Surprise is the overwhelming sense of this rhetorical question, but it is difficult to be certain of its tone.[157] There is probably a note of delight, of gladness to see her back.[158] Family and friends would be keen to catch up with her news—what has been going on in her life in the intervening years. Perhaps there is even a note of

---

152. Cf. 1 Samuel 4:13, "The whole town [*kol-hā'îr*] cried out."

153. It could be a *niphal* of *hmm* or *hwm* (see GKC §§67t, 72v) or a *qal* of *hwm* (see GKC §72h).

154. See F. Stolz, "*hmm*," *TLOT* 1:378; H. -P. Müller, "*hmm*," *TDOT* 3:419–22; Harry F. van Rooy, "*hûm*," *NIDOTTE* 1:1018–20; W. R. Domeris, "*hmh*," *NIDOTTE* 1:1041–43; R. H. O'Connell, "*hmm*," *NIDOTTE* 1:1046–48.

155. Cf. Morris, *Ruth*, 262; *Midr. Ruth Rab.* 3:6: "In the past, [Naomi] used to go in a litter, and now she walks barefoot. . . . In the past she wore a cloak of fine wool, and now she is clothed in rags. . . . Before her countenance was ruddy from abundance of food and drink, and now it is sickly from hunger."

156. The women do not address Naomi directly; cf. 1 Kgs 18:7, 17.

157. See B. Jongeling, "*hz't n'my* (Ruth I 19)," *VT* 28 (1978): 474–77.

158. Campbell, *Ruth*, 75.

## 1:19B–22 TOWN GATE: NAOMI LAMENTS BEFORE THE TOWNSWOMEN

criticism since she and her family left these people in their time of need.[159] A note of shock or disbelief, however, probably predominates because of her haggard appearance.[160] The women immediately noticed the absence of her family members. She left Bethlehem with a husband and two sons; she now returns with a foreign childless widow.

Although the whole town is astir when the two women arrive, the astonished question is about Naomi. It is not so much that Ruth goes unnoticed, since the whole town is abuzz because of *them*, but the focus of the women's attention is on Naomi. The question reveals the informal women's network of the town—which were probably widespread in ancient Israel.[161] The question is on the lips of the women who would have been her social group, one in which she was well known, friends with whom she chatted as they went about their daily tasks, such as baking bread around a common oven. These are the women who first recognize her, as expressed in their question. Will they help her resettle into life in Bethlehem, or is there some lingering resentment toward her?

**20** As much as Naomi might have mentally rehearsed her return "home," nothing would have fully prepared her for the familiar sights and sounds and smells. After more than a decade, the recognition of place and people triggered a flood of emotions. And comparing her personal circumstances when she left with what they are now would have been overwhelming.

Her response is poignant and semi-poetic, with the orderly structure belying its strong emotions. She rejects her name with two statements (A and A'), each followed by reasons based on what God had done to her (B and B'):

> She said to them,
> A  "Do not call me 'Naomi' ['Pleasant']. Call me 'Mara' ['Bitter']
>     B  because *Shaddai* [the Almighty] has made me very bitter.
>        (v. 20)
>        I went away full,
>        but empty <u>Yahweh</u> has returned me.
> A'  Why should you call me Naomi?
>     B'  <u>Yahweh</u> has testified against me.
>         *Shaddai* has brought disaster upon me." (v. 21)

---

159. Cf. Ronald T. Hyman, "Questions and Changing Identity in the Book of Ruth," *USQR* 39 (1984): 192–93; Grossman, *Ruth*, 114.

160. Cf. Sakenfeld, *Ruth*, 35; LaCocque, *Ruth*, 55. Amazement at deterioration is also found in Isa 14:16; Lam 2:15.

161. Carol L. Meyers, "'Women of the Neighbourhood' (Ruth 4.17): Informal Female Networks in Ancient Israel," in *Ruth and Esther: A Feminist Companion to the Bible*, ed. Athalya Brenner (Sheffield: Sheffield Academic Press, 1999), 120.

## THE BOOK OF RUTH

The focus of Naomi's response is herself, as shown by the repetition of "me" and "I."[162] But she rejects her name because of what she says God has done to her, as evidenced in the chiastic arrangement of Shaddai-Yahweh-Yahweh-Shaddai.

The women were speaking to one another, but, overhearing their words, Naomi speaks to them directly (*said to them*). Her outburst cuts through their chatter and dispels any uncertainty about her identity. The change in Naomi was not only external, it was also internal, as symbolized by the rejection of her name: *Do not call me 'Naomi.'* If a name reflects character and personality rather than simply being an identifier,[163] then "Naomi" ("Pleasant," see comment on v. 2) was no longer suitable for her. With a prominent citizen as a husband and two sons in her household, she could easily live up to her name. Now deprived of all that could make her "pleasant," she feels only bitterness, and hence the personal identifier "Mara" is more appropriate for her current situation and state of mind.[164] "Mara" is not only appropriate because Shaddai has embittered her life but also because it has associations with misfortune ( Job 3:20; 7:11; 10:1; 21:25) and even death (1 Sam 15:32; Isa 38:17).[165] Hence, to continue to call her Naomi would have been akin to mockery. Naomi changes her name because she feels it does not reflect her character and situation, but the narrator continues to call her Naomi (starting in v. 22), which hints that Naomi's understanding of her situation is flawed or incomplete.[166]

Naomi's repudiation of her name expresses the intense shame she suffered. She felt completely empty because she had lost her husband, sons, and material possessions. Yet she also felt she had lost her reputation before her peer group—she has lost "face." She felt devalued in her own eyes, and in the eyes of the townswomen. She felt flawed and hence a sense of being unworthy of belonging, of disconnection from her former social group. So the reputation and honor that was an integral part of her previous name she now rejects. Socially, she cannot fall any further. And she feels that there is no way out of her pit. In her eyes, her situation is completely hopeless. Yet the rejection of her former identity promulgates and entrenches her in her situation. By rejecting her former name, she alienates herself from her

---

162. She refers to herself with *lî* ("me"; 5×), *bî* ("me"; 1×), and *'ănî* ("I"; 1×).

163. Cf. BDB, 1027; *IDB* 3:500–508.

164. Heb. *mārā'* derives from the root *mrr*, "to be bitter"; BDB, 600; *HALOT* 2:638. It is probably the adjective *mr* with a feminine ending, which usually produces *mrh* (Gen 27:34; 2 Sam 2:26; Ezek 27:30; Prov 5:4; Job 21:25; Esth 4:1). This explains the reading *mrh* instead of *mr'* in multiple MSS; *BHS* critical apparatus. But the use of ' to mark a feminine noun ending is found for other roots (Num 11:20; Isa 19:17; Ps 127:2; Lam 3:12); see GKC §80h.

165. Fischer, *Rut*, 151. Cf. Campbell, *Ruth*, 76–77.

166. Cf. Saxegaard, *Character*, 78–79.

## 1:19B–22 Town Gate: Naomi Laments before the Townswomen

former close social network. By demanding they no longer call her Naomi, she implies that she is not the same woman they knew a decade ago. Hence, they cannot relate to her as they used to. Owing to her loss of husband and sons, with the resultant loss of social status, perhaps there is a sense that she cannot relate to them or, conversely, that they cannot relate to or empathize with her experience. It may be a combination of these, with the outcome that she isolates herself. By keeping her social group at arm's length, she ends up perpetuating her marginal status.

The derivation and meaning of *šadday* are uncertain,[167] but more pertinent is its contextual usage in Old Testament texts. The divine epithet Shaddai (or the full form, *'el šadday*; "El Shaddai") is primarily associated with power: he is the awesome ruler of the world (e.g., Num 24:4, 16; Ezek 1:24; 10:5; Ps 68:15[14]). Influenced by *pantokratōr* (LXX translation of *šadday* elsewhere in the Old Testament) and *omnipotens* (Vulg.), *šadday* is usually translated "the Almighty" in EVV (but NJPS "Shaddai"; NET "Sovereign One"). Naomi's use of "Shaddai" also evokes ideas of fertility, since the appearance of "Shaddai" in Genesis is related to the blessing of the patriarchs (e.g., Gen 17:1; 28:3; 35:11; 48:3–4). This association is strengthened by alliteration, as, for instance, in Gen 49:25 ESV, "Shaddai [*šadday*], who will bless you with blessings of heaven above, blessings of the deep that crouches beneath, blessings of the breasts [*šādayim*] and of the womb." In the Ruth narrative, *šadday* alliterates with *śadê*, "fields," of Moab (1:1, 2, 6).[168] Naomi and her family left Bethlehem because of its infertile fields to seek the fertile fields of Moab. But now Shaddai has made Naomi bitter instead of blessed: her sons died without producing children, and she is not fertile anymore (vv. 11–13).

Naomi's use of Shaddai thus evokes another association. Since he is all powerful, he not only blesses, he also judges and punishes (e.g., Isa 13:6; Joel 1:15; Job 6:4; 23:16; 27:14–23). Apart from the patriarchal narratives,[169] the second major cluster of the epithet is in the book of Job.[170] In Job, the divine epithet is associated with justice (Job 8:3; 24:1; 27:2), punishment or discipline (e.g., Job 5:17; 6:4; 23:16; 27:14–23), and vindication (Job 8:5; 13:3; 31:35). Yet Shaddai's ways are inscrutable (Job 11:7). Like Job, Naomi formerly enjoyed a life blessed by Shaddai, but they both lost their children

---

167. Some suggestions include: (1) "God of the mountain," cf. Akk. *šadu*; (2) "The Strong One" or "Almighty," cf. Arabic *sdd*; (3) "God of the field/wilderness," cf. Heb. *śadeh*; (4) "Breasted One," cf. Heb. *šadday*; and (5) "God of protection," cf. Akk. *šēdu*, "demon." For discussion and references, see E. A. Knauf, "Shadday," *DDD*, 749–53; G. Steins, "*šadday*," *TDOT* 14: 419–46.

168. Also *śādeh* in 1:22, 2:2, 3 (2×), 6, 8, 9, 17, 22; 4:3 (2×), 5.

169. See below. Shaddai thus recalls an earlier historical period.

170. The book of Job contains thirty-one of the forty-eight references in the Old Testament. This book is also set in the patriarchal period.

# THE BOOK OF RUTH

and possessions.[171] Instead of enjoying the blessing of fertility from Shaddai, they experienced bitterness. It is thus fitting they lament similarly: "Shaddai has made my soul bitter" (Job 27:2). As she had done previously (v. 13), Naomi attributes the cause of her bitterness to God.[172] She referred to him as Yahweh (1:8, 9, 13), but now she uses Shaddai. In her eyes, this divine ruler of the world is responsible for her bitterness.

In the Old Testament, "Shaddai" is associated with a basic plot structure: a threat to patriarchal land and lineage, then deliverance from that threat.[173] In the Pentateuch, the divine name is used in the context of the covenant with Abraham, and threats to that covenant. God identifies himself as "El Shaddai" when initiating the covenant of circumcision with Abram (Gen 17:1), although lineage is under threat because of Abram and Sarah's advanced age. Isaac refers to God as "El Shaddai" as he passes on the blessing of Abraham to Jacob (Gen 28:3–4). Then God refers to himself with the same name as he reassures Jacob of his covenant blessing when he returns from Paddan-aram (35:11–12). Jacob uses the name "El Shaddai" as he prays for his sons (43:14) and "Shaddai" as he blesses Joseph (49:25). When Abraham's descendants are under threat in Egypt, God again uses the name to reaffirm the covenant by declaring to Moses that he will deliver his people (Exod 6:3). When Israel is under threat from Balak, Balaam sees "the vision of Shaddai" (Num 24:4, 16) and ends up blessing Israel instead of cursing them. In the book of Job, "Shaddai" is not only associated with a threat to Job's land and lineage, he also restores by giving Job twice as much as he had (Job 42:10). With this Old Testament plot structure in mind, Naomi invoking the name "Shaddai" in the context of a threat to land and lineage links the Ruth narrative to the patriarchal narratives and foreshadows a resolution along similar lines to those narratives.

The epithet Shaddai features prominently in the mouths of foreigners from east of Israel. The prophet Balaam from Pethor of Mesopotamia (Num 22:5; Deut 23:5[4]) is not Moabite but is hired by Balak, a Moabite king (Num 22–24). The prophet uses Shaddai in his third and fourth oracles (Num 24:4, 16; cf. *šdyn* in the eighth century BC inscription from Deir ʿAllā in Jordan[174]). The epithet is used by all the dialogue partners in the book of Job,[175] which is set in

---

171. Later in the narrative, it will be revealed that she still has a plot of land (Ruth 4:3).

172. The *hiphil* (causative) form of the root *mrr* reinforces her point.

173. For the ideas in this paragraph, I am indebted to Terrance R. Wardlaw Jr., "Shaddai, Providence, and the Narrative Structure of Ruth," *JETS* 58 (2015): 33–40.

174. See "The Deir ʿAlla Plaster Inscriptions," trans. Baruch A. Levine (*COS* 2.27:140–45).

175. It is used with increasing frequency toward the culmination of the dispute (Job 22:3, 17, 23, 25–26; 23:16; 24:1; 27:2, 10–11, 13; 29:5; 31:2, 35; 32:8; 33:4; 34:10, 12; 35:13; 37:23); see Steins, "*šadday*," *TDOT* 14:437–41.

## 1:19B–22 TOWN GATE: NAOMI LAMENTS BEFORE THE TOWNSWOMEN

the Transjordan region, east of Israel proper.[176] God responds to Job by referring to himself using this epithet (40:2). Shaddai is active in the Transjordan in Job and, as Naomi says, in Transjordan Moab in her life.

**21** Naomi then explains God's role in her bitterness. The antithetically parallel clauses show the conflict between Naomi and God:

> *I* went away <u>full</u>
> but <u>empty</u> *Yahweh* has returned me.

Naomi says she *went away full*, yet we wonder if she is overstating her case since she left because of famine. Her fullness must refer to her complete family when she departed—a husband and sons. Nonetheless, the narrative will return to the other sense of emptiness (3:17). Naomi omits reference to God as the source of her blessing of family, which sounds a dissonant note with the mention of God as provider (v. 6). However, she attributes her suffering to God: *but empty Yahweh has returned me.* The fronting of the adjectives *məlēʾâ*, "full," and *rêqām*, "empty" (both used adverbially) highlights the contrast between Naomi's situation when she left and when she returned to Bethlehem. The sentence structure pits Naomi against God: she went away full but Yahweh has caused her to return empty.[177]

The basis on which Naomi considers herself empty is the lack of male family members. This underlines the reality for women living in ancient Israel: without a man for provision and protection, a woman is destitute and vulnerable. Nonetheless, we know Ruth has returned with her, so she is not completely empty. Ruth was so determined not to abandon her mother-in-law that she vowed to take on Naomi's God and people, forming an irreversible kinship bond (vv. 16–18; cf. 4:15). And the narrator stated that "the two of them returned" (v. 19), a reality emphasized in the next verse. Ironically, Naomi complains of being "empty" when she is accompanied by someone whose name means "satiation."

Naomi's failure to acknowledge Ruth's presence might betray resentment or embarrassment. The repetition of "me" and "I" in Naomi's response points to self-absorption, perhaps due to grief or self-pity triggered by the overwhelming emotions of returning "home." Perhaps she did not want to draw attention to her strange daughter-in-law. No matter the strength of Naomi and Ruth's relationship before entering Bethlehem, it would be understandable

---

176. For a discussion of the location of Uz, see Francis I. Andersen, *Job: An Introduction and Commentary* (Leicester: Inter-Varsity, 1976), 59, 77; David J. A. Clines, *Job 1–20*, WBC 17 (Grand Rapids: Zondervan, 1989), 10.

177. In Hebrew: "*I* full went away but empty he has returned me *Yahweh*." Cf. Porten, "Scroll," 31.

# THE BOOK OF RUTH

for Naomi to feel ashamed to return to her hometown and face her former social group. For the contrast could not have been starker: her "full" family has been replaced by a foreign daughter-in-law—and a Moabite one at that.

Naomi rejects her name again, this with a rhetorical question, *Why should you call me Naomi?* This question parallels Naomi's previous statement ("Do not call me . . ."), with the "why" (*lāmmâ*) having a sense of prohibition.[178] Again she continues with reasons to support the rejection of her name. But whereas the previous reasons were presented as antithetically parallel clauses ("full . . . empty"), these clauses are synonymous. There is some ambiguity with the verb *'ānâ*, as reflected in the versions and English translations.[179] The verb seems to have primarily a legal sense, "to testify,"[180] although the meaning "to afflict" or "to humble" is also appropriate in this context. And the possible wordplay between *'ānâ bî* and *no'ŏmî*[181] would not only heighten the poetic quality of Naomi's speech, but also strengthen the association between her name and her suffering. Perhaps the verb was also chosen for its polysemantic nature.[182] If so, Naomi says that God's testimony against her has left her humiliated. Does the use of "Yahweh" hint that she has broken the covenant, and that God is testifying against her on this basis? No charge is mentioned, so we cannot be sure, but we can be sure that no one can refute God's testimony in a court of law.

Naomi gives the second parallel reason for rejecting her name: *Shaddai has brought disaster upon me.* The *hiphil* verb *hēra'* means "to cause disaster or distress, to bring misfortune."[183] When used regarding God's action, "Yahweh" is normally used, not "Shaddai." The verb *hēra'* (e.g., Josh 24:20) and the cognate noun *rā'â*, "disaster, misfortune," describe God's judgment against his people's disobedience or evil by bringing disaster (e.g., 1 Kgs 14:10; 21:29; Isa 47:11; Ezek 6:10),[184] which may hint at Naomi's culpability.[185] But

---

178. Cf. "Why (*lāmmâ*) would you go with me?" (v. 11).

179. In the MT[L] *'ānâ bî*, "testified against me," reflects a *qal* verb (*'ānâ*) in the MT[L], whereas LXX, Vulg., and Syr. read a *piel* verb (*'innâ*) from the homonymous root *'nh*, "to humble, afflict." Some EVV translate the former (e.g., ESV, NASB), while others the latter (e.g., NIV, NJPS, NRSV). The verb *'ānâ* simply means "to respond, answer" (cf. 2:6, 11). The preposition *bǝ* following the *piel* is not biblically attested.

180. When *'ānâ* is followed by the preposition *bǝ* it usually has a legal connotation, "to bear witness" (e.g., Exod 20:16; Deut 5:20; 1 Sam 12:3; Mic 6:3), or "to testify against" (e.g., Num 35:30; Deut 19:16, 18; Job 15:6; Prov 25:18); consult C. J. Labuschagne, "'nh," TLOT 2:926–30. Only in Ruth 1:21 is Yahweh described as testifying against someone.

181. H. H. Witzenrath, *Das Buch Rut: Eine literaturwissenschaftliche Untersuchung* (Munich: Kösel, 1975), 20; Sasson, *Ruth*, 36; Hubbard, *Ruth*, 122n14.

182. See Michael S. Moore, "Two Textual Anomalies in Ruth," *CBQ* 59 (1997): 234–38.

183. BDB, 948–49. It derives from the root *r'*, "to be evil, bad."

184. See Dohmen, "*r'*," *TDOT* 13:586.

185. Cf. Block, *Discourse*, 103–4.

116

## 1:19B-22 Town Gate: Naomi Laments before the Townswomen

the verb is used by people to question God's purposes in bringing calamity upon them (e.g., Exod 5:22; Num 11:11; 1 Kgs 17:20), which may hint that Naomi considers her suffering unjust. Perhaps both senses are invoked here, but the thrust of Naomi's final statement is that the ultimate cause of her bitter misfortune is God.

Does Naomi take responsibility for her suffering, or does she lay the blame solely at God's feet? On the one hand, she seems to say it is all God's fault: "Shaddai has made me very bitter. Yahweh has brought me back empty. Yahweh has testified against me. Shaddai has brought disaster upon me" (vv. 20–21). On the other hand, there may be hints she takes some responsibility for her suffering. In a patriarchal society such as ancient Israel, we expect that power is primarily held by males. This is at least true in the public realm, where, with only a few exceptions, the Israelite leaders were men. But in the private realm, we find glimpses where females also held power and influence. We are not told how much input Naomi had in the decision to leave the promised land. As the family departs, Elimelech is the subject of the verbs: he decides, and his family follows. By the end of the chapter, however, Naomi states, "*I* went away" (1:21), not "*We* went away." Naomi seems to accept some responsibility for leaving Israel.[186] If so, this family's departure was not solely a husband's decision.[187]

Despite the bitterness of Naomi's complaint, we can detect a flicker of faith. Theologically, she is correct: God is behind not just blessing but also barrenness. He does not stand behind good and evil symmetrically,[188] but if Shaddai is sovereign over all creation, how could it be otherwise? In a time of suffering, lament and complaint can be an honest expression of faith. In this chapter, Naomi does not speak directly to God in lament; rather, she addresses her complaints to her daughters-in-law (1:13) and the townswomen (1:21). This may reflect her sense of abandonment by God, and some might detect a lack of faith. Yet, at another level, we can understand Naomi's complaint as also addressed to God.[189] Those without faith might turn against God altogether, throw their hands in the air, and not bother with God at all. Those with faith continue to wrestle with God and their understanding of

186. Cf. Barry G. Webb, *Five Festal Garments: Christian Reflections on the Song of Songs, Ruth, Lamentations, Ecclesiastes, Esther*, NSBT (Leicester: Apollos, 2000), 42; Zakovitch, *Rut*, 103.

187. Examples of a wife's influence in decision-making are found throughout the Old Testament, including Eve (Gen 3:6), Rebekah (Gen 27:46–28:5), Samson's wife (Judg 14:15–20), Bathsheba (1 Kgs 1:11–31), and Job's wife (Job 2:9–10). Naomi also would have had some say in finding wives for her sons.

188. See D. A. Carson, *A Call to Spiritual Reformation: Priorities from Paul and His Prayers* (Grand Rapids: Baker Academic, 1992), 158.

189. Cf. Sakenfeld, "Naomi's Cry," 141.

his treatment of them. We hear their laments in both the Old Testament and the New Testament—Job, the psalmists, Jeremiah, Jesus. Reading Ruth with Job, we notice the similar laments on the lips of Naomi and Job, who both suffer under the hand of the Almighty. Job protests his innocence; Naomi's culpability is ambiguous. Job's faith may be more robust than Naomi's, but both point to a right response when God and his purposes seem hidden and perplexing. Believers do not always need to speak to God in a controlled and sanitized way. Christians can address him as "our Father in heaven" (Matt 6:9), so we can communicate honestly, expressing our heartfelt emotions. Lament is an expression of faith, not its lack. Nonetheless, care must be taken that complaints do not turn to bitterness or resentment toward God. He is both almighty and good; we need to trust he has good intentions for us (Rom 8:28–29).

Naomi's speech also highlights how poverty leads to shame and social isolation.[190] To fully take part in a society requires having the material resources considered normal for that society. Lacking such resources, the common response is that of Naomi's—to withdraw from society, which itself is a typical response to shame. Yet such a response limits opportunities to break free from poverty and can lead to a perpetuating cycle. She needs someone to step in to break her out of the cycle.

In Naomi's speech we find three typical ways to avoid dealing maturely with shame.[191] First, she begins to "withdraw" by severing the connection with her former social group to avoid their judgment, real or imagined. Second, she "attacks self" by changing her name in an attempt to regain control of the situation by at least controlling the self-condemnation. Third, she "attacks other"—God—by shifting blame to him. These three responses to shame are maladaptive because they do not require Naomi to examine herself and then address what the shame highlights about her or her behavior. Yet, all is not lost: she seems to accept some responsibility and, more significantly, she draws God into the discussion. Naomi effectively questions God's honor by pointing the finger at him for her suffering. In contrast to other biblical laments in which the supplicant seeks the restoration of honor to God's name,[192] Naomi's self-centered lament signals that she only seeks relief for herself. The restoration of God's honor is often before the nations and their

---

190. See Robert Walker and Grace Bantebya-Kyomuhendo, *The Shame of Poverty* (Oxford: Oxford University Press, 2014); Elaine Chase and Grace Bantebya-Kyomuhendo, *Poverty and Shame: Global Experiences* (Oxford: Oxford University Press, 2014).

191. Donald L. Nathanson, *Shame and Pride: Affect, Sex, and the Birth of the Self* (New York: Norton, 1992), 305–77. The fourth response is "avoidance."

192. See esp. Jerry Hwang, "'How Long Will My Glory Be Reproach?' Honour and Shame in Old Testament Lament Traditions," *OTE* 30 (2017): 684–706.

## 1:19B-22 TOWN GATE: NAOMI LAMENTS BEFORE THE TOWNSWOMEN

gods,[193] and so it is here: she even referred to God as "Yahweh" in front of her foreign daughters-in-law when speaking of his causing her bitterness (v. 13). Ruth had since pledged her allegiance to Yahweh, but this missional element forms a tension. He need not act because Naomi called his reputation into question, but will he act to restore his honor before "the nations," since his honor is intrinsically tied to that of his people?

**22** The concluding narrative statement of this scene summarizes the return of two people and anticipates their future in Bethlehem. The verb *šûb*, "return," is one of the *Leitworte* or leading words in this chapter, with different forms of the Hebrew word occurring twelve times (6, 7, 8, 10, 11, 12, 15 [2×], 16, 21, 22 [2×]).[194] The use of the word at the beginning and end of the chapter forms an *inclusio*, completing the journey motif. The first return is that of the central character: *So Naomi returned.* She just highlighted the state in which God returned her (v. 21), so the focus shifts to the second returnee. The women of the town focused on Naomi; Naomi overlooked her loyal daughter-in-law, but the narrator ensures that we do not miss her significance: *and Ruth the Moabite her daughter-in-law with her, who returned from the territory of Moab.* The awkward sentence structure not only draws Ruth back into the spotlight[195] but also makes us reflect on the paradox of the return of "the Moabite" from "the territory of Moab." This is the first of six times that she will be referred to by her ethnic descriptor (also 2:2, 6, 21; 4:5, 10). But Ruth had declared her allegiance to Naomi and her people and God (1:16), so we begin to wonder about the validity of her vow. For her mother-in-law spoke as if she is alone, and the narrator indicates that she is still viewed as a Moabite by the people of Bethlehem. Will her vow be accepted by Naomi and the townspeople? Will this Moabite be accepted into the people of God, and if so, on what basis?

"Return" usually means a person going back to a previous place. Orpah returns to her homeland, her people, and her gods; Naomi returns to her homeland, her people, and her God. But Ruth has never been to Bethlehem so her "return" does not seem to make sense. Yet, there are three ways we can understand Ruth's "return." Physically, she "returns" to Bethlehem as a family unit with Naomi, so they can be thought of as returning to the land of Israel together. But the singular pronoun "who" might weaken this reading.[196] Genealogically, Ruth as a Moabite "returns" to the people of Israel.

---

193. The parade example in the Old Testament is the "recognition formula," found over seventy times in Ezekiel: "Then they [Israel or the nations] will know that I am Yahweh." See esp. Walther Zimmerli, *I Am Yahweh*, trans. Douglas W. Stott (Atlanta: John Knox, 1982).

194. It is only used three times in the rest of the book (2:6; 4:3, 15).

195. Holmstedt, *Handbook*, 100–101.

196. The referent for a relative marker is usually the nearest appropriate antecedent, so *haššābâ*, "who returned," in this verse is most likely Ruth, not Naomi (ESV; contra NIV,

THE BOOK OF RUTH

According to Gen 19:30–38, the Moabites are closely related to the Israelites through Lot, Abraham's cousin. In pledging her loyalty to Naomi's people (1:16), Ruth symbolizes a return to the fold of God's people after generations of estrangement. Spiritually, in pledging her allegiance to Naomi's God, Ruth changes direction: she "turns" her back on the Moabite god(s) and "turns" toward Yahweh (1:16–17). Her primary loyalty to Naomi does not invalidate her pledge of allegiance to Yahweh. Hers is a change from placing her trust in Moabite deities to a sole trust in Yahweh. And it is from this new relationship that blessings can flow.

This spiritual sense for *šûb* is also relevant for Naomi. From a canonical viewpoint, departure from and return to the land is often more than just a physical departure. When Moses foresees Israel's disobedience leading to their expulsion, he also foresees their restoration, but only after the people of Israel return to God or repent (*šûb*; Deut 30:1–5).[197] "Return" is also regularly used in the Prophets for repentance. Amos's indictments particularly resonate with the Ruth narrative. The prophet indicts Israel for not repenting (*šûb*), despite God having sent famine, pestilence, and the sword (Amos 4:6–11). Amos states that God deliberately withheld rain in Israelite towns to induce Israel to repent, but they did not (4:7–8). These biblical texts, one from the Law and one from the Prophets, suggest that Naomi's return is not only physical; it is also spiritual, a repentance from sin, a turning back to, and a renewed trust in, God. Hers was a return to the sphere of God's blessing.

The idea of a physical return would have been especially relevant for audiences outside the promised land. During the exile, many would have longed to return to the land and the times of God's abundance. Although estranged from the land, the prophets still called on God's people to "return" to Yahweh—to turn from wickedness and walk rightly with him (e.g., Isa 50:10; 55:6–7; Ezek 14:6; 18:30–31). By the postexilic period, many had settled outside the promised land with no intention of returning (see the book of Esther). Only a minority returned (Ezra 2). Set in the early restoration period, Ezra-Nehemiah defines the people of God as "the returned exiles" along with those who turned to Yahweh from their uncleanness (Ezra 6:19–21; cf. Neh 10:29–30 [Eng. 28–29]).[198] Other books, such as Daniel and Esther, show that the diaspora can still have a place in God's plans. In the New Testament, Jesus says we find our "rest" in him (Matt 11:28–29) by repenting and

---

NJPS). As such, it distinguishes between Orpah and Ruth, since the former returned to the territory of Moab.

197. Nonetheless, the initiative lies with Yahweh, who enables repentance through a circumcision of the heart (Deut 30:6); see Paul A. Barker, *The Triumph of Grace in Deuteronomy: Faithless Israel, Faithful Yahweh in Deuteronomy* (Carlisle: Paternoster, 2004), 163–68.

198. See Peter H. W. Lau, "Gentile Incorporation into Israel in Ezra–Nehemiah?," *Bib* 90 (2009): 356–73.

## 1:19B–22 TOWN GATE: NAOMI LAMENTS BEFORE THE TOWNSWOMEN

pledging our loyalty to him. Yet we also look forward to a promised eternal rest, the ultimate promised land, when Christ returns. In the meantime, as diaspora and strangers in this world (1 Pet 1:1; cf. Jas 1:1), we persevere in obedience to ensure we enter that rest (Heb 4:1–11).

The final clause adds the detail of when they arrived and anticipates what might lie ahead: *They came to Bethlehem at the beginning of the barley harvest.* The mention of Bethlehem and harvest not only forms an inclusio for this scene (with v. 19) but also for the act. The narrative began with a famine in Bethlehem and a departure, it ends with a harvest and a return. "They arrived" reminds us that Naomi and Ruth made the journey together and shifts the focus from Naomi to both of them.[199] They were both the focus in v. 19, but from the end of v. 19 to the beginning of v. 22 only Naomi was in view. Their arrival together means they can both anticipate the blessing of the barley harvest. Naomi had heard that God had broken the famine (v. 6), and they arrive just as it is time to gather the barley. According to the tenth-century BC Gezer Calendar, the barley harvest is in late April or early May.[200] It was the first crop to be harvested in the year, so Naomi and Ruth could look forward to various produce from the land.[201] The question of how this new migrant and repatriate would access the crops is laid aside as we watch the barren and empty return to the house of bread in a time of fullness. God is not mentioned, but perhaps we catch a glimpse of his providential timing.

As this scene closes, the audience might have mixed feelings because there is no mention of where the widows lodged. Naomi had decried her destitution but no relative or friend had offered hospitality.[202] Was it because they felt rejected or isolated by Naomi's speech? Was their reluctance because a Moabite accompanied Naomi? In any case, Naomi and Ruth have "returned" but, like us the audience, do not feel settled. The blessing of food is near, but the obstacles for their other problems seem insurmountable. Naomi's yearning for a full family and to continue her husband's family line is stymied

---

199. The subject pronoun is redundant with a finite verb, so its presence indicates a shift in topic (in distinction to marking focus), from Naomi to Naomi and Ruth; Holmstedt, *Handbook*, 101.

200. This calendar lists the months of the year according to agricultural activity: (1) olive harvest; (2) planting grain; (3) late planting; (4) pulling up flax; (5) barley harvest; (6) wheat harvest and feasting; (7) vine-tending; and (8) summer fruit. See *ANET*, 320; and "The Gezer Calendar," trans. P. Kyle McCarter (*COS* 2.85:222). The Tg. specifies the timing of their arrival: "And they entered Bethlehem on the eve of Passover, and on that day the children of Israel began to harvest the omer of the elevation-offering, which was of barley." The Israelites were to bring the sheaf of the first grain of their harvest to the priest as an offering (Lev 23:10–11).

201. Ruth would glean the barley and wheat harvests (2:23).

202. For the expected hospitality protocol, see Matthews, *Judges/Ruth*, 68–69.

## The Book of Ruth

by her barrenness. Ruth's need for rest in the house of a husband is hindered by her foreignness. Yet Ruth's determined voice is hard to forget (vv. 16–17), and the narrator's insistence on her presence (v. 22) hints that this foreign daughter-in-law will play a key part in the resolution of these problems.[203] From an honor-shame perspective, the restoration of Naomi's name and status from her current social disgrace is the core problem for this central character. We lean forward to listen to how these problems will be resolved.

---

203. A wordplay strengthens this connection: Naomi returned with *kallātāh*, "her daughter-in-law," *bitḥillat*, "at the beginning," of the barley harvest.

## ACT 2: SEEKING SHORT-TERM SECURITY (2:1-23)

The spotlight was primarily on Naomi in act 1, but it now shifts to Ruth and will remain on her until act 4. Naomi is the central character; hers are the crisis and the emptiness. But the audience is about to find out the crucial role her daughter-in-law will play in the plot. This Moabite had returned with Naomi from the "fields" of Moab to Bethlehem just as the harvest began (1:22). She now sets off to the field to take part in reaping the harvest to seek short-term security (2:2–3).

Act 2 divides into three scenes, framed by conversations between Naomi and Ruth (vv. 1–3, 18–23). The central scene details the interaction between Ruth and Boaz (vv. 4–17).

|          | Characters      | Location      | Action                    |
|----------|-----------------|---------------|---------------------------|
| 2:1–3    | Naomi and Ruth  | Naomi's home  | Naomi accepts Ruth's plan |
| 2:4–17   | Ruth and Boaz and workers | Boaz's field | Public encounter between Ruth and Boaz |
| 2:18–23  | Naomi and Ruth  | Naomi's home  | Naomi and Ruth debrief    |

While this scene exhibits an introspective chiastic structure (A-B-A'), there is also plot progression. For instance, the act begins and ends with mentions of Boaz. He is introduced as a new character in the narrative (v. 1), but by the end of the act, he is established as Naomi and Ruth's benefactor (v. 23). Ruth takes the initiative in the first scene, while Naomi seems withdrawn, but by the last scene, Naomi is excited in response to Ruth's haul of grain. The act describes the proceedings of one day—from morning to evening—then the narrative summary telescopes the plot to the end of the barley and wheat harvests (v. 23).

## D. HOME: NAOMI ACCEPTS RUTH'S PLAN (2:1-3)

*[1] Now Naomi had[a] a relative[b] of her husband's, a man of great worth[c] from the clan of Elimelech, and his name was Boaz.*

*[2] Ruth the Moabite said to Naomi, "Let me go[d] to the field[e] so that I may glean[f] the ears of grain[g] after him in whose eyes I find favor."[h] She said to her, "Go,[i] my daughter."*

*[3] When she went, arrived,[j] and gleaned in the field after the harvesters, by chance she came upon[k] the portion of the field belonging to Boaz,[l] who was from the clan of Elimelech.*

# THE BOOK OF RUTH

a. Heb. *ûlənā'ŏmî*, "Now Naomi had," begins a non-*wayyiqtol* clause that presents circumstantial information.

b. Either the *qere, môda'* ("close acquaintance, friend") or the *ketiv, məyuddā'* ("relative") is possible. The *ketiv* seems to be a *pual* participle of *yd'* (2 Kgs 10:11; Pss 31:12[11]; 55:14[13]; 88:9, 19[8, 18]; Job 19:14). The *qere* reads a construct form from the same root (*yd'*), and only occurs in Prov 7:4, where it is in parallel with *'āḥôt*, "sister" (cf. *môda'tānû*, 3:2, with note). The meaning "relative" fits this proverbial context best rather than "friend." Moreover, since Naomi later describes Boaz in familial terms, "close" (*qārôb*; 2:20; cf. 3:12; 2 Sam 19:43[42]; Neh 13:4), and a "kinsman-redeemer" (*gō'ēl*; 2:20; 3:9, 12, 13), the *ketiv* reading, "relative," is preferred. This reading is supported by the Vulg. (*consanguineus*), while the LXX and Tg. read "acquaintance." Most EVV read "relative" or "kinsman" (including ESV, NIV, NJPS).

c. I read *'iš gibbôr ḥayil* as a noun, *'iš* ("man"), followed by an adjective, *gibbôr* ("mighty," "great"), bound to another noun, *ḥayil* ("strength," "power"), which modifies the first noun, so "a man of great worth." Cf. LXX *anēr dynatos*, "a mighty/powerful man."

d. Heb. *'ēlkâ-nā'* is a singular cohortative with particle *nā'*, and this combination is usually used by inferior persons to address superior persons (e.g., *DCH* 5:576; exception 2 Kgs 7:12), and along with the cohortative *'ălaqqăṭâ* (*piel*, although lacking the *dagesh* in *qoph* to mark gemination; MT^A and MT^Y read *'ălaqqăṭâ*, while MT^L and Tiberian manuscripts read *'ălaqăṭṭâ*) is best read as a polite request, "Let me go . . . glean" (e.g., Deut 3:25; Exod 4:18; 2 Sam 15:7; cf. 2:7; so ESV, NIV). Some read the cohortative with *nā'* as a declaration of intention, "I am going"; e.g., Hubbard, *Ruth*, 136n1; NJPS; cf. *IBHS* §34.7a. However, to be read as a declaration, an imperfect is expected rather than a cohortative, and the cohortative with *nā'* is declarative only when addressed to the self (Gen 18:21; Exod 3:3; 2 Sam 14:15; Isa 5:1; Song 3:2; 1 Chr 22:5). Moreover, Naomi's reply is best understood as a response to a request from Ruth. For recent discussions of the particle *nā'*, see Bent Christiansen, "A Linguistic Analysis of the Biblical Hebrew Particle *nā'*: A Test Case," *VT* 59 (2009): 379–93; Peter Juhás, *Die biblisch-hebräische Partikel* נָא *im Lichte der antiken Bibelübersetzungen* (Leiden: Brill, 2017).

e. Heb. *haśśādeh* is singular but either refers collectively to "the fields," or generically to "a field" or "some field" that Ruth will find; cf. Holmstedt, *Handbook*, 107.

f. The *waw* with the cohortative, *wa'ălaqqăṭâ*, connects the previous cohortative and syntactically indicates purpose rather than sequence, "so that I may glean." The *piel* rather than the *qal* might lend a frequentative nuance; see *IBHS* §24.5a–b.

g. The use of the preposition *bə* in *baśibbŏlîm* is difficult to interpret, with at least three possibilities; see *IBHS* §11.2.5b, f. Locative: "among the ears of grain" (LXX); however, one gleans ears of grain, not among ears of grain (e.g., Isa 17:5; cf. Lev 19:9; 23:22). Partitive: "some of the ears of grain" (Hubbard, *Ruth*, 136n3); however, *min* instead of *bə* seems more natural. Stylistic: although unusual, *bə* can mark the object, so "glean the ears of grain." Ernst Jenni, *Die hebräischen Präpositionen*, 3 vols. (Stuttgart: Kohlhammer, 1992–2000), 1:272, classifies this usage as "Arbeit/Zerstörung an Naturdingen" ("work/destruction of objects of nature"), citing Zech 11:1, "Open your doors, O Lebanon, so that fire may devour your cedars" (*wətō'kal 'ēš ba'ărāzêkā*). This last possibility is most likely and is probably an alternative way of describing gleaning grain. Holmstedt, *Handbook*, 107–8, suggests that the unusual grammar marks Ruth's speech as of a slightly different dialect or her understanding of Hebrew.

h. A word-for-word translation of *'aḥar 'ăšer 'emṣā'-ḥēn bə'ênāyw* would be "after him who I find favor in his eyes." This takes *'ăšer* to have an implicit antecedent, which is clarified by the third-person masculine singular suffix on *bə'ênāyw*, "his." Pace Sasson, *Ruth*, 42–43,

124

## 2:1-3 HOME: NAOMI ACCEPTS RUTH'S PLAN

who takes *'aḥar 'ăšer* as "after that," so "after that I may find favor in his [Boaz's] eyes." That is, Ruth set out to glean in Boaz's field to gain his favor. However, at this point in the narrative, there is no evidence that Ruth was aware of Boaz (cf. 2:19-20).

i. The imperative *ləkî*, "Go," is one of permission, not command (e.g., Gen 50:6; 2 Sam 18:23; 2 Kgs 2:17; *IBHS* §34.4b).

j. LXX, Syr., and Vulg. do not have the word translated as "she arrived"; the MT[L] is supported by Tg.

k. Heb. *wayyiqer miqrehā*, "her chance chanced upon" (cf. Eccl 2:14). This phrase begins a *wayyiqtol* clause that fills in details of the situation just described in 2:3a; see *IBHS* §33.2.2a.

l. Heb. *ḥelqat haśśādê ləbōʻaz* can either be read as "the portion of the field(s) [collective; cf. 2:2] belonging to Boaz," or "the field belonging to Boaz" (cf. 2 Kgs 9:25-26; H. H. Schmid, "*ḥlq*," *TLOT* 1:432). The following clause renders the former marginally more likely. Elimelech held the usufruct to some arable land his clan had apportioned to him from their inheritance. For *ḥelqat haśśādê* see also Gen 33:19; Josh 24:32; 2 Sam 23:11; 1 Chr 11:13; Ruth 4:

This section evidences a concentric structure:

> A  Naomi had a relative, Boaz of the clan of Elimelech (v. 1).
> B  Ruth requests to go to the field (*haśśādeh*) to glean after
>   (*'aḥar*) him in whose eyes she finds favor (v. 2a).
> B' Naomi grants her request to go, Ruth goes and gleans in the
>   field (*haśśādeh*) after (*'aḥar*) the harvesters (v. 2b-3a).
> A' Ruth happens upon the field (*haśśādeh*) of Boaz of the clan of
>   Elimelech (v. 3b).

This scene is enclosed by mentions of Boaz, from the clan of Elimelech (A-A'). The way he is described heightens audience expectations (A), which are even higher by the end of the scene because Ruth has stumbled into the portion of his *field* (A'). The central pair in the chiasm contains the dialogue between Ruth and Naomi, where Ruth requests to glean in a *field* (B-B'). Other repeated words strengthen the pair, including "go," "glean," and "after." Moving from B to B', the audience may be disappointed that "*after* him in whose eyes I find favor" is in parallel to "*after* the harvesters." However, by the end of the scene, the expectation is that Boaz (A') will replace "the harvesters."

**1** In this verse, story time stops as the narrator introduces a new character. He is described in four ways, alternating between the social and personal aspects of his identity. First, since Naomi is the central character, the new character is introduced in relation to her: *a relative of her husband's*. Naomi has someone who might intervene in her life, but he is only related through her husband. Israelite clans were patrilineal, so the death of her husband and sons makes her connection to an Israelite clan precarious. Since she married into Elimelech's clan, Naomi was to an extent considered an outsider.[1] Only

---

1. Cf. Edmund R. Leach, *Culture and Communication* (Cambridge: Cambridge University

## THE BOOK OF RUTH

when a woman produces a son is she concretely and irrevocably part of the clan; she has contributed to the building up of the clan.[2] If a woman is left as a widow without sons, she can be sent back to her father's house (e.g., Gen 38:11; Lev 22:13) or mother's house (1:8).[3]

This leaves Naomi (and Ruth) in an insecure position, no longer tangibly connected to Elimelech's clan.[4] The narrator's introduction of Boaz is suggestive of this situation (Ruth 2:1). He is a potential benefactor or patron, but he is from the clan of Elimelech, so he is not Naomi's blood relative. Direct kinship obligations are deflected by the descriptor "relative" (*môda'*; *qere*) rather than "kinsman-redeemer" (*gō'ēl*, cf. 2:20; 3:9, 12)—one with more defined kinship responsibilities. Boaz is a relative (we never learn how Boaz is related to Elimelech), but the benefits of clan membership are no longer freely available. She (or, as it turns out, Ruth) will need to work hard to eke them out.

Second, he is *a man of great worth*. In the Bible, *hayil* has the basic meaning "strength, power," and is used with *gibbôr* in four contexts: military (mighty warrior; e.g., Josh 6:2–3; Judg 6:12; 2 Sam 17:8; 2 Kgs 24:16; 2 Chr 13:3); material (wealthy man; 2 Kgs 15:20); moral (virtuous person; 3:11; cf. 1 Kgs 1:42, 52); and social (influential or capable person; e.g., 1 Kgs 11:28; 1 Chr 9:13; 26:6, 31).[5] Reading Ruth after Judges, we associate Boaz with Gideon or Jephthah, each described as a "mighty warrior" (*gibbôr hayil*; Judg 6:12; 11:1). Reading Ruth with 1 Samuel, we associate Boaz with Kish, a man of prominence and wealth (1 Sam 9:1), and David, a brave warrior (16:18). Reading Ruth within the Megilloth, we think of *hayil* denoting a person of high character (Prov 31:10).[6] Later in the Ruth narrative, Ruth is described as an *'ēšet-hayil*, "a worthy woman" (3:11). At this point in the Ruth narrative, it is not clear which of the four connotations is intended. As the narrative unfolds in act 2, we find that he is a man of wealth, then also of virtue. Act 4 reveals

---

Press, 1976), 74. Adaptation to a new household is lessened when a marriage is arranged within clans (cf. Num 36:6–9) since they would have shared a common cultural and territorial heritage. See Carol L. Meyers, "The Family in Early Israel," in *Families in Ancient Israel*, ed. Leo G. Perdue et al. (Louisville: Westminster John Knox, 1997), 36.

2. Cf. Leach, *Culture*, 74–75.

3. From Naomi's perspective, she encourages her widowed daughters-in-law to return to their *mothers* instead of remaining with their *mother-in-law*; cf. Porten, "Scroll," 26. The use of "mother's house" provides a glimpse into the power held by women in the household sphere (cf. Gen 24:28; Song 3:4; 8:2); see Meyers, "'To Her Mother's House,'" 39–51; Levine, "Ruth," 80.

4. The tenuous connection is illustrated in the fictional story of the wise woman of Tekoa (2 Sam 14:1–7).

5. See BDB, 298; *HALOT* 1:311–12; H. Eising, "*hayil*," *TDOT* 4:348–55.

6. "A worthy woman ['*ēšet-hayil*] who can find?"

## 2:1–3 HOME: NAOMI ACCEPTS RUTH'S PLAN

that he is also a man of influence within society. Thus, in the context of the Ruth narrative, the description of Boaz as *hayil* encompasses the last three senses, and *gibbôr* indicates that Boaz is a particularly fine example.[7] "A man of substance" also covers the senses in the Hebrew word.[8]

In Israelite society, reputation was important, as in any ancient society. It was important to secure recognition and respect from others. So far, the main characters have been shamed and have lost "face," especially Naomi. But now we meet a man with an impeccable reputation, since "a man of great worth" holds connotations of wealth, social standing, good character, and virtuous action. We have high expectations that he will act honorably as a relative of Naomi's husband.

Third, he is *from the clan of Elimelech*. In ancient Israel, an individual is a member of four kinship groups: people/nation, tribe, clan, and father's house. For example, Saul the son of Kish is an Israelite from the tribe of Benjamin, the Matrite clan, and the father's house of Abiel (1 Sam 10:20–21; see also the listing of Achan's and Gideon's kinship groups; Josh 7:16–18; Judg 6:15).[9] The clan of Elimelech and Boaz was probably that of the Ephrathites (1:2), although they were probably distantly related. Land was given as an inheritance according to clans (Num 33:54) rather than tribes, and Elimelech and Boaz each held a portion of the clan's field (2:3; 4:3). Membership of each of the Israelite kinship groups entailed certain roles and responsibilities. Clan members, which included uncles and cousins (Num 27:11; Lev 25:48–49), were expected to perform the role of a kinsman-redeemer, which included maintaining land within the clan (Lev 25:23–28). The levirate responsibility (Deut 25:5–10) usually operated at the father's house level, the closest kinship group.

Fourth, the new character is finally named: *Boaz*. We might expect his personal name to head the list of his descriptors, similar to the sequence in the description of Elimelech and his family (1:2). Its placement at the tail thus heightens audience curiosity and adds emphasis. Yet placing his name, an individual descriptor, after his social relations makes sense within a collectivist society like ancient Israel.[10] His membership in the "clan of Elimelech" also entailed the social responsibilities just listed above. If Boaz is to maintain

---

7. H. Kosmala, "*gābar*," *TDOT* 2:373, comments that *gibbôr* is an intensive form, and thus means "a particularly strong or mighty person who carries out, or has carried out great deeds, and surpasses others in doing so." Cf. J. Kühlewein, "*gbr*," *TLOT* 1:299–302; BDB, 1368; *HALOT* 1:172.

8. Campbell, *Ruth*, 90.

9. For a discussion of this kinship structure with references, see Lau, *Identity and Ethics*, 33–37.

10. In some societies today, a person's surname comes first, e.g., in Chinese, my name is Lau Hon Wan.

127

# THE BOOK OF RUTH

his reputation and honor within society, he will need to display loyalty to his kin. His kinship identity provides a sense of morality.

The origin and meaning of the name Boaz elude us. It only occurs in the book of Ruth and genealogies (1 Chr 2:11–12; Matt 1:5; Luke 3:32). An audience from the late monarchy onward would be aware of the northern pillar in the Solomonic temple named Boaz (1 Kgs 7:21; 2 Chr 3:17), and most earlier translations and interpreters make a connection between Boaz and "strength."[11] Considering the close apposition of Boaz with "a man of great worth," the most appropriate translation is "a pillar of society,"[12] which also conveys an allusion to the temple. Not only is Boaz described as "a man of great worth," his name itself symbolically reflects his worth. Given the author's penchant for wordplay with personal names (e.g., Naomi, Mahlon, Chilion, Orpah, and Ruth), the consonants of the name *bʿz* could play on *ʿzb*, "to abandon.[13] The author has alerted the audience to this motif already via the mouth of Ruth (1:16), and it will appear again later in this chapter, in the mouth of Boaz (v. 11) then Naomi (v. 16). In the last verse, *ʿzb* is juxtaposed with Boaz's identity.

**2** From the third verse of the Ruth narrative, Naomi has been the central character—the primary actor and speaker. Now *Ruth* takes the initiative by asking permission from Naomi: *Let me go to the field.* Acutely aware of their need for food and their lack of a provider, Ruth shows resourcefulness. We do not know why Naomi did not take the initiative to ask Ruth to glean or join her in gleaning. We can speculate that Naomi needed to rest after the exertions of journeying to Bethlehem or that she was still adjusting to the shock of her return to her hometown. Perhaps she felt depressed and wanted to withdraw from social interaction (cf. 1:19–20). Perhaps her older age precluded her from hard labor (cf. 1:12). In any case, Ruth shows filial piety by requesting permission from her mother-in-law to glean. And her willingness to seek food is an outworking of her commitment to Naomi (1:16–17). She gleans not just for herself but also her mother-in-law.

Coming after the introduction of Boaz, the initiative of Ruth is somewhat jarring. Why did he not take the initiative to provide for these widows?[14] The structure reinforces the contrast between the initiative of Ruth (B-B') and

---

11. The transliterations of the name in LXX and Vulg. as *Boos* support this meaning; Hubbard, *Ruth*, 134. For a discussion, see Saxegaard, *Character*, 144–46, who also finds "strength" a suitable meaning of Boaz.

12. So Fewell and Gunn, *Compromising*, 40.

13. Moshe Garsiel, *Biblical Names: A Literary Study of Midrashic Derivations and Puns*, trans. Phyllis Hackett (Ramat Gan: Bar-Ilan University Press, 1991), 252.

14. Although there is no textual evidence, Flavius Josephus, *Jewish Antiquities*, trans. William Whiston (Cambridge: Harvard University Press, 1966), 145, writes that Boaz showed Naomi and Ruth hospitality as soon as they arrived in Bethlehem.

## 2:1–3 HOME: NAOMI ACCEPTS RUTH'S PLAN

the inaction of Boaz (A-A'). Yet his lack of planning heightens the feeling of serendipity that Ruth gleans in Boaz's field. This is reflected in the chiastic structure of vv. 1–3 (see above), where Boaz's name and designation ("clan of Elimelech") is repeated in his introduction and at the "chance" meeting of Boaz and Ruth.

The narrator identifies Ruth as *the Moabite*, here and in five other places (1:22; 2:6, 21; 4:5, 10). She was one of the "Moabite" wives of Naomi's sons (1:4), and she was identified as "the Moabite" when she arrived in Bethlehem (1:22). The mention of her ethnic status again (2:2) perhaps only shows that her ethnic status has not changed since her arrival. But since the narrator also refers to her simply as "Ruth" (1:14, 16; 2:8, 22; 4:13), we suspect that the use of the ethnic designation is deliberate. Our suspicions are confirmed as the narrative continues, as the designation brackets this chapter (2:21). Also, the young overseer mentions Ruth's foreign status twice: "the Moabite woman who came back with Naomi from Moab" (v. 6). The designation keeps Ruth's foreign origin at the forefront of an audience's mind. We wonder: how will a foreigner get on in an unfamiliar field? How will the locals treat a foreigner wanting to glean in their field? Our perspective on Ruth is colored by her ethnic designation, and we view her as those in the field (the overseer, Boaz, and his workers) would have viewed her.

Ruth's ethnic designation also creates tensions in our minds. We know Ruth has committed herself to Naomi, her people, and her God (1:16–17). How is this going to play out as she enters Naomi's land and interacts with her people? From the Old Testament, we know that the stereotype of a Moabite is negative—from the etiology of Moab to the history of relations between Moab and Israel.[15] Stereotyped as a member of the Moabite outgroup, Ruth would have been viewed with suspicion by Bethlehem's residents, whether or not she deserved it. For Ruth, favor in a foreign field will be hard to find.

Ruth requests to go to *the field* to glean, which is the same Hebrew word for "country" of Moab (1:1, 2, 6, 22). An Israelite family found sustenance in Moab; we now anticipate a Moabite will find sustenance in one of the fields around Bethlehem. The land was subdivided among the townspeople into plots (2:3; 4:3). In the ancient Near East, to maximize the arable land, unobtrusive demarcations were in place.[16] Each field, however, was identified by the name of its owner, most likely in relation to the owners of adjacent plots, and demarcated with boundary stones.[17] The lack of clear boundaries

---

15. See comment on 1:1.

16. Natural boundaries would have included features such as rivers and ditches.

17. Bernard S. Jackson, "Ideas of Law and Legal Administration: A Semiotic Approach," in *The World of Ancient Israel: Sociological, Anthropological and Political Perspectives*, ed. Ronald E. Clements (Cambridge: Cambridge University Press, 1989), 190. God allotted

# The Book of Ruth

will become significant for Ruth (v. 3). She intended *to glean the ears of grain,* to gather up those already cut by the harvesters then inadvertently dropped (cf. vv. 3, 7, 9). Gleaning is a key motif in this chapter, as indicated by the repetition of the root *lqṭ* (2:2, 3, 7, 8, 15 [2×], 16, 17 [2×], 18, 19, 23; not found elsewhere in the book). The harvesters would use a sickle to cut off grain from the stalk, then lay down the ears of grain beside the standing stalks for the women gleaners to bundle together.

Ruth says she wants to glean *after him in whose eyes I find favor.* To find favor or grace (*ḥēn*) in the eyes of (*bəʿênê*) someone is a common expression in the Old Testament. People find favor in the sight of God (e.g., Gen 6:8; Exod 33:12), although most of the uses of this idiom are in the context of human relations between a superior and an inferior. It is commonly used by supplicants addressing rulers or kings (e.g., 1 Sam 16:22; 27:5; 2 Sam 14:22; 16:4; 1 Kgs 11:19; Esth 5:2, 8; 7:3), and in other human interactions between a weaker and a superior party (e.g., Gen 32:6[5]; 39:4, 21).[18] The one seeking favor depends on the generosity or grace of the other. Here Ruth's words reveal that she knows her gleaning in another's field will be a privilege granted by the landowner or his workers. Israelite law made provision for the needy (esp. Lev 19:9–10; 23:22; Deut 24:19–22), namely the resident alien, the fatherless, and the widow—those with absent or tenuous connections to an Israelite family, and hence no access to the produce from the land. Ruth qualifies under two of these categories, although we do not know if Ruth was aware of the law. It is possible that gleaning was a privilege extended to the underprivileged in the ancient Near East.[19] In any case, there was often a lamentable gap between the law and its application, a gap we expect would be wider in the time of the judges (Judg 17:6; 21:25).

We noted earlier that poverty can lead to shame and social isolation. Free handouts can worsen feelings of humiliation. The wisdom of the gleaning laws is that it requires the needy to collect the scraps of the crops. They have the chance to work to alleviate their suffering by sharing in God's blessings, for he is the true landowner (Lev 25:23). The gleaning law is an honorable way to address poverty; in working, a gleaner maintains some dignity. Moreover, working in the fields places the needy in a social context—that of the gleaning community. This raises the possibility of social re-integration and acceptance.

---

land to Israel as their inheritance, based on tribes, clans, and father's houses. These were permanent inheritances, so a person could not move a neighbor's boundary marker (Deut 19:14; 27:17; Prov 22:28; 23:10). Prophets railed against a disregard of these laws (e.g., 1 Kgs 21:17–19; Hos 5:10; Mic 2:1–5).

18. See H. J. Stoebe, "*ḥnn*," *TLOT* 1:439–47; Edwin Yamauchi, "*ḥēn*," *TWOT* 1:303.

19. References to gleaning in Sumerian and Egyptian texts show that the practice was not uncommon; see David L. Baker, "To Glean or Not to Glean . . .," *ExpTim* 117 (2006): 406.

## 2:1–3 HOME: NAOMI ACCEPTS RUTH'S PLAN

Ruth's use of the expression "in whose eyes I find favor" has two further implications. First, it characterizes her as one who is more concerned with favor and kindness than legal convention. The law may have provision for people like her, but she still seeks someone who will show her favor by allowing her to glean. It is thus not insignificant that she will use "favor" (*ḥēn*) twice in conversation with Boaz (vv. 10, 13). In other words, she looks for someone like herself, for in gleaning she again shows kindness to her mother-in-law, as she did when she loyally returned to Bethlehem with her. Second, the expression puts us, the audience, on watch for a gracious patron for herself and Naomi. Ruth seeks a patron who would provide protection and material benefits. As a client, Ruth would also gain honor by association with a patron. Since Boaz has already been introduced, we expect it will be he, but the (dramatic) irony is that we have information Ruth does not yet have. If he takes on the patron role, he will gain honor through societal recognition of his generosity. Our expectations of him are raised to another level.

Naomi grants Ruth permission to glean with two rhyming words, *ləkî bittî*, "Go, my daughter." Calling Ruth "my daughter" (cf. 1:13) is an appropriate form of address from a senior, and Boaz will also use the same with Ruth (2:8; 3:10, 11). In this verse, it reflects a more intimate relationship than "daughter-in-law" (1:22), and their kinship endures through the whole narrative (cf. 1:11, 12, 13; 3:1, 18). Without a centralized system of welfare and support for the elderly, the younger generation, in particular sons, were responsible for providing care and security for their parents in their old age (cf. 4:15).[20] In the absence of sons, the expectation would be for daughters to fulfill this role. In providing for her mother-in-law, Ruth is going beyond what is required of her as a daughter-in-law;[21] she is taking on an offspring's role, although she is neither son nor daughter.

What Naomi does not say is a little surprising. Following the introduction of Boaz (v. 1), we wonder why she does not direct Ruth into his field. And given the setting in the days of the judges (1:1), what were the chances of her finding "favor" in the fields? Our feeling of trepidation for a single foreign woman venturing into the open fields is later confirmed by Boaz and Naomi (vv. 9, 15–16, 21–22). For now, we wonder if Naomi's gloom clouds her judgment. Perhaps she is experiencing repatriation stress and reverse culture shock, so having to deal with her foreign daughter-in-law's request overwhelms her. All she can do is utter two words. A more sympathetic reading, although less likely in my opinion, is that she trusts God to guide and protect Ruth. In any case, with Naomi's terseness, the narrator moves the

---

20. In ancient Israel, most daughters would leave their family to join the family of their husband; cf. Fischer, *Rut*, 253.

21. Cf. Jon L. Berquist, "Role Differentiation in the Book of Ruth," *JSOT* 57 (1993): 27–28.

131

# THE BOOK OF RUTH

action along without delay and highlights the relative inaction of Naomi (cf. 2:18–22; 3:1–4).

3 With three successive verbs, the narrator proleptically summarizes the scene: *When she went, arrived, and gleaned in the field after the harvesters.*[22] This removes some of the tension since we are told what she did, yet we still want to find out how she does so. The summary immediately transports us to the field, where Ruth gleans after the harvesters. Perhaps from her perspective, she found favor in their eyes but following vv. 1–2, we still anticipate a landowner's favor. The narrator then shifts our focus to how Ruth arrived in the field: *by chance she came upon* (*wayyiqer miqrehā*). This redundant expression with a verb and noun from the same root *qrh* ("to happen, meet") could be translated "by chance she chanced upon." Elsewhere the noun *miqreh* denotes an event that occurs without the intent of the person affected.[23] The Philistines attribute their disaster to either Yahweh or "coincidence" (1 Sam 6:9), and Saul thinks David's absence is because "something has happened to him" (1 Sam 20:26). In Ecclesiastes, *miqreh* refers to fate or destiny (Eccl 2:14–15; 3:19 [3×]; 9:2–3), but it is to be understood within the context of God's sovereignty (3:1–15; 7:13–14; 8:16–9:1; 11:5). "Luck"—a random occurrence of chance—is a concept prevalent in many cultures, but not in Old Testament thinking about God. He is viewed as ultimately behind all events that take place in the world: good and bad, big and small (e.g., Amos 3:6; Lam 3:37–38; Isa 45:1–8). Even as the dice are rolled, God is behind the outcome (Prov 16:33). Similarly, when Abraham sends his servant to find a wife for Isaac (Gen 24:12–27), the servant prays that God would grant him success (*hiphil* of *qārâ*; 24:12) in his task. As the servant thanks God for fulfilling his request afterward, the clear understanding is that God has superintended the outcome (24:26–27).

Consistent with the style of the book of Ruth—where God's actions are mentioned indirectly (4:13 is the exception), either by the narrator or via the speech of the characters—the phrase "by chance she came upon" obliquely hints at God's providence.[24] Throughout the narrative, there is a delicate interplay between God's design and the characters' actions, with the focus on the latter. Here the phrase underlines Ruth's unintentional action, yet as we read the phrase, we can almost see the narrator winking at his audience.

---

22. For the same combination of *hlk* ("go") and *bô'* ("come"), see 1 Sam 22:5; 2 Kgs 4:25; 8:14.

23. Ringgren, "*qārâ*," *TDOT* 13:161–62.

24. "Chance" or "coincidence" is a major theme in the book of Esther, another book with a female protagonist. God is not explicitly mentioned in Esther, but his fingerprints are found throughout, especially in the "coincidences" at key points in the narrative. See, e.g., David J. A. Clines, *The Esther Scroll: The Story of the Story* (Sheffield: JSOT Press, 1984), 153–58; Jon D. Levenson, *Esther*, OTL (Louisville: Westminster John Knox, 1997), 18–22.

## 2:4–17 BOAZ'S FIELD: ENCOUNTER BETWEEN RUTH AND BOAZ

Of all the cultivated fields outside Bethlehem, the newcomer Ruth just happens to stumble upon *the portion of the field belonging to Boaz, who was from the clan of Elimelech.* "The portion of the field" (cf. 4:3) belonging to Boaz refers to his piece of the arable land, which the clan apportioned to him as his inheritance.[25] Since Yahweh owns the land (e.g., Deut 12:10), Boaz does not own his plot, he only holds its usufruct. Ruth has no intention to seek Boaz's field since she does not even know him. We have expectations of Boaz (v. 1), and surprise! Ruth ends up in his field. We already know he is "from the clan of Elimelech," so the repetition of this phrase (vv. 1, 3) further supports our reading of divine providence. Since Boaz is a "worthy man" with kinship responsibilities to Ruth's mother-in-law, we wonder if and how he might show favor to Ruth.

### E. BOAZ'S FIELD: ENCOUNTER BETWEEN RUTH AND BOAZ (2:4–17)

Naomi had lost her family in Moab and, although she felt empty upon her return to Bethlehem (1:21), the narrator had introduced us to a relative of her husband (2:1). In a practical display of her commitment to her mother-in-law (1:16–17), Ruth had taken it upon herself to glean in a field where she would find favor (2:2). We have high expectations that Naomi's miserable lot in life is about to improve because Ruth has just stumbled into Boaz's field (v. 3). This scene narrates what happens when Ruth the Moabite meets Boaz the honorable from Elimelech's clan.

⁴*And look! Boaz arrived*ᵃ *from Bethlehem. He said to the harvesters, "May Yahweh be with you!"*ᵇ *They said to him, "May Yahweh bless you."*ᶜ

⁵*Boaz said to his male servant who was set over the harvesters, "Whose young woman is this?"*

⁶*The male servant who was set over the harvesters*ᵈ *answered and said, "She is a young Moabite woman,*ᵉ *who returned with Naomi from the territory of Moab.*ᶠ

⁷*She said, 'Let me glean*ᵍ *and gather among the sheaves*ʰ *after the harvesters.'*ⁱ

*So she entered, and remained from then, the morning, until now,*ʲ *this . . . her sitting . . . the hut . . . a little."*ᵏ

⁸*Boaz said to Ruth, "Haven't you heard, my daughter? Don't go to glean in another field; in fact,*ˡ *don't leave this one,*ᵐ *but stay close*ⁿ *to my female servants here.*ᵒ

---

25. Cf. Tsevat, "*chālaq*," *TDOT* 4:449.

# The Book of Ruth

[9]*Let your eyes be on the field that they harvest,[p] and go after them [the female servants]. Haven't I commanded the male servants not to touch you? And when you are thirsty, you may go[q] to the vessels and drink from whatever[r] the male servants draw.*"

[10]*Then she fell on her face and bowed to the ground. She said to him, "Why have I found favor in your eyes, that you have paid attention to me, although I[s] am a foreigner?"*

[11]*Boaz answered and said to her, "It has been fully reported to me: all that you have done for[t] your mother-in-law after your husband died—how you abandoned[u] your father[v] and mother and your native land, and went to[w] a people you didn't know before.[x]*

[12]*May Yahweh repay your deed, and may your wages be complete from[y] Yahweh, the God of Israel, under whose wings you came to seek refuge.*"

[13]*She said, "May I continue to find favor in your eyes, my lord, for you have comforted me and spoken to the heart of your maidservant, although I'm not[z] like one of your maidservants."*

[14]*Then Boaz said to her[aa] at mealtime,[ab] "Come here[ac] and eat some of the bread and dip your morsel in the vinegar." So she sat beside the harvesters, and he handed her roasted grain. She ate until she was full, and she had some left over.*

[15]*When she rose to glean, Boaz commanded his male servants,[ad] "Even among the sheaves let her glean, and do not humiliate her.[ae]*

[16]*In fact,[af] even pull out[ag] for her some stalks from the handfuls and abandon them that she may glean them.[ah] Do not rebuke her."[ai]*

[17]*So she gleaned in the field until evening. She beat out what she had gleaned, and it was about an ephah of barley.*

a. Heb. *bā'* could be a participle (Boaz "was coming") or a perfect ("Boaz "came"). The versions support both the former (Vulg., Syr.) and the latter (LXX, Tg.). A participle would indicate that Boaz arrived at or around the same time as Ruth, which is unlikely based on the overseer's statement (2:6–7). Thus, the perfect is preferred.

b. Heb. *yhwh 'immākem* is a null copula clause, "Yahweh . . . with you," without an explicit verb. As a greeting, it has an optative force, functioning as a wish, "Yahweh be with you," or "May Yahweh be with you." Cf. Judges 6:12 where *yhwh 'imməkā* is indicative, "Yahweh is with you"; JM §163b.

c. The verb-subject order of the clause *yəbārekā yhwh* indicates that the verb is modal, a jussive, so the clause expresses a wish, "Yahweh bless you," or "May Yahweh bless you." The *piel* of *brk* is used in speech to mean "to greet" (e.g., 1 Sam 13:10; 25:14; 2 Kgs 4:29; 10:15); C. A. Keller, "*brk*," *TLOT* 1:271. Similar to Boaz's greeting, only in Ruth 2:4 is the greeting used between people (cf. Jer 31:23). Perhaps greetings (*brk*) consisted of "May Yahweh bless you"; so J. Scharbert, "*brk*," *TDOT* 2:291.

d. Vulg. and Syr. omit "who was set over the harvesters."

e. LXX and Syr. read "the Moabite," while Vulg. supports the MT reading, "a Moabite." Most EVV translate with the definite article, although NJPS is an exception.

134

## 2:4–17 Boaz's Field: Encounter between Ruth and Boaz

f. For a discussion of the *h*-relative clause *haššābâ 'im-no'ŏmî miśśdēh mô'āb*, and *haššābâ* as a *qatal* instead of a participle, see note on 1:22.

g. The singular cohortative *'ălaqŏṭâ* with particle *nā'* is best understood as a request rather than a resolute declaration; see note on v. 2.

h. Heb. *wə'āsaptî bā'ŏmārîm*, "and gather [them] into sheaves," is absent in Syr. and Vulg, but supported by LXX and Tg.

i. Heb. *'aḥărê haqqôṣərîm*, "after the harvesters," is both spatial (positioned behind the harvesters) and temporal (gleaning after the harvesters have finished); cf. *IBHS* §11.2.1a.

j. LXX "until evening" (cf. 2:17). Other versions support the MT.

k. The versions reveal the difficulty in interpreting the MT: LXX "she did not rest a bit in the field"; Vulg. "and has not gone home even for a moment." For a discussion of this sentence, see comments.

l. Heb. *wəgam* ("in fact") conjoins this phrase with the preceding, and adds emphasis and focus; see Holmstedt, *Handbook*, 118–19.

m. Syr. "Haven't you heard what the proverb says: 'Do not glean in a field that is not yours.'" Tg. interprets "don't leave this one" as don't go to another "people" or "nation," which seems to read "this one" as Bethlehem or Israel.

n. The verb *dbq*, "to cling," or "stay close" (cf. 1:14; 2:8, 21, 23) occurs only with the preposition *'im* in Boaz's speech (2:8) or a quotation of his speech (2:21). Elsewhere in the Old Testament, it usually occurs with the preposition *bə*, including by the narrator in 1:14; 2:23. This may simply be a grammatical irregularity, but it would be consistent with the rest of the book for this linguistic irregularity to contribute to the characterization of Boaz. Hebrew *tidbāqîn*, "cling" or "stay close," has a paragogic *nun* (see *IBHS* §31.7.1), which some scholars view as an indication of an older text. Yet if the paragogic *nun* is from an earlier period, it is difficult to discern if it is a genuine archaism or intentional archaizing, that is, the author/editor used it to make the text appear older. Moreover, since the paragogic *nun* is found in biblical texts covering a range of historical periods, it is better to view its usage as stylistic. In the Ruth narrative, we find this linguistic feature on the lips of those from the older generation: Boaz (2:8, 9 [2×]) and Naomi (3:4, 18). The only other occurrence is Ruth's (mis) quotation of Boaz's speech (2:21). The paragogic *nun* thus sprinkles a generational flavor.

o. Heb. *wəgam* has an emphatic ("indeed") rather than additive ("and also") function; cf. *HALOT* 1:195. The adverb *kōh* can indicate manner, place, or time; BDB, 462. In this context, place is the best sense. See comments.

p. Both "harvest" and "draw" contain a paragogic *nun*; see comment on 2:8.

q. MT^L misspells *wəhālakti* while MT^AY spells *wəhālakt*.

r. MT lacks an object, but "water" is included in Tg.

s. MT^L misspells *wə''ānôkî* (with two alephs) while MT^AY spells *wə'ānôkî*. Ruth uses *'ānôkî* rather than *'ănî*. E. J. Revell, "The Two Forms of First Person Singular Pronouns in Biblical Hebrew: Redundancy or Expressive Contrast?," *JSS* 40 (1995): 199–217, observes that *'ănî* is the default pronoun used by individuals when speaking to someone of the same or lower social status, while *'ānôkî* is the default pronoun used by individuals when speaking to those of higher status. Ruth's use of *'ānôkî* in her speech is thus typical (she similarly uses *'ānôkî* in v. 13 and 3:9). There are exceptions to this general tendency. For instance, Revell notes that *'ănî* is also used in situations where the speaker has a right to expect attention because of status difference or the importance of their speech. Naomi uses *'ănî* when addressing the townswomen (her peers; 1:21) as she speaks with emotion, reflecting her personal interest.

# The Book of Ruth

t. Here the preposition *'et* ("for") is used with the verb *'āśâ* ("to do, make"), while elsewhere the preposition is *'im* ("with"; 1:8; 2:19). Since we find the former in Boaz's speech and the latter in Naomi's, it seems best to understand this as linguistic variation to mark the idiosyncrasies of these characters. Similarly, the narrator uses the preposition *bǝ* with the verb *dābaq* ("to cling, keep close"; 1:14; 2:23), while the preposition *'im* is used in the speech of Boaz and Naomi (2:8, 21, respectively). See Holmstedt, *Handbook*, 48, 49, 127.

u. In the context of this verse, the *waw* in *watta'azbî* does not indicate chronological sequence. Rather, it functions to explain or specify what Ruth did for her mother-in-law (JM §118j); hence, the translation "how." See, similarly, Gen 31:26; 1 Sam 8:8; 1 Kgs 2:5; 18:13.

v. MT^L misspells *''ābîk* (with two alephs) while MT^AY spells *'ābîk*.

w. Although the verb *hālak* with the preposition *'el* (to) can take the less common meaning of "to come" (BDB, 230), the usual meaning of "to go" is preferred since it makes sense here (*pace* most EVV). The verbs *hālak* (1:1, 7, 8, 11, 12, 16 [2×], 18, 19, 21; 2:2 [2×], 3, 8, 9 [2×], 11; 3:10) and *bô'* ("to come"; 1:2, 19 [2×], 22; 2:3, 4, 7, 12, 18; 3:4, 7 [2×], 14, 15, 16, 17; 4:11, 13) are key words in the Ruth narrative.

x. Heb. *tǝmôl šilšôm*, "yesterday, three days ago" idiomatically means "previously" or "before" (*HALOT* 4:1546). See, e.g., Gen 31:2; Exod 5:8; Josh 3:4; 1 Sam 4:7; 2 Kgs 13:5.

y. The compound preposition *mē'im* can mean "from," indicating source or origin, including from God, as is the case here (see also, e.g., 1 Kgs 2:33; 12:15; Isa 7:11; 8:18; 28:29; Ps 121:2). LXX reads "from" (*para*), and Tg. reads "from before" (*min qŏdām*). It can also mean "from with" or "from among" after verbs of departing or removing, as in 4:10 (see also, e.g., Gen 13:14; 26:16; 1 Sam 10:2, 9; 14:17). See BDB, 768–769; *HALOT* 2:840.

z. While the LXX, Syr., and Old Latin seem to read the negative particle *lō'* ("not") as *lû* ("surely" or "indeed"), thus producing an opposite meaning to MT. The MT, however, makes sense as it is, expressing well her self-abasement, and the MT is supported by Vulg. and Tg.

aa. Heb. *lāh*, "to her," lacks a *mappiq* in the *h*; cf. Num 32:42; Zech 5:11; GKC §23k; JM §§25a, 103f. The expected form is found later in this verse and elsewhere (1:10; 2:2, 11, 16, 18–20, 3:1, 16; 4:13).

ab. The clause *lǝ'ēt hā'ōkel*, "at mealtime," can be understood as the beginning of Boaz's speech (so LXX, Vulg.) or as the words of the narrator (so most modern commentators and EVV, incl. ESV, NIV, NJPS). The syntax and Masoretic accents allow for either interpretation, but the slightly stronger disjunctive accent on *hā'ōkel* and the flow of the narrative favor the latter. For an argument for the former, see Holmstedt, *Handbook*, 132–33.

ac. The imperative *gōšî* is unusual since *gǝšî* is expected. But such anomalies with the imperative are attested; see GKC §66c.

ad. The masculine plural *nǝ'ārāyw* can be translated "his male servants" or "his servants." See comment on v. 15.

ae. Modal or jussive *yiqtol* with the nuance of permission ("let her"), followed by *lō'* + modal *yiqtol*, which expresses obligation ("do not").

af. Syr. omits v. 16, possibly triggered by the particle *gam* or assuming the verse is a repetition of v. 15.

ag. Infinitive absolute followed by *yiqtol* of the same root (*šll*) for emphasis.

ah. Two modal *qatal* verbs: the first continues the nuance of obligation of the previous clause, while the second continues this nuance with the sense of permission.

ai. Heb. *lō'* + modal *yiqtol*, which expresses obligation ("do not"); cf. vv. 8, 15.

This scene contains three parts, enveloped by a narrative introduction and conclusion. The introduction is marked by *wǝhinnēh*, "and look!" and draws

## 2:4–17 BOAZ'S FIELD: ENCOUNTER BETWEEN RUTH AND BOAZ

our attention to the arrival of the first main character in this scene, Boaz (v. 4a). The conclusion describes the last actions of the second main character in this scene, Ruth, and the abundant barley she would take home (v. 17). The bulk of the scene comprises three parts:

> A   Boaz's conversations with his workers (vv. 4b–7)
> B   Boaz's conversations with Ruth (vv. 8–14)
> A'  Boaz's conversation with his workers (vv. 15–16)

There is some overlap with the timing of parts B and A', as Boaz's second conversation with Ruth (v. 14) and Boaz's second conversation with his workers (A'; vv. 15–16) occur at mealtime. Direct speech predominates this scene, with Boaz uttering most of the words. This reflects his status and authority in relation to the other characters, but we should not miss the focus on Ruth's kindness at the center of the chiasm (vv. 11–12). Boaz notes what she "had done," while this scene highlights what she continues to do.[26] The structure also contrasts the attitude of Boaz to Ruth (B) with that of his workers (A and A').

**4** *And look! Boaz arrived from Bethlehem*, which would have been within walking distance.[27] We cannot determine the exact amount of time between the arrivals of Ruth and Boaz. Based on the overseer's description of Ruth's work (2:7),[28] it is more likely hours than seconds.[29] The narrative's focus is not on precise timing but the surprise of Boaz's arrival.[30] The alliteration of the letter *b* draws further attention to Boaz's arrival.[31] Scholars suggest the *hinnēh* clause represents the point of view of Ruth or the harvesters. Both are unlikely because Ruth would not be able to identify Boaz at this point in the narrative, and the harvesters have not been mentioned yet.[32] *Look!*

---

26. Apart from the verbs of speech ("to say," vv. 4 [2×], 5, 6, 7, 8, 10, 11, 13, 14; "to answer," vv. 6, 11; "to command," v. 15), most of the verbs describe Ruth's actions ("and she fell," "and she bowed down," v. 10; "and she sat," "and she ate," "and she was satisfied," "and she had some left over," v. 14; "and she rose," 15), with just two verbs describing Boaz's ("he came," v. 4; "and he passed," v. 14); Block, *Discourse*, 125nn28, 30, 31.

27. His home would be in the town and his field outside the town.

28. His speech is difficult to interpret, which adds to the uncertainty of timing.

29. So, respectively, Jan de Waard and Eugene A. Nida, *A Handbook on the Book of Ruth*, 2nd ed., UBS Handbook Series (New York: United Bible Societies, 1992), 27; Sasson, *Ruth*, 46.

30. Heb. *hinnēh*, "look," functions as an exclamation (traditional EVV, "And behold") to draw attention to a surprising, unexpected, or coincidental event (e.g., Gen 24:15; Exod 2:13). In the Ruth narrative, it is used in direct discourse (1:15; 3:2) or as an indicator of point of view (3:8; 4:1).

31. Heb. *Bō'az bā' mibbêt leḥem*; cf. Porten, "Scroll," 33.

32. For further discussion, see Berlin, *Poetics*, 94–95; Robert S. Kawashima, *Biblical Narrative and the Death of the Rhapsode* (Bloomington: Indiana University Press, 2004),

137

THE BOOK OF RUTH

thus addresses the reader and draws attention to the coincidental arrival of Boaz. The narrator flagged his presence (v. 1), Ruth seeks someone in whose sight she might find favor (v. 2), she happens to stumble upon Boaz's field (v. 3), and it just so happens that Boaz appears—at the same place while she is there (v. 4). This series of events points to the implicit providence of God. Similar to elsewhere in the Old Testament, *wahinnēh* here also introduces a new character after a scene has started.[33]

The first words of a character often reveal important information about their personality.[34] Boaz says, *May Yahweh be with you!* He is a godly man who makes the effort to greet his harvesters. His words are consistent with the narrator's introduction of him as a noble man (2:1). We could read his words as a regular greeting, such as "Shalom!"[35] But since the wording of Boaz's greeting is not found in the rest of the Old Testament, we are invited to ponder this departure from the norm.[36] So far in the Ruth narrative, the narrator has not stated explicitly that God has done anything. But he has dropped hints in the narrative, so, as the audience, we are attuned to God's presence. Naomi heard he came to the aid of his people by breaking the famine (1:6). Based on this hearsay that God was present to bless, she returned to Bethlehem. God was also on the lips of Naomi, invoked in a blessing (1:8) and named as the cause of her calamity (1:13). God was also on the lips of Ruth the Moabite. She pledges loyalty to God and invokes a self-imprecation based on the personal name of God (1:16–17). And as the widows return to Bethlehem, we find a clear sign of God's presence to bless—a barley harvest (1:22). In this context, Boaz's greeting is loaded with theological meaning.

The connection between presence and blessing is underscored by the harvesters' reply to Boaz, *May Yahweh bless you!* Their response shows they respect him and indicates a cordial relationship between landowner and workers. This could be a formulaic blessing used as a greeting since the *piel* of *brk* can mean "to greet, salute" (e.g., 1 Sam 13:10; 2 Kgs 4:29; 10:15).[37] How-

---

120–22; Gary Yamasaki, *Perspective Criticism: Point of View and Evaluative Guidance in Biblical Narrative* (Eugene, OR: Cascade, 2012), 48; Konstantin Nazarov, *Focalization in the Old Testament Narratives with Specific Examples from the Book of Ruth* (Carlisle: Langham, 2021), 173–75.

33. E.g., Numbers 25:5–6; Judg 4:21–22; 1 Sam 11:4–5; 1 Kgs 12:33–13:1.

34. See comment on 1:9.

35. See Judg 6:23; 1 Sam 25:6; 2 Sam 18:28.

36. The phrase is used elsewhere but not as a greeting, e.g., Josh 1:17; Judg 6:12.

37. The greeting could have consisted of "Yahweh bless you"; Scharbert, "*brk*," *TDOT* 2:291. Cf. *brktk lyhwh*, "I bless you by Yahweh," in Arad 16:2–3 and 21:3–4; F. W. Dobbs-Allsopp et al., *Hebrew Inscriptions: Texts from the Biblical Period of the Monarchy with Concordance* (New Haven: Yale University Press, 2005), 32, 44. Hubbard, *Ruth*, 144, suggests the formulaic blessing was used at harvest time for greeting and to ask God for a bountiful crop.

ever, in the Ruth narrative, the greetings' mention of God's presence to bless his people in Bethlehem contrasts with Naomi's declaration that Yahweh has afflicted her (1:21). And her assertion that God has brought her back empty creates a tension with the greetings that seeks a resolution. In the wider Old Testament, "Yahweh bless you" recalls the priestly blessing (Num 6:24; cf. Jer 31:23; Ps 128:5), a prayer that God would grant his presence and care to his people.[38] One manifestation of this in the Ruth narrative would be a plentiful harvest in Bethlehem. The narrator does not directly speak of God acting, but the characters remind the audience that he is. We thus read the "chance" event in a different light (v. 3).

**5** Boaz noticed someone out of place in his field. He directs his question to his harvest overseer, *his male servant who was set over the harvesters*. While *naʿar* primarily refers to males from newborn to a young man of marriage-able age ("boy," "lad," "youth"), it also refers to servants or attendants (e.g., Gen 18:7; 22:3; 41:12; Num 22:22; Judg 7:10; 19:3; 1 Sam 9:3; 2 Sam 13:28; 16:1; 2 Kgs 4:19; Job 1:15; Neh 6:5; 13:19), which is the sense in this verse.[39] This Israelite was hired by Boaz to oversee his reapers. The choice of *naʿar* (originally "young man") rather than *ʿebed* ("servant") may reflect the age difference between him and Boaz (cf. 3:10), but it also allows for the interplay between *naʿar* and *naʿărâ* in this chapter, starting with Boaz's question.

*Whose young woman is this?* translates *ləmî hannaʿărâ hazzōʾt*, "to whom does this young woman belong?"[40] This question might sound inappropriate to many ears today since most people would ask "who" instead of "whose." But it was a more natural question in a collectivist and patriarchal society like that of the Old Testament. A person's social identity was primary—who they were related to, and which groups they were members of. A woman in the ancient Near East was usually attached to a man: before marriage, her father or an uncle; after marriage, her husband.[41] This reality could leave widows in a desperate situation (see comment on 1:5). The noun *naʿărâ* is the feminine equivalent of *naʿar*, with a similar semantic range, most commonly denoting a girl or young unmarried woman, but also a maid, attendant, or servant (e.g., Gen 24:61; Exod 2:5; 1 Sam 25:42; Prov 31:15; Esth 2:9; 4:4).[42] Boaz could thus be inquiring about Ruth's kinship connection or marital status (cf. Tg. "From which people is this girl?") or about the identity of her

---

38. Timothy R. Ashley, *The Book of Numbers*, NICOT (Grand Rapids: Eerdmans, 1993), 149.

39. See BDB, 654–55; *DCH* 5:708.

40. Whereby *ləmî* is a genitive (e.g., Gen 38:25; Exod 32:24; 2 Sam 3:12).

41. Cf. Bush, *Ruth, Esther*, 113. This situation continues in many parts of the world today; see, e.g., Mercy A. Oduyoye, *Beads and Strands: Reflections of an African Woman on Christianity in Africa* (Carlisle: Paternoster, 2002), 69.

42. See BDB, 655; *DCH* 5:711.

# THE BOOK OF RUTH

master (cf. Gen 32:18–19[17–18]; 1 Sam 30:13). Perhaps there was a special quality in Ruth that caught his eye,[43] or, more likely, his was a routine question after noticing a newcomer. Unlike other women in the Old Testament, Ruth is not described as physically beautiful (cf. Gen 24:16), either because she was not, or, if she was, perhaps to focus on her inward beauty (3:10, 11; 4:15). Boaz's inquiry characterizes him as an attentive landowner, concerned about each worker in his field.

Boaz's use of *na'arâ* for Ruth hints at an age gap between them, just like between him and his *na'ar*. Based on Boaz's inquiry about her marital status, some also speculate about his romantic interest, but the corresponding terms hint at a possible rivalry. If a romantic undercurrent can be detected, the narrator has kept it firmly in the background, perhaps to highlight Boaz's other motivations, which will be revealed as the scene continues.

**6** The harvest overseer provides a long answer to Boaz's question, not just outlining her identity but also her activity. The narrator's extended introduction (*the male servant who was set over the harvesters answered and said*) to the overseer's response underscores its importance. To introduce direct speech, a pronoun and a verb suffices, e.g., "he answered" or "he said." The repetition of his full identity and the use of two verbs raises audience expectation that the overseer's speech will contribute to plot or characterization.[44] His answer recalls events from earlier in the narrative and focuses on aspects of her social identity. First, he says *she is a young Moabite woman*. The narrator has already mentioned her ethnicity twice after she arrived in Bethlehem (1:22; 2:2), and now we hear the perspective of a resident. The word order of the overseer's sentence further foregrounds her ethnicity.[45] Second, she *returned with Naomi from the territory of Moab*. In a small town, the word spread quickly about Naomi's return with a foreign young woman (1:22). The overseer does not mention Ruth's name—perhaps he does not know it, but his response details her relationship and group membership, just as Boaz focused on the social aspect of her identity. The overseer says she is attached to Naomi, not a man, but he does not specify that she is Naomi's daughter-in-law. He ends his response to Boaz's question by recalling a

---

43. Suggestions include her beauty, her character, her clothing, and her behavior; see Hubbard, *Ruth*, 125–26n25. Eskenazi and Frymer-Kensky, *Ruth*, 32, suggest that Ruth could have made herself conspicuous to gain the landowner's favor (cf. v. 2).

44. Grossman, *Ruth*, 147. Cynthia L. Miller-Naudé and Jacobus A. Naudé, "The Translation of Quotative Frames in the Hebrew Bible," *FO* 52 (2015): 254, observes that multiple-verb frames usually introduce "the most salient or important speech in a dialogue."

45. The predicate-subject null-copula clause is of classification ("she is *a* young Moabite woman," rather than of identification, "she is *the* young Moabite woman"; see *IBHS* §8.4), or it signals focus ("she is a young *Moabite* woman"). Whichever the case, her ethnic background is emphasized.

## 2:4–17 BOAZ'S FIELD: ENCOUNTER BETWEEN RUTH AND BOAZ

previous event: she returned from the territory of Moab (1:22). Ruth did not return to Bethlehem because she did not leave it, but the close connection between her and her mother-in-law meant the overseer understood them as both returning.

Boaz's inquiry and the overseer's response raise the question of Ruth's identity. In this scene, the narrator has already highlighted her Moabite ethnicity, and it is reinforced by the overseer's words. His mention of her association with Naomi is bracketed by foreign descriptors. The individual aspects of her identity are muted, and the social aspects accented, especially her Moabite ethnicity and origin. She is an outsider. We know she ends up gleaning (v. 3), but how does a Moabite outsider receive such favor in the harvesting community? And since this outsider "returned"—physically to Israel and spiritually to Yahweh—what part will this change play in her acceptance or otherwise by the Bethlehem community?

7 The overseer had already answered Boaz's question, but he continues by reporting Ruth's request when she entered the field. His is a quotation of Ruth's speech (*she said*), so we must keep in mind the possibility that it is not accurate.[46] Since her direct request is not recorded, his words may be a misrepresentation of her actual words. He quotes Ruth as saying, *Let me glean and gather* bā'ŏmārîm *after the harvesters.* The plural noun 'ŏmārîm only occurs here and v. 15, and means sheaves—harvested grain bundled for transport to the threshing floor.[47] The difficulty is understanding the meaning of the preposition *b* in *bā'ŏmārîm.* There are two possibilities. First, Ruth asked to *glean* the ears of grain *and gather* them into sheaves or bundles.[48] This is consistent with her intention as she set out (v. 2), and more pertinently, under Israelite law it would have been an acceptable request. In which case, why would Ruth need to ask for permission?[49] More likely is the second understanding: the overseer says Ruth asked to *glean* and *gather* the ears of grain *among the sheaves.*[50] A gleaner like Ruth would usually gather the remnants of the harvest, either the ears of grain left behind by the harvesters or those dropped on the ground (Lev 19:9–10; 23:22). This second understanding paints Ruth not just as resourceful but also audacious. The overseer says Ruth asked to "gather," not just "glean," which suggests that Ruth was

---

46. Grossman, *Ruth*, 149, understands Ruth's speech as her thoughts rather than her speech to the overseer. Cf. Rashi's commentary: "And she said—in her heart."

47. The singular, "sheaf," occurs in Lev 23:10, 11, 12, 15; Deut 24:19; Job 24:10.

48. Cf. Bush, *Ruth, Esther*, 114, who reads *bā'ŏmārîm* as specifying the goal, "into sheaves," rather than the location, "among the sheaves." So also Schipper, *Ruth*, 119–20.

49. Eskenazi and Frymer-Kensky, *Ruth*, 33, suggest it is because she asks to glean immediately behind the reapers to get the first pickings. If this is the case, the overseer's refusal is understandable.

50. So also, e.g., Hubbard, *Ruth*, 148–50; LaCocque, *Ruth*, 66.

## The Book of Ruth

presumptuous, if not greedy.[51] Yet Ruth said to her mother-in-law she only intended to glean (v. 2), which is supported by the narrator's description (v. 3). And although Ruth has acted with initiative and independent thinking (e.g., 1:16–17; 2:2–3), this request is too bold for someone who also displays due deference (2:2, 7). In short, it seems that the overseer wants Boaz to view Ruth's request as inappropriate, which explains his prohibition on her gleaning, as we will soon see.[52]

The overseer continues: *So she entered, and remained from then, the morning, until now.* She "entered" is straightforward (cf. v. 3), but what is the precise meaning of the overseer's second verb *'āmad*? It can mean almost opposite actions in this situation. Basically, *'āmad* means "stand," but it can mean either "stand still" or "remain, continue."[53] If Ruth stood still, this implies that the overseer did not grant her permission to glean, either because he adjudged her request as inappropriate or beyond his authority to grant. She had thus waited from the morning until Boaz's arrival. But if Ruth "remained," the overseer implies he allowed her to remain in the field instead of sending her away, where she has continued to glean and gather. She had thus been gleaning from her arrival until Boaz's arrival. Since the former meaning of *'āmad* is much more common than the latter (see, e.g., Gen 45:9; Josh 10:19; 1 Sam 20:38), "stand still," waiting for a response to her request is the overseer's likely intended meaning. However, his use of *'āmad* could have been intentional—to leave a scrap of uncertainty in Boaz's (and our) mind.

The fragmentary nature of the overseer's next statement, however, betrays the overseer's anxiety: *this . . . her sitting . . . the hut . . . a little.* Bible translations all down the ages have tried to make sense of these words by smoothing over the grammar and syntax. Yet, since broken sentences can indicate emotion (e.g., 1 Sam 9:12–13),[54] it seems best to first try to make sense of the text as it is, rather than to revocalize or emend it.[55] "This" (*zeh*) is masculine singular, so although the MT accents join "this" with "her sitting" (*šibtāh*), it does not make grammatical sense. The closest reference for "this" seems to be "the hut" (*habbayit*; masculine singular).[56] "Her sitting" translates the MT

---

51. Grossman, *Ruth*, 151, notes that the verb "to glean" (*lāqaṭ*) is precise, while "to gather" (*'āsap*) is haphazard, a contrast found in Num 11:7–8, 32.

52. At least the overseer's report of her misinterpretation of the law would make sense following his double mention of her foreign origin (v. 6).

53. For nineteen different interpretations of this phrase, see Daniel Lys, "Résidence ou repos? Notule sur Ruth ii 7," *VT* 21 (1971): 497–99.

54. Gary A. Rendsburg, "Confused Language as a Deliberate Literary Device in Biblical Hebrew Narrative," *JHebS* 2 (1999): 1–8, also lists these examples: Gen 37:28, 30; Judg 18:14–20; 1 Sam 14:21; 17:38. Irregular syntax is also found in Ruth 1:9.

55. Avi Hurvitz, "Ruth 2:7–'A Midrashic Gloss'?," *ZAW* 95 (1983): 121–23.

56. Cf. Lys, "Résidence ou repos?," 500, who suggests that "this" refers to "field" (2:3).

## 2:4–17 BOAZ'S FIELD: ENCOUNTER BETWEEN RUTH AND BOAZ

vocalization, which is supported by the Tg (Aram. root *ytb*, "to sit, dwell").[57] "The hut" is then presumably a temporary shelter in the field (cf. Job 27:18), to provide shade for rest or drinking or eating meals (2:14).[58] "A little" (*maʿāṭ*) is a substantive, here probably meaning "a little while." As it is written, the speech reflects the overseer's vacillation:

| | |
|---|---|
| this | |
| | her sitting |
| the hut | |
| | a little while |

I imagine seeing him turn his attention to the hut, Ruth's location ("this"), where he sees her activity ("her sitting"), then he considers the location again ("the hut"), then how long she has been sitting ("a little while").

My tentative reconstruction of the overseer's speech (v. 7) is as follows. He first reports her request, which he presents as inappropriate under Israelite law. At this point in the conversation, I see Boaz raising an eyebrow. Since she asked for more than the law permits, he states she has stood waiting for permission to glean. The overseer chose *ʿāmad* because of its double meaning: he did not grant permission, but at least he allowed her to remain in the field. Boaz sees she has not gleaned, so now I see a bemused look on Boaz's face, and the overseer also finds a hint of disapproval. The narrator introduced Boaz as a wealthy, virtuous, and godly man, well respected by his workers. His overseer now realizes he has not been as generous as his boss would have been and would have expected of an overseer of his field. So the overseer reports that, at Boaz's arrival, Ruth had been sitting in the hut a short time. He intended to save some face: she had been waiting around since morning, and now that the sun was high in the sky, at least he allowed her to shelter for a while. But his anxiety at his boss's disapproval of his prohibition to glean is betrayed by the fragmentary nature of his explanation of Ruth's sitting in the hut. The overseer's speech only breaks down at the end as his misjudgment dawns on him. And perhaps he feels nervous as he sees his boss does not believe his misrepresentation of Ruth's intent.[59] The overseer's

57. LXX takes *zeh* as a negative and reads "she has not rested" (reflecting the verb *šbt*, "to cease, rest"). The Vulg. also takes *zeh* as a negative and reads "she has not returned home" (reflecting the verb *šûb*, "to return").

58. In Job 27:18, *bayit*, "house," is in parallel with *sukkāh*, "booth, hut," made from branches or reed mats, to provide shade from the sun (Isa 4:6; Jonah 4:5), and shelter at night for watchmen in the field (Isa 1:8) and for livestock (e.g., Gen 33:17). Booths were used in military camps, and Ben-Hadad, the king of Syria, drank in one of these with his allies (1 Kgs 20:12, 16); cf. *HALOT* 2:753; Kronholm, "*sākak*," *TDOT* 10:244–45.

59. Cf. Block, *Discourse*, 128.

143

## The Book of Ruth

speech thus provides insight into his character, especially his attitude toward Ruth, since Boaz only inquired about her identity (v. 5).[60]

Many interpreters view the overseer more positively, but I contend that the above reading makes the best sense of the narrative.[61] We could interpret the overseer's anxiety as due to him permitting too much rather than too little (gleaning as well as sitting in the workers' hut), but my restrictive reading makes more sense considering Boaz's generous character. This contrast between Boaz and the overseer would be consistent with major characters and their foils in the Ruth narrative: Ruth and Orpah, Boaz and the nearer kinsman-redeemer. The overseer would be among those whom Boaz warns against harming Ruth (vv. 9, 15, 16), presumably because she is a foreigner, as he emphasized (v. 6). His omission of Ruth's kinship connection to Naomi reinforces her foreign status. Boaz's effusive response (v. 8) makes more sense as an answer to her request if she has been waiting for hours rather than if she had been gleaning already. Finally, if there was any hint of romantic possibility between the young overseer and Ruth,[62] how he deals with her ends it, leaving the spotlight solely on Boaz.

**8** Boaz does not press his overseer for details. He does not even answer the overseer, but immediately turns his attention to Ruth. His speech can be structured as:

### First Set of Instructions

| | |
|---|---|
| **Negative question as affirmative** | Haven't you heard, my daughter? |
| **Negative instruction** | Don't go to glean in another [*aḥēr*] field; |
| **Negative instruction** | in fact, don't leave this one, |
| **Instruction** | but stay close to my female servants here (v. 8). |
| **Instruction** | Let your eyes be on the field that they harvest, |
| **Instruction** | and go after [*aḥar*] them. |
| **Negative question as affirmative** | Haven't I commanded the male servants not to touch you? |

### Second Instruction

| | |
|---|---|
| **Instruction** | And when you are thirsty, you may go to the vessels and drink from whatever the male servants draw (v. 9). |

60. My reconstruction reads beyond what is explicit in the text, but in my filling of the narrative gaps I have tried to remain faithful to the original text and culture.

61. My reading is in the same vein, but not the same in details as Grossman, *Ruth*, 151–56 and Block, *Discourse*, 126–29.

62. So Porten, "Scroll," 33: "The careful notice which this 'boy' [*na'ar*] has taken of that 'girl' [*na'ărâ*] makes us apprehensive lest *they* be paired and not she and Boaz" (emphasis original).

## 2:4–17 Boaz's Field: Encounter between Ruth and Boaz

We could understand Boaz's negative question as rhetorical, but what has Ruth already heard? Boaz has just arrived on the scene, and nothing has been mentioned about any information or instructions from him. So it is better to understand the negative question as a strong affirmative: "Listen carefully, my daughter." This is the case in Ruth (2:9; 3:1, 2), and elsewhere in the Old Testament (e.g., Gen 27:36; 2 Kgs 19:25; Isa 37:26).[63] Like Naomi, Boaz addresses Ruth with "my daughter," which shows their age difference and suggests his care and concern for her, yet dampens romantic expectations. This intimate familial address is surprising, coming straight after the overseer's description of Ruth as an outsider to all Israelite kinship groups. The narrator hints that Boaz does not primarily see her as "Ruth the Moabite" by introducing his speech with *Boaz said to Ruth*. Her foreignness was flagged by the narrator (v. 2) and detailed by the overseer (v. 6), but Boaz views her simply as "Ruth." His warm greetings with his harvesters revealed the narrower hierarchical distance between them, but now, against cultural expectation, he breaks through that structure. And his use of "my daughter" hints that he is beginning to draw Ruth—the destitute widowed Moabite—into his household.

Now that Boaz has Ruth's attention, he makes three specifying statements, probably accompanied by gestures. We can imagine him first extending his arm to motion beyond his field as he instructs her, *Don't go to glean in another field*. We can then imagine him pointing out the boundaries of his field as he commands her, *In fact, don't leave this one*.[64] This detail is necessary because in ancient Israel the boundaries were either not marked or difficult to discern (see comments on v. 2). Then we can see him directing her attention to a group of reapers as he instructs her, *but stay close to my female servants here*. Boaz uses double reinforcement with increasing specificity to make sure Ruth stays in his field.

> Don't glean in another field
> Don't go beyond this one
> Stay close to my female servants here

Although Boaz does not respond to his overseer, his speech shows he heard what he said. The overseer reported that she asked for permission to glean and gather (v. 7); Boaz grants permission indirectly by telling her to

---

63. See GKC §150e.

64. Heb. *wəgam* ("in fact") in conjunction with *lōʾ taʿăbûrî* ("don't leave") indicates the increasing emphasis with which Boaz speaks. Heb. *lōʾ* + *yiqtol* is more emphatic than preceding *ʾal* + jussive (*ʾal-tēləkî*; "do not go"); see GKC §107o.

145

# The Book of Ruth

stay in his field to glean. He then instructs her to stick with (*dbq*) his female servants. Based on the structure for Boaz's first set of instructions, this is the central instruction. The repetition of a key word from act 1 draws a subtle link between the acts (1:14; 2:8, 21, 23), and we wonder: is Ruth's clinging (*dbq*) to Naomi about to pay dividends? For staying close to the female servants provides Ruth protection (vv. 9, 15–16, 22). The overseer reported that Ruth asked to glean among the sheaves, that is, probably at a distance behind or away from them after they had bundled the grain into sheaves. Yet Boaz allows Ruth to stick with his female servants; that is, she can glean at a location and at a time closer to the harvesters than that usually available to gleaners. Now she can identify with the female servants, she begins to move up the social ladder. No longer a rank outsider, she has made her first step to integrate into the Israelite community. Ruth is not only protected she is now privileged.

**9** Boaz continues his instructions with more explanations. Since his next phrase (*'ênayik baśśādeh*) is grammatically bare, it could be translated as "your eyes on the field" (LXX). The context, however, favors a jussive sense, "May your eyes be on the field," or *Let your eyes be on the field* (supported by Tg).[65] Boaz already directed Ruth's visual attention to three locations (v. 8). He now instructs her to look at the field in which his harvesters work. Previously "eyes" had been used to convey the idea of finding favor (v. 2), and the same idea will be repeated by Ruth (vv. 10, 13). In this verse, keeping eyes fixed on the field means looking with single-mindedness or determination (cf. Ps 25:15 and Prov 4:25). He does not want her eye wandering to other fields, which would predispose her to be led astray.[66] Ruth is to make sure she focuses her attention on the field in which she has found favor. Boaz may not necessarily refer to a single field; he may mean consecutive fields. He may mean his portion of field allotted from the clan inheritance as a whole, or he may mean whichever field in which his reapers work. The latter is more likely if barley and wheat were grown in different fields (cf. Lev 19:19), and one harvest followed the other (Ruth 2:21, 23). This being the case, Boaz allowed Ruth to glean not just for a day, nor just for a harvest, but for the entire harvest season.

Opinion is split over the first referent in Boaz's instruction, *Let your eyes be on the field that they harvest* [yiqṣōrûn; masculine plural], *and go after them* (feminine plural). Since *yiqṣōrûn* is masculine plural, it can refer to either the

---

65. Such a null-copula clause is similar to the greetings in 2:4, "(May) Yahweh be with you" and "(May) Yahweh bless you." See JM §§154n, 163b.

66. Lot's wife looked astray, in particular, backward (Gen 19:17, 26). See Davies, *Lift Up Your Heads*, 58.

146

## 2:4–17 Boaz's Field: Encounter between Ruth and Boaz

male harvesters (e.g., NIV) or all the harvesters.[67] The latter is more likely in this context. The collective (male and female) is most likely the sense in the summary description (v. 3) and Boaz's greeting (v. 4), almost definitely the sense in the overseer's title (vv. 5, 6; "male servant who was set over the harvesters"), probably the sense in Ruth's question (v. 7), and most likely the sense at mealtime (v. 14). Thus, Ruth was instructed to see where the harvesting was done by all of Boaz's workers and to follow the female harvesters. Previously she was told to "stay close" to the female harvesters (v. 8), now she is told specifically to "go behind [*'aḥar*] them." Naomi urged Ruth to return after (*'aḥar*) her sister-in-law, but Ruth countered, "Do not urge me to return from following [*'aḥar*] you" (1:15–16). At the beginning of the day, Ruth set out to glean after him in whose eyes she might find favor, and she was successful (2:2, 3; cf. v. 7). Yet now she is granted the privilege of gleaning right behind the female harvesters (v. 9). One can imagine that this would increase her yield compared to other gleaners who collected further away, after the harvesting crew had finished. Favor follows favor after favor.

Boaz rounds off his first set of instructions with another question, *Haven't I commanded* [ṣiwwîtî][68] *the male servants not to touch you?* As with his first question to Ruth (v. 8), this one is best understood as an affirmative statement. Yet the perfective *qatal* (*ṣiwwîtî*) is difficult to interpret. Even with narratorial selective representation of events, it seems highly unlikely to be a past action. Boaz has just arrived, and for the audience to understand that he has already issued this command "off stage" is too jarring.[69] We could also interpret the perfective as expressing the speaker's view that an action is completed although it is still imminent.[70] The sense may be similar here: Boaz tells Ruth he will surely issue the command, and actually does so after mealtime (v. 15).[71] Most likely is the performative interpretation of the perfective: in Boaz's declaration, he is issuing the command.[72] This presumes

---

67. Biblical Hebrew uses masculine plural to refer to mixed-gender groups.

68. The verb *ṣwh* describes a "command" or "order" given by a superior to a subordinate. Here the former is more apt since a "command" has lasting validity beyond a unique situation (2:9, 15; also, e.g., Amos 2:12b), while an "order" can be fulfilled and thus rendered obsolete (3:6; also, e.g., 2 Sam 13:28–29). Consult G. Liedke, "*ṣwh*," *TLOT* 2:1062–63.

69. Schipper, *Ruth*, 129, floats the less likely possibility that Boaz had not issued the command but tells Ruth "what he thinks she wants to hear."

70. Often prophets speak of God's actions in the future as completed events, given the certainty that the actions will happen. See GKC §106n.

71. Cf. Hubbard, *Ruth*, 158. Against this interpretation is the time lag between Boaz's statement and the issuing of the command, and the difference between "touch" and "insult"; Bush, *Ruth, Esther*, 121–22.

72. See JM §112g, which translates the perfective in 2:9 as "Behold, I order." Cf. LXX: "Look, I have commanded."

## The Book of Ruth

that at least some harvesters are within earshot. His repetition of a not too dissimilar command at mealtime is then necessary because not all his harvesters would have heard it the first time. Thus, the sense is: "Am I not commanding the male harvesters not to touch you?"[73] as we imagine Boaz also addressing the nearby harvesters.

Although the basic meaning of *nāgaʿ* is "to touch," here it probably has a more sinister tinge—to touch intending to harm. A prohibition is only necessary against physical contact that would make Ruth uncomfortable or bring her harm. Since Boaz's command is addressed to the males, it could refer to sexual assault (e.g., Gen 20:6; Prov 6:29), but more likely given the public context is physical harm or harassment in general (e.g., Gen 26:11, 29; Josh 9:19; 2 Sam 14:10).[74] This would be consistent with Boaz's instruction to stick close to his female harvesters (vv. 8–9) and his later commands to his male harvesters not to humiliate or rebuke her (vv. 15–16). Naomi's words to Ruth upon her return reveal the level of physical danger to Ruth, as an unattached female foreigner working in the field (v. 22).[75] The word *nāgaʿ* might allude to the patriarchal motif of protecting the matriarch.[76] Sarah and Rebekah were foreigners outside the promised land when they were protected from physical harm (*nāgaʿ*; Gen 20:6; 26:29). How might Ruth's protection align with the story of the matriarchs?

The allusions might extend to the scene as a whole. Robert Alter identified the concept of betrothal type-scenes, classically at wells outside the promised land.[77] Jacob meets Rachel at a well in Haran (Gen 29:1–12) and Moses meets Zipporah at a Midianite well (Exod 2:15–22). A variation is Rebekah meeting Abraham's servant, rather than the potential bridegroom himself, at a well in Aram-Naharaim[78] (Gen 24:11–18). A greater variation of the betrothal type-scene is found in the Ruth narrative: the protagonist is female instead of male; she is Moabite, so her meeting with a potential spouse takes place not at a foreign well, but near a well in Judah. One way God's working in Israelite history is revealed is through the betrothal type-scenes. Is the meeting of Ruth and Boaz a nod to divine destiny? Will they end up in the illustrious covenantal line of the patriarchs and Moses? Yet these raised courtship expectations are dampened by Boaz's address, "my

---

73. Tg. supports MT: "Have I not commanded?"

74. *HALOT* 2:668; M. Delcor, "*ngʿ*," *TLOT* 2:718–19. Physical harm, not simply physical contact, is the reading of these versions: Tg., Syr., Vulg.

75. See also David Shepherd, "Violence in the Fields? Translating, Reading, and Revising in Ruth 2," *CBQ* 63 (2001): 444–63.

76. Hubbard, *Ruth*, 160.

77. For ideas in this paragraph, I am indebted to Alter, *Biblical Narrative*, 51–62.

78. Mesopotamia.

2:4–17 Boaz's Field: Encounter between Ruth and Boaz

daughter," and Ruth's determination to provide for her mother-in-law rather than find a husband.

The variation in the type-scene in Ruth also draws attention to the extraordinary nature of Boaz's permission. Harvesters might have drawn water from a well or cistern on their way from the town to the fields, such as the well near the gate of Bethlehem (2 Sam 23:16 // 1 Chr 11:17). The water would be stored in vessels (*kēlîm*), clay jars (or maybe animal-skin water bags)[79] probably placed on the harvest field to satisfy the thirst of the workers.[80] Boaz makes the refreshment available not just for his workers but also for Ruth, a gleaner. Boaz's permission goes against two conventions. Normally, women draw water for men (Gen 24:11, 13; 1 Sam 9:11); here, Ruth can drink from the water the male servants[81] have drawn. Foreigners were expected to draw water for Israelites (Deut 29:11; Josh 9:21–27); here, a Moabite drinks water drawn by Israelites. And this permission is granted without prior request.

The last part of Boaz's speech might also indirectly be in response to his overseer's report. He permits Ruth to *go to the vessels and drink from whatever the male servants draw* when she is thirsty. The overseer was probably nervous about Ruth's sitting in the hut because of how it would reflect upon him. If so, although Boaz's offer for Ruth to drink water from the vessels is directed to her, it might also be designed to indirectly allay his overseer's concerns about her presence in the hut. It was a privileged place for refreshment; Boaz permits Ruth refreshment from water.

**10** In response to Boaz's favor, Ruth *fell on her face and bowed to the ground*; that is, she probably dropped to her knees[82] and bowed with her face low to or touching the ground.[83] In the ancient Near East, such actions showed profound respect or a strong emotional response; thus, it was commonly used to worship deities but also used between humans. That Ruth "fell" (*nāpal*) on her face suggests a fast action[84] (cf. Gen 17:3; 44:14; Josh 5:14), an immediate expression of her gratitude and respect before someone of higher social status (e.g., Gen 48:12; 2 Sam 14:22; 2 Kgs 4:37). Her verbal response expresses her surprise and disbelief: *Why have I found favor in your eyes?* Ruth set out to glean in the

---

79. Heb. *kəlî* can denote a range of vessels from small flasks to large jars. See Edwin C. Hostetter, "*kəlî*," *NIDOTTE* 2:654–56.

80. Oded Borowski, *Agriculture in Iron Age Israel* (Winona Lake, IN: Eisenbrauns, 2002), 61.

81. Although *hannəʿārîm* could refer to either "the male servants" or "the servants" in general, in the flow of Boaz's speech, the former is more likely.

82. One knee might have been drawn back, with the other forward, to aid in standing again; see the pictures of obeisance, from Egypt and Nineveh, respectively, in Davies, *Lift Up Your Heads*, 79, 81.

83. Cf. H.-P. Stähli, "*ḥwh*," *TLOT* 1:398–400.

84. Davies, *Lift Up Your Heads*, 78.

## THE BOOK OF RUTH

field of anyone in whose sight she would find favor (*ḥēn*; 2:2). She received the overseer's permission, but she finds (*māṣā'*) Boaz's favor. The mention of "finding" recalls Naomi's farewell to Ruth and Orpah: "May you find [*māṣā'*] rest in the home of another husband" (1:9). In Boaz, Ruth has found "favor" (*ḥēn*), not "rest" (*mənûḥâ*), but perhaps her finding "rest" is not too far off.[85]

Ruth then outlines the result of Boaz's favor or the way his favor is expressed, *that you have paid attention to me*.[86] Ruth is amazed that Boaz would "notice" or "pay attention" (from Heb. *nkr*) to her, as evidenced in the special privileges she has been granted.[87] The overseer had already noticed her (vv. 6–7), and Boaz was concerned about the malevolent attention that she would receive from the male harvesters (v. 9). Yet, Boaz's attention is of the benevolent kind, regarding Ruth for good (cf. Jer 24:5).

Later in the narrative *nkr* will hold the nuance of "to recognize" (3:14), but perhaps some of that nuance is in the background of Ruth's words here. In her thinking, Boaz might grant special favor to someone he knows. But she cannot understand why he would treat her with such generosity, as she says, *although*[88] *I am a foreigner*. The wordplay and assonance (*ləhakkîrēnî wə'ānōkî nokrîyâ*; "you have paid attention to me although I am a foreigner")[89] is based on almost opposite meanings from the same Hebrew root (*nkr*). To bring out the wordplay, it might be translated, "you have recognized someone who should not be recognized as your own."[90] This draws further attention to the dissonance in Ruth's mind: How can he treat her as someone who has special standing in his sight, even though she has just arrived from a foreign land? How can he treat her as a relative or a friend even though she is just a "foreigner"?

Ruth identifies herself not as a "sojourner" or "resident alien" (*gēr*) but a "foreigner" or "stranger" (*nokrî*). In the Old Testament, *nokrî* refers to people who are ethnically other to Israel, that is, non-Israelites (e.g., 2 Sam 15:19; 1 Kgs 11:1, 8; Ezra 10:2, 10; Neh 13:26), although less often it refers to those outside the family or clan (e.g., Gen 31:15; Exod 21:8; Ps 69:9[8]; Job 19:15).[91]

---

85. The Hebrew words *ḥēn* and *mənûḥâ* share two consonants, which lends mild support to this reading.

86. Heb. *lə* with the *hiphil* infinitive construct, *ləhakkîrēnî*, indicates the result or consequence of Boaz's favor (*IBHS* §36.2.3d).

87. See BDB, 648; *HALOT* 2:699–700.

88. Heb. *wə'ānōkî nokrîyâ* is a nominal clause following a verbal clause, which in this context is circumstantial, highlighting a contradictory expectation to the previous verbal clause (see *GKC* §141e; e.g., Gen 18:27; 48:14). The *waw* is thus translated "although."

89. Cf. Campbell, *Ruth*, 98.

90. Cf. Goslinga, *Joshua*, 531–32, "respect a reject." Similar meanings from the root *nkr* are also found in Gen 42:7, where Joseph "recognized" (*hiphil*) his brothers but treated them as "strangers" (*hithpael*). See Marvin R. Wilson, "*nkr*," *TWOT* 2:580.

91. R. Martin-Achard, "*nēkār*," *TLOT* 2:740. Heb. *nokrî* is also used to describe Israel as a "wild" vine (Jer 2:21) and God's work as "strange" or "alien" (Isa 28:21).

The distinction is significant because in Old Testament texts a foreigner has a different standing, with different rights, from a sojourner. Foreigners are on the fringes of Israelite society, while sojourners were partly assimilated into it. Foreigners maintained an independent sense of identity, while sojourners could enjoy some privileges of native Israelites. Many Old Testament texts indicate a cautious or defensive attitude toward foreigners (e.g., Judg 19:12), although not all texts (e.g., 1 Kgs 8:41–43 // 2 Chr 6:32–33; Isa 56:3, 6). Primarily, this attitude derives from the temptation posed by foreign religions and gods (e.g., Gen 35:2; Deut 31:16; Josh 24:20, 23; Judg 10:16; 1 Sam 7:3; Jer 5:19; Mal 2:11; Ps 81:10[9]; Dan 11:39; 2 Chr 33:15). By contrast, those sojourners willing to assimilate into Israelite society could take part in Israelite religious life, including festivals (e.g., Exod 12:48; Deut 16:11, 14) and covenant renewal (Deut 29:11; 31:12).[92] Also, along with widows and orphans, sojourners could glean from Israelite land (Lev 19:9–10; 23:22; Deut 24:19).

So Ruth self-identifies as a "foreigner," but is she? In the Old Testament, "foreigner" denotes the stranger who is only temporarily residing in a foreign country, who has not given up their original home.[93] Elimelech and his family departed Judah to sojourn, to live for a while, in Moab. But Ruth had severed all connections with her homeland and pledged allegiance not only to Naomi but also to her God (1:16–17).[94] Thus, considering the events in the narrative so far, Ruth's self-identification is incorrect. Perhaps her use of "foreigner" betrays her self-consciousness about her alien status, heightened after the overseer's double mention of her Moabite ethnicity (2:6). Or perhaps her use of the term is intentional since "foreigner" may be less likely to provoke hostility than "sojourner."[95]

Nonetheless, placed beside Num 25:1–18, an audience might view Ruth as a foreign woman, with the attendant dangerous or hostile connotations. And the warnings against the *nokrîyâ* in Proverbs (e.g., 2:16; 5:20; 6:24), where it refers not to a non-Israelite but an "adulteress" (ESV) or "wayward woman" (NIV), only heighten the danger of Ruth's presence. As such, the

---

92. As the external sign of membership in the covenant community (Gen 17:10), those male sojourners willing to assimilate into Israelite society were circumcised, along with their household (Exod 12:48). Sojourners can choose to assimilate or not; Kenton L. Sparks, *Ethnicity and Identity in Ancient Israel: Prolegomena to the Study of Ethnic Sentiments and Their Expression in the Hebrew Bible* (Winona Lake, IN: Eisenbrauns, 1998), 240–41. Along with slaves, sojourners could be part of an Israelite household (e.g., Exod 20:10).

93. Michael Guttmann, "The Term 'Foreigner' (נכרי) Historically Considered," *HUCA* 3 (1926): 1. Cf. B. Lang, "*nkr*," *TDOT* 9:427.

94. Cf. Tg: "Why have I found favor in your eyes that you should befriend me since I am *from a* foreign *people, from the daughters of Moab, who are not purified to enter into the congregation of the Lord?*" (words in italics not found in the MT).

95. Victor H. Matthews, "The Determination of Social Identity in the Story of Ruth," *BTB* 36 (2006): 51.

THE BOOK OF RUTH

audience would expect that Boaz would treat her with caution. Hence, Ruth's surprise (and ours as the audience) at Boaz's indifference to her foreigner status is understandable. Boaz's acts of generosity beyond legal and social expectations are the embodiment of kindness (*ḥesed*). Noticing the outsider is the first step to acknowledging one's social responsibility. And for Ruth, Boaz's acknowledgment is a crucial step in her journey of integration into Bethlehemite society.

**11** Boaz responds to Ruth in two parts: an explanation and a blessing. Ruth thinks Boaz would not recognize her and thus should not pay any attention to her. He responds, *It has been fully reported to me: all that you have done for your mother-in-law after your husband died.* The source of Boaz's knowledge is not stated. From the narrative, however, we know that although the entire town was "stirred" at her arrival, Naomi conversed with the women of the town, including those who knew her previously (1:19–21). It seems likely that information about Naomi and her daughter-in-law would have been "gossiped" through this informal network (or networks), which is again mentioned toward the end of the narrative to speak to Naomi (4:14) and to name Ruth's son (4:17).[96] Naomi probably provided further information about Ruth to her immediate female neighbors, and through them, that information spread to Boaz.[97] This would explain why Boaz did not press his overseer for more details about Ruth.

Boaz says that what Ruth did has been *fully reported* (*huggēd huggad*) to him. The *hophal* infinitive absolute followed by the perfect verb of the same root (*ngd*) intensifies the verb.[98] The infinitive absolute could modify the degree of certainty ("It has surely been reported to me"), extent ("It has been thoroughly reported to me"), or manner ("It has been carefully [or clearly] reported to me") of the information that Boaz received. Elements of all three could be in play here: Boaz can assure Ruth of his knowledge because it seems he fully investigated the circumstances of her return with Naomi.[99] He says he knows everything Ruth has *done for* Naomi after the death of her husband (1:5).[100] Presumably, this includes her remaining with

96. Gossip can be defined as "the exchange of information about absent third parties." For a social-scientific understanding of gossip, with references, see Philip F. Esler, "'All That You Have Done . . . Has Been Fully Told to Me': The Power of Gossip and the Story of Ruth," *JBL* 137 (2018): 646–49.

97. Esler, "The Power of Gossip," 662.

98. See *IBHS* §35.3.1–2.

99. The same phrase in Josh 9:24 is also semantically open-ended.

100. At this point in the narrative, it is not clear whether Ruth was married to Mahlon or Chilion. Boaz might have known already, but it is only revealed to the audience in 4:10.

## 2:4–17 Boaz's Field: Encounter between Ruth and Boaz

Naomi before her vow of commitment on the road to Bethlehem (1:18–19) and her returning with Naomi to Bethlehem.

Given the thoroughness of Boaz's report about Ruth, he almost certainly also knew of Ruth's familial relationship to Naomi and hence to him through the clan of Elimelech. His response, however, is framed in such a way that he does not mention *to Ruth* that she is a member of his clan. At the same time, there is enough evidence for *an audience* to infer that he is in effect correcting her false understanding of her foreign status (esp. after his introduction in v. 1). This being the case, we find dramatic irony: the reader knows she is a fellow clansperson, whereas Ruth at this stage is in the dark.

Boaz's explanation for his favor is that it is in response to the kindness Ruth had shown her mother-in-law. He continues by specifying what she did: *how you abandoned your father and mother and your native land*. Boaz (*bō'az*) says that Ruth abandoned (*'āzab*) her parents instead of her mother-in-law, contrary to Naomi's pleading (1:16). Boaz praises Ruth for her personal sacrifice and, based on the wordplay, we wonder if Boaz will go to the same lengths for Ruth and her family.[101] He has made a promising start. His mention of Ruth leaving her father and mother reminds us of Gen 2:24, the only other place in the Old Testament the collocation of words occurs.[102] Even when her husband died and Naomi released her from family obligation (1:11–13), she remained devoted to her new family (1:16–18). Ruth also left her native land, the place where she belongs, the land of her kin (Jer 22:10; 46:16; Ezek 23:15).[103] The use of "native land" (*'ereṣ môledet*) draws the Ruth narrative into the orbit of two groups of Old Testament texts: patriarchal and exilic. We are reminded of the narrative of Abraham (Gen 11:28; 24:7); yet Ruth's decision to leave her family and "native land" not only finds parallels with, but perhaps even exceeds Abram's similar decision (Gen 12:1; cf. 24:7), since Ruth leaves without a word or a promise from God. We are also reminded of the narrative of Jacob, whom God asked to return to his "native land" (Gen 31:13). In the second group of Old Testament texts, we are reminded of how bitter life can be outside one's "native land" (Jer 22:10; 46:16; cf. Ezek 23:15), an experience perhaps still raw for an audience of the book of Ruth in the exilic or post-exilic period.

---

101. Cf. Garsiel, *Names*, 252.

102. In the New Testament, Gen 2:24 is quoted by Jesus (Matt 19:5; Mark 10:7) and Paul (Eph 5:31).

103. Heb. *'ereṣ môladtēk* can also be translated "land of your birth" or "land of your kindred"; *HALOT* 2:556; BDB, 409. The noun is derived from the root *yld*, "to give birth," which connects back to the loss of Naomi's two "sons" or "children" (1:5; cf. 1:12), and forward to the "birth" of Obed (4:13, 15, 16, 17; cf. 4:12). The motif of birth is also found in the genealogy at the end of the narrative ("these are the *generations*" [*tôlǝdôt*]; 4:18–22).

THE BOOK OF RUTH

Boaz says Ruth not only left her people and her land, but *went to a people you didn't know before*. The use of *'am* (commonly translated "people") instead of *gôy* (commonly translated "nation") brings to the fore kinship and familial ideas (cf. 1:10, 16), as well as hints of covenant relationship (cf. 1:16; 2:12).[104] Often *'am* denotes an ethnic group, and here Boaz refers to the Judean or Israelite ethnic group. The phrase "people/nation not known before" often describes a strange, foreign threat, usually a people that God uses to judge his own people (e.g., Deut 28:33, 36; 2 Sam 22:44; Jer 9:15[16]; Zech 7:14). Since Moab neighbors Israel, Ruth would have at least had some general knowledge of Israel. She would have gained more specific knowledge through her relationship with her husband's family. Through this family, she would have learned something of Israelite history, language, culture, and religion. Yet now that Ruth has come to live among the people of Israel, she gains a personal, experiential knowledge of them.[105] In short, there is a progression: Ruth left her parents (smallest kinship group) and the land of her kin (largest kinship group) to go to a foreign people (largest non-kinship group).

We can detect Boaz's implied values behind his explanation.[106] Boaz and those involved in "gossip" prioritize loyalty to family, people, and God. In group-oriented cultures, loyalty is highly prized, while disloyalty is frowned upon. Indeed, harmonious relationships are based on loyalty, while disloyalty can tear apart a society. In turning her back on her relationships in Moab, Ruth forfeits any hope of future benefit from her former society. We can thus understand Boaz's admiration for Ruth's loyalty to Naomi because she is a mother-in-law, kin only through marriage, in fact, a marriage bond already broken. And we can understand his eagerness from the concept of reciprocity in a communal society: favor begets favor, so loyalty deserves a reward. Actions have consequences, and Boaz's next words of blessing reveal that retributive justice is prominent in his thinking (v. 12). Yet, unlike most "gossip," in this instance, Ruth does not fail to live up to this societal virtue; rather, she embodies it. Boaz effectively praises Ruth—a foreigner—for exemplifying an Israelite value.[107]

Concerning Ruth's question to Boaz about his motivations, three inferences that can be drawn from the narrative context are almost more revealing than his reply. First, he may obey the gleaning law because he is a "man

---

104. Israel is known as *'am yhwh*, a people with whom God is in familial and covenant relationship. Cf. A. R. Hulst, "*'am/gôy*," *TLOT* 2:905–6.

105. Cf. W. Schottroff, "*yd'*," *TLOT* 2:514. Words based on the root *yd'* are found in chapters 2 (vv. 1, 11) and 4 (v. 4), but cluster in chapter 3 (vv. 2, 3, 4, 11, 14, 18).

106. Cf. Esler, "The Power of Gossip," 661.

107. Boaz will later describe this action of Ruth's as one of *ḥesed* (3:10).

## 2:4-17 Boaz's Field: Encounter between Ruth and Boaz

of great worth," which is how we are introduced to him (2:1). As such a man, generosity and kindness might mark all his behavior toward the needy.[108] Second, some suggest that Boaz is sexually attracted to Ruth at first sight and that the sexual overtones continue in his speech throughout this chapter.[109] While sexual attraction is possible, the narrator's description of Boaz as a "man of great worth," especially its moral component, renders this less likely as the primary motivation for his actions. It would be better to view his actions as a response to her past actions and a concern for those working in his field. The allusions to the betrothal type-scene, however, flag the *romantic potential* between Ruth and Boaz. Third, as a relative, Boaz is obligated to provide for Ruth. He says to her that he knows "all that you have done *for your mother-in-law*," which suggests he shows favor because she is a member of his clan. One may counter that Boaz would not feel any kinship obligation toward Ruth: she is a widow without a son to bind her to the clan; she is a foreigner from a vilified country; he had not met her before. Yet, the narrative highlights Boaz's kinship relation to Naomi. That he is from the same clan as Naomi's deceased husband Elimelech has already been mentioned twice in the chapter (2:1, 3). The overseer's description of Ruth as "the Moabite who came back from Moab with Naomi" (2:6 NIV) also highlights Ruth's relation to Naomi. Within the narrative context, then, Boaz seems to be primarily motivated by kinship responsibility, while the other two factors remain in the background.

**12** Boaz follows his explanation with a prayer of blessing. He showed favor to Ruth because of her loyalty to her mother-in-law; now he invokes further favor from Yahweh. Boaz's blessing can be viewed as one blessing in two parts (A and B), followed by an image of Ruth's protection under Yahweh (C):

> A  May Yahweh repay [*yašallēm*][110] your deed,
> A'  and may your wages be complete [*šəlēmâ*, adjective] from Yahweh,
> B  the God of Israel, under whose wings you came to seek refuge.

In lines A and A', Yahweh encloses the reward for Ruth's action. In Boaz's mind, Ruth deserves more than what he has provided for her. He says, *May*

---

108. Nonetheless, it seems unlikely that he would treat all needy persons with such generosity. Indeed, Ruth is the only person eating with Boaz and his workers and having food offered to her at mealtime (2:14-15).

109. See, e.g., Fewell and Gunn, *Compromising*, 40-41; Linafelt and Beal, *Ruth & Esther*, 30-31.

110. The verb-subject word order, *yašallēm yhwh*, indicates a modal/jussive clause, in the same way as *ûtəhî maškurtēk* in the next line.

# THE BOOK OF RUTH

*Yahweh repay* [yᵊšallēm, piel] *your deed.* The verb *šlm* means "to complete, to make whole," and is based on the same root as the noun *šālôm*, "peace, wholeness, well-being."[111] The *piel* form of the verb is often used in legal and cultic contexts to mean "repay, compensate" a debt (e.g., 2 Kgs 4:7), or figuratively, the payment of a thanksgiving offering (Pss 56:13[12]) or a vow (22:26[25]; Hos 14:3[2]).[112] The concept is also applied to God's dealings with humankind: he will repay each person according to their actions. Good deeds will be rewarded, bad deeds will be punished. As Saul says to David, "May Yahweh reward you with good for what you have done" (1 Sam 24:20[19] ESV); in contrast, as David says to the people, "May Yahweh repay the evil-doer according to his evil deeds" (2 Sam 3:39). In this way, Boaz views Ruth's act of loyalty to Naomi (v. 11) as putting God in debt to Ruth. The word for "deed" (*pōʿal*)[113] is mainly used in poetic texts and is often linked with God's recompense for actions, both good and bad (e.g., Jer 25:14; 50:29; Job 34:11; Ps 28:4; Prov 24:12, 24:29).[114] In short, Boaz desires that Yahweh "repay" or "reward" (*yᵊšallēm*) Ruth's good action.

In line A', Boaz essentially prays the same as line A, except in reverse order: *May your wages be complete from Yahweh.* Yet the use of "wages" (*maśkōret*) leads the reader to another web of texts—patriarchal rather than poetic. Laban tells Jacob that he must pay him wages for working for him (Gen 29:15), although Jacob complains that his father-in-law changed his wages ten times (31:7, 41). Ruth did not render services to her mother-in-law that required monetary wages, but in Boaz's mind, she deserves payment for her loyal service to Naomi. Boaz prays that this payment from Yahweh would be *šᵊlēmâ*, "full, complete," an adjective which forms a wordplay based on the same root as the verb *yᵊšallēm* in line A. As a sign of her transfer of allegiance, Ruth previously vowed on the personal, covenant name of God (1:17); now Boaz prays that Yahweh would act as the rewarder.

This is the second time an Israelite has prayed that Yahweh would reward Ruth for her past actions. On the road to Bethlehem, Naomi had prayed that Yahweh would deal kindly with her, just as she had dealt with Naomi's family. This was followed by Naomi's prayer that she would find rest in the house of another husband, back in Moab (1:8–9). Now in Bethlehem, Boaz similarly prays that Yahweh would reward Ruth's actions, but a significant difference is found in the last line of Boaz's prayer (B): he adds that Ruth had sought protection from *the God of Israel.*[115] These prayers not only link the attitudes and

---

111. BDB, 1022.

112. Consult G. Gerleman, "*šlm*," *TLOT* 3:1340–41.

113. It is synonymous with *maʿăśēh*, "deed, work"; see BDB, 821.

114. Cf. J. Vollmer, "*pʿl*," *TLOT* 2:1016.

115. Boaz's use of "Yahweh" encloses his prayer, and at the same time, "Yahweh" is also in apposition to "the God of Israel."

## 2:4–17 BOAZ'S FIELD: ENCOUNTER BETWEEN RUTH AND BOAZ

hopes of the Israelite characters in the Ruth narrative, they also remind us of God's quiet providence working behind and through the human characters.

Within the narrative, Boaz's statement adds veracity to Ruth's vow of loyalty to Yahweh (1:16–17). She made her vow only before Naomi and God; here Boaz acknowledges and accepts the genuineness of her commitment. She had turned from Chemosh, the god of Moab (1 Kgs 11:33), to Yahweh, the God of Israel. Having entered the land of Israel, she could all the more expect to "find refuge" (*ḥāsâ*) under the God of Israel's wings. While *ḥāsâ* can refer to seeking physical shelter (e.g., Isa 4:6; 25:4; Job 24:8), it more often denotes seeking refuge, and thus placing trust in a god (e.g., Deut 32:37), or in a nation, such as Egypt (Isa 30:2; cf. Judg 9:15). Relying on God for "refuge" (*maḥseh*) is often found in the Psalter, especially Book I, beginning with Ps 2:12 ("Blessed are all who take refuge in him" [ESV]).[116] In the Psalter, seeking refuge in God is characteristic of the righteous (e.g., Pss 15; 24; 34; 37), who trust in him rather than in humans or human rulers (Ps 118:8–9; cf. Pss 142:5–6[4–5]; 146:3).[117] Ruth can be viewed as an embodiment of such a person.

The metaphor of Yahweh's wings probably derives from the tender image of a mother bird protecting her chicks under her wings (cf. Deut 32:11; Isa 31:5; Matt 23:37; Luke 13:34).[118] This image is especially prominent in the Psalms (17:8; 36:8[7]; 61:5[4]; 63:8[7]; 91:4), where it is a metaphor for God's protection of his people.[119] A comparison with Ps 91:4, the other occurrence of the phrase "refuge under his wings,"[120] confirms the meaning "wings" rather than "skirt" (cf. Ruth 3:9),[121] and the surrounding context of Ps 91 enfolds ideas of divine help and defense (also Ps 17:8; 57:2[1]; 63:8[7]). God's "kindness" (*ḥesed*) is almost always mentioned with his "wings" in the Psalter (Pss 17:7–8; 36:8[7]; 57:2, 4[1, 3]; 61:5, 8[4, 7]; 63:4, 8[3, 7]).[122] One

---

116. See Jerome F. D. Creach, *Yahweh as Refuge and the Editing of the Hebrew Psalter*, JSOTSup 217 (Sheffield: Sheffield Academic, 1996), 77–80.

117. In worship, individuals often confess, "in you, Yahweh, I take refuge" (or similar, e.g., Ps 7:2[1]; 16:1; 25:20, etc.); E. Gerstenberger, "*ḥsh*," *TLOT* 2:465.

118. The other possible derivation for this image is a winged god, but this is unlikely because there is no known association between protection and the gods' wings. Also unlikely is a reference to asylum in the sanctuary for this image, symbolized by the cherubim's wings in the temple (e.g., Ps 36:8[7]). See Joel M. LeMon, *Yahweh's Winged Form in the Psalms: Exploring Congruent Iconography and Texts*, OBO 242 (Göttingen: Vandenhoeck & Ruprecht, 2010), 83–94; A. S. van der Woude, "*kānāp*," *TLOT* 2:619.

119. See G. Kwakkel, "Under Yahweh's Wings," in *Metaphors in the Psalms*, ed. Pierre van Hecke and Antje Labahn, BETL (Leuven: Peeters, 2010), 141–65.

120. A similar image is "to seek refuge in the shadow (*ṣēl*)/shelter (*sēter*) of [Yahweh's] wings" (Pss 17:8; 36:8[7]; 57:2[1]; 61:5[4]; 63:8[7]).

121. The parallel in Ps 91:4 is "He will cover you with his *pinions*, and under his *wings* you will find refuge" (the same parallel is found in Ps 68:14[13]; Deut 32:11). See also BDB, 489.

122. Psalm 91:4 associates "wing" with God's "faithfulness" (*ʾĕmet*), and is also found in Pss 57:4, 11[3, 10] and 61:8[7].

# The Book of Ruth

way in which Yahweh protects is through the structure of ancient Israelite society. As discussed previously, one reason Boaz showed favor, including granting her protection in his field, is that they belong to the same clan through Naomi's husband. By going beyond the strict requirements of the gleaning law in protecting Ruth in his field, Boaz was in a real sense displaying Yahweh's kindness by acting as his wings.

This speech of Boaz is the climax of the scene, and it highlights important shifts in the narrative. Remarkably, in the middle of a scene that presents a litany of Boaz's generosity, the author focuses our attention on Ruth's kindness. Boaz has already given permission, protection, and provision for Ruth (vv. 8–9), and more is to come (vv. 14–16). Within this swirl of extravagant actions, however, Boaz's words cast our minds back to Ruth's firm loyalty to her mother-in-law. She committed herself not just to Naomi, but also to Naomi's people and God (1:16–17). The consequences of that decision are now developing. She views herself as a foreigner, but Boaz is integrating her into Bethlehemite society by treating her as one of his workers. And the significance of her devotion to Israel's God is underscored by Boaz: Yahweh will now notice and reward her actions. God does not turn a blind eye to those who seek refuge under his wings. Indeed, he will grant recompense for actions borne of kindness. Ruth's kindness to Naomi will redound with kindness from God. As the audience, we look forward to seeing how God will bless Ruth in Bethlehem.

**13** Ruth's response expresses both her request for Boaz to continue his favor and her gratitude to him. Her mention of finding favor in his eyes links to a motif mentioned twice by her—before she left to glean (v. 2) and once to Boaz already (v. 10). Some read this phrase as a statement of what has happened ("I have found"; e.g., ESV), but the verb is better read as a desire or a subtle request—*May I continue to find* (e.g., NIV).[123] Although Ruth does not explicitly thank Boaz, her words of self-abasement can be read as expressing gratitude.[124] She respectfully addresses him as "my lord/master" (*'ădōnî*),[125] and says she is *your maidservant, although I'm not like one of your maidservants.* From an honor-shame perspective, she reduces her "face" and

---

123. The *yiqtol 'emṣā'* has a modal nuance here. Holmstedt, *Handbook*, 130, suggests, "Why do I find favor in your eyes," but this is unlikely because it requires an unmarked interrogative (with an indicative *yiqtol*).

124. For the following, I am indebted to Edward J. Bridge, "Self-Abasement as an Expression of Thanks in the Hebrew Bible," *Bib* 92 (2011): 255–73.

125. This term indicates social order, and in speech "my lord" is used deferentially in opposition to terms such as "your servant" (*'abdəkā*; e.g., Gen 32:5[4]; 44:18; 1 Sam 29:8) or "your maidservant" (*šipḥātekā*; e.g., 1 Sam 25:27; 2 Sam 14:15). See E. Jenni, "*'ādôn*," *TLOT* 1:25.

## 2:4–17 Boaz's Field: Encounter between Ruth and Boaz

increases Boaz's "face" to highlight Boaz's generosity.[126] Her self-abasement also means that she avoids expressing obligation to Boaz, which is normally the case when gifts are accepted. This is consistent with her low social position in society as a gleaner who depends on the favor of generous landowners, a provision within the law (Lev 19:9–10; Deut 24:19–20).

Ruth expresses her desire for Boaz to continue his favor by describing the effect he has had on her already.[127] First, she appreciates how Boaz has *comforted* her. The *piel* of *nḥm* often refers to comforting or consoling those at the occasion of death (e.g., Gen 37:35; 2 Sam 10:2) or sorrow (e.g., Gen 50:21). In Gen 50:15–21, Joseph speaks "to comfort" or "to bring relief" to his brothers, for they feared retribution for the harm they had done to him. We can imagine the fear Ruth felt as she ventured into the field as a destitute, unattached foreign woman. Boaz reassured her by his provision and protection. Practical help is associated with the *piel* of *nḥm* elsewhere, where it is used of God assisting his people (e.g., Pss 23:4; 71:21; 86:17).[128] Other contexts of the *piel* of *nḥm* suggest the nuance of (re)establishing a social relationship, such as when God comforts his people after a time of judgment (e.g., Isa 12:1). In this sense, Boaz had also comforted Ruth by drawing her into a relationship with him and the social network of those working in his field. Second, Ruth appreciates that Boaz had *spoken to [her] heart*. The idiom "to speak to the heart," when used with the *piel* of *nḥm* (Gen 50:21; Isa 40:1–2) indicates a deep, heartfelt comfort,[129] spoken by a person who is compassionate and engaged, not just glib words spoken by a well-meaning but disinterested person. The idiom is also used in romantic contexts to mean "to speak tenderly," "to persuade to win affection" (Gen 34:3; Judg 19:3), which is most clearly seen when the idiom is in parallel to "allure" (*pth*; Hos 2:16[14]). This romantic possibility lingers in the background of Ruth's speech.[130] In short, Ruth's description of the two effects of Boaz's kindness on her would encourage him to do so all the more. Not surprisingly, we find him doing just that (vv. 14–16).

Her self-designation *maidservant* (*šipḥâ*) is significant for her changing identity. Previously she was amazed that Boaz would treat her well as a "foreigner" (v. 10). Now she is amazed that he would treat her as a "maidservant,"

---

126. Self-abasement to express gratitude is also found in Gen 32:11[10]; 1 Sam 25:41; 2 Sam 7:18; 9:8; 14:22; 16:4; 1 Kgs 3:7; Ps 116:16.

127. The modal *yiqtol* ("may I continue to find") is followed by two *qatal* verbs ("comforted" and "spoken" to the heart), which provide the basis for her request.

128. H. J. Stoebe, "*nḥm*," *TLOT* 2:736. These are linked in Ps 86:17: "For you, Yahweh, have helped and comforted me."

129. H. J. Stoebe, "*nḥm*," *TLOT* 2:735.

130. A female participant in one of my Ruth classes suggested Ruth is "flirting" with Boaz in 2:13.

# THE BOOK OF RUTH

*although*[131] *[she] is not like one of [his] maidservants.*[132] In this chapter, Boaz's female workers are called *naʿărôt,* "young women" or "female servants" (vv. 8, 23; cf. *nəʿārîm,* "male servant"; e.g., 2:9, 15), which is a general term, with no denotation of social rank. By referring to herself as a "maidservant," Ruth is in effect placing her foot on the social ladder at the lowest rung. As a "foreigner," she was not even on the ladder; now, she at least has a start. Later, she will call herself an *ʾāmâ* ("handmaid") which in many contexts is synonymous with *šipḥâ,* including in deferential speech (e.g., 1 Sam 1:12–18; 25:24–31; 2 Sam 14:4–19).[133] However, outside Genesis *ʾāmâ* is the preferred term for female servants in marital contexts,[134] which is the situation in 3:9. She will thus continue to climb the social ladder with her self-designation at the threshing floor, but in this verse, she is amazed that Boaz would provide her such succor. She does not know that he is related to her by marriage, and maybe the use of *šipḥâ* here hints at that kinship link. Given the use of assonance and wordplay throughout the Ruth narrative, *šipḥâ* creates an aural link to *mišpāḥâ* ("clan"), mentioned by the narrator at the beginning of this act (2:1, 3). Perhaps *šipḥâ* plays on this dramatic irony: she cannot understand how Boaz treats her (better than) a *šipḥâ* even though she is not even a *šipḥâ,* but we are reminded that she is in fact from Boaz's *mišpāḥâ.*

**14** Boaz continues his dialogue with Ruth, but this second conversation occurs *at mealtime.*[135] This is the midday meal, so some hours have elapsed between vv. 13 and 14—between Boaz's granting permission to glean and his invitation to eat. The mealtime exchange enhances Boaz's reputation as a man of great worth, as he showers Ruth with more acts of generosity and kindness.

This is a congenial scene with food and fellowship, the landowner Boaz eating with his workers after the morning's labor. Boaz asking Ruth to *come here* shows that she had politely kept her distance. She might have found Boaz's favor, but she was not presuming upon it. It is remarkable that Boaz would invite a Moabite outsider to join his working party to a meal, but then again, in the short time since his arrival on the scene, we have already come

---

131. The fronting of the pronoun *ʾānōkî* in this context signals the shift from Boaz (who is the one who "spoke" in the previous clause) to Ruth as the subject.

132. Reading the *yiqtol ʾehyê* with a present progressive, rather than with a futuristic nuance.

133. In some passages, "female slave" is a better translation than "female servant" or "maidservant" (e.g., Exod 21:20; Deut 28:68; Esth 7:4), where *ʿebed* is the male equivalent.

134. See Edward J. Bridge, "Female Slave vs Female Slave: *ʾāmâ* and *šipḥâ* in the HB," *JHebS* 12 (2012): 1–21.

135. The phrase "at mealtime" can be attached to the words of the narrator or Boaz (see notes on v. 14). But Boaz inviting her to eat with him and his harvesters directly after his instructions to glean (v. 13) would render the narrative too disjointed.

## 2:4–17 Boaz's Field: Encounter between Ruth and Boaz

to expect such open-mindedness and -handedness. He previously offered her water (v. 9), now he invites her to partake of the food (*eat some of the bread*)[136] prepared for his workers and to *dip [her] morsel in the vinegar*. Her "piece, morsel" (*pat*) is probably shorthand for "morsel of bread" (*pat leḥem*; Gen 18:5; Judg 19:5; 1 Sam 2:36; 28:22; 1 Kgs 17:11; Prov 28:21).[137] The word *ḥōmeṣ* could refer to a sour drink (cf. Num 6:3),[138] but since she is invited to dip her piece of bread in it, it is more likely a sour sauce derived from spoiled wine.[139] It would moisten dry bread or add flavor and thus enjoyment to her meal. Boaz not only gives her food out of charity; he also wants her to eat as well as the rest of his company.

Ruth accepts his lunch invitation: *she sat beside the harvesters*. Her position "beside" (*miṣṣad*) instead of "among" the reapers might show her modesty and her transitional status, but the key point is that she is now part of the group. We should not underestimate the significance of this for a newly arrived foreigner, an outsider who had left her family behind. Similar to today, eating together in biblical times held social significance beyond partaking in food. People ate and drank to celebrate special occasions (e.g., Ps 23:5; Matt 22:1–14), to express hospitality (e.g., Gen 18:1–8), to culminate covenants (e.g., Gen 31:51–54; Exod 24:1–11), and to express fellowship or acceptance (e.g., Luke 15:1–32; 10:1–10; Gal 2:11–14). Ruth, a foreign gleaner, who was not one of Boaz's maidservants (vv. 10, 13), is accepted into the fold of Boaz's broader household.

His next action is even more intimate than his words: *and he handed her roasted grain*. The narrator's choice of the verb *ṣābaṭ* draws further attention to Boaz's action since it is the only time it is found in the Old Testament. In Mishnaic Hebrew, *ṣbt* means "to seize, grab, to handle," in relation to a vessel or jar,[140] which is similar to Akkadian *ṣabātum* and Arabic *ḍabaṭa*. It could also be related to the Ugaritic noun *mṣbtm*, "tongs."[141] The LXX and Vulg. read "to heap, pile up," perhaps from Heb. *ṣbr* instead of *ṣbt* (cf. v. 16, *ṣebet*, "bundle,

---

136. In *min-halleḥem* the *min* is partitive, and the definite article indicates that the bread was specifically prepared for the workers. The noun *leḥem* could be a synecdoche for "food" (cf. 1:8) but taken with the next phrase, "bread" is better.

137. Heb. *pat* also refers to bread in 2 Sam 12:3; Job 31:17; Prov 23:8.

138. Vinegar, *ḥōmeṣ*, can be as unpalatable as poison (Ps 69:22 [21]; cf. Matt 27:34, 48; Mark 15:36; Luke 23:36; John 19:29–30), setting teeth on edge (Prov 10:26).

139. For further discussion, see D. Kellermann, "*ḥmṣ*," *TDOT* 4:490–92. Nathan MacDonald, *What Did the Ancient Israelites Eat? Diet in Biblical Times* (Grand Rapids: Eerdmans, 2008), 22–23, suggests that wine was the principal drink in ancient Israel, and when spoiled, was used as an adjunct to bread.

140. Marcus Jastrow, *A Dictionary of the Targumim, the Talmud Babli and Yerushalmi, and the Midrashic Literature* (Peabody, MA: Hendrickson, 1926), 1258.

141. *HALOT* 3:997.

# The Book of Ruth

heap, handful").[142] So here it could mean "to pile up" or "to hand over, pass," but since a surplus is described at the end of the verse, the latter seems the better translation, with the idea that he handed her more than she could eat. The hapax legomenon *ṣābaṭ* could have been chosen to alliterate with another hapax legomenon, *haṣṣəbātîm* ("the bundles, handfuls," v. 16). Even within this verse, word sounds bind Boaz's words to his action. Three consonants in the verb *wəṭābaltə* (*t-b-l*), "and you dip," reoccur in the expression *wayyiṣbāt-lāh* (*b-t-l*), "he handed to her."[143] Likewise, the repetition of the *ṣ* sound gently binds together Boaz's words (*bahōmeṣ*, "in the vinegar"), Ruth's action (*miṣṣad haqqôṣərîm*, "beside the harvesters"), and Boaz's action (*wayyiṣbāt-lāh*; "he handed to her"). Boaz's words and actions ensure Ruth does not eat scraps as a beggar; instead, she eats as a special guest because Boaz does not personally serve food to his other workers. Ruth's response to this special treatment is not recorded, but we can imagine her astonishment.

The ears of wheat and barley could be eaten fresh (2 Kgs 4:42) or the fresh grain roasted in the fire (Lev 2:14; Josh 5:11). Boaz hands Ruth *roasted grain*, which was a common food in ancient Israel (1 Sam 17:17; 25:18; 2 Sam 17:28). He was so generous that *she ate until she was full, and she had some left over*. In the context of survival subsistence, such an abundance of food is rarely mentioned in the Old Testament. Ruth went to the field to glean for her mother-in-law and herself because they had no food. Now, through the largesse of Boaz, things are turning around for them. Indeed, his actions are characterized by *ḥesed*—acts of kindness beyond expectation, performed within a covenant/kinship context. Previously, Boaz prayed that Yahweh would repay Ruth for the loyalty shown to her Israelite mother-in-law and provide Ruth a full reward (v. 12). In the Old Testament, eating until satisfaction (the verbs *'ākal*, "to eat," and *šāba'*, "be sated, satisfied") is usually due to God's generosity (e.g., Deut 6:11; 8:10; 11:15; 31:20; Joel 2:26; Ps 22:27[26]; 78:29; Neh 9:25; 2 Chr 31:10), as is eating and having some left over (the verbs *'ākal*, "to eat," and *yātar* [*hiphil*], "to have abundance, left over," 2 Kgs 4:43–44; 2 Chr 31:10). Thus, we can understand Boaz's generosity as reflecting God's lavish provision. In other words, God's reward to Ruth is being given through Boaz.

**15** Refreshed and with a full stomach, Ruth *rose to glean*. Her action seems to trigger another *command* from Boaz to *his male servants*, who presumably were still gathered around.[144] His speech can be structured as orders alternat-

---

142. Vulg. "she heaped up for herself."

143. My thanks to Gary Rendsburg for this observation, personal communication on Oct. 16, 2019.

144. If they were still eating, it would present Ruth as eager to glean; Hubbard, *Ruth*, 175–76.

## 2:4–17 BOAZ'S FIELD: ENCOUNTER BETWEEN RUTH AND BOAZ

ing between permission and prohibition: what the harvesters were to allow her to do and what they were not to do.

> A  Even among the sheaves let her glean,
>   B  and do not humiliate her (v. 15).
> A  In fact, even pull out for her some stalks from the handfuls
>   and abandon them that she may glean them,
>   B  and do not rebuke her (v. 16).

The noun *nəʿārāyw* is masculine plural, so it could be translated "male servants" or all the servants. But since Boaz previously warned the male servants not to harass Ruth (v. 9), it is more likely that Boaz addresses them here as well. Of course, any female servants present would have overheard, so his command applies to them too. Boaz's first warning was indirect; now, it is direct and emphatic. As in my translation, *among the sheaves* is fronted for focus, and Boaz's words begin with an emphatic particle *gam*, "even, indeed." The double stress was needed because of the extraordinary location—among the piles of harvested grain, which would significantly increase the amount she would glean. This is the same location that the overseer reported Ruth as requesting when she arrived in the field (v. 7). She most likely did not make that request, but now, perhaps in response to the overseer's words, Boaz allows her to glean there. Given Ruth's Moabite background, the overseer's attitude is perhaps understandable, but, by contrast, Boaz's kindness shines all the more brightly.

A prohibition follows Boaz's permission: *do not humiliate her*. The verb *kālam* has the sense of "to shame, disgrace, humiliate," and Boaz wants to prevent this outcome for Ruth, either from molestation by his male servants (vv. 9, 22) or rebukes by his male or female servants (v. 16).[145] Danger lurked in the fields for a poor, single, foreign woman, but it seems that Boaz detected additional animosity toward her, not just in his overseer but also in his harvesters. In a group-oriented society, they probably did not understand why this foreigner should receive special privileges. And perhaps they did not want this "Moabite woman" (v. 6) to take advantage of Israel's gleaning laws. We can speculate on other reasons for their wariness: they were hired, whereas she arrived uninvited; and they wanted to protect their boss's field from an outsider. Knowing that Ruth would have already felt shame because she was a foreign outsider (v. 10), Boaz is quick to ensure her shame is not compounded. He had granted her a sense of belonging within the gleaning community and hence granted her ascribed honor. Prohibiting his

---

145. Cf. Wagner, "*klm*," *TDOT* 7:188. The nuance of "harm" (*HALOT* 2:480; 1 Sam 25:7) is brought out in the parallel clause (v. 16).

## The Book of Ruth

workers from humiliating her is a way of asking them to recognize her fledgling social standing in the community. But he is not done yet with his show of generosity.

**16** Boaz's final command is strongly worded, as signaled by the introductory *wəgam* (*in fact*, cf. v. 8). He tells his harvesters to *even pull out for her some stalks from the handfuls*. Further emphasis is signaled by the infinitive absolute followed by the *yiqtol* of the same root, probably *šll* (reflected in the translation with "even").[146] This hapax legomenon means "to pull out," perhaps related to the Arabic cognate *šll*, "to draw out (a sword from a scabbard)."[147] What the harvesters were to pull out is difficult to know for certain, since *ṣəbāṭîm*, translated "handfuls," only occurs here in the Old Testament. In Arabic, *dabtat* means "handful, sheaf," so here it seems to refer to the handfuls of ears of grain held in one hand by a reaper (the other hand held the sickle). "Pull out" does not have an object, so does Boaz ask his harvesters to pull out "ears of grain from the handfuls" or "some of the handfuls"?[148] The former is more likely, given our understanding of the verb "pull out." As noted above, it may be that the *hapax legomenon haṣṣəbāṭîm*, "the handfuls," was chosen to assonate with *wəṭābalta*, "and he handed"; the exceptional Hebrew words reflect Boaz's exceptional provision.

We might not be able to pin down the specifics of Boaz's instructions, but the implications are clear: Ruth is granted the convenience of gleaning grain without cutting or pulling from the stalk. He also tells the harvesters to *abandon* the handfuls of cut grain in their hands *that she may glean them*, thus making sure that she collects even more. Within the Ruth narrative, *ʿāzab*, "to abandon, leave behind," described Ruth's leaving her family and homeland (1:16), as reiterated by Boaz (2:11). Now he blesses Ruth for her decision by "leaving" grain for her, which will lead to Naomi identifying Yahweh/Boaz as not "abandoning" his kindness (2:20).

Prohibition again follows permission because Boaz anticipates that his superabundant generosity would generate bitterness in his servants. This bitterness would not be taken out on him, but on Ruth, so he commands them, *do not rebuke her*. The verb *gāʿar* means "to scold, rebuke,"[149] and, similar to the connotation of harm found in *kalam* (v. 15), brings out the hostility Ruth could have faced in the fields. For *gāʿar* here has the sense of the harvesters

---

146. Cf. Bush, *Ruth, Esther*, 126, "In fact, be sure you pull out."

147. BDB, 1021; *HALOT* 4:1531.

148. The object of the verb "pull out" can be understood from the context—"stalks" or "ears of grain." Most commentators take this line of interpretation, although the lack of an object for the verb means that the *min* in *min-haṣṣəbāṭîm* could be read as partitive, i.e., Boaz instructs his harvesters to leave entire handfuls of grain rather than just stalks from the handfuls of grain; so Joüon, *Ruth*, 61; cf. Vulg.

149. See G. Liedke, "*gʿr*," *TLOT* 1:322.

2:4–17 Boaz's Field: Encounter between Ruth and Boaz

driving Ruth away with angry cries, stopping her from gleaning in an otherwise forbidden location.[150] Again, Boaz is quick not only to provide for but also to protect Ruth.

In these last commands to his harvesters (vv. 15–16), Boaz is generous beyond the requirement of the gleaning laws. His allowances for Ruth can be structured chiastically:

> A  Permission to glean in his field (v. 8)
>> B  Protection from male harvesters (v. 9)
>>> C  Provision of water (v. 9)
>>> C'  Provision of food (v. 14)
>> B'  Protection from male harvesters (vv. 15–16)
> A'  Permission to glean at a privileged location in his field (vv. 15–16)

Under the law, Boaz was only obliged to allow Ruth to glean in his field (v. 8). Landowners were to leave the corners of their fields unharvested for the poor (Lev 19:9-10; 23:22) and were not to return for unharvested sheaves (Deut 24:19-21). To this basic legal requirement, Boaz added protection (vv. 9, 15–16) and provision (vv. 9, 14) and special permission (vv. 15–16), all triggered by the overseer's report of Ruth's request (v. 7) and spurred on by her encouraging responses (vv. 10, 13). This greatly anticipated "man of great worth" has lived up to his billing. His actions are evidence of his virtuous character—marked by compassion, kindness, and charity. Yet within the Old Testament, Boaz's actions recall the kindness and generosity of God, who had first blessed him. As such, we can see Boaz as the one through whom God is beginning to "reward" Ruth for taking shelter under Yahweh's wings (v. 12).

**17**  Refreshed by her meal, Ruth *gleaned in the field until evening*. She had arrived in the field in the morning (v. 7) but did not start gleaning until Boaz gave her permission (v. 8). So she diligently worked until the end of the day to make the most of Boaz's generosity. Then she *beat out* the collected grain from its stalk, probably using a stick or rod (cf. Isa 28:27).[151] The amount of grain was extraordinary—*about an ephah*[152] *of barley*. The word *'êpâ* is an Egyptian loanword, a unit of dry measure, especially grains (Amos 8:5;

150. Caquot, "*gā'ar*," *TDOT* 3:50; similarly, James M. Kennedy, "The Root *G'R* in the Light of Semantic Analysis," *JBL* 106 (1987): 62.

151. The verb *ḥābaṭ*, "beat out," refers to threshing small quantities of grain and to "beating" trees to shake out the fruit (e.g., olives, Deut 24:20). Gideon "beats out" wheat in a winepress to hide from the Midianites (Judg 6:11). Large quantities of grain were threshed on an open floor with cattle (e.g., Isa 28:27, 28); BDB, 286.

152. Heb. *kə'êpâ* could mean "about an ephah" (reading the *kaph* as a mark of approximation) or "exactly an ephah" (*kaph* as a mark of precision; *kaph veritas*); see Campbell,

# THE BOOK OF RUTH

Mic 6:10).[153] It was equal to the liquid measure bath (Ezek 45:11) and ten omers (Exod 16:36; Ezek 45:11). The exact amount in modern equivalents is hard to estimate because ancient societies probably had differing measuring norms based on local customs, and the size may have changed from the pre-exilic to post-exilic periods.[154] Estimates range from 22 to 40 liters (5.8 to 10.6 gallons), with a weight from 13.6 to 22.7 kilograms (30 to 50 pounds).[155] For comparison, an omer of manna fed a person for a day (Exod 16:16), David brought an ephah of parched grain and ten loaves for his three brothers (1 Sam 17:17), and the ration for a male worker at Mari (Old Babylonian period, nineteenth century BC) was 0.45 to 0.9 kilograms (1 to 2 pounds) per day.[156] In a day, Ruth probably collected enough grain to feed herself and Naomi for at least a week. In this verse, Ruth's large gleanings show that Boaz's workers followed his commands and that Ruth worked hard.

The amount Ruth gleaned creates literary links. Within the narrative, the word *'êpâ* creates a soundplay with the word *'êpōh*, "where," two verses later (see comment on v. 19). "An ephah" also draws an inner-biblical link between the Ruth narrative and the narrative of Hannah and Elkanah (1 Sam 1–2). There is already a connection between Ruth and Hannah since Samuel is the son of the latter and the anointer of the first two kings, including David. Both narratives thus concern the coming monarchy. And their similar expressions about being better than seven/ten sons (Ruth 4:15 and 1 Sam 1:8; see comments on 4:15) reinforces the connection. Given these inner-biblical links, the use of "an ephah" brings out a contrast.[157] Ruth offers "an ephah" to her mother-in-law, while Hannah offered "a three-year-old bull, one ephah of flour and a skin of wine" to God, to give thanks for her son (1 Sam 1:24). Ruth has the same amount of barley but no son. She has the fruit of the land but still waits for the fruit of the womb.

Before we move onto the next scene, we will consider Boaz's application of the law. His is a generous application according to the principle of kindness, based not on the letter of the law but the moral logic underlying it. Boaz protects and provides for her way beyond the minimal requirements

---

*Ruth*, 104. In this verse, it does not make much difference to our understanding of the large amount Ruth collected.

153. It also refers to a vessel ("basket") of the same measure (e.g., Zech 5:6–10).

154. For discussions, see R. Fuller, "*'êpâ*," *NIDOTTE* 1:382–88; M. A. Powell, "Weights and Measures," *ABD* 6:897–908.

155. Eighth-century BC vessels from Tell Beit Mirsim and Lachish marked *bt* ("bath") contained approximately twenty-two liters. Josephus (*Ant.* 3.8.3 §197) suggests the higher end of the range; cf. forty liters, *HALOT* 1:43; BDB, 144.

156. For the Mari evidence, see Sasson, *Ruth*, 57.

157. After Grossman, *Ruth*, 173–74.

of the gleaning law (Deut 24:19–22). Like his field overseer, Boaz could have applied the law restrictively by viewing Ruth as an outsider because of the Moabites' previous inhospitality and their tempting of Israel into idolatry (Deut 23:1–6). And perhaps some hostility toward Ruth the Moabite can be detected in Boaz's commands for his male servants not to harm her. Boaz's kindness is even more remarkable against the backdrop of lawlessness that marks the judges, the historical period in which the Ruth narrative is set. He knows Ruth had pledged her allegiance to Yahweh, so she will not seduce him into idolatry. He also knows she had shown hospitality to Naomi's family in Moab. Thus, the law excluding Moabites did not apply in Ruth's case.[158]

Although Boaz was "a man of great worth," which also includes his material wealth, this does not mean he would have automatically shared his wealth. This can be deduced from the laws commanding generosity toward the poor and needy, both fellow Israelites and sojourners. These laws not only outline the requirements but also provide motivations for obedience. God's people are a redeemed people, freed to serve him who places ethical demands on them. They have been redeemed from oppressive bondage under Pharaoh to become slaves of God (Lev 25:42, 55). In response, they were to act generously and with compassion toward sojourners (e.g., Deut 10:19), indentured servants (e.g., Deut 15:13–15), and the marginalized and the underprivileged (e.g., Deut 24:17–21). God's people must not repeat the oppression of their former masters; instead, a redeemed people must seek to redeem others through generosity (Deut 24:18, 22). God's people are to give from what God has blessed them with (e.g., Deut 15:14). They are commanded to not be tight-fisted but open-handed toward the needy, presumably because stinginess was the attitude of many. Such an attitude is understandable in a subsistence agricultural society, where generosity requires trust in God, even for the relatively wealthy. And, in Boaz's assertion that Ruth's kind loyalty to Naomi deserved reward from God, we find an echo of a motivation to be generous in the law: "Give freely . . . because for this Yahweh your God will bless you in all that you undertake" (Deut 15:10). Boaz understands this virtuous cycle of blessing, and as someone who has been richly blessed by God, his generous attitude is manifested in his acts of kindness beyond legal requirement. In the New Testament, the apostle Paul says that Christians have experienced an even greater redemption in Jesus Christ. We thus have even greater motivation to be cheerful, generous givers to those in need (cf. 2 Cor 8:1–15; 9:7), but especially to others who have sought refuge under God's wings, those of the household of faith (cf. Gal 6:10).

---

158. See section "Applying the Law" in the introduction.

# The Book of Ruth

## F. HOME: NAOMI AND RUTH DEBRIEF (2:18–23)

The location and actors for this final scene of act 2 are the same as the first, but the mood cannot be more different. Naomi's despondency is transformed as she sees Ruth returning home from the field with an enormous haul of grain (v. 18). This scene draws out the significance of Ruth's encounter with Boaz (vv. 4–17) and flags future events. Ruth set out to glean in a field where she would find favor (2:2), the audience knows Boaz has lived up to his reputation (cf. v. 1), but now we share in Naomi's elated surprise at Ruth's reveal of Boaz's identity (v. 19). As Naomi's accusation against God (1:20–21) turns to praise and gratitude (2:20), we are reminded of God's hand working through human actors (cf. v. 12). Boaz's acts of kindness included provision, protection, and inclusion for Ruth (vv. 21–23), yet there is a hint of more to come: Boaz is not just a relative (v. 1), not just a *close* relative, he is a "kinsman-redeemer" (v. 20). Ruth gleaning "until the end of the barley and wheat harvests" (v. 23) draws a thread back to the end of act 1, when Naomi and Ruth arrived in Bethlehem "at the beginning of the barley harvest" (1:22). We can draw the thread back even further, to the mention of God breaking the famine (1:6). The harvest provision is God's providence and blessing.

¹⁸*She carried it*ᵃ *and entered the town. Her mother-in-law saw*ᵇ *what she had gleaned. She also brought out and gave her what she had left over from her full meal.*ᶜ

¹⁹*Her mother-in-law said to her, "Where did you glean today? Where did you work?*ᵈ *May he who took notice of you be blessed." So she reported to her mother-in-law whom she worked with. She said, "The name of the man whom I worked with today is Boaz."*

²⁰*Naomi said to her daughter-in-law, "May he be blessed by Yahweh, who has not abandoned his kindness to the living and the dead!" Then Naomi said to her, "The man is our close relative, he is one of our kinsman-redeemers."*ᵉ

²¹*Ruth the Moabite*ᶠ *said, "Also, he even said to me, 'Cling to the male servants*ᵍ *who are mine until they have finished all the harvest that is mine.'"*

²²*Naomi said to Ruth, her daughter-in-law, "It is better,*ʰ *my daughter, that you go out with his female servants, so they will not assault you in another field."*ⁱ

²³*So she clung to Boaz's female servants to glean until the barley and wheat harvests were finished. And she lived*ʲ *with her mother-in-law.*

a. The implied object of the verb *nāśāʾ*, "to lift, carry," is the threshed grain from the previous verse.

b. Heb. *wattēreʾ*, "she saw" (*qal*). Two Kennicott MSS (18 and 109; *BHQ*, 53–54*) read the verb as a *hiphil*, and add a direct object marker before "her mother-in-law," which produces "she [Ruth] showed her mother-in-law" (supported by Syr. and Vulg.). This reading avoids a change in subject, from Ruth to Naomi to Ruth. However, the MTᴸ is preferred because

## 2:18-23 HOME: NAOMI AND RUTH DEBRIEF

of the lack of a direct object marker, subject switching is found elsewhere (e.g., 4:13), and it is the more difficult reading (supported by LXX, 2QRuth[a], and Tg.).

c. Heb. *miśśāba'āh* can be read as an infinitive construct with a feminine suffix, and the *min* marks the cause of the situation (the so-called ablative use of *min*, *IBHS* §11.2.11d; e.g., 2 Sam 3:37; Ezek 28:18), so "because of her fullness." Or it could be read as the noun *śōba'*, "satisfaction, fullness," and the *min* has a temporal function (see *IBHS* §11.2.11c; e.g., Ps 73:20; Hos 6:2), so "after her fullness." The former is preferred in this context, although it does not make much difference to the meaning of the verse. MT[L] *miśśāba'āh* is supported by LXX and Tg., whereas 2QRuth[a], supported by Vulg., reads *bśb'h*, which is consistent with the ablative sense of *min* in MT[L].

d. The root *'śh* here and elsewhere in this verse means "work"; *HALOT* 2:891.

e. Heb. *miggō'ălēnû* looks like a singular noun with the preposition *min*. In this context, the *min* is partitive, which requires a plural reading, "one of our kinsman-redeemers" (so LXX, Syr., and Vulg.). The reconstruction of 2QRuth[a] supports MT[L]. It may thus be a shortened spelling for the plural (see GKC §91k).

f. LXX, Syr., OL, and Vulg. omit "the Moabite," with the first three adding "to her mother-in-law." 2QRuth[a] and Tg. support the MT[L].

g. Heb. *hanna'ărîm* could refer to both male and female servants or just male servants; see comment on v. 21. For further discussion, see Lim, "Otherness," 103–6.

h. The adjective *tôb* could be understood in an absolute ("good"; Tg., LXX), comparative ("better"; Vulg.), or superlative ("best") sense; see *IBHS* §14.4–5; JM §141g. Since Naomi is correcting Ruth's misconception, either of the latter two senses is in view. The comparative sense is found in 1 Sam 27:1; 2 Sam 18:3 and is preferred here.

i. Syr. "in the field of someone you do not know."

j. A few Heb. MSS read *wattāšāb*, "and she returned." This reading is supported by Vulg., which takes this clause as the beginning of the next chapter. LXX, Syr., and Tg. support the MT[L], which is to be retained.

This scene can be structured as a chiasm:[159]

> A   Ruth carries gleanings to town, her *mother-in-law* sees what she has *gleaned*, she gave her what she had left over because of her <u>fullness</u> (v. 18)
>
> > B   *Naomi* asks <u>where</u> Ruth gleaned and blesses the one who took notice of her
> >
> > > C   *Ruth* tells Naomi that she <u>worked with Boaz</u> (v. 19)
> > >
> > > > D   *Naomi* blesses <u>Boaz</u> because of his and/or Yahweh's unceasing kindness
> > > >
> > > > D'   *Naomi* tells Ruth that <u>Boaz</u> is a relative and redeemer (v. 20)
> > >
> > > C'   *Ruth* tells Naomi that <u>Boaz told her to stay with his servants</u> until the end of the harvest (v. 21)

---

159. Modified from Bush, *Ruth, Esther*, 131–32.

## THE BOOK OF RUTH

> B' *Naomi* tells Ruth to <u>stay with Boaz's female servants</u> because
> she might be assaulted in another field (v. 22)
>
> A' Ruth clung to Boaz's female servants to *glean* until the barley and
> wheat harvests were <u>finished</u>. She lived with her *mother-in-law*
> (v. 22).

This third and final scene is mostly a dialogue, which takes place with the same speakers at the same location as the first of act 2. The scene is enclosed by a narrative introduction and conclusion that describe the actions of Ruth and include "her mother-in-law" (*ḥămôtāh*), "glean" (*laqqēṭ*), and the idea of fullness or completion (A-A'). Each of the three paired elements contains the verb *'āmar*, "to say." Naomi initiates the conversation and has the last say (B-B'). In this pair of speeches, she focuses on the location of Ruth's gleaning, first with questions, then with a warning (B-B'). Ruth does not speak until spoken to, her first speech revealing with whom she worked, and the second revealing with whom Boaz said she should work until the end of the harvest (C-C'). The central elements are Naomi's benediction on Boaz and her revelation that he is a kinsman-redeemer of the two women. This structure highlights the predominance of Naomi's speeches and the crucial importance of her words in D-D'. Apart from Ruth's last designation ("the Moabite"), the rest foreground the mother- and daughter-in-law relationship. Ruth's respect for her mother-in-law (filial piety) is reflected in this dialogue, and Naomi dominates the discussion as the head of her family unit.

There are similarities between this Naomi-Ruth dialogue (vv. 19–22) and the Boaz-Ruth dialogue (vv. 8–14).[160]

| Boaz (vv. 8–9) | Naomi (v. 19a) |
|---|---|
| Ruth (v. 10) | Ruth (v. 19b) |
| Boaz (v. 11–12) | Naomi (v. 20) |
| Ruth (v. 13) | Ruth (v. 21) |
| Boaz (v. 14) | Naomi (v. 22) |

As an Israelite landowner in his field, Boaz dominates the discussion, like Naomi as head of her Israelite household at her home. Although Naomi and Boaz never meet in the narrative, the core of Naomi's speeches focus on the significance of Boaz (v. 20), and the core of Boaz's speeches outline the significance of what Ruth had done for Naomi as the trigger for his generous response (vv. 11–12). Both Boaz and Naomi invoke a blessing—Boaz on Ruth, and Naomi on Boaz (vv. 12, 20). And Boaz's initial concern for Ruth's safety and instruction to stay close to his maidservants (vv. 8–9) form an inclusio

---

160. After Zakovitch, *Rut*, 125.

## 2:18–23 HOME: NAOMI AND RUTH DEBRIEF

with Naomi's final concern and instruction for the same (v. 22). The similarities reinforce the stature of Boaz and Naomi—Israelites from the older generation—and their shared concern for Ruth the Moabite.

**18** There is a quick shift in location, from the field to the town. *Ruth carried* the collected grain, which would have taken some effort since it weighed up to 22.7 kilograms (50 pounds). The first time *she entered the town*, her mother-in-law complained that she was empty, although her daughter-in-law was beside her (1:19–22). This time Ruth enters alone, with a huge bundle of grain (perhaps in a shawl slung over her shoulder) to give to her mother-in-law. Naomi immediately *saw what she had gleaned*, and we can imagine her astonished look, perhaps with a gaping mouth. For a day which had begun with uncertainty had finished with plenty. But there was more—her daughter-in-law also brought out and gave her the surplus roasted grain from her lunch. No doubt this was a surprise for Naomi (as it is a surprise for us) since it was not mentioned that she stashed away her leftovers. The Hebrew is chiastic: Ruth ate until she was full and had some left over (*wattiśbaʿ wattōtar*, v. 14), now she brings out to give to her mother-in-law what she had left over after eating her fill (*hôtirâ miśśābǝʿāh*). Boaz handed her roasted grain, some of which she had kept to pass on to her mother-in-law. Even as she was filling her stomach, she was thinking of her mother-in-law. Previously, Naomi was left without (*wattiśśāʾēr min*) her two children and her husband (1:5); now she enjoys the leftovers from (*hôtirâ min*) Ruth.[161]

**19** Naomi's amazement at seeing what Ruth carried and the leftovers she brought out is reflected in her two parallel questions. First, *Where did you glean today?* Naomi's question begins with a relatively rare word *ʾêpōh*, "where," which forms a soundplay with *ʾêpâ*, "ephah," two verses earlier. For a reader of the ancient Hebrew text, it would have been written the same way.[162] We are to make the connection between Ruth's massive grain haul and Naomi's question, and perhaps the interrogative particle was triggered by Naomi's estimation of the amount Ruth gleaned.[163] Second, *Where did you work?* The word *ʾānâ* is also relatively rare, also meaning "where" (e.g., 2 Kgs 6:6; Isa 10:3).[164] The redundancy of this second question reflects Naomi's excitement, and we can imagine her face and mood transformed from despondency to delight.

Naomi's two breathless questions about location are followed by an exclamation of benediction on the benefactor, *May he who took notice of you be blessed!*

---

161. Cf. Joüon, *Ruth*, 62; 1 Kgs 9:21.

162. The reader thus would have enjoyed the visual and the aural effect; Rendsburg, *How the Bible Is Written*, 209.

163. So Hubbard, *Ruth*, 183.

164. The word is comprised of the locative interrogative and the directional suffix *he*, usually meaning "where to?" (e.g., Gen 16:8; Josh 2:5); *HALOT* 1:69.

# The Book of Ruth

She knows that Ruth's huge haul and roasted grain are not primarily because of the field in which Ruth gleaned but the generosity of the field owner. If the word order of this blessing is unusual,[165] it would emphasize "he who took notice." The blessings of Naomi and Boaz (2:12) draw another thread between them.

In Naomi's blessing, we sense a significant change in her. First, she asked God to bless her daughters-in-law (1:8–9), then she accused God of cursing her (1:13, 20–21), but now she returns to asking God to bless. Her use of the participle *makkîrēk*, "he who took notice of you," from the verb *nkr*, points to those responsible for this transformation. Ruth spoke of Boaz as the one who "paid attention" to her (v. 10), and although Naomi does not know it yet, she referred to the same person. Boaz acknowledged Ruth without her knowing the kinship connection, and Naomi blesses Ruth's benefactor without knowing the kinship connection. For Ruth, Boaz taking notice of her meant that she had found favor in his eyes (v. 10), the very thing she set out to seek at the beginning of the day (2:2). Yet Ruth returned with more than just grain. Her loyalty triggered a Godward reflex in Boaz (2:9), and now Naomi experiences the same.

There have been attempts to amend the redundancy in the rest of v. 19, but it is best explained stylistically. Naomi's double questions about location were followed by a blessing on Ruth's unnamed benefactor. The narrator tells us that Ruth *reported to her mother-in-law whom she worked with*. Then Ruth says, *The name of the man whom I worked with today is Boaz*. The LXX and Syr. read "where she worked," which not only removes the redundancy but also answers Naomi's "where" questions. Yet the Tg. and Vulg. support the MT, so if we retain the MT, why the redundancy? First, the repetition slows the narrative pace and creates suspense for Ruth's revelation. Second, just as Naomi's excitement was heard in her two questions, so Ruth's excitement may be heard in the repetition. This repetition is punctuated by the alliteration of *shin*, the gutturals *aleph* and *ayin*, and *mem*:[166]

- *'ăšer-'āśətâ 'immô*, "whom she worked with"
- *šēm hā'îš 'ăšer 'āśîtî 'immô hayyôm*, "the name of the man whom I worked with today."

Both the narrator and Ruth state that she worked "with him" (*'immô*) rather than, say, "in his field."[167] Yet, there is no description of Boaz working

---

165. See 1 Kgs 10:9 = 2 Chr 9:8; Prov 5:18; Jer 20:14; cf. Gen 27:33; Deut 7:14. Those who find the verb-subject word order significant emphatic include Campbell, *Ruth*, 134; Block, *Discourse*, 144; and those who do not include Bush, *Ruth, Esther*, 133–34; Holmstedt, *Handbook*, 140.

166. Cf. Porten, "Scroll," 36; Hubbard, *Ruth*, 185n24.

167. "With whom she/I worked" is better English grammar (so most EVV), but I translate "whom she/I worked with" to reflect the surprising Hebrew preposition "with."

172

## 2:18–23 HOME: NAOMI AND RUTH DEBRIEF

in the field, and Ruth stays close to his servants to glean (vv. 8, 21). This may be a way of saying that she worked "under the authority of" Boaz,[168] or, given his tender generosity, may intimate the closeness she felt to him.[169] They did not work side-by-side in his field, but they did share a meal and the harvest of his field.

Ruth's answer is indirect but follows the flow of the conversation. Although Naomi twice asked about location, Ruth answers about identity. In a sense, to name the field owner reveals where she gleaned, but Ruth's reply also follows the sequence of the conversation because Naomi shifted her focus from field to field owner. Like Naomi, Ruth realized that "who" or "with whom" was the crucial factor. Ruth's reply shifted the focus to her benefactor, and she delayed naming him for as long as possible, teasingly perhaps, even to the last word in her sentence: *Boaz*.[170] In response to her mother-in-law's "today" (*hayyôm*) in her first question, Ruth adds *today*, although it is unnecessary. All this adds to the suspense for Naomi and the pleasure for us, the audience. We were conspiratorially introduced to him before the action began (v. 1), and Ruth met him face-to-face in his field (v. 3). Now Naomi is let in on the secret. As the reality dawns on her, we can feel her world shifting, and we anticipate her response to this revelation.

**20** Naomi's next words are the turning point of the conversation, as reflected in the chiastic structure above. Upon hearing that the benefactor was Boaz, Naomi revealed his dual significance for them, marked out by the repetition of *Naomi said*. For the first time in this scene, she is named, and her foregrounding prepares us for her important words. First, she again breaks out with a spontaneous blessing (cf. v. 19), *May he be blessed by Yahweh*. In the phrase *layhwh*, the *lamed* could be read to indicate the goal of the action, so "may he be blessed to Yahweh," but it is better to read it as the source of the blessing, so "may he be blessed by Yahweh." At this point, Naomi has not revealed that Boaz is their kinsman, so her blessing is solely based on his generosity, not on family responsibility. The latter might have played a part (cf. 2:11–12), but the dominant note is the former because he went much beyond the requirement of the law.

Naomi's next clause, *who has not abandoned his kindness to the living and the dead*, has stimulated much discussion. First, is *ḥasdô*, "his kindness," the subject or object of the verb *'āzab*, "abandoned"? The former would yield the translation "whose kindness has not abandoned," while the latter "who has not abandoned his kindness." Although the latter is the better reading in

---

168. Jeremy Schipper, "Translating the Preposition *'m* in the Book of Ruth," *VT* 63 (2013): 665–66.

169. So also Grossman, *Ruth*, 176.

170. The narrator employs the same dramatic effect in 1:1–2 and 2:1.

## THE BOOK OF RUTH

this context because it has a personal subject (cf. Gen 24:27; LXX),[171] both are possible and convey a similar meaning.

Second, who is the referent for the "who"?[172] Naomi could refer to Boaz's kindness or Yahweh's. The reasons for Boaz include: (1) Ruth 1:8 and 3:10, where similar phrases refer to people showing kindness; (2) 2 Sam 2:5, where people show kindness, not Yahweh;[173] (3) the absence of God showing kindness to the dead elsewhere in the Old Testament;[174] (4) if *'zb*, "abandoned," is an anagram of *b'z*, Boaz's name,[175] it would point to him as the subject; and (5) Boaz is the subject of Naomi's succeeding speech.[176] The reasons for Yahweh include: (1) the nearest grammatically acceptable antecedent is usually the referent of a relative clause;[177] (2) Ruth 4:14, where the women of the town refer to Yahweh using a similar blessing formula; and (3) Gen 24:27, where God has "not abandoned his kindness."[178] It is hard to choose one or the other option, although the context slightly favors Boaz. To my mind, it is a case of intentional ambiguity: that is, the phrase "has not abandoned" refers to both Yahweh and Boaz.[179] This reflects the underlying theology of the Ruth narrative. God is the ultimate source of kindness, and he does not cease to bless the living and the dead. He does so here through Boaz's acts of kindness (cf. v. 12).

Who are "the living and the dead"? The phrase could be a merism for "everyone," but in the Ruth narrative it more likely refers to all the family members. Earlier, Naomi asked God to show kindness to her daughters-

---

171. See Hubbard, *Ruth*, 185–86.

172. The *'ăšer* can function here as a relative pronoun ("who") or as a causal connective indicating the grounds for the blessing ("for" or "because"). On the latter, see GKC §158b; JM §170e.

173. Syntactically, 2 Sam 2:5 is the closest blessing in the Old Testament: "Blessed be you by Yahweh, because you have shown this kindness with my lord Saul and have buried him."

174. See especially Glueck, *Hesed*, 40–42; Basil Rebera, "Yahweh or Boaz? Ruth 2.20 Reconsidered," *BT* 36 (1985): 317–27.

175. Porten, "Scroll," 36.

176. LXX and Vulg. read Boaz as the referent of the *'ăšer* clause. He is the referent in NIV, NET, NLT, CEV.

177. Holmstedt, *Handbook*, 141–42.

178. Yahweh is the referent in NJPS, ESV, HCSB, NRSV, NASB. Genesis 24:27 is the only other narrative occurrence of "who has not abandoned his kindness" (cf. Jonah 2:9[8]). In this verse, God "has not abandoned his kindness" from Abraham, as evidenced in his arranging the meeting between Abraham's servant and Rebekah. Similar to the Ruth narrative, human initiative is also important since she kindly gives Abraham's servants and camels water to drink (24:15–21).

179. Cf. Eskenazi and Frymer-Kensky, *Ruth*, 44: "Instead of God's abandoning (*'-z-bh*) [sic] his *ḥesed*, there is now Boaz (*b-'-z*)." Ruth also showed loyalty by refusing to "abandon" (*'zb*) her mother-in-law (1:16).

in-law because of the kindness they had shown to "the dead and with me [Naomi]" (1:8). "The dead" were Elimelech, Mahlon, and Chilion,[180] so if we take the phrase to refer to the same in this verse, "the living" would be Naomi and Ruth. How did God through Boaz show kindness to the dead? First, the provision of grain and leftover food for Naomi and Ruth expressed "loyalty" to "the dead." As noted above in 1:8, *ḥesed* is a key word in the Ruth narrative, a word pregnant with meaning, unable to be captured by one English word. Here *ḥesed* has ideas of generosity and kindness, but also loyalty and faithfulness. In group-oriented societies, loyalty is a core value. God through Boaz was being faithful to Elimelech's line by showing generosity to Naomi and Ruth. Second, the use of similar words recalls Naomi's prayer in 1:8. Hearing 1:8 and 2:20 together reveals a chiastic pattern: dead–living–living–dead.[181] We wonder if Naomi's prayer for kindness for her daughters-in-law is now being fulfilled, raising hopes for the future restoration of the line of "the dead."

This is the major turning point of the Ruth narrative. Naomi's spirits began to lift as she saw Ruth's haul of grain. Now she connects Boaz's generosity with Yahweh's blessing. From ascribing her bitterness to Yahweh, she now proclaimed blessing upon Yahweh and Boaz. Her theological realization will lead to her initiating a plan (3:1–4). The repetition of *Naomi said* without reporting a response from Ruth introduces a brief pause and keeps the focus on Naomi. It also suggests an afterthought, whereby Naomi realizes the significance of her previous words.[182] She outlined what Boaz did for them; now she reveals his kinship relation, and hence what he could do for them. Although we as the audience knew the significance of Boaz (2:1), Ruth did not. Only now Naomi reveals *the man is our close relative* (Heb. "close to us"). Naomi does not refer to Boaz by name, but as *hā'îš*, "the man," which highlights his social role and hence his significance for them. Boaz was described as a "relative" (2:1), and "close to us" is also a kinship term, which can refer to an immediate family member (Lev 21:2–3) or a relative from the same clan (Num 27:11; cf. Lev 25:25).[183] The former applies in this verse. Naomi's subsequent identification of Boaz as *one of our kinsman-redeemers* sharpens his significance.

Drawn from Israelite family law, a kinsman-redeemer is a relative who restores to wholeness that which has been lost, usually at personal cost.[184]

---

180. Elimelech "died" in 1:3, and his sons in 1:5. Ruth is described as "the wife of the dead," i.e., Mahlon (4:5), and "the name of the dead" is mentioned twice, referring to Mahlon.

181. Cf. Zakovitch, *Rut*, 128.

182. Cf. Gen 30:27–28; 41:39–41; Num 32:2–5.

183. In Exod 32:27, the term could mean "fellow Israelite"; see Gane/Milgrom, "*qārab*," *TDOT* 13:144–45.

184. For a longer discussion of the kinsman–redeemer, including tracing the theme through to the New Testament, see Lau and Goswell, *Unceasing Kindness*, 117–39.

## THE BOOK OF RUTH

The duties were at the clan level and included: (1) buying back property that was lost outside the clan for an indebted relative (Lev 25:25–30); (2) buying back a relative who had sold themselves into slavery (Lev 25:47–55); (3) executing murders of relatives as an "avenger of blood" (Num 35:12, 19–27; Deut 19:6, 11–13); (4) receiving restitution money on behalf of a deceased relative (Num 5:8); and (5) mediating for a relative in lawsuits (Job 19:25; Ps 119:154; Prov 23:11; Jer 50:34). The relative who needed redemption could not help themselves, and the redeemer acts because of family solidarity—every Israelite is linked by a series of widening networks: father's house, clan, tribe, and nation. If a relative was in need, there was an obligation to help: the closer the relation, the stronger the obligation.

Naomi says that Boaz is "one of" their kinsman-redeemers, which suggests there is more than one relative who could help them. It is significant that not only is her mood and view on life improving, she now has a clear option—redemption through a kinsman. She sees this redemption as not only for Ruth, who has formed a relationship with Boaz, but for her also: "the man is *our* close relative, he is one of *our* kinsman-redeemers." When Naomi proclaimed she was "empty" upon her arrival in Bethlehem although Ruth was by her side (1:21–22), we wondered if she resented the presence of her foreign daughter-in-law. And even though Naomi addressed Ruth as "my daughter," the narrator kept reminding us they were mother-in-law and daughter-in-law. But here Naomi speaks of Ruth as a member of her family and hence holds out the potential for the redemption of her family.

Yet, it is not clear how Boaz will act as a redeemer. Naomi and Ruth do not fall under one of the five family law situations outlined above. According to the law, marriage was not a role for a kinsman-redeemer but assisting a relative in a lawsuit was not mentioned in the law either.[185] Isaiah 54:4–5 might provide additional background to this custom. These verses describe Yahweh as the redeemer who marries "a widow" (*'almānâ*), a woman without the protection and security provided by a male (husband, son, or brother). Ruth is not described as an *'almānâ*, but we might recall Naomi's view that Ruth's security is to be found in the home of another husband (1:9). It seems likely that the law outlined the basic obligations for a kinsman-redeemer, but the real-life application was broader. It included helping a clansperson in whatever way required, including mediating in lawsuits and marrying widows. In any case, the audience now wonders how Boaz might act in his role as a redeemer.

**21** In response to Naomi's excitement, Ruth adds information not previously disclosed. Yet, the narrator calling Ruth *the Moabite* is unexpected. She had been accepted into Boaz's field, she had worked alongside his servant

---

185. The latter is not drawn from the law but from instances in the Writings and a prophetic text; see point (5) above.

2:18–23 Home: Naomi and Ruth Debrief

girls, and had been invited to eat with him and his workers. Naomi had just disclosed that Boaz was one of their kinsman-redeemers. Yet the audience is reminded of her foreign status, recalling her arrival in Bethlehem (1:22) and before she went out to glean (2:2). There are three possible reasons for this reminder. First, despite all that she had achieved in Boaz's field, she remained an outsider. Her integration into Israelite society had started, and she would have felt some belonging among the workers in Boaz's field, but it was only the beginning. Boaz had accepted her, but it is unlikely the overseer and rest of the workers viewed her as kindly. It would take a lot more for her to be integrated into the wider Israelite society. Second, it highlights the magnitude of her success in Boaz's field.[186] By "chance" she stumbled into his field (v. 3) and became the recipient of his generosity. Might Yahweh have more in store for this foreigner who had taken refuge under his wings (v. 12)? Third, it prepares the audience for what Ruth says next.

She reports that Boaz told her, *Cling to the male servants who are mine*, although Boaz said to cling to his female servants (v. 8). The masculine plural can refer to all of Boaz's workers, and maybe Ruth is conflating Boaz's two instructions in verses 8 and 9. She might even include Boaz's later instructions to his male servants to allow her to glean among the sheaves (vv. 15–16). But in the context of the more specific use of the masculine plural noun in verses 9 and 15, it is more likely that the narrow meaning is meant here (cf. Naomi's use of *na'ărôtāyw*, "his female servants," v. 22). If so, it is consistent with Ruth's foreignness: Boaz told Ruth to stay close to the female harvesters, but in her charming naivety the Moabite misunderstood the instructions.[187] She does not know the farming etiquette in Bethlehem.

And perhaps she has not fully digested all the information. For in response to Naomi's excitement, her speech also has an excited tone, as reflected in her awkwardly phrased sentence. She begins with *gam kî*, "also (it is) that," which signals a disjointed addition, *also . . . even*.[188] Her words do not follow naturally from Naomi's, nor her own previous words, and are emphatic ("even"). Then her sentence fronts *'im-hannə'ārîm*, "with/to the male servants," which draws our attention to this group. The relative clause *'ăšer-lî*, "who are mine," is periphrastic, and since Boaz used the simpler "my" previously (*na'ărōtāy*, "my female servants," v. 8), we wonder if Ruth relays Boaz's meaning but expresses it in her own words. If it is a reliable quotation of Boaz, it is consistent

186. Hubbard, *Ruth*, 190.

187. Cf. Lim, "Otherness," 109, who suggests that Ruth's misunderstanding is due to "unevenness in her facility in the Hebrew language."

188. This combination of words occurs only seven times elsewhere, meaning "moreover, when . . ." (Josh 22:7; Prov 22:6) or "even though" (Isa 1:15; Hos 8:10; 9:16; Ps 23:4; Lam 3:8). But this is the only verse where a *paseq* separates the two words, indicating they are not to be read together; Holmstedt, *Handbook*, 143.

# THE BOOK OF RUTH

with his slightly stilted speech elsewhere,[189] perhaps part of his characterization as from the older generation.[190] Either way, the emphasis of the wordy "who are mine" is on Boaz's possession, here of the servants.[191] So, she says, "Also, he even said to me, 'Cling to the male servants who are mine.'" If these words are a rephrase of Boaz's words, it reflects an excited mind in which the information has not quite settled. This would be expected after the multitude of new things Ruth had experienced that day.

Ruth then ends her speech by revealing how long she was permitted to harvest. She can cling to Boaz's harvesters *until they have finished all the harvest that is mine*. The combination of *'ad* and *'im*, "until," is rare and seems superfluous.[192] Since the narrator later uses *'ad-kəlôt*, "until (they were) finished" (v. 23), either this is another example of Boaz's stilted speech or the product of Ruth's excited mind. The entire harvest will include the barley and wheat harvests (v. 23). We hear of this extended permission for the first time here. Placing these words in Ruth's mouth emphasizes the implications for her and her mother-in-law, and leads the scene to end on an even higher note. It is no wonder that Ruth begins her words with, "Also, he even said to me."

There are two implications of Ruth's speech. First, previously Ruth "clung" to Naomi, which meant loyalty to her mother-in-law and their kinship relationship. Now that she is to "cling" to Boaz's male servants, the narrative flags a possible shift in her loyalty. But the emphasis is on Boaz, not the male servants, as the relative clause "who belong to Boaz" especially highlights. And since Boaz is from the clan of Naomi's husband, perhaps she can also maintain her loyalty to her mother-in-law? Second, Boaz's generosity was not just for a day, it was for a season. He will continue to provide for Ruth and Naomi from his harvest, "the harvest that is mine." Not just a part of the harvest, but the entire harvest. Given his largesse for a single day, this signals that Ruth and Naomi would be sustained for many months.

**22** Naomi closes their conversation by correcting Ruth's misunderstanding. Her words echo those of Boaz's (vv. 8–9) with the same parental tone, underscored here by the narrator's mention of *Ruth, her daughter-in-law* and Naomi's address to Ruth ("my daughter"). She redirects Ruth by telling her *it is better* to do two things. First, whereas Ruth reported that Boaz said "cling to" the male servants, Naomi instructs Ruth to *go out with his female servants*. Since the word translated "male servants" can mean servants in general (both

---

189. Cf. Campbell, *Ruth*, 107: "Boaz is depicted to us as a man of rather turgid speech."

190. See note on 1:8.

191. See JM §130e and references there.

192. The combination only occurs elsewhere in Gen 24:19, 33; Isa 30:17. To express the same sense, Naomi uses *'ad 'ăšer* (1:13; 3:18) and *'ad* with an infinitive (3:3), while the narrator only uses the latter (1:19; 2:23).

male and female), Naomi is quick to clear up any confusion. Second, Naomi uses the verb *yṣ'*, "to go out," since she wants to avoid the kinship associations of "cling to." Perhaps there is a hint that Naomi only wants Ruth to "cling to" Boaz.[193] "Go out with" (*tēṣə'î 'im*) might also imply leaving the town with the group of female workers,[194] thus providing further safety for Ruth. For Naomi reinforces Boaz's understanding that the open field is dangerous for an unattached foreign woman.

Naomi gives the reason for her restriction: *so they will not assault you in another field*. Boaz commanded his male workers not to molest (v. 9) or humiliate (v. 15) or rebuke her (v. 16). It is better for Ruth to stay in his field because it is highly unlikely that she would be afforded the same protection in another field. The phrase *pāga' bə-* has a broad range of meaning. The basic meaning is "to meet, encounter," but it can have the sense of "to entreat, urge" (cf. 1:16), and the more hostile sense of "to fall upon, attack."[195] Considering Boaz's warning and commands, the last sense is most likely here. This sense of *pg'* recalls its use in the book of Judges (8:21; 15:12; 18:25), the disordered and often depraved historical period in which the Ruth narrative is set (Ruth 1:1). As such, a whole range of assaults are in view here—verbal, physical, and even sexual. Like Boaz, Naomi wants to protect Ruth from these.

This raises the question of why Naomi did not warn Ruth of such dangers when Ruth left for the field in the morning. Some view Naomi with a jaundiced eye: she is ambivalent about having a foreign daughter-in-law lingering with her in Bethlehem so that she only becomes concerned about Ruth's welfare when she realizes the benefit of having her around.[196] For, as it is argued, Ruth had become the breadwinner, and, moreover, Naomi detects the potential in Ruth's newly formed association with Boaz. Since human motivations are complex, often with an amount of self-interest intermingled with altruism, this is a possible reading of Naomi's motives. Yet, I prefer a reading more sympathetic to Naomi's situation. She had returned "home" empty and bitter, with no family and no food. She also had to deal with the stresses of repatriation with the added stress of having to look after a daughter-in-law that she had encouraged to return to her own mother's house. We might even speculate that her grief and repatriation triggered an adjustment disorder with depressed mood,[197] so she could only bring herself

---

193. Cf. Grossman, *Ruth*, 184.

194. So Hubbard, *Ruth*, 182n11.

195. For references, see comment on 1:16.

196. See, especially, Fewell and Gunn, *Compromising*, 76–77.

197. An adjustment disorder is "the development of emotional or behavioral symptoms in response to an identifiable stressor(s) occurring within 3 months of the onset of the stressor(s)." See "adjustment disorders," in American Psychiatric Association, *Diagnostic and Statistical Manual of Mental Disorders*, 5th ed. (Arlington: American Psychiatric Publishing,

## THE BOOK OF RUTH

to utter a one-word assent to Ruth's request to glean (2:2). Naomi's words reveal that she knew of the dangers in the field, but her unmotivated state is only broken by Ruth's day-end report of her activities. Her success in the field shakes Naomi out of her inertia, as she now takes on the role of mother-in-law, or even mother, to Ruth. Not only is Naomi becoming comfortable with the presence of Ruth, she is also waking up to the responsibility and promise of Ruth's presence.[198]

**23** The narrator closes the act and scene with a summary that also anticipates events in the next act (as the mention of "the beginning of the barley harvest" in 1:22 prepares for act 2). Ruth followed Naomi's and Boaz's instruction: *she clung to Boaz's female servants*, perhaps hinting that she had nothing to do with the male servants,[199] hence removing the romantic potential. She stayed close to them *to glean until the barley and wheat harvests were finished*. This is the "entire harvest" Boaz mentioned (v. 21), lasting around seven weeks, which in the modern calendar runs from April until early June.[200] Although the narrator does not report further contact between Boaz and Ruth, this seems inevitable during these weeks in his field. She would have collected and stored enough of the two grains to last for months. Thus, the food needs of these two widows are supplied for the short to medium term. But that is all. Something needs to be done to secure their long-term provision.

The narrator hints as much in his conclusion: *and she lived with her mother-in-law*. The harvest was completed, but Ruth still lived with Naomi. She had formed ties with Boaz's household in his field, but she was still living in her mother-in-law's household, under her authority, not Boaz's. The end of the harvests also means the end of contact with Boaz, and hence the end of the opportunity to develop their relationship. Naomi's wish was for her daughters-in-law to find rest in the home of a husband, but now this is fast fading. The resonances with the end of act 1 invite comparison. Act 1 ended with the widows "returning" (from *šûb*) to Bethlehem at the beginning of the "barley harvest." The "barley and wheat harvests" have ended, but she

---

2013). My diagnosis is tentative since it is based on sparse textual evidence: her outburst in response to the townswomen's question (1:19–20) and her response to Ruth (2:2). It is hard to establish a baseline for Naomi's behavior to compare with those found in act 2, but she functions as a mother-in-law on the road to Bethlehem, urging her daughters-in-law to return to find a husband (1:8–9, 11–13, 15). There is a marked contrast with initiative-taking Naomi on the road with withdrawn and verbally restricted Naomi in her Bethlehem home. However, a definitive diagnosis requires an extensive interview with a patient.

198. Cf. Johanna W. H. Bos, "Out of the Shadows: Genesis 38; Judges 4:17–22; Ruth 3," *Semeia* 42 (1988): 59.

199. Porten, "Scroll," 37.

200. Cf. Deut 16:9; Miller II, "Judges and the Early Iron Age," 183–84.

still lives (from *yšb*) with Naomi.[201] There has been some progress from act 1, but it has now halted. Each scene had raised audience expectation higher, especially for a relationship between Boaz and Ruth, and a reversal of the widows' emptiness and isolation and shame, but the act ends anticlimactically. And so, the stage is set for the next scene.

In our age of globalization, there has been an unprecedented movement of people.[202] People move to and between cities, states, and countries. People migrate for several reasons, which can be broadly classified as "push" and "pull." "Push" factors are difficulties in migrants' home country that make it difficult or impossible to live there, such as famine, war, or oppression. "Pull" factors are circumstances in a destination country that make it a more attractive place to live than their home country, such as work opportunities, a better quality of life, or being united with family members. The former is the case for Elimelech and his family at the beginning of act 1; the latter is the case for Naomi and Ruth at the end of act 1. Ruth is an immigrant, someone who seeks refuge under the wings of Yahweh and in his covenant community in Bethlehem (2:12). The responses of the receiving community and the immigrant are both instructive. There are solidarity and mutuality, both ministry to and of the immigrant.

Boaz exemplifies an ideal response to an immigrant in the covenant community. His first step is to recognize the stranger and to seek after her attachments and identity. He recognizes Ruth as a person, not just as an anonymous member of an amorphous grouping of "Moabite," "foreigner" or "foreign worker" or "outsider" or "refugee."[203] This recognition of her personhood and her membership in Israelite society triggers Boaz's sense of responsibility toward the poor and weak. The wealthy and influential in all societies should use their physical resources and social capital to help the needy. This is still relevant for Christians, whose first responsibility is to the household of faith (Gal 6:10), then all others who might come across our path. After all, in the parable of the good Samaritan, Jesus said that our neighbor is anyone in need, especially those we can help (Luke 10:25–37). Set against an undercurrent of suspicion and hostility toward outsiders in the Ruth narrative, Boaz

---

201. Cf. 3:18, where *yšb* will mean "sit" or "wait, sit tight."

202. In 2019, the number of international migrants was estimated to be 272 million, 3.5% of the world's population; see "World Migration Report 2020," International Organization for Migration, accessed 11 May, 2020, https://publications.iom.int/system/files/pdf/wmr_2020.pdf.

203. The modern definition of a refugee is "a person who has been forced to leave their country in order to escape war, persecution, or natural disaster"; *Oxford English Dictionary*, 2nd ed., s.v. "refugee." Unless Ruth would have faced persecution for turning to Yahweh, she does not fit this definition. She is a refugee, however, in the sense that she went to Israel and sought refuge under Yahweh's wings (2:12).

THE BOOK OF RUTH

manifests the covenant ideal by taking up his responsibilities as expressed in his acts of kindness to Ruth. And Boaz's acceptance of Ruth in his gleaning community opens the path to her sense of belonging in Bethlehem.

Yet, the responsibility is not one-sided; an immigrant can also contribute. Ruth does not passively wait for a handout as if it were her right; instead, she takes the initiative to go out to glean. Her response to Boaz as her patron is ideal: she expresses her gratitude and gives him due respect. The patron-client relationship is unequal, but there is still reciprocity. With her words and actions, she seizes the opportunity to secure Boaz's patronage, not just for a day but for a whole harvest season. She works hard in the field to improve her lot, as well as that of Naomi. Boaz ministers to this refugee but the refugee also has much to give. She gives due honor to Boaz, enhancing his reputation in Israelite society and Naomi's eyes. She also ministers to her Israelite mother-in-law by assuaging her hunger and helping her break out of despondency. By the end of the narrative, this singular Moabite will contribute immeasurably more to the house of Israel.

The migratory impulse pervades the Bible's story line.[204] God told Adam and Eve to be fruitful, multiply, and spread throughout the earth (Gen 1:28), and because of their sin they were forced out of the garden of Eden (Gen 3:23–24). Abraham was a migrant called by God, whose life was punctuated by movement (e.g., Gen 12:1). The same can be said of Abraham's descendants Isaac, Jacob, and Joseph, and indeed, the people of Israel. After the exodus from Egypt, Israel finds "rest" in the promised land (Josh 21:43–45). Yet the three annual pilgrimage festivals—journeys to Yahweh's sanctuary—perhaps reminded them they were historically a people on the move. This movement continues when the kingdom of Judah is forcibly deported out of Canaan to Babylon and again when a remnant returns to the promised land. In the New Testament, God himself becomes a migrant and a refugee. Jesus leaves his heavenly home and becomes a refugee with his family in Egypt (Matt 2:13–15). In his ministry, he would withdraw from ministry in primarily Jewish areas to gentile regions.[205] In his self-sacrificial death, he journeyed to the realm of the dead, then back to the realm of the living. Finally, he would ascend back to heaven, where he awaits his followers to join him in a new heaven and earth. And after the coming of the Holy Spirit, the New Testament church was scattered (Acts 1:8; 8:1; 11:19).

Not surprisingly, then, Christians are called "sojourners" and "aliens" or "strangers" in this world (Phil 3:20; Heb 11:13–16; 1 Pet 2:11). We are encour-

---

204. For an introduction to immigration in the Bible, see M. Daniel Carroll R., *The Bible and Borders: Hearing God's Word on Immigration* (Grand Rapids: Brazos, 2020).

205. See, e.g., Paul Hertig, "Jesus' Migrations and Liminal Withdrawals in Matthew," in *God's People on the Move: Biblical and Global Perspectives on Migration and Mission*, ed. vanThanh Nguyen and John M. Prior (Eugene, OR: Wipf and Stock, 2014), 46–61.

182

aged to persevere on our journey to our final promised rest (Heb 4:1–13). We are "sojourners" who find our refuge in God through the work of Christ. As such, we must recognize the sojourner and foreigner in our midst—the migrant worker, the undocumented foreigner, the new migrant, the refugee, and the asylum seeker among them—and live out our responsibility to them. And if we are one of these people, we can look for opportunities to contribute to improving our situation and that of our community. This is nothing less than what God commands in his law, as exemplified by Boaz and Ruth. Of course, the best example is Jesus. Although his mission was first to the Jews, he still shows compassion and concern for the female outsider, including the foreigner (e.g., the Syrophoenician woman; Matt 15:21–28; Mark 7:24–30) and the despised (e.g., the Samaritan woman; John 4:3–42). We would do well to imitate Jesus, because in serving the needy and poor and marginalized, we are serving him: "For I was hungry and you gave me food, I was thirsty and you gave me drink, I was a stranger and you welcomed me. . . . Truly, I say to you, as you did it to one of the least of these my brothers, you did it to me" (Matt 25:35, 40).

# The Book of Ruth

## ACT 3: SEEKING PERMANENT SECURITY (3:1–18)

The end of the harvest seasons also meant the end of contact between Ruth and Boaz. Ruth still lived with her mother-in-law, which was not the outcome Naomi had hoped for. Now shaken out of her despondency, Naomi decides to do something about their long-term security. The events in this act span from one evening to the next morning.

Structurally, act 3 balances act 2, although there is a contrast in the action.

| | Characters | Location | Action |
|---|---|---|---|
| 2:1–3 | Naomi and Ruth | Naomi's home | Naomi accepts Ruth's plan |
| 2:4–17 | Ruth and Boaz and workers | Boaz's field | Public encounter between Ruth and Boaz |
| 2:18–23 | Naomi and Ruth | Naomi's home | Naomi and Ruth debrief |
| 3:1–5 | Naomi and Ruth | Naomi's home | Ruth accepts Naomi's plan |
| 3:6–15 | Ruth and Boaz | Threshing floor | Private encounter between Ruth and Boaz |
| 3:16–18 | Naomi and Ruth | Naomi's home | Naomi and Ruth debrief |

Ruth initiated the action in act 2 and Naomi responded, whereas Naomi initiates the action in act 3 and Ruth responds. Ruth sought food, Naomi now seeks a home and husband. Ruth assuaged their immediate need; Naomi seeks permanent security. Boaz is mentioned as "a relative," and "our relative," in the first scenes of both acts (2:1; 3:2), but his role is different in the second scenes. He still dominates the action and speaks most of the words, but he responds to the initiatives of Naomi and Ruth. In the final scenes of both acts, Naomi and Ruth discuss Boaz's actions—what he did and continued to do (act 2) and what he will do (act 3). In both acts, Ruth is the mediator; Naomi and Boaz do not meet.

## F'.  HOME: RUTH ACCEPTS NAOMI'S PLAN (3:1–5)

[1]*Naomi her mother-in-law said to her, "My daughter, shouldn't I seek rest for you, where it would go well for you?*[a]

[2]*Now, isn't Boaz our relative,*[b] *whose female servants you were with? Look, he is winnowing barley tonight*[c] *at the threshing floor.*[d]

[3]*Wash, rub on some oil,*[e] *and put on your best clothes.*[f] *Then go down*[g] *to the threshing floor. Don't make yourself known to the man until he has finished eating and drinking.*

184

## 3:1–5 Home: Ruth Accepts Naomi's Plan

[4]*When he lies down, take note of the place where he lies. Then enter and uncover the place of his feet and lie down.*[h] *He will tell you what to do."*
[5]*And she*[i] *said to her, "All that you say to me*[j] *I will do."*

a. It is best to read the *'ăšer* as introducing a relative rather than a purpose clause: "where it would go well" (cf. NIV, NJPS) rather than "so that it would go well" (cf. ESV, CSB, NRSV). So also Block, *Discourse*, 167; Holmstedt, *Handbook*, 148; *pace* Campbell, *Ruth*, 116; Bush, *Ruth, Esther*, 144–45.

b. Heb. *mōda'tānû* ("our relative") is unusual in two respects: (1) it is a feminine form; (2) the suffix is -*ānû* instead of the expected -*ēnû*. For possible reasons for the latter, see JM §94h.

c. LXX, OL, Syr., and Vulg. read "this night" for MT[L] *hallāylâ*, "tonight." The meaning is the same.

d. Tg. "He is winnowing at the barley threshing floor in the night wind."

e. Heb. *wāsakt*, "anoint (yourself)" with oil. Here the *qal* verb has a reflexive sense; BDB, 691–92.

f. The *ketiv* has the singular *śimlātēk*, "your garment," while the *qere* has the plural *śimlōtayik*, "your garments" (cf. 2QRuth[a], Syr., Vulg., Tg.). I read the *ketiv* as a singular collective noun, "your clothes" (e.g., Deut 10:18; 22:5; Isa 3:7), probably including at least a shawl and a cloak (the latter mentioned in v. 15). The noun can refer to a specific piece of clothing (mantle or cloak; cf. v. 15) or an outer garment in general. See *HALOT* 3:1337–38; Niehr, "*śimlâ*," *TDOT* 14:159. It is also used as a covering at night (e.g., Exod 22:25–26[26–27]). In the context of the previous two verbs, "best clothes" is the most likely sense (cf. Tg. "your finery"), keeping in mind that Ruth probably did not have many changes of clothes.

g. The *qere* corrects the *ketiv* to be consistent with the previous three *qatal* modal verbs. The *ketiv yāradtî* looks like a first-person singular verb, "I will go down," which does not seem to make sense after Naomi tells Ruth to get ready; but see Brian P. Irwin, "Removing Ruth: *Tiqqune Sopherim* in Ruth 3.3–4?," *JSOT* 32 (2008): 331–38. If we want to maintain the first-person singular verb, an explanation is that it reflects Naomi's nervousness; so Block, *Discourse*, 165n4. Alternatively, it could be an archaic second-person feminine form, "you go down," which is used to characterize the speech of Naomi and Boaz, who are both from the older generation (cf. Jer 2:33; Ezek 16:18; see GKC §44h and comments on 2:8). It is only used in the fourth verb of a four-verb sequence (the same sequence in v. 4 with *šākābtî* as the fourth verb), which Holmstedt, *Handbook*, 152–53, suggests adds distinctiveness to Naomi's speech without sacrificing clarity (the first three verbs establish that all the verbs are to be understood as second-person feminine singular). The LXX reads "go up" but "go down" for the same verb in v. 6, perhaps indicating the threshing floor's elevation relative to the surrounding area but still below the town. The versions do not support LXX.

h. Heb. *wəšākābtî* looks like a first-person singular verb but is more likely an archaic second-person feminine form; see note on v. 3.

i. LXX specifies the speaker as Ruth.

j. The *qere* adds vowel points *ē a* without the consonants *'ly*, indicating that *'ēlay*, "to me," is to precede *'e'ĕśeh*, "I will do." This is probably a case of parablepsis, whereby the scribe skipped from the *aleph* that begins *'ēlay* to the *aleph* that begins *'e'ĕśeh*. LXX, OL, and Syr. support the *qere*, while Vulg. omits "to me."

This scene is framed by two narrative statements: "Naomi . . . said to her" (v. 1) and "She said to her" (v. 5). These statements are followed by, respectively, Naomi's proposal and Ruth's assent to Naomi's proposal. Naomi dominates

# The Book of Ruth

this scene. She initiates the conversation and the volume of her words (fifty-three words) far outweighs that of Ruth's (four). She is firmly discharging her role as "mother-in-law" with her "daughter" (v. 1); after a short interruption (2:1–2), normal functioning has firmly resumed (cf. 1:8–15; 2:19–22).

In our chiastic structure of the Ruth narrative, this scene (3:1–5; F') corresponds to 2:18–23 (F). The characters and location are the same, and although one is the end of an act and the other the beginning, plot progression indicates that the scenes comprise the narrative's turning point: Naomi saw the potential of the relationship between Ruth and Boaz (2:18–23), and now she takes action to realize that potential (3:1–5). Boaz is one of Naomi's and Ruth's kinsman-redeemers (2:20); Naomi now details her plan to nudge him into taking up that role to provide long-term security for the widows.

The structure of Naomi's speech is:

Two parallel rhetorical questions (vv. 1–2a)

> My daughter,
> shouldn't [*hălō'*] I seek rest for you,
> where [*'ăšer*] it would go well for you? (v. 1)

> Now, isn't [*hălō'*] Boaz our relative,
> whose [*'ăšer*] female servants you were with? (v. 2a)

Instructions (vv. 2b–4)

> A He [*hû'*] is winnowing barley tonight at the threshing floor. (v. 2b)
>   B Bathe, anoint, dress, go down.
>     C Don't make yourself known [from *yd'*] to the man. (v. 3)
>     C' Take note [from *yd'*] of the place where he lies.
>   B' Go, uncover, lie down.
> A' He [*hû'*] will tell you what to do. (v. 4)

Based on this structure, Naomi's focus is on the man—where he is (A) and what he will tell Ruth to do (A'). Nonetheless, Naomi has an important role for Ruth. She gives her four instructions (B) in parallel with three instructions (B'). These commands bracket the central component (C), which turns on "knowing" (C'). Naomi's plan is a ruse with two actors, involving withholding and giving knowledge.

**1** Soon after the events of act 2,[1] Naomi initiates a plan for Ruth. She was despondent when she returned to Bethlehem (1:20–21) and passive

---

1. The specific timing is not given, but since Boaz and the men were processing the harvested sheaves (v. 2), it was soon after the harvest season.

## 3:1–5  HOME: RUTH ACCEPTS NAOMI'S PLAN

when Ruth took the initiative to glean (2:2). Now, with her hope renewed (2:18–22), she initiates the action. Yet the narrator's reference to Naomi as "her mother-in-law" and "to her" ensures that our focus remains on Ruth: *Naomi her mother-in-law said to her*. Naomi's address to Ruth as *my daughter* expresses a closer bond than the in-law relationship just mentioned by the narrator (so also 2:2, 22; cf. 1:11, 12, 13 [plural]). It also shows the generational difference between them, as had Boaz's use of the term previously (2:8). Both Boaz and Naomi use rhetorical questions, indicating their authority, and here Naomi poses a rhetorical question to Ruth (cf. Boaz's in 2:8, 9): *shouldn't I*[2] *seek rest for you?* Naomi prayed that her daughters-in-law would find *mənûḥâ*, "rest" or "security" in the household of another husband back in Moab (1:9). But Ruth clung to Naomi and remained in her household. As her de facto parent, Naomi seeks *mānôaḥ*, "rest" or "a resting place" in the household of an Israelite husband, who will protect and provide for her. It was a place *where it would go well for* Ruth. The clause contains an implicit comparison: home with a husband would be better than her current situation, in which she does not have a place of rest.[3] As a foreigner, Ruth also does not have a sense of belonging. The clause "go well for you" echoes that found in the Old Testament, especially Deuteronomy. There it refers to God's blessing of a good life in the promised land: material abundance, long life, and generations of descendants (Deut 4:40; 5:16, 33; 6:3). Naomi wants Ruth to enjoy these covenant blessings as an accepted member of God's people.

Not all, however, agree that Naomi is primarily motivated by altruism.[4] Some argue that Naomi's plan aims to improve her own situation or to provide an heir for Elimelech's line. Certainly, human motivations are often mixed, so other reasons might have been in the back of her mind. And her plan does put Ruth in danger. But Naomi's words suggest that she primarily wants what is best for Ruth: "Shouldn't I seek rest *for you*, where it would go well *for you*?" Her words express the same sentiment as on the road to Bethlehem, when she urged her daughters to find rest with a husband in Moab (1:9). Naomi wants to reverse the destitution and disgrace of Ruth's widowhood, not to fulfill her own emptiness or to continue Elimelech's line. Naomi's words express an unchanging concern for her daughter-in-law.

As expected for the ancient Israel context, the premise is that the key to security and belonging is found in a man. Yet even in this narrative, a woman will play a vital role in finding security and fullness for Naomi, so much so that she will be described as "better than seven sons" (4:15). And Naomi's initiative to formulate a plan plays no small role in the outcome. Nonetheless,

---

2. Naomi uses a *yiqtol* modal form ("shouldn't I"), whereas Boaz used a *qatal* form ("haven't I").

3. Holmstedt, *Handbook*, 148.

4. Cf. Fewell and Gunn, *Compromising*, 77–78.

some see her planning as wresting the initiative from God.[5] She prayed that God would grant her daughters-in-law rest, but now she seeks rest for Ruth without reference to God. But perhaps Naomi's use of "go well with you" signals that she acknowledges the source of "rest." So instead of viewing Naomi's actions as independent of God's, we can see a delicate interplay between God's sovereignty and human responsibility. An acknowledgment of God's providence does not lead to paralysis; rather, it forms the basis and motivation for action. Then, as now: prayer does not preclude action; or viewed from the other perspective, God's will is often enacted through people.

**2** Having raised the problem and stated her intention, Naomi begins to detail her solution (*Now*). But her speech is ambiguous, indirect. She uses another rhetorical question, which parallels her previous question:

> My daughter,
> shouldn't [*hălō'*] I seek rest for you,
> where [*'ăšer*] it would go well [*yîṭab*] for you? (v. 1)

> Now, isn't [*hălō'*] Boaz our relative,
> whose [*'ăšer*] female servants you were with? (v. 2)

The implication is that she identifies Boaz as one in whom she will find "rest"—in a husband and a home. On first reading, the qualifying phrase "whose servant girls you were with" seems redundant. Ruth already knows who Boaz is. Within the narrative, however, it recalls Boaz's wealth and honorable status. As Naomi's and Ruth's patron, he provided food and protection for them by asking Ruth to cling to his servant girls (2:8). Moreover, it recalls Naomi's words from the end of the previous scene: "It is *better* [*ṭôb*], my daughter, that you go out with *his female servants*" (2:22). The given reason was that Ruth would find protection in Boaz's field, but the implication now is that remaining in Boaz's field raised the possibility of finding security and belonging. By the end of the harvest season, nothing had eventuated, so Naomi seizes the initiative before it is too late.

Naomi's question—*isn't Boaz our relative?*—is rhetorical because she had already revealed their relation (2:20). The noun is related to *mōyda'*, "relative" (2:1), both unusual forms of the verbal root *yd'*, "to know." Naomi had specified that Boaz was "one of our kinsman-redeemers" (2:20), but now she does not refer to him as such. It seems what she has in mind does not entail him functioning in that role. She also mentions nothing about a levirate role (cf. 1:11–13). Nonetheless, in a collectivist society, being a "relative" entailed

---

5. Cf. Block, *Discourse*, 168.

## 3:1–5 Home: Ruth Accepts Naomi's Plan

a range of obligations to kin. Naomi views Ruth as part of her kinship group ("our relative"); Boaz is not just a relative of Naomi's family.

Naomi first draws attention to his location and action. *Look* does not imply that Boaz's location is visible; rather, it indicates Naomi's understanding of local agricultural practices and prescience of Boaz's activities. She says *he is winnowing barley tonight at the threshing floor,* perhaps in contrast to the wheat threshing floor. But since she and the narrator only mention "threshing floor" subsequently, it is more likely there was only one (vv. 3, 6). The Hebrew reads "he is winnowing the threshing floor of barley," whereby the threshing floor is a metonym for the barley on or from the threshing floor (cf. 2 Kgs 6:27; Job 39:12).[6] The point is that Naomi knows Boaz is at a threshing floor and he is winnowing barley there. The participle *zōreh,* "to scatter, winnow,"[7] denotes the action of throwing threshed grain[8] into the air with a shovel or fork so the wind can blow away the chaff and stalks (cf. Hos 13:3), leaving the grain to fall back to the floor. Although Naomi says Boaz is winnowing tonight, the sense is probably "this evening," since winnowing needs a favorable breeze (cf. Tg.). In the Bethlehem region, the wind typically rises early- to mid-afternoon, then drops toward sunset and the evening. But since the timing and strength of the wind are variable (it cannot be too weak or too gusty), this may be the reason Naomi specifies "tonight," meaning "this evening" (cf. Josh 2:2). Or perhaps Boaz was not on duty every night, but Naomi heard he was "tonight," which included winnowing and staying the night to guard the grain from thieves or animals.

The threshing floor was located outside (cf. v. 15) and downhill from (vv. 3, 6; cf. 4:1) the town. It was a large, flat space where landowners and workers could thresh harvested sheaves and winnow the threshed grain. Unlike other threshing floors, this one seems to be a common facility rather than one owned by Boaz (cf. 2 Sam 6:6; 24:16; 2 Chr 3:1). Over time, this communal setting could have held business, judicial (1 Kgs 22:10), and worship activities.[9] It was associated with fertility, and as a liminal space with easy access and privacy, it was also a place of transgression (Hos 9:1).

**3** Having set the scene, Naomi instructs Ruth to prepare herself: *wash, rub on some oil, and put on your best clothes.* The three modal *qatal* verbs are instructions for Ruth, and, taken together, are loaded with symbolism. Naomi asks her to bathe and anoint herself with oil, perhaps olive oil with

---

6. Joüon, *Ruth,* 66–67.

7. BDB, 279.

8. The grain would have been previously threshed by beating, trampling, or crushing (Mic 4:13; Isa 28:28) to remove the husk from the kernels.

9. See Matthews, *Judges/Ruth,* 232–33. A threshing floor becomes the site of the Jerusalem Temple (1 Chr 21:1–22:1; cf. 2 Sam 24).

## The Book of Ruth

fragrance (cf. Prov 27:9), which was used for festive or special occasions (Eccl 9:7–8). Although applying oil was also part of the normal ablutions for men and women (cf. Deut 28:40; Mic 6:15; Dan 10:3; 2 Chr 28:15),[10] as a widow, abstaining from application was probably part of the mourning process (2 Sam 14:2). In an honor-shame society, Ruth would also need to make these preparations to show respect as she approached someone of higher social standing. Since Ruth was poor, her "best clothes" were probably a change of clothes from her daily workwear, including placing aside garments marking her widowhood and perhaps suggesting the end of her mourning period. Significantly, in the Old Testament, the sequence of these three verbs symbolized a change in a person's life. When David ends his mourning period for his son, he "washed and anointed himself and changed his clothes" (2 Sam 12:20; *śimlâ*, the same word Naomi used for Ruth's clothing). His actions signaled his readiness to return to normal activities. Tamar also takes off her widow's garments before she meets Judah (Gen 38:14, 19). Understood in this way, Ruth signals the end of her mourning period for her husband and her readiness for marriage.[11] This understanding of her actions is reinforced by Ezek 16:8–12, where God metaphorically bathed, applied oil, and clothed Jerusalem as part of a betrothal ceremony. In short, Naomi instructs Ruth to look her best to show respect to Boaz, and to indicate the end of her mourning and her readiness for marriage.

Naomi then tells Ruth to *go down to the threshing floor*, since Bethlehem is situated at a high point for defensive purposes. Her use of a modal *yiqtol* verb marks the first of her two core instructions: *Don't make yourself known to the man*. Since it would be unusual for women to be beyond the protection of the city wall at night, Naomi tells Ruth to hide from Boaz and the other men. The core of this episode turns on the verb *yd'*, "to know"—first, withholding knowledge. The *qal* form of the verb is used to refer to sexual intercourse, so the *niphal* form here somewhat deflects this understanding. However, the repetition of the verb (vv. 3, 4, 11, 14, 18) is highly suggestive, especially in combination with reference to Boaz as "the man"[12] and Ruth as "the woman." This focus on gender adds to the mystery and ambiguity of the scene but also makes the audience wonder: what is going to happen between this man and this woman in the secrecy of the threshing floor?

Timing will be important: Ruth is told not to reveal herself *until he has finished eating and drinking*. After winnowing, the men would share a meal,

---

10. R. Patterson, "*sûk*," *TWOT* 2:619.

11. Cf. Laura Quick, *Dress, Adornment and the Body in the Hebrew Bible* (Oxford: Oxford University Press, 2021), 169–70.

12. At the end of the act, "the man" will carry a different nuance (v. 18).

## 3:1-5 Home: Ruth Accepts Naomi's Plan

at this time to celebrate the harvest.[13] With a full stomach, Boaz would be more receptive to Ruth's advances. Previously Boaz and Ruth had shared a meal as an expression of his generosity and her belonging. Now Ruth must wait until he has finished his meal to make her move to request further generosity and entrench her belonging in society. "Drinking" would most likely include wine, and for an audience this might recall the encounter between Lot and his daughters (Gen 19:30-38). They plied their father with wine before having sexual relations with him, so will Ruth the Moabite repeat the behavior of her forebears?

**4** Naomi then tells Ruth what to do *when he lies down*. She should *take note of the place* (Heb. "you will know [wəyādaʻat] the place") *where he lies* because darkness would be descending, and she would not want to approach the wrong man. He is not to "know" that she is there, but she is to "know" his location. Since Boaz was a landowner, he might have slept apart from the workers. Naomi then details four things Ruth should do at this location. First, when he is asleep, she should *ûbāʼt*, "enter," perhaps indicating that he slept in a shelter or a tent.[14] Second, she should *uncover the place of his feet*. This phrase is doubly suggestive. Forms of the verb, "to uncover," are used to refer to nakedness (e.g., Lev 18:6-19; 20:11, 17-21; Ezek 22:10) or to illicit sex (e.g., Deut 23:1 [22:30]; 27:20). But the verb is also used in non-sexual contexts, such as uncovering an eye (e.g., Num 22:31) or an ear (e.g., Ruth 4:4; 1 Sam 9:15). Nonetheless, in the context of Naomi's instructions, especially in conjunction with what Ruth is told to uncover, the verb evokes sexual connotations. Yet what exactly is Ruth told to uncover?[15] The noun *margəlōtāyw* contains a *mem* prefix, which usually indicates location; hence, "place of his feet," just as in English we might say "foot end," or more loosely, "foot of the bed."[16] *Margəlôt* is found once elsewhere, where it is in parallel with "arms," so it most likely is referring to "legs," although "feet" is also possible (cf. Dan 10:6). "Feet" can be used euphemistically for genital organs (e.g.,

---

13. The Gezer calendar lists "harvesting and feasting" after the barley harvest; see *ANET*, 320; "The Gezer Calendar," trans. P. Kyle McCarter (*COS* 2.85:222).

14. Block, *Discourse*, 171.

15. Nielsen, *Ruth*, 69-70, suggests that Ruth uncovered herself and lay down at his feet. This is unlikely because the *piel* form of the verb used here requires a direct object. The reflexive sense would be *hithpael* (Gen 9:21) or *niphal* (Exod 20:26; 2 Sam 6:20). See Bush, *Ruth, Esther*, 153.

16. Cf. Heb. *məra'ăšôt*, which means "at the place of the head" (Gen 28:11, 18; 1 Sam 26:7, 11, 12, 16; 1 Kgs 19:6). The versions support MT^L (Tg., 2QRuth^a), or have a locative interpretation, e.g., "uncover the place at his feet" (LXX), "uncover the garment which hides the place of his feet" (Vulg.).

## The Book of Ruth

Exod 4:25; Judg 3:24 [all male]; Deut 28:57; Ezek 16:25 [all female]),[17] and even the use of *margəlôt* does not remove all sexual connotations. However, *margəlôt* instead of the more explicit *regel/raglayim*, "foot"/"feet," makes more general the region being referred to, and deflects a more sexual understanding. Naomi tells Ruth to uncover Boaz's feet, probably up to the knee. This would give time for Boaz to fall asleep, then be awakened by the cool night air on his feet.

Third, Ruth should *lie down* but Naomi does not specify the location. The verb *škb*, "to lie," is also suggestive. Although it can be used without sexual connotation, especially to lie down to sleep,[18] it often has sexual connotation when a woman is involved, such as in this situation. The verb is used eight times in this chapter (vv. 4 [3×], 7 [2×], 8, 13, 14), and also clusters in the episodes of Lot and his daughters (Gen 19:30–38 [7×]), Joseph and Potiphar's wife (Gen 39:6–18 [4×]), David and Bathsheba (2 Sam 11–12 [8×]) and Amnon's rape of Tamar (2 Sam 13:1–22 [6×]). Since a sexual meaning is usually clearly indicated by the use of a preposition, *'et* or *'im*, "with" (cf. Eng. "to lie with" or "sleep with" someone),[19] the lack of such a preposition here diffuses the sexual explicitness.

Recent scholars have suggested that Naomi's plan amounts to seduction, with a view to entrapment.[20] That is, her plan was to present Ruth as attractively as possible to entice Boaz to impregnate her to force his hand in marriage (cf. Exod 22:16), or at least own up to the pregnancy and receive a payoff (cf. Gen 38).[21] Certainly, the location and circumstances of Naomi's plan invite speculation. And her plan is vague and many of her key words hold double meanings, imbued with sexual innuendo—know, lie, enter, uncover, and (place of the) feet. In this context, eating and drinking could even have sexual overtones since these verbs are found in the episodes of David

---

17. Urine is called "water of the feet" (2 Kgs 18:27//Isa 36:12), and defecation is referred to as "covering the feet" (Judg 3:24; 1 Sam 24:3 [4]).

18. E.g., Samuel and Eli (1 Sam 3:2–15, *škb* used eight times). For other nuances of this verb, see W. Williams, "*škb*," *NIDOTTE* 4:100.

19. With the exception of Gen 30:15–16 and 2 Sam 11:11, "to lie with" refers to illicit sexual relations; see, e.g., Lev 20:11, 12, 13, 18, 20; Deut 22:25; 27:20–23. Approved sexual relations are usually described by *yd'*, "to know," or *bô' 'el*, "to go into/enter."

20. See esp. Charles Halton, "An Indecent Proposal: The Theological Core of the Book of Ruth," *SJOT* 26 (2012): 30–43, and for the alternative view from an African (Bowa people of Mali) perspective, see Schadrac Keita and Janet W. Dyk, "The Scene at the Threshing Floor: Suggestive Readings and Intercultural Considerations on Ruth 3," *BT* 57 (2006): 17–32. Halton argues that Naomi's plan is "an attempt at sexual entrapment." This would be similar to Tamar's manipulation of Judah (Gen 38). If this is the case (which I do not think it is), Ruth shows initiative by deviating from Naomi's plan and *not* taking advantage of Boaz, but instead requesting marriage.

21. Fewell and Gunn, *Compromising*, 78.

## 3:1–5 HOME: RUTH ACCEPTS NAOMI'S PLAN

and Bathsheba (2 Sam 11:11; 12:3)[22] and Joseph and Potiphar's wife (Gen 39:6, 8–9). The combination of verbs is also found on the lips of the foolish woman in Prov 9:17.[23] It seems that Naomi's plan is for Ruth to seduce Boaz.

But seduction is unlikely on textual and cultural grounds. As noted above, while Naomi's words can hold sexual nuances, how they are used in her speech skirt around such meanings. The words are suggestive without making the sexual meaning explicit. The masterful use of words elsewhere in the Ruth narrative would indicate that this is intentional. Naomi's three instructions—wash, oil, dress—signal the end of her mourning period and readiness for marriage but not necessarily with the aim of seduction. A demure reading also finds support from the honor-shame context of the ancient Near East. In the law prohibiting a woman from seizing the "private parts" (*mabûšîm*) of a man (Deut 25:11–12), the word translated "private parts" is a euphemism deriving from *bôš*, "shame."[24] Removing clothing to expose the genitals evoked a feeling of shame, as one's dignity is removed with the clothing.[25] It left the person feeling defenseless and impotent. The exposure and sight of the genitals were condemned (Gen 9:20–27; Lev 20:17–21; 2 Sam 6:20), and such exposure served as a metaphor for personal or collective punishment (e.g., Isa 20:4; 47:2–3; Mic 1:11; Nah 3:5–6). Living in such a culture, Naomi and Ruth would have understood this shame code and would not have subjected Boaz to this humiliation, even in the dark. Exposing the foot region of a patron was already an audacious act, not to mention lying down in the zone of his personal space.

Nonetheless, at this point in the evening, we wonder how Ruth the Moabite would understand Naomi's inexplicit plan. It was customary for parents to arrange marriages for their children (e.g., Gen 21:21; 24; 34; 38; Exod 2:21; Judg 14:2–3, 10), and Naomi as a mother-in-law has taken on the responsibility. Although seemingly unlikely, was such an approach Israelite but not Moabite,[26] or was it Moabite so Ruth did not need further explanation? Or would Ruth the Moabite misinterpret Naomi's plan, including the Hebrew double meanings, and try to seduce Boaz? All this adds to the intrigue and the suspense of the narrative, as we, the audience, are kept in the dark about the specifics of Naomi's plan.

---

22. Gow, *Ruth*, 67n9.

23. See also Exod 2:20–21.

24. Cf. Seebass, "*bôš*," *TDOT* 2:50.

25. For ideas in this paragraph, I am indebted to John H. Elliott, "Deuteronomy—Shameful Encroachment on Shameful Parts: Deuteronomy 25:11–12 and Biblical Euphemism," in *Ancient Israel: The Old Testament in Its Social Context*, ed. Philip F. Esler (Minneapolis: Fortress, 2006), 169–70.

26. Cf. Morris, *Ruth*, 284.

THE BOOK OF RUTH

The vagueness and suggestiveness evoke the sexually charged milieu.[27] A woman from an ethnic background associated with sexual promiscuity (Gen 19:30–38; Num 25) prepares herself to look and smell attractive. Under the cloak of darkness, she steals to a location at a time associated with prostitution (Hos 9:1), seeking a midnight rendezvous with a man who has drunk wine and would be receptive to her advances. They are alone; no one knows they are there. And so, we the audience begin to feel the sexual tension and the temptation for them, especially for the man. Will he succumb like elder men in similar situations, like Lot and Judah? Both continued their family lines in similar situations, so will the same happen here?

Much rests with Boaz because Naomi concludes her speech with her fourth instruction: *he will tell you what to do*. He had not taken the initiative to secure the widows' long-term future, so Naomi wants to force his hand. The interplay between knowing and not knowing continues, as Naomi says Boaz will "tell you" or "reveal to you" (*yaggîd*)[28] what to do. This seems quite a leap since Boaz was not in on Naomi's plan. But it shows Naomi's trust in Boaz's character and his relationship to them—he is a man of worth who had already shown partiality toward them, and he is their relative (2:1; 3:2)—so he will act toward Ruth honorably. Perhaps we can detect a hint of Naomi's trust in God, although she does not mention him. In any case, she trusts Ruth will not be harmed or taken advantage of.

Naomi's threshing floor scheme is risky and dangerous. It is unconventional. It transgresses physical and social boundaries. Such a strategy to secure rest through marriage is neither prescribed in Old Testament law nor described in narrative. Marriage was usually arranged by at least one parent, with one Old Testament narrative example the betrothal type-scene at the well.[29] Naomi's scheme is born of desperation. The widows' hopes for obtaining long-term security were evaporating with the end of the wheat and barley harvests. No relative had assumed ongoing responsibility for the widows. Naomi's plan was fraught with risk, but we can understand its necessity under their circumstances. And her knowing Boaz's character mitigates the risk. Hers was a calculated risk, intermingled with faith.

In a small town such as Bethlehem, we can presume Naomi was aware of the nearer kinsman. But since she (and Ruth) had formed a patron-client relationship with Boaz and not the nearer kinsman, she was obliged to show loyalty and make the request to Boaz first. But why didn't Naomi, as the de facto parent, approach Boaz herself during daylight hours to arrange a

27. Cf. Moshe J. Bernstein, "Two Multivalent Readings in the Ruth Narrative," *JSOT* 50 (1991): 15–20.

28. Forms of this verb are found in 2:11 [2×], 19; 3:4, 16; 4:4 [3×].

29. See comment on 2:9 for the variations in the Ruth narrative.

194

## 3:1-5  HOME: RUTH ACCEPTS NAOMI'S PLAN

marriage with Ruth? And why didn't Naomi send Ruth to Boaz to request marriage during daylight hours? Within an honor-shame society such as ancient Israel, showing respect is crucial. It would have been too forward for Naomi to approach Boaz directly to request marriage because it would have put Boaz "on the spot." For if he was not willing to marry Ruth, Naomi would have caused him, her patron, to feel unease or embarrassment. He would "lose face," and his good name would be tarnished. And since Ruth was a "foreign" gleaner, or one of his "servant girls" at best (2:22), to request marriage directly would have been out of the question. The gulf in social standing would render a direct approach from Ruth impossible. This explains Naomi's choice of an indirect way to preserve the relationship with Boaz. Moreover, an indirect approach is often more persuasive because the one approached will not feel disrespected or shamed. Indeed, we will see that Boaz feels honored (v. 10).

**5** Ruth's response to Naomi's plan is surprising: *All that you say to me I will do.* She promises to obey everything Naomi instructs her ("all that you say to me"[30]; vv. 2–4). The *yiqtol* verb *tō'marî*, "you say," signals an ongoing commitment to obey Naomi (cf. 3:11; 2 Sam 9:11; 2 Kgs 10:5; Jer 42:5), not just obedience to Naomi's plan (which would be signaled by a *qatal* verb, "you said"; cf. Num 32:31; Josh 1:16). Ruth does not complain. She does not ask for further explanation. All we hear is her quiet trust in her mother-in-law's plan and we recall her vow of commitment on the road to Bethlehem (1:16–17). Yet we need to be careful not to misinterpret Ruth's obedience as blind or unquestioning.[31] Her ability for independent thinking was heard in her vow of commitment, which came after she refused to accept Naomi's directive to return to Moab (1:8–15). She chose to go out to glean in the fields and worked hard to secure provision for herself and Naomi. And as we will soon see, Ruth's execution of her mother-in-law's plan requires her to take initiative when an opportunity is presented to her. Ruth chooses to obey.

It is thus hard not to think that Ruth knew the risks she was taking. Going beyond the protection of the town gates after nightfall, she was at risk of physical assault (cf. Song 5:7). If Boaz misunderstands her approach as solicitation, she would be at risk of sexual assault. Since Boaz could misunderstand her intentions as seduction, he could send her away in shame, and so her reputation was at risk. She is willing to take these risks, but how will Boaz respond?

---

30. This clause is fronted for focus.

31. For the dangers of oppression and abuse from (mis)reading Ruth's obedience in an Asian family context, see Anna May Say Pa, "Reading Ruth 3:1-5 from an Asian Woman's Perspective," in *Engaging the Bible in a Gendered World: An Introduction to Feminist Biblical Interpretations in Honor of Katherine Doob Sakenfeld*, ed. Linda Day and Carolyn Pressler (Louisville: Westminster John Knox, 2006), 47-59.

# THE BOOK OF RUTH

Boaz's need to respond to the widows' initiative raises other questions. Why didn't he take the initiative in the first place? Why didn't Boaz do more to secure the long-term security of Ruth and Naomi?[32] Although he had been generous, by the end of the harvests their predicament was essentially unchanged. If Boaz had taken further initiative, Naomi's risky threshing floor scheme would have been unnecessary. At least three factors could have contributed to his inaction. First, Ruth had probably been wearing her mourning garb for the weeks she gleaned in his field.[33] Clothing has symbolic and social functions, and Ruth's clothing signaled that she was not ready for remarriage. Thus, Boaz was used to seeing her as a bereaved widow. This all changes when Naomi tells Ruth to wash, perfume, and change out of her mourning attire.

The next two hindering factors will be discussed here, although they do not become clear until the scene at the town gate (4:1–6). The second, Boaz states, is the presence of the nearer kinsman, who had the first right of redemption (3:12–13). But if Boaz did not want to usurp his kinsman's privilege, he could have pressed him to redeem the field, or he could have offered to Naomi to redeem the field if the nearer kinsman did not approach her. The third hindering factor could have been his personal situation. In this particular situation, if, in Boaz's mind, the redemption and levirate roles are inseparable, and he redeemed the land, he would need to marry the dowager—Naomi.[34] If he was single and without an heir, this course of action would preclude his producing a son to perpetuate his own "name" (Naomi is post-menopausal; 1:11–13). This being the case, should Boaz have encouraged the nearer kinsman to exercise his right of redemption? Yet if the nearer kinsman-redeemer redeemed the field and married Naomi, this would end Elimelech's family line. Boaz, keenly attuned to his social obligations, would be unlikely to allow this to happen. Thus, Boaz is caught in a bind. He can only escape if Naomi removes the possibility of levirate marriage to her, which she does by sending Ruth to the threshing floor.[35]

We, the audience, feel a sense of uncertainty as we hear Naomi's plan. Seeing things from Naomi's and Ruth's perspective grants us an appreciation of their vulnerable situation. This scene thus raises awareness in audiences— both ancient and modern—of those at risk in society. Awareness followed by initiative and intervention can forestall risks taken by vulnerable persons. Ruth's willingness to obey Naomi's risky plan was another sign of her

---

32. This paragraph is modified from Lau, *Identity and Ethics*, 83–85.

33. We cannot be sure because we do not know for how long widows (Israelite or Moabite) wore mourning clothes.

34. Marriage was not specified in the law as a role of a kinsman-redeemer but within a communal society, it could have fallen within their remit or wider sphere of responsibility (depending on the circumstances).

35. Ruth's substitution for Naomi is reinforced by the townswomen's ascription of Obed to Naomi (4:17).

196

## 3:6–15 THRESHING FLOOR: ENCOUNTER BETWEEN RUTH AND BOAZ

kindness. Those in a position to help can show kindness by protecting and providing for those in need, including sojourners, widows, and orphans in their affliction (e.g., Deut 24:17–22; 26:12–13; cf. Jas 1:27), thereby reflecting God's character (Deut 10:17–18).

## E'. THRESHING FLOOR: ENCOUNTER BETWEEN RUTH AND BOAZ (3:6–15)

Naomi has outlined her audacious scheme, to which Ruth assented without question (vv. 1–5). Since this scene opens with the narrator stating that Ruth followed her mother-in-law's instructions (v. 6), the audience focuses not on *if* but *how* she does so. We might be surprised by what we observe of Ruth's words and actions.

This scene parallels and contrasts scene 2 of the previous act. In both scenes, Boaz speaks in response to Ruth's action, although in this scene she is more directive. In their first recorded meeting, Ruth "chanced" upon Boaz's field; this time their meeting on the threshing floor is planned. The first takes place during the day in public; the second at night in private. The speeches in the field were heard and overheard by all; this time their hushed interchange is secret and kept secret. The theme of redemption mentioned by Naomi at the end of act 2 (2:20) is now developed in relation to Ruth and Boaz, its implication and a complication exposed. Again, the action is driven by Boaz's acts of generous kindness, and again the scene and the act hinge on his words about Ruth—her loyal kindness (2:11) and her public reputation as a "worthy woman" (3:11). Boaz takes a request in secret and gives an indication of Ruth's true worth. She takes his words about "wings" (2:12) and uses them to ask him to spread his "wing" over her as a kinsman-redeemer (3:9). Much is revealed under the cover of darkness.

⁶*So she went down to the threshing floor and did according to all*ᵃ *her mother-in-law had ordered her.*ᵇ

⁷*And Boaz ate and drank, and his heart was happy. Then he entered to lie down at the end of the grain heap. And she entered secretly and uncovered the place of his feet and lay down.*

⁸*In the middle of the night, the man trembled and turned over, and look! A woman lying at the place of his feet!*

⁹*He said,*ᶜ *"Who are you?"*ᵈ *And she answered, "I am Ruth, your handmaid. Spread the wing of your garment*ᵉ *over your handmaid, for you are a kinsman-redeemer."*

¹⁰*And he said, "May you be blessed by Yahweh, my daughter. You have made this last kindness better than the first by not going after young men, whether poor or rich.*

197

## THE BOOK OF RUTH

[11]*And now, my daughter, do not fear. All that you say*[f] *I will do for you, for all the assembly of my people*[g] *know that you are a worthy woman.*

[12]*And now*[h] *it is certainly true that I am a kinsman-redeemer. But there is a kinsman-redeemer nearer than I.*

[13]*Lodge*[i] *tonight, and in the morning, if he will redeem you, good;*[j] *let him redeem. But if he is not willing to redeem you, then I will redeem you—as Yahweh lives. Lie down until the morning."*

[14]*So she lay at the place of his feet*[k] *until the morning, but arose before*[l] *a man could recognize another. For he thought,*[m] *"Let it not be known that the woman*[n] *came to the threshing floor."*[o]

[15]*And he said, "Hold out*[p] *the cloak that is on you and grasp it." So she grasped it, and he measured out*[q] *six amounts of barley*[r] *and put them*[s] *on it.*[t] *And he*[u] *entered the town.*

---

a. A few Hebrew manuscripts, along with Syr. and Vulg., read *kōl* instead of *kəkōl*, most likely because of haplography. LXX and Tg. support MT[L].

b. The verb *ṣiwwattâ*, "she had ordered her," has a dagesh in the final *tav* because of the assimilation of *he* from the feminine suffix. The *he* does not have a *mappiq* because it is a mater lectionis; see GKC §59g; Holmstedt, *Handbook*, 157–58.

c. LXX[L], supported by Vulg. and Syr., reads "he said to her." Other LXX MSS and Tg. support MT[L].

d. MT[L] misspells the feminine pronoun by omitting the *shewa* under the *tav*. MT[A] has the correct spelling.

e. The consonants *knpk* could be read as a singular or a shortened dual form. MT *ketiv* Babylonian reads the former (supported by MT[L] *qere*, LXX, and Syr.), while the MT Tiberian *ketiv* reflects the latter (*BHS* critical apparatus). The singular, "wing of your garment," is the better reading in this context in light of the Hebrew idiom in other biblical texts; see comment on v. 9.

f. For the translation of this *yiqtol* form, see comment on v. 5. A few medieval MSS, supported by some LXX MSS, Syr., Tg., and Vulg., include *'ēlay*, "to me," after "you say." However, most Hebrew MSS and LXX MSS lack "to me." Its inclusion in some versions is most likely an interpretive addition (cf. v. 5).

g. Heb. "all the gate of my people."

h. "And now" is omitted in LXX.

i. In some Hebrew manuscripts either the *lamed* or *nun* is enlarged in *lînî*, which draws attention to the word, but for unknown reasons.

j. I read *tôb* as a finite verb with an indefinite subject, so "(it is) good." Some Jewish sages understood "Tob" as the name of the nearer kinsman (see, e.g., *Midr. Ruth Rab.* 6:3), but he is not referred to by this name in chapter 4.

k. MT[L] misspells "at the place of his feet" as *margəlōtāô*, while the MT[A] and MT[Y] have *margəlōtāw*. The *qere* reads *margəlōtāyw*, supported by 2QRuth[b].

l. The *ketiv* misspells "before" as *baṭerewm*, with the *qere* and multiple manuscripts reading *baṭerem*.

m. The third-person masculine singular *wayyiqtol wayyō'mer* is a shift from the preceding third-person feminine singular verbs, referring to Ruth. The verb most commonly means "to say," but if Boaz is speaking (LXX and Vulg.), the addressee is not clear. It cannot be

## 3:6–15 THRESHING FLOOR: ENCOUNTER BETWEEN RUTH AND BOAZ

Ruth (Vulg.), because the *niphal* jussive is third-person masculine singular, and he would not address her as "the woman" (*hā'iššâ*). In the Tg., Boaz speaks to "his servant" and in the *Midr. Ruth Rab.* 7:1 he addresses God. The Syr. reads "she said to him," that is Ruth speaks to Boaz. It is best to read the verb *'mr* as denoting "internal speech," which is found with the *yiqtol*, *wayyiqtol*, and *qatal* forms of *'mr* when introducing direct speech without a specific addressee. The Hebrew idiom *'mr blb*, "to say in the heart/mind," denotes internal speech (e.g., Gen 17:17; 27:41; Isa 47:10; Hos 7:2; Obad 3), but *'mr* by itself denotes the same elsewhere (e.g., Gen 20:11; 26:9; Exod 3:3; Judg 16:20; 1 Sam 18:11; 20:26; cf. Ruth 4:4). See BDB, 56; Wagner, "*'āmar*," *TDOT* 1:333.

n. 2QRuth[b] reads "she" instead of "the woman." The Tg. and LXX ("a woman") support MT[L].

o. Vulg. reads "here" but 2QRuth[b], Tg., Syr., and LXX support MT[L]: "the threshing floor."

p. The imperative *hābî* from the root *yāhab* can be an exhortation like "come!" (e.g., Gen 11:3, 7; 38:16; Exod 1:10; 2 Sam 11:15) or it can mean "give" (e.g., Gen 29:21; 30:1; 47:15; Judg 1:15; 1 Sam 14:41; Pss 60:13[11]; 108:13[12]; similarly in cognate languages, see *HALOT* 1:236). In this verse, it is the latter meaning, and since it generally expresses the desire for one person to provide something, a suitable translation is "hold out," especially since Ruth does not hand over ("give") the shawl to Boaz.

q. 2QRuth[b] reads "there" (*šm*) after "measured out," but the Vulg, Tg., and LXX support MT[L].

r. The Hebrew reads "and he measured six of barley" (*wayāmād šēš-šə'ōrîm*), omitting the unit of measurement (cf. v. 17). MT[L] implies six unspecified measures (supported by LXX and 2QRuth[b]), and Vulg. and Syr. translate "six measures." Only Tg. specifies "seahs" as the unit of measurement.

s. From the previous clause, the portions of barley ("them") are the object of the verb "put."

t. The suffix in *'ālêhā* ("on it/her") could refer to either the cloak (feminine noun) or Ruth. Boaz is more likely to place the portions of barley on the cloak since it is the closest prior referent.

u. Multiple Heb. manuscripts, Syr., and Vulg. read a feminine subject for the verb *bô'*, "enter," while Tg. ("Boaz") and LXX support MT[L]. The latter is preferred because the former would create a redundancy with the same verb (*wattābô'*) in the next clause. Boaz as the subject also maintains continuity with the previous two verbs.

This central scene takes place on the threshing floor. It is enveloped by descriptions of Ruth's going down to (v. 6) and Boaz's departure from (v. 15) this location. The initiative has passed from Naomi and Ruth to Boaz, but this occurred over three episodes based on time:

> A Early evening: Ruth arrives and waits (vv. 6–7)
>    B Middle of the night: Ruth proposes, Boaz responds (vv. 8–13)
> A' Early morning: Boaz gives Ruth grain, then departs (vv. 14–15)

The first episode contains narrative, the second is predominantly speech, and the third a mixture of the two. The parallels between the outer elements

## THE BOOK OF RUTH

(A-A') include "lying down," "the place of his feet," and secrecy (vv. 7, 14), and are strengthened with other words and wordplays (vv. 7, 15):

| he ate, | drank [*wayyēštə*], . . . | entered . . . | the grain heap [*hā'ărēmâ*] |
|---|---|---|---|
| he measured out six amounts of barley, | put [*wayyāšet*], . . . | entered . . . | the town [*hā'îr*].[36] |

As is often the case, the parallel elements are complementary:

| Ruth went down to the threshing floor on Naomi's command (v. 6) | Ruth prepares to return to the town after receiving an instruction from Boaz (v. 15) |
|---|---|
| Boaz eats and drinks (v. 7) | Boaz gives food to Ruth (v. 15) |
| Ruth comes secretly, uncovers his feet, and lies down (v. 7) | Ruth lies at his feet until morning, then prepares to leave secretly (vv. 14–15) |

The central element comprises the precipitant of the conversation and Boaz's question (vv. 8–9a). Ruth identifies herself (v. 9b) and presents her proposal, to which Boaz responds point-by-point:

Ruth: Spread the wing of your garment over your maidservant. (v. 9c)
Boaz: May you be blessed for this last kindness. I will do what you ask. (vv. 10–11)

Ruth: For you are a kinsman-redeemer [*gō'ēl*]. (v. 9d)
Boaz: I am a kinsman-redeemer but there is a closer kinsman-redeemer. If he will not redeem you, I will. (vv. 12–13)[37]

Similar to the previous act (2:11–12), at the center of the central scene we find Boaz praising Ruth's kindness and asking God to bless her (3:10–11). Kindness is a central character trait, expressed in her actions in daylight and darkness. It should not surprise us that Boaz recognizes this in Ruth since he too performs acts of kindness (2:20). In the Ruth narrative, both are channels of God's kindness (cf. 1:8; 2:20).

**6** After the conversation between Naomi and Ruth, the narrator inserts a statement with a Janus function. This verse confirms that Ruth acts according to her word (v. 5) and advances the narrative to the next location—the threshing floor. The dramatic tension is thus not in seeing whether Ruth

---

36. Porten, "Scroll," 39.

37. Boaz repeats *g'l* six times, twice in the same form (*gō'ēl*), four times in forms of the verb *gā'al*, "to redeem" (vv. 12–13).

## 3:6–15 Threshing Floor: Encounter between Ruth and Boaz

is true to her word and obeys her mother-in-law, but *how* her obedience is enacted and the outcome of her obedience. That Ruth *went down to the threshing floor* is consistent with her going down from the higher location of Bethlehem town (see comment on v. 2). Some, however, observe a difference in the sequence between Naomi's instruction (v. 3a) and Ruth's reported actions (v. 6). Did Ruth go down to the threshing floor and then execute her mother-in-law's commands (wash, perfume, put on garments)?[38] It is unlikely that Ruth could have washed at the threshing floor, and the three steps are closely connected. More likely is that Ruth's obedience to the three-step preparation is presumed in v. 6, which focuses on Ruth's obedience to Naomi's commands after her preparations (vv. 3b–4). Ruth's obedience was absolute: she did *according to all her mother-in-law had ordered her.*[39] The word for "order," *ṣiwwat*, can be softened to "instruct," but "order" better reflects the authority of Naomi in her relationship with Ruth. It is the word used for Boaz's "commands" to his workers (2:9, 15), and in the Old Testament for a household head's instructions to household members (e.g., Gen 27:8; 49:29; 50:16; 1 Sam 17:20; 1 Kgs 2:1; Jer 35:6, 8, 10; Esth 2:10, 20). Ruth said to Naomi, "All you *say* I will do," but the narrator says that Ruth did everything her mother-in-law *ordered* her. Ruth honors her mother-in-law's authority and views her words as orders.

7 Nonetheless, a comparison between Naomi's orders and Ruth's execution of said orders is instructive:

| | |
|---|---|
| Don't make yourself known to the man until he has finished eating and drinking. (v. 3) | And Boaz ate and drank, and his heart was happy. |
| When he lies down, take note of the place where he lies. | Then he entered to lie down at the end of the grain heap. |
| Then enter and uncover the place of his feet and lie down. | And she entered secretly and uncovered the place of his feet and lay down. (v. 7) |
| He will tell you what to do. (v. 4) | Startled, Boaz asks who she is and Ruth tells him what to do. (vv. 8–11) |

Ruth had prepared herself and was waiting at the threshing floor. As Naomi anticipated, *Boaz ate and drank, and his heart was happy.* Boaz had feasted, presumably with the other workers, and now he felt content and

---

38. Rashi suggests that Ruth adorned herself after she went to the threshing floor so she would not be mistaken for a prostitute.

39. Elsewhere *kakōl 'ăšer* with the verb *ṣāwâ* means following commands completely or thoroughly (e.g., Gen 7:5; Exod 31:11; Deut 1:41; 26:14; 1 Kgs 9:4; 2 Kgs 21:8; Jer 35:10; 36:8; 50:21; Ruth 3:6; 2 Chr 7:17). The preposition *kə* is taken as a *kaph veritatis*; see *IBHS* §11.2.9b.

# THE BOOK OF RUTH

perhaps mellow. The phrase *wayyîṭab libbô*, "his heart was good," when combined with drinking can indicate intoxication, so a person's judgment is impaired (e.g., 1 Sam 25:36; Esth 1:10) or they cannot defend themselves (2 Sam 13:28). But it can also indicate a relaxed or cheerful mood (Judg 18:20; 1 Kgs 8:66; Prov 15:15; Eccl 9:7). The ambiguity leaves some uncertainty about how Boaz might respond,[40] although the latter reading is more consistent with the mood of this scene. Even if he was tipsy, he is about to sleep it off. Understood this way, this detail gives us a sense of optimism that Naomi's plan is about to work out well. As does the next detail: *Then he entered to lie down at the end of the grain heap.* Where Boaz lies down is specified, and Ruth has taken note of it. The verb *wattābō'*, "he went in, entered," might suggest a shelter or tent, although the object of the verb is left implied.[41] In any case, tired after winnowing and with a full stomach after feasting, Boaz lies down to sleep in good spirits. The end of the grain heap is from Ruth's perspective and is an ideal location because it is away from prying ears. So far, so good.

The only difference between the next step of Naomi's plan and Ruth's implementation is the word *ballāṭ*, "secretly." The alliteration between *ballāṭ* and *wayyîṭab libbô*, "his heart was good," reminds us of Boaz's condition as Ruth approaches him.[42] In the episode of Sisera, Jael "secretly" approaches (*wattābō' . . . ballā'ṭ*; Judg 4:21) the sleeping army general to drive a tent peg through his skull. Nothing so violent is expected here; in fact, quite the opposite. Jael approached Sisera to end their brief association; Ruth seeks to make hers with Boaz permanent. The collocation of *ballāṭ*, *kānāp*, and *regel* is reminiscent of David's stealthy approach of Saul, when he cut off the "wing" of Saul's garment while the latter was "covering his feet" (relieving himself) in a dark cave (1 Sam 24:1–4). In both the Ruth and Samuel episodes, the younger honors the elder, who invokes a blessing on the younger. And Saul's concern for the continuation of his family line is suggestive for the situation between Ruth and Boaz.

So, Ruth enters Boaz's sleeping place without him knowing and uncovers his leg region. She waits for the cool night air to disturb his sleep. Everything is going to plan. For now.

**8** In the Bible, *the middle of the night* is the time for pivotal events, often with an element of defenselessness and surprise. The exact phrase (*wayəhî baḥăṣî hallaylâ*) is used for when the Egyptian firstborn were killed (Exod 12:29), and "the middle of the night" was when Samson outwitted the Philistines by pulling out Gaza's city gates (Judg 16:3).[43] On the threshing floor,

---

40. Cf. Campbell, *Ruth*, 122, who sees Boaz's condition as another obstacle to overcome.
41. Holmstedt, *Handbook*, 160, suggests a "half-filled granary."
42. The sounds *t-b-l* recur in *b-l-t*; see Rendsburg, *How the Bible Is Written*, 210.
43. See also 1 Kgs 3:20; Job 34:20; Matt 25:1–13; Acts 16:25–26; 27:27.

## 3:6–15 Threshing Floor: Encounter between Ruth and Boaz

events are about to reach a crescendo. Boaz's actions do not correspond to any of Naomi's orders, so we are especially alert to what will happen. The rapid-fire verbs reflect the speed of his actions: *the man trembled and turned over*. The verb *ḥrd*, meaning "to tremble,"[44] refers to Boaz's involuntary physical reaction which disturbs his sleep. Most likely, it was because of the cool night air on his feet, and so he "shivered,"[45] although he could have been "startled" by the sense of another person nearby or by a sound Ruth might have made. Trembling in the Bible is predominantly associated with fear (e.g., Exod 19:16; 1 Sam 14:15; 28:5; Isa 32:11),[46] and, despite the associations with the middle of the night, an element of fear is not necessarily present here.[47] The next verb *wayyillāpēt* means "and he turned" or "and he groped." The verb alliterates with *wayyîṭab libbô* and *ballāṭ*,[48] linking Boaz's action with Ruth's action and Boaz's response. After the man's sleep is disturbed, he either turns over or gropes for his covering.[49] The reflexive sense of the *niphal* verb[50] and the external point of view of the narrative[51] make the former more likely. Yet the ambiguity of the verbs used to describe Boaz's actions adds to the mystery of the encounter.

Boaz's actions are in staccato, but his response is reported in legato: *And look!*[52] *A woman lying at the place of his feet!* We now see things from Boaz's perspective. What a surprise to wake and turn over to find a woman nearby! He can tell that it is "a woman" (*'iššâ*), perhaps by what he can make out in the moonlight or by her scent, but he cannot identify her. The participle conveys the action in progress—we gain a sense of immediacy; we are in the moment with Boaz with the woman lying at his legs—and we wonder how he will respond. Her location, "at the place of his feet," rather than beside him, is suitable for someone of lower social status, especially someone who makes a request of a patron. The location "at the feet" elsewhere denotes following

---

44. *HALOT* 1:350.

45. Jacob describes the cold of the night preventing his sleep (Gen 31:40).

46. Consult Baumann, "*ḥārad*," *TDOT* 5:167–68.

47. Fear is also probably absent in Isaac's response to Jacob's deception (Gen 27:32–33); see Edward Allen Jones III, "'Who Are You, My Daughter [מי את בתי]?' A Reassessment of Ruth and Naomi in Ruth 3," *CBQ* 76 (2014): 659–60.

48. The voiceless labial *p* corresponds to the voiced labial *b* in the former words; Rendsburg, *How the Bible Is Written*, 210.

49. LXX and Vulg. read "troubled."

50. The root only occurs elsewhere to describe the "twisting" path of caravans (Job 6:18; *niphal*) and Samson "grasping" the pillars of the temple (Judg 16:29; *qal*); consult BDB, 542; *DCH* 4:564. For a discussion of this verb, see Sasson, *Ruth*, 78–80.

51. At this point, the narrative is externally focalized, giving support to "trembled" and "turned over." The next clause will shift to Boaz's perspective. See Nazarov, *Focalization*, 194–95.

52. For *hinnēh*, "look!" see the comment and note on 2:4.

## The Book of Ruth

that person, and hence dependency and submission to another's authority (e.g., Exod 11:8; Judg 4:10; 8:5; 1 Sam 25:24; 1 Kgs 20:10; 2 Kgs 3:9).[53] According to Naomi's plan, Boaz is now meant to tell Ruth what to do. But Naomi did not mention his midnight surprise and grogginess, so will he respond unexpectedly? Will she?

**9** The slightly off-script nature of events continues with Boaz's understandably brusque question, *Who are you?* Naomi said he will tell Ruth what to do, but now he asks her to identify herself. In the presence of others, Boaz's question to his field overseer was "Whose young woman is this?" (2:5), but now his question is reduced to its simplest form. Face-to-face with this woman, the man wants to hear her direct response. He previously viewed her as belonging to someone (2:5), now his question presents an opportunity for her to express her understanding of who she is. Previously, the overseer's answer highlighted her Moabite ethnicity and her relationship to Naomi (2:6). Previously, she was a "young woman"; now she is a "woman." This undercover mission, with its language of knowing and noting, revealing and concealing, has been leading to this point of identity crisis.

And she says, *I am Ruth.* Others might view her as a "foreigner," a designation she used on her first encounter with Boaz (2:10). She felt like an outsider, but after weeks in Boaz's field working among other harvesters, she feels some sense of belonging. She is not "the Moabite," just "Ruth." And she does not add, "widow of Mahlon" (4:10). Instead, she refers to herself as *'ămātekā*, "your handmaid." In Boaz's field, she referred to herself as a *šipḥâ*, which in many passages is synonymous (see comment on 2:13). Yet in narrative texts outside Genesis, *'āmâ* is the preferred term for a female slave who is a wife or in a conjugal relationship with her master (Judg 9:18; 19:19; 2 Sam 6:20–22).[54] If, as seems likely, there are different shades of meaning in the Ruth narrative, it would be that *šipḥâ* is the lowest form of female servant, while *'āmâ* includes those who are wives or concubines. Ruth is not in a conjugal relationship with Boaz when she makes her request, but her self-designation of *'āmâ* reveals what she aspires to be. If *šipḥâ* is the lowest rung of the social ladder, she now lifts her foot to the next rung with her use of *'āmâ*. Her use of *'ānōkî*, the deferential form of "I,"[55] and *'ămātekā* signals that she gives due respect to her social superior. Yet she also reveals her personal name to Boaz, which is consistent with the intimate nature of their encounter and her hopes of where their relationship will end up. She moves within the confines of the social structure, yet she does not feel bound by them.

---

53. *HALOT* 3:1185; Stendebach, "*regel*," *TDOT* 13:317.

54. Cf. Bridge, "Female Slave vs Female Slave," 17–18.

55. See note on 2:10.

204

## 3:6–15 Threshing Floor: Encounter between Ruth and Boaz

For, given that Ruth had intended to follow Naomi's plan and the report of Ruth doing so (vv. 5–6), it is startling to find that she *seems* not to. Rather than wait for Boaz to tell her what to do, she says, *Spread the wing of your garment over your handmaid*. She uncovered his feet and now asks him to cover her with *kənāpekā*, "your wing." Boaz prayed that Yahweh would richly reward her for taking shelter under *kənāpāyw*, "his wings" (2:12),[56] so by echoing the same word she is essentially asking him to act as the human agent through whom Yahweh will answer his prayer.[57] And it adds extra incentive for him to accept her request. But what exactly is she asking of Boaz? In light of its previous usage in the Ruth narrative, she could be asking for protection, like the English idiom, "to take her under his wing." Here "wing" probably refers to the corner of Boaz's garment, so we might think that Ruth simply asks Boaz to shield her from the cool night air. Some suggest she asks Boaz to literally cover her because she has disrobed.[58] But she is almost certainly asking him to marry her since this is the meaning elsewhere in the Old Testament (Ezek 16:8;[59] cf. Deut 23:1 [22:30]; 27:20) and the Near East.[60] The gesture of a groom covering his bride with his garment symbolizes the consummation of the marriage and the husband's authority over, and protection and provision for his wife. Although some understand Ruth's proposal as a sexual advance,[61] a marriage proposal is more likely. Indeed, Boaz will take her words as such (vv. 10–13).

Ruth continues by stating the reason for her request: *for you are a kinsman-redeemer*. Just as she echoed Boaz's own word ("wing"), she now echoes Naomi's. Her mother-in-law said that Boaz was "one of our kinsman-redeemers" (2:20), and now she uses this morsel of information to her advantage. In her plan, Naomi mentioned that Boaz was *mōda'tānû*, "our relative" (v. 2, cf. 2:1); Ruth now tells Boaz that he is a *gō'ēl*, "kinsman-redeemer." She does not say "the redeemer" but "a redeemer," likely because she had listened carefully to Naomi (2:20). Yet marriage is not one of the responsibilities of a kinsman-redeemer listed in the Old Testament. As such, some commentators understand Ruth to be adding the levirate responsibility to that of the kinsman-redeemer, and that at least part of her motivation is to provide an heir for

---

56. See comment on 2:12.

57. Cf. W. S. Prinsloo, "The Theology of the Book of Ruth," *VT* 30 (1980): 337.

58. E.g., Nielsen, *Ruth*, 68–70; Schipper, *Ruth*, 143.

59. See Paul A. Kruger, "The Hem of Garment in Marriage: The Meaning of the Symbolic Gesture in Ruth 3:9 and Ezek 16:8," *JNSL* 12 (1984): 79–86; Campbell, *Ruth*, 123. Cf. Rashi's comment on 3:9.

60. W. Robertson Smith, *Kinship and Marriage in Early Arabia*, Repr. ed. (Boston: Beacon Press, 1903), 105; D. R. Mace, *Hebrew Marriage: A Sociological Study* (London: Epworth, 1953), 181–82; Quick, *Dress*, 31.

61. E.g., D. R. G. Beattie, "Ruth III," *JSOT* 5 (1978): 41–43.

# THE BOOK OF RUTH

Mahlon.[62] Not only is such a reading unlikely,[63] it is unnecessary because the Old Testament most likely only outlines some, not all, of a kinsman-redeemer's responsibilities. Based on kinship solidarity, a kinsman-redeemer would be obligated to do whatever is required to help a family member in need. Maintaining and gaining greater honor was achieved by performing actions for the benefit of family members, and going beyond the minimum requirements of the law is worthy of greater ascribed honor. A kinsman-redeemer's role is to restore to wholeness that which has been lost, in this case, "rest" and ongoing security for Ruth and Naomi and the attendant restoration of their honor. It is thus best to understand Ruth's use of *gō'ēl* in its general sense of a kinsman who has responsibility for the well-being of fellow family members. Ruth is not requesting marriage with reference to levirate marriage or redemption of land. She has just revealed her identity and now confronts Boaz with his: you are a kinsman-redeemer. Play the part.

Ruth's proposal is not evidence, however, for an alteration to Naomi's plan. She has not misunderstood her mother-in-law's instructions.[64] Instead, Ruth's proposal is best understood as her taking the initiative when a small gap opens up with Boaz's inquiry: "Who are you?" (3:9). She answers his question but does not stop at that. We can imagine Ruth anxiously waiting for Boaz to awake (cf. v. 11), rehearsing different scenarios, and when the moment finally arrives, blurting out all that is on her heart. She replies by telling him who he is and what he is to do,[65] and her clever selection of the words "wing" and "redeemer" maximizes the chances that he will accept her proposal. For Naomi's plan only sketches the steps Ruth is to take up to the point of conversation with Boaz; it does not provide the words she is to say.

Furthermore, by beginning with a question rather than telling Ruth what to do, Boaz has gone outside Naomi's script.[66] Yet Ruth's words are still

---

62. These include Gray, *Ruth*, 395; Matthews, *Judges/Ruth*, 234; cf. Rashi's comment on 3:9.

63. Bush, *Ruth, Esther*, 168–69, lists three reasons: (1) The expressed sole purpose of the plan is the provision of "home and husband" for Ruth (3:1–4). Naomi does not mention the provision of an heir for Elimelech and Mahlon. (2) The previous usage of *gō'ēl* (2:20) was in its general non-legal sense. Since nothing has changed between that point in the narrative until chapter 3, it is unlikely Ruth is now using *gō'ēl* in its legal sense of asking Boaz to redeem land. (3) Ruth does not identify herself as "wife of the deceased," or "wife of Mahlon," implying she must raise an heir for her deceased husband's property. Instead, she calls herself an *'āmâ*, one who is socially eligible for marriage. Sakenfeld, *Ruth*, 61, adds another reason against reading a reference to property or offspring: it is unlikely that Ruth, as a new immigrant, would have technical knowledge of Israelite laws.

64. E.g., Berlin, *Poetics*, 90: "Naomi sent her on a romantic mission but she turned it into a quest for a redeemer." Cf. Zakovitch, *Rut*, 141, who suggests that Ruth disobeys Naomi's command.

65. The reversal is also noted by, inter alios, LaCocque, *Ruth*, 97; Campbell, *Ruth*, 121.

66. Cf. Sakenfeld, *Ruth*, 57: "Boaz has moved the encounter away from Naomi's anticipated scenario."

## 3:6–15 THRESHING FLOOR: ENCOUNTER BETWEEN RUTH AND BOAZ

consistent with the overall aim of the scheme: to provide her with security through a marriage partner (3:1; cf. 1:9). Her words are best understood as the climactic culmination of her actions immediately before and during the encounter on the threshing floor. They do not contravene the express plan of her mother-in-law; instead, they reveal Ruth's determination and ability for independent thought in seizing the initiative within the small window of opportunity presented to her by both Naomi and Boaz. She shows remarkable calmness and wisdom in her words and actions.

Nonetheless, Ruth's initiative is not without risk. Perhaps we think Ruth is reducing the risk by stating upfront that she is looking for marriage instead of a one-night stand. Yet by taking the initiative to tell Boaz what to do, the risk is magnified. He might reject her proposal out of hand due to shock: remember, he is not expecting this. She is also breaking several social taboos: she is a young female, he is an older man; she is a fringe-dwelling foreigner, he is a pillar of society; she lives off the scraps of the land, he is a wealthy landowner. We have reached the second key turning point of the narrative. How will Boaz respond to Ruth's audacity? Will he be angry? Will he reject her and send her away?

**10** He does none of the above. Instead, he says, *May you be blessed by Yahweh, my daughter.* Boaz's mention of Yahweh recalls his words to his harvesters ("May Yahweh be with you"; 2:4) and shows that he has regained his composure. His patriarchal benevolence is expressed in the way he addresses her again as "my daughter" (cf. 2:8), and he calls on Yahweh to bless Ruth (cf. 2:12). From the same generation as Boaz, Naomi addressed Ruth as "my daughter" (2:2, 22; 3:1). She also invoked a similar blessing on Boaz:

Naomi: *bārûk hû' layhwh*, May he be blessed by Yahweh. (2:20)
Boaz: *bərûkâ 'att layhwh*, May you be blessed by Yahweh. (3:10)

We are relieved that Boaz does not view Ruth's words as proposition or solicitation. Yet compared to his open generosity in the field, his generosity on the threshing floor is measured. Boaz's response comprises three parts:

*Blessing:* May you be blessed by Yahweh.
*Explanation:* This is a better kindness because you have not pursued more eligible men (v. 10).

*Promise:* And now [*wə'attâ*] all that you say I will do for you.
*Explanation:* For all my fellow townsmen know that you are a worthy woman (v. 11).

*Complication:* And now [*wə'attâ*] there is a nearer redeemer.
*Explanation:* Stay the night but if he will not redeem you, I will (vv. 12–13).

207

# THE BOOK OF RUTH

The harvesters' blessing was spoken to Boaz and, although they meant their words, functioned more as a greeting (2:4). Naomi's blessing for Boaz was not spoken in his presence (2:20). Boaz's blessing is spoken directly to Ruth and, canonically, is doubly significant.[67] First, she is one of only seven women in the Old Testament who are directly blessed. The others are Rebekah (Gen 24:60), Leah and Rachel (Gen 32:1[31:55]), Jael (Judg 5:24), Hannah (1 Sam 2:20), and Abigail (1 Sam 25:32–33). Second, she is the only woman who is blessed by invoking God's name, which recalls the paradigmatic Old Testament blessing invoking God's name: "Yahweh bless you and keep you; Yahweh make his face to shine upon you and be gracious to you; Yahweh lift up his countenance upon you and give you peace" (Num 6:24–26). The Aaronic blessing was spoken to God's people; remarkably, Boaz's blessing connects Ruth directly to Yahweh, strengthening her standing as a member of the covenant community, worthy of Yahweh's blessing.

Boaz invokes God's blessing, but his words are spoken to a person—Ruth. Yet Boaz wants God to act in response to his blessing. Again, in the Ruth narrative we see the interplay of God's sovereignty and human action. When Boaz blesses Ruth, he believes God is the decisive actor but also that God uses humans to carry out his blessing. Even in the act of blessing Boaz becomes part of how Ruth is blessed.

Boaz explains his blessing: *You have made this last kindness better than the first.* Ruth's first act of "kindness" (*ḥesed*) was shown to Naomi when she gave up the security of her homeland, people, and gods for those of her mother-in-law (cf. 2:11). In contrast to Orpah, Ruth ignored Naomi's urging to remain in Moab and committed herself to Naomi. But the reason for her choice of Boaz for a marriage partner as a greater act of kindness than the first is not as clear. Because of their previously established relationship, it would seem to be an understandable, if not a natural choice; this would hardly represent an act of kindness.

Yet Boaz says her act is better because she did not go *after young men, whether poor or rich.* The phrase *hālak 'aḥărê*, "to go after, follow," is used to describe relationships of allegiance and dependence, including worship of Yahweh (e.g., Deut 13:5[4]; Jer 2:2) or other gods (Deut 4:3; 6:14; 1 Kgs 18:21; cf. Ruth 1:15), and between a wife and her husband (Gen 24:5, 8, 39, 61; 1 Sam 25:42; Song 1:4). It can describe a passionate pursuit (e.g., Prov 7:22; Hos 2:7[5]),[68] as is appropriate here. Boaz describes the other potential husbands as "the choice young men" (*habbaḥûrîm*)[69] in contrast to his more

---

67. Cf. Eskenazi and Frymer-Kensky, *Ruth*, 61.

68. The illicit nature of the relations in these verses is not in view in this context.

69. The word is derived from *bḥr*, "to choose," and refers to men in their prime. See BDB, 104; H. Wildberger, "*bḥr*," *TLOT* 1:210.

## 3:6–15 THRESHING FLOOR: ENCOUNTER BETWEEN RUTH AND BOAZ

mature status. His age is not mentioned in the narrative but his style of language and the way he addresses Ruth indicate that he is at least Naomi's generation.[70] His statement that Ruth was free to choose from all the eligible bachelors in town reveals that she was under no obligation to marry a relative of her deceased husband (3:10). Indeed, she was released from all familial responsibilities (1:8–9). In one sense, Ruth's marriage to any Israelite could be viewed as an act of kindness because it makes permanent her relationship with Naomi in Israel, and thus her continued provision for Naomi.

Boaz's description of Ruth's action as one of kindness needs to take into account two other factors, the second of which will be discussed later (see comment on v. 13). First, her choice of Boaz means she sets aside personal preferences. As Boaz notes, she could have chased after a host of young men, either poor or rich (3:10). That is, she could have married for love or money, but she chose loyalty to Naomi and her family instead.[71] Boaz seems delighted and even flattered that Ruth would choose him. Hence, Ruth is understood to be showing further kindness to him by selecting him, despite his more elderly status. But we wonder what a Moabite widow's marriage prospects would have been in Bethlehem. Naomi thought they were so bleak that she told her daughters-in-law to return to Moab, and hints that their best chance would be if she bore more sons (1:9–13). The townswomen's response to Ruth on her arrival was underwhelming at best (1:19), and the field overseer emphasized her outsider status (2:6). It is unlikely that the Israelite men would have seen this Moabite widow as an attractive marriage partner (but cf. Boaz's assessment in v. 11). By his words, Boaz is showing Ruth kindness.[72]

But Boaz is too self-deprecating. Although he may be older than other potential marriage partners, he also has attractive qualities. He is a man of great worth—he is well respected and honorable, he is wealthy and generous. And if Boaz was single and without an heir, her choosing him would be a kindness because it would raise the possibility of offspring for him. The narrative does not mention his personal circumstances. He could have been married with children[73] or unmarried without children. The latter is more likely in his socio-historical situation, and since he is older, he could have been a widower.[74] The

---

70. Both Naomi (2:2, 22; 3:1, 16, 18) and Boaz (2:8; 3:10–11) call Ruth "my daughter." The Jewish interpretation suggesting that Boaz is eighty years old exaggerates his age (*Midr. Ruth Rab.* 6:2) since he can still protect his pile of grain on the threshing floor at night.

71. Hubbard, *Ruth*, 214–15. Zakovitch, *Rut*, 142, suggests that given Boaz's elderly status, Ruth acts independently of her heart's desire.

72. Cf. Grossman, *Ruth*, 229.

73. Assumed by, e.g., Millar Burrows, "The Marriage of Boaz and Ruth," *JBL* 59 (1940): 452.

74. Cf. Eryl W. Davies, "Inheritance Rights and the Hebrew Levirate Marriage: Part 2," *VT* 31 (1981): 259; H. H. Rowley, "The Marriage of Ruth," in *The Servant of the Lord and Other Essays on the Old Testament* (Oxford: Blackwell, 1965), 192; Morris, *Ruth*, 312.

209

# THE BOOK OF RUTH

probably low incidence of polygamy, combined with Naomi's choice of Boaz as a husband for Ruth, suggests Boaz was single (cf. comment on 4:12).

Nonetheless, from Ruth's perspective, a younger groom would have been more beneficial. If she wanted the kinship benefits, she could have chosen the other kinsman-redeemer, who was probably younger than Boaz.[75] In a close community, it is unlikely Naomi and Ruth were unaware of the nearer kinsman-redeemer's presence (cf. 1:19; 2:6; 3:11). Although, as a younger man, he would be more concerned to secure his financial stability, at least he would have a longer timeframe in which to provide for Ruth.[76] And as a younger man, there is a higher chance for Ruth to conceive. These may be pertinent reasons for Boaz's view that her proposal is a greater act of kindness: choosing him means there is a lower chance of bearing children and a higher chance she would be widowed again before any children are self-sufficient.[77]

**11** The second part of Boaz's response comprises a promise and an explanation. Echoing Naomi (v. 2), Boaz begins to outline his promise with *and now* (*wə'attâ*), which has the sense of "this is what I'm going to do" in light of preceding events (e.g., Gen 12:19), namely, Ruth's marriage request. The way he addresses Ruth, as *my daughter*, assures her that his concern for her will continue (cf. 2:8). He also calms her anxiety: *do not fear.* These words of reassurance are commonly used in the Old Testament (e.g., Gen 26:24; 35:17; Deut 1:21; 1 Sam 4:20; 2 Kgs 6:16), and Yahweh uses them in his role as redeemer (see Isa 41:13–14). Here Boaz acknowledges that fear would have been a natural response for someone in Ruth's position: destitute and without security, widowed and without children. He would have detected the quiver in Ruth's voice and the risk in her words. Although Naomi was confident of Boaz's favorable reaction, events had unfolded slightly differently to her plan, and there is always uncertainty with human interactions. And Boaz's reassurance shows he recognizes that Ruth's presence was daring and her proposal risky.

Most reassuring for Ruth is his promise: *All that you say I will do for you.* His promise is almost the same as Ruth's to Naomi: "All that you say to me I will do" (v. 5). Again, "all that you say" is fronted for focus, and the *yiqtol* verb *tō'mərî*, "you say," signals an ongoing commitment to act for Ruth, rather than what she has just requested (*qatal* verb). And their similar state-

---

75. See comment on 4:6.

76. For the comparative anthropological evidence from contemporary kinship-based societies, see Timothy M. Willis, *The Elders of the City: A Study of the Elders-Laws in Deuteronomy* (Atlanta: SBL, 2001), 238–50.

77. Cf. Willis, *Elders*, 264–65. One strand of Jewish thought has Boaz dying on the day after the wedding; *Ruth Zuta* 55, as mentioned in Louis Ginzberg, *The Legends of the Jews*, vol. 4, trans. Henrietta Szold, Paul Radin and Boaz Cohen (Philadelphia: Jewish Publication Society of America, 1928), 34.

## 3:6–15 THRESHING FLOOR: ENCOUNTER BETWEEN RUTH AND BOAZ

ments present Ruth and Boaz as similar in character—both loyal and generous. Although in effect he is committing to Naomi's plan, he commits to act *for you*, for Ruth. This is a reversal of what Naomi had anticipated: she said Boaz will tell her what to do, but here she is telling Boaz what to do and he commits to it! Boaz's response is startling from an honor-shame perspective and testament to his self-assurance since this man of great honor is willing to obey this self-designated "handmaid."

Boaz's explanation for his promise is *for all the assembly of my people know that you are a worthy woman*. The phrase *kol-ša'ar 'ammî*, "all the gate of my people," is a synecdoche for the appointed elders who assembled at the town gate to make political and legal decisions (cf. Deut 16:18), who in turn represent all the people of the town (cf. 4:11; Deut 22:15–16; 25:7).[78] The town gate was not only the way in and out, it also contained chambers where town business could be transacted, and the mention of the "gate" foreshadows the next act (4:1). As a public space, the decisions could be witnessed by the townspeople. Most likely, Boaz was one of the elders who met at the town gate (cf. 4:2), and so he knew of Ruth's reputation among his people. Arriving as a poor foreigner, Ruth had little ascribed honor (cf. 2:6). Her claims to honor stopped at "handmaid," but, according to Boaz, the public court of reputation had assessed her worth as much higher.[79]

Indeed, Boaz says that all the townspeople think highly of her, that she is an *'ēšet ḥayil*, "a worthy woman." Elsewhere, this phrase only occurs in Proverbs. In Prov 12:4, it describes a wife who is "the crown of her husband" (ESV) instead of a wife who brings shame. In Prov 31:10, the phrase *'ēšet ḥayil* introduces an acrostic (vv. 10–31) singing the praises of an invaluable wife: hardworking, capable with home duties, capable trading goods, generous to the needy, and trusted by her husband. Apart from the aforementioned, these characteristics are reminiscent of the Ruth narrative: a worthy woman is good with land management (v. 16); her husband is known in the gates, where he sits among the elders (v. 23); she teaches kindness (*ḥesed*; v. 26); and her works praise her in the gates (v. 31).[80] This proverbial acrostic fills in the picture of an excellent wife, and the placement of the book of Ruth after Proverbs in the Writings (in the Leningrad Codex) suggests that Ruth is an embodiment of this exemplary woman.[81] In the Ruth narrative, Boaz

---

78. Tg.: "all who sit at the gate of the Great Sanhedrin."

79. For a recent discussion of acquired and ascribed honor, and the public court of reputation, see Zeba Crook, "Honor, Shame, and Social Status Revisited," *JBL* 128 (2009): 591–611.

80. See Samuel T. S. Goh, "Ruth as a Superior Woman of ליח? A Comparison between Ruth and the 'Capable' Woman in Proverbs 31.10–31," *JSOT* 38 (2014): 487–500. For a recent minority view, that the book of Ruth problematizes conventional biblical wisdom, see Laura Quick, "The Book of Ruth and the Limits of Proverbial Wisdom," *JBL* 139 (2020): 47–66.

81. See Lau and Goswell, *Unceasing Kindness*, 37–52.

THE BOOK OF RUTH

is called *'îš gibbôr ḥayil*, "a man of great worth," i.e., a wealthy, virtuous, and honorable man. For Ruth, the word refers to her virtue and honor, and the proverbial background hints that she is the ideal wife—especially for Boaz, the "man of great worth." Based on virtuous character, they are a perfect match. What a transformation, from overlooked foreigner by the townspeople to a woman accepted by the townspeople and viewed as an ideal wife for Boaz! One from a shameful background is now capable of bringing great honor to her husband.

We must not overlook the place of public opinion in Boaz's thinking. Perhaps he would have given his promise to Ruth irrespective of the valuation of his townspeople, but the reason he gives is "for all the assembly of my people know that you are a worthy woman." High public praise indeed for a recently arrived Moabite. Gossip is a form of group sanction which influences conformity to community values.[82] Here, the Bethlehemite's high view of Ruth stems from her conformity to the norms of their society, especially kindness (*ḥesed*), and this gives Boaz a potent reason to marry her without risk to his reputation. If opinion is not uniform in Bethlehem society, the attitude of the elders assembled at the town gate represents the positive view, while Boaz's field overseer represents the more negative (2:6). The elders at the gate are more influential, so going beyond the minimum obligations of a kinsman would gain Boaz greater ascribed honor. And the positive public opinion of Ruth will help him carry out his plans.

As the central section of this act, verses 10–11 cast the spotlight on Ruth's character. As he had in the core of the previous act (2:11–12), Boaz praises Ruth's act of kindness and kinship loyalty, and calls on God to bless her in response. But there is a development: before, she was viewed as an immigrant and foreign outsider; now, she is an eligible woman in Israelite society, and recognized by the town elders as a worthy woman.[83] Despite hiding in the darkness, Boaz has identified her true character.

But notice what Boaz does not say: Yes, I will marry you. Because he cannot until a complication is removed.

**12** The obstacle is introduced by a second "and now" (*wə'attâ*, cf. v. 11). Boaz first gives an emphatic affirmation: *it is certainly true that I am a kinsman-redeemer*. He thus accepts the identity Ruth gives him and confirms he can fulfill the role. Boaz's use of *'ānōkî*, "I," instead of *'ănî* (see note on 2:10) may indicate that Boaz views her as on the same social level as himself,[84]

---

82. For ideas here I am indebted to Esler, "Power of Gossip," 664.

83. Boaz's response to Ruth reinforces my chaste reading of this scene. It would be incongruous for Boaz (also a man of worth/honor; 2:1) to praise Ruth for her kindness (v. 10) and worthy character (v. 11) if she approached to seduce or entrap him.

84. See Holmstedt, *Handbook*, 167.

## 3:6–15 THRESHING FLOOR: ENCOUNTER BETWEEN RUTH AND BOAZ

which is consistent with his description of her as "a worthy woman" (v. 11). Or Boaz could use *'ānōkî* here to speak to Ruth on a personal level.[85] Yet the clause *kî 'omnām kî 'im*, "it is certainly true that," is awkward. The *ketiv* has the consonants *'m* but is unpointed, while the *qere* suggests the word should be "written, not read."[86] The usual meaning of *kî 'im*, "unless, except for," does not make sense here.[87] Thus, many view the *kî 'im* as a dittography and remove it.[88] But if we maintain the MT, it would be another case of form following content, similar to the overseer's comment (2:7). The disjointed and overloaded syntax in Hebrew would reflect Boaz's dawning realization that there is *a kinsman-redeemer nearer than* him. Perhaps the *'im*, "if," betrays a hint of uncertainty and hesitation in Boaz's mind because of the existence of this kinsman.[89]

Naomi said to Ruth that Boaz was "close" to them, one of their kinsman-redeemers (2:20). Boaz now explains there is a nearer kinsman-redeemer, who holds the priority of redemption. In a small town, Naomi would have known about this nearer kinsman. It is thus likely Naomi chose Boaz based on his character and the relationship that had developed between him and Ruth, confident that Boaz would deal with the legal impediment of the nearer kinsman's priority. We do not know the exact kinship relation of Boaz or the nearer kinsman to Elimelech,[90] but the duty of a redeemer fell to the nearest male relative, then to the next nearest male relative if he declined.[91] Although Boaz has pledged personal responsibility to Ruth, he does not let his promise override his social obligations to the nearer kinsman. Perhaps Boaz had not acted earlier to secure Naomi and Ruth's future because of the presence of this nearer kinsman. Harmony and maintaining "face" in an honor-shame society could have deterred Boaz from confronting the nearer kinsman to perform his duty.

**13** The last part of Boaz's explanation can be structured as:

> A  Lodge tonight, and in the morning,
> > B  if he will *redeem* you, good;
> > let him *redeem*.

---

85. God uses *'ānōkî* in similar circumstances; see Revell, "Two Forms," 212–13.

86. There are seven other occurrences of this type of *qere* (2 Sam 13:33; 15:21; 2 Kgs 5:18; Jer 38:16; 39:12; 51:3; Ezek 48:16).

87. For a discussion, see Holmstedt, *Handbook*, 165–67.

88. LXX, Vulg., and Syr. do not translate the *kî 'im*.

89. Cf. LaCocque, *Ruth*, 100.

90. Rashi suggests the nearer kinsman was a brother of Elimelech, while Boaz was a nephew.

91. Regarding redemption of land, the order of responsibility was brother, uncle, cousin, then any other blood relation (Lev 25:48–49).

# The Book of Ruth

> B' But if he is not willing to *redeem* you,
>> then I will *redeem* you—as Yahweh lives.
> A' Lie down until the morning.

Boaz's plan to resolve the complication (B-B') is enveloped by his instruction to stay the night on the threshing floor (A-A').

Ruth had pledged that she would "lodge" wherever Naomi lodged (1:16). Boaz's use of the same word deflects a more sexual reading of his intentions. Boaz's invitation anticipates a shift of Ruth's primary allegiance, from her mother-in-law to Boaz; here it is only for *tonight*, in the future, it would be permanent.[92] By telling Ruth not to return to town alone, he takes on the role of a protector—he takes her "under his wing" (cf. 2:12; 3:9). He protects her from physical harm since it could be dangerous for a single woman to wander around at night, especially outside the town gate (cf. Song 5:7). He also protects her from public disgrace since she could be mistaken for a prostitute (cf. Hos 9:1). His honor is also at stake if people misunderstand their nocturnal actions and hence, also the outcome of Boaz's plans.

For Boaz is keen to help Ruth: *in the morning* he will offer the right of redemption to the nearer kinsman. The fourfold use of "redeem" in Boaz's speech ensures that neither Ruth nor we, the audience, miss the importance of this concept. Ruth asked Boaz to marry her on the basis that he would act in a general sense as a kinsman-redeemer. Although "redemption" as applied to marriage is unattested elsewhere in the Old Testament, Boaz accepts this general sense of his role because he says "redeem you" three times to Ruth. Redemption in Boaz's mind is not primarily of land nor Naomi,[93] although she is the Judahite widow of Elimelech. If kinsman-redeemer marriage was specified under the law, we would expect that marriage would be to Naomi, not Ruth the Moabite. But Boaz is still willing to restore to wholeness what had been lost to the clan by marrying Ruth.

Boaz may be eager to marry Ruth, but he is still aware of the nearer kinsman's "first right of refusal." He says, *if he will redeem you, good; let him redeem.* It is not that Boaz is sanguine about the prospect of the nearer kinsman marrying Ruth; rather, his words reflect his respect for the nearer kinsman's rights. Boaz's heart pulls in one direction, but his willingness to uphold the law constrains him. Again, he lives up to his reputation as "a man of great worth" (2:1)—everything must be done in a right and honorable way.

---

92. Naomi's first use of *hallaylâ*, "tonight," had sexual connotations (1:12) but not her second (3:2).

93. As it turns out, Ruth's marriage to a kinsman-redeemer is inextricably linked to the redemption of land (4:3–10).

## 3:6–15 THRESHING FLOOR: ENCOUNTER BETWEEN RUTH AND BOAZ

Boaz continues: *if he is not willing to redeem you, then I*[94] *will redeem you.* So far, there has been no mention of preserving Elimelech's family line, but this may be in the back of Boaz's mind. The aim of Naomi's plan was to find "rest" for Ruth in a husband and home, with Boaz as the chosen man (vv. 1–2). In response to Ruth calling him a redeemer, he speaks of redeeming her. The phrase *wə'im-lō' yaḥpōṣ*, "but if he is not willing," only occurs in one other place in the Old Testament, concerning a release from the levirate duty: "But if the man is not willing to take his sister-in-law" (Deut 25:7). Boaz does not say "if he is not willing to *take* you," but "if he is not willing to *redeem* you." Boaz's allusion to the levirate law[95] not only strengthens the link between redemption and marriage, it also hints that Boaz is thinking about the broader consequences of his marriage. In this sense, his speech has come full circle: he began by praising Ruth's choice of him as a "better" (*hêṭabtə*) kindness, and now he declares it is "good" (*tôb*) that she will be redeemed. She might not have linked marriage with any legal responsibilities of a kinsman-redeemer, but this is how Boaz understands her request. Ruth simply requested marriage, but Boaz sees the wider consequences of her request—not clear at this point in the narrative, but eventually also involving the redemption of land and the perpetuation of Elimelech's line. This is the second reason Boaz considers Ruth's marriage request as an act of better kindness than her first.

Boaz's promise is conditional on the response of the nearer kinsman, but he affirms it by swearing an oath: *as Yahweh lives.*[96] Usually, the oath precedes the declaration,[97] but here its position emphasizes Boaz's promise—he is determined to keep it. The mention of Yahweh's name forms an inclusio with Boaz's blessing that opened his speech (v. 10). Here Boaz invokes Yahweh as a witness to his promise and the punisher if he does not keep it. The mention of Yahweh's name also reminds us of God's sovereignty. As the characters invoke God's name in blessings and oaths (1:8–9; 2:4, 12, 20), they also do their utmost to fulfill what they have promised or requested. As we play our part, we are often the instruments through whom God brings blessing to others.

Boaz again instructs Ruth to remain on the threshing floor: *Lie down until the morning.* The verb *škb*, "to lie down," can have sexual connotations and its use adds to the suggestiveness of this scene (see comment on v. 4). But

---

94. Boaz continues to use *'ānōkî* rather than *'ănî* (cf. v. 12).

95. Cf. LaCocque, *Ruth*, 102: "One will appreciate Boaz's Freudian slip by which, instead of quoting the text of Deuteronomy literally ('desire to take [a woman]'), he hides his feelings by saying, 'desire to redeem.'"

96. On oath exclamations, see *IBHS* §40.2.2; JM §165e. See also Moshe Greenberg, "The Hebrew Oath Particle *ḥay/ḥē*," *JBL* 76 (1957): 34–39.

97. Only here and 1 Sam 20:21 does the oath follow the declaration.

215

## The Book of Ruth

in the context of Boaz's speech, the plain sense is more likely: Boaz invites Ruth to lie down on the ground and, by extension, to go to sleep, as he had done earlier (v. 7; cf. v. 4). It is highly unlikely Boaz would promise before Yahweh that he would ensure her redemption through marriage, and then act as if they were already married. If there is an additional sense to *škb*, it is that it foreshadows her future permanent rest with Boaz, in contrast with "lodging." In any case, Boaz's second mention of "the morning" is reassuring for Ruth. The first mention was followed by his statement that he would first offer her redemption to the nearer kinsman; this time it follows his guarantee that he would redeem her if the nearer kinsman declines. Either way, her redemption is certain. Nonetheless, Boaz's diligent concern for her welfare, as expressed in his asking her to stay under his protection until daybreak—after the dangers of the night have passed—signals to us, the audience, that he is likely to be the redeemer. She first entered Boaz's field in "the morning" to work (2:7); now, she will rest "until the morning" to learn the outcome of their relationship that developed.

**14** Ruth followed Boaz's instructions: *she lay at the place of his feet until the morning*. Naomi had mentioned this location (v. 4), she had lain there before the encounter with Boaz (vv. 7, 8), and now after. Although she had requested marriage, they were not yet, and so she remains "at the place of his feet." This location symbolizes dependence and submission (cf. v. 8)—she lies at the place of a supplicant instead of by his side as his wife. Their indeterminate relational status and the imminent resolution of the same motivate their following actions. Ruth rises at daybreak, *before a man could recognize another*. A whiff of scandal would scupper negotiations at the town gate, so she prepares to return home unseen. Her desire not to be recognized is conveyed by the *hiphil* of *nkr*, which contrasts with her delight in the opposite by Boaz (2:10), a joy shared by her mother-in-law (2:19). This is in keeping with the mystery and the concealing and revealing of identity in this scene. She does not want to be recognized by "a man" (*'îš*), and Boaz thinks, *Let it not be known that the woman came to the threshing floor*. In referring to Ruth, Boaz de-identifies her to "the woman" (*hā'iššâ*) since public presumption of an inappropriate visit would make her lose face—she would lose her status as "a worthy woman." He is probably also concerned to protect his own reputation from damage if his fellow townsmen misunderstood the nature of his midnight encounter with "the woman."

With the first light creeping onto the threshing floor, we begin to make out Boaz's emerging identity. Reference to him as an anonymous "man" (vv. 3, 8, 16, 18) hides a deeper development in his identity. The previous evening Boaz went to the threshing floor as an honored and honorable member of Bethlehem society, a relative of Elimelech, and by extension of Naomi and Ruth. He is a wealthy landowner used to giving commands but

## 3:6-15 THRESHING FLOOR: ENCOUNTER BETWEEN RUTH AND BOAZ

on the threshing floor, Ruth tells him who he is and what he should do. For a brief moment, he is caught off guard, but quickly gains his equanimity to take up the role requested of him. Kin he is, but Ruth wants him to be more. She requests marriage and wants him to be her redeemer, a special task for the nearest relative. His desire stirs and he catches a glimpse of his new identity—as Ruth's husband and redeemer. Hers is the most drastic identity development in the narrative, but the identity of others will not be left unchanged in her wake.

**15** Similar to act 2, Ruth returns to Naomi with grain from Boaz. The grain might simply be another act of generosity, but the extended description of his giving of the grain invites us to consider other potential meanings. Boaz first instructs Ruth to *hold out the cloak that is on you and grasp it* firmly.[98] The word for cloak (*miṭpaḥat*) only occurs elsewhere in Isa 3:22, where it is one of four in a list of women's fine clothes. Although different words are used, the use of *miṭpaḥat* supports the reading that Ruth put on her "best clothes" (*śəmālōt*; v. 3) to meet Boaz. It would have been an outer garment, probably either a cloak or a shawl, that Boaz asks Ruth to make available to measure *six amounts of barley* into.[99] The Hebrew is *šēš-śə'ōrîm*, "six barleys," but since Boaz asks for her cloak to contain them, it must be that the unit of measure is not stated[100] because six grains of barley only require her hand to hold them. As such, we can only guess the amount of barley, although it may have been known by ancient audiences. Recent interpreters' estimates have ranged from six grains to six seahs (27–45 kilograms or 60–100 pounds).[101] The exact amount is not important, but following Boaz's concerns to protect her and his reputations (v. 14), it would need to be large enough to be visible to observers to provide a cover for Ruth's presence. They would presume that, because of her poverty, she had gone to the threshing floor at night to collect grain.[102] Based on our current understanding of ancient measurements, six omers (18–29 pounds or 8.2–13.2 kilograms) is most likely.[103] But perhaps,

---

98. The verb *'āḥaz* can have the nuance of "hold fast" or "grasp." For instance, one can hold fast to heels (Gen 25:26), a snake's tail (Exod 4:4), the doors of a city gate (Judg 16:3), the ark (2 Sam 6:6 = 1 Chr 13:9), a beard (2 Sam 20:9), or the horns of the altar (1 Kgs 1:51); see H. H. Schmid, "'ḥz," *TLOT* 1:81–82.

99. Cf. Judg 8:25, where a garment (*śimlâ*) is used to store earrings.

100. The omission of units of measurement is fairly common in the Old Testament; see JM §142n; GKC §134n; *IBHS* §15.2.2b. The Tg. interprets the six measures as symbolizing David, Daniel and his companions, and the King Messiah.

101. Six grains would not need a cloak to carry, while six seahs seem too large an amount to fit and carry in a cloak. Ephahs were mentioned previously (2:17), but six ephahs (between 82–132 kilograms or 180–290 pounds) would be too heavy for Ruth to carry.

102. Humbert, "Art et leçon de l'historie de Ruth," 279–80.

103. An omer is a tenth of an ephah. Moreover, since Boaz placed the grain onto Ruth's

## The Book of Ruth

given the circumstances, Boaz simply scooped six cupped handfuls of grain, or six measures of grain with a nearby implement into Ruth's cloak.

Clothing could have further symbolic meaning, as it has previously in this act. In scene 1, Naomi told Ruth to put on her "best clothes" (v. 3) to indicate her period of mourning was over and her availability for marriage. In scene 2, Ruth asked Boaz to spread the corner of his garment over her (v. 9), an act symbolizing marriage. In this scene, Boaz sending Ruth back with grain in an item of clothing that signaled her availability for marriage perhaps hints he will play a central role in securing "rest" for her. He will ensure that she will be redeemed.[104] The lingering description of this exchange adds weight to the interpretation that the exchange symbolizes and foreshadows his giving of another "seed"—to produce a child.[105] This symbolism is reinforced if Boaz scoops the grain into her cloak she is holding in front of her, which would form a bulge in front of her stomach.[106] Some interpreters understand Boaz as placing the six measures of grain on her back, but the garment is the more likely referent for "on it/her" (‘ālêhā) since it is the nearest referent and it will be how she will transport the grain.[107] This exchange is indeed pregnant with meaning.

After Boaz placed the grain onto Ruth's cloak, he entered (yābō’) the town. Careful to avoid any suspicions of wrongdoing between himself and Ruth, he left by himself. With daybreak, there was no further need for him to protect the grain piles,[108] and anyway, he was eager to find a solution to the issue that Ruth has raised. He could have returned home or gone straight to the town gate; either way, Boaz and Ruth do not return to town together.

In this verse, Boaz acts efficiently after he determines that Ruth's presence on the threshing floor should not become known. He spoke, he measured, he placed, he left. This rapid sequence of verbs not only bustles the plot along, it also presents Boaz as a man of purposeful action. As he leaves the scene, we eagerly anticipate what he will do next.

---

cloak, not onto her (so CSB; contra ESV, NIV, NJPS), a larger amount is possible but not as necessary; see translation note.

104. Ruth will give another reason for Boaz's gift (v. 17).

105. Cf. Barbara Green, "The Plot of the Biblical Story of Ruth," *JSOT* 23 (1982): 63–64. But cf. 4:12, where Ruth is described as giving "seed" or offspring to Boaz.

106. Similarly, Timothy J. Stone, "Six Measures of Barley: Seed Symbolism in Ruth," *JSOT* 38 (2013): 197–98; Nehama Aschkenasy, "Language as Female Empowerment in Ruth," in *Reading Ruth: Contemporary Women Reclaim a Sacred Story*, ed. Judith A. Kates and Gail T. Reimer (New York: Ballantine Books, 1994), 117; Porten, "Scroll," 40. For a picture of Ruth carrying the barley in front, see the thirteenth-century French Gothic "Crusader Bible," MS M.638, fol. 18v, accessed May 22, 2021, https://www.themorgan.org/collection/crusader-bible/36.

107. Cf. Holmstedt, *Handbook*, 172–73.

108. Presumably, other workers remained on the threshing floor that night.

## 3:16–18 Home: Naomi and Ruth Debrief

This central scene of act 3 hums with tension. The combination of the location, the biblical backstory, the mood, the double entendres, and the taut plot makes for a heady cocktail reflecting the tension and sexual temptation felt by the characters, especially Boaz. We feel uneasy reading or hearing this scene, as many audiences before us have.[109] It reaches a climax with Boaz's speech, the high point of tension not just in this act but the Ruth narrative overall. Boaz releases some of the tension by acknowledging Ruth's virtuous character and assuring her that he will fulfill her request (vv. 10–13). He acts with honor, as befits his reputation as a worthy man (2:1). Others before him had fallen into temptation in similar circumstances (including his forefather Judah; Gen 38). As we, the audience, experience the action from Boaz's perspective, the narrative raises the question: how would we respond in his situation? For, in the heat of the moment, Boaz has the presence of mind to invoke God's presence—to bless and as a witness to his promise. Indeed, Boaz is a man of his word: in act 2, he spoke big and backed up his words with generosity; now, he gives his word, and we know he will act with integrity. He does not take advantage of Ruth's vulnerability but recognizes her kindness and responds with loyalty. Acts of kindness engender kindness in return.

### D'. HOME: NAOMI AND RUTH DEBRIEF (3:16–18)

Naomi's risky plan (vv. 1–4) has been successful—to an extent. Boaz accepted Ruth's proposal, but he also raised a complication (vv. 9–13). Ruth surreptitiously returns to her anxious mother-in-law to report all that happened. Similar to the last scene of act 2, Ruth returns with a gift of grain from Boaz and reports what he had said and done. There is a definite end in sight for Ruth's and Naomi's destitution, and Boaz's recognition of Naomi's hand in the midnight encounter foreshadows greater honor she will receive. The complete reversal of the widows' shame is imminent.

[16] *When she came to her mother-in-law, she said, "Who are you,*[a] *my daughter?" And she told her all that the man had done for her.*

[17] *And she said, "These six measures of barley he gave to me, for he said to me,*[b] *'You must not come empty-handed to your mother-in-law.'"*

---

109. For instance, the Tg. at 3:4 makes Naomi's instructions less open-ended: "You shall ask advice from him, and in his wisdom he will tell you what to do." Rabbinic traditions reduce the sensual element by commenting that "washing" was to remove the soiling of idolatry, and "anointing" was with "mitzvot and righteousness" (*Midr. Ruth Rab.* 5.13). It reduces the risky element by suggesting Boaz's heart was merry because he was engaged in the words of the Torah (*Midr. Ruth Rab.* 5.15; 3:7).

# THE BOOK OF RUTH

[18]*She said,[c] "Sit tight,[d] my daughter, until you know[e] how the matter[f] turns out, because the man won't rest unless[g] he finishes the matter today."[h]*

a. The question *mî-'att* is omitted in the LXX. 2QRuth[b] (*mâ*) and Vulg. (*quid*) read "What are you?" Tg. and Syr. read "who," with Ruth answering in the latter, "I am Ruth."

b. In the same way as 3:5, MT[L] *qere* adds vowel points *ē a* without the consonants *'ly*, indicating that *'ēlay*, "to me," is to precede *'al-tābô'î*, "you must not." This is probably another case of parablepsis, whereby the scribe skipped from the *aleph* that begins *ēlay* to the *aleph* that begins *'al-tābô'î*. LXX, Tg. and Syr. support MT[L] *qere*, while the Vulg. omits "to me."

c. Vulg. specifies "Naomi" as the subject and Syr. "her mother-in-law."

d. The basic meaning of the verb *yāšab* is "to sit, sit down," but it can also mean "to stay, dwell" or "to wait." See comments and Görg, "*yāšab*," *TDOT* 6:424–30; *HALOT* 2:444–45.

e. MT[L] *tēd'în*; for the paragogic *nun*, see note on 2:8.

f. MT[L] lacks a definite article with *dābār* ("matter"; cf. LXX *rhēma*), although it is present later in this verse (*haddābār*). For instances where the definite article is omitted, see JM §137p.

g. Reading the *kî-'im* clause as exceptive; see GKC §163c; JM §173b. It can also be read adversatively, "The man will not rest but will finish the matter today"; so Holmstedt, *Handbook*, 177.

h. Vulg. omits "today."

The end of the previous scene was marked by Boaz's return to the town, the start of this scene is marked by Ruth's return to her mother-in-law. But this scene does not end with a narrative conclusion; rather, its openness points forward. Similar to the last scene of the previous act, Ruth responds to Naomi's question (2:19; 3:16). Boaz's action is the focus of this scene — first summarized by the narrator (v. 16) then refracted through Ruth's words (v. 17). Our attention is focused on the significance of Boaz's gift. Then the conclusion of this act echoes that of the previous act:

> Boaz . . . until the . . . harvests were finished [*kəlôt*] . . . she lived [*wattēšeb*]. (2:23)
> Sit tight [*šəbî*] . . . the man . . . unless he finishes [*killâ*]. (3:18)[110]

The previous act ended with hope then disappointment because the solution was only temporary. This act ends with hope and expectation.

In our chiastic structure of the Ruth narrative, this scene (3:16–18; D') parallels and contrasts with Naomi's acceptance of Ruth's plan (2:1–3; D). The characters and location are the same for both scenes, and although there are similarities with the last scenes of both acts (2:18–23 and 3:16–18), this scene better corresponds to the first scene of act 2. That scene opened by mentioning Boaz and closed with Ruth entering his field. This scene opens with an inquiry about Ruth's relationship to Boaz and what he had done for

110. Cf. Porten, "Scroll," 42.

220

## 3:16–18 HOME: NAOMI AND RUTH DEBRIEF

her on the threshing floor, and closes with an anticipation that he would secure their future that day. Ruth set out to find food for her and her mother-in-law for at least one day (2:1–3); now she returns with barley from Boaz as both a gift and a guarantee he will keep his promise to secure her future (3:17–18). Thus, from a plot perspective, this scene forms an inclusio with 2:1–3—a sense of hope raised by the presence of Boaz has now developed into a certain expectation that he will fulfill that hope.

**16** Just as Ruth was sent out into the night by "her mother-in-law" (v. 1), and Ruth followed the plan of "her mother-in-law" (v. 6), she now comes back to *her mother-in-law*, who was awaiting her return. The narrator may well be hinting that Ruth's kinship status has not changed just yet.[111] Naomi's seemingly simple question to Ruth bristles with potential meaning. The Hebrew is *mî-'att bittî, Who are you, my daughter?* but this does not seem to make sense since Naomi's question about identity ("Who are you?") is followed by an address ("my daughter") that reveals she knows whom she is speaking to. Most English versions change the question from one of identity to an inquiry about welfare, e.g., "How did you fare, my daughter?" (ESV).[112] This is consistent with Ruth's reply, but an inquiry solely about welfare misses the resonances of the Hebrew text.

An alternative rendering of the Hebrew is, "Is that you, my daughter?"[113] We can imagine that Naomi would be anxiously awaiting Ruth's return from her fraught nocturnal encounter. Boaz was also anxious for Ruth to leave the threshing floor unnoticed. The hint of uncertainty about Ruth's identity would then indicate that Ruth returned before sunrise, when the light was still murky. More specifically, this rendering indicates that Naomi knew the person approaching her was female,[114] but that Naomi was uncertain about her identity. She addresses her as "my daughter" because she was eagerly awaiting Ruth's return. An inquiry to clarify a person's identity would be similar to the question posed by the elderly dim-eyed Isaac when Jacob approached him: *mî 'attâ bənî,* "Who are you, my son?" (Gen 27:18). Isaac knew it was one of his sons, but he did not know which one. This inner-biblical allusion foregrounds the use of a shady scheme by a mother/mother-in-law to gain a blessing from an elderly man.[115]

Yet Naomi's inquiry about identity links it more closely to a nest of other questions in the Ruth narrative. Ruth heard the same question just hours

---

111. Hubbard, *Ruth*, 223.

112. "How did it go, my daughter?" (NIV); "How is it with you, daughter?" (NJPS). So also, e.g., Eskenazi and Frymer-Kensky, *Ruth*, 66–67; *IBHS* §18.2d.

113. So NKJV; see also Basil Rebera, "Translating Ruth 3.16," *BT* 38 (1987): 234–37.

114. "You" (*'att*) is feminine.

115. For other similarities with Gen 27:1–40, see Jones III, "'Who Are You, My Daughter . . . ,'" 653–64; Ben-Zion Ovadia, "The Scene of Ruth's Encounter at the Threshing-Floor, in Light of the Story of Jacob's Deception of Isaac (Genesis 27)," *Beit Mikra* 65 (2020): 88–106 (Heb.).

# THE BOOK OF RUTH

ago, on the lips of Boaz in the middle of the night (3:9). He did not add "my daughter" because he was unsure of the identity of this female. But he addressed her as "my daughter" before (2:8) and directly after he finds out her identity (3:10, 11). Boaz also inquired about Ruth's identity when he first saw her in his field (2:5). If these three questions chart the development of Ruth's identity to this point, Naomi's question could be read as, "Who are you now?"[116] or better, "Whose are you?"[117]

> 2:5    *ləmî hanna'ărâ hazzō't* / "Whose young woman is this?"
> 3:9    *mî-'ātt* / "Who are you?"
> 3:16    *mî-'att bittî* / "Whose are you, my daughter?"

After all, Naomi had sent out her daughter-in-law to find a husband and home with Boaz (3:1–2), so now Naomi is essentially asking her whether she was successful.[118] As expected for such a question, Ruth does not respond with, "I am Ruth" (as she would to "Who are you?"; cf. 3:9; Gen 27:18–19) but by laying out what Boaz had done for her.

We, the audience, are meant to understand the narrator's report of Ruth's reply, detailing *all that the man had done for her*, as an accurate summary of the night's events. However, consistent with the tenor of the nocturnal encounter, it is somewhat vague. It still even refers to Boaz as "the man," as he had been previously (3:3, 8; cf. 14), just as Ruth had been de-identified to "a/the woman" (vv. 8, 14; cf. 11), reminding the audience of the riskiness of Naomi's scheme. Curiously, the summary mentions what Boaz had *done* since the main thing he did was to *speak* about what he would do in the future. He provided Ruth protection and barley, but his main activity was to promise to do all Ruth asked (v. 11), and that he would redeem her if the nearer kinsman declined (v. 13). Thus, the forward-leaning aspect of what the man "had done," or more specifically promised he would do, pushes the audience to anticipate what he will do next. By not repeating the details of the night, the narrator swiftly moves the action on and shifts the emphasis to Ruth's next words (v. 17).

We can understand Ruth's focus on Boaz's actions from an honor-shame perspective, and it adds to our understanding of her character. Naomi anticipated that Boaz would tell Ruth what to do, but, as it turned out, Ruth took the initiative to tell Boaz who he is and what he should do. Ruth omitted her role in starting the conversation and leading it in a particular direction, for

---

116. So also Sasson, *Ruth*, 101.

117. For this genitive sense of *mî*, see Gen 24:23, 47; 1 Sam 12:3; 17:55, 56, 58; Jer 44:28; GKC §137b.

118. Similarly, *Midr. Ruth Rab.* 7:4; Sasson, *Ruth*, 100.

## 3:16-18 HOME: NAOMI AND RUTH DEBRIEF

to do so would cause Naomi to "lose face." We can imagine Ruth thinking it is better not to mention something if it is unnecessary or if it could cause disharmony in her relationship with her mother-in-law. Ruth's focus on Boaz's actions also reflects her self-effacing nature. She could have claimed credit for adapting Naomi's plan to draw out a promise from Boaz, all without any impropriety. Instead, she gives the credit to Boaz (and indirectly to Naomi for her plan), thus again manifesting her generosity (*ḥesed*).[119]

Kindness is a core aspect of Ruth's personal identity, but the inquiries into her identity show how quickly her social identity is changing. She arrived in Bethlehem as an anonymous person, a *persona non grata* (1:19–21). In response to Boaz's question, "Whose young woman is this?" the overseer replies she is a Moabite who returned with Naomi, but unattached to any man (2:6). At the threshing floor, Boaz asks, "Who are you?" and she replies, "I am Ruth, your handmaid" (3:9). She has risen to be in a position to be Boaz's wife if he takes up the role of her redeemer, as she has challenged him to do. Naomi's question, "Who are you?" asks if she is Boaz's future wife or if she remains a widow. Ruth the Moabite stands between these two older Bethlehemites,[120] and her identity changes through her interaction with them. Yet her identity is not passively shaped by them; instead, her initiative manifests throughout the narrative—on the road to Bethlehem, at home with Naomi, in Boaz's field, and on the threshing floor—and is crucial to her emerging social identity.

**17** Having explained what Boaz had done for her, presented as indirect speech, Ruth's direct speech to Naomi now reports what Boaz did for her mother-in-law. Boaz's previous actions are summarized with the focus on his last action (v. 15), as marked by *and she said*.[121] Just as she had adapted Naomi's plan, she now goes beyond what Naomi had just asked her. The structure of the Hebrew sentence emphasizes *These six measures of barley*, which the audience is aware of from v. 15, but its significance was not mentioned. Ruth now states the gift is for Naomi, *for he said to me, 'You must not come empty-handed* [rêqām] *to your mother-in-law.'* Some suggest this is Ruth's interpretation of Boaz's silent gesture or her interpretation of Boaz's words, but the phrase "for he said to me" indicates that what follows is her quotation of Boaz's direct speech. Even if Boaz did not say the words, placing these words in Ruth's mouth characterizes her as someone whose primary concern is for her mother-in-law. Naomi's plan and its execution had focused on Ruth. But as she reports Boaz's words, she says the benefit is for her *mother-in-law*. Her

---

119. Cf. Eskenazi and Frymer-Kensky, *Ruth*, 67.

120. Cf. Hyman, "Changing Identity," 199.

121. "And she said" is repeated, although there is no interruption to her words; Grossman, *Ruth*, 242.

# THE BOOK OF RUTH

character is marked by *ḥesed*, "loyalty and kindness": she committed herself to Naomi (1:16–17), she saved parched grain for her (2:18), and she now gives her the six measures of grain. The audience hearing the purpose of the gift for the first time now[122] underlines this aspect of Ruth's character because it presents Boaz's words from her perspective. While Naomi and Boaz plot to secure her future, her steadfast concern is for her mother-in-law.

Why did Boaz give the gift to Naomi? Is it simply another typical action of this worthy Israelite man, who does not send away widows empty-handed (*rêqām*; cf. Job 22:9)? The gift of barley probably sends at least two messages to Naomi.[123] First, it expresses Boaz's appreciation to Naomi for her plan. Boaz's location and actions at night on the threshing floor (vv. 1–4) were local or personal knowledge to Naomi; either way, his movements would have been unknowable to a newcomer to Bethlehem of a few months. Through the gift of grain, Boaz signals his gratitude to Naomi for her initiative in sending Ruth to the threshing floor. Second, from an honor-shame perspective, the gift giver not only accrues honor, gift-giving also confers honor; in this case, Boaz honors Naomi with his gift. Reciprocity is important in such a society: Naomi sent Ruth, so he feels obligated to send a gift of grain.[124] Thus, his gift also strengthens their existing relationship and anticipates the possibility of a new relationship, since the grain also shows Boaz's intention to carry out the purpose for which Naomi had sent Ruth (v. 1). He promised to do all Ruth asked (v. 11), including acting as redeemer if the nearer kinsman is not willing (v. 13). The six measures of barley are his tangible down payment, guaranteeing that he will be true to his word.[125]

The sweep of the Ruth narrative loads the gift of barley with even greater significance. When Naomi returned to Bethlehem, her bitter cry was, "I went away full, but empty [*rêqām*] Yahweh has returned me" (1:21). She was impoverished, bereft of family (husband and sons) and food. By the end of Ruth's first day of gleaning, Boaz had provided enough food to fill Naomi for the short term (2:17–18). In this scene, he again sends Ruth back with grain, but this gift foreshadows a comprehensive filling—both the provision

---

122. This literary device of postponed information is found throughout the Bible, including in Ruth (2:7, 11, 21). Consult Berlin, *Poetics*, 96–99; Sternberg, *Poetics*, 186–229.

123. For an overview of gifts in antiquity, see Gary Stansell, "The Gift in Ancient Israel," *Semeia* 87 (1999): 65–90; John M. G. Barclay, *Paul and the Gift* (Grand Rapids: Eerdmans, 2015), 1–65.

124. That is not to say that Ruth is viewed as an object for exchange: Boaz primarily responds to Naomi's *plan* to send Ruth, and his gift is given in the context of a relationship.

125. Some suggest that Boaz's gift can be understood as a *mōhar*, a "bride-price," usually paid at the time of betrothal (Gen 34:12; Exod 22:16[17]; 1 Sam 18:25); recently, Block, *Discourse*, 192. But this would be too presumptuous an act on Boaz's part because of the presence of the nearer kinsman. For more on *mōhar*, see Lipinski, "*mōhar*," *TDOT* 8:147–49.

of food long-term, as well as a child and family. Naomi's prayer for "rest" for her daughter-in-law (1:9) is about to be answered. Bitterness and shame accompanied Naomi's physical emptiness; joy and honor are not far away. And since Naomi attributed her emptiness to Yahweh, the hint is that the reversal of her emptiness will also be from Yahweh. Yet this filling will come through human agents, Boaz and Ruth.

Placing these words of Boaz in Ruth's mouth as her last words in the narrative is particularly poignant. Naomi lamented that she returned empty, but Ruth was by her side, ignored and unappreciated (1:19–22). She heard her mother-in-law's lament, which was unanswered from then until now. It is thus significant that the Moabite daughter-in-law who returned with her announces the end to her emptiness. Ruth focuses on the reversal of circumstances for her mother-in-law, but of course, the reversal is also for her. Like Naomi, she returned bereft of family and food; although, unlike Naomi, she had not lost children. However, she left behind her kin, whereas Naomi was returning to her kin. Thus, Ruth also would have felt "empty." Yet the focus of her words again shows primary concern for her mother-in-law's welfare over against her own.

Reading the word *rêqām*, "empty-handed," beyond the book of Ruth infuses it with additional figurative meaning.[126] The manumission law requires that a Hebrew man or woman must not be released from debt bondage "empty-handed" (Deut 15:12–15). They must be given generous provisions. Naomi is about to be released from her bondage to poverty, so she is given her due. But the law is based on a deeper theological reality. God had blessed his people in releasing them from Egyptian slavery, so Israelites were to do the same to others (Deut 15:14–15). The time reference, "in the middle of the night," and other narrative elements further link the exodus with Ruth's encounter with Boaz on the threshing floor.[127] In the exodus redemption, God's people did not depart "empty-handed" (Exod 3:21; 12:35–36),[128] and neither did Ruth. Just as the Israelites were to bless slaves upon their release as God had blessed them at their redemption, so Boaz's gift of grain foreshadows Ruth's redemption. This reciprocal dynamic of blessing and obedience is even stronger for Christians. God's greater redemption in Christ compels God's people today to be even more generous givers (2 Cor 8:9; 9:6–15; 1 Tim 6:17–19).

**18** Naomi is reassured by Ruth's report of her encounter with Boaz. In contrast to her counsel at the beginning of this act, she now advises Ruth

---

126. For further figurative uses, see Kedar-Kopfstein, "*rêqām*," *TDOT* 13:482–83.

127. Grossman, *Ruth*, 245–47, also includes the fulfillment of the command, dismissal/invitation to stay, taking food upon departure, and the explanation for the bounty.

128. Cf. *Midr. Ruth Rab.* 7:5.

# The Book of Ruth

to rest. Ruth has been a blur of action from the time she left her homeland, but now her mother-in-law tells her to *sit tight* (*šəbî*) and wait for an event to occur (cf. Gen 38:11; 1 Sam 1:23). Ruth journeyed to Judah, she gleaned in the field, she descended to the threshing floor, she returned to Naomi. Finally, after months of activity, she can sit down and take a rest because someone else will be busy on her behalf. The verb *yāšab* can refer to a temporary or permanent stay. Naomi and her sons "stayed" in Moab (*yēšbû*; 1:4) for about ten years. In act 2, Ruth was full of industrious action in Boaz's field, except her "sitting" in the hut for a short time (*šibtāh*; 2:7), and when she "sat" beside the harvesters at mealtime (*tēšeb*; 2:14). By the end of the act, we are told that she "stayed" with her mother-in-law until the harvest seasons were "finished" (*kəlôt*; 2:23). Similarly, in act 3, Ruth was on the go but again paused to "lodge" on the threshing floor (*lîn*; 3:13). At the end of the act, she is told to "sit" or *sit tight* to wait until the matter is "finished" (*killâ*). Yet there is more to Ruth's "sitting" and waiting.

Naomi's plan of action was aimed at securing "rest" for Ruth (*mānôaḥ*; 3:1), a more permanent dwelling in Boaz's household. Her stays in Boaz's hut and with his harvesters—his household—were only temporary, and her overall stay ceased with the end of the barley and wheat harvests. From this perspective, Naomi can be understood to ask Ruth to "stay" in her household until the matter is completed. Ruth will not leave for another household until she has married, settled into another household. In fact, the *hiphil* of the verb *yāšab* takes a meaning of "to cause to dwell" or "to marry" in post-exilic texts (see Ezra 10:2, 10, 14, 17; Neh 13:23, 27).[129] The matter of marriage has been raised by Ruth (3:9), and now that it is in process, she stays to await the outcome of whether she is about to set up a new household.

Naomi tells Ruth to wait *until you know*. The verbal root *yd'* ties this act together and is used here for the last time.[130] Naomi said Boaz was "our relative" (*môda'tānû*) who would be winnowing barley on the threshing floor (v. 2). Naomi's use of "knowing" was suggestive, Ruth was not to make herself "known" to the man until the right time, then she was to "observe" where Boaz lay (vv. 3–4). After revealing her identity and telling Boaz his, he says all the townspeople "know" that she is a worthy woman (v. 11). Then he sends her back at first light so that no one will "know" that she came to the threshing floor (v. 14). The women initiated the "knowing," the man took over the control of information, and the women wait to "know" the outcome of their plotting (*how the matter turns out*; Heb. "how the matter will fall"), now that it is left in the hands of their relative. The verb *nāpal* ("fall") is combined with the noun *dābār* ("matter, word, thing") in situations where

---

129. Cf. Görg, "*yāšab*," *TDOT* 6:426–27.
130. It will be used again in 4:4.

226

## 3:16–18 Home: Naomi and Ruth Debrief

two outcomes are possible, either failure or fulfillment (e.g., Esth 6:10). In particular, these two words are often used of God not allowing a promise or prophecy to go unfulfilled (e.g., Josh 21:45; 23:14 [2×]; 1 Sam 3:19; 1 Kgs 8:56; 2 Kgs 10:10), or of God speaking a word then it happening (e.g., Isa 9:7[8]). How things "fall" can point to God's hand in guiding events, such as casting lots. People cast (*hiphil* "cause to fall") lots for guidance in secular settings (e.g., Esth 3:7; 9:24), as well as to determine God's will (e.g., 1 Sam 14:42; Neh 10:35[34]; 11:1; 1 Chr 24:31; 25:8; 26:13). In both cases, the outcome is determined by God (Prov 16:33). So, in this verse, the audience hears an echo of God's quiet working[131] in the lives of these two widows through the actions of Boaz. Although the lot falls according to the will of God, the watchers do not know the outcome—including Naomi and Ruth and the audience. Will Naomi's plan be successful? And will Ruth end up marrying Boaz or the nearer kinsman-redeemer?

Whatever the outcome, Naomi expects that *the man won't rest unless he finishes the matter today*. Naomi does not use Boaz's name but refers to him as *hāʾîš*, "the man," highlighting his social role and his capacity to act in the public realm (cf. 2:19; 3:3). Again, Naomi knows more about Boaz's character than she has let on previously (cf. vv. 2–4). She had focused on his kinship relation to them (2:20; 3:2) and his kindness (2:20). Yet she was confident enough of his trustworthiness to send her daughter-in-law to him in the danger of night, certain that he would tell her what to do (3:4) instead of taking advantage of her. Now Naomi is confident of his diligence to settle the matter of Ruth's redemption, even that very day. No doubt Ruth's report of the events on the threshing floor, especially Boaz's promises, would have reinforced Naomi's view that Boaz would act swiftly and decisively. She says that he will not allow himself to "rest" (*šāqaṭ*) until he has completed his promised obligation as a kinsman-redeemer. Often the word *šāqaṭ* is used to describe a town ( Judg 18:7, 27) or land (e.g., Judg 3:11, 30; 5:31) at peace, without military threat, where inhabitants can live a "quiet" and secure existence. Boaz will not cease activity and be at peace until he has pursued the matter to its completion (*killâ*, from the same word in 2:21, 23; 3:3). In this way, he shadows the pattern of God's work, for God also does not rest until he has completed his work.[132] Unlike Boaz, others will not always keep their word, but God will.

Ruth has spoken her last words, and now these are Naomi's. The repetition of "my daughter" and "rest" brings us back to the beginning of the act,

---

131. Cf. Tg., in which Naomi tells Ruth to wait for the decree from heaven.

132. God "rests" (*šāqaṭ*) after he completes his work of vindication and salvation (Isa 62:1), and after his wrath is satisfied (Ezek 16:42). Cf. God's "rest" (*šābat*) after he completed (*yəkal*) the work of creation (Gen 2:2–3).

# THE BOOK OF RUTH

with Naomi plotting for Ruth's "rest," that it may be well for her (v. 1). She anticipated what Boaz would be doing "tonight," just as she anticipates what he will do "today." The time for covert conversation is over; the matter is about to be completed in the broad light of day. Act 1 ended with a note of hope amid the gloom: the beginning of the barley harvest. Act 2 ended with muted expectations: the barley and wheat harvests had ended, but Ruth still lived with her mother-in-law. Act 3 ends with a new day and a new hope that Naomi's prayer will finally be answered. The repetition of sounds and words and themes also brings us back to Naomi's first words in the narrative (1:8–9, 11–12). At that time, she told her "daughters" to "return" (*šōbnâ*) and find "rest" in the house of "her husband" (*'îšāh*). Now she tells Ruth her "daughter" to "sit" (*šəbî*) for "the man" (*hā'îš*) will not "rest" but will resolve the matter today. Before, she urged her daughters to return to Moab to find a husband; now, she tells Ruth to sit and wait in Bethlehem for her husband to be revealed. What a reversal! Then, Naomi could not envision her daughters-in-law finding security in a husband in Israel; now, this security is as clear as the morning light. Rest and wellness (cf. v. 1) for Ruth the Moabite also means provision and protection, abundance and children, belonging and honor. If she waits, they will be hers. And so, Naomi's final words hearken back and reach forward.

It takes wisdom to know when to act and when to wait. Ruth took the initiative to glean when they arrived back in Bethlehem (2:2). Naomi was passive then, but grasped the opportunity presented by Ruth's interaction with Boaz in his field. Her initiative led to the calculated risk of sending Ruth to Boaz at the threshing floor at night (3:1–4). Ruth's willingness to obey her mother-in-law, then improvise in her encounter with Boaz, led to their current expectant waiting. Their initiative led to their inaction, as they now put their outcome in the hands of Boaz. He will work restlessly for them, and it is wise to put their trust in him. He is a man of his word; he is trustworthy.

Yet standing behind Boaz is one who is even more trustworthy.[133] Naomi chose to return to God's land and his people, and so did Ruth (1:6, 16). Boaz recognized that Ruth had taken refuge in Yahweh, the God of Israel (2:12). Yahweh is a God who cares for the marginalized: the widows, the fatherless, and the immigrants. His law makes provision for all these people—someone just like Ruth. And there are hints in the narrative that God is working behind the scenes to bring Ruth and Boaz together (e.g., 2:1–3). Naomi says as much when she realizes that God's kindness has not forsaken them, as manifest in the generosity of Boaz (2:20). Boaz is someone who takes up the cause of the widow and the orphan (Isa 1:17; Jer 7:6; 22:3; Zech 7:10). But behind Boaz's

---

133. For ideas in this paragraph, I am indebted to Barry G. Webb, *Judges and Ruth: God in Chaos* (Wheaton: Crossway, 2015), 270.

## 3:16–18 HOME: NAOMI AND RUTH DEBRIEF

word is God's word, that he will provide for the refugee, the helpless, and the impoverished. And so, to trust in Boaz's promise is to trust in God's promise. Without God, there is no law, no redeemer, and no rest. Just as Naomi's advice to Ruth to sit and wait is wise, it is wise to "wait" upon a trustworthy God (Ps 27:14; Isa 40:31). In the New Testament, to those who seek Jesus and put their trust in him, he promises eternal rest (Matt 11:28). In him is found true wellness: abundance, belonging, and honor.

As we read or listen to this chapter, we experience the risk that the characters take. Naomi's scheme is not only risky, it is risqué. Yet it is constructed on trust in Boaz's integrity and generosity, and perhaps also in God's superintendence. If so, the risk is mitigated. Ruth, surprisingly, executes her mother-in-law's scheme without question or word of protest. Naomi schemes, but Ruth bears the brunt of the risk—physically, sexually, and reputationally. Yet, she ends up escalating the risk by telling Boaz what to do instead of waiting for Boaz to tell her what to do. Boaz also takes risks, by allowing Ruth to remain on the threshing floor until the morning and allowing the nearer kinsman to have the first right of refusal. How the chapter is crafted helps us experience these risks, through elements such as the mood, the tension, the wordplays, and the de-identification of Boaz and Ruth to "the man" and "the woman." We not only feel the risk but also the weight of the temptation for Boaz. As he encounters Ruth in secret, a vulnerable female is at his mercy. That both characters can pass through the night without a hint of impropriety allows them to leave the encounter with their reputations not just intact but enhanced.

This chapter dramatically presents the risky aspect of kindness. Someone has said that *kin*dness is treating people as *kin* even though they are not. Everything is shared with family, inconveniences are endured because the other is family, the extra mile is taken for the sake of family. These things are done willingly because "we are family." Boaz treats a foreigner as family even though those in his society view her with suspicion and her mother-in-law at times is ambivalent toward her. Ruth treats her mother-in-law as kin even though her husband died, and Naomi released her from family obligations. Boaz continues to act in kindness (cf. 2:20); likewise, Ruth's second act of kindness is even greater (3:10). Jesus's parable of the good Samaritan demonstrates how to show kindness (Luke 10:25–37). The man who was beaten and left for dead is bypassed by two of his kin. The one who shows him kindness is not kin. He is willing to bind and anoint and carry the needy man at the risk to his own person and possessions. He is willing to pay whatever it costs to the innkeeper at the risk to his own wealth. In kindness, the good Samaritan shows mercy,[134] at risk to himself.

---

134. The word for "mercy" (*eleos*) in Luke 10:37 is the same word for *ḥesed* in LXX Ruth (1:8; 2:20; 3:10).

# The Book of Ruth

Sometimes to act in kindness will involve risk in treating others as kin. There is the risk of wasted effort, or time, or resources. There is a risk to one's reputation. There is a risk that kindness will not even be accepted. However, reflection on God's infinite kindness in Jesus Christ (Eph 2:7; Titus 3:4–7) impels action in kind—lives marked by risky kindness.

## ACT 4: REDEMPTION AND FULLNESS (4:1–22)

Naomi has come a long way. Physically, she traveled from Bethlehem to Moab and back again, but more important has been her social and spiritual journey. From a mother of a full house to empty, destitute, and shamed, she is now on the cusp of achieving fullness, security, and inclusion. Her permanent honor and dignity are nearly restored, but even she would not have imagined its final degree and extent. And her social journey is inextricably linked to her spiritual journey, for it all started when she "returned" to Yahweh's promised land. Ruth, her daughter-in-law, the Moabite who was overlooked on their return to Bethlehem, has been crucial in the reversal of Naomi's situation. Through her acts of loyal and risky kindness, she has won widespread recognition—both in private and in public. In particular, Boaz, the man of great worth, discerned and acknowledged Ruth's virtue and worth. He, too, has been instrumental in Naomi's and Ruth's reversal. Behind the being and doing of all the characters, however, stands another character. So far, the narrator has only described God's action once (and even then, it was hearsay; 1:6), but the speeches and prayers of the characters consistently recall his presence to the audience's mind. His is the gentle guiding hand behind the reversal; the characters enact and reflect his kindness. We will see his decisive intervention in this act.

Structurally, act 4 plays out differently from the short-long-short scenic (D-E-F // F'-E'-D') rhythm of the previous two acts. The central acts were circular in that they began and ended with Naomi and Ruth at home. This act, like the first, is linear, with one scene progressing to the next and the next. This act contains a long scene followed by two shorter scenes and balances act 1.

| | Characters | Location | Action |
|---|---|---|---|
| A 1:1–6 | Elimelech's family | Bethlehem then Moab | The end of a family line in Moab |
| B 1:7–19a | Naomi, Orpah, and Ruth | En route: Moab to Bethlehem | Naomi, Orpah, and Ruth dialogue |
| C 1:19b–22 | Naomi and Ruth | Town gate | Naomi laments before the townswomen |
| C' 4:1–12 | Boaz, nearer kinsman-redeemer, witnesses | Town gate | Boaz redeems before the elders |
| B' 4:13–17 | Boaz, Ruth, Obed, townswomen, Naomi | Home of Boaz and Ruth | Naomi and the women dialogue |
| A' 4:18–22 | Boaz's extended family | N/A | The beginning of a royal line in Israel |

# THE BOOK OF RUTH

Act 1 presented the crises that set the narrative in motion. Death, emptiness, and return (act 1) are balanced by redemption, birth, and fullness (act 4). The grave opening family history (A) is revived surprisingly and gloriously (A'). A seeming dead end now breaks the bounds of the Ruth narrative and Bethlehem to extend to the greater biblical narrative with universal significance. Just as Naomi dialogued with her daughters-in-law (B), she now dialogues with the women of Bethlehem (B'), who celebrate Naomi's reversal of fortune. But whereas Naomi lamented before the townswomen of Bethlehem (C), Boaz now redeems before the elders of Bethlehem (C'). The balanced scenes of act 1 and act 4 reflect the reversal motif in the Ruth narrative. Yet, despite this structural symmetry, the plot is not entirely symmetrical because the narrative ends in greater honor for Naomi and a more hopeful future for Israel.[1]

There are contrasts between acts 3 and 4. Act 3 was initiated by women and centered on a whispered conversation without witnesses. It took place in darkness, in private. Act 4 is initiated by Boaz, centered on a legal discussion with witnesses. It takes place in daylight, in public. The focus for most of the narrative was on the female perspective (1:3b–3:18), but it now shifts back to the male perspective (cf. 1:1–3a). The different gender roles and concerns seem to be in tension. In the male sphere, Boaz speaks of redeeming landed inheritance and the establishing of a name. The witnesses wish for perpetuation and fame. Ostensibly, men are concerned about ongoing existence and fame. In the female sphere, the townswomen speak of a redeemer who will restore and nourish an elderly woman's life. They give him a name that means "servant." Ostensibly, the women are concerned about domestic security and family wholeness.

Yet these gender concerns intersect and function cooperatively.[2] At the town gate, Boaz speaks of male concerns—land and heir—but this does not exclude his care for the well-being of Naomi and Ruth. In a legal setting, he uses the language of public discourse. He had promised to ensure the long-term security of the widows, and at the town gate, he enacts his promise with words appropriate for the context. The townswomen focus on Obed's significance for Naomi's welfare but also wish that "his name be proclaimed in Israel" (4:14). The men wish for regional renown (Ephrathah, Bethlehem, and Judah; v. 11), the women raise the stakes to national renown. Perhaps Obed, the product of a male/female union, personifies the potential of gender cooperation. He fulfills the concerns of both genders: perpetuity and provision. This is consistent with the gender interaction in the rest of the Ruth narrative. Ruth sought short-term sustenance in the field, which she gained with Boaz's assistance and provision. Naomi and Ruth sought long-term sustenance on the threshing floor, which they gained with Boaz's

---

1. Set in a chaotic period without a king (1:1), the narrative ends with King David (4:17, 22).
2. Cf. Bauckham, "Book of Ruth," 39.

## 4:1–12 Town Gate: Boaz Redeems before the Elders

promise. Boaz sought the approval of the gathering at the town gate, which he gained as the legal agent of Naomi and Ruth. One cannot function without the other, and their cooperation led to an extraordinary fulfillment. Even the patrilineal genealogy can be viewed as raising the honor of women; Obed, who becomes the grandfather of King David, is Naomi's "son" (v. 17), the offspring of her Moabite daughter-in-law.

## C'. TOWN GATE: BOAZ REDEEMS BEFORE THE ELDERS (4:1–12)

The stage is set for the showdown between Boaz and the nearer kinsman-redeemer. Naomi had hatched an audacious plan, Ruth had executed it to perfection, but Boaz raised a complication. Yet with the widows, we rest assured that Boaz's promise would ensure Ruth's redemption one way or the other. The last scene ended with Naomi saying that the man would settle the matter that day (3:18); this scene opens with Boaz busying himself at the town gate (4:1). Although there have been intimations of the levirate custom in the Ruth narrative, its mention in this scene and its association with the right of redemption is unexpected for an audience of the narrative. After all, there has been no hint that Naomi owns land that needs to be redeemed. Perhaps we are to feel as surprised and off-balance as Mr. So-and-So at Boaz's nimble maneuverings.

[1]*Boaz went up to the gate*[a] *and sat down there. And look! The kinsman-redeemer was passing by, of whom Boaz had spoken! He said, "Turn aside, sit here, Mr. So-and-So." So he turned aside and sat.*

[2]*Then he*[b] *took ten men from the elders of the town and said, "Sit here," and they sat.*

[3]*He said to the kinsman-redeemer, "The portion of the field that belongs to our brother Elimelech, Naomi, who returned from the territory of Moab, is hereby transferring.*[c]

[4]*So I thought*[d] *I would uncover your ear by saying, 'Acquire [it] in front of those sitting here, in front of the elders of my people.' If you will redeem, redeem.*[e] *But if you will not redeem,*[f] *tell me so I may know,*[g] *for there is no one except you to redeem, and I am after you." He said, "I will redeem."*

[5]*Boaz said, "On the day you acquire the field from the hand of Naomi, also*[h] *Ruth the Moabite, the wife of the dead man, you acquire*[i] *to establish the name of the dead man upon his inheritance."*

[6]*The kinsman-redeemer said, "I'm not able to redeem for myself, in case I ruin my own inheritance. Redeem for yourself . . . you . . . my right of redemption, for I'm not able to redeem."*

# The Book of Ruth

[7](Now this was [the custom][j] formerly in Israel regarding redemption and exchange, to establish any [such] matter: a man would slip off his sandal and give it to his companion. This was the manner of witnessing in Israel.)

[8]The kinsman-redeemer said to Boaz, "Acquire [it] for yourself,"[k] and he slipped off his sandal.[l]

[9]Then Boaz said to the elders and all the people, "You are witnesses today that I hereby acquire all that belonged to Elimelech and all that belonged to Chilion and Mahlon from the hand of Naomi.

[10]Also Ruth the Moabite, the wife of Mahlon, I hereby acquire for myself as a wife, to establish the name of the dead upon his inheritance, so that[m] the name of the dead may not be cut off from among his brothers and from the gate of his place.[n] You are witnesses today."

[11]All the people who were at the gate and the elders said,[o] "[We are] witnesses. May Yahweh make the woman[p] coming into your house like Rachel and Leah, who built, the two of them,[q] the house of Israel. And act worthily[r] in Ephrathah and proclaim a name in Bethlehem.

[12]May your house be like the house of Perez, whom Tamar bore for Judah, from the seed that Yahweh will give to you from this young woman."

a. Syr. reads "the gate of the city," while Tg. reads "sat there with the elders."

b. LXX and Vulg. specify Boaz as the subject, but Tg. supports MT[L].

c. LXX reads "was given to Naomi" instead of "Naomi . . . is hereby transferring." The other versions support MT[L].

d. In this context, the first-person common singular qatal verb 'āmartî indicates "internal speech," so the translation "I thought"; see note at 3:14.

e. Similar to qnh ("acquire"), the object of the verb g'l is assumed to be Elimelech's land. Alternatively, g'l could have an intransitive meaning, "to serve as kinsman-redeemer."

f. MT[LA] read "but if he (yig'al; third-person masculine singular) will not redeem," whereas multiple Kennicott and de Rossi manuscripts, as well as LXX, Syr., Tg., and Vulg. read "but if you (tig'al; second-person masculine singular) will not redeem." As Wilhelm Rudolph, *Das Buch Ruth, das Hohe Lied, die Klagelieder*, KAT 17 (Gütersloh: Mohn, 1962), 59, notes, it is difficult to explain a y for a t as a scribal error. Against most commentators, Sasson, *Ruth*, 103, 118, maintains the third-person masculine singular and interprets the clause as Boaz's aside to the elders before turning back to the kinsman-redeemer. Yet such a device seems unlikely in a narrated story, and an aside is too disruptive of Boaz's seemingly focused address to the kinsman-redeemer. Thus, it is best to read the verb in parallel with "if *you* will redeem"; so all EVV. See also the discussion in *BHQ*, 55*.

g. The qere (wə'ēd'â) marks the first-person yiqtol as a jussive, but contextually the ketiv (wə'ēda') can also be read as a jussive.

h. The word ûmē'ēt can be read as "and from" or "and/also." For a discussion of readings, see comment on v. 5.

i. MT[L] ketiv reads qānîtî, "I acquire," while the qere reads qānîtā, "you acquire." For a discussion of readings, see comment on v. 5.

j. MT[L] reads wəzō't ləpānîm bəyiśrā'ēl, "this was formerly in Israel," which LXX adds dikaiōma, "right/statute/ordinance" after "this" (similarly Tg, Syr., and Vulg.). The versions probably specify the implied meaning of MT[L] (hammišpāt or a similar term; cf. Jer 32:7, 8),

234

## 4:1–12 Town Gate: Boaz Redeems before the Elders

since this terseness is found elsewhere in the Ruth narrative (e.g., 2:7, 9, 14; 3:4, 15). The feminine demonstrative *zō't* refers to something abstract, in this case, the sandal custom; see *IBHS* §6.4.2, 6.6d.

k. LXX adds "my right of redemption" as the object for *qnh* ("acquire"), which is followed by Joüon, *Ruth*, 87. However, the transaction involves not just the land but also Ruth; see comment on v. 8. The Vulg. has Boaz taking off the nearer redeemer's shoe.

l. After this clause LXX adds "and gave it to him," which would be based on *wayyittēn lô* in MT[L] (cf. v. 7). If this is the case, it would be an instance of elision because of homoioteleuton, whereby the scribe's eye passes from the first *lô* to the second; so emended by Joüon, *Ruth*, 88; Rudolph, *Ruth*, 60. However, the emendation is unnecessary because the audience can fill in the details based on the explanation in v. 7. The curt description is consistent with the nearer redeemer's curt statement in this verse.

m. I read the *wāw* as an "epexegetical *wāw*"; see *IBHS* §39.2.4.

n. LXX reads "tribe of his people" (cf. 3:11). The phrase "gate of his place" (*miššaʿar məqômô*) only occurs elsewhere in Deut 21:19. Campbell, *Ruth*, 151, suggests that the choice of this phrase in this verse might be explained by its assonance with *ləhāqîm* (earlier in this verse) and *ləqayyēm* (v. 7). I would add that there is assonance (albeit weaker) with "Chilion and Mahlon" (*kilyôn ûmaḥlôn*; v. 9).

o. In LXX, the people say "Witnesses," while the elders pronounce the blessing. The Vulg., OL, Tg. support MT[L], although Tg. reads "gate of the Sanhedrin and the elders." It is best to maintain the MT[L], since in v. 9 the two groups act together (*BHQ*, 56*). The Syr. places "elders" before "people," probably to maintain consistency with v. 9, but the reversal of order might have a stylistic reason; see comment on v. 11.

p. Tg., Vulg., and Syr. read "this woman," while LXX reads "your wife." MT[L] allows for a double meaning (see comment on v. 11).

q. Heb. *šəttēyhem* ("the two of them") is another instance of gender mismatch; see note on 1:8.

r. LXX reads "they produced might," referring to Rachel and Leah (cf. Syr.), while Vulg. reads "she may be an example of virtue" (presumably referring to Ruth). The masculine singular imperative in MT[L] fits well the chiastic structure of the blessing (see comments on vv. 11–12) and is supported by Tg.

In our chiastic structure of the Ruth narrative, this scene (C′) parallels and contrasts with 1:19b–22 (C). Both take place at the town gate, a public scene with townspeople witnessing the events. Both involve two characters (Naomi and Ruth; Boaz and the nearer kinsman-redeemer) and a subset of the townspeople (townswomen; the elders). While Naomi laments before the townswomen about Yahweh "testifying" against her (1:21), a word with legal overtones, Boaz redeems before a legal quorum of (male) town elders. And Boaz acquiring the land from Naomi and marrying Ruth are crucial steps in filling the "emptiness" Naomi experienced (1:21).

Repeated words tie this scene to the preceding: "know," "sit," "say," "man/ men"; as well as the wordplay *haśśəʿōrîm*, "the barleys," and *haššaʿar*, "the gate."[3] The repetition of *gāʾal*, "redeem," or words from the same root signals one of the central concerns of both acts 3 and 4.

---

3. Porten, "Scroll," 14.

# THE BOOK OF RUTH

This scene can be structured as a chiasm:[4]

> A  Boaz gathers the witnesses (vv. 1–2)
> > B  Boaz's proposal to the nearer kinsman-redeemer (vv. 3–5)
> > > C  The nearer kinsman-redeemer declines Boaz's proposal (vv. 6–8)
> > B'  Boaz's declaration to the elders (vv. 9–10)
> A'  The witnesses bless Boaz (vv. 11–12)

Framing this scene are mentions of "the gate" (vv. 1, 11) and "the elders" (vv. 2, 11), as well as Hebrew wordplays—*haššaʿar*, "the gate," and *ʿăśārâ*, "ten" (vv. 1, 2); *hazzeraʿ*, "the seed" and *hannaʿărâ*, "the young woman" (v. 12).[5] The public location and key participants are present in both outer elements (A-A'). The focus of this scene is the nearer kinsman-redeemer's refusal to accept Boaz's offer of redeeming the field and marrying Ruth (C). His response is set in contrast with Boaz's, which envelops it (B-B'). Boaz makes it clear that he will step in if Mr. So-and-So declines (B), then makes a public declaration when Mr. So-and-So does (B'). Similar to most of the Ruth narrative, this scene mostly comprises dialogue: Boaz dominates, with a blessing by the witnesses and some short responses from the nearer kinsman-redeemer. Apart from the verbs introducing speech, the narrator sets the scene (v. 1) and interjects with a description of the sandal custom (v. 7).

**1** Act 3 ended with Naomi assuring Ruth that Boaz would settle the matter that day (3:18). As act 4, begins we find Boaz beginning to do just that. He had entered the town (3:15), and this verse picks up the action. He could have gone up to the town gate[6] before, during, or after Ruth and Naomi's conversation.[7] He could have returned home first or gone straight to the town gate after leaving Ruth. If he waited at the town gate, the subsequent events would have taken place after the women's conversation because Ruth returned before sunrise, and people would pass through the town gate to pursue their activities, especially working in the fields, after sunrise.

Boaz *went up* to the gate because towns were generally built on high geographical points for defensive purposes. He went up from the threshing floor,

---

4. Cf. Block, *Discourse*, 198.

5. Porten, "Scroll," 43.

6. Although the English word "gate" can be used in domestic settings, *šaʿar* ("gate") often referred to the gate in the wall surrounding a town or city (also a temple or palace), as in this verse. See Otto, "*šaʿar*," *TDOT* 15:368.

7. The lack of a *wayyiqtol* to begin this verse indicates that the event in this clause does not necessarily follow the preceding events.

## 4:1-12 TOWN GATE: BOAZ REDEEMS BEFORE THE ELDERS

which is usually situated lower than a town (3:3, 6).[8] The town gate of Bethlehem would have been a major thoroughfare since it was probably the only way in and out of the town. And it would have been peak hour early in the morning. Moreover, the town gate was not only a thoroughfare, it was also the location for administrative and legal proceedings (see, e.g., Deut 21:19; 22:15; Josh 20:4; Isa 29:21; Amos 5:15).[9] Today, we might say it was like a town hall.

Beyond its practical function, the town gate holds symbolic significance in three ways. First, it highlights the gender interplay. Boaz *sat* at the town gate and waited at the town gate, while Ruth was sitting and waiting at home (3:18). The public gathering at the town gate is a man's domain, although it is the women at home who have precipitated the negotiations.[10] In the Ruth narrative, power is not always just found in obvious places or people. Second, the gate represents the interface between a household (a father's house, or here, a mother's house) and the wider kinship group.[11] The interconnected communal structure of ancient Israel renders it appropriate for Boaz to bring a household matter for adjudication by the wider kinship group. Third, the gate symbolizes Ruth's entrance into the community as a legally recognized member of Bethlehem.[12] She passed through the gate as a *persona non grata* (1:19–22), and her path to belonging has required chance, hard work, and risk. Boaz's early acceptance of her was crucial, and, while apparently she has already received public recognition (3:11), she now is on the cusp of receiving legal recognition.

Boaz was waiting at the town gate, *And look!* he suddenly sees the *kinsman-redeemer* passing by. For a moment, the audience sees things through Boaz's eyes, and at the same time, is introduced to a new character—the nearer kinsman, the one *of whom Boaz had spoken* (3:12–13). Just as Boaz arrived in the field Ruth "happened" to stumble into (2:4), the nearer redeemer arrives at the right place at the right time. Considering his earlier mention and the invoking of Yahweh's name by Boaz (3:12–13), the nearer redeemer's arrival points to a divine appointment, not just coincidence. Although the audience might expect a greeting (cf. 2:4), Boaz does not utter one here; instead, he is all business: *Turn aside, sit here.* With two curt commands, Boaz changes the course of the nearer kinsman's day, as he tells him to sit, possibly at a bench

---

8. Ruth "went down" (3:6) to the threshing floor as instructed by Naomi (3:3).

9. See Natalie N. May, "Gates and Their Functions in Mesopotamia and Ancient Israel," in *The Fabric of Cities: Aspects of Urbanism, Urban Topography and Society in Mesopotamia, Greece and Rome*, ed. Natalie N. May and Ulrike Steinert (Leiden: Brill, 2014), 95–100.

10. Cf. Trible, "Comedy," 182.

11. Cf. Eskenazi and Frymer-Kensky, *Ruth*, 70.

12. Cf. Grossman, *Ruth*, 262.

# The Book of Ruth

in a chamber of the town gatehouse[13] or a bench in the city plaza inside the gate.[14] The nearer kinsman obeys Boaz without any fuss.

Curiously, Boaz is not reported to address the nearer kinsman by his given name. *Mr. So-and-So* translates the rhyming phrase *pelōnî 'almōnî*; which is used by the narrator to obfuscate, not because Boaz did not know his name.[15] The phrase is used elsewhere in the Old Testament to denote an undisclosed location—"such and such" a place (1 Sam 21:3; 2 Kgs 6:8). In a small town with a collectivist culture such as Bethlehem, it is highly unlikely that Boaz would not know the name of a fellow member of his clan. He mentions him to Ruth at the threshing floor, and he easily identifies him as he passes through the town gate. Boaz would have called him by his personal name. But unlike other characters in the narrative, the narrator keeps Mr. So-and-So nameless. This loss is especially significant in a chapter concerned with names: to establish or restore a name upon an inheritance (vv. 5, 10), to proclaim a name far and wide (v. 14), to name a newborn (v. 17), and to name descendants (vv. 18–22). The nearer kinsman fades into anonymity.

However, the concealment of Mr. So-and-So's name also has a protective effect. If he was identified by name in the narrative, there would be some shame attached to it—for him and his descendants. The shame would not be to the same degree as someone who refused to perform the levirate duty because he was not a brother dwelling together (Deut 25:5) with Elimelech. But his reputation, and that of those who would follow him, would be damaged. The withheld name also ensures there is no ongoing shame.

**2** Boaz's authority is also seen in what he does next. He *took ten men from the elders of the town*, either as they were also about to exit through the town gate on their way to daily business or he had brought them to form an assembly. The change of verb[16] slightly favors the latter interpretation, but either way, their acceptance indicates Boaz's authority and the importance the men placed in the eldership role. He commands them to *Sit here*, and, like the nearer kinsman, they also do so without any ado. The elders of Bethlehem represented the entire town and were the community's authoritative body

---

13. Chambered gatehouses were common in the ancient Near East during the Iron II period. They consisted of a broad gate passage (4.2m wide on average) with chambers on each side (ranging from two to six chambers). The Bethlehem gatehouse was probably at the modest end of the spectrum. Plastered benches within the chambers could be used as seating. See Daniel A. Frese, "Chambered Gatehouses in the Iron II Southern Levant: Their Architecture and Function," *Levant* 47 (2015): 75–92.

14. So Campbell, *Ruth*, 154–55; see photographs of gates at Dan and Gezer on pp. 100–101.

15. In English, there are similar rhyming phrases, such as "hocus pocus," "helter skelter," and the name "Joe Blow."

16. Boaz asked the nearer kinsman to *sûrâ*, "turn aside," while he *wayyiqqaḥ*, "procured," the elders to form the legal assembly; see Bush, *Ruth, Esther*, 197–98.

## 4:1–12 Town Gate: Boaz Redeems before the Elders

that was involved in governing (e.g., Josh 20:4; 2 Kgs 10:1, 5), judging (e.g., Deut 21:18–21; 1 Kgs 21:8–12),[17] advising (e.g., 2 Sam. 17:15; 1 Kgs 20:7–8), and dealing with outsiders (1 Sam 16:1–5).[18] The elders administered and maintained legal and societal standards and were thus important for preserving the integrity of the community.[19] Assemblies of elders were summoned when needed, and they usually did not get involved in cases unless it affected more than one father's house,[20] as is the case in Ruth. The town elders probably comprised the heads of the clans in the town, and it is from this group[21] that Boaz procures *ten men*. The ten elders represent a legal assembly; Boaz now has a legal quorum.[22] The efficient description of Boaz's actions lends him an air of control, so we anticipate subsequent proceedings with a sense of optimism.

**3** Mr. So-and-So remains anonymous, but his designation is again *gōʾēl, the kinsman-redeemer* (cf. v. 1). Boaz's speech to him to start proceedings evidences parallelism:[23]

> The portion of the <u>field</u>
> that belongs to our brother *Elimelech*
> *Naomi* is hereby transferring,
> who returned from the <u>field</u>[24] of Moab.

This structure conveys two contrasts. First, "our brother" Elimelech is contrasted with Naomi "who returned." "Our brother" (*ʾāḥînû*) does not

---

17. Judicially, town elders are involved in cases of murder (Deut 19:1–13; 21:1–9; Josh 20:1–9), rebellious children (Deut 21:18–21), levirate marriage (Deut 25:5–10), and adultery (Deut 22:13–21).

18. The town elders probably comprised the heads of the clans of the town. On elders, see Conrad, "*zāqēn,*" *TDOT* 4:122–31; Kenneth T. Aitken, "*zāqēn,*" *NIDOTTE* 1:1137–39; Willis, *Elders.*

19. See, e.g., Victor H. Matthews and Don C. Benjamin, *Social World of Ancient Israel 1250–587 BCE* (Peabody, MA: Hendrickson, 1993), 126–31.

20. E.g., Deut 21:18–21, where the case of a stubborn and rebellious son is brought before the elders since the well-being of one family affects that of the entire community; see Christopher J. H. Wright, *Deuteronomy,* NIBCOT 4 (Peabody, MA: Hendrickson, 1996), 235–36.

21. The *min* in *mizziqnê hāʿîr* is partitive, "some of the elders of the town." The phrase *ʾănāšîm mizziqnê,* "men from the elders of" is also found in Jer 26:17; Ezek 14:1; 20:1.

22. Ten was often the smallest effective group of people in the Old Testament (Judg 6:27; 1 Sam 25:5; 2 Sam 18:15; 20:3). In later Jewish tradition, ten is the minimum number of adults, a *minyan,* required to form a community.

23. For this structure and the following observations, cf. Linafelt and Beal, *Ruth & Esther,* 66; Grossman, *Ruth,* 270–71.

24. I have translated *śādēh* as "field" to highlight the parallelism, but "territory" is more accurate, as distinct from Israelite territory. See translation note on 1:1.

## THE BOOK OF RUTH

necessarily mean that Boaz, the nearer kinsman, and Elimelech were sons of the same father,[25] since *'āḥ*, "brother" can also refer to second and third-generation relatives (e.g., Gen 13:8; Lev 10:4). "Brother" can also refer to those from the same tribe (e.g., Num 16:10; 25:6; Judg 14:3) or even Israelites in general ("brothers of Israel," e.g., Exod 2:11; Ezek 11:15).[26] Boaz's relation to the family of Elimelech has only been described in general terms in the narrative; he is a *môdā'*, "relative" or "kinsman" (2:1; 3:2; cf. 2:20, *qārôb lānû*, "our close relative"). The word *'āḥ* is found in both the redemption (Lev 25:23–55) and levirate laws (Deut 25:5–10), so its usage here also foreshadows these legal associations. Elimelech's kinship with Boaz and Mr. So-and-So forms the basis of the land transaction at hand. Yet, the contrast also reminds the audience of the beginning of the narrative and Elimelech's demise. He no longer possesses the field, and he did not return from Moab, in contrast to his widow Naomi who now does and did. The second contrast is between the "fields." Elimelech left his "field" because of famine in Bethlehem to seek food in the "field of Moab." Now, ironically, his wife has returned in a time of fertility but needs to transfer the field to survive. Bethlehem is blessed again, but she does not fully share in the bounty. She has "returned" from the fields of Moab, but she has not yet fully reintegrated into Bethlehem society or her husband's clan.

Between the two mentions of "fields," Boaz surprises the audience by bringing up new information about Elimelech's field. Unexpectedly, its transfer is the first item on the agenda. For, in response to Ruth's marriage proposal, Boaz had promised to do all she asked and to ensure her redemption (3:11–13). Even though he mentioned the nearer kinsman-redeemer, the audience expects that, as a man of action (3:18), Boaz would settle the matter of her marriage—not of Naomi's field—as soon as possible. Moreover, so far in the narrative, the impression has been that the widows were destitute; they are so poor that Ruth had to go out to glean in another's field. Yet, Boaz's promise to redeem Ruth was vague enough to encompass redemption of kinship inheritance, although it was not mentioned explicitly.[27] And perhaps Boaz's mention of Naomi's property would not have been as unexpected for an Israelite audience since redemption of property is a duty outlined in the law (Lev 25:25). Both the narrator and Boaz have the situation in hand, and now they pull out a surprise tactic from their playbook.

Much hinges on our understanding of Boaz's use of the verb *mākərâ*, often used of commercial transactions, and usually translated "to sell" (e.g., Neh 10:32[31]; 13:15, 20; Prov 31:24). The verb can also mean "to transfer

---

25. So, e.g., the Babylonian Talmud, B. Bat. 91a.
26. See E. Jenni, "*'āḥ*," *TLOT* 1:73–77; Ringgren, "*'āḥ*," *TDOT* 1:188–93.
27. Hubbard, *Ruth*, 238.

240

4:1–12 Town Gate: Boaz Redeems before the Elders

the right of usage" without transferring ownership. For instance, if a person fell into debt, both land (e.g., Lev 25:23–28; 27:20, 24) and persons (e.g., Lev 25:39–42, 47–54; Deut 15:12; Jer 34:14) could be "handed over" to a creditor for their use or service for a limited time.[28] Concerning land, the technical term is "usufruct," from *usus* "a use" plus *fructus* "fruit"—the right to enjoy the use of another's property without destroying it.[29] The purchaser buys the usufruct of the land, and since the property will be returned at the next Jubilee Year, the price is adjusted accordingly (Lev 25:13–16). Israelites were forbidden to buy and sell land in perpetuity because God is the land-owner (Lev 25:23). A more metaphorical usage of *mākərâ* is found close to the narrative setting of Ruth, where Yahweh "hands over" the Israelites be-cause of their disobedience, also for a limited time ( Judg 3:8; 4:2; 10:7). In short, Naomi is not "selling" (most EVV) but "transferring" the land. From this verse, it is not clear what it is about the land Naomi is transferring, but as Boaz continues his speech, it becomes clear he is transferring the right to redeem the field's usufruct (v. 4), not its possession.

This raises questions of ownership since women rarely possessed land in the Old Testament. The categorization of widows with orphans and so-journers as groups of people who required special protection and provision suggests that widows did not ordinarily inherit property (e.g., Deut 10:18; 24:19–21; 26:12–13). God gave the land to his people as an inheritance (e.g., Josh 14:1–5), to remain within the tribe and clan, passed down through the male line (e.g., Deut 21:15–17). Elimelech and his sons died while they were outside the land of Israel, effectively leaving the land in trust to Naomi. Under normal circumstances, at Elimelech's death the land would pass to the next heir in his line (including to a daughter if there are no sons) or, failing that, to a male relative in his clan (Num 27:8–11; 36:1–12).[30] Now that Naomi has returned and the forlorn state of Elimelech's line has come to light, Boaz takes action on Naomi's behalf to restore the usufruct of Elimelech's land. The benefit would be for those Elimelech has left behind. Since Naomi was away when the males in her family died, she could not have "sold" or "transferred" the land already. Hence, a present tense understanding of the verb *mākərâ* is best, *Naomi . . . is hereby transferring*, and is both grammatically possible[31] and situationally appropriate.

---

28. Cf. Lipinski, "*mkr*," *TDOT* 8:292; *DCH* 5:271; Babylonian Talmud Baba Metz 79a–b.

29. Cf. "Usufruct," in Lexico.com, Oxford University Press, accessed July 14, 2020, https://www.lexico.com/definition/usufruct.

30. As a widow, Naomi probably held these rights until she passed the property onto a suitable heir, married again, or died. The proverbial ideal woman buys and sells land (Prov 31:16), but she probably does so on behalf of her husband since her industriousness and efficiency reflect well on him (31:23).

31. The *qatal* verb is a "performative perfective," with the situation or action occurring

# THE BOOK OF RUTH

We are not told how Boaz knows Naomi wants to transfer the land now. The narrative does not mention Boaz and Naomi meeting, let alone discussing the land sale. Perhaps, since only selected events are included in the narrative, Naomi mentioned the land transfer to Boaz "offstage." More likely, since only a few hours have passed since Ruth's marriage request, Boaz concocted this scheme in response to Ruth's request. Based on our understanding of the transfer of property as outlined above, Naomi did not need to tell Boaz she wants to transfer the land because it would have been common knowledge.

There are two main ways to understand the transaction Boaz proposes:

(1) *A redemption of land that has been alienated from the clan.* In this case, the usufruct of the land was transferred to someone outside Elimelech's clan. Since this required a male to execute the transaction, presumably Elimelech did it before he and his family left for Moab. Perhaps during the famine, he fell on hard times, forcing him to sell part or all of the usufruct of his land. Since the next stage of the poverty cycle would be selling himself (or a family member) into indentured service to a fellow Israelite (cf. Lev 25:23–55), perhaps Elimelech chose sojourn rather than servitude. If so, during his absence, the land was cultivated by the one who owned the right to use it. Now Naomi has *returned from the territory of Moab*, and the harvest season is over, the time is ripe for the field to be returned to the clan's fold. Naomi does not have the means or ability, so a kinsman from her husband's clan must assume responsibility for the redemption.

(2) *A preemptive redemption to prevent the land from being alienated from the clan.* Because of her destitution, Naomi wants to sell the use of the land to ensure her long-term survival. In this case, the use of the land was not transferred to another person when Elimelech and his family left for Moab. He did not sell the usufruct, presumably, because of famine, the amount he would have received was meager, or there were no buyers. The land could have lain fallow, or since more than a decade passed and no one knew if Elimelech would return to claim the land, a clan member worked the field. In either case, Boaz now offers the right of the land for pre-emptive purchase to prevent a non-clan member from acquiring the right. This right of redemption by purchase would be similar to Jeremiah's acquisition of his cousin Hanamel's field (Jer 32:1–15). Hanamel asked Jeremiah to "acquire" (*qənēh*) the "field" (*śādeh*) since the prophet had the

---

instantaneously with Boaz's declaration (see *IBHS* § 30.5.1d; see also Ruth 4:9; 2 Sam 24:22–23; Jer 40:4). The use of "hereby" aims to bring out this understanding of the verb.

## 4:1–12 Town Gate: Boaz Redeems before the Elders

"right [*mišpāṭ*] of possession [*yəruššâ*] and redemption [*gə'ullâ*]." Jeremiah buys the field with seventeen shekels of silver, and the transaction is executed in the presence of witnesses.

The first option is more likely. There is an overlap of terminology between the Ruth narrative and the case of preemption in Jeremiah: "acquire," "field," and "redemption." However, "right" and "possession" are not found in the Ruth narrative. More importantly, the description in the Ruth narrative is not consistent with other land "purchases" in the Old Testament, either outright ownership (see Gen 23:4–18; 33:19; 2 Sam 24:24; 1 Kgs 16:24) or possession and usufruct (Jer 32).[32] The seller is not present, no price is mentioned in the transaction, and no money is exchanged.[33] In short, Boaz is not "selling" the land but "transferring the right of redemption" of it.

Boaz is careful to perform the transaction in public, ratified by the town elders. As we will see later, it may well be that he performs this transaction in the presence of elders and the general public because the subsequent transaction he proposes does not strictly follow legal obligation.

**4** Having raised the issue of land transfer, Boaz discloses his role and interest in the transaction. He first arouses the nearer kinsman's interest: *I thought I*[34] *would uncover your ear*. As in 3:14, the verb *'mr* ("to say") most likely indicates internal speech, so *'āmartî* means "I thought." *Uncover your ear* indicates the disclosure of information, often important and confidential (e.g., 1 Sam 20:2, 12–13; 22:8, 17).[35] This vivid idiom probably derived from the gesture of sweeping back hair, then whispering information into the ear of a recipient. In its two other occurrences after "uncover your ear," *lē'mōr* ("by saying")[36] introduces new information through direct speech (1 Sam 9:15; 2 Sam 7:27). However, here it precedes Boaz's challenge to the nearer kinsman to *acquire* [the land]. It thus introduces a consequence of what Boaz has already revealed.[37]

---

32. Bush, *Ruth, Esther*, 214–15.

33. A legal document—a *sēper hammiqnâ*, "deed of purchase"—is included in the case of the preemptive purchase, signed by the witnesses (Jer 32:11, 12, 14).

34. The first-person pronoun *'ănî* ("I") is syntactically unnecessary with a finite verb. Here it probably marks a shift in topic, from Naomi to Boaz (so also Holmstedt, *Handbook*, 187) rather than emphasis (*pace*, e.g., Hubbard, *Ruth*, 236n4). Boaz's use of *'ănî* rather than *'ānōkî* in speaking to his peers probably also expresses the importance of his subsequent words, thus deserving attention from his addressees (similar to Naomi's use of *'ănî* in 1:21). See translation note on 2:10.

35. See G. Liedke, "*'ōzen*," *TLOT* 1:71; Zobel, "*gālâ*," *TDOT* 2:480.

36. This is a rare instance of the gerundive use of the infinitive with *lamed, lē'mōr* ("by saying"); see *IBHS* §36.2.3e.

37. Cf. Wagner, "*'āmar*," *TDOT* 1:334–35.

# THE BOOK OF RUTH

Ruth has not been mentioned so far in the negotiations, but Boaz's words remind the audience of her actions and presence. Boaz's "uncovering" (*glh*) of the kinsman-redeemer's ear recalls Ruth's "uncovering" (*glh*) of Boaz's feet (3:4, 7).[38] Her first proposal has led to Boaz's current proposal. And the alliteration between "uncover" (*glh*) and "redeem" (*g'l*) foreshadows the theme of redemption. Five times in this verse, Boaz will use forms of the verb *g'l*. This theme will form the center of the negotiations between Boaz and Mr. So-and-So, and we wait to see how Boaz will fulfill his promise to ensure Ruth's redemption (3:13).

Rather than speak of redemption, Boaz first uses the verb *qānâ*, which means "buy" in commercial situations,[39] but here has its general meaning, "to take possession of" or "acquire."[40] He asks the nearer kinsman to *acquire* the right to redeem Elimelech's land. There is no monetary payment, no exchange of goods for the land purchase (see also vv. 7–8). Boaz already stated Naomi is "transferring" (*mākrâ*) the right of redemption; now he asks Mr. So-and-So to take up or claim the right.

The transaction would take place *in front of those sitting here*, which may be a different group from *the elders of my people*. If the former group are the elders whom Boaz has asked to sit down (v. 2), who are the latter group? Some suggest they are people who have gathered around to observe the proceedings (cf. 4:9, 11). However, Boaz asked the elders to sit, and with limited seating, onlookers would probably be standing. It is better to understand the two phrases as referring to the same group, with the second phrase specifying who belongs to the group.[41] In any case, the mention of "the elders of my people" recalls Boaz's words to Ruth on the threshing floor: "all the assembly of my people know that you are a worthy woman" (3:11). The moment of truth has arrived: it is time for the elders to manifest their alleged recognition of Ruth with action. Underlying the legal acceptance, Boaz seeks social acceptance.[42]

Boaz then makes it clear to the nearer kinsman that to acquire the field of Elimelech, he must redeem it. Forms of the verb *gā'al*, "to redeem," are used

---

38. Cf. Sasson, *Ruth*, 116.

39. That is, to acquire by monetary payment (Gen 33:19; Lev 22:11; Josh 24:32; 2 Sam 24:24; 1 Kgs 16:24; Isa 43:24; Jer 32:9, 25, 44; 1 Chr 21:24) or other form of compensation (Gen 47:19–20; Prov 4:7); Lipinski, "*qānâ*," *TDOT* 13:59.

40. Cf. W. H. Schmidt, "*qnh*," *TLOT* 3:1149. See also comment on v. 5.

41. The second phrase could be translated, "that is, the elders of my people." The *waw* between the appositional phrases is "epexegetical" or "explicative"; see *IBHS* §39.2.4; David W. Baker, "Explicative Waw," in *Encyclopedia of Hebrew Language and Linguistics*, ed. G. Khan et al. (Leiden: Brill, 2013), 1:890–92.

42. Cf. Grossman, *Ruth*, 274–75.

## 4:1–12 Town Gate: Boaz Redeems before the Elders

five times in Boaz's proposal, replacing the verb "acquire." The wording Boaz uses reminds the audience of his promise to Ruth on the threshing floor:[43]

> If you will redeem, redeem.
> But if you will not redeem, tell me so I may know. (4:4)

> If he will redeem you, good; let him redeem.
> But if he is not willing to redeem you, then I will redeem you. (3:13)

Reading with 3:13, we expect Boaz is getting to the heart of the matter, but the surprise is that the land is now the object of redemption, not Ruth. Boaz's wording hints that Ruth and the land are closely intertwined, so we eagerly anticipate how they will be extricated by Boaz. As we will see, Boaz is expanding the implications of the redemption law. And although Boaz said Ruth's redemption by the nearer kinsman is "good," his omission of this assessment to the nearer kinsman betrays his preference that he himself will redeem Ruth.[44] But to the nearer kinsman and before the elders, Boaz hides his interest by saying, "so I may know" rather than "so I may redeem."

Boaz is keen to hear the nearer kinsman's response to his offer, *for there is no one except you to redeem, and I am after you.* Boaz tells Mr. So-and-So he has the first right of refusal to redeem the land, but if he declines, there is a fallback option. Narrowing it down to a friendly[45] two-horse race may also bring out the nearer kinsman's competitive side.[46] Nonetheless, Boaz seems careful not to pit himself against the nearer kinsman as a direct competitor. Observe how Boaz avoids applying the word "redeem" to himself:[47]

| Boaz says to Ruth (3:13) | Boaz says to the nearer-kinsman (4:4) | Boaz does *not* say to the nearer-kinsman |
|---|---|---|
| But if he is not willing to redeem you, | But if you will not redeem, | |
| then I will redeem you. | tell me so I may *know*, for there is no one except you to redeem, | tell me so I may *redeem* |
| | and I am after you. | and I am after you *to redeem.* |

43. Following the observation by Hubbard, *Ruth*, 241.

44. Cf. Zakovitch, *Rut*, 156.

45. Boaz uses *'ānōkî* ("I") instead of *'ănî* ("I"), which might indicate deference (cf. v. 4; 2:10; 3:12). The nearer kinsman similarly uses *'ānōkî* in his response.

46. Hubbard, *Ruth*, 242.

47. After Grossman, *Ruth*, 275.

# THE BOOK OF RUTH

Boaz does not state he would take up the right to redeem, but reading with 3:13, that is what the audience expects. His avoidance of the word "redeem" does not mean he will not do so; rather, it hints he has in mind more than *just* land redemption. The dramatic irony is acute: Boaz echoes his words from the threshing floor but substitutes the field for Ruth. He leads Mr. So-and-So into thinking that redemption is only of the field, but he is about to spread the redemption responsibility to cover Ruth.

The narrative now reaches a point of exquisite tension. We wait with bated breath for the nearer kinsman's response, which is swift and short: *I will redeem*.[48] The nearer kinsman's eagerness to accept the responsibility of land redemption shows it was also a privilege. Although an amount had to be paid to the current leaseholder and there was the added burden of providing materially for Naomi, the usufruct of the land would offset this cost. Since Naomi had no descendants, the land could not be redeemed from him, and the law of Jubilee would not have affected him.[49] Furthermore, if Mr. So-and-So already had children, the land would enlarge their inheritance. And in a group-oriented society, taking on this kinship responsibility would increase his social standing. For these reasons, the benefits outweigh the costs; it is an overwhelmingly attractive proposal. Yet the nearer kinsman does not say *gāʾaltî*, "I hereby redeem," in a declarative sense, which leaves the door ajar for further proposals from Boaz.[50]

Now the tension of the plot is ratcheted up another level. The nearer kinsman has accepted the offer, but what of Ruth? There has been no mention of her so far in the legal proceedings, so the audience wonders: does Boaz have something else up his sleeve?

**5** He does. Having settled the land issue, Boaz pulls out his trump card. The redemption of the field comes with a stipulation, and this second part of Boaz's proposal ends up being the deal breaker. Boaz says, "on the day" (*bəyôm*),[51] which puts the pressure on the nearer kinsman: he must decide on the spot, in front of the elders, and the offer is about to take on a different form altogether. But at least from the time of the scribes, people have found it hard to understand and interpret what Boaz says. The points of contention center on two loci:[52]

---

48. The first-person singular pronoun *ʾānōkî* ("I") before the verb *ʾegʾāl* indicates focus (the nearer kinsman instead of Boaz) rather than emphasis.

49. Sasson, *Ruth*, 118.

50. The perfect form would indicate that the case was settled; Joüon, *Ruth*, 83; JM §112f. Cf. Heb. *qānîtî*, "I hereby acquire" (vv. 9, 10).

51. More generally, *bəyôm* means "at the moment of," or "when"; Sasson, *Ruth*, 119; JM §129p.

52. For further discussion, see Lau, *Identity and Ethics*, 67–74.

## 4:1–12 TOWN GATE: BOAZ REDEEMS BEFORE THE ELDERS

On the day you acquire the field from the hand of Naomi [*ûmē'ēt*] Ruth the Moabite, the wife of the dead man, [*qānîtāy/qānîtî*] to establish the name of the dead man upon his inheritance.

There are two main possibilities for the two words:

(1) *ûmē'ēt*

    (a)  "And from,"[53] so that the field is to be acquired from both Naomi and Ruth.[54] Against this reading is that it leaves the verb "acquire" without an object, and it requires a shift in the disjunctive accent mark.[55] Moreover, Ruth was not mentioned as an owner in v. 3, nor is she mentioned as such in v. 9 or v. 10.[56] While it is possible for Naomi and Ruth to each possess rights over portions of the field,[57] it is unlikely they were co-possessors of the undivided field of Elimelech.

    (b)  "And/also," so that the acquisition of the field and the acquisition of Ruth are separate transactions. This is the majority view, either via an emendation of the Hebrew text,[58] or with-

---

53. This analyzes *ûmē'ēt* as *waw* + *min* + *'ēt* ("and" + "from" + direct object marker); cf. Num 35:8; Lev 16:5; Zech 6:10.

54. Some who read "and from" detect a distinction in the Hebrew: the portion of the field is acquired from the "hand of Naomi" (*miyyad no'ŏmî*) but only "from Ruth" (*mē'ēt rût*). This distinction is possible, but *miyyad* and *mē'ēt* with *qnh* ("acquire") are also used interchangeably in Lev 25:14–15 within the context of property acquisition.

55. In MT[L] the *'atnāḥ* marks a major pause in the verse and would need to be moved from "Naomi" to "Moabite." If the women are named as co-sellers, then the referent for "the wife of the dead man" would be somewhat ambiguous (but Ruth is the nearest referent); for the implications of this reading, see Holmstedt, *Handbook*, 191.

56. Cf. Rudolph, *Ruth*, 59. I would add that, within the Old Testament context, it seems unlikely that a foreign woman would be allowed ownership or control over a portion of the promised land. She is referred to as such in the legal transaction (vv. 5, 10).

57. So, e.g., Zevit, "Dating Ruth," 597. As discussed above, Naomi probably inherited the field of Elimelech only in the sense of usufructuary rights and the right to transfer it within the clan of Elimelech. So also, e.g., Bush, *Ruth, Esther*, 204; E. Lipiński, "Le mariage de Ruth," *VT* 26 (1976): 125–26. As a widow, Naomi probably held these rights until she passed the property onto a suitable heir, she remarried or died.

58. Either *ûmē'ēt* is read *gam 'et* (following Vulg.), with the *waw* read as a scribal error for *gimel*, or read as *wəgam 'et*, which harmonizes the reading in 4:10.

247

# THE BOOK OF RUTH

out an emendation.[59] The latter is the preferred reading[60] and it places emphasis on the second transaction.[61]

(2) *qānîtāy/qānîtî*

    (a)  "I acquire" (*qānîtî; ketiv*). Those who read the Hebrew in this way understand Boaz's words as "an obligatory statement of intent,"[62] a strategy designed at discouraging the buyer,[63] or a slip of the tongue.[64]

    (b)  "You acquire" (*qānîtâ; qere*).[65] Along with most versions,[66] commentators,[67] and EVV,[68] this is the preferred option because it is consistent with vv. 9–10, where Boaz states that Ruth is part of the package.

Combining the two preferred readings yields:

---

59. This reads the *mem* as enclitic: *waw* plus enclitic *mem* plus *'ēt* ("and" plus emphasizing conjunction ["indeed, even"] plus direct object marker). "Enclitic" refers to a word pronounced with so little emphasis it is shortened and forms part of the preceding word, e.g., *n't* in *can't*. For further discussion, see Bush, *Ruth, Esther*, 215–17. See also Constance Wallace, "*WM-* in Nehemiah 5:11," in *Eblaitica: Essays on the Ebla Archives and Eblaite Language*, ed. Cyrus H. Gordon, Gary A. Rendsburg and Nathan H. Winter (Winona Lake, IN: Eisenbrauns, 1987), 31; Gary A. Rendsburg, "Eblaite *U-MA* and Hebrew *WM-*," in *Eblaitica: Essays on the Ebla Archives and Eblaite Language*, ed. Cyrus H. Gordon, Gary A. Rendsburg and Nathan H. Winter (Winona Lake, IN: Eisenbrauns, 1987), 38. While his discussion of the enclitic *mem* is compelling, our opinions diverge on the second clause of Ruth 4:5, and hence I disagree with his translation of *ûmē'ēt* with "but, however." Ellen F. Davis and Margaret Adams Parker, *Who Are You, My Daughter? Reading Ruth through Image and Text* (Louisville: Westminster John Knox, 2003), 101, creatively reads the *mem* as a throat-clearing "ahem," reflecting his nervousness.

60. This reading maintains the integrity of MT^L.

61. Cf., e.g., ESV, NASB, NRSV.

62. Zevit, "Dating Ruth," 595–97.

63. Cf. Olivier J. Artus, "Les frontières de la communauté judéenne à la lumière du livre de Ruth," *Transeu* 37 (2009): 15.

64. LaCocque, *Ruth*, 130: "No Freudian slip could better indicate Boaz's nervousness and also his feeling to have stymied his opponent." Scholars who have recently argued for *qānîtî* include Block, *Discourse*, 212–14, and, tentatively, McKeown, *Ruth*, 92–95.

65. Reading *qānîtâ* as a second-person masculine form with the final *ā* vowel written with a mater lectionis *h*, rather than as a second-person masculine form with a feminine object, "you shall acquire her." The latter is the reading of, inter alios, Schipper, *Ruth*, 166.

66. LXX, Vulg., and Tg.

67. Recently, Hawk, *Ruth*, 118–20; Schipper, *Ruth*, 166.

68. E.g., ESV, NIV, NKJV, NJPS, NRSV.

4:1–12 Town Gate: Boaz Redeems before the Elders

> On the day you acquire the field from the hand of Naomi, also Ruth the Moabite, the wife of the deceased, you acquire in order to restore the name of the dead upon his inheritance.[69]

On this reading, Boaz links redemption of land with marriage, but the burning question is: on what basis? In Old Testament law, there is no explicit connection between redeeming a field and marrying a widow.[70] Therefore, Boaz is probably extending the obligations of a redeemer beyond the roles found in the law. Previously we noted that, in a collectivist society, roles are not clearly defined. A kinsman-redeemer's role would include whatever is required to help a needy family member, to mend the breach in the kinship structure.[71] If so, Boaz here includes among the redemptive role not just redemption of property and persons (Lev 25), but also marriage and preservation of a deceased kin's name and patrimony.[72] The reason he raises land redemption first is there is legal precedence (Lev 25:23–34).

We need to keep in mind the close linkage between name, offspring, and land in the Old Testament (esp. Gen 48:6; Num 27:4; Deut 25:5–10; 2 Sam 14:1–7; Ps 113:9). The "name" of a man was primarily preserved through the inheritance of his property by his descendants. Indeed, one of the worst fates for a person was to have their name "cut off" from his people (e.g., Lev 20:3) or the face of the earth (e.g., Josh 7:9).[73] A name (*šēm*) not only indicated identity, reputation, and social connections, in some sense, it also made the named present.[74] That is why the transmission of names through descendants is important: it ensured the postmortem existence of the deceased through their children (cf. Num 27:4; 1 Sam 24:22[21]; Isa 56:5).[75] In the Ruth narrative, "to restore/maintain the name of the dead

---

69. EVV that follow these two interpretive options include ESV, NASB, NIV, NRSV.

70. For a recent discussion of the redemption and levirate laws in Ruth, see Brad Embry, "Legalities in the Book of Ruth: A Renewed Look," *JSOT* 41 (2016): 31–44. He suggests the regulation regarding Zelophehad's daughters (Num 27; 36) resolves some of the legal curiosities in Ruth 4, but I do not think it fully applies since it is unlikely that Ruth, as a foreign widow, inherited land.

71. See comment on 3:9.

72. Cf. Matthew J. Suriano, "Death, Disinheritance, and Job's Kinsman-Redeemer," *JBL* 129 (2010): 63–64.

73. See also comment on v. 10.

74. For a discussion of the word, see A. S. van der Woude, "*šēm*," *TLOT* 3:1348–67.

75. For a recent study of this issue, see Steffan Mathias, *Paternity, Progeny, and Perpetuation: Creating Lives after Death in the Hebrew Bible*, LHBOTS 696 (London: T&T Clark, 2020), esp. 94–123.

THE BOOK OF RUTH

on his inheritance" (vv. 5, 10) involved the closely intertwined notions of property and offspring.

In this case, the redemption of property works in tandem with levirate marriage so that the name of the dead can be raised on his inheritance. The land by itself can be redeemed, but if this is the only transaction, then a name from its rightful line of inheritance is not attached to it. However, the ideal in ancient Israel was for the name of the dead to be established with the land. A practical implication of this is when the alienated land belongs to a childless widow, redemption of it "triggers the levirate duty."[76] This is because the principle undergirding both institutions is the same: redemption restores to the family property that is lost (or is at threat of being lost) by alienation; the levirate institution "restores a family to its property from which it is separated by extinction of the male line."[77] Both redemption and the levirate institutions thus restore wholeness to a family that had suffered a rupture. In the book of Ruth, this restoration of "shalom" requires both redemption and levirate roles.

Some commentators do not consider the levirate custom to be in play in the Ruth narrative.[78] However, the collective allusions to this practice indicate that this is how we are to understand the marriage between Ruth and Boaz. The phrase *'ēšet-hammēt*, "the wife of the dead," only occurs elsewhere in the description of the levirate law (Deut 25:5). This describes a woman who remains under the authority and protection of her husband's household, rather than returning to her birth household as a "widow" (*'almānâ*, cf. Gen 38:11; Lev 22:13).[79] Boaz's designation of Ruth as Mahlon's wife also situates her within Elimelech's household. She is thus linked to the patrimony. Moreover, the phrase "to establish the name of the dead man upon his

76. Raymond Westbrook, *Property and Family in Biblical Laws*, JSOTSup 113 (Sheffield: Sheffield Academic, 1991), 67. Cf. Brichto, "Kin," 15–16; David Daube, *Ancient Jewish Law: Three Inaugural Lectures* (Leiden: Brill, 1981), 38. Eryl W. Davies, "Ruth IV 5 and the Duties of the *Go'el*," *VT* 33 (1983): 233, "By insisting that the kinsman should undertake the double obligation of marrying the widow and redeeming the property, Boaz was simply making explicit what had always been implicit in the levirate duty."

77. Westbrook, *Property*, 64. Adele Berlin, "Legal Fiction: Levirate cum Land Redemption in Ruth," *Journal of Ancient Judaism* 1 (2010): 13, views the combination of the levirate and land redemption as reflecting the situation faced by postexilic Judeans.

78. Eskenazi and Frymer-Kensky, *Ruth*, 76, note that the term for levirate marriage is not used in the Ruth narrative, and list four explanations: (1) Boaz refers to contemporary customs of levirate unions (supposing that the practice changed over time); (2) Boaz alludes to levirate marriage (although it does not quite apply) as a way of extending moral responsibilities; (3) Boaz alludes to levirate marriage (although it does not quite apply) to justify his marriage with Ruth; and (4) Boaz is not referring to marriage but to taking economic responsibility as a redeemer. Eskenazi and Frymer-Kensky adopt (3).

79. Unlike Orpah, Ruth refused to return to her birth household as an *'almānâ* (1:14–17).

## 4:1–12 TOWN GATE: BOAZ REDEEMS BEFORE THE ELDERS

inheritance," is similar to the language in Deut 25:5–7, which describes the responsibility of a brother to produce a child with his dead brother's wife. In the Old Testament, "to establish" (ləhāqîm) means to restore or make something endure, including a reign or a lineage (e.g., Deut 29:12; 2 Sam 3:10; 1 Kgs 15:4; Isa 49:6).[80] The latter is the meaning here (also v. 10), and the verb is used in the two other texts related to levirate marriage in the Old Testament (Gen 38:8; Deut 25:7). From the immediate context, the referent for "the name of the dead" is most likely Ruth's husband, Mahlon, but Boaz had mentioned that Naomi was disposing of Elimelech's land (v. 3). By continuing Mahlon's line, Boaz would continue Elimelech's line and establish not just the name of Mahlon but also Elimelech's on the patrimony.

Apart from the two above allusions, there are at least seven other possible allusions to the levirate institution in the Ruth narrative: 1:11–13; 2:20; 3:9–13; 4:7–8, 9–10, 11–12, 16–17.[81] Taken individually, each allusion might not be sufficient evidence to establish the case for a levirate link but taken as a whole, their cumulative force is strongly in favor of this link. Certainly, the circumstances in the Ruth narrative do not fulfill the formal requirements for levirate marriage (Deut 25:5–10).[82] Yet Boaz extends the levirate obligation in this case to maintain the name of the dead on his inheritance.

The unique circumstances in the Ruth narrative also explain the only use of the verb qnh, "acquire," in the context of marriage. It is used regarding both the field and Ruth (vv. 4, 5, 8, 9, 10). The word has a wide range of meanings, and in commercial contexts, it refers to the purchase of objects, such as a field or a threshing floor (Gen 33:19; 2 Sam 24:21), or people (e.g., Gen 39:1; Neh 5:8).[83] Especially relevant to the case at hand is the use of qnh in texts related to redemption: the redemption of land and the purchase of slaves (Lev 25) and Jeremiah's redemption of family land (Jer 32:1–15). Ruth refers to herself as "your handmaid" (ʾămātekā; 3:9), and although Boaz is not "buying" her in the same way as described in Lev 25:44 (also ʾāmâ), perhaps the use of qnh in the Ruth narrative was influenced by Lev 25:44.[84] Rabbinic texts will use qnh in association with marriage (including levirate),

---

80. Gamberoni, "qûm," TDOT 12:596; S. Amsler, "qûm," TLOT 3:1139.

81. See Gow, Ruth, 143–82.

82. The underlying principle was to continue the lineage of a deceased man, but it is manifested differently in the Old Testament. The usual application of the principle is found in the levirate law, which describes a brother marrying the widow and carrying out the duty (Deut 25:5–10). In Genesis 38, the deceased's brother intentionally failed in his duty, but the father fulfilled it unknowingly without marrying the deceased's widow. I would suggest that the Ruth narrative is another manifestation of the principle, with someone outside the immediate household taking up the duty.

83. See W. H. Schmidt, "qnh," TLOT 3:1149.

84. So Schipper, Ruth, 166.

## The Book of Ruth

especially in contexts where there are other transactions in which *qnh* is used for a "purchase."[85] In any case, it is unlikely this is a payment of a "bride-price."[86] Previously, *qnh* meant to claim the redemption right for Elimelech's land, which did not require monetary payment (v. 4).[87] Hence, the use of *qnh* here to refer to marriage is contextual because of the immediately preceding use of *qnh* to refer to the purchase of the field (v. 5, also vv. 9–10). Indeed, it seems likely that Boaz uses "acquire" instead of "redeem" regarding the field so Ruth can be added as an acquisition: "On the day you *acquire* the field . . . also Ruth . . . you *acquire*."[88] Boaz presents the responsibility to the nearer kinsman as a land and wife package.[89]

The inseparability of land and offspring necessitated the tandem functioning of the redemption and levirate responsibilities. Boaz began with the land issue first because it had legal precedent. And Boaz was obliged to offer it to the nearer kinsman because he had priority. He accepted. Now that Boaz raises the connected issue of marriage and potential offspring, the audience is about to see the extent of the nearer kinsman's kinship loyalty.

**6** When the levirate obligation is introduced, the nearer kinsman has second thoughts. He says, *I'm not able to redeem for myself.* He does not say "I will not" but the stronger "I cannot" or "I'm not able" (*lōʾ ʾûkal*).[90] He also strongly states his reason for refusing: *in case I ruin* [ʾašḥît] *my inheritance.* Often used in the context of war, the verb *šāḥat* (in the *hiphil*) means "to destroy" (e.g., Gen 6:13; Jer 6:5) or "to ruin" (e.g., Judg 6:4; 1 Sam 6:5).[91] Some scholars thus view his statement as an exaggeration,[92] but even if it might not be fully grounded in reality, it still reveals his anxiety about his potential loss if he marries Ruth. The word *ʾašḥît*, "I ruin," recalls the story of Onan, who refused to impregnate his deceased brother's wife. Instead, he "ruined/

---

85. See David H. Weiss, "The Use of *qnh* in Connection with Marriage," *HTR* 57 (1964): 244–48.

86. For references and a comprehensive discussion, see Bush, *Ruth, Esther*, 217–18.

87. Commercial language is used elsewhere to refer to marriage (Gen 31:15; Hos 3:2). As noted by Sasson, *Ruth*, 123, however, the words used in those contexts are *mkr* ("to sell") and *krh* ("to barter"), and, moreover, are used sarcastically.

88. So also Grossman, *Ruth*, 281–82. The meaning of *qnh* is thus "to acquire a wife" (see also vv. 10, 13, and comment there).

89. Brad Embry, "'Redemption-Acquisition': The Marriage of Ruth as a Theological Commentary on Yahweh and Yahweh's People," *JTI* 7 (2013): 257–68, observes the words "redeem" and "acquire" only occur together elsewhere explicitly in Exod 15:13–16 and Ps 74:2, and implicitly in Deut 32:6 and Isa 11:11. He suggests the Ruth narrative is emblematic of Yahweh redeeming Israel in the exodus to acquire them as his chosen people.

90. Cf. Morris, *Ruth*, 304.

91. See D. Vette, "*šḥt*," *TLOT* 3:1317–19; Conrad, "*šāḥat*," *TDOT* 14:583–95.

92. E.g., Joüon, *Ruth*, 84.

## 4:1–12 Town Gate: Boaz Redeems before the Elders

wasted (*wašiḥēt*) his seed on the ground" (Gen 38:9).[93] Both Onan and the nearer kinsman refused to perform their levirate obligation. Although the nearer kinsman states his refusal strongly, *how* marrying Ruth would endanger his inheritance is opaque.

This has prompted many proposed reasons for his refusal. Those that are primarily arguments from silence are less likely:

(1) Mr. So-and-So's statement is "courteous circumlocution for the thought that he did not wish to marry Ruth."[94]

(2) Ruth's presence would cause too much friction with an incumbent wife.[95]

(3) He could not maintain both his current property and the additional property.[96] Yet, he had already agreed to it before Boaz adds the levirate stipulation.

(4) He did not want to "soil [his] estate by perpetuating the name of Mahlon upon it" because Mahlon's was a family of "traitor-emigrants."[97] This is plausible, although we cannot be certain because the nearer kinsman does not explicitly state this. And might not raising up the name of such a disgraced relative on his inheritance enhance his own reputation?

(5) Ruth is a Moabite.[98] This is also plausible. Boaz includes this designation in his revised proposal to Mr. So-and-So (4:5). Ruth's foreign status is certainly highlighted in the Ruth narrative, mainly in the first half of the narrative, as she first arrives in Bethlehem (1:22; 2:2, 6, 21).[99] Boaz says "Ruth the Moabite" twice (4:5, 10),[100] both times in conjunction with her widow status, which suggests that either the designation is used for legal precision,[101] or to recall her "doubly unfortunate" status—Ruth's non-Israelite ethnicity along

---

93. Cf. Zakovitch, *Rut*, 159.

94. Frants Buhl, "Some Observations on the Social Institutions of the Israelites," *AJT* 1 (1897): 736. Cf. Joüon, *Ruth*, 84. This suggestion does not explain his statement.

95. Targum to Ruth 4:6.

96. Gray, *Ruth*, 399.

97. Grossman, *Ruth*, 288.

98. E.g., *Midr. Ruth Rab.* 7:7, 10; Rashi. Zakovitch, *Rut*, 159, suggests that Mr. So-and-So cannot reveal his genuine reasons because they would also apply to Boaz, who has already announced that if he refuses, he will redeem Ruth.

99. As mentioned previously, this probably reflects how the people of Bethlehem view Ruth.

100. Campbell, *Ruth*, 160, correctly notes that if it was only used at 4:5, the case for this understanding would be stronger.

101. Hubbard, *Ruth*, 243, 255.

## The Book of Ruth

with her tragic widowhood.[102] This suggestion is not completely an argument from silence, but since the reason is not stated by Mr. So-and-So, it reduces the likelihood of it being the primary reason for his refusal.

We are left to draw a reason from Mr. So-and-So's response, which involves understanding *how* a levirate union with Ruth would impair his inheritance. The maintenance of Ruth, Naomi, and any potential offspring he might sire, along with the needs of any current family, would add to his production requirements from his fields in the short term. If we factor in the extra burden of repaying the cost for the additional field, along with the vagaries of subsistence agriculture, we can understand why Mr. So-and-So would decline. If he were to find himself overextended because of the upkeep for his enlarged number of dependents, he might enter the downward spiral of poverty (see Lev 25).[103] In this way, he would impair his landed inheritance. It thus appears his refusal is the most prudent course of action.[104]

Mr. So-and-So might also be considering the fate of his inheritance after he passes away. This hinges on his marital status, and more importantly, on whether he has heirs.[105] Many commentators presume he is married or at least has children.[106] This is a sound presumption in his cultural context, but since it is not stated in the narrative, we cannot be sure. We will thus consider the two possibilities.

The first possibility is that Mr. So-and-So is without an heir. In a levirate marriage with Ruth, their first son will be regarded as Mahlon's, not his. The land he redeemed at his own expense would be inherited by this son, along with his own land, unless he has further children.[107] Thus, it would not only

---

102. Hubbard, *Ruth*, 256; Campbell, *Ruth*, 160.

103. See Jacob Milgrom, *Leviticus 23–27*, AB 3B (New York: Doubleday, 2000), 2191–241.

104. Nonetheless, two factors mitigate the risk. First, Mr. So-and-So has at least one clansman who is "a man of great worth" (ethically and financially), and thus able and willing to assist him if he fell into economic straits, especially considering the concern he has already displayed for the widows. Second, it seems unlikely he cannot afford the extra cost because the only additional factor to his initial acceptance is he would have to feed two widows in the short term, along with any offspring in the future. The usufruct of Elimelech's field should offset the additional demand. Thus, while the inability to meet production needs potentially leading to debt and the alienation of his land may be sufficient motivation, the aforementioned factors should diminish this concern for Mr. So-and-So.

105. Rashi, commenting on his name *pelōnî 'almōnî*, suggests he is called *'almōnî* because he was a widower. He also suggests he had offspring.

106. Including, inter alios, Josephus, *Ant.* 5.332 (Thackeray, LCL); Thomas Thompson and Dorothy Thompson, "Some Legal Problems in the Book of Ruth," *VT* 18 (1968): 98; Rudolph, *Ruth*, 67.

107. If he is a bachelor and were to have children, most likely it would be with Ruth.

## 4:1–12 Town Gate: Boaz Redeems before the Elders

become an issue of property inheritance but also the perpetuation of his name upon his property. His land would not be alienated from the clan if he produced one son, but he would face personal extinction unless he had subsequent sons. Also lurking in the background is the possibility that Ruth did not bear children because she is infertile. Mr. So-and-So would have known that Ruth was previously barren for up to ten years (1:4–5), and her remaining reproductive time is limited. This would be advantageous if Mr. So-and-So already has offspring, but if he lacks an heir, the threat to his name and inheritance is further magnified.

The second possibility is that Mr. So-and-So already has offspring. He would still bear the cost of redeeming the property in addition to the upkeep of Naomi, Ruth, and any offspring produced with Ruth. The usufruct from the redeemed land should offset the increased needs, but there is still a risk from unpredictable crop production. Eventually, the first son from the levirate union would inherit the redeemed land. Perhaps, as some suggest, this son would also inherit a share of Mr. So-and-So's estate, diluting the inheritance for each of his own children.[108] I think this is less likely since the firstborn son would be regarded as Mahlon's (cf. Deut 25:6). Nonetheless, there is still considerable risk in accepting the levirate responsibility for Mr. So-and-So and his household. In short, if Mr. So-and-So is without an heir, levirate marriage to Ruth presents a greater long-term risk (to the perpetuation of his "name") than short-term risk (to his landed property while he is alive). If he has an heir, levirate marriage presents a greater short-term than long-term risk.[109]

This consideration of the potential reasons behind Mr. So-and-So's refusal to accept the levirate responsibility finds them reasonable and predictable. While we do not know the specific personal circumstances of Mr. So-and-So's refusal of the responsibility, his general motivation is clear enough: he wants to preserve his own inheritance. Perhaps his explanation is deliberately opaque because his reasons would apply to Boaz also, who has already announced he would take up the responsibility if he refused.[110] Whether we read "you acquire" (*qere*) or "I acquire" (*ketiv*) the levirate custom still applies. Since the firstborn son of Ruth (with either Boaz or Mr. So-and-So) would be considered the heir and descendant of Elimelech, he would in-

---

Although polygamy was permissible in ancient Israel, the cost of maintaining more than one wife was probably prohibitive, not to mention the family tensions it could cause, as illustrated in the patriarchal narratives (e.g., Abraham with Hagar and Sarah, and Jacob with Leah and Rachel). Both narrative and legal texts draw attention to its undesirability. See, e.g., the discussion in Wenham, *Story*, 84–87.

108. E.g., Davies, "Duties," 234; Thompson and Thompson, "Legal," 98; Rudolph, *Ruth*, 67.

109. *Pace* Joüon, *Ruth*, 84, who avers that Mr. So-and-So exaggerates the condition he would find himself in; and Bush, *Ruth, Esther*, 246.

110. Zakovitch, *Rut*, 159.

255

# THE BOOK OF RUTH

herit the redeemed land when the nearer redeemer died. Thus, his refusal is the way a normal, responsible family man would be expected to act.[111] Like Orpah, he began by taking the right action but ended up falling short; he too is a foil for the extraordinary actions of a protagonist. Yet there is limited shame attached to his refusal. In fact, the kinsman-redeemer's excuse enables him to withdraw with his honor intact.[112]

Nevertheless, Mr. So-and-So's actions contrast with those of Boaz. The structure of Mr. So-and-So's response brings this out:

> I'm not able to redeem for myself,
> in case I ruin my own inheritance.
> Redeem for yourself ... you ... my right of redemption,
> for I'm not able to redeem.

In the first and last clauses, Mr. So-and-So reiterates his inability to redeem,[113] and, in the third clause, the transfer of his right of redemption to Boaz. These two complementary actions are brought into stronger relief by the emphatic syntax of his words in the first and third clauses.[114] Mr. So-and-So's primary consideration for himself is also underlined by his multiple self-references (he says "I," "my," or "myself" six times), compared with no references to those who would stand to gain or lose the most from the transaction—Ruth and Naomi.[115] The apposition of the second and third clauses clearly shows the transfer of the right of redemption from Mr. So-and-So to Boaz. Whatever Mr. So-and-So's family circumstances were, he was not willing to place himself or his immediate family at risk for the sake of the interests of his wider kinship group. But, unlike Onan, he passes the levirate responsibility to someone willing and able to carry it out.

Questions remain: Was Mr. So-and-So aware of the linkage between the redemption and levirate duties? If so, why did he first agree to redeem the

---

111. Cf. Würthwein, *Megilloth*, 22; Hubbard, *Ruth*, 247. *Pace* Rudolph, *Ruth*, 67.

112. Cf. Hawk, *Ruth*, 129.

113. The repetition of his refusal to redeem is emphatic; *pace* Zakovitch, *Rut*, 159, who views it as a marker of his uncertainty.

114. The "ethical dative" is used in both the first ($l\hat{\imath}$) and third clauses ($l\partial k\bar{a}$), further enhancing the contrast (See GKC §119s), and the independent pronoun (*'attâ*) in the third clause in apposition to the pronominal suffix places further emphasis on the transference of the redemption right (GKC §§135d–g); see Bush, *Ruth, Esther*, 229, 33. Hubbard, *Ruth*, 246, adds that the statement is made more emphatic by the same derivation of both the imperative (*gə'al*) and its object (*gə'ullâ*).

115. Mr. So-and-So does not specify an object for the redemption, so he most likely has the land principally in mind, although the more general understanding of "redeem" in the narrative allows for Naomi and Ruth as a secondary consideration. Cf. Hubbard, *Ruth*, 237–38n12; Bush, *Ruth, Esther*, 229.

## 4:1–12 Town Gate: Boaz Redeems before the Elders

land? It seems Mr. So-and-So was aware of the linkage. When Boaz presents the linkage, the nearer kinsman does not argue that it is an invalid connection, and neither do the observing elders. Mr. So-and-So is probably unaware of *with whom* the levirate marriage will apply.[116] Presuming that the widow would be Naomi, who is beyond child-bearing age, he accepts the offer of redemption because it was economically attractive. Mr. So-and-So only declines when Boaz reveals the levirate obligation would apply to pre-menopausal Ruth.[117] The substitution of Ruth for Naomi may also contribute to the need for the transaction to take place at the town gate. Since levirate marriage would be a moral rather than a legal obligation (especially to Ruth instead of Naomi), it is conceivable Mr. So-and-So could have objected to Boaz's proposal that he also marry Ruth. Therefore, a public forum provides social pressure to stifle any objections Mr. So-and-So might have about the substitution, and the observing elders can also ratify the outcome.

7 This verse is an aside,[118] in which the narrator addresses the audience to explain an old custom before it takes place in the narrative (cf. 1 Sam 9:9). An explanation is required because the procedure was no longer practiced, but it is unknown how long it had fallen out of use. *Formerly* can refer to within a generation or so (Judg 3:2; Neh 13:5), hundreds of years (1 Chr 9:20) or even further back (Ps 102:26[25]) in Israel's history. The custom was about legalizing a transaction—*redemption and exchange*. The noun gə'ûllâ is the same as in v. 6, where the nearer kinsman renounced his "right of redemption." Although the rarely used word təmûrâ can mean "substitute" (Lev 27:10, 33; Job 28:17) or "recompense" (Job 15:31), in the commercial/legal context of this verse, it primarily means "exchange" (cf. Job 20:18): the transfer of the right of redemption.[119] In which case, "the redemption and exchange"

---

116. Cf. Davies, "Duties," 233–34.

117. It is improbable that Mr. So-and-So was unaware of the existence of Ruth, and her relation to the clan of Elimelech (see 1:19; 2:11; 3:11). The substitution of Ruth for Naomi is the most likely factor that caught Mr. So-and-So off guard and caused him to change his mind; so, e.g., Rudolph, *Ruth*, 67; Campbell, *Ruth*, 159; Bush, *Ruth, Esther*, 232. While it is presented within the narrative as an accepted practice, there is no consensus regarding the basis for the substitution. Joüon, *Ruth*, 10, and Lipiński, "Le mariage," 127, suggest it is similar to the custom that allowed servants to be substituted for infertile patriarchal wives (e.g., Gen 16:1–3; 30:1–6, 9–13). Thompson and Thompson, "Legal," 98, suggest that, as a daughter-in-law, Ruth was dependent on Elimelech's estate and was thus presumed to have "a claim on the estate for a potential heir." If this is the case, we would expect that this principle would be common knowledge, and thus also known to Mr. So-and-So. Therefore, the most likely suggestion is that of Davies, "Duties," 233–34, who suggests Naomi voluntarily renounced her right as a widow because of her advanced age, as indicated by her sending Ruth to Boaz to propose marriage.

118. The absence of *wayyiqtol* to begin the verse indicates it is outside the narrative sequence.

119. Cf. the English idiom, "to exchange contracts"—to make a legal contract binding.

257

# THE BOOK OF RUTH

is a hendiadys for "the transfer of the right of redemption."[120] The unusual word *təmûrâ* might have been chosen to create assonance with *tāmār*, Tamar (4:12), whose union with Judah was one of levirate-type substitution. If "substitution" is an intended secondary nuance, it foreshadows the replacement of the nearer kinsman with Boaz. In any case, the following procedure was probably *to establish any [such] matter*, not all legal transactions.[121] The infinitive of *qûm* (*ləqayyēm*; "to establish") is the same word that Boaz used to "establish" the name of the dead upon his inheritance (v. 5; cf. v. 10), thus drawing a thread between what Boaz is aiming to achieve, the sandal custom, and the levirate custom (Deut 25:6 and Ruth 4:10). The sandal procedure "confirms" or "establishes" the verbal agreement.[122]

To relinquish his right of redemption, *a man would slip off his sandal and give it to his companion.* The verb *šālap*[123] usually describes the unsheathing or drawing out of a sword (e.g., Judg 3:22; 1 Sam 17:51), but it is used here for "removing" or "drawing off" of a sandal. Only in this verse is *šālap* used with sandal rather than *ḥlṣ* (e.g., Deut 25:9, 10; Isa 20:2) or *nšl* (Exod 3:5; Josh 5:15). I translate *šālap* with "slip off" because the unusual English word reflects the rare usage of the Hebrew word as well as the onomatopoeic effect produced in the Hebrew phrase.[124] The noun *na'al* can refer to "shoes," but mostly it refers to a "sandal"—a wooden or leather sole strapped to a foot with thongs (Gen 14:23; Isa 5:27).[125] In the Old Testament (e.g., Josh 10:24; 1 Kgs 5:17[3]; Ps 8:7[6]) and ancient Near Eastern literature, the foot represents power and authority,[126] and this symbolic meaning is transferred

---

120. So also Bush, *Ruth, Esther*, 234, following Brichto, "Kin," 18.

121. In MT[L] the *zaqef qaton* on *dābār* indicates this phrase is connected to the preceding phrase; Sasson, *Ruth*, 142. There is no biblical evidence this procedure was enacted for every transaction or transfer; *pace* Eskenazi and Frymer-Kensky, *Ruth*, 79.

122. The noun *dābār* can mean word or matter, as reflected in the LXX, "to confirm every word/agreement" [*logon*]."

123. The modal *qatal šālap* expresses habitual activity in the past (e.g., 1 Sam 9:9); Bush, *Ruth, Esther*, 236.

124. By contrast, Aramaic Targums use *šlp* to translate *ḥlṣ* and *nšl*. This may be evidence that 4:7 was an addition, or Aramaic borrowing, and hence a later date for the composition of *Ruth*. However, given the assonance elsewhere in the narrative, as well as in this verse, I posit another explanation: the author chose *šlp* for the sounds produced in the phrase *šālap 'îš na'ălô* (we can almost hear a sandal being "slipped" off). Support for this explanation can be drawn from the levirate law, where the refusing brother's statement (*lō' ḥāpaṣtî ləqaḥtāh*; "I don't want to marry her"; Deut 25:8) alliterates more with the widow's response (*wəḥāləṣâ na'ălô*; "and draw off his sandal"; v. 9) if *ḥlṣ* is used rather than *šlp*.

125. Ringgren, "*na'al*," *TDOT* 9:465.

126. In the Old Testament, to "set foot" on land was associated with its ownership (Deut 1:36; 11:24; Josh 1:3; 14:9).

4:1–12 Town Gate: Boaz Redeems before the Elders

to the sandal by metonym.[127] In Ps 60:10[8] the sandal could symbolize possession of land, so it may do so in the sandal custom, although here it is the right to redeem the land and not the land itself. In ancient Israel, witnesses and ritual actions confirmed legal agreements. A sandal is convenient for such usage because it was not too costly (cf. Amos 2:6; 8:6) and could be removed without leaving the giver too inconvenienced.

Yet strangely for an aside meant to explain a disused custom, the description and meaning are not immediately clear. Unfortunately, no extrabiblical usage of sandals in legal transactions has been found to shed light on the custom.[128] We are left with lingering questions:[129] Who removed his sandal and gave it to his companion? What does the giving represent? The ambiguous nature of the aside has led some to consider other purposes for its insertion at this point in the narrative.

Indeed, it is worth considering the well-crafted literary quality of this aside. For an audience, the similar phrases enveloping it ("Now this was [the custom] formerly in Israel" [wəzō't ləpānîm bəyiśrā'ēl] and "This was the manner of witnessing in Israel" [wəzō't hattə'ûdâ bəyiśrā'ēl]) signal the aside's beginning and end, respectively. The assonance of the key words "redeeming," "exchanging," and "witnessing" (haggə'ûlâ, hattəmûrâ, hattə'ûdâ) not only provides aural pleasure for a listener but also binds the verse together. The repetition of a key word from the previous verse (gə'ûllâ) allows the verse to segue naturally, while the assonance with words in surrounding verses not only prepares hearers for future narrative events (e.g., təmûrâ and tāmār, v. 12; ləqayyēm and məqômô, v. 10),[130] they also help to embed the aside into the story as an organic part of it. On a narrative level,[131] the aside functions as a pause between the negotiation (vv. 3–6) and the outcome and declaration (vv. 8–10), allowing an audience to reflect on the momentous outcome of the negotiation. It also gives the following declaration an added solemn and legal feel (vv. 9–10). In short, this aside interrupts the plot but nonetheless fits snugly into its narrative surroundings.

Moreover, the aside subtly links proceedings with the levirate institution as well as intimates some differences. Forging a link is necessary because of two main points of divergence between the levirate institution and the situa-

127. See Åke Viberg, *Symbols of Law: A Contextual Analysis of Legal Symbolic Acts in the Old Testament*, ConBOT 34 (Stockholm: Almquist & Wiksell International, 1992), 161–63. When Mr. So-and-So removes his sandal, he abstains from using his authority as a kinsman-redeemer.

128. For discussions of potential ANE parallels to the shoe custom with references, see Bush, *Ruth, Esther*, 235–36; Viberg, *Symbols of Law*, 146–47.

129. See comment on v. 8.

130. The latter assonance is noted by Campbell, *Ruth*, 151; see comment on v. 10.

131. The following narratological reflections are from Hubbard, *Ruth*, 248.

## THE BOOK OF RUTH

tion in the Ruth narrative. First, the specific circumstances of the levirate law (Deut 25:5–10) do not attain in the Ruth narrative: neither Boaz nor Mr. So-and-So is "brother" of the deceased men, and they do not "dwell together" on an undivided estate. In Deuteronomy, the widow brings the case to the elders at the gate, but in the Ruth narrative, both Naomi and Ruth are absent from the scene.[132] The phrase "redeeming and exchanging" affirms that not only is this a case of land redemption (Lev 25:23–28), it also hints that it is a case of "substitution" (the secondary meaning discussed above). The levirate institution at its core is based on substitution—the replacement of a deceased man with his "brother" to continue the deceased's line; however, in the Ruth narrative, we are about to see the substitution taken to the next degree—the substitution of the substitute. The second point of divergence is the sandal ceremony. In Deuteronomy, when the brother refuses, his brother's widow enacts a shame-inducing ritual: she draws off his sandal, spits in his face, and says, "So shall it be done to the man who does not build up his brother's house" (Deut 25:9). Because Mr. So-and-So does not fulfill the criteria outlined above (he is not a brother-in-law living on an undivided estate), there is not the same level of obligation for him to act as the levir.

These two divergences explain the necessity for the aside. It affirms the connection with the levirate law but also indicates that, because of the different circumstances, its application will be different in the Ruth narrative. In particular, the drawing off of the sandal will be enacted by one of the men involved in the transaction (we cannot be certain which man it is until the next verse), and there will be no shame-inducing rituals because the nearer kinsman is not a brother-in-law of Ruth.[133] Mr. So-and-So declines his right or privilege, whereas the brother-in-law (Deut 25:5–10) refuses to perform his duty. Boaz has already alluded to the levirate law (4:5), so this aside tempers any audience expectation of a full enactment of its rituals.

**8** Based on the aside, it was uncertain who would remove his sandal and pass it to whom. It is revealed now, but only by the end of the verse. First, *the kinsman-redeemer* resumes his speech *to Boaz*. The kinsman-redeemer was the last to speak, but the aside distracted the audience's attention. Both characters might have been specified here (the only place it occurs in the proceedings, vv. 1–6) because it prepares the hearer for the scene's climax.[134]

132. There is no evidence in the narrative that Ruth can or even wants to take this course of action. After all, she was released from her duties to her family-in-law and not required to marry within the family (1:8–13; 3:10).

133. Contra Josephus, *Ant.* 5.335 (Thackeray, LCL), who adds that Ruth removed Mr. So-and-So's shoe and spat in his face.

134. So Hubbard, *Ruth*, 252. It also raises the tension by slightly delaying the nearer kinsman's speech.

## 4:1–12 TOWN GATE: BOAZ REDEEMS BEFORE THE ELDERS

There might also be some irony here:[135] "the redeemer" does not redeem; instead, the right of redemption is passed to Boaz.

The kinsman-redeemer's response lacks an object for *acquire* (*qǝnēh-lāk*, "acquire for yourself"). In v. 4, the referent was "the field," the same object as the only other use of the clause *qǝnēh-lāk* (Jer 32:7, 8, 25). In both contexts, the acquisition of the field is by a kinsman taking up the right of redemption.[136] Thus, in this verse, the implied object seems to be "redemption right," and the kinsman-redeemer used "redeem" to refer to the field. But now he echoes Boaz in using "acquire," which previously referred to "the land" (vv. 4, 5; cf. vv. 9–10) and "Ruth the Moabite" (v. 5; cf. v. 10). He is correct to use "acquire" because, legally, the transaction is not just a redemption of the land but an acquisition of the land and Ruth.[137]

The kinsman-redeemer has already firmly declined the offer to redeem the land based on the effect it would have on his own inheritance (v. 6), so hearing his response after the narrator's aside[138] colors our impression that it is not primarily for financial reasons he declines the offer, but for marital reasons. And the curtness of the nearer-kinsman's last departing words (just two words in Hebrew) leaves an impression that he finds marriage to "Ruth the Moabite" impossible to imagine, or perhaps even distasteful.[139]

Then *he slipped off his sandal*. Since the masculine subject of the verb and the owner of the sandal is covert, there have been several suggestions about who took off whose sandal and what the sandal symbolizes.[140] However, since the nearer kinsman had just spoken and there is no explicit change in the subject, it is most likely that he removed his sandal[141] and then presumably passed it to

---

135. So Campbell, *Ruth*, 149.

136. The verb *qnh* ("to acquire") also lacks an explicit object in Lev 25:14–15, but again the object in that context is landed property, or more specifically, the usufruct of the land (see comment on v. 3).

137. Cf. Grossman, *Ruth*, 283.

138. It was suggested that "redeeming" and "exchanging" refers to the redemption and levirate institutions, respectively; see comment on v. 7.

139. Boaz stated that his fellow townsmen know Ruth is a worthy woman (3:11), but we do not know if this included the nearer kinsman. In any case, her status as a Moabite might still have precluded marriage to her in the minds of anyone other than Boaz.

140. For instance, LXX specifies that "a man would take off his sandal and give it to his neighbor who was acquiring his right of redemption." *Midr. Ruth Rab.* 7:12 suggests that Boaz removes his shoe because the transaction is a purchase. Campbell, *Ruth*, 148, raises the possibility that the giving was reciprocal.

141. This reading would be supported if the verse can be structured as three parallel lines:
The kinsman-redeemer said to Boaz,
"Acquire it for yourself,"
and he slipped off his sandal.

261

# THE BOOK OF RUTH

Boaz (v. 7).[142] If so, the sandal represents the transfer of his right of redemption of the field, which triggers the acquisition of Ruth. The divergences with the levirate law were discussed above, but if the sandal symbolizes the transfer of the right of redemption, the similarity now becomes apparent: in both cases, the removal of the sandal represents a refusal of kinship responsibility.[143]

The uncovering of the kinsman-redeemer's foot recalls the uncovering of Boaz's feet at the threshing floor.[144] In private, Ruth exposed Boaz's feet as a gesture of approach; in public, the kinsman-redeemer exposes his feet as a gesture of retreat. Ruth lies down at the place of Boaz's feet in recognition of his authority; the kinsman-redeemer removes his sandal to symbolize the relinquishing of his right to acquire the field and Ruth to Boaz. Ruth's action and request stretched the boundary of the law; the nearer-kinsman's action is a customary act attesting to the law's fulfillment. There are two exposures, but the exposer's contexts and motivations are opposites.

**9** Having officially gained the right of redemption from the nearer kinsman-redeemer, Boaz immediately speaks to the elders and all the people. His declaration outlines his inseparable roles of redeemer (v. 9) and levirate (v. 10), and is similar to his proposal to the nearer kinsman (v. 5):

| v. 5 | vv. 9–10 |
|---|---|
| Boaz said, | Then Boaz said to the elders and all the people, |
| "On the day | "You are witnesses today |
| you acquire the field | that I hereby acquire all that belonged to Elimelech |
| | and all that belonged to Chilion and Mahlon |
| from the hand of Naomi, | from the hand of Naomi. |
| also Ruth the Moabite, | Also Ruth the Moabite, |
| the wife of the dead man, you acquire | the wife of Mahlon, I hereby acquire for myself as a wife, |
| to establish the name of the dead man upon his inheritance." | to establish the name of the dead upon his inheritance, |
| | so that the name of the dead may not be cut off from among his brothers |
| | and from the gate of his place. |
| | You are witnesses today." |

---

142. Since the procedure has just been explained, the passing to Boaz need not be detailed for the audience.

143. Cf. Hawk, *Ruth*, 130.

144. For ideas in this paragraph, I am indebted to Grossman, *Ruth*, 292.

## 4:1–12 Town Gate: Boaz Redeems before the Elders

Boaz's first speech is brief, and while the second has the same basic content, it adds more detail.

He first addresses *the elders and all the people* at the town gate to formally ratify his transaction. The elders were the ten who constituted the legal assembly (vv. 1–2), and now it seems a crowd has also gathered to observe the proceedings. Boaz's address to everyone present, *You are witnesses today*, enlists them all as witnesses of his proposal.[145] The repetition of this statement at the beginning and end of his speech makes it clear what they are witness to (vv. 9, 10). The ten elders sufficed as representatives of the people, but a wider range of witnesses is important for and foreshadows the acceptance of Ruth the Moabite into the broader Bethlehem community (vv. 11–12). In an oral culture, verbal attestation was required instead of a signature on a written document (cf. Jer 32:9–15). The confirmation of the witnesses is similar to that of the witnesses in the covenant ceremony in Josh 24:22, "We are witnesses" (v. 11).[146] The use of *today* indicates the transaction's legal consummation and ongoing validity.[147]

Compared to his previous proposals to the nearer kinsman (vv. 3, 5), Boaz is more comprehensive. Certainly, his brevity was appropriate for a legal proposal. But perhaps Boaz also only presented the minimum detail required, being careful not to make his proposal more attractive than it need be.[148] Boaz proposes he not only acquires the field, but *all that belonged to Elimelech and all that belonged to Chilion and Mahlon*. Now that the kinsman-redeemer has declined, Boaz speaks with more detail, perhaps also dictated by the legal need for full disclosure. Yet, since his expansiveness is consistent with his speech elsewhere, we get the sense he was holding back in v. 5. In any case, his more extensive description reflects the wide-ranging significance of his proposal. He redeems the patrimony of Elimelech, as well as that of his sons, *from the hand of Naomi*. She was holding the estate "in trust" and was the one who put it up for "sale" (vv. 3, 5). It is not clear here, but a particular owner of the estate will be specified in the next verse. The mention of Elimelech, Chilion, and Mahlon casts our minds back to the beginning of the narrative (1:3–5).[149] Their demise not only triggered a crisis for Naomi

---

145. Heb. "witnesses you (are) today," which fronts "witnesses" to contrast their role as witnesses with any other potential role; so Holmstedt, *Handbook*, 199.

146. Cf. 1 Sam 12:5; Isa 43:9–10, 12; 44:8.

147. See Gene M. Tucker, "Witnesses and 'Dates' in Israelite Contracts," *CBQ* 28 (1966): 44–45.

148. Cf. Zakovitch, *Rut*, 162; Hubbard, *Ruth*, 255.

149. Interestingly, the son's names are in reverse order to that in 1:2, 5. This may be chiastic, or perhaps Mahlon is mentioned last because he is most relevant to the continuing narrative. Campbell, *Ruth*, 14, lists other such chiasms: 1:3/5; 1:8/12; 1:9/14; 1:20–21a/21b; 4:9/11.

# THE BOOK OF RUTH

but also left Elimelech's family line without descendants on their inheritance. Boaz's speech signals that resolution is now at hand.

**10** *Also Ruth the Moabite, the wife of Mahlon,* is emphatically placed at the beginning of the second part of Boaz's speech.[150] This stands out even more strongly when contrasted with the normal word order in the previous clause, the first part of Boaz's speech, and hints that acquiring Ruth was Boaz's main aim. Boaz's choice of words— *I hereby acquire for myself as a wife*—contrasts with the kinsman-redeemer's curt "acquire it for yourself" (*qənēh-lāk*, v. 8): there is an intimate, personal significance side to this "transaction" for Boaz.[151] And if there is any significance of the use of "as a wife" (*lə'iššâ*) rather than "as my wife" (*lə'ištî*) it would be to foreshadow Ruth's greater role: to raise up Mahlon's name and to preserve it on his patrimonial estate (v. 10).[152]

Boaz's double designations for Ruth—"the Moabite" and "the wife of Mahlon"—might have been required for legal precision. Nonetheless, the mention of marriage to a Moabite surely would have raised eyebrows in the audience. As mentioned previously, the Israelites viewed the Moabites as an outgroup, frowned upon because of their incestuous origin (Gen 19:30–38) and their idolatrous practices (esp. Num 25). Throughout Israel's history, there was animosity between these two nations, including during the narrative context of Ruth (Judg 3:12–30). It is only during the time of David that there was anything close to cordial relations. Perhaps the greatest tension in Boaz's announcement is with Deut 23:4(3), which states, "No Ammonite or Moabite may enter the assembly of Yahweh" (ESV). Yet we can resolve this tension by examining the underlying reason for the prohibition and considering the crucial importance of Ruth's vow (1:16–17).[153] Despite her vow, the continuing usage of "the Moabite" might indicate the community's perception of her, or even the way they referred to her; if so, although they accepted Ruth, her Moabite ethnicity persisted.

Boaz's second designation for Ruth, the wife of Mahlon, is the first time it is specified who Ruth was married to. This was not specified at the beginning of the narrative, and since Mahlon is listed before Chilion, and Orpah before Ruth (1:2, 4, 5), we might have presumed Ruth was married to Chilion. Her identification as Mahlon's widow might have been required because she was

---

150. The object "Ruth the Moabite, the wife of Mahlon" is placed before the verb *qānîtî*, "I hereby acquire." Boaz's designations for Ruth in this verse are the same as v. 5, except "the dead" is replaced with "Mahlon." While there was ambiguity when Boaz said *ûmē'ēt* (v. 5), in this verse, the meaning of *wəgam 'et-rût*, "also Ruth," is clear—she is the second part of the transaction.

151. Cf. Zakovitch, *Rut*, 163.

152. So Block, *Discourse*, 224.

153. For further discussion, see section "Applying the Law" in the introduction.

## 4:1–12 TOWN GATE: BOAZ REDEEMS BEFORE THE ELDERS

legally a substitute widow for Naomi (v. 5).[154] In any case, the significance of Boaz listing the brothers in the ownership of the estate now becomes clear: as the wife of one of the brothers, marriage to her forms the link between their land and their lineage (cf. v. 5). Only here in the Old Testament is the verb *qnh*, "acquire," used in the context of marriage. The usual verb is *lqḥ*, "to take" (4:13) or less commonly *nś'*, "to lift, carry" (1:4).[155] As discussed above, Boaz most likely uses "acquire" because he just mentioned "acquiring" the estate of Elimelech, Chilion, and Mahlon (v. 9; see comment on v. 5), and he views the land and marriage as a package. Here, Boaz acquires Ruth as his wife; the marriage proper will take place shortly (v. 13).

Boaz's declaration is significant from a narrative and thematic perspective. When Naomi sent her daughters-in-law back to their mother's houses, she prayed that Yahweh would grant them rest in the home of a new husband (1:8–9). In the field, Boaz prayed that Yahweh would reward Ruth for her loyalty (2:12). Naomi's express purpose for sending Ruth to the threshing floor was to obtain rest through a union with Boaz (3:1). His declaration ties up these narrative loose ends. God heard and now answers those prayers— through the plans and efforts of those same people. Thematically, God's providence and human action are interwoven.

After announcing his "acquisition" of Ruth, Boaz then details its significance in parallel—first positively, then negatively:

> Also Ruth the Moabite, the wife of Mahlon [*maḥlôn*],
> I hereby acquire for myself as a wife,

> *Positively:*   to establish [*ləhāqîm*] the name of the dead
>                 upon his inheritance [*naḥălātô*],
> *Negatively:* so that the name of the dead may not be cut off from
>                 among his brothers
>                 and from the gate of his place [*məqômô*].

For an audience hearing this verse, alliteration draws a tighter connection between Mahlon (*maḥlôn*) and his inheritance (*naḥălātô*). If the meaning of his name ("sickly") pointed to his fate, this wordplay points to a better future. Alliteration also ties the positive significance to the negative, with "to establish" (*ləhāqîm*) at the beginning and "his place" (*məqômô*) at the end. Given the author's penchant for alliteration, the choice of the word *məqômô*

---

154. Hubbard, *Ruth*, 255–56.
155. See comments on the respective verses.

## The Book of Ruth

might have been influenced by its similar sounds with *ləhāqîm*, and perhaps *ləqayyēm*, "to establish" (v. 7).[156]

Boaz's detailing of the negative significance of his acquisition of the land and Ruth fills out the basic content of his proposal to the nearer kinsman-redeemer (v. 5) and clarifies the previous phrase. Boaz wants to ensure that the name of the dead will *lō'-yikkārēt, not be cut off* in two senses. First, *from among his brothers*.[157] Here *'eḥāyw*, "his brothers," refers to Mahlon's kinsmen, in particular, the relatives from his clan in Bethlehem. The use of the verb *krt*, "to cut off," in Leviticus sheds some light on its sense in this verse.[158] There it refers to the termination of a person's lineage and also to a person not being united with their ancestors in death, often described with a phrase such as "gathered to his people." This idiom (only found in the Pentateuch) reflects a belief in an immortal element that continues after clinical death,[159] where a person is united with their ancestors with whom they would rest and find peace (e.g., Gen 15:15; 25:8; 35:29; Num 27:13).[160] Mahlon's lineage is threatened, and he was not physically gathered to his people because he died in Moab (cf. the burial of Jacob, Gen 49:28–33; 50:12–14).[161] In the concern for separation in death, we hear an echo of Ruth's commitment to Naomi, even to the point of wanting to be buried with her (1:17). "To cut off a name" is a disastrous fate, one of several idioms that speaks of the annihilation of a person's reputation, and the cutting off of posthumous existence (e.g., Josh 7:9; 1 Sam 24:22[21]; Isa 14:22; 48:19; Zeph 1:4). The concept is found in the concern of the daughters of Zelophehad, that their father's name not be taken away (verb *gāra'*) from his clan (Num 27:4). And Boaz's words recall the levirate law, where the son bears the name of the deceased "so that his name may not be wiped out [verb *māḥâ*] from Israel" (Deut 25:6 NASB). Boaz's concern is for the threat to Mahlon's lineage (and, by extension, Elimelech's) and his separation from his wider family.

Second, Boaz is concerned that Mahlon's name is not cut off *from the gate of his place*. Most commentators understand "gate of his place" as a metonym for "the assembly at the gate" (cf. "all the assembly of my people"; 3:11).[162]

---

156. Also Campbell, *Ruth*, 151.

157. For "brother," see comment on v. 3.

158. See Jacob Milgrom, *Leviticus 1–16*, AB 3 (New York: Doubleday, 1991), 457–60.

159. Nahum M. Sarna, *Genesis*, JPS Torah Commentary (Philadelphia: JPS, 1989), 174.

160. Some suggest ancient Israelites believed that interment in the family tomb on ancestral land manifested the integration of the dead into the realm of the ancestors; for a recent discussion of ancient Israelite burial with references, see Mathias, *Paternity*, 71–79.

161. But note that Abraham (Gen 25:8–10), Aaron (Num 20:26–28), and Moses (Deut 32:50; 34:5–6) were not buried with their ancestors.

162. See the discussion in Daniel A. Frese, *The City Gate in Ancient Israel and Her Neighbors: The Form, Function, and Symbolism of the Civic Forum in the Southern Levant* (Leiden:

## 4:1–12 Town Gate: Boaz Redeems before the Elders

The setting of this scene, a legal assembly at the town gate, suggests such a reading. Further evidence can be drawn from Deut 21:19, where "gate of his place" is in parallel with "the elders of his town." This is a possible reading, but the structure above suggests another reading. If "to establish the name of the dead" is in parallel with "so that the name of the dead may not be cut off from among his brothers," then "upon his inheritance" is in parallel with "and from the gate of his place." In which case, "the gate of his place" could be the gate at a family compound, or more symbolically, the household that lived within a family compound, of which Mahlon would be the patriarch.[163] Both readings are possible—assembly at the town gate or gate of his family compound—although based on the above structure I lean toward the latter.

Boaz's declaration to the throng at the town gate (vv. 9–10) repeats and embellishes his proposal to the nearer kinsman-redeemer (v. 5). The repetition is primarily to legalize his proposal and apply it to himself, but it also has the effect of reinforcing his character as a man of his word.[164] He says something, then he does it. He promised Ruth that he would do all she asked, then confirmed his pledge by giving her barley (3:11, 15). At that time, it was unclear what he would do or how he would do it, but it involved giving the nearer kinsman-redeemer the first opportunity of redeeming her. Now Boaz has kept his word—redeemed the field and married Ruth. Integrity is another virtue of this "man of great worth" (2:1), one that should characterize the people of God. As a quality of God (e.g., Num 23:19), it is enjoined for his people in oath-taking (e.g., Num 30:1–2), and Jesus raises the expectation for honesty for Christians in the New Testament (e.g., Matt 5:33–37).

Some suggest that Boaz's stated motivation at the gate is at odds with his motivation at the threshing floor.[165] There, his concern was for Ruth's welfare (3:10–13); here, his concern is to perpetuate the name of the deceased (4:10). These motivations need not be in conflict; a person can have multiple motivations for one action. The difference is partly due to the circumstances: a private conversation with Ruth, compared with a public discussion about the primarily male concerns of land and legacy.[166] By marrying Ruth and acquiring the land he achieves both purposes, which resolves the dual narrative crises of a family's extinction (1:1–5) and a widow's security (1:8–9). A wordplay reinforces this connection. Ruth's name or reputation is recognized at the town gate, "for all the assembly of my people [*šaʿar ʿammî*] know that you

---

Brill, 2020), 205–6. Schipper, *Ruth*, 170, suggests it refers to the assembly of elders at the gate (cf. v. 2) and Mahlon's deceased ancestors.

163. So also Block, *Discourse*, 224, who reads the *waw* epexegetically ("that is") rather than as a conjunction ("and").

164. Cf. Holmstedt, *Handbook*, 200.

165. E.g., Linafelt and Beal, *Ruth & Esther*, 73.

166. Cf. Trible, *Sexuality*, 192.

## The Book of Ruth

are a worthy woman" (3:11), while the aim at the town gate is for the name of the dead to not be "cut off from among his brothers and from the gate of his place [*ûmiššaʿar məqômô*]" (v. 10).[167] Ruth's loyalty to Naomi's family (3:10) is reciprocated by Boaz's loyalty to Ruth (3:11–13; 4:10).

Boaz concludes his declaration by repeating his refrain from the beginning, *You are witnesses* (cf. v. 9). The repetition is emphatic, and the throng's response reveals that this statement functions as a challenge, one they willingly accept (v. 11). In hearing and accepting the legal declaration, they would attest to its validity in the case of future challenge (cf. Josh 24:27). *Today* points to the declaration's legal validity from the time of the throng's acceptance. Within the narrative, "today" also reminds us of Naomi's words: "for the man won't rest unless he settles the matter today" (3:18). Boaz and Naomi do not meet in the narrative, but once again the words they speak are similar (also, e.g., "my daughter"). Boaz is not only a man of his word (3:11–13), he is a man of action.

Before we move on to the throng's response, we will consider two aspects of redemption brought out in this scene at the town gate.[168] The first is the costly nature of redemption. When first offered the right of redemption, the nearer redeemer jumps at the opportunity. But when Boaz reveals that redemption would trigger a levirate marriage with Ruth, he reneges. The initial cost of redeeming the property was not the issue: he was willing to pay that price (4:4). His concern was the ruin of his inheritance (4:6). The ongoing cost of feeding Naomi, Ruth, and any children produced with Ruth was a risk for him and his family in a time of subsistence agriculture. This initial and ongoing cost would have no ultimate benefit for Mr. So-and-So, since the property would be inherited by any son produced with Ruth. When the property is transferred to this heir, Mr. So-and-So would lose the produce of the land. Moreover, this son would continue Elimelech's family line, not the nearer redeemer's. The nearer redeemer thus functions as a foil for Boaz, who is willing to redeem Elimelech's property and marry Ruth. One might counter that it was easier for Boaz to make that decision because he found Ruth attractive. This is true: he had voiced his appreciation of her virtuous character (3:10–11). And if Rahab was an ancestor of Boaz (so Matt 1:5),[169] this might have predisposed him to act in kindness toward foreigners, including Ruth. Yet, Boaz's decision still entails significant risk, as the nearer

---

167. Grossman, *Ruth*, 295.

168. For another two aspects of redemption, see section "Ruth and the New Testament" in the introduction.

169. Most scholars accept that the Rahab listed in the Matthean genealogy is the same as in the Joshua narrative (Josh 2; 6:17, 23–25). See esp. Raymond E. Brown, "*Rachab* in Mt 1,5 Probably Is Rahab of Jericho," *Bib* 63 (1982): 79–80.

## 4:1–12 TOWN GATE: BOAZ REDEEMS BEFORE THE ELDERS

redeemer states (4:6). If Boaz did not already have an heir, he risks his own perpetuity by marrying Ruth since she had not borne children in up to ten years of marriage (1:4–5). Despite knowing the risk and the cost, Boaz follows through on his commitment.

The second aspect of redemption revealed in this scene is thus the character of the redeemer. Boaz acts for the benefit of others who are in need. He is willing to risk his immediate security in providing for Naomi and Ruth, and his future legacy by marrying Ruth. As he states, he acts for the sake of his fellow clansman, to raise up Mahlon's name and ongoing existence (4:10). Such generosity and selflessness are closely aligned with kindness. Acts of kindness often go beyond obligation or requirement[170] and often contain inherent risk. Such is the character of a redeemer.

In the context of the Old Testament, Boaz's act of redemption echoes that of God, the great Redeemer.[171] The exodus was his foundational act of redemption, an event drawn upon in every section of the Old Testament. In this event, God releases his people from physical bondage. In the return from exile (often viewed as a second exodus), God redeems his people from both physical and spiritual bondage. As Boaz redeems the land and releases Naomi and Ruth from poverty, he can be viewed as acting on behalf of God. As redeemer, kindness is one of God's core characteristics (Exod 34:6, 7). He acts generously on behalf of those who cannot help themselves. God's kindness in redemption finds ultimate fulfillment in the New Testament, where God redeems through Jesus. As the apostle Peter says, Jesus ransoms (or redeems) not with silver or gold, but with "the precious blood of Christ" (1 Pet 1:18–19). His once-and-for-all self-sacrifice redeems all humanity (Heb 9:12).

**11** The group of people then respond to Boaz's declaration. Instead of repeating the description of the people verbatim ("the elders and all the people"; v. 9), the narrator reverses the order and adds *who were at the gate* (*'ăšer-baššaʿar*) between the two groups.[172] This might simply be repetition with variation, but a reference to "the gate" so soon after Boaz's concern for the continuation of his kinsman's name at "the gate of his place" (*šaʿar məqômô*; v. 10) would make a listener anticipate what these people "at the gate" are about to say. If we remember that Boaz has already asserted that some, or even a majority of these people ("all the gate of my people"; *kol-šaʿar ʿamî*; 3:11) think highly of Ruth, we expect they will respond by saying something positive about her. Moreover, the mention of "the gate" and "el-

---

170. In the Old Testament, *ḥesed* has a strong element of benevolence over obligation; Andersen, "Yahweh, the Kind and Sensitive God," 44.

171. For more detail and references, see section "Ruth and the New Testament" in the introduction, and Lau and Goswell, *Unceasing Kindness*, 128–31.

172. As noted above, Campbell, *Ruth*, 152, suggests the reversal forms a chiasm with v. 9.

THE BOOK OF RUTH

ders" recalls the beginning of this scene, when Boaz assembled the witnesses (4:1–2). Thus, repetition of the location and participants signals to an attentive listener the scene is ending. This fits nicely with the content of these verses—legal affirmation, then blessing from the same participants (along with "all the people who were at the gate").

This throng first responds to Boaz's declaration by expressing their agreement. They had observed the legal proceedings at the usual location, and now they provide their legal assent to the outcome. Their one-word statement, *ʿēdîm*, [*We are*] *witnesses*, corresponds with the same word Boaz used at the beginning and end of his declaration (vv. 9, 10). Since Biblical Hebrew has no equivalent of the English word "yes," the throng's use of "witnesses" directly affirms Boaz's concluding statement, "You are witnesses today" (v. 10; cf. Josh 24:22).

Those assembled at the gate then proclaim a three-part benediction for Boaz, structured as a chiasm (vv. 11b–12):

> A  May Yahweh make the woman coming into your house
> > B  like Rachel and Leah, who built, the two of them, the house of Israel.
> > > C  And act worthily in Ephrathah
> > > C'  and proclaim a name in Bethlehem.
> > B'  May your house be like the house of Perez, whom Tamar bore for Judah,
> A'  from the seed that Yahweh will give to you from this young woman.

The first and third parts (A–B and B'–A') are benedictions for Boaz's wife and Boaz's house, respectively. The central part (C–C') is a benediction for Boaz, based on place names.

Naomi prayed that Yahweh would grant (*yittēn yhwh*) rest to her daughters-in-law in the house of another husband (1:9), and now the townsfolk pray that Yahweh would make (*yittēn yhwh*) *the woman coming into* Boaz's household *like Rachel and Leah*. One can imagine the joyful chorus of people asking God to make Ruth like the matriarchs of Israel, *the two of them* the progenitors of the twelve tribes of Israel.[173] Just as Rachel and Leah *built . . . the house of Israel*, so the townspeople wish for Ruth to build up the house of Boaz by producing children.[174] Rachel was barren then bore children, so

---

173. Bilhah and Zilpah also produced children, but since they were the maidservants of Rachel and Leah, they bear children on behalf of their masters (see Gen 30). Gunkel, "Ruth," 86, compares the people to the chorus in a Greek tragedy.

174. "To build a house" metaphorically means "to found a family," "to have descendants"

270

## 4:1–12 Town Gate: Boaz Redeems before the Elders

we anticipate that Ruth will follow the same trajectory. There are delightful wordplays to match the people's delight: they wish that *the woman*, Boaz's soon-to-be wife (*hā'iššâ*; cf. 1:1, 4, 5; 4:10, 13),[175] who is coming into his *house* or household will build up his *house* or lineage (*bayit*; cf. 1:8, 9).[176] The people may simply wish for God to enable Ruth to produce a foundational lineage for Boaz, comparable to Rachel and Leah and the house of Israel.[177] If we widen our focus, however, we can discern further Old Testament allusions. The phrase "build a house" recalls its first usage in the Old Testament, where a nearest kinsman "does not build up his brother's house" (Deut 25:9). An allusion to the levirate law is even more likely when this blessing is read with the third part of the blessing (v. 12; see below). And since "build a house" is famously associated with David (2 Sam 7:27; 1 Kgs 11:38; 1 Chr 17:25), there is perhaps an anticipation of the foundation of a royal dynasty (vv. 17–22).

The Bethlehemites' acceptance of Ruth is even more amazing because Ruth is a self-proclaimed foreigner (2:10), as were the matriarchs Rachel and Leah in at least one sense (see comment on v. 12). Jacob chose them (at least he chose Rachel!), but Ruth herself chose to identify with Israel's people and Israel's God (1:16). We cannot know if the people of Bethlehem ever considered her a full Israelite. The lack of the ethnic label "the Moabite" when she marries Boaz (v. 13; cf. 1:22; 2:2, 8, 21) might suggest that at least some members of the Bethlehem community did not only see her as a foreigner. In any case, she truly belonged among God's people. Naomi's prayer for Ruth was answered; will the townsfolk's prayer of blessing also be answered?

The people's prayer prompts a consideration of the God to whom they pray. By asking Yahweh to bless Ruth, the people imply that they share the same God.[178] Yahweh's provision of refuge for this foreign immigrant shows his acceptance of "outsiders" who place their trust in Yahweh (1:16; 2:12). In fact, it is the same trust that is required of those who are ethnically Israelite.[179] Ruth is one of a handful of foreigners incorporated into God's people in the

---

(Gen 16:2; 30:3 [both *niphal*]); A. R. Hulst, "*bnh*," *TLOT* 1:246. For further connotations, see below.

175. See N. P. Bratsiotis, "*'îš*," *TDOT* 1:224–25; F. Stolz, "*'iššâ*," *TLOT* 1:187–88.

176. See Hoffner, "*bayit*," *TDOT* 2:113–15; E. Jenni, "*bayit*," *TLOT* 1:235.

177. Perhaps "Israel" refers to Jacob rather than the nation; so Tg. and Sasson, *Ruth*, 154. This would be consistent with the parallel to Judah in the third part of the benediction (v. 12), as well as the genealogies in Chronicles (1 Chr 1:34; 2:1; 5:1, 3; 6:23[38]; 7:29). Nonetheless, it is difficult to separate the patriarch from the nation he founds, so both are probably referred to here.

178. Hubbard, *Ruth*, 256.

179. For a recent exploration of this theme, see David G. Firth, *Including the Stranger: Foreigners in the Former Prophets*, NSBT (Downers Grove, IL: InterVarsity, 2019).

# THE BOOK OF RUTH

Old Testament.[180] Yet, her acceptance foreshadows the wider incorporation of non-Israelites into the people of God, a theme mentioned elsewhere in the Old Testament, and which finds full fruition in the New Testament.[181]

The throng blesses Boaz in the second, central, part of their benediction, which comprises two complementary exhortations. These exhortations at first seem out of place in a benediction, but it is best to read them as wishes directed at Boaz.[182] Their poetic nature[183] resists specific meanings; indeed, it allows for a wider range of blessings. Following from the prayer that Ruth would produce children to build up the house of Israel, *act worthily* (*'ăśēh-ḥayil*) could mean "to produce worthy offspring," with the same character as Boaz. The elders would be wishing that this worthy man and woman (2:1; 3:11) produce offspring of similar character. Other nuances of *act worthily* are possible also, such as "to make wealth," "to prosper," or "to act in strength." However, from the way *ḥayil* has been used in the narrative so far, the foremost nuance is probably "to act worthily/honorably."

If the first exhortation outlines how Boaz is to act in *Ephrathah/Bethlehem*,[184] the second specifies what he is to do. Again, there is a range of ways to understand *qərā'-šēm*. It can mean to name a child at birth, such as the women do for Obed (4:17b), or to honor a person or to proclaim ("call out") their name, such as the women pray for and then do so themselves after Obed's birth (4:14; 17a).[185] In the latter case, since the people and elders do not mention a name in their blessing, we cannot know for certain whose name is to be honored—Boaz's or another.[186] Since Boaz has twice mentioned that he wants to establish the name of the dead (*ləhāqîm šēm-hamēt*; 4:5, 10), it seems most natural to understand that the wish is

---

180. Among others, some include Rahab (Josh 6:25), Naaman (2 Kgs 5:1–14), and perhaps some in the Persian Empire (Esth 8:17; 9:27); cf. "the mixed multitude" (Exod 12:38). See also Lau, "Gentile," 356–73.

181. E.g., Isa 49:6; 56:3–7; Zech 8:23; Matt 28:18–20; Acts 1:8; Eph 2:11–22. See section "Mission" in the introduction.

182. The second part of the townspeople's benediction contains two masculine singular imperatives— "act" and "proclaim." These two imperatives are enveloped by two jussives in the first and third parts of the townspeople's benediction—*yittēn* and verb-subject word order ("May he make") and *yəhî* and verb-subject word order ("May it be"; v. 12).

183. The two imperatives of the second part of the benediction form a parallel poetic couplet.

184. Ephrathah is in parallel with Bethlehem, and elsewhere they are synonymous (Gen 35:19; 48:7; cf. Mic 5:2); see comment on 1:2. The mention of Ephrathah recalls the place to which Jacob was traveling when Rachel died and thus also links to the first part of the throng's benediction.

185. For "proclaim a name" (*qərā'-šēm*) concerning God, see Exod 33:19; Deut 32:3.

186. Although unlikely in this context, a person can proclaim their own name, as Yahweh does in Exod 33:19.

## 4:1–12 TOWN GATE: BOAZ REDEEMS BEFORE THE ELDERS

for either Elimelech or Mahlon's name to be proclaimed. In Old Testament thinking, mentioning a person's name expresses their continued existence (e.g., Gen 48:16), while not mentioning the name of the dead means they cease to exist (e.g., Isa 14:20).[187] As such, "proclaiming the name" is akin to perpetuating the family line of Elimelech/Mahlon, which dovetails with the first and third elements of the people's benediction. In short, the people wish for Boaz to act worthily by proclaiming the name of the dead in Ephrathah/ Bethlehem. By doing so, he would also enjoy the blessing of the proclamation and perpetuation of his own name.

This mention of Ephrathah and Bethlehem forms an inclusio with 1:2. The problem with Bethlehem, "house of bread," was that there was no bread, and this precipitated a family crisis that left Elimelech's "house" empty. We have now come full circle. Naomi's emptiness has been filled with bread,[188] and the throng's repetition of "house" in their prayer anticipates a dynastic fulfillment. Thus, the people prompt us to consider God's grace in reviving a family that was all but extinct.

**12** The third part of the benediction is upon Boaz's house. The throng prays that his would be *like the house of Perez*. Although not particularly large, the clan of Perez gained prominence in the tribe of Judah over those of his older and younger brothers (Gen 46:12; Num 26:20–21; 1 Chr 2:3–6; 4:1). It was the clan from which Elimelech and Boaz and most of his audience in Bethlehem had descended (vv. 18–22). Thus, the people wish that Boaz's house would be as distinguished in Judah. He will perpetuate the line of Elimelech (v. 5, 10, 11), but the people recognize that the offspring of Boaz and Ruth would also build *his* house. The offspring would belong to Naomi (v. 17), and hence continue Elimelech's line, but also to Boaz (which foreshadows v. 21).

The people's description of Perez, *whom Tamar bore for Judah*, draws in a rich network of associations. Most likely, the primary allusion is to the levirate nature of the union between Boaz and Ruth. Hints of the levirate custom have bubbled beneath the Ruth narrative, and even in this chapter, the aural similarity between "exchange/substitution" (*təmûrâ*) and Tamar[189] adds to the strength of the association.[190] But now, the levirate custom is brought to the surface since the union between Judah and Tamar is its only

---

187. C. J. Labuschagne, "*qr'*," *TLOT* 3:1162. A similar Hebrew construction ("call" [*qr'*, *niphal*] + "name" [*šēm*] + "in" [*bə*] + proper name) is found in the levirate law, where a shame-inducing name is attached to a brother-in-law who refuses to perform the levirate duty: "And his name shall be called in Israel, 'the house of the removed sandal'" (Deut 25:10).

188. Ruth's marriage secures ongoing sustenance for Naomi, initially through Boaz, potentially through Obed (4:15).

189. This instance of assonance is noted by Schipper, *Ruth*, 177.

190. See comment on v. 7.

## THE BOOK OF RUTH

clear instance in Old Testament narrative (Gen 38). Judah was left without an heir after two of his sons failed to produce offspring. He refused to give Tamar, the widow of his eldest son, Er, to his last remaining son. So Tamar took matters into her own hands, and through deception, managed to get herself impregnated by her father-in-law to produce an heir for him. This was scandalous, but Judah's outrage turns to penitence, as, in a moment of disarming insight, he declares, "[Tamar] is more righteous than I" (Gen 38:26 ESV).[191] The "rightness" of that union, despite its morally dubious nature,[192] intimates that the union between Boaz and Ruth the Moabite (cf. Deut 23:3–6) can also be considered "right." God's blessing on the union is evidenced in Tamar bearing twins to continue Judah's line, one of whom is Perez. His name means "a breach" or "a break," and the midwife gave him this name because he pushed in front of his brother to come out of the womb (Gen 38:27–30). Perez, not his brother Zerah, becomes the ancestor of a royal line (Ruth 4:18–22). In his name, we find that a breach in protocol can be used within God's plans, and perhaps a hint that a marriage with an outsider can be considered "right."[193]

The two offspring from the union of Judah and Tamar may also allude to Boaz's personal situation. If he was a widower without an heir (cf. comment on 3:10), the throng is wishing Boaz not just an heir to inherit the "name" of Elimelech, but also another to inherit his own "name." And so, their mention of *your house* and *the seed that Yahweh will give to you* may indicate that Boaz was without an heir.[194]

The throng's blessing ends similarly to its beginning—acknowledging that the building of Boaz's "house" will depend on God's blessing. Although not the forebear of the royal line, Zerah's presence is recalled with the mention of *the seed (hazzera') that Yahweh will give* to Boaz. Consistent with ancient Israelite thinking, the people know that pregnancy is ultimately an act of God. Yet their use of "the seed" recalls the barren matriarchs who only conceive when God enabled them, including Sarah (Gen 21:1), Rebekah (25:21), and Rachel (30:22). Closer to the time of the audience of the book of Ruth, God also enabled conception for Manoah's wife (Judg 13) and Hannah (1 Sam 1:19). "Seed" is also evocative of God's promise to the patriarchs, including Abraham (Gen 12:7; 13:15, 16), Isaac (26:3, 4, 24), and Jacob (28:13–14), and later his promise to David (2 Sam 7:12).

---

191. Similar to *ḥesed*, *ṣādqâ* ("righteousness") can exceed obligatory behavior; cf. K. Koch, "*ṣdq*," *TLOT* 2:1051.

192. This case is the female equivalent to Lev 18:17, which forbids a man from having sexual relations with a woman and her daughter.

193. Eskenazi and Frymer-Kensky, *Ruth*, 84–85.

194. Morris, *Ruth*, 312, comments that the first son would be heir to Boaz and Mahlon.

274

4:1–12 Town Gate: Boaz Redeems before the Elders

Moreover, in the Ruth narrative, the "seed" is attributed to a female, Ruth. She is referred to as *this young woman* (*hanna'ărâ hazzō't*), which brings us full circle to Boaz's first words concerning Ruth, "Whose young woman is this?" (*ləmî hanna'ărâ hazzō't*; 2:5), reminding us how far Ruth has come from the first time she was in Boaz's presence. The use of the word *na'ărâ* ("young woman") accentuates her nubility and potential fertility (perhaps in contrast to the elderly Naomi) and complements *the woman* in the first part of the throng's blessing (v. 11). Our attention is drawn to the fertility aspect of "young woman" by the assonance between "from the seed" (*min-hazzera'*) and "from the young woman" (*min-hanna'ărâ*). In the Old Testament, "seed" or offspring are usually attributed to men, so Ruth stands alongside other women to whom "seed" is attributed, such as Eve (Gen 3:15) and Rebekah (24:60).[195] Thus, we anticipate that Boaz's "seed" or offspring through Ruth will join the ranks of foundational, honored ones.

Juxtaposing Tamar with Rachel and Leah also highlights their common "foreign" element. Just as Judah took a Canaanite wife, so his son's wife Tamar is probably also a Canaanite (Gen 38:1–6). Since the genealogy in Matthew's gospel includes Tamar among other gentile women (Rahab and Ruth),[196] the assumption is that she is also non-Israelite (Matt 1:1–6).[197] She is thus ethnically "foreign." In contrast to Esau, Jacob is prevented from marrying a Canaanite by being sent to find a wife from the daughters of Laban, his mother's brother. Laban is identified as an Aramean (28:5), and in later biblical tradition, even Jacob is described as "a wandering Aramean" (Deut 26:5). Hence, the kinship is close, although there are clear markers of differentiation. In terms of religion, Laban practices divination and his family worship household gods, gods that Rachel was reluctant to relinquish (Gen 30:27; 31:19). In terms of geography, Jacob is sent from his people and country to go to Paddan-aram, to another country, "to the land of the people of the east" (29:1; cf. 28:20–21). When God tells Jacob to return, he says, "go out from this land and return to the land of your kindred" (31:13). For an ancient Israelite audience of the Ruth narrative (in the monarchic period and later), Arameans were distinctly non-Israelite. Rachel and Leah were kin to Jacob, yet they were geographically and religiously "foreign." And when placed side-by-side in the same blessing with Tamar and Ruth, their

195. Other examples include Hagar (Gen 16:10), and more symbolically, Zion (Isa 54:3). By contrast, a priest's childless daughter is described as "without seed" (Lev 22:13).

196. "The wife of Uriah" is also listed in the Matthean genealogy. Bathsheba is an Israelite (2 Sam 11:3; 23:34), but her designation highlights her foreign connection since Uriah was a Hittite (2 Sam 11:3; 23:39).

197. See R. T. France, *The Gospel of Matthew*, NICNT (Grand Rapids: Eerdmans, 2007), 36–37; Leon Morris, *The Gospel According to Matthew* (Grand Rapids: Eerdmans, 1992), 23.

## The Book of Ruth

"foreignness" becomes especially prominent.[198] Thus, we can consider the four women, although in slightly different senses, as "foreigners" who join and build up the Israelite line.

Looking at the people's blessing as a whole, we find interdependence between men and women. The focus of the blessing is Boaz—that he act worthily by perpetuating the name of his dead male relatives (C-C'). Yet this cannot take place without the enveloping blessings that focus on Ruth's fertility—that she will produce offspring to build up his house, just like the Israelite ancestresses Rachel and Leah (A-B) and Tamar (B'-A'). Indeed, the people highlight the contribution of women in building up the house of Israel. And the future greatness and honor of this man of worth are dependent on a woman, in particular, her ability to produce children (especially a son). This is suggested by the description of Ruth giving a "seed" or "offspring" (v. 12), a reversal of Boaz's giving of "seed" so far in the narrative (2:14–18; 3:15, 17).[199]

This is an important corrective, but it does not amount to a subversion of patriarchy. The women in the Ruth narrative worked within the patrilineal system to secure their own future, similar to Rachel, Leah, and Tamar.[200] Within the patriarchal society of ancient Israel, as expressed in Old Testament texts, women are mainly presented as essential and valuable in their reproductive capacity and their loyalty to their men.[201] The Ruth narrative provides a balancing perspective, shining the light on the woman's perspective and experience, their fears and hopes, their initiative and independence, and their indispensable place in the whole social structure.[202] We can take this gynocentric perspective to read other Old Testament texts in which this perspective is not clearly presented.[203]

As we find elsewhere in the Ruth narrative, God's sovereign action is interwoven with human action in the townspeople's blessing. The extension of lineages and the building of dynasties is ultimately the work of God (the first and third parts of the blessing), but it also requires people to act—in this case, virtuously (the second part of the blessing). For in honoring the dead

---

198. Rachel and Leah's great-grandfather was Nahor, Abraham's brother. Since Haran, Lot's father, is also Abraham's brother, Ruth is distantly related to Rachel and Leah (for the generations of Terah, see Gen 11:26–32).

199. Linafelt and Beal, *Ruth & Esther*, 75.

200. See James Black, "Ruth in the Dark: Folktale, Law and Creative Ambiguity in the Old Testament," *Literature and Theology* 5 (1991): 20–36.

201. Cf. Mathias, *Paternity*, 247.

202. See, e.g., Irmtraud Fischer, "The Book of Ruth: A 'Feminist' Commentary on the Torah?," in *Ruth and Esther: A Feminist Companion to the Bible*, Second Series, ed. Athalya Brenner (Sheffield: Sheffield Academic Press, 1999), 24–49.

203. Bauckham, "Book of Ruth," 29–45.

## 4:13-17 HOME: NAOMI AND THE WOMEN DIALOGUE

by perpetuating their name, Boaz will also be blessed. And ultimately, God's faithfulness will be recognized by all.

With the crowd's blessings, Boaz leaves the narrative spotlight bathed in honor and potential greater future renown. And deservingly so. He showed kindness—favor and generosity—to a foreigner (albeit a distant relative by marriage) who "just happened" to stumble into his field (act 2). At the threshing floor, he gave his word to Ruth that he would redeem her when she asked for his hand in marriage (act 3). At the town gate, he kept his word through a series of nimble socio-psychological and legal maneuverings (4:1-12). Because of his enacted kindness—his loyalty and self-sacrifice—he is worthy of more honor than the nearer kinsman, just as Ruth is worthy of more than Orpah. And now, the spotlight is about to shift back to the character whose crisis set the narrative in motion.

## B'. HOME: NAOMI AND THE WOMEN DIALOGUE (4:13-17)

Based on our chiastic structure of the Ruth narrative, this scene (B') parallels and contrasts with 1:7-19a (B). In both, Naomi "dialogues" with women: Ruth and Orpah; and the townswomen and neighborhood women. In both, Naomi's dialogue partners reduce—from Orpah and Ruth to just Ruth (1:14), from the townswomen (4:14) to just the neighborhood women (4:17). While the first scene took place on the way to Bethlehem, the corresponding scene is presumably set in Boaz's and Ruth's home. While Naomi's words dominated the dialogue with her daughters-in-law, she is described as a silent dialogue partner with the women of Bethlehem. The bewailing of her emptiness and bitterness is now replaced with a quiet contentment, as she listens to the townswomen. In contrast to Naomi's complaint about Yahweh's hand going out against her (1:13), the women speak of Yahweh's blessing of a redeemer (4:14). In contrast to Naomi's lament that she could not bear any more sons (1:11-13), the neighborhood women proclaim that a "son" has been born to her (4:17). The value of Naomi's loyal daughter-in-law (1:16-18) is now revealed to be more than seven sons (4:15)! And Naomi's concern for rest in the house of a husband for her daughters-in-law (1:9) is fulfilled for Ruth. Naomi's words of loss and grief are replaced by the women's words of joy and celebration.

In her bitterness and shame, Naomi rejected her name (1:20); now she is more than happy to receive it back. Her dignity and social status restored, she can live up to her name, she is comfortable with others calling her "pleasant." Previously, a name was rejected (Naomi); now, one is given (Obed). This denouement ties up the loose threads in the narrative and resolves the problems raised by Naomi's crisis in act 1.

# THE BOOK OF RUTH

[13]*And Boaz took Ruth, and she became his wife, and he came in to her,[a] and Yahweh gave her conception, and she bore a son.*

[14]*Then the women said to Naomi, "Blessed be Yahweh,[b] who has not left you without a redeemer today. May his name be proclaimed[c] in Israel.*

[15]*May he become[d] your restorer of life[e] and nourisher when you are gray-haired, because your daughter-in-law, who loves you,[f] bore him—she who is better for you than seven sons."*

[16]*And Naomi took the child and placed him in her bosom[g] and she became his nanny.*

[17]*And the neighborhood women[h] gave him a name, saying, "A son has been born for Naomi," and they named him Obed. He was the father of Jesse, the father of David.*

a. LXX[B] lacks "and she became his wife" and "and he came in to her," possibly because of haplography triggered by the *waw* in "and she became" and "and Yahweh gave"; so Schipper, *Ruth*, 178. Or the clauses were omitted because of a misunderstanding of their function; so Sasson, *Ruth*, 161.

b. The phrase *bārûk yhwh*, "blessed be Yahweh," expresses human thankfulness or praise. Humans "bless" God by speaking of his goodness, i.e., by praising him. The basis of the praise is often introduced with *'ăšer*, as in this verse (also Gen 14:20; 24:27; Exod 18:10; 1 Sam 25:32, 39; 2 Sam 18:28; 1 Kgs 1:48; 5:21[7]; 8:15 = 2 Chr 6:4; 1 Kgs 8:56; 10:9 = 2 Chr 9:8; Ps 66:20; Ezra 7:27; 2 Chr 2:11[12]). See C. A. Keller, "*brk*," *TLOT* 1:269–70; M. L. Brown, "*bārak*," *NIDOTTE* 1:766. Elsewhere in the Ruth narrative, characters ask God to bless others (2:19, 20; 3:10); here, the women bless God.

c. LXX has "your [*sou*] name," referring to Naomi, and Syr. has "you will call his name." Tg. supports MT[L], although it reads "may his name be proclaimed among the righteous of Israel."

d. The *weqatal* verb *wəhāyâ* can be read as an indicative, so "he will," with the subject more likely to be Yahweh who had provided Naomi with a redeemer (v. 14). However, following the modal *weqatal* verb *wəyiqqārē'*, "may [his name] be proclaimed" (v. 14), and since the next clause makes it clear the subject is the child ("she bore him"), it is best to read a modal verb, "May he become." So also Holmstedt, *Handbook*, 208; Block, *Discourse*, 235–36.

e. The word *nepeš* here means "life force, vitality, somewhere between the meanings "soul" and "life"; C. Westermann, "*nepeš*," *TLOT* 2:748.

f. MT[L] reads *'ăhēbatek*, "she loves you," instead of *'ăhēbātek*, as found in many Heb. manuscripts. The meaning is the same. See GKC§ 59g.

g. Syr. lacks the clause "and placed him in her bosom," perhaps due to haplography.

h. The noun *šəkēnôt* is the feminine plural form of the verb *škn* ("to dwell, inhabit"). The feminine form only occurs elsewhere in Exod 3:22, where Israelite women ask their female Egyptian "neighbors" for articles of silver and gold and clothing. The masculine form refers to either an "inhabitant" (e.g., Isa 33:24; Hos 10:5) or a "neighbor" (e.g., Exod 12:4; Jer 6:21; 2 Kgs 4:3; Prov 27:10).

This scene can be divided into two parallel parts:[204]

204. Cf. Bush, *Ruth, Esther*, 250–52. This structure is more organic to the text than chiastic proposals, e.g., Gow, *Ruth*, 81–82; Luter and Davis, *Ruth and Esther*, 76.

278

### 4:13–17 HOME: NAOMI AND THE WOMEN DIALOGUE

A Narrative: Boaz *took* Ruth, she *became his* wife, and *she bore a son* (v. 13).

   B Women's speech: May *his name be proclaimed (called)* in Israel (vv. 14–15).

A' Narrative: Naomi *took* the child, she *became his* nanny (v. 16).

   B' Women's speech: They *named him (called his name)* Obed, *"A son has been born* for Naomi" (v. 17)

Framing this scene are the phrases "and she bore a son" (v. 13) and "a son has been born" (v. 17). Each narrative action triggers speeches from women. Yahweh granting and Ruth giving birth (A) triggers words of praise to Yahweh, wishes for Yahweh and the son, and praise of Ruth (B). Naomi taking the child and becoming his nanny triggers a proclamation that a son has been born to Naomi and the naming of the child (B'). Although this scene exhibits synonymous parallelism in form and content, there is also a shift in focus from Ruth to Naomi. Although Ruth gives birth to the son (A), the women speak to Naomi, although they also speak words of appreciation for Ruth (B). As Naomi takes the son, we might be surprised that the women proclaim his significance for Naomi, not Ruth. Yet this is consistent with the narrative's presentation of Naomi as the central character—hers was the crisis that set the narrative in motion (1:3–5). The structure of this scene is consistent with the trajectory of the plot: Ruth's actions are essential to the reversal of Naomi's situation, but now that she has played her part, the spotlight shifts to Naomi.

This scene departs from the typical "birth report" found in biblical narratives.[205] A birth report consists of a setting and the birth report proper. The report proper comprises the following elements: (1) conception; (2) birth; (3) naming; and (4) etiology.[206] Similar to other birth report settings,[207] the Ruth narrative states that Boaz "took" Ruth, but it is unique because it adds, "and she became his wife."[208] This birth report proper is unusual in at least four ways. First, the naming is delayed until after the women's speech (vv. 14–15) and after Naomi takes the child (v. 16).[209] This adds resonance to the unusual content of the women's speech in outlining the significance of the child for Naomi, instead of the mother. And in the naming, they state that a

---

205. E.g., Gen 4:1–2; 16:15; Judg 13:24; 1 Sam 1:19–20; Isa 8:3–4. For a full list, see Timothy D. Finlay, *The Birth Report Genre in the Hebrew Bible*, FAT 2.12 (Tübingen: Mohr Siebeck, 2005), 24.

206. Finlay, *Birth Report*, 32–36. See also Roland E. Murphy, *Wisdom Literature: Job, Proverbs, Ruth, Canticles, Ecclesiastes, and Esther*, FOTL (Grand Rapids: Eerdmans, 1981), 94.

207. Genesis 25:20; 38:2; Exod 2:1; 2 Sam 11:4; and Hos 1:3.

208. For ideas in this paragraph, I am indebted to Finlay, *Birth Report*, 209–16.

209. Elsewhere only in Exod 2:1–10.

THE BOOK OF RUTH

"son has been born for Naomi." Second, Yahweh's granting of "conception" is unique. In other birth reports, Yahweh is described as enabling children by remembering or opening wombs.[210] The unusual description here underscores God's providence, which only explicitly surfaces elsewhere in 1:6 (yet it is implicit throughout the narrative). Third, this is the only occasion in the Bible where neighborhood women name a child rather than a mother or father. This is consistent with the female perspective found in the book. Fourth, instead of an etymological association with Obed's name, there is a note about Obed's etiological significance as an ancestor of David. This draws another parallel with the etiological note that concludes the narrative of Lot's daughters (Gen 19:37–38). The narrator has adapted the conventional birth narrative report to emphasize themes and associations.

**13** Consistent with the rest of the Ruth narrative, the delicate interplay between human action and God's providence is found in this verse. The five *wayyiqtol* clauses can be structured as:

> A And Boaz took Ruth,
> > B and she became his wife,
> A and he came in to her,
> > > C and Yahweh gave her conception,
> > B and she bore a son.

The clauses alternate with Boaz and Ruth as the subjects (A-B), the neat pattern broken by God's action (C). Boaz and Ruth do their part, but it takes God's crucial intervention for their actions to be successful. In this verse, we also find the fulfillment of many of the throng's just-voiced wishes (vv. 11–12). The reporting of the events is compact: at least nine months are covered in this one verse—more time than that covered in the preceding narrative.

Boaz had spoken of "acquiring" Ruth as his wife (v. 10), but now *Boaz took [wayyiqqaḥ] Ruth*, the more common verb for marriage (e.g., Gen 25:20; 28:9).[211] Elsewhere, "to take" (*lāqaḥ*) carries the connotation "to take home" (Deut 20:7), perhaps reflecting the processing to the groom's home in the marriage ritual (cf. Gen 24:67).[212] If so, this would echo the language of the throng when they said, "the woman coming into your house" (v. 11). Taken together with the previous phrase, *and she became his wife* underlines the legality of their marriage. Yet, strictly speaking, the phrase "she became his

---

210. E.g., Gen 29:31; 1 Sam 2:21.

211. "He took" may or may not include "as wife" (e.g., Exod 2:1; 1 Kgs 3:1; Hos 1:3). Previously in the Ruth narrative, *nś'* was used for marriage; see comment on 1:4.

212. For additional biblical references, see *DCH* 4:573.

## 4:13-17 Home: Naomi and the Women Dialogue

wife" is not essential (see Hos 1:3).[213] It clearly signals her change in status, from "daughter" (as she is referred to by Naomi and Boaz, indicating their parental concern) to Boaz's wife. Since the phrase places Ruth as the subject, it may also reflect her consent to marriage, since other uses of the idiom are in situations when a woman exercises some independent agency.[214] These situations include either a widow remarrying (Abigail to David, 1 Sam 25:42; Bathsheba to David, 2 Sam 11:27) or a woman who is not under the authority of a male (Zelophehad's daughters choosing their own husbands, Num 36:11).[215] Even in the marriage of Isaac and Rebekah ("And he took Rebekah, and she became his wife," Gen 24:67 NASB1995; cf. v. 51), Rebekah had voiced her consent (24:58). In fact, the closely similar Hebrew phrasing draws a fine thread between Ruth and another matriarch, Rachel.[216]

A further point of comparison between the marriage of Isaac and Rebekah with that of Boaz and Ruth might cause us to consider the level of emotional attachment in the latter. The marriage of the former is followed by "and he loved her" (Gen 24:67) but is lacking in the description of the marriage of Boaz and Ruth. An intentional allusion is more likely if we can demonstrate clear parallels between the Ruth narrative and the search for a wife for Isaac.[217] But even if there is a clear parallel, we need to take into consideration the fact that expressions of romantic "love" are rare in Old Testament narrative. Jacob is the parade exception (Gen 29:18, 20), but apart from him, there is only a smattering of other descriptions of male romantic affection (Gen 34:3; Judg 16:4; 1 Sam 1:5; 1 Kgs 11:1; 2 Chr 11:21; Esth 2:17).[218] The lack of this description in the Ruth narrative is thus not unusual. One factor that might give us pause before we move on, however, is the later mention of Ruth's "love" for Naomi (v. 15). Does this suggest that Ruth's marriage is devoid of love?[219] Not necessarily: based on Old Testament precedent, we cannot infer that it was lacking (cf. Deut 21:15, 16). Rather, in this context, the description from the mouth of the townswomen emphasizes particularly Ruth's manifest love for her mother-in-law (see comments below).

---

213. Holmstedt, *Handbook*, 205, suggests that "and she became his wife" is an explicit intertextual link with Naomi's denial that she can provide her daughters with husbands. If this is the case, this link highlights God's ability to achieve what Naomi could not.

214. This understanding is also reinforced by the reciprocal structure of this verse.

215. So Eskenazi and Frymer-Kensky, *Ruth*, 87.

216. This is the only other time in the Old Testament the phrase is used, namely, "and he took [*wayyiqqaḥ*] [name of man][name of woman], and she became his wife [*watthî-lô lə'iššāh*]."

217. For parallels, see Grossman, *Ruth*, 35–37; Zakovitch, *Rut*, 54–55.

218. For other descriptions of female love, along with those of non-romantic love in the Old Testament, see the comment on v. 15.

219. So Grossman, *Ruth*, 306.

# THE BOOK OF RUTH

Not to be lost in this tapestry of associations is the basic equality evidenced in the first two clauses. A man willingly takes a willing wife; yet they are a perfect match based on virtue,[220] as the narrative has already hinted (2:1; 3:11). We must not miss the remarkable ascension of Ruth, of which her marriage is the culmination. Her social status has changed from "foreigner" (2:10) to "maidservant" (2:13) to "handmaid" (3:9) and now to "wife." No longer a widow ("the wife of the dead man," v. 5), she can now hope to have children again. She is simply called "Ruth," without the designation "the Moabite," perhaps a hint that she has been accepted into the Bethlehemite community as "one of them." Even if she cannot be fully transformed into an Israelite, at least she can feel that she belongs, more as a "resident-alien" than as a fringe-dwelling "foreigner." Note the reversals from act 1: she was left bereft, bereaved, and outside the people of God. And as we recall Naomi's prayer for Yahweh to grant her daughters-in-law rest in the home of a husband (1:9), we discern God's quiet working, and we wonder if the throng's prayer for fecundity (vv. 11–12) might also be answered. Of course, we also recognize the part Boaz plays in Ruth's social transformation, beginning with a single word to her, "my daughter" (2:8). Yet his generosity was in response to what he had heard of Ruth's kind loyalty to her mother-in-law (2:11–12). Indeed, Yahweh rewards his refugees (2:12), often through his own people.

Boaz *came in to her* (*wayyābō' 'ēlêhā*) is a Hebrew euphemism for sexual intercourse (e.g., Gen 29:23; 30:4; 38:2; Judg 16:1; 2 Sam 12:24), and perhaps here, as in other instances, also includes the connotation of a man entering a woman's room or bridal chamber (e.g., Judg 15:1; 2 Sam 12:24). Similar English idioms include "made love to her"[221] or better, "came to bed with her,"[222] but my more wooden translation brings out the Hebrew wordplay with the throng's description of Ruth as "the woman coming into your house (*habbā'â 'el-bēytekā*)" (v. 11).[223] They prayed that the woman coming into Boaz's house would build it through bearing children, and now Boaz comes in to Ruth to conceive a child. The audience might feel a pang of uncertainty upon recalling Ruth's prior childlessness, but this tension is quickly dispelled.

The quick succession of verbs not only hurries the plot along but also points to God's keenness to act. *And Yahweh gave her conception* stands out not only because it breaks the reciprocal pattern in this verse, but because simply "and she became pregnant and bore a son" can follow "and he came

---

220. Cf. the Midrash: "One and the same willingly joins each other—a righteous woman to a righteous man" (Lekach Tov).

221. NIV.

222. Robert Alter, *Strong as Death Is Love: The Song of Songs, Ruth, Esther, Jonah, and Daniel, A Translation with Commentary* (New York: W. W. Norton & Company, 2015), 81.

223. This "pun" is noted by Schipper, *Ruth*, 182.

## 4:13–17 Home: Naomi and the Women Dialogue

in to her" (Gen 38:2–3; cf. 16:4). In the Old Testament, all pregnancies and births are viewed as a gift from God (e.g., Gen 4:1; 21:2; 25:21; 29:32, 33; Judg 13:3; 1 Sam 1:20; Pss 127:3; 139:13–16), but in this verse, God's intervention is particularly highlighted. God's gift of pregnancy is presented as swift and perhaps also as miraculous. Like Isaac and Jacob, and Samuel and Samson, this child might also have a special destiny.[224] The form of the word for conception, *hērāyôn*, only occurs elsewhere in Hos 11:1. The alternative "and she conceived" (*wattahar*) is widely used,[225] but *hērāyôn* could have been chosen in this verse to draw a connection to the similar-sounding Mahlon (*mahlôn*) and Chilion (*kilyôn*).[226] We have just been reminded of them as the former inheritors of the land to be transferred, and Mahlon as the former husband of Ruth (vv. 9, 10). But the more poignant and pertinent connection is as husbands who could not achieve conception. Mahlon and Ruth had been married for up to ten years without having children, so perhaps we are to attribute the childlessness to him.[227] Yet the stronger note here is that God grants conception to a previously barren womb. Ruth is not described as "barren";[228] nonetheless, her difficulty in conceiving further links her to the matriarchs who shared the same experience—Sarah, Rebekah, Leah, and Rachel (Gen 21:1; 25:21; 29:31; 30:17; 22, 23).[229] Indeed, conception granted (verb *ntn*) by God is no less than what the throng had just prayed that God would "grant" (verb *ntn*; vv. 11–12). And so, with great expectation we anticipate the outcome for this *son*.[230]

This is all the more so when we ponder further God's intervention. In the book of Ruth, this conception is the only explicitly stated action of God. While in Moab, Naomi heard that Yahweh had broken the famine in Israel (1:6). Strictly speaking, this was hearsay, although other Old Testament texts

---

224. Cf. Hubbard, *Ruth*, 97.

225. It is found twenty-eight times in the Old Testament (Gen 4:1, 17; 16:4; 21:2; 25:21; 29:32, 33, 34, 35; 30:5, 7, 17, 19, 23; 38:3, 4, 18; Exod 2:2; 1 Sam 1:20; 2:21; 2 Sam 11:5; 2 Kgs 4:17; Isa 8:3; Hos 1:3, 6, 8; 1 Chr 4:17; 7:23).

226. It also forms an aural link to three names in the genealogy (4:18–22)—Hezron, Nahshon, and Salmon. See comments on vv. 18–21.

227. And perhaps we are to view their childlessness as God's judgment; see comment on 1:5.

228. The word *'ăqārâ*, "barren," is used to describe three matriarchs: Sarah (Gen 11:30), Rebekah (25:21), and Rachel (29:31).

229. God granting conception to previously infertile women is a motif also found in the books surrounding Ruth in the Christian canon. He grants conception to Manoah's wife (Judg 13) and Hannah (1 Sam 1:19–20), both of whom were *'ăqārâ*, "barren" (Judg 13:2, 3; cf. 1 Sam 2:5).

230. Daughters only inherit land when a man dies without producing sons (Num 27:1–11; 36:1–12).

THE BOOK OF RUTH

support the statement's veracity based on the construction of the phrase[231] and the association of "visit" (*pāqad*) with Yahweh's direct action.[232] In both interventions of God in the Ruth narrative, God provides fertility—for the land, for Ruth's womb. As God "attended to" his people to break the famine (1:6), he "attends to" Ruth as a member of his people.

Perhaps the barren matriarch motif in Genesis anticipates the barrenness of the land in Israel's experience, impressing upon God's people the need for continual obedience to and trust in him for fertility and life (e.g., Deut 7:11–15; 11:8–15; 28:1–14). Yet the related motif of "seed" in Genesis is much richer, especially since "offspring" is an integral part of God's promise to Abraham (12:2, 7).[233] God intervenes with Sarah to honor his promise of descendants and again and again with the subsequent matriarchs. His intervention with Ruth points to the continuation of his purposes through Boaz and Ruth. God's intervention can also be viewed as a sign of his approval. The marriage of Ruth and Boaz received legal authorization, God now gives his approval through the blessing of conception,[234] and soon the townswomen will give their approval (v. 14–15, 17).

**14** That the women now speak to Naomi is remarkable for several reasons. Since naming usually follows directly after childbirth, the break in the sequence alerts the audience that something surprising is afoot. It will turn out that producing a son ends up being the last action involving Boaz and Ruth. They leave the scene for the last time, as the focus turns to Naomi (vv. 14–17). The townswomen[235] speak about the significance of the birth for Naomi, not Ruth. The blessing of the throng at the town gate focused their attention on Boaz—praying that Ruth would build his house and that he would act worthily (vv. 11–12). It was primarily a male perspective. By contrast, when Naomi first arrived back from Moab, the chorus of women expressed the sentiment of the townswomen, and here they again express the women's perspective.

The speech is bound together by alliteration, four words with similar-sounding consonants in Hebrew (vv. 14–15).[236]

---

231. Intertexts in which characters act after hearing reliable information include Gen 43:25 and 1 Kgs 5:1; Zakovitch, *Rut*, 83.

232. Yahweh "visiting" his people can be in a positive sense ("to come to aid of"; e.g., Gen 50:24; Exod 4:31; 1 Sam 2:21) or a negative sense ("to punish," e.g., Exod 20:5; Num 14:18; Deut 5:9–10); BDB, 824–25. See comment on 1:6.

233. God's promise is repeated to Abraham (15:1–20; 17:1–14; 22:15–18), and then to Isaac (26:24) and Jacob (28:13–14).

234. Cf. Eskenazi and Frymer-Kensky, *Ruth*, 87–88.

235. Or perhaps the midwives at Ruth's confinement (Exod 1:15–20); so Zakovitch, *Rut*, 168.

236. The alliteration is based on combinations of the consonants *š-ś-b*, with the first and third words also sharing *t*, and the second and fourth also sharing *m*.

## 4:13–17 Home: Naomi and the Women Dialogue

Blessed be Yahweh,
who has not left you without (*hišbît*) a redeemer today.
May his name be proclaimed in Israel.
May he become for you a restorer (*ləmēšîb*) of life
and nourisher when you are gray-haired (*śêbātēk*),
because your daughter-in-law, who loves you, bore him—
she who is better for you than seven (*miššibəʿâ*) sons.

By saying *Blessed be Yahweh* the women honor and give thanks to God, thus underlining God's gracious role in the conception and birth of the son (v. 13). The basis of their praise is God's manifest action. It is phrased negatively, *not left you without* (Heb. "he has not ceased [*hišbît*] for you"),[237] rather than positively, "has provided a redeemer for you." Since the *hiphil* of the verbal root *šbt* is rare in Old Testament prose,[238] the phrase is likely constructed partly for its alliterative effect. The negative phrase also recalls a time when Naomi was without—without a husband, sons, provision, and even hope. Feeling empty, she had laid the blame squarely at Yahweh's feet (1:20–21). Yet God had not ceased working for Naomi, even though it felt that way for her. Now the women give voice to Yahweh's role in this reversal in Naomi's life, for he has provided *a redeemer* for her *today*. Although the women specify it is a redeemer that God has blessed Naomi with, as we recall her initial destitution, we recall the many stages that have led to this turnaround. And as we look back, we see God's hand in all the precarious and delicate and risky places. We hear an answer to the prayers and benedictions, not least among which is the first prayer, that of Naomi's. She prayed that Yahweh would deal kindly with her daughters-in-law (1:8). God answered it for Ruth (Orpah's fate is unknown), and God's blessing for Ruth also means blessing now for Naomi. Naomi's prayer for others has now returned to her with interest.

On first hearing, we might think the *redeemer* is Boaz. So far in this chapter, the term referred to the nearer kinsman-redeemer, then Boaz when he assumed the role. Previously, Naomi stated that Boaz "is one of our kinsman-redeemers" (2:20), but the interpretive clue is in the women's use of the word *today*, which indicates they are referring to the newborn child. This is the only case in the Old Testament where the redeemer is not an adult male; the narrator has added a broader nuance to this term. In the context of this scene,

---

237. The *hiphil hišbît*, "cause to cease, put an end to," refers to the cessation of a previous activity or to the completion of a process, not just a process that is interrupted temporarily; E. Haag, "*šābat*," *TDOT* 14:385. It is derived from the verbal root *šbt*, "to cease, come to an end," as God did on the last day of creation (Gen 2:2). Cf. NJPS: "Not withheld . . . from you."

238. It mostly appears in poetry and prophecy, and in prose only five times (Exod 5:5; 12:15; Josh 22:25; 2 Kgs 23:5, 11). For details, see F. Stolz, "*šbt*," *TLOT* 3:1298–99.

THE BOOK OF RUTH

Boaz spoke of restoring Elimelech's family line by producing an offspring with Ruth (vv. 9–10), an aim which was reinforced by the blessing of the throng (vv. 11–12). The son thus "redeems" by restoring Elimelech's name on his property. The women will soon add their perspective by detailing other benefits of this redeemer for aged Naomi (v. 15).

But first, the women break out with a spontaneous wish that *his name be proclaimed* (Heb. "his name be called"). Whose name? For a first-time audience, it could be Yahweh or the newborn child since they were both mentioned in the previous clause. If it is Yahweh, proclaiming his name is by proclaiming his kindness toward Naomi and her family.[239] The wish, then, is for God's good reputation to be spread far and wide because he perpetuated the family name of Naomi's family. However, the closest referent in the clause is the newborn child. And a repeat audience would know that the women speak of him in the next verse. The women thus wish for the boy's name to become famous or to continue to be proclaimed after his death by his descendants (a task previously entrusted to Boaz; see comment on v. 11). The scope of the proclamation is among the people *in Israel*, not just Bethlehem, which foreshadows the ending of the narrative (vv. 17–22).[240]

**15** The women then wish two things of the boy for Naomi. First they wish that he will *become* for her a *restorer of life*. The rare usage of the *hiphil* participle form of the verb *šûb*[241] allows for the crafting of an alliteration (vv. 14–15, see above), which connects the string of four words. God, who did not cease to work for Naomi's good, provided a boy who will "return" Naomi's "spirits." Elsewhere, the *hiphil* participle of *šûb* with *nepeš* refers to "reviving the spirits" or "refreshing the soul" (Ps 19:8[7]; Prov 25:13). The word *šûb* draws a connection with the leitmotif of act 1 (1:6–8, 10–12, 15–16, 21–22; cf. 2:6; 4:3), and the *hiphil* form in this verse recalls its only other use in the Ruth narrative (1:21). When Naomi returned to Bethlehem bereft of husband and sons, she lamented, "I went away full, but empty Yahweh has returned me [*hĕšîbanî*]." Her life was seemingly empty and devoid of hope. But her hope has returned with the birth of the newborn, and thus her spirits have been revived. We also recall the efforts of Boaz, whose gift of barley and words conveyed through Ruth anticipated Naomi's filling: "You must not come empty-handed to your mother-in-law" (3:17).

---

239. As argued by Holmstedt, *Handbook*, 206–7.

240. This may be another case of intentional ambiguity (similar to 2:20): the women wish for both the child's and Yahweh's names to be proclaimed. So Campbell, *Ruth*, 163–64.

241. It appears only two other times in narrative (Gen 20:7; 38:29), with the other occurrences in prophecy (Isa 38:8; 44:25; Jer 28:3–4; Ezek 9:11) or poetry (Job 20:18; Prov 17:13; 18:13; 24:26; Lam 1:16).

4:13–17 HOME: NAOMI AND THE WOMEN DIALOGUE

The women's second wish for the boy is that he will be for Naomi a *nour-isher when you are gray-haired* (*śêbātēk*).[242] The unusual word *śêbātēk* is chosen rather than a form of the word Naomi used previously (*zāqēn*, "old"; 1:12), most likely because of its similar sounds with the other three words in the women's speech. Their first wish spoke about the newborn's effect on her now, the second speaks about him sustaining her in the future. The *pilpel* of *kûl* has the meaning "to nourish, provide with food" (e.g., Gen 47:12; 50:21; 1 Kgs 4:7), and the *pilpel* form might have a frequentative sense, a regular provision.[243] Again, this recalls Naomi's former emptiness (act 1), this time regarding food. When the boy is grown, the women expect he will provide nourishment for Naomi, and more generally, that he will support or sustain her in her old age.[244] This task is usually entrusted to sons, although if they do not perform it, daughters and daughters-in-law can step into the breach (as Ruth does). Since Boaz is presented in the narrative as being in the same generation as Naomi, perhaps there is a hint he might not always be around to provide for her. Perhaps also it foreshadows that this boy takes the place of her sons (vv. 16–17). In any case, the women wish that Naomi will enjoy fullness of life into her old age, that the reversal of her emptiness will be permanent.

The women then present the basis for their confidence in the boy—his mother. The choice of the infinitive *ləkalkēl* ("nourish") instead of the participle *məkalkēl* (Mal 3:2) in the previous clause may partly be explained by its closer sound to *kallātēk* ("daughter-in-law").[245] If so, this stronger assonance intimates that the boy will indeed discharge his duty to nourish and provide for his grandmother in her old age because he is the son of Ruth. The thinking would be along the lines of "like mother, like son." Just as Ruth is indispensable to the blessings for Boaz (vv. 11–12), so she is to these blessings for Naomi. The irregular Hebrew word order[246] signals the surprising nature of a *daughter-in-law*[247] producing a child redeemer for Naomi—not her sons,

---

242. Following the Hebrew syntax, a more literal translation would be "to nourish your gray hair." But since this does not reflect the sense of the phrase, I have opted for "nourisher when you are gray-haired." Unfortunately, however, my translation does not bring out the difference in syntax between this phrase (which uses a participle, *mēšîb*) and the previous parallel phrase (which uses an infinitive, *ləkalkēl*). Apart from Jer 44:19, this is the only instance of a participle followed by *l* + infinitive construct. A possible explanation for this combination in this verse is presented below.

243. Baumann, "*kûl*," *TDOT* 7:87–88.

244. "Old age" was probably between sixty and seventy years (cf. Ps 90:10). For a discussion of old age in the Old Testament and the ANE, see Fabry, "*śêbâ*," *TDOT*, 14:79–84.

245. The consonants *l-k-l-k-l* assonate more closely with *k-l-l-t-k* than *m-k-l-k-l*.

246. Heb. *kallātēk*, "your daughter-in-law," is focus-fronted.

247. Significantly, the women do not refer to Ruth's foreign roots but her relation to

# THE BOOK OF RUTH

not even Boaz, the kinsman-redeemer father. (Should it not be "like father, like son"?) She is the one who *bore him* (*yəlādattû*; cf. vv. 18–22). Amazingly, one not related by blood, and even after she has remarried, can produce kin and a redeemer.

But this is no ordinary daughter-in-law; she is one who *loves* (*'āhab*) her mother-in-law. In personal human relationships, men and women are said to love one another, along with parents and children.[248] It is also a covenantal term: because God loved his people (e.g., Deut 7:7–8), they are to love him with complete devotion and commitment (see esp. Deut 6:5). God's people are also enjoined to love their neighbors (Lev 19:18), including resident-aliens (Lev 19:34; Deut 10:19).[249] We could argue the case for "love" between Boaz and Ruth, but it is not explicitly stated in the narrative. Kindness or loyalty (*ḥesed*) is emphasized instead: Boaz praises Ruth for her *ḥesed* when she proposes marriage (3:9–10), and Boaz remains true to his word to her in securing her hand in marriage (4:10). Ruth is described as loving her mother-in-law, which is even more remarkable because only rarely is the love of a woman described,[250] and in the Old Testament only here of a daughter-in-law's love for her mother-in-law. She has expressed her love and commitment to Naomi through her many acts of kindness,[251] which are more noteworthy because it is a resident-alien showing love to a native-born. It is this love that, in the minds of the women, will ensure the boy will fulfill his role as Naomi's "son" when her hair is gray.[252]

Yet, the women reserve their highest praise for last. They declare to Naomi that her daughter-in-law is *better for you than seven sons*.[253] The use of the word *ṭôbâ*, "better," is the culmination of a minor motif in the Ruth narra-

---

Naomi. The designation "daughter-in-law" (*kallâ*) stands out further in this verse when we realize that this is the only time in the narrative that a character has used this term. All other instances are by the narrator (1:6, 7, 8, 22; 2:20, 22). LaCocque, *Ruth*, 142, draws parallels between Tamar and Judah: Tamar is also referred to as "your daughter-in-law" (Gen 38:24), and Obed is also the offspring of a man old enough to be his grandfather.

248. "Love" famously characterized the friendship of Jonathan and David (1 Sam 18:1, 3; 20:17; 2 Sam 1:26).

249. For the meaning of "love" in Deuteronomy, see Bill T. Arnold, "The Love-Fear Antinomy in Deuteronomy 5–11," *VT* 61 (2011): 552–62.

250. Rebekah loved her son Jacob (Gen 25:28), Michal loved David (1 Sam 18:20, 28), and the woman in the Song of Songs declares her love (Song 1:7; 3:1, 2, 3, 4).

251. Her love and loyalty were first expressed in her vow to Naomi on the road to Bethlehem (1:16–17), and then evidenced in kind actions such as returning with her mother-in-law (act 1), gleaning in the field to secure food (act 2), and going to the threshing floor at night to propose a marriage with Boaz (act 3).

252. For a description of the often-fraught relationship between mother-in-law and daughter-in-law in Confucian-influenced cultures, see Lin, "Cross-Textual Reading," 47–55.

253. Campbell, *Ruth*, 164, observes that the word *ṭôb* is the culmination of a motif, with

## 4:13–17 HOME: NAOMI AND THE WOMEN DIALOGUE

tive, with forms of *tb/ytb* found throughout the Ruth narrative (2:22; 3:1, 7, 10, 13).[254] To Naomi, Ruth is better than seven sons, with "better" having the sense of "more to" or "means more." After losing her own sons, Naomi said she could not bear any more sons, and her life was bitterly empty because of her loss (1:12–13). Her daughter-in-law has stepped in the breach to bear a "son," but it is not this son the women praise, it is her daughter-in-law. Seven is the number of completeness,[255] and in the next book in the Christian canon, Hannah will proclaim that the barren woman will bear seven children, a sign of God's blessing of fertility (1 Sam 2:5). Hannah's husband, Elkanah, also asks, "Am I not better to you than ten sons?" (1 Sam 1:8), which suggests that the numbers seven and ten are somewhat interchangeable (cf. Prov 26:16 with Eccl 7:19; Gen 15:19–21 with Deut 7:1).[256] Ruth was married for ten years without bearing any children (1:4–5), and the numbers seven and ten will carry significance in the upcoming genealogy (4:18–22). Job's blessed family has the ideal seven sons (along with three daughters for a total of ten children; Job 1:2; 42:13),[257] so it is remarkable—especially in a patriarchal culture that so values sons—that Ruth, a daughter-in-law, is esteemed more than seven sons. That she is a Moabite daughter-in-law makes it even more remarkable.

**16** After the women finish their blessing, the spotlight shifts to Naomi. Her action and its outcome in this verse are reminiscent of v. 13:

V. 16: And Naomi took the child . . . and she became his nanny
(*wattiqqaḥ noʿŏmî ʾet-hayyeled . . . watthî-lô ləʾōmenet*).

V. 13: And Boaz took Ruth, and she became his wife
(*wayiqqaḥ bōʿaz ʾet-rût watthî-lô ləʾiššâ*).

In both cases, there is a change in social status after "taking," but in Naomi's case, there is an additional gesture.[258] Another difference is that Naomi's

---

forms of *tb/ytb* found throughout the Ruth narrative (2:22; 3:1, 7, 10, 13). For the range of meanings for *tōb*, see BDB, 374.

254. As observed by Campbell, *Ruth*, 164.

255. See Otto, "*šebaʿ*," *TDOT* 14:341–60.

256. Zakovitch, *Rut*, 169–70. Word choice could have been influenced by the sound of the word *miššibəʿâ*, since it forms an alliteration with three other words in the women's speech (see comment on v. 14).

257. Haman the Agagite had ten sons (Esth 9:10, 12–14), a number of which he was proud (5:11).

258. At the beginning of the chapter, Boaz also "takes" (verbal root *lqḥ*) ten elders, and they form a legal quorum (4:2).

# THE BOOK OF RUTH

status changed after the "taking," while Ruth's status changed after having been "taken."[259]

Naomi's taking of *the child* (*hayyeled*) brings us as the audience back to the fateful beginning of the narrative, when Naomi was left without *her children* (*yəlādêhā*, 1:5). She was left feeling completely empty, but now her taking this newborn in her hands represents the return of fullness of life (cf. v. 15). In fact, the dearth of sons and hence descendants at the beginning of the narrative will give way to an abundance by its end, as reinforced by the repetition of various derivatives from the root *yld* in every verse until the end of the narrative.[260] After actively taking the child, Naomi *placed*[261] *him in her bosom.* The word *ḥêq*, "bosom" (sometimes translated "lap"; Prov 16:33) refers to the chest or breast, and is used to describe the intimate relationship between mother and child (e.g., 1 Kgs 3:20; 17:19; Lam 2:12), and between husband and wife (e.g., Deut 13:7[6]; 28:54, 56).[262] Used in reference to both males (e.g., 2 Sam 12:3, 8; Isa 40:11) and females, it is the usual location for holding a child (Num 11:12) and never refers to the female breast at which a child is fed.[263] Naomi's embrace expresses her affection and willingness to bond with the child, a "son" who symbolically replaces those she lost (v. 17).[264]

*And she became his nanny* is the outcome of her taking and embracing, and poignantly symbolizes the child as a replacement for the children she has lost. The word *'ōmenet*, "caregiver" or "nanny," is a *qal* feminine participle from *'mn* ("to support, be firm"), and in its only other occurrence means "caregiver" or "nurse" for Mephibosheth (five years old; 2 Sam 4:4). The masculine participle form refers to male caregivers or guardians (e.g., Num 11:12; 2 Kgs 10:1; Esth 2:7; Isa 49:23). This further supports the view that Naomi did not breastfeed the child as his "wet nurse."[265] She is too old to perform this task. Also, it is best not to view Naomi's actions as an adoption ritual, since in ancient Israel she most likely would have lived with Boaz and Ruth in a family compound, and thus would have had an integral role in looking after the child already (especially since Ruth was a first-time mother).

---

259. As discussed above, "and she became his wife" probably indicates Ruth's consent to the marriage.

260. *Qal* passive *yullad*, "has been born" (v. 17), noun *tôlədôt*, "generations" (v. 18), *hiphil* perfect *hôlîd*, "fathered" (9× in vv. 18–22). Earlier in this chapter: *qal* perfect *yālədâ*, "she bore" (v. 12) and *qal wayyiqtol wattēled*, "and she bore" (v. 13).

261. Only here is the verb *šît* ("to place, set") used with *ḥêq* ("bosom").

262. For further discussion, see André, "*ḥêq*," *TDOT* 4:357.

263. Hence my translation, "in her bosom" rather than "at her breast."

264. Cf. Viberg, *Symbols of Law*, 166–76, who views the act as symbolizing both affection and the legitimation of Obed as Naomi's "son."

265. As Bush, *Ruth, Esther*, 259, points out, "wet-nurse" is expressed by the *hiphil* participle *mynqt*, from *ynq*, "to suck" (e.g., Exod 2:7).

## 4:13–17 HOME: NAOMI AND THE WOMEN DIALOGUE

Moreover, there is no known biblical precedent for an Israelite woman to adopt a child by themselves,[266] and even if it were possible, it would be unusual for a grandmother to do so while the parents are still alive. And since Boaz had just legally acquired the redemption right on behalf of Mahlon (4:10), adoption is unnecessary for hereditary purposes. Instead, Naomi takes up the roles of caregiver and grandmother, both senses of which are nicely captured by the word "nanny" (esp. in informal British English).[267]

Understanding Naomi's new status within the context of the narrative and the broader sweep of the Old Testament prevents us from viewing it as mushy sentimentalism. This is more than just a grandmother displaying her affection for a grandchild. For the bosom that had been emptied of both husband and children is now full again. She does not take up the same role as at the beginning of the narrative, though. Then, she was wife and mother; in between, she was mother-in-law to Ruth; now, she is nanny or caregiver to her grandson. This child will look after her in the future, but in the meantime, she will help look after him. Naomi's initial cry of lament now receives a response from God. Not all complaints of suffering made to God will receive an explanation (cf. book of Job). And although it might seem that God has hidden his face (e.g., Ps 88:14), he is in fact present to act for his good purposes and his glory. His response to lament might even be to give the one who continues to trust in him a new status and task, such as we see with Elijah, Jeremiah, and even Job.[268] The new task must be taken and embraced, for only God knows the outcome of faithful labor (vv. 17–22; cf. Matt 1:1–16).

**17** The setting becomes more intimate as *the neighborhood women* speak. Previously, all the people at the gate and the elders spoke (vv. 11–12), then the women (v. 14). Now it is narrowed down to the women who lived nearby. This is probably another glimpse of the informal women's networks in ancient Israel, in which women provided mutual social support and practical help (cf. 1:19).[269] Yet what they say is surprising in three ways. First, these local women *named* the child. This is the only time in the Old Testament that someone other than the parents name a child. Second, the sequence of explanation–naming is the reverse of what we find in the rest of the Old Testament. Third, the typical birth announcement is made to the father. These three anomalies have triggered much discussion.[270] I view these anomalies as the author's way of prompting the audience to reflect on the

---

266. The closest is Pharaoh's daughter, who "adopts" Moses (Exod 2:10).

267. I note in passing that there is assonance between *no'ŏmî* and *'ōmenet*, which is reflected somewhat with "Naomi" and "nanny."

268. Following Campbell, *Ruth*, 167–68.

269. See Meyers, "Informal Female Networks," 120–27.

270. For an overview, see Bush, *Ruth, Esther*, 259–62.

THE BOOK OF RUTH

extraordinary significance of the child. To my mind, reading these verses as the logical outcome of the women's perspective begun in v. 14 provides the interpretive key.

The naming of the child can be structured:

> A  And the neighborhood women *gave him a name*, saying,
>> B  "A son has been born for Naomi,"
> A'  and they *named him* Obed.

As reflected in my English translation, "gave him a name" is expressed slightly differently than "named him" in Hebrew. Since the second clearly refers to naming Obed, it is tempting to read the first clause differently, such as "proclaimed his name" or "proclaimed his significance." On the one hand, this alternative is possible because of the semantic range of *qrh*, and the phrase could thus be read as the fulfillment of the women's recently expressed hope for the child (v. 14; cf. v. 11). On the other hand, since repetition with variation is a well-documented Hebrew stylistic feature, variation in expression does not necessarily indicate a different meaning. However, it seems more likely that if the author intended the sense of "proclaimed his name," he would have used the same expression as v. 14[271] for us to draw the link. This leaves us with the question: Why is the naming by the neighborhood women repeated (A-A')? Probably because this is a climactic moment. Naomi's emptiness has now been fully reversed, and the repetition gives time for the audience to savor its significance. All the more so because the explanation (A-B) is surprising—*a son has been born for Naomi!*[272] The birth announcement, "A son has been born for X!" is usually directed at the father of a child (Jer 20:15; cf. Isa 9:5[6]),[273] We expect the announcement would be that Ruth has given birth to a son for the father Boaz, her husband (cf. v. 12). Or, recalling the previous scene, we might even expect that Ruth would give birth to a son for Mahlon (vv. 5, 10).

Yet a son for Naomi has been foreshadowed. Ruth substituted for postmenopausal Naomi in the levirate marriage with Boaz (vv. 5, 10), and thus not only bears a son for Boaz (v. 21) but also a substitute son for Naomi. The son not only preserves Mahlon's name on his inheritance, he also continues and preserves Elimelech's name. In this sense, the benefit of the son is for

---

271. Heb. *wayyiqtol* + *šəmô*, "his name."

272. Perhaps another reason for the repetition of the naming by the neighborhood women is its uniqueness. It needs to be stated twice to ensure that an audience hears it correctly.

273. The *qal* passive form of *yld* + *l-* prefix predominantly refers to a father (Gen 4:26; 10:21, 25; 35:26; 41:50; 46:22; 1 Chr 1:19; Jer 20:15), with the exception of "the giants" (2 Sam 21:20) and "us" (Isa 9:5[6]).

## 4:13–17 Home: Naomi and the Women Dialogue

Mahlon and Elimelech, and, by extension, Naomi. The child is also described as taking on the role of sustainer, a role typically ascribed to sons (v. 15). Naomi's taking up the role of nanny might also hint at her taking care of her grandson as if he were a replacement son. This is another reversal for Naomi: she lamented the loss of her sons and her inability to produce another (1:11–13, 20–21) but now has one! She is no longer childless. The ascription of the son to Naomi is even more amazing because this child is not related to her by blood since it is the offspring of her daughter-in-law and a kinsman-redeemer from her husband's clan. The naming of the child by the neighbor women is consistent with the women's perspective in this scene, and their naming reinforces the significance of the child for Naomi.

The birth of a son to Naomi recalls the end of the book of Job.[274] The connection is strengthened when we parallel Naomi's initial loss and the wording of her accusation against "Shaddai" (1:20–21) with Job's initial loss and accusation. Just as Job was blessed again with children after maintaining his faith in God, so Naomi (and Ruth) is blessed with a son after "returning" to their faith in God. Job receives seven sons from God (Job 42:13), while Ruth is described as "better than seven sons" for Naomi. Also, a "redeemer" plays a prominent part in both narratives. Job cries out for a redeemer to plead his case before God (Job 19:25), while in the Ruth narrative, God blesses Naomi (and Ruth) through a kinsman who discharged his role as a redeemer. If there was a broader meaning of "redeemer" in Job as a kinsman who assisted in a lawsuit,[275] it is extended even further with the application of "redeemer" to a child. In both narratives, God seemed absent or silent, but by the end he shows his hand.

The naming of the child also reverses "naming" in act 1. The names of Naomi's sons were associated with death and destruction (v. 2), perhaps reflecting the conditions in which they were born, but also anticipating their fate. Naomi's new "son" is associated with revival and sustenance, indicating the present effect on her condition, but also anticipating the role he will play in her future. As such, Naomi's name can be restored to her. When she arrived in Bethlehem, the women asked, "Is this Naomi?" She responded by changing her name to Mara to reflect her bitter circumstances without a response from the townswomen (1:19–21). Now they speak: "A son has been born for Naomi." These are not only the last spoken words in the book; they can also be understood as the last word on Naomi's reversal. From pleasant to bitter to pleasant again: Naomi–Mara–Naomi. She has finally returned to fullness and completion. If she felt her bitterness was from the hand of God (1:21), surely now she views her happiness as a sign of God's blessing.

---

274. Cf. LaCocque, *Ruth*, 141.

275. See comment on 2:20.

# THE BOOK OF RUTH

After the climactic explanation follows the naming proper (A'): *and they named him Obed.* It is consistent with the flow of the scene for the women to name the child and thus unnecessary to amend "they" to "she" or "he."[276] It would have been unlikely for all the women to be involved in the explanation and name-giving, but plausible for the closer women of Naomi's local social network. It is reminiscent of the midwife at the birth of Perez who said, "'What a breach you have made for yourself!' Therefore his name was called Perez" (Gen 38:29 ESV). This woman voiced the circumstances of Perez's birth, but she is not explicitly described as naming the child. Further social background for understanding neighbors and naming is found in the account of John's birth (Luke 1:57–63). Elizabeth's neighbors and relatives suggested they name the child after his father, but Elizabeth demurred and insisted they name him "John." If these two accounts reflect ancient naming customs, the neighborhood women were involved in naming the child, but Ruth and Boaz (or at least one of them) were probably also part of the process (see esp. Gen 35:17–18 for the naming of Benjamin). In fact, the parents most likely decided the name. Yet, the author's reticence to specify Ruth's role in naming may be because the neighborhood women attribute a "son" to Naomi in this verse. Indeed, the name "Obed" means "servant" and thus nicely encapsulates the significance of the birth of the child for Naomi, as viewed from the women's perspective (vv. 13–17). These women do not focus on the impact of the child's birth for the predominantly male concerns of descendants and inheritance (vv. 3–12);[277] instead, Obed is a "redeemer" who will "serve" Naomi by reviving and caring and sustaining.

The rarity of the explanation (A-B) then naming (A') sequence also draws attention to similar accounts. Rebekah wanted to give Benjamin the name Ben-Oni, "son of my sorrow," because of the difficulty of her labor, which subsequently led to her death (Gen 35:16–19).[278] And the name Zerah is given after the explanation of the scarlet thread on his hand (Gen 38:30). With these accounts another fine link is drawn between the Ruth narrative and the patriarchal narratives, a hint in particular that this child continues Judah's line (cf. vv. 11–12; 17–22).

---

276. A minority of LXX witnesses have a singular verb; Campbell, *Ruth*, 167. "She" assumes Naomi is the subject, while "he" assumes Boaz. For the former, see, e.g., Joüon, *Ruth*, 95.

277. That is not to say that women are unconcerned about descendants and inheritance. The case of Zelophehad's daughters shows they are concerned about the continuation of their father's name on an inheritance (see Num 27:1–12; 36:1–13). Patriarchal structures are not undermined in the book of Ruth; instead, we catch an insight into how a woman might view things within that structure. See also Bauckham, "Book of Ruth," 29–45.

278. Bush, *Ruth, Esther*, 260.

## 4:13–17 Home: Naomi and the Women Dialogue

Since Obed's name is tied to his service of Naomi, there is a suggestion his name should be Obednoam, "servant of Naomi."[279] And since Obadiah, "servant of Yahweh," is a more common name than Obed, others suggest Obed might be a shortened form.[280] Nonetheless, Obed is the name of at least four other people in the Old Testament, including warriors and gatekeepers (1 Chr 11:47; 26:7), some of which are described similarly to Boaz: "mighty men" or "men of great worth" (*gibbôrê ḥayil/gibbôrê haḥăyālîm*; 1 Chr 11:26; 26:6).[281] Thus, his name is common enough to be accepted as his actual name (so also named in 1 Chr 2:12).

Even if his name had a longer form, the shorter form in this verse allows for an association with the next phrase: *He was the father of Jesse, the father of David.*[282] In this deft description, the audience is jolted from the past to the present, as the broader implications of this gentle story about this seemingly insignificant family are revealed. It is only from this vantage point in the narrative that we can see the earlier hint: this family and David are both Ephrathites from Bethlehem in Judah (1:2; 4:11; 1 Sam 17:12). God will often refer to Obed's esteemed grandson as "my servant David" (2 Sam 3:18; 7:5, 8; 1 Kgs 11:32; 14:8; 2 Kgs 19:34; 1 Chr 17:4, 7; Isa 37:35; Ezek 34:23–24; 37:24), someone truly after God's own heart.[283] Obed serves Naomi, but he also serves God's wider purposes: to restore her, to continue her husband's family line, and to produce Israel's greatest king. The collective naming by the women rather than by the parents is at least consistent with the national influence that Obed's descendant will have.

If there was an ironic tinge to Elimelech's name—"my God is king," although he leaves the king's land—it is revised by the presence of King David, who lived under God's rule, not that of other gods. And in Isaiah an even greater servant king emerges, one with a task for all humanity and with a reign over the whole world (Isa 42:1–4; 49:1–6; 50:4–9; 52:13–53:12). Similarly, the prophet Micah envisages a ruler over Israel from Bethlehem Ephrathah, who will shepherd in the strength[284] of Yahweh (Mic 5:1–4[2–5]). His

---

279. D. R. Ap-Thomas, "The Book of Ruth," *ExpTim* 79 (1968): 371. Cf. Abinoam (e.g., Judg 4:6; 5:12) and Ahinoam (1 Sam 14:50; 25:43); Obed-edom (e.g., 2 Sam 6:10, 12) and Ebed-melech (e.g., Jer 38:7, 8, 10, 11).

280. E.g., Bush, *Ruth, Esther*, 261. Thirteen men bear the name Obadiah in the Old Testament, and it is also found in extrabiblical inscriptions; see *DCH* 6:229–31.

281. Others named Obed also include the father of Jehu (1 Chr 2:37–38) and the father of Azariah (2 Chr 23:1).

282. For this genealogy, see 1 Chr 2:12, 15 and the discussion below.

283. God also uses "my servant" with others, including Moses, Caleb, Job, Jacob/Israel, but most often regarding David; for a discussion of "servant of Yahweh," see Ringgren, "'ābad," *TDOT* 10:394–96.

284. Interestingly, the word *bǝ'ōz*, "in the strength," has the same letters as "Boaz."

# THE BOOK OF RUTH

greatness will reach the ends of the earth, and he will embody peace. In the New Testament, we find fulfillment in Jesus the Messiah, born in Bethlehem (Matt 2:6; cf. John 7:42). God is king, and amid disorder and death (1:1–5) he will preserve his royal line.

The townswomen play an important social role in this scene. Upon her return, Naomi changed her name, indicating a disavowal of her former identity and those associated with it. She withdrew from society, including from the women of her former social network. In acts 2 and 3, she only interacted with her daughter-in-law, a foreigner who was also marginalized. Even after Ruth's marriage and the birth of a son, the townswomen acknowledge her continuing bond to Naomi as her "daughter-in-law." The townsmen had legally authorized the marriage of Ruth to Boaz, and hence through the levirate custom, tied Ruth to Elimelech's family. If the men speak in legal and formal tones, the women speak in social and emotional tones. The townswomen recognize both Naomi and Ruth as finally belonging to Bethlehemite and Israelite society. Their marginalization is now over, as Naomi is enfolded into the tight-knit community of women. Just as Ruth's marriage to Boaz and the birth of Obed signal Ruth's assimilation into Israelite society, so Naomi's reassimilation is dependent on the birth of Obed.[285] Their period of childless widowhood is over, and through their motherhood they receive honor and blessing.[286] This child's name will be proclaimed "in Israel" as both Ruth and Naomi are now accepted as members of the motherhood of Israel.[287]

Yet, that is not to say that Ruth's foreignness is completely removed. Some view the attribution of Obed as Naomi's son to imply that Ruth's foreign status is problematic. According to this line of thinking, Obed needs legitimization through an Israelite mother;[288] his Moabite mother must be hidden from view. Some scholars suggest that Ruth cannot be trusted to raise the son in the Israelite way,[289] and she is not suitable to be an ancestress of King David. Such an interpretation misreads a central thrust of the narrative—to promote *ḥesed* living. That this ideal for God's people is ironically promoted by a foreigner highlights this virtue even more. The point of this

---

285. Cf. Southwood, "Naomi's Nation," 120; Smith, "Family," 258: "In 4:16–17, Ruth helps to give family to Naomi, just as Naomi accepts Ruth's terms of family in 1:16–17."

286. For further on the barrenness theme in the Ruth narrative, see Janice Pearl Ewurama De-Whyte, *Wom(b)an: A Cultural-Narrative Reading of the Hebrew Bible Barrenness Narratives* (Leiden: Brill, 2018), 252–69.

287. Cf. Grossman, *Ruth*, 322.

288. Gillis Gerleman, *Ruth. Das Hohelied*, BKAT 18 (Neukirchen-Vluyn: Neukirchener Verlag, 1965), 37–38; also Nielsen, *Ruth*, 94; Block, *Discourse*, 240.

289. E.g., Bonnie Honig, "Ruth, the Model Emigrée: Mourning and the Symbolic Politics of Immigration," in *Ruth and Esther: A Feminist Companion to the Bible*, Second Series, ed. Athalya Brenner (Sheffield: Sheffield Academic, 1999), 60.

## 4:13–17 HOME: NAOMI AND THE WOMEN DIALOGUE

verse is not to expunge Ruth's motherhood but to add to motherhood Naomi's role as grandmother and to impute the child to Naomi as her "son." Readings that problematize Ruth's foreignness are also unnecessary because Ruth had already pledged her allegiance to Naomi, her people, and her God (1:16–17), and then proved herself a worthy member of the people of Yahweh. Moreover, the throng assembled at the town gate had already compared Ruth to the Israelite matriarchs, indicating Ruth's acceptance within the Israelite community.

Nonetheless, those who view Ruth as a Moabite mother are correct in identifying that a vestige of her foreignness remained. She was still referred to as a Moabite at the legal proceedings. This designation might have been for legal precision, but the plainer reading is this is how she was still viewed by the community (vv. 5, 10). Moabite and Israelite were ethnically similar, but they were viewed as distinct groups, as shown in the Old Testament accounts. And collective identity has a long memory.[290] Ruth's foreignness need not be downplayed or removed. For it highlights all the more the extraordinary nature of her acceptance by the Bethlehemite community: a foreign woman not only belongs as a member of God's people but can even contribute to building the Davidic dynasty.[291]

As we reflect on this scene, we observe that God is vindicated. In her laments, Naomi pointed the finger at Yahweh for her suffering: his hand went out against her, he dealt bitterly with her, he brought her back empty, he testified against her, he brought calamity against her (1:13, 20–21). God's name and honor were brought into question, not just before his people, but also before "the nations," as represented by Orpah and Ruth (v. 13). Yet Naomi also affirmed that God is characterized by *hesed* (2:20), and his actions in the Ruth narrative demonstrate that he is true to his nature by reversing all of Naomi's accusations. His kindness and loyalty can be found in the way he works behind the scenes and through the words and actions of his people. His *hesed* was expressed twice in his granting fertility—to his people's fields and Ruth's womb (1:6; 4:13). Yahweh did not leave Naomi without a redeemer (4:17); in fact, he provided two—Boaz and Obed. He also showed kindness to Israel, for Obed's grandson would bring blessing to the whole nation. Everyone who hears Naomi's story will spread abroad the greatness of God's name for perpetuating her family name (v. 14). And thus, God vindicates his name in Israel; his reputation is upheld before the nations.

---

290. The Israelites recalled the exodus as formative in their collective identity; the inclusion of the narratives of Moabite wrongdoing toward the Israelites (Num 22–25; cf. Deut 23:3–6) indicates their collective view of the Moabites.

291. For the continuation of this trajectory into the New Testament, see "Matthean Genealogy" in the introduction.

THE BOOK OF RUTH

## A'. THE BEGINNING OF A ROYAL LINE IN ISRAEL (4:18–22)

Many scholars view this genealogy (vv. 18–22) as a later editorial addition.[292] Some reasons include:

(1)   the narrative is finished at v. 17, and it repeats information from that verse,

(2)   genealogies are characteristic of the "priestly" (P) source, and

(3)   the intent in the narrative is to establish the name of the dead on his inheritance, but paternity is ascribed to Boaz in the genealogy.

But structural evidence suggests that the genealogy is original to the book:[293]

(1)   The Ruth narrative has an overall symmetrical structure, with parallels between acts 2 and 3, and acts 1 and 4. The genealogy (A') corresponds to the "family history" at the beginning of the narrative (1:1–6; A). Three people die before the main action (Elimelech, Mahlon, Chilion), and the narrative ends with three generations born after the main action (Obed, Jesse, David).[294]

(2)   Each of the three previous acts contained three scenes. Without the genealogy, act 4 would only have two.

(3)   The first scene of the book of Ruth mentions ten years without progeny in Moab (1:4), while the final scene details ten generations in Israel.[295]

The number seven also links this scene with the previous. Ruth is "better . . . than seven sons" (4:15) and marries the seventh-listed ancestor. The townspeople at the gate had wished that Boaz's house would be like the house of Perez (v. 12).

[18]*Now these are the descendants*[a] *of Perez: Perez fathered*[b] *Hezron,*[c]
   [19]*Hezron fathered Ram,*[d] *Ram fathered Amminadab,*
   [20]*Amminadab fathered Nahshon,*[e] *Nahshon fathered Salmon,*[f]
   [21]*Salmon fathered Boaz, Boaz fathered Obed,*
   [22]*Obed fathered Jesse, and Jesse fathered David.*

292. E.g., Campbell, *Ruth,* 172–73; Nielsen, *Ruth,* 96; Schipper, *Ruth,* 186. See the discussion in Sasson, *Ruth,* 178–87.

293. For further arguments for its originality, see Bush, *Ruth, Esther,* 10–16; Hubbard, *Ruth,* 15–21; Zakovitch, *Rut,* 172–73.

294. Cf. Bar-Efrat, "Some Observations," 156–57.

295. Porten, "Scroll," 47–48.

### 4:18–22 The Beginning of a Royal Line in Israel

a. The plural form *tôlǝdôt* is related to the *hiphil* verb *hôlîd*, "cause to give birth," and so it means "people who are related": "descendants" or "generations." For its meaning in other contexts, see Schreiner, "*tôlǝdôt*," *TDOT* 15:582–83.

b. The verb *hôlîd* is from the root *yld*, a different root from *'ăbî*, "the father of" (v. 17). "Begat" is thus preferable (cf. BDB, 409), but it has dropped out of common usage.

c. Some versions have "Hezrom" (OL, Vulg., some LXX manuscripts), which probably influenced its spelling in the New Testament (*Esrōm*, Matt 1:3; Luke 3:33). The MT[L] spelling "Hezron" is supported by Tg., LXX[B], and Syr. It is the same spelling as in 1 Chr 2:9 and fits with the spelling of other names in the book of Ruth—Mahlon, Chilion, Nahshon, and Salmon. The interchange of *m* and *n* is found in other biblical names: Gershom/Gershon; Zetham/Zethan.

d. MT[L] and Tg. spell this name "Ram." Other versions begin the name with an *a*-class vowel, although they differ on spelling the rest of the name, e.g., Aram (Vulg., Syr.; Matt 1:3–4), Arran (LXX[BA]), and Arni (Luke 3:33). The spelling "Ram" in both MT[L] Ruth and 1 Chr 2:9–10 suggests an interdependence of these two genealogies; Campbell, *Ruth*, 171.

e. LXX and Vulg. spell this name "Naassōn"/"Naasson." The MT[L] spelling is supported by Tg.

f. In MT[L], this name is spelled *śalmâ* (v. 20) and *śalmôn* (v. 21), supported by Tg. In 1 Chr 2:11 the name is spelled *śalmā'* (cf. 1 Chr 2:51, 54). Most LXX manuscripts have *Salmōn* in both verses (Matt 1:4, 5), although LXX[B] has *Salman* in both verses. The Vulg. has *Salma*, OL *Salam*, and Syr. *sl'* in both verses. Since these are alternative spellings for the same person, to avoid confusion I have maintained the same spelling in both verses and followed most LXX manuscripts against MT[L].

The formula "Now these are the descendants of" signals that scene 3 of act 4 is a genealogy, a different form from the narrative in the rest of the book. A genealogy is the record of the descent of an individual or group from an ancestor or ancestors.[296] There are two types in the Old Testament:

(1)  Linear genealogies list the line of descent of an individual, with one name for each generation.

(2)  Segmented genealogies outline the kinship relations within a specific generation and from generation to generation. It thus shows the relationships between families, clans, tribes, and nations.[297]

A genealogy is not simply a list of names. It holds significance for identity, territory, and relationships. For ancient (and many modern) writers and audiences, "the names of ancestors, towns, and groups were of special relevance . . . because their genealogical connections defined [each group's]

---

296. For an overview of Old Testament genealogies, see Yigal Levin, "Understanding Biblical Genealogies," *CurBS* 9 (2001); Philip E. Satterthwaite, "Genealogy in the Hebrew Bible," *NIDOTTE* 4:654–63.

297. The presence of segmented genealogies distinguishes the Old Testament from genealogical material in the ancient Near East, which is almost always linear; Robert R. Wilson, *Genealogy and History in the Biblical World*, YNER 7 (New Haven: Yale University Press, 1977), 196.

# THE BOOK OF RUTH

position in relation to others."[298] Moreover, the mention of David bestows great honor on Boaz, and by extension all who were involved in his birth—Ruth and Naomi. The genealogy in Ruth is linear, and these usually legitimate the political, religious, or juridical role of the last-named person by connecting him to the lineage founder.[299] The Ruth genealogy links David to Perez and hence to the tribe of Judah. Yet, the genealogy has further significance in the book of Ruth and the Old Testament.

The relation between the genealogies in 1 Chr 2:5–16 and Ruth 4 cannot be determined with certainty.[300] The genealogical formula in Ruth is closer to the pentateuchal form than 1 Chronicles, which uses the phrases "these are the sons of" (e.g., 1 Chr 2:1; 3:1) or "the sons of" (e.g., 1 Chr 1:5, 6). Nonetheless, a comparison reveals the prominence given to the line of Perez in both Chronicles and Ruth. A comparison also shows the selectivity of the Ruth genealogy: ancestors have been omitted to craft a ten-generation model.[301] Five of the ancestors were mentioned in the Ruth narrative, but the reason for the selection of the other five is not clear. One suggestion for three of the five names (Hezron, Nahshon, and Salmon) is to rhyme with Mahlon and Chilion and the word for Ruth's "conception" (*hērāyôn*).[302]

The telescoping of the Ruth genealogy presents Israel's history in two periods: Perez to the generation of Moses (Nahshon; see below) and from the next generation (Salmon) to David, five generations who experienced the exodus (starting with the patriarchs, Gen 46:8–12) and five from the exodus to the formative years in the promised land.[303] This echoes the movement of the Ruth narrative, from the journey out of the promised land to the return and resettlement. Consistent with other Old Testament lists, the ten-generation genealogy places Boaz and David at prominent positions—

---

298. Gary N. Knoppers, "Intermarriage, Social Complexity, and Ethnic Diversity in the Genealogy of Judah," *JBL* 120 (2001): 18.

299. See Wilson, *Genealogy*, 38–45.

300. The direction of influence could be either way, or they could have originated separately or from a common source. However, the close parallel between 1 Chr 2:10–12 and Ruth 4:19–22, including the otherwise rare formula in Chronicles, *X hôlîd 'et-Y*, favors a Ruth to Chronicles direction of influence; so Sasson, *Ruth*, 188–89; Hubbard, *Ruth*, 282n10.

301. Israel spent about 400 years in Egypt (Gen 15:13; Acts 7:6; cf. Exod 12:40; Gal 3:17), and Solomon began building the temple 480 years after the exodus (1 Kgs 6:1). So the Ruth genealogy spans about 800 years.

302. Schipper, *Ruth*, 187.

303. Compare the genealogy of Jesus, which comprises three periods of fourteen generations: Abraham to David; David to the Babylonian exile; and the exile to the Christ (Matt 1:17).

## 4:18-22 The Beginning of a Royal Line in Israel

seventh (cf. "seven sons" in 4:15) and tenth.[304] In ancient Near Eastern king lists the tenth position is most prestigious[305] and is thus suitable for David.

**18** *Now these are the descendants of* signals the beginning of a genealogy, and the use of this formula here is the only time it is found outside the Pentateuch. The formula links the Ruth narrative especially to the patriarchal narratives (Gen 6:9; 10:1; 11:10, 27; 25:12, 19; 36:1, 9; 37:2; also Gen 2:4; Num 3:1).[306] "Descendants" (*tôlədôt*) comes from the root *yld*, "to bring forth (children),"[307] and it culminates and brings to a climax a motif in the Ruth narrative. It spans from the death of Naomi's "children" (1:5) to the "child" that takes their place (4:16) to this child's position in the "generations" of Perez (v. 18), including the ancestors who "fathered" the next generation, to this child's own royal "descendant" (v. 22). The concluding genealogy ends with the same three names mentioned in the previous verse (v. 17; Obed, Jesse, David) and begins with *Perez*. Curiously, it begins with him instead of his more illustrious father Judah. Perez might have been chosen to achieve the ten generations, but since the genealogy is selective, it could have begun with Judah. Perez is mentioned three times in the book of Ruth (also v. 12), compared to Judah's single mention (v. 12), which suggests that the choice of his name is significant. Perhaps he was chosen to underline the levirate link since the only other narrative occurrence of this custom resulted in his birth (Gen 38), just as the Ruth narrative ends with the birth of Obed. Perhaps he was chosen because his name represents both breach and blessing, and these motifs may be a key to interpreting the book.[308] Whatever the reason for choosing Perez (and each may be a contributing factor), his mention ties nicely with the narrative as the answer to the throng's prayer that Boaz's house would be like the house of Perez (4:12). The book of Ruth points to him as the ancestral head in both the narrative and the genealogy.

*Hezron* was the son of Perez and the grandson of Judah (Gen 46:12; 1 Chr 2:5).[309] Like Joseph's sons (Gen 46:27), he could have been born in Egypt. His descendants constituted the Hezronite clan (Num 26:21; cf.

---

304. For instance, Enoch and Noah occupy the seventh and tenth positions (Gen 5), as do the Amorites and the Jebusites (Gen 15:19–21); Gary A. Rendsburg, "Notes on Genesis XV," *VT* 42 (1992): 269.

305. See Abraham Malamat, "King Lists of the Old Babylonian Period and Biblical Genealogies," *JAOS* 88 (1968): 170–73.

306. Critical scholars note these are all Priestly (P) texts; Schreiner, "*tôlədôt*," *TDOT* 15:582–83.

307. See Schreiner, "*yālad*," *TDOT* 6:76.

308. Eskenazi and Frymer-Kensky, *Ruth*, 94. See comment on v. 12.

309. First Chronicles 4:1 lists Hezron as the son of Judah.

1 Chr 2:9–33). He is listed in both versions of Jesus's genealogy (Matt 1:3; Luke 3:33).

**19** *Ram* means "high, exalted," and is also spelled "Aram" (Matt 1:3, 4; Luke 3:33). He was probably the second son of Hezron (1 Chr 2:9). Ram's son was *Amminadab*, which means "my kin is generous, noble."[310] He was the father of Nahshon (Num 1:7; 2:3; 7:12, 17; 10:14; 1 Chr 2:10; Matt 1:4; Luke 3:33) and Elisheba, Aaron's wife (Exod 6:23).[311]

**20–21** *Nahshon* probably means "little snake" (*nāḥāš*, "snake" [Gen 3:1; 49:17; Exod 4:3; Num 21:6] plus diminutive *-ôn*),[312] and he was the brother-in-law of Aaron. He represented Judah in assisting Moses with the first census (Num 1:7) and led the tribe during the wilderness wanderings. He is given the title *nāśî'*, "tribal chief, leader" of the people of Judah in 1 Chr 2:10 and Num 2:3. On behalf of the tribe of Judah, he was the first to present an offering at the dedication of the tabernacle (Num 7:12, 17). When Israel left Sinai, he was their leader (Num 10:14).

*Salmon* probably means "garment," and the name takes two forms in the Ruth genealogy—*śalmâ* (v. 20) and *śalmôn* (v. 21).[313] It is spelled *śalmā'* in 1 Chr 2:11, and the variant spellings of the name suggests scribal flexibility with the endings of names.[314] Perhaps the author chose *śalmôn* in v. 21 to rhyme with Hezron and Nahshon. He was the son or grandson of Nahshon,[315] and he could have been a contemporary of Elimelech.[316] Salmon fathered *Boaz* (1 Chr 2:11), who fathered *Obed* (1 Chr 2:11–12).[317] Boaz is only mentioned elsewhere in the Old Testament in 1 Chr 2, which does not list any other sons.[318] In the genealogy in Matthew, Salmon is the father of Boaz by Rahab (Matt 1:5), most likely the prostitute from the book of Joshua (2; 6:17, 23–25).[319]

Since the narrative is concerned to raise and preserve the name of the dead, it is surprising that Boaz is inserted in the genealogy. He stated that

---

310. BDB, 770; *HALOT* 2:844.

311. There are two other individuals named Amminadab in the Old Testament: a son of Kohath (1 Chr 6:7[22]); and a son of Uzziel (1 Chr 15:10).

312. *HALOT* 2:691. For other possible meanings, see Sasson, *Ruth*, 189.

313. The noun *śalmâ* shares the same root letters with the more common *śimlâ*, "garment, cloak" (Ruth 3:3); see Niehr, "*śimlâ*," *TDOT* 14:158–59.

314. Cf. David's father, whose name is spelled *yiśay* and *'îśay* in consecutive verses (1 Chr 2:12–13); Sasson, *Ruth*, 190.

315. Hubbard, *Ruth*, 283.

316. Block, *Discourse*, 254, speculates that he was Elimelech's brother.

317. On Boaz, see comment on 2:1, and on Obed, see comments on 4:17, 22.

318. One Jewish Rabbinic tradition suggests that Boaz died on the night Obed was conceived; Ruth Zuta 4:13.

319. So most scholars, e.g., France, *Matthew*, 36; John Nolland, *The Gospel of Matthew*, NIGTC (Grand Rapids: Eerdmans, 2005), 74.

4:18–22 THE BEGINNING OF A ROYAL LINE IN ISRAEL

he did not want the name of the dead to be cut off (4:10), but this seems to be what is happening. Based on the legal fiction of paternity and patrimony, we expect either Mahlon's or Elimelech's name in the genealogy. They are absent, and in the narrative Naomi is listed as an ancestor in Obed's line (a "son" is born to her, 4:17) rather than the men in the family. Is this seeming dissonance further evidence for the insertion of the genealogy by a later editor? We need to consider how ancient genealogies functioned.

Boaz occupies the seventh position, a place of honor in ancient genealogies.[320] This genealogical custom partly explains why Boaz is inserted instead of Mahlon. Boaz was already a well-respected member of society (2:1), and his actions elevated his status even further. His acts of kindness beyond the requirements of the law restored to wholeness the lives of Naomi, Ruth, and Elimelech's family line. The insertion of his name in the genealogy brings him further honor and thus encourages the virtue of kindness in the audience.[321] There are only two applications of the levirate custom in the Old Testament, and in both genealogies the son is ascribed to the biological father, not the man who died without an heir (Gen 46:12; 1 Chr 2:3–4; Ruth 4:12, 21).[322] In one contemporary society where the levirate custom is practiced, the man from the senior generation and with higher social status is placed in the genealogy.[323] Not only are Judah and Boaz the biological fathers, they also fit the two aforementioned criteria. To my mind, the higher status of Judah and Boaz is a plausible explanation for the perceived conflict in the intent of the narrative (to establish the name of the dead on his inheritance, 4:5, 10) with the genealogy.

It may be that Obed was reckoned as both Boaz's and Mahlon's.[324] Since we only have two Old Testament instances of levirate unions, we cannot be certain. The redemption and levirate laws work in tandem in the Ruth narrative to preserve name, land, and progeny, so there are other ways Boaz might have practically perpetuated "the name of the dead on his inheritance." In the Old Testament, individuals were described by a given name followed by their father's or mother's name, so Obed could have been referred to as "Obed the son of Mahlon." And since landed property was marked with boundary markers (Deut 19:14; 27:17), a marker for the redeemed property could have been inscribed with "property of Obed the son of Mahlon." These two proposals are speculative, but the point is that the name of the dead

320. See discussion before comments on vv. 18–22.

321. Cf. Eskenazi and Frymer-Kensky, *Ruth*, 83–84.

322. In the New Testament, Boaz is listed as the father of Obed (Matt 1:5; Luke 3:32). But Matthew identifies Joseph as the father of Jesus (Matt 1:16), while Luke points out the legal fiction: "He was the son, as was supposed, of Joseph" (Luke 3:23).

323. See Gow, *Ruth*, 180–81, who draws on the practice of the Tswana people in Africa.

324. Cf. Campbell, *Ruth*, 172.

# THE BOOK OF RUTH

could have been practically perpetuated in ancient Israel other than through a genealogy. Indeed, the presence of a son was the key element to perpetuate the existence of the deceased, and land allows "a form of materiality" to be attached to the name.[325] Mahlon's/Elimelech's omission in the genealogy is not necessarily evidence against a levirate union between Boaz and Ruth or that the genealogy is an addition.

**22** The information in this verse repeats that found at the end of v. 17. *Obed* only occurs elsewhere in genealogies in the Old Testament (1 Chr 2:12) and New Testament (Matt 1:5; Luke 3:32). He fathered *Jesse*,[326] the meaning of whose name is uncertain.[327] Jesse was from Bethlehem and called an Ephrathite (1 Sam 17:12; cf. Ruth 1:2). He had two daughters (1 Chr 2:13–16) and eight sons (1 Sam 17:12), the youngest of whom was David (1 Sam 16:1–13).[328] David is sometimes referred to as "the son of Jesse," without mention of his personal name (e.g., 1 Sam 20:27, 30; 22:7–9; 1 Kgs 12:16).[329] Isaiah would prophesy about a messianic ruler who would sprout from the "stump" or "root" of Jesse (Isa 11:1, 10; cf. Rom 15:12).

The meaning of the name *David* is uncertain, perhaps deriving from a root meaning "beloved/darling" or "paternal uncle."[330] Similar to the names of the patriarchs, David is the only person in the Old Testament with this name. He is the second and greatest of Israel's kings, a man according to God's heart—chosen by God and faithful to him (1 Sam 13:14; cited Acts 13:22).[331] Along with Moses, he ranks as one of the two most revered individuals in the Old Testament. He is the most illustrious Israelite king. Known for his military leadership, he brings rest and peace to a united Israel. He defeats the Philistines and captures Jerusalem (2 Sam 5:20–25), and his reign lasts forty years (2 Sam 5:4–5; 1 Kgs 2:11; 1 Chr 3:4). God ensures his legacy by making a foundational covenant with him to establish his royal dynasty forever (2 Sam

---

325. Mathias, *Paternity*, 242. Monuments function similarly (see, e.g., 2 Sam 18:18; Isa 56:4–5).

326. Heb. *yišāy* or *'išay* (see 1 Chr 2:12–13).

327. For a discussion of possible etymologies, see Sasson, *Ruth*, 190.

328. David is listed as Jesse's seventh son in 1 Chr 2:13–15, but the Chronicler probably abbreviated his list to place David in the favored seventh position. In addition to the seven sons listed in 1 Chr 2:13–15, Elihu is mentioned as David's brother in 1 Chr 27:18.

329. In direct discourse in 1–2 Samuel, this patronym is often used in a derogatory sense (e.g., Sheba's call to revolt; 2 Sam 20:1). The full name "David son of Jesse" is rarely used (2 Sam 23:1; 1 Chr 10:14; 29:26; cf. Ps 72:20; Acts 13:22).

330. For a discussion of etymology, see Carlson, "*dāwid*," *TDOT* 3:157–59. The spelling of the name David in the book of Ruth is *dāwid*, while in Ezra-Nehemiah and Chronicles it is spelled *dāwîd* (including in the corresponding genealogy, 1 Chr 2:15).

331. For a discussion of the phrase *kilbābô*, "like/according to his heart," see Jason S. DeRouchie, "The Heart of YHWH and His Chosen One in 1 Samuel 13:14," *BBR* 24 (2014): 467–89.

7:8–16). His son builds the temple, but David purchases the site (1 Chr 21:18–22:1; 2 Chr 3:1). He is the gold standard against which subsequent kings are measured (e.g., 1 Kgs 3:6; 9:4; 11:4; 14:8; 15:3; 2 Kgs 18:3; 22:2), and his dynasty remained on the throne until the fall of Jerusalem and the Babylonian exile (2 Kgs 24; 2 Chr 36:17–21). Yet after the return from exile, there is no king from the line of David. In the New Testament, the fulfillment of God's covenant with David is in Jesus Christ, the "Son of David,"[332] whose kingship will never end (Luke 1:31–33).

If the author of Ruth borrowed the genealogy form, he also adapted it. Elsewhere genealogies precede the narratives, introducing characters whose lives are then detailed (including Gen 11:27–32; 25:19–26).[333] The placement after the narrative in the book of Ruth maintains the suspense[334] and allows an audience to suspend judgment on the book's intention until the end.[335] Its placement points forward to the life of David, especially his succession to the throne, as told in the books of Samuel.[336] Moreover, its placement highlights the wider significance of the Ruth narrative by reinforcing its link to David (who was already mentioned in v. 17). The genealogy also fills in the gap between the prayer in vv. 11–12 and the three generations listed in v. 17.[337] The throng prayed that God would make Boaz's house like that of Israel/Jacob, and Judah and Perez. But since Boaz is not mentioned at the end of v. 17, his place in the lineage is unclear, along with the answer to prayer. The genealogy makes clear the link between Perez and Boaz; the prayer is answered. The genealogy also underscores the significance of Boaz: he (not Mahlon) is the father of Obed, and he is connected to the line of Judah. This is Boaz's esteemed place within the wider patrilineal framework. From a theological perspective, God's quiet providence is revealed again: he has heard and answered another prayer.

The ten-generation model is significant in three other ways, apart from being typical of ancient royal genealogies. First, in the Ruth narrative, the ten years without progeny in Moab correspond to the ten generations in Israel.[338] The death of Elimelech's sons seems to end his line, but it is re-established in the genealogy. Second, in the Old Testament, the ten-generation model con-

---

332. Matthew 1:1; 9:27; 12:23; 15:22; 20:30–31; 21:9, 15; Mark 10:47–48; 12:35; Luke 3:31; 18:38–39; 20:41.

333. The only other place the genealogy comes after the narrative is Gen 2:4, where it is used metaphorically of the *tôlǝdôt*, the "generations" or "descendants" of "the heavens and the earth."

334. Block, *Discourse*, 250n2.

335. Gow, *Ruth*, 138.

336. Linafelt, *Ruth*, xx.

337. Similarly, Schipper, *Ruth*, 187–88; Bush, *Ruth, Esther*, 267–68.

338. Cf. Porten, "Scroll," 47–48. Ten elders are also selected to form a legal quorum (4:2).

305

THE BOOK OF RUTH

nects the Ruth narrative, the founding of the Davidic dynasty, to the founding of humanity. Ten generations are listed between Adam and Noah (Gen 5) and from Noah to Abraham (Gen 11). Perhaps, similar to the accounts of Noah and Abraham, the account of the birth of David leads us to understand the dawn of a new and better age. Looking at the events at the end of the book of Judges, things could not have been much worse. In these ways, the Ruth genealogy testifies again to God's mercy and providence. He was faithful to his people at a time when they were not faithful to him (some characters in the Ruth narrative excepted). Third, the ten-generation model draws the Ruth narrative into dialogue with two Old Testament laws. Moabites are prohibited from entering "the assembly of Yahweh . . . even to the *tenth generation*" (Deut 23:3 NIV).[339] Indirectly related is the law forbidding intermarriage with Canaanites, including Moabites, since they served "other gods" (7:1–4). If these two laws are in dialogue with the ten-generation genealogy, Ruth the Moabite's marriage to an Israelite and her acceptance into the community of God's people present a nuanced application of the law.

There are other ways the genealogical formula connects the genealogy in Ruth to those in Genesis (e.g., Gen 2:4; 5:1; 6:9; 10:1).[340] The last of these detailed the line of Jacob (37:2), with none of his sons' family trees detailed. The effect is to present one main line of the people of Israel after Jacob. Thus, the genealogy in Ruth continues the narrative from Gen 38, with special significance now attached to the line of Judah. Yet the linkage is even broader: the genealogy connects the Ruth narrative to the main narrative of the Old Testament from Genesis to 2 Kings. The continuity is from Perez in the patriarchal period to King David (whose last years are recorded in 1 Kgs 1–2). Yet the exact sequence of the formula, "These are the generations of," followed by the phrase "X fathered Y," is only found elsewhere in Gen 11:27–32 and 25:19–26.[341] These genealogies mark the start of the Abraham and Jacob narratives, emphasizing the special importance of these fathers of the nation of Israel. The mention of barrenness in the wives of these patriarchs soon after the genealogy (11:30; 25:21) forges an even stronger link with the Ruth narrative. The significance of these similarities further connects the Ruth genealogy to those of the significant patriarchs. God's reversal of initial barrenness in their wives, just like Ruth, adds to the sense of God's hand in the lineage's continuation.

We can thus view the Ruth narrative as God working his grand purposes for his people in one family. God's foundational promise to Abraham of land,

339. See "Applying the Law" in the introduction.

340. Irmtraud Fischer, "The Book of Ruth as Exegetical Literature," *European Judaism* 40 (2007): 142.

341. As observed by Gow, *Ruth*, 187.

offspring, and blessing (Gen 12:1–7) is sorely tested but is found to hold firm. A family experiences famine in the promised land and is exiled to a foreign land. The ravaged family returns to the promised land, but their hold on their plot of land is under threat. The absence of offspring means their lineage is also under threat. But through redemption and substitution, land is restored to the family with an ongoing name attached. Moreover, blessing is found by a foreigner who had blessed this Israelite family while they were in exile. Blessing comes to Moab, and they become part of the genealogy of God's people again. God can be trusted because he is unwaveringly faithful to his covenant, even to a family who might not have been completely faithful to him. The Ruth narrative is God's plan for and history of his Old Testament people writ small.

This is not a complete history and the ending points to the greater that is to come. It is the small beginnings of the kingdom of David, the greatest Israelite king. Perhaps we find an anticipation of the interweaving of the Abrahamic and Davidic covenants. One who would have Moabite in his veins would finally realize God's promise to Abraham but will also be promised a temple and an eternal royal line (2 Sam 7:1–17). Sadly, by the end of the Old Testament, God's people have broken the covenant, resulting in the covenant curses falling upon them, and they are deported and exiled from the promised land. God restores them to the land, and they partially experience the blessings of the Abrahamic covenant again. But what of the Davidic covenant? For no Davidic king sits on a royal throne in post-exilic Yehud. For Christians, the end of this plot is found in King Jesus, who would fulfill not just the Abrahamic covenant, but also the Davidic—in ways far beyond those imagined in the Old Testament.

# Index of Authors

Aitken, K. T., 239
Alba, R., 49
Alexander, T. D., 26, 54
Alter, R., 10, 20, 28, 85, 89, 148, 282
American Psychiatric Association, 179
Amsler, S., 251
Andersen, F. I., 87, 115, 269
André, G., 290
Ap-Thomas, D. R., 295
Arnold, B. T., 288
Artus, O. J., 248
Aschkenasy, N., 218
Ashley, T. R., 139

Baker, D. L., 130
Baker, D. W., 244
Bantebya-Kyomuhendo, G., 118
Barclay, J. M. G., 224
Bar-Efrat, S., 2, 20, 298
Barker, P. A., 120
Bartholomew, C. G., 54, 76
Bauckham, R., 87, 232, 276, 294
Baumann, A., 203, 287
Baylis, C. P., 69
Beal, T. K., 2, 18, 155, 239, 267, 276
Beattie, D. R. G., 205
Beckwith, R. T., 29, 30
Beekman, J., 23

Beeston, A. F. L., 97
Benjamin, D. C., 239
Berger, Y., 24, 25
Berlin, A., 1, 9, 20, 23, 137, 206, 224, 250
Bernstein, M. J., 194
Berquist, J. L., 131
Bertman, S., 2
Beyse, K.-M., 90
Black, J., 276
Blackburn, W. R., 55
Block, D. I., 1, 11, 14, 28, 36, 69, 98, 116, 137, 143, 144, 172, 185, 188, 191, 224, 236, 248, 264, 267, 278, 296, 302, 305
Bogaert, P.-M., 28
Bons, E., 34
Borowski, O., 149
Bos, J. W. H., 180
Botte, P., 28
Brady, C. M. M., 106
Bratsiotis, N. P., 271
Brichto, H. C., 102, 250, 258
Bridge, E. J., 158, 160, 204
Brown, C. A., 15
Brown, M. L., 278
Brown, R. E., 268
Buhl, F., 253
Burrows, M., 209

## Index of Authors

Bush, F. W., 4, 9, 17, 18, 21, 23, 36, 69, 74, 80, 82, 84, 99, 101, 139, 141, 147, 164, 169, 172, 185, 191, 206, 238, 243, 247, 248, 252, 255, 256, 257, 258, 259, 278, 290, 291, 294, 295, 298, 305

Callaham, S. N., 97
Callow, J., 23
Campbell, E. F., 10, 11, 14, 17, 36, 70, 80, 81, 83, 92, 98, 104, 110, 112, 127, 150, 165, 172, 178, 185, 202, 205, 206, 235, 238, 253, 254, 257, 259, 261, 263, 266, 269, 286, 288, 289, 291, 294, 298, 299, 303
Caquot, A., 165
Carlson, D., 304
Carroll R., M. D., 49, 103, 182
Carson, D. A., 117
Cassuto, U., 24
Chase, E., 118
Cheung, S. C.-C., 91
Chisholm, R. B., Jr., 69
Christiansen, B., 124
Clark, G. R., 87
Clements, R. E., 72
Clines, D. J. A., 115, 132
Conrad, E. W., 239, 252
Craigie, P. C., 48
Creach, J. F. D., 157
Crook, Z., 211
Cuddon, J. A., 9
Culp, A. J., 91

Dagley, K. D., 50
Darr, K. P., 36
Daube, D., 250
David, M., 16
Davies, E. W., 209, 250, 255, 257
Davies, J. A., 55, 90, 146, 149
Davis, B. C., 2, 15, 36, 278
Davis, E. F., 21, 248
Dearman, J. A., 2, 68
Delcor, M., 148

DeRouchie, J. S., 304
De-Whyte, J. P. E., 296
Dobbs-Allsopp, F. W., 138
Dohmen, C., 116
Domeris, W. R., 110
Dommershausen, W., 21
Donaldson, L. E., 98
Driesbach, J., 15
Durham, J. I., 55
Duvall, J. S., 37
Dyck, J. E., 23
Dyk, J. W., 192

Ehrensvärd, M., 18
Eising, H., 126
Elliott, J. H., 193
Elliott, M. W., 36
Embry, B., 249, 252
Epstein, I., 30
Eskenazi, T. C., 13, 27, 36, 69, 73, 102, 140, 141, 174, 208, 221, 223, 237, 250, 258, 274, 281, 284, 301, 303
Evans, M. J., 15
Exum, J. C., 97

Fabry, H.-J., 287
Fentress-Williams, J., 6, 15
Fewell, D. N., 96, 107, 128, 155, 179, 187, 192
Finlay, T. D., 279
Firth, D. G., 11, 271
Fisch, H., 26
Fischer, I., 14, 32, 61, 112, 131, 276, 306
France, R. T., 275, 302
Frese, D. A., 238, 266
Frevel, C., 13
Frymer-Kensky, T., 13, 27, 36, 69, 73, 102, 105, 140, 141, 174, 208, 221, 223, 237, 250, 258, 274, 281, 284, 301, 303
Fuller, R., 166

Gamberoni, J., 251
Gane, R., 175

## Index of Authors

Garsiel, M., 128, 153
Gerleman, G., 156, 296
Gerstenberger, E., 157
Ginzberg, L., 210
Glanville, L., 56
Glanville, M. R., 56
Glanzman, G. S., 15
Glover, N., 49
Glueck, N., 87, 174
Goh, S. T. S., 211
Goheen, M. W., 54
Gordis, R., 13, 16
Görg, 220, 226
Goslinga, C. J., 16, 150
Goswell, G., 23, 30, 31, 46, 54, 58, 67, 75, 175, 211, 269
Gow, M. D., 2, 14, 15, 16, 21, 193, 251, 278, 303, 305, 306
Gray, J., 21, 206, 253
Green, B., 218
Greenberg, M., 215
Grossman, J., 2, 22, 64, 65, 69, 77, 111, 140, 141, 142, 144, 166, 173, 179, 209, 223, 225, 237, 239, 244, 245, 252, 253, 261, 262, 268, 281, 296
Gunkel, H., 8, 270
Gunn, D. M., 96, 107, 128, 155, 179, 187, 192
Guttmann, M., 151

Haag, E., 285
Habel, N. C., 90
Hals, R. M., 16, 36, 41
Halton, C., 192
Harris, J. G., 15
Hausmann, J., 104
Hawk, L. D., 13, 23, 96, 107, 248, 256, 262
Hays, J. D., 37
Hertig, P., 182
Hirsch, E. D., 8
Hoffner, H., 75, 271

Holmstedt, R. D., 18, 65, 80, 81, 83, 91, 96, 106, 109, 119, 121, 124, 135, 136, 158, 172, 174, 177, 185, 187, 198, 202, 212, 213, 218, 220, 243, 247, 263, 267, 278, 281, 286
Honig, B., 296
Hostetter, E. C., 149
Hubbard, R. L., 2, 14, 22, 26, 65, 70, 72, 73, 81, 83, 87, 106, 108, 116, 124, 128, 138, 140, 141, 147, 148, 162, 171, 172, 174, 177, 179, 209, 221, 240, 243, 245, 253, 254, 256, 259, 260, 263, 265, 271, 283, 298, 300, 302
Hulst, A. R., 99, 154, 271
Humbert, P., 21, 217
Humphreys, W., 9
Hurvitz, A., 17, 142
Hwang, J., 118
Hyman, R. T., 111, 223

Irwin, B. P., 185

Jackson, B. S., 129
Jackson, J., 15
Jastrow, M., 83, 161
Jenni, E., 95, 96, 124, 158, 240, 271
Jobling, D., 28, 87
Jones, E. A., III, 14, 203, 221
Jongeling, B., 110
Joüon, P., 22, 164, 171, 189, 235, 246, 252, 253, 255, 257, 294
Juhás, P., 124

Kawashima, R. S., 137
Kedar-Kopfstein, B., 225
Keita, S., 192
Keller, C. A., 134, 278
Kellermann, D., 161
Kennedy, J. M., 165
Knauf, E. A., 113
Knoppers, G. N., 300
Koch, K., 274
Kopesec, M. F., 23

## INDEX OF AUTHORS

Korpel, M. C. A., 2, 13, 15, 16
Kosmala, H., 127
Köstenberger, A. J., 54
Kroeze, J. H., 65
Kronholm, T., 143
Kruger, P. A., 205
Kühlewein, J., 75, 127
Kwakkel, G., 157
Kwok, P.-L., 97

Labuschagne, C. J., 116, 273
LaCocque, A., 1, 13, 15, 16, 17, 105, 111,
    141, 206, 213, 215, 248, 288, 293
Lang, B., 151
Laniak, T. S., 6
Lau, P. H. W., 12, 17, 20, 23, 30, 31, 46,
    54, 56, 58, 67, 75, 90, 98, 106, 120,
    127, 175, 196, 211, 246, 269, 272
Leach, E. R., 125, 126
Leggett, D. A., 21
Lehmann, M. R., 104
LeMon, J. M., 157
Levenson, J. D., 132
Levin, Y., 299
Levine, A.-J., 87, 126
Liedke, G., 147, 164, 243
Lim, T. H., 30, 80, 169, 177
Lin, Y., 90, 107, 288
Linafelt, T., 2, 18, 24, 28, 155, 239, 267,
    276, 305
Lipiński, E., 224, 241, 244, 247, 257
Long, V. P., 11
Longman, T., III, 32, 95
Luter, A. B., 2, 15, 36, 278
Lys, D., 142

MacDonald, N., 161
Mace, D. R., 205
Malamat, A., 301
Martin-Achard, R., 150
Mathias, S., 249, 266, 276, 304
Matthews, V. H., 18, 121, 151, 189, 206,
    239

Mattingly, G. I., 99
May, N. N., 237
McKeown, J., 26, 59, 248
Meinhold, A., 16
Meyers, C. L., 87, 111, 126, 291
Milgrom, J., 175, 254, 266
Miller, R. D., II, 11, 180
Miller-Naudé, C. L., 140
Moore, M. S., 15, 116
Morris, L., 16, 85, 99, 104, 110, 193,
    209, 252, 274, 275
Müller, H.-P., 99, 110
Murphy, R. E., 279
Myers, J. M., 10

Nathanson, D. L., 118
Naudé, J. A., 65, 140
Nazarov, K., 138, 203
Nee, V., 49
Nida, E. A., 137
Niditch, S., 16
Niehr, H., 185, 302
Nielsen, K., 2, 3, 14, 15, 17, 191, 205,
    296, 298
Niggemann, A. J., 51
Nolland, J., 302
Nu, R., 56, 93

O'Connell, R. H., 110
Oduyoye, M. A., 139
Oeste, G., 68
Olyan, S. M., 102
Ott, C., 54
Otto, 236, 289
Ovadia, B.-Z., 221

Pa, A. M. S., 195
Parker, M. A., 248
Patterson, R., 190
Payne, J. D., 57
Peters, G. W., 57
Pfeiffer, R. H., 13
Phinney, D. N., 90

## Index of Authors

Pilch, J. J., 7
Plevnik, J., 7
Polzin, R., 17
Porten, B., 2, 64, 78, 87, 115, 126, 137, 144, 172, 174, 180, 200, 218, 220, 235, 236, 298, 305
Powell, M. A., 166
Powell, S. D., 97
Pressler, C., 15, 18
Preuss, H. D., 89
Prill, T., 57
Prinsloo, W. S., 205

Queen-Sutherland, K., 14
Quick, L., 190, 205, 211

Rebera, B., 174, 221
Reid, D. G., 95
Rendsburg, G. A., 1, 100, 102, 142, 162, 171, 202, 203, 248, 301
Revell, E. J., 135, 213
Rezetko, R., 18
Ringgren, H., 132, 240, 258, 295
Rooker, M. F., 18
Roop, E. F., 15
Rooy, H. F. van, 110
Routledge, B., 68
Rowley, H. H., 209
Rudolph, W., 234, 235, 247, 254, 255, 256, 257
Rust, E. C., 16

Sakenfeld, K. D., 15, 18, 23, 27, 38, 69, 87, 105, 111, 117, 206
Sarna, N. M., 266
Sasson, J. M., 8, 14, 70, 82, 88, 92, 98, 116, 124, 137, 166, 203, 222, 234, 244, 246, 252, 258, 271, 278, 298, 300, 302, 304
Satterthwaite, P. E., 299
Saxegaard, K. M., 9, 14, 69, 107, 112, 128
Scharbert, J., 134, 138

Schibler, D., 93
Schipper, J., 14, 81, 83, 104, 141, 147, 173, 205, 248, 251, 267, 273, 278, 282, 298, 300, 305
Schmid, H. H., 125, 217
Schmidt, W. H., 83, 244, 251
Schottroff, W., 154
Schreiner, J., 299, 301
Seebass, H., 72, 193
Shepherd, D., 148
Smalley, B., 3
Smith, M. S., 104, 105, 296
Smith, W. R., 205
Southwood, K. E., 49, 296
Sparks, K. L., 151
Stager, L. E., 102
Stähli, H.-P., 149
Stansell, G., 224
Steins, G., 113, 114
Stendebach, F. J., 204
Sternberg, R., 20, 224
Stoebe, H. J., 130, 159
Stolz, F., 89, 110, 271, 285
Stone, T. J., 28, 218
Strauss, S. J., 54
Sun, C., 54
Suriano, M. J., 249
Swete, H. B., 28

Tennent, T. C., 54
Thambyrajah, J. A., 49
Thomas, N. J., 55
Thompson, D., 254, 255, 257
Thompson, T., 254, 255, 257
Tigay, J. H., 47
Toorn, K. van der, 83
Tov, E., 33, 35
Triandis, H. C., 8
Trible, P., 6, 88, 237, 267
Tsevat, M., 133
Tucker, G. M., 16, 263
Tully, E. J., 35

## INDEX OF AUTHORS

Ulrich, E., 34

Van Der Merwe, C. H. J., 65
Vanhoozer, K. J., 54
Vesco, J.-L., 13
Vette, D., 252
Viberg, Å., 259, 290
Vollmer, J., 156

Waard, J. de, 34, 137
Wagner, S., 163, 199, 243
Walker, R., 118
Wallace, C., 248
Wallis, G., 96
Wardlaw, T. R., Jr., 114
Webb, B. G., 4, 117, 228
Wechsler, M. G., 34, 83
Weinfeld, M., 14
Weis, R. D., 33
Weiss, D. H., 252
Wenham, G. J., 46, 97, 255
West, M., 97
Westbrook, R., 250
Westermann, C., 278
Wetter, A.-M., 83
Whedbee, J. W., 6
Wilch, J. R., 15
Wildberger, H., 72, 208

Williams, W., 192
Williamson, P. R., 104
Willis, T. M., 210, 239
Wilson, L., 76
Wilson, M. R., 150
Wilson, R. R., 299, 300
Witzenrath, H. H., 116
Woude, A. S. van der, 95, 106, 157, 249
Wright, C. J. H., 54, 106, 239
Wright, N. T., 54
Wu, D., 6
Würthwein, E., 8, 256

Yamasaki, G., 138
Yamauchi, E., 130
Young, I., 18
Younger, K. L., 15, 18, 69

Zakovitch, Y., 8, 13, 16, 32, 117, 170, 175, 206, 209, 245, 253, 255, 256, 263, 264, 281, 284, 289, 298
Zenger, E., 13, 14
Zevit, Z., 13, 18, 82, 247, 248
Ziegert, C., 34
Ziegler, Y., 103, 105, 106
Zimmerli, W., 119
Zobel, H.-J., 243

# Index of Subjects

adoption, 290, 291. *See also* Naomi: as nanny

alliteration, 64, 78, 113, 137, 162, 172, 202, 203, 244, 258n124, 265, 284, 285, 286, 289n256

allusions, 13, 17, 22, 26, 47, 74, 85, 87–88, 92–93, 94, 103, 128, 148, 155, 215, 221, 250, 251, 260, 271, 273, 274, 281

Aramaisms, 13, 18, 82, 83, 258

archaisms, 80, 135, 185

assonance, 64, 78, 84, 150, 160, 164, 235, 258, 259, 273n189, 275, 287, 291n267

Bethlehem, 3, 11, 27–28, 61, 63, 66–67, 71, 77, 78, 121, 149, 189, 190, 194, 201, 238, 272–73

betrothal type-scene, 26, 148, 155, 190, 194, 224n125

birth announcement, report, 279–80, 291–92

blessings, benediction, 37–38, 39, 41, 42–45, 54–55, 138–39, 155–56, 170–72, 174, 207–8, 215, 270, 271, 272, 273, 274, 276–77, 285, 307

Boaz: age of, 135, 139–40, 208–10; and application of the law, 166–67; cleverness of, 46–47, 239, 242–52,

263; garment of, 185, 205, 218; generosity and kindness of, 39–40, 46, 55, 58, 144–46, 148, 152, 163–65, 177–78, 228–29; and gifts of food and drink, 149, 162, 171, 217–18, 224n125, 225; as God's instrument, 43, 138, 158, 162, 172, 174–75; as honored ancestor, 52, 300, 302–3, 305; marriage of, 47–48, 214–15, 280, 296; as model, 9, 21, 57, 160–62, 181–83; motivation of, 150, 155, 167; name, 128; prayer of, 155–58; relationship of, with Ruth, 51, 126, 145, 175–76, 187–89, 212–13; reward of, 276–77; and risk taking, 58, 228–29, 268–69; showing favor, 150, 172; social status of, 127–28, 133, 137, 188, 211–12, 303 (*see also* honor-shame culture); as type of Christ, 58; values of, 154

burial customs, 11, 71–72, 102, 266

chiasm, 4, 99, 125, 137, 169, 236, 263n149, 269n172, 270

childlessness, 26, 33, 74, 250, 275n195, 282–83, 296

Chilion, 4, 22, 70, 72n37, 73, 74, 128, 152n100, 175, 235, 263, 264, 265, 298, 299, 300

# INDEX OF SUBJECTS

city gate. *See* gate

clan, 46, 125–26, 127–28, 176, 242, 266

David: continuity of, from patriarchal period, 306; dynasty, covenant, 20, 27, 28, 105, 297, 306, 307; genealogy of, 9, 11, 21–22, 26, 28, 30, 52–53, 280, 295, 300, 305; name of, 304; receiving divine providence, 25, 26–27, 28, 31; similarities of, with Ruth, 10, 24, 88, 103–7, 190, 202

elders, 211–12, 235–36, 238–39, 243–46, 263, 267, 272, 289, 291, 305n338

Elimelech, 36, 69, 71–72, 127, 240, 241–42, 263

Ephah, 165–66, 171, 217n101, 217n103

Ephrathah, Ephrathites, 24, 71, 272, 273, 295, 304

ethnicity, foreigner, 22, 47–52, 72, 119, 129, 140, 141, 150–52, 154, 181, 253–54, 264, 271, 275, 296, 297

Ezra and Nehemiah, 16, 19, 22, 120

famine, 64, 66–69, 75–76, 78, 242

favor, finding of, 125, 130–32, 147, 172. *See also* ḥesed

fertility, 36, 113, 275, 284

fields: of Bethlehem, 124, 129–30, 133, 146, 240; danger of, 163–65, 179; of Moab, 61, 66–67, 123, 240

food and drink, 40, 46, 64, 78, 110n155, 143, 149, 160–62, 180, 183, 224–25

foreigners. *See* ethnicity, foreigner; Moab, Moabite identity

gate, 211, 236–37, 238, 257, 260, 263, 267–68

gender mismatch, 80, 81, 82, 84, 109, 235

genealogy, of Jesus Christ, 11n37, 52–53, 300n303, 301–2

Gezer calendar, 121, 191n13, 238n14

gleaning, 32, 46, 56, 124, 130–31, 142, 144, 163–67

God: as cosmic ruler (*see* theology: God's sovereignty); as covenant God, 35, 46, 55, 58–59, 78, 100n117, 114 (*see also* theology: covenant); and foreigners, 35, 52, 54, 56, 183, 307 (*see also* theology: mission); as giver of life, 41, 43, 45, 286; as king, 36, 69, 295–96; as Naomi's enemy, 7, 95, 111–18; providence of (*see* providence); as refuge, 25, 31, 157–58, 167, 181, 183, 228–29, 271, 282; as rewarder (*see* theology: reward); Shaddai, 35, 112, 113–15, 116–17, 293. *See also* theology

greetings, 38, 90n75, 134, 138–39, 145, 146n65

harvest, 5, 32, 121, 123, 146, 168, 178, 180, 184, 188, 191, 242

Hebrew, dual forms, 80, 81, 198

ḥesed, 42–44, 87–88, 157, 162, 175, 288, 296, 297

Hezron, 301–2

honor-shame culture, 6–8, 51, 67–68, 69, 70, 71, 75, 88, 90, 91, 97–98, 100, 102–3, 107, 112, 118–19, 122, 127, 130, 131, 158–59, 163, 182, 190, 193, 195, 201, 202, 206, 211–14, 219, 222, 224, 233, 238, 256, 260, 272, 273, 275, 276–77, 300, 303

*inclusio*, 119, 121, 170, 215, 221, 273

Israelite-Moabite relations. *See* Moab, Moabite identity

Ittai the Gittite, 27, 106–7

Jesse, 66, 298, 301, 304

Job, 10, 76, 113–15, 118, 291, 293

Joseph Story (Gen. 37–50), 10, 14, 72n33, 114, 150n90, 159, 182, 192–93, 301

## INDEX OF SUBJECTS

Josiah, 14, 17, 20

Judah (patriarch), 10–11, 25–26, 53n185, 93, 190, 192n20, 194, 219, 258, 273–75, 288n247, 294, 301, 303, 305

judges: role of, 62; time of, 10, 11, 12, 15–16, 19, 28, 43–44, 64–66, 68, 69, 130, 167

kinsman-redeemer: duty of, 21, 46–47, 127, 175–77, 205–6, 246, 250n76, 250n78; Jesus as our, 59; nearer, Mr. So-and-So, 4–5, 7, 22, 35, 37, 44, 58, 196, 210, 213–16, 236–46, 252–53, 257–58, 267. *See also* Boaz; shoe ceremony (4:7–8)

land: inheritance of, 127, 130n17, 146, 241, 250, 254–56, 283n230; redemption of, 46–47, 56, 57–59, 176, 196, 197, 213, 214–16, 233–37, 240, 242–46, 249–52, 256–58, 260–62, 268–69, 307

Leah, 25, 208, 235, 255, 270–71, 275–76, 283

legal process, procedure, 11, 13, 45–48, 165, 167, 232–33, 235, 237, 239, 243, 247n56, 257–59, 263, 267, 270, 289n258, 305n338

levirate marriage. *See* marriage: levirate

literary devices: ambiguity, 10, 39, 116, 174, 190, 202, 203, 264n150, 286n240; dialogues, 10, 84–85, 109–10, 125, 160, 170, 231, 232, 236, 277; flashbacks, 2; rhyming words, 70, 94, 131, 238, 300, 302; suggestive language, 72, 126, 190–94, 215, 226; summaries, 2, 65, 109, 119, 123, 132, 180, 220, 222, 223; surprises, 71, 110, 133, 137, 149, 152, 168, 171, 197, 202–4, 233, 240, 245, 279; understatement, 38

literary structure, 2–3, 5–6, 19, 24n110, 36, 39, 64, 74, 76, 81, 84, 85, 86, 89, 91, 99–100, 109, 111, 114, 115, 119, 123, 125, 128, 129, 137, 144, 145, 162–63, 165, 169–70, 173, 186, 213–14, 220, 223, 235, 236, 239, 256, 267, 270, 277, 278–79, 280, 292, 298. *See also* chiasm

Mahlon, 70, 72n37, 73, 74, 206, 251, 253, 263, 264–67, 269, 273, 283, 291, 292, 303–4

marriage: as act of kindness, 209; anti-marriage, 22, 261; and change of status, 187–88, 282 (*see also* honorshame culture); comparison of, with Isaac and Rebekah, 281; consent, 281, 290n259; intermarriage, 19, 20n88, 22, 26, 27, 46, 47–48, 50, 51, 72–74, 96, 261, 264, 274, 306; levirate, 21, 196, 214, 250–51, 255, 257, 268, 292; marriageable age, eligibility for, 139, 206, 218; redemption as result of, 57–59, 176, 190, 214, 215, 216, 249, 265; remarriage, 42, 51, 75, 95, 196; rest as result of, 194, 207, 273 (*see also* rest); ritual, 280; Ruth's proposal of, 32, 40, 192–93, 195, 205, 210, 215–17, 288

midrash, 21, 32, 35, 47n174, 106, 110n155, 198, 199, 209n70, 219n109, 222n118, 225n128, 253n98, 261n140, 282n220

Moab, Moabite identity: customs of, 86–87; and David, 11, 19–20, 21, 24; deity and religion of, 67, 78, 98n110, 99; difficulty living in Israel, 93, 163, 209, 261; land of, 2, 62–64, 66–68; as Naomi's residence, 73–74; negative portrayal of, 47–48, 67, 69, 129, 163; positive portrayal of, 13, 22, 307; references in the Torah, 47–48,

317

## INDEX OF SUBJECTS

120, 129, 167, 264, 274, 306; relationship of, to Israel, 65n5, 67, 149, 167; as Ruth's description, 48–52, 53, 119, 129, 140–41, 151, 155, 157, 176–77, 204, 253–54, 264, 271, 297; Ruth's rejection of, 44, 50, 103, 105, 154 (*see also* Ruth: as "convert"). *See also* ethnicity, foreigner

Nahshon, 283, 299, 300, 302
name, Hebrew concept of, 69–71, 112–13, 238, 249–51, 266–68, 273, 274, 286
naming, 279–80, 284, 291–94, 295
Naomi: as central character, 1, 4–7, 72, 77, 125, 128, 279; covenant of, with Ruth, 104–6; and dealing with shame, 118–19 (*see also* honor-shame culture); farewell speech of, 86–90, 91–96, 98–99, 100; as honored ancestress, 233, 296, 300; as mother-in-law, family matriarch, 73, 92, 95–96, 131, 148, 178–80, 187; motivation of, 187–88, 194–95; name of, 70, 109, 112–13, 116–17; as nanny, 290–93; relation of, to Boaz, 124, 126, 175–76, 188; return of, 77–78, 84–86, 107, 110–12, 119–21; reversal of fortune of, 5–7, 171–75, 224–25, 285–87, 292–94, 296; scheme of, 186, 188–95, 196, 219, 221–23, 226, 229; troubles of, 74–77, 93–94, 95, 109, 112–18, 126

oaths, 35, 48, 50, 85, 103–7, 215, 267
Obed: as blessing to Naomi and Ruth, 43, 45, 58, 273, 295–96, 302; genealogical relations, 9, 23, 233, 303–5; name of, 277, 292–95
old Latin version, 35, 82, 136, 169, 185, 235, 299
Orpah, 4, 72–73, 89–91, 96–98
overseer, 129, 139–46, 149–50, 163, 177

patriarchal motifs, 86, 117, 139, 148, 156, 276, 289
patriarchal narratives, 17, 24–26, 28, 35, 67, 69, 77, 102, 113, 114, 255n107, 294, 301
Perez, 4, 24, 25, 26, 52, 55, 234, 273–74, 294, 298, 300, 301, 305, 306
priestly source, 13, 298, 301n306
providence, 25–29, 36–41, 42, 43, 44, 45, 57, 89, 121, 132–33, 138, 157, 168, 188, 280, 305–6

Qumran manuscripts, 18, 29, 34

rabbinic tradition, 31, 32, 47n174, 82, 106n144, 219n109, 302n318
Rachel, 25, 31, 49n179, 71, 148, 208, 235, 255n107, 270–71, 272n184, 274, 275, 276, 281, 283
Ram, 299, 302
Rashi, 106n144, 141n46, 201n38, 205n59, 206n62, 213n90, 253n98, 254n105
reapers, reaping, 123, 139, 141n49, 145, 146, 161, 164
repetition, of words and statements, 48, 50, 76, 78, 91, 92, 93, 99, 105, 112, 115, 125, 129, 130, 133, 140, 146, 148, 172, 173, 175, 190, 200n37, 223n121, 227, 228, 235, 256n113, 259, 263, 267, 268, 269, 270, 273, 290, 292
rest, 25, 29, 39, 41, 42, 43, 81, 88–89, 90, 101, 120–21, 122, 143n57, 150, 182, 183, 187–88, 194, 206, 215, 216, 226, 227–29, 265, 266
Ruth: and Abraham, 54–55, 101; as "convert," 53, 99–102, 103, 105, 106n144, 120, 157; courage of, 91, 210; encounters of, with Boaz, 133–65, 204–17; ethnicity of (*see* Moab, Moabite identity: as Ruth's description); and execution of Naomi's plan, 197–202, 204–7; as honored

318

# INDEX OF SUBJECTS

ancestress, 296, 305–7; industrious action of, 31, 226; kindness and loyalty of, to Naomi, 42–43, 87–88, 96–99, 102–6, 107, 158; marriage proposal of (*see* marriage: Ruth's proposal of); as mediator, 184; as model, 9, 21, 31, 48, 88n71, 154, 211–12; name of, 73; possible barrenness of, 36, 74, 76, 255, 283–84; rise of, in status, 51, 211–12, 280–81, 282, 296 (*see also* honor-shame culture); as wife of Mahlon, 250–51, 264–66, 283; as "worthy woman," 27, 31–32, 52, 126, 211–13, 216, 226

Ruth, book of: and dating of, 12–20, 21n89, 83, 258; and David, 14–16, 19–20

Salmon, 34, 283n226, 299, 300, 302

Septuagint (LXX), 27n119, 30, 32, 33, 34n149, 35, 62, 63, 64, 80, 81, 82, 83, 84, 108, 109, 113, 116n179, 124, 125, 128n11, 134, 135, 136, 143n57, 146, 147n72, 161, 169, 172, 174, 185, 191n16, 198, 199, 203n49, 213n88, 220, 229n134, 234, 235, 248n66, 258n122, 261n140, 278, 294, 299

Shaddai. *See* God: Shaddai

shoe ceremony (4:7–8), 12, 13n43, 19, 34, 235, 257–62, 273n187

Solomon, 14, 16, 20, 27, 28, 31, 300n301

Syriac version, 34, 35, 62, 63, 73n40, 80, 81, 82, 83, 84, 108, 116n179, 125, 134, 135, 136, 148n74, 168, 169, 172, 185, 198, 199, 213n88, 220, 234, 235, 278, 299

Talmud, 12, 29, 30, 65, 240n25, 241n28

Tamar, 10, 12, 17n73, 25, 53, 93, 190,

192, 258, 259, 273, 274, 275, 276, 288n247

Targum to Ruth, 35, 63, 80, 81, 82, 83, 84, 106n144, 109, 121, 124, 125, 134, 135, 136, 139, 148, 169, 172, 185, 189, 191, 198, 199, 211n78, 217n100, 219n109, 220, 227, 234, 235, 248n66, 253n95, 258, 271n177, 278, 299

theology: and book's purpose, 20–29, 55; covenant, 27, 44–45, 48, 58–59, 75–76, 78, 100n117, 104–6, 154, 181, 208, 288, 304–5, 307; divine-human interaction, 39–41, 42, 43, 89, 188, 208, 225, 265, 276, 280; God's kindness, blessing, 36–39, 42–45, 55–58, 87–88, 157–58, 165, 167, 173–74, 197, 229–30, 269, 285–86; God's sovereignty, 35, 45, 57, 69, 76, 88, 113–14, 132, 215; mission, 53–57, 183, 272n181; redemption, 57–59, 167, 225, 269; reward, 21, 25, 38, 40, 43–44, 76, 88, 106, 154–56, 158, 162, 165, 167, 205, 282. *See also* God

threshing floor, 53, 141, 185, 189, 190, 197–219, 226, 246, 251

*toledoth* formula, 26

towns' layout, 149, 189, 211, 236–38

Ugaritic, 70n26, 70n28, 72n38, 161

wages of workers, 156

weight and measures, 166, 171, 217

widow, widowhood, 47, 48, 75, 86, 89, 103, 130, 139, 190, 240–41, 260

winnowing, 189–91

wordplay, 40, 116, 122n203, 128, 150, 153, 156, 160, 200, 229, 235, 236, 265, 267, 271, 282, 295n284

young women, 75, 95, 139, 140, 160, 204, 207, 275

# Index of Scripture and Other Ancient Texts

**OLD TESTAMENT**

**Genesis**

| | | | | | |
|---|---|---|---|---|---|
| 1:28 | 182 | 9:21 | 191 | 13:9 | 104 |
| 2:2 | 285 | 10:1 | 26, 301, 306 | 13:11 | 104 |
| 2:2–3 | 227 | 10:21 | 292 | 13:14 | 104, 136 |
| 2:4 | 26, 301, 305, 306 | 10:25 | 72, 292 | 13:15 | 274 |
| 2:10–14 | 69 | 11 | 306 | 13:16 | 274 |
| 2:23 | 97 | 11:3 | 199 | 14 | 26 |
| 2:23–24 | 97 | 11:7 | 77, 199 | 14:1 | 65 |
| 2:24 | 96, 97, 100, 153 | 11:8 | 84 | 14:20 | 278 |
| 3 | 76 | 11:10 | 26, 301 | 14:23 | 258 |
| 3:1 | 302 | 11:26–32 | 276 | 15:1–20 | 284 |
| 3:6 | 117 | 11:27 | 26, 301 | 15:7 | 67 |
| 3:15 | 275 | 11:27–32 | 10, 305, 306 | 15:7–17 | 104 |
| 3:23–24 | 182 | 11:28 | 153 | 15:13 | 300 |
| 4:1 | 283 | 11:30 | 283, 306 | 15:15 | 102, 266 |
| 4:1–2 | 279 | 12:1 | 44, 67, 153, 182 | 15:19–21 | 289, 301 |
| 4:17 | 283 | 12:1–3 | 54, 72, 76, 101 | 16 | 17 |
| 4:20–21 | 70 | 12:1–5 | 26 | 16–17 | 26 |
| 4:20–22 | 69 | 12:1–7 | 307 | 16:1–3 | 74, 257 |
| 4:26 | 292 | 12:2 | 284 | 16:2 | 271 |
| 5 | 301, 306 | 12:3 | 47, 53 | 16:4 | 283 |
| 5:1 | 306 | 12:4–5 | 107 | 16:8 | 108, 171 |
| 6:8 | 130 | 12:7 | 67, 72, 274, 284 | 16:10 | 275 |
| 6:9 | 26, 301, 306 | 12:10 | 26 | 16:15 | 279 |
| 6:13 | 252 | 12:10–20 | 67 | 17:1 | 113, 114 |
| 7:5 | 201 | 12:10–13:1 | 24 | 17:1–14 | 284 |
| 7:23 | 72 | 12:11 | 31 | 17:3 | 149 |
| 9:20–27 | 7, 193 | 12:14 | 31 | 17:5 | 70 |
| | | 12:17 | 26 | 17:8 | 67 |
| | | 12:19 | 210 | 17:10 | 151 |
| | | 13:8 | 240 | 17:17 | 70, 199 |

320

## INDEX OF SCRIPTURE AND OTHER ANCIENT TEXTS

| | | | | | |
|---|---|---|---|---|---|
| 17:19 | 70 | 24:15–21 | 174 | 27:33 | 172 |
| 18:1–8 | 161 | 24:16 | 140 | 27:34 | 112 |
| 18:5 | 161 | 24:19 | 178 | 27:36 | 145 |
| 18:7 | 139 | 24:23 | 222 | 27:41 | 199 |
| 18:11 | 84 | 24:26–27 | 132 | 27:46–28:5 | 117 |
| 18:12 | 70 | 24:27 | 174, 278 | 28:3 | 113 |
| 18:21 | 124 | 24:28 | 26, 87, 126 | 28:3–4 | 114 |
| 18:27 | 150 | 24:30 | 108 | 28:5 | 275 |
| 19 | 17 | 24:33 | 178 | 28:9 | 280 |
| 19:2 | 101 | 24:39 | 208 | 28:11 | 101, 191 |
| 19:17 | 146 | 24:47 | 222 | 28:13–14 | 274, 284 |
| 19:18 | 94 | 24:51 | 281 | 28:13–15 | 67 |
| 19:26 | 146 | 24:58 | 281 | 28:18 | 191 |
| 19:30–38 | 67, 120 | 24:60 | 208, 275 | 28:20–21 | 275 |
| 19:37–38 | 191, 192, 194, | 24:61 | 139, 208 | 29 | 73 |
| | 264, 280 | 24:67 | 280, 281 | 29:1 | 275 |
| 20 | 26 | 25:8 | 102, 266 | 29:1–12 | 148 |
| 20:1–18 | 63 | 25:8–10 | 266 | 29:11 | 81 |
| 20:3 | 26 | 25:12 | 26, 301 | 29:14 | 97 |
| 20:6 | 26, 148 | 25:19 | 26, 301 | 29:15 | 156 |
| 20:7 | 286 | 25:19–26 | 10, 305, 306 | 29:17 | 31 |
| 20:11 | 199 | 25:20 | 279, 280 | 29:18 | 281 |
| 21:1 | 63, 78, 274, 283 | 25:21 | 26, 274, 283, 306 | 29:20 | 281 |
| 21:1–2 | 26 | 25:26 | 217 | 29:21 | 199 |
| 21:2 | 283 | 25:28 | 288 | 29:23 | 282 |
| 21:21 | 73, 77, 193 | 26 | 26 | 29:31 | 26, 36, 280, 283 |
| 21:22–34 | 26, 63 | 26:1 | 26, 67 | 29:32 | 283 |
| 22:3 | 139 | 26:3 | 274 | 29:33 | 283 |
| 22:15–18 | 284 | 26:3–4 | 67 | 29:34 | 283 |
| 22:21 | 70 | 26:4 | 274 | 29:34–35 | 36 |
| 23 | 26 | 26:6–16 | 63 | 29:35 | 283 |
| 23:4–18 | 243 | 26:7–11 | 26 | 30 | 26, 270 |
| 23:8 | 100 | 26:7–17 | 67 | 30:1 | 199 |
| 24 | 10, 26, 73, 193 | 26:9 | 199 | 30:1–6 | 257 |
| 24:5 | 208 | 26:11 | 148 | 30:3 | 271 |
| 24:7 | 153 | 26:16 | 136 | 30:4 | 282 |
| 24:8 | 208 | 26:24 | 210, 274, 284 | 30:5 | 283 |
| 24:11 | 149 | 26:29 | 148 | 30:7 | 283 |
| 24:11–18 | 148 | 27:1–40 | 221 | 30:9–13 | 257 |
| 24:12 | 132 | 27:8 | 201 | 30:15–16 | 192 |
| 24:12–27 | 132 | 27:18 | 221 | 30:17 | 26, 283 |
| 24:13 | 149 | 27:18–19 | 222 | 30:19 | 36, 283 |
| 24:15 | 137 | 27:32–33 | 203 | 30:22 | 26, 36, 274, 283 |

# INDEX OF SCRIPTURE AND OTHER ANCIENT TEXTS

| | | | | | |
|---|---|---|---|---|---|
| 30:23 | 26, 283 | 37:28 | 142 | 43:25 | 284 |
| 30:27 | 275 | 37:30 | 142 | 44:14 | 149 |
| 30:27–28 | 175 | 37:35 | 159 | 44:18 | 158 |
| 31:2 | 136 | 38 | 10, 17, 24, 26, 52, | 44:22 | 100 |
| 31:7 | 156 | | 93, 192, 193, 219, | 45:9 | 142 |
| 31:9 | 80 | | 251, 274, 301, 306 | 45:15 | 81 |
| 31:13 | 153, 275 | 38:1–6 | 275 | 46:2–4 | 67 |
| 31:15 | 150, 252 | 38:2 | 279, 282 | 46:3 | 76 |
| 31:19 | 275 | 38:2–3 | 283 | 46:8–12 | 300 |
| 31:26 | 136 | 38:3 | 283 | 46:12 | 273, 301, 303 |
| 31:28 | 96 | 38:4 | 36, 283 | 46:21 | 70 |
| 31:30 | 83, 98 | 38:8 | 98, 251 | 46:22 | 292 |
| 31:40 | 203 | 38:9 | 253 | 46:27 | 301 |
| 31:41 | 156 | 38:10 | 76 | 47:4 | 67 |
| 31:51–54 | 161 | 38:11 | 86, 126, 226, | 47:12 | 287 |
| 32:1[31:55] | 208 | | 250 | 47:15 | 199 |
| 32:5[4] | 158 | 38:13–16 | 53 | 47:19–20 | 244 |
| 32:6[5] | 130 | 38:14 | 190 | 47:29–31 | 72 |
| 32:11[10] | 159 | 38:16 | 199 | 48 | 26 |
| 32:18–19[17–18] | 140 | 38:18 | 283 | 48:3–4 | 113 |
| 33:4 | 90, 96 | 38:19 | 190 | 48:6 | 249 |
| 33:10 | 94 | 38:24 | 288 | 48:7 | 71, 272 |
| 33:17 | 143 | 38:24–26 | 93 | 48:10 | 90 |
| 33:19 | 26, 125, 243, | 38:25 | 139 | 48:12 | 149 |
| | 244, 251 | 38:26 | 274 | 48:14 | 150 |
| 34 | 8, 26, 193 | 38:27–30 | 274 | 48:16 | 273 |
| 34:3 | 96, 97, 159, 281 | 38:29 | 286, 294 | 49:17 | 302 |
| 34:12 | 224 | 38:30 | 294 | 49:25 | 113, 114 |
| 35:2 | 151 | 39:1 | 251 | 49:28–33 | 266 |
| 35:11 | 113 | 39:4 | 130 | 49:29 | 201 |
| 35:11–12 | 114 | 39:6 | 193 | 49:29–33 | 72 |
| 35:16–19 | 294 | 39:6–18 | 192 | 50:1 | 81 |
| 35:17 | 210 | 39:8–9 | 193 | 50:6 | 125 |
| 35:17–18 | 294 | 39:21 | 130 | 50:12–14 | 266 |
| 35:18–20 | 71 | 41:12 | 139 | 50:13 | 102 |
| 35:19 | 71, 272 | 41:34 | 80 | 50:15–21 | 159 |
| 35:26 | 292 | 41:39–41 | 175 | 50:16 | 201 |
| 35:29 | 266 | 41:45 | 26 | 50:20 | 41, 76 |
| 36:1 | 26, 301 | 41:49 | 84 | 50:21 | 159, 287 |
| 36:9 | 26, 301 | 41:50 | 292 | 50:24 | 63, 78, 284 |
| 36:26 | 70 | 41:50–52 | 26, 72 | 50:24–26 | 72, 102 |
| 37–50 | 10 | 42:7 | 150 | 50:25 | 63, 78 |
| 37:2 | 26, 301, 306 | 43:14 | 114 | | |

322

# Index of Scripture and Other Ancient Texts

**Exodus**

| | | | | | |
|---|---|---|---|---|---|
| 1:10 | 199 | 12:40 | 300 | 11:44–45 | 46 |
| 1:15–20 | 284 | 12:48 | 151 | 16:5 | 247 |
| 2:1 | 279, 280 | 13:9 | 95 | 18:6–19 | 191 |
| 2:1–10 | 279 | 15:13 | 58 | 18:17 | 274 |
| 2:2 | 283 | 15:13–16 | 252 | 19:3 | 107 |
| 2:5 | 139 | 16:16 | 166 | 19:9 | 124 |
| 2:7 | 290 | 16:36 | 166 | 19:9–10 | 46, 130, 141, |
| 2:10 | 291 | 18:3–4 | 72 | | 151, 159, 165 |
| 2:11 | 240 | 18:10 | 278 | 19:18 | 288 |
| 2:13 | 89, 137 | 19:1 | 32 | 19:19 | 146 |
| 2:15–22 | 148 | 19:4–6 | 55 | 19:32 | 107 |
| 2:17 | 80 | 19:6 | 55 | 19:34 | 288 |
| 2:20–21 | 193 | 19:16 | 203 | 20:3 | 249 |
| 2:21 | 193 | 20:5 | 284 | 20:11 | 191, 192 |
| 3:3 | 124, 199 | 20:10 | 151 | 20:12 | 192 |
| 3:5 | 258 | 20:12 | 7, 107 | 20:13 | 192 |
| 3:21 | 225 | 20:16 | 116 | 20:17–21 | 191, 193 |
| 3:22 | 278 | 20:26 | 191 | 20:18 | 192 |
| 4:3 | 302 | 21:6 | 83 | 20:20 | 192 |
| 4:4 | 217 | 21:8 | 150 | 21:2–3 | 175 |
| 4:18 | 124 | 21:20 | 160 | 22:11 | 244 |
| 4:22–23 | 58 | 22:16 | 192 | 22:12 | 82 |
| 4:25 | 192 | 22:16[17] | 224 | 22:13 | 86, 126, 250, 275 |
| 4:31 | 284 | 22:25–26[26–27] | 185 | 23:10 | 141 |
| 5:3 | 100 | 23:16 | 32 | 23:10–11 | 121 |
| 5:5 | 285 | 24:1–11 | 161 | 23:11 | 141 |
| 5:8 | 136 | 31:11 | 201 | 23:12 | 141 |
| 5:22 | 117 | 32:8 | 73 | 23:15 | 141 |
| 6:3 | 114 | 32:24 | 139 | 23:15–16 | 32 |
| 6:6–7 | 58 | 32:27 | 175 | 23:15–21 | 32 |
| 6:23 | 302 | 32:32 | 81 | 23:22 | 32, 124, 130, 141, |
| 9:1–3 | 95 | 32:34 | 63, 78 | | 151, 165 |
| 9:22–25 | 66 | 33:12 | 130 | 25 | 249, 251, 254 |
| 11:2 | 73 | 33:19 | 272 | 25:13–16 | 241 |
| 11:8 | 204 | 34:6 | 58, 269 | 25:14–15 | 247, 261 |
| 12:4 | 278 | 34:6–7 | 43, 87 | 25:23 | 130, 241 |
| 12:11 | 86 | 34:7 | 58, 269 | 25:23–24 | 249 |
| 12:12 | 98 | 34:22 | 32 | 25:23–28 | 127, 241, 260 |
| 12:15 | 285 | 34:28 | 71 | 25:23–55 | 240, 242 |
| 12:29 | 202 | | | 25:25 | 175, 240 |
| 12:35–36 | 225 | **Leviticus** | | 25:25–30 | 46, 176 |
| 12:38 | 86, 272 | 2:14 | 162 | 25:39–42 | 241 |
| | | 10:4 | 240 | 25:42 | 167 |

## INDEX OF SCRIPTURE AND OTHER ANCIENT TEXTS

| | | | | | |
|---|---|---|---|---|---|
| 25:44 | 251 | 23:19 | 267 | 4:34 | 95 |
| 25:47–54 | 241 | 24:4 | 77, 113, 114 | 4:35 | 99 |
| 25:47–55 | 46, 176 | 24:16 | 113, 114 | 4:39 | 99 |
| 25:48–49 | 127, 213 | 25 | 194, 264 | 4:40 | 187 |
| 25:48b–49 | 46 | 25:1–3 | 67 | 5:9–10 | 284 |
| 25:55 | 167 | 25:1–18 | 151 | 5:16 | 107, 187 |
| 26:14–39 | 104 | 25:5–6 | 138 | 5:20 | 116 |
| 26:18–20 | 75 | 25:6 | 240 | 5:33 | 187 |
| 26:19–20 | 45 | 26:20–21 | 273 | 6:1 | 62 |
| 26:36 | 72 | 26:21 | 301 | 6:3 | 187 |
| 26:39 | 72 | 27 | 249 | 6:5 | 288 |
| 27:10 | 257 | 27:1–11 | 283 | 6:11 | 162 |
| 27:20 | 241 | 27:1–12 | 294 | 6:14 | 208 |
| 27:24 | 241 | 27:4 | 249, 266 | 7:1 | 48, 289 |
| 27:33 | 257 | 27:8–11 | 241 | 7:1–4 | 306 |
| | | 27:11 | 127, 175 | 7:3–4 | 47, 76 |
| **Numbers** | | 27:13 | 266 | 7:4 | 48 |
| 1:7 | 302 | 30:1–2 | 267 | 7:7–8 | 288 |
| 2:3 | 302 | 32:2–5 | 175 | 7:9 | 48 |
| 3:1 | 26, 301 | 32:31 | 195 | 7:11–15 | 284 |
| 5:8 | 46, 176 | 32:42 | 136 | 7:14 | 172 |
| 6:3 | 161 | 33:54 | 127 | 8:10 | 162 |
| 6:24 | 139 | 35:8 | 247 | 9:6 | 73 |
| 6:24–26 | 45, 208 | 35:12 | 46, 176 | 9:13 | 73 |
| 7:12 | 302 | 35:19–27 | 46, 176 | 10:17–18 | 197 |
| 7:17 | 302 | 35:30 | 116 | 10:18 | 185, 241 |
| 10:14 | 302 | 36 | 249 | 10:19 | 167, 288 |
| 10:31 | 100 | 36:1–12 | 241, 283 | 10:20 | 96 |
| 11:7–8 | 142 | 36:1–13 | 294 | 11:8–15 | 284 |
| 11:11 | 117 | 36:6–9 | 126 | 11:15 | 162 |
| 11:12 | 290 | 36:11 | 281 | 11:22 | 96 |
| 11:20 | 112 | | | 11:24 | 258 |
| 14:18 | 284 | **Deuteronomy** | | 11:32 | 142 |
| 16:10 | 240 | 1:21 | 210 | 12:9 | 89 |
| 20:26–28 | 266 | 1:36 | 258 | 12:10 | 62, 133 |
| 21:6 | 302 | 1:41 | 201 | 13:5[4] | 208 |
| 21:29 | 99 | 2:13–15 | 95 | 13:7[6] | 290 |
| 22–24 | 67, 114 | 3:25 | 124 | 14:29 | 75 |
| 22–25 | 297 | 4:3 | 208 | 15:10 | 167 |
| 22:5 | 114 | 4:3–4 | 67, 96 | 15:12 | 241 |
| 22:22 | 139 | 4:14 | 62 | 15:12–15 | 225 |
| 22:31 | 191 | 4:27 | 72 | 15:13–15 | 167 |

324

## Index of Scripture and Other Ancient Texts

| Ref | Page | Ref | Page | Ref | Page |
|---|---|---|---|---|---|
| 15:14 | 167 | 24:19 | 141, 151 | 29:25 | 100 |
| 15:14–15 | 225 | 24:19–20 | 159 | 30:1–5 | 120 |
| 16:3 | 86 | 24:19–21 | 165, 241 | 30:6 | 120 |
| 16:9 | 180 | 24:19–22 | 46, 130, 167 | 30:20 | 96 |
| 16:9–12 | 32 | 24:20 | 165 | 31:6 | 100 |
| 16:11 | 151 | 24:22 | 167 | 31:12 | 151 |
| 16:14 | 151 | 25 | 12 | 31:16 | 151 |
| 16:16 | 32 | 25:5 | 93, 238, 250 | 31:20 | 162 |
| 16:18 | 211 | 25:5–7 | 251 | 32:3 | 272 |
| 19:1–13 | 239 | 25:5–10 | 47, 58, 93, 127, | 32:6 | 252 |
| 19:6 | 46, 176 | | 239, 240, 249, 251, | 32:11 | 157 |
| 19:11–13 | 46, 176 | | 260 | 32:16–17 | 99 |
| 19:14 | 130, 303 | 25:6 | 255, 258, 266 | 32:21 | 99 |
| 19:16 | 116 | 25:7 | 98, 211, 215, 251 | 32:37 | 157 |
| 19:18 | 116 | 25:8 | 258 | 32:39 | 95, 99 |
| 20:7 | 280 | 25:9 | 98, 258, 260, 271 | 32:50 | 266 |
| 21:1–9 | 239 | 25:10 | 258, 273 | 34:5–6 | 266 |
| 21:10–14 | 48 | 25:11–12 | 193 | | |
| 21:15 | 281 | 26:5 | 275 | **Joshua** | |
| 21:15–17 | 241 | 26:12–13 | 197, 241 | 1:1 | 65 |
| 21:16 | 281 | 26:14 | 201 | 1:2 | 62 |
| 21:18–21 | 7, 239 | 27:17 | 130, 303 | 1:3 | 258 |
| 21:19 | 235, 237, 267 | 27:20 | 191, 205 | 1:14 | 62 |
| 22:5 | 185 | 27:20–23 | 192 | 1:16 | 195 |
| 22:13–21 | 239 | 28:1–14 | 284 | 1:17 | 138 |
| 22:15 | 237 | 28:15–68 | 104 | 2 | 268, 302 |
| 22:15–16 | 211 | 28:18 | 76 | 2:1 | 53 |
| 22:20–21 | 75 | 28:20–24 | 75 | 2:2 | 189 |
| 22:25 | 192 | 28:23–24 | 45 | 2:5 | 171 |
| 23:1[22:30] | 191, 205 | 28:32 | 76 | 2:12–14 | 55 |
| 23:1–6 | 167 | 28:33 | 154 | 2:16 | 100 |
| 23:3 | 47, 306 | 28:36 | 154 | 3:1 | 101 |
| 23:3–6 | 67, 274, 297 | 28:40 | 190 | 3:4 | 136 |
| 23:4[3] | 47, 264 | 28:49 | 77 | 5:11 | 162 |
| 23:4–6 | 47 | 28:49–51 | 66 | 5:14 | 149 |
| 23:4–7[3–6] | 47 | 28:54 | 290 | 5:15 | 258 |
| 23:5[4] | 114 | 28:56 | 290 | 6:1 | 108 |
| 23:7[6] | 47 | 28:57 | 192 | 6:2–3 | 126 |
| 24:2 | 82 | 28:68 | 160 | 6:17 | 268, 302 |
| 24:17–21 | 167 | 29:11 | 149, 151 | 6:23–25 | 268, 302 |
| 24:17–22 | 197 | 29:12 | 251 | 6:25 | 53, 272 |
| 24:18 | 167 | 29:17 | 99 | 7:9 | 249, 266 |

# INDEX OF SCRIPTURE AND OTHER ANCIENT TEXTS

| | | | | | |
|---|---|---|---|---|---|
| 7:16–18 | 127 | 4:6 | 295 | 15:12 | 100, 179 |
| 9:19 | 148 | 4:10 | 204 | 16:1 | 282 |
| 9:21–27 | 149 | 4:14 | 95 | 16:3 | 202, 217 |
| 9:24 | 152 | 4:21 | 202 | 16:4 | 281 |
| 10:19 | 142 | 4:21–22 | 138 | 16:20 | 199 |
| 10:24 | 258 | 5:4 | 95 | 16:28–30 | 44 |
| 14:1–5 | 241 | 5:12 | 295 | 16:29 | 203 |
| 14:9 | 258 | 5:24 | 208 | 17–21 | 33, 41, 65, 66 |
| 19:15–16 | 66 | 5:31 | 227 | 17:1 | 62 |
| 20:1–9 | 239 | 6:3–5 | 66 | 17:6 | 24, 33, 43, 65, 68, |
| 20:4 | 237, 239 | 6:4 | 252 | | 130 |
| 21:43–45 | 182 | 6:11 | 165 | 17:7 | 66 |
| 21:45 | 227 | 6:12 | 126, 134, 138 | 17:8–9 | 27 |
| 22:3 | 100 | 6:15 | 127 | 17:9 | 66 |
| 22:5 | 96 | 6:23 | 138 | 18:1 | 24, 33, 65, 68 |
| 22:7 | 177 | 6:27 | 239 | 18:2 | 101 |
| 22:17 | 67 | 7:10 | 139 | 18:7 | 227 |
| 22:25 | 285 | 8:5 | 204 | 18:14–20 | 142 |
| 23:12 | 96 | 8:21 | 100, 179 | 18:20 | 202 |
| 23:14 | 227 | 8:22–23 | 69 | 18:24 | 83, 98 |
| 24:20 | 100, 116, 151 | 8:25 | 217 | 18:25 | 179 |
| 24:22 | 263, 270 | 8:31–9:57 | 63 | 18:27 | 227 |
| 24:23 | 151 | 9:2 | 97 | 19:1 | 24, 33, 65, 66, 68 |
| 24:27 | 268 | 9:15 | 157 | 19:1–2 | 27 |
| 24:32 | 102, 125, 244 | 9:18 | 204 | 19:3 | 139, 159 |
| | | 10:6 | 67, 100 | 19:4 | 101 |
| **Judges** | | 10:7 | 241 | 19:5 | 161 |
| 1 | 65 | 10:16 | 151 | 19:10–12 | 66 |
| 1:1 | 65 | 11:1 | 126 | 19:10–30 | 66 |
| 1:15 | 199 | 11:24 | 98 | 19:12 | 151 |
| 2:15 | 95 | 12:8 | 66 | 19:13 | 101 |
| 2:16 | 62 | 12:8–10 | 65 | 19:15 | 101 |
| 3:2 | 257 | 12:10 | 66 | 19:18 | 66 |
| 3:8 | 241 | 13 | 26, 274, 283 | 19:19 | 204 |
| 3:11 | 227 | 13:2 | 283 | 19:23 | 94 |
| 3:12–30 | 67, 264 | 13:3 | 283 | 20:4 | 72 |
| 3:15–29 | 10 | 13:24 | 279 | 21 | 28 |
| 3:22 | 258 | 14:1–3 | 73 | 21:2 | 90 |
| 3:24 | 192 | 14:2–3 | 193 | 21:23 | 72 |
| 3:29 | 67 | 14:3 | 240 | 21:25 | 24, 33, 43, 65, 68, |
| 3:30 | 227 | 14:10 | 193 | | 130 |
| 4:2 | 241 | 14:15–20 | 117 | | |
| 4:4–5 | 62 | 15:1 | 282 | | |

326

## INDEX OF SCRIPTURE AND OTHER ANCIENT TEXTS

**Ruth**

| | |
|---|---|
| 1 | 40 |
| 1:1 | 3, 4, 11, 12, 13, 15, 26, 27, 61, 62, 63, 65–69, 71, 73, 74, 77, 78, 106, 107, 109, 113, 129, 131, 136, 179, 232, 271 |
| 1:1 (LXX) | 62 |
| 1:1–2 | 6, 173 |
| 1:1–3a | 232 |
| 1:1–4 | 66 |
| 1:1–5 | 3, 19, 24, 76, 79, 267, 296 |
| 1:1–6 | 34, 61, 62–78, 231, 298 |
| 1:1–12 | 34 |
| 1:1–22 | 61–122 |
| 1:1b–2 | 109 |
| 1:2 | 11, 24, 62, 63, 66, 67, 69–71, 74, 78, 79, 85, 108, 113, 127, 129, 136, 263, 264, 273, 293, 295, 304 |
| 1:2 (LXX) | 63 |
| 1:2–3 | 74 |
| 1:2–5 | 74 |
| 1:3 | 4, 63, 71–72, 74, 106, 107, 175, 263 |
| 1:3–4 | 48 |
| 1:3–5 | 52, 263, 279 |
| 1:3–22 | 6 |
| 1:3b–3:18 | 232 |
| 1:4 | 11, 63, 66, 69, 72–74, 77, 96, 129, 226, 264, 265, 271, 298 |
| 1:4–5 | 4, 76, 96, 255, 269, 289 |
| 1:5 | 26, 63, 74–77, 103, 107, 152, 153, 171, |

| | |
|---|---|
| | 175, 263, 264, 271, 290, 301 |
| 1:6 | 2, 4, 5, 35, 36, 37, 38, 39, 42, 43, 45, 50, 63, 66, 67, 77–78, 79, 85, 88, 89, 92, 108, 113, 115, 119, 121, 129, 138, 168, 228, 231, 280, 283, 284, 288, 297 |
| 1:6 (LXX) | 63–64 |
| 1:6–8 | 1, 286 |
| 1:6a | 62 |
| 1:6b | 63 |
| 1:7 | 50, 63, 67, 77, 79, 84, 85–86, 92, 107, 108, 109, 119, 136, 288 |
| 1:7–19a | 61, 79–107, 231, 277 |
| 1:8 | 26, 27, 32, 39, 42, 43, 50, 63, 75, 77, 80, 82, 86–88, 89, 92, 98, 99, 101, 107, 108, 109, 114, 119, 126, 136, 138, 161, 174, 175, 200, 263, 271, 285, 288 |
| 1:8 (LXX) | 80, 229 |
| 1:8–9 | 10, 35, 37, 38, 45, 51, 57, 81, 89, 92, 95, 96, 97, 156, 172, 180, 209, 215, 228, 265, 267 |
| 1:8–9a | 84 |
| 1:8–13 | 260 |
| 1:8–15 | 186, 195 |
| 1:8–18 | 27, 79 |
| 1:9 | 25, 39, 41, 42, 75, 80, 83, 86, 87, 88–90, 96, 101, 114, 142, 150, 176, |

| | |
|---|---|
| | 187, 207, 225, 263, 270, 271, 277, 282 |
| 1:9 (LXX) | 81 |
| 1:9–13 | 209 |
| 1:9b | 84 |
| 1:10 | 77, 83, 90–91, 92, 100, 108, 119, 136, 154 |
| 1:10–12 | 286 |
| 1:10–13 | 84 |
| 1:11 | 50, 74, 77, 80, 91–93, 98, 99, 101, 108, 116, 119, 131, 136, 187 |
| 1:11–12 | 228 |
| 1:11–13 | 4, 45, 47, 96, 97, 98, 113, 153, 180, 188, 196, 251, 277, 293 |
| 1:12 | 35, 50, 74, 77, 82, 92, 93–94, 95, 98, 99, 101, 108, 119, 128, 131, 136, 153, 187, 214, 263, 287 |
| 1:12 (LXX) | 82 |
| 1:12–13 | 289 |
| 1:12–13a | 91, 93 |
| 1:12–15 | 34 |
| 1:13 | 35, 37, 39, 45, 50, 57, 80, 85, 91, 92, 93, 94–96, 98, 104, 114, 117, 119, 131, 138, 172, 178, 187, 277, 297 |
| 1:13 (LXX) | 82, 83 |
| 1:13b | 92, 94 |
| 1:14 | 4, 50, 83, 84, 90, 96–98, 129, 135, 136, 146, 263, 277 |
| 1:14 (LXX) | 83 |
| 1:14–17 | 250 |
| 1:15 | 50, 73, 77, 83, 98–99, 102, 105, |

327

## INDEX OF SCRIPTURE AND OTHER ANCIENT TEXTS

108, 119, 137, 180, 208
1:15 (LXX) 83–84
1:15–16 147, 286
1:15–18 84
1:16 19, 35, 77, 84, 97, 99–102, 108, 119, 120, 128, 129, 136, 153, 154, 164, 174, 179, 214, 228, 271
1:16–17 22, 26, 27, 31, 43, 44, 48, 50, 83, 104, 120, 122, 128, 129, 133, 138, 142, 151, 157, 158, 195, 224, 264, 288, 296, 297
1:16–18 115, 153, 277
1:17 11, 35, 48, 53, 80, 97, 100, 102–6, 156, 266
1:18 63, 106–7, 136
1:18 (LXX) 84
1:18–19 153
1:19 3, 4, 61, 63, 80, 115, 121, 136, 178, 209, 210, 257, 291
1:19–20 128, 180
1:19–21 152, 223, 293
1:19–22 171, 225, 237
1:19a 79, 84, 107, 108, 109
1:19b 84, 109, 110
1:19b–c 110–11
1:19b–20 108–9
1:19b–22 61, 108–22, 231, 235
1:19c–21 109
1:20 111–15, 277
1:20–21 2, 31, 35, 39, 45, 70, 104, 117, 168, 172, 186, 285, 293, 297

1:20–21a 263
1:21 1, 23, 35, 37, 41, 77, 108, 109, 111, 115–19, 133, 135, 136, 139, 224, 235, 243, 286, 293
1:21 (LXX) 116
1:21–22 176, 286
1:21b 263
1:22 32, 38, 45, 49, 50, 53, 62, 63, 66, 67, 77, 80, 81, 108, 109, 110, 112, 113, 119–22, 123, 129, 131, 136, 138, 140, 141, 168, 177, 180, 253, 271, 288
2 40
2:1 1, 37, 50, 69, 71, 123, 125–28, 131, 133, 138, 153, 154, 155, 160, 168, 173, 175, 184, 188, 194, 205, 212, 214, 219, 240, 267, 272, 282, 303
2:1 (LXX) 124, 128
2:1–2 132, 186
2:1–3 4, 123–33, 184, 220, 221, 228
2:1–15 65
2:1–23 123–83
2:1–3:18 7
2:2 4, 31, 34, 39, 49, 50, 53, 67, 113, 119, 125, 128–32, 133, 136, 138, 140, 141, 142, 145, 146, 147, 150, 158, 168, 172, 177, 180, 187, 207, 209, 228, 253, 271
2:2 (LXX) 124
2:2–3 123, 142

2:2a 125
2:2b–3a 125
2:3 37, 67, 71, 113, 127, 129, 130, 132–33, 136, 138, 139, 141, 142, 147, 155, 160, 173, 177
2:3 (LXX) 125
2:3a 125
2:3b 125
2:4 35, 37, 38, 45, 134, 136, 137–39, 146, 147, 207, 208, 215, 237
2:4 (LXX) 134
2:4–17 4, 123, 133–67, 168, 184
2:4a 137
2:4b–7 137
2:5 5, 137, 139–40, 144, 147, 204, 222, 275
2:6 49, 50, 53, 63, 67, 77, 81, 108, 109, 113, 116, 119, 129, 137, 140–41, 142, 144, 145, 147, 151, 155, 163, 204, 209, 210, 211, 212, 223, 253, 286
2:6 (LXX) 135
2:6–7 134, 150
2:7 5, 31, 34, 81, 124, 129, 130, 136, 137, 141–44, 145, 147, 163, 165, 213, 216, 224, 226, 235
2:7 (LXX) 135, 143
2:8 26, 51, 83, 96, 113, 129, 130, 131, 135, 136, 137, 144–46, 147, 160, 164, 165, 173, 177, 187, 188,

328

## Index of Scripture and Other Ancient Texts

207, 209, 210, 222, 271, 282
2:8–9   43, 148, 158, 170, 178
2:8–14   137, 170
2:9   26, 41, 113, 130, 131, 135, 136, 144, 145, 146–49, 150, 160, 161, 163, 165, 172, 177, 179, 187, 201, 235
2:9 (LXX)   146, 147
2:10   5, 34, 35, 50, 53, 106, 131, 137, 146, 149–52, 158, 159, 161, 163, 165, 170, 172, 204, 212, 216, 245, 271, 282
2:10–11   212
2:10–12   26
2:11   26, 34, 39, 43, 50, 97, 100, 116, 128, 136, 137, 152–55, 156, 164, 194, 197, 208, 224, 257
2:11 (LXX)   136
2:11–12   2, 27, 38, 51, 137, 170, 173, 200, 212, 282
2:12   22, 25, 30, 31, 32, 35, 40, 43, 44, 45, 48, 57, 136, 154, 155–58, 162, 165, 168, 170, 172, 174, 177, 181, 197, 205, 207, 214, 215, 228, 265, 271, 282
2:12–13   35
2:13   51, 131, 135, 137, 146, 158–60, 161, 165, 170, 282
2:13–3:8   34
2:14   137, 143, 147, 154,

160–62, 165, 170, 171, 226, 235
2:14 (LXX)   136, 161
2:14–15   155
2:14–16   158, 159
2:14–18   276
2:15   130, 136, 137, 141, 144, 147, 160, 162–64, 177, 179, 201
2:15–16   5, 131, 137, 146, 148, 165, 177
2:16   100, 128, 130, 136, 144, 161, 162, 163, 164–65, 179
2:16–23   65
2:17   31, 113, 130, 135, 137, 165–67, 217
2:17–18   224
2:18   5, 31, 39, 50, 108, 130, 136, 168, 169, 171, 224
2:18 (LXX)   169
2:18–20   136
2:18–22   132, 187
2:18–23   4, 5, 39, 123, 168–83, 184, 186, 220
2:19   38, 50, 69, 130, 136, 166, 168, 169, 171–73, 194, 216, 220, 227, 278
2:19 (LXX)   172
2:19–20   125
2:19–21   2
2:19–22   170, 186
2:19a   170
2:19b   170
2:20   5, 9, 25, 26, 27, 35, 38, 39, 40, 42, 45, 47, 50, 51, 57, 87, 100, 124, 126, 164, 168, 169, 170,

173–76, 186, 188, 197, 200, 205, 206, 207, 208, 213, 215, 227, 228, 229, 240, 251, 278, 285, 286, 288, 297
2:20 (LXX)   169, 174, 229
2:21   35, 49, 53, 83, 96, 119, 129, 135, 136, 146, 169, 170, 173, 176–78, 180, 224, 227, 253, 271
2:21 (LXX)   169
2:21–22   131
2:21–23   168
2:22   26, 39, 41, 50, 100, 113, 129, 146, 148, 163, 170, 171, 177, 178–80, 187, 188, 195, 207, 209, 288, 289
2:22 (LXX)   169
2:23   32, 50, 83, 96, 121, 123, 130, 135, 136, 146, 160, 168, 178, 180–83, 220, 226, 227
2:23 (LXX)   169
3   25, 40, 206
3:1   25, 41, 50, 88, 131, 136, 145, 185, 186–88, 207, 209, 221, 224, 226, 228, 265, 289
3:1–2   215, 222
3:1–2a   186
3:1–4   9, 73, 132, 175, 206, 219, 224, 228
3:1–5   4, 5, 39, 40, 184–97
3:1–18   184–230
3:2   124, 137, 145, 154,

329

## Index of Scripture and Other Ancient Texts

184, 186, 188–89, 194, 205, 210, 214, 226, 227, 240
3:2 (LXX) 185
3:2–3 32
3:2–4 195, 227
3:2a 186
3:2b 186
3:2b–4 186
3:3 154, 178, 186, 189–91, 201, 216, 217, 218, 222, 227, 237, 302
3:3 (LXX) 185
3:3–4 226
3:3a 201
3:3b–4 201
3:4 35, 135, 136, 154, 185, 186, 190, 191–95, 201, 215, 216, 227, 235, 244
3:4 (LXX) 191
3:5 34, 185, 195–97, 198, 200, 210, 220
3:5–6 205
3:6 50, 147, 185, 189, 197, 199, 200–201, 221, 237
3:6 (LXX) 198
3:6–7 199
3:6–15 4, 25, 184, 197–219
3:7 35, 136, 192, 200, 201–2, 216, 244, 289
3:7–8 5
3:7–15 26
3:7–16:31 66
3:8 35, 137, 192, 202–4, 216, 222
3:8 (LXX) 203
3:8–9a 200

3:8–11 201
3:8–13 199
3:9 5, 25, 34, 40, 51, 57, 124, 126, 135, 157, 160, 197, 198, 204–7, 214, 218, 222, 223, 226, 251, 282
3:9 (LXX) 198
3:9–10 288
3:9–13 47, 57, 219, 251
3:9b 200
3:9c 200
3:9d 200
3:10 2, 25, 27, 35, 38, 41, 42, 43, 45, 51, 57, 87, 131, 136, 139, 140, 154, 174, 195, 207–10, 212, 215, 222, 229, 260, 268, 274, 278, 289
3:10 (LXX) 229
3:10–11 200, 209, 268
3:10–13 205, 219, 267
3:11 26, 31, 34, 51, 52, 126, 131, 140, 154, 190, 195, 197, 206, 207, 209, 210–12, 213, 222, 224, 226, 235, 237, 244, 257, 261, 266, 267, 268, 269, 272, 282
3:11 (LXX) 198
3:11–13 240, 268
3:12 91, 124, 126, 212–13, 215, 245
3:12 (LXX) 198, 213
3:12–13 5, 37, 196, 200, 207, 237
3:13 35, 101, 124, 192, 213–16, 222, 224, 226, 244, 245, 289

3:13 (LXX) 198
3:13–14 32
3:13–18 34
3:14 5, 34, 136, 150, 154, 190, 192, 200, 216–17, 222, 226, 243
3:14 (LXX) 199
3:14–15 199, 200
3:15 34, 136, 185, 189, 199, 200, 217–19, 223, 235, 236, 267, 276
3:15 (LXX) 199
3:15–17 5
3:16 34, 50, 136, 194, 209, 216, 220, 221–23
3:16 (LXX) 220
3:16–17 2
3:16–18 4, 184, 219–30
3:17 34, 41, 50, 115, 136, 199, 218, 220, 222, 223–25, 233, 276, 286
3:17 (LXX) 220
3:17–18 221
3:18 37, 50, 131, 135, 154, 178, 181, 190, 209, 216, 220, 225–30, 233, 236, 237, 240, 268
3:18 (LXX) 220
3:18–4:1 2
4 40, 125, 198, 249, 300
4:1 37, 110, 137, 189, 211, 233, 236–38, 239
4:1–2 236, 263, 270
4:1–6 57, 196, 260
4:1–12 1, 7, 11, 31, 231, 233–77

## Index of Scripture and Other Ancient Texts

4:1–22 231–307
4:2 211, 236, 238–39, 244, 267, 289, 305
4:2 (LXX) 234
4:3 26, 63, 77, 81, 108, 109, 113, 114, 119, 127, 129, 133, 239–43, 247, 251, 263, 286
4:3 (LXX) 234
4:3–4 34, 46
4:3–5 236
4:3–6 259
4:3–10 214
4:3–12 294
4:4 34, 58, 154, 191, 194, 199, 226, 241, 243–46, 251, 252, 261, 268
4:4 (LXX) 234
4:5 28, 34, 35, 51, 53, 58, 69, 113, 119, 129, 175, 238, 246–52, 253, 258, 260, 261, 262, 263, 264, 265, 266, 267, 272, 273, 282, 292, 297, 303
4:5 (LXX) 248
4:6 22, 252–57, 261, 268, 269
4:6–8 236
4:7 11, 12, 13, 34, 235, 236, 257–60, 262, 266
4:7 (LXX) 234, 258, 261
4:7–8 47, 244, 251
4:8 4, 251, 260–62, 264
4:8 (LXX) 235
4:8–10 259

4:9 26, 235, 242, 244, 246, 247, 251, 258, 262–64, 265, 268, 269, 270, 283
4:9–10 4, 47, 236, 248, 251, 252, 259, 261, 262, 267, 286
4:10 28, 34, 51, 53, 58, 69, 72, 119, 129, 136, 152, 204, 238, 246, 247, 250, 251, 253, 258, 259, 261, 262, 263, 264–69, 270, 271, 272, 273, 280, 283, 288, 291, 292, 297, 303
4:10 (LXX) 235
4:10–13 26, 32
4:11 31, 34, 36, 49, 51, 69, 80, 136, 211, 232, 236, 244, 263, 268, 269–73, 275, 280, 282, 292, 295
4:11 (LXX) 235
4:11–12 25, 31, 38, 45, 47, 57, 236, 251, 263, 280, 282, 283, 284, 286, 287, 291, 294, 305
4:11–14 35
4:11b–12 270
4:12 24, 26, 49, 153, 218, 236, 258, 259, 271, 272, 273–77, 290, 292, 298, 301, 303
4:13 4, 5, 25, 26, 36, 38, 40, 43, 45, 49, 51, 72, 129, 132, 136, 153, 169, 265, 271, 279, 280–84, 285, 289, 290, 297

4:13 (LXX) 278
4:13–16 7
4:13–17 4, 53, 231, 277–97
4:14 45, 58, 69, 109, 110, 152, 174, 232, 238, 272, 277, 278, 284–86, 291, 292, 297
4:14 (LXX) 278
4:14–15 4, 31, 38, 279, 284, 286
4:14–17 4, 284
4:15 28, 31, 49, 50, 51, 77, 97, 108, 115, 119, 131, 140, 153, 166, 187, 273, 277, 281, 286–89, 290, 293, 298, 301
4:16 75, 153, 279, 289–91, 301
4:16–17 47, 251, 287, 296
4:17 1, 4, 12, 15, 23, 51, 62, 69, 152, 153, 196, 232, 238, 273, 277, 279, 284, 290, 291–97, 298, 299, 301, 303, 304, 305
4:17–22 7, 9, 11, 23, 24, 33, 40, 43, 271, 286, 291, 294
4:17a 19, 272
4:17b 272
4:17b–22 23, 24, 26
4:18 24, 26, 290, 301–2
4:18 (LXX) 299
4:18–22 4, 13, 15, 19, 26, 28, 69, 75, 231, 238, 273, 274, 283,

## Index of Scripture and Other Ancient Texts

| | |
|---|---|
| | 288, 289, 290, |
| | 297, 298–307 |
| 4:19 | 302 |
| 4:19 (LXX) | 299 |
| 4:19–22 | 300 |
| 4:20 | 34, 299, 302 |
| 4:20 (LXX) | 299 |
| 4:20–21 | 302–4 |
| 4:21 | 34, 273, 292, 299, |
| | 302, 303 |
| 4:22 | 4, 12, 62, 232, |
| | 301, 304–7 |

**1 Samuel**

| | |
|---|---|
| 1–2 | 33, 166 |
| 1:1 | 62, 65 |
| 1:5 | 281 |
| 1:8 | 28, 166, 289 |
| 1:12–18 | 160 |
| 1:19 | 274 |
| 1:19–20 | 26, 279, 283 |
| 1:20 | 283 |
| 1:23 | 226 |
| 1:24 | 166 |
| 2:5 | 283, 289 |
| 2:10 | 33 |
| 2:20 | 208 |
| 2:21 | 280, 283, 284 |
| 2:36 | 161 |
| 3:2–15 | 192 |
| 3:17 | 103 |
| 3:18 | 80 |
| 3:19 | 227 |
| 4:5 | 110 |
| 4:7 | 136 |
| 4:13 | 110 |
| 4:20 | 210 |
| 5:9 | 95 |
| 6:5 | 252 |
| 6:9 | 132 |
| 7:3 | 151 |
| 7:13 | 95 |

| | |
|---|---|
| 7:15 | 28 |
| 8:8 | 136 |
| 9:1 | 126 |
| 9:3 | 139 |
| 9:9 | 257, 258 |
| 9:11 | 149 |
| 9:12–13 | 142 |
| 9:15 | 191, 243 |
| 10:2 | 136 |
| 10:9 | 136 |
| 10:20–21 | 127 |
| 11:4–5 | 138 |
| 11:7 | 104 |
| 12:3 | 116, 222 |
| 12:5 | 263 |
| 12:23 | 84 |
| 13:10 | 134, 138 |
| 13:14 | 304 |
| 14:15 | 203 |
| 14:17 | 136 |
| 14:21 | 142 |
| 14:41 | 199 |
| 14:42 | 227 |
| 14:44 | 103 |
| 14:50 | 295 |
| 15:27 | 25 |
| 15:28 | 25 |
| 15:32 | 112 |
| 16 | 22 |
| 16:1–4 | 27 |
| 16:1–5 | 239 |
| 16:1–13 | 304 |
| 16:13 | 25 |
| 16:18 | 25, 126 |
| 16:22 | 130 |
| 17:12 | 24, 66, 71, 295, |
| | 304 |
| 17:17 | 162, 166 |
| 17:20 | 201 |
| 17:38 | 142 |
| 17:51 | 258 |
| 17:55 | 222 |

| | |
|---|---|
| 17:56 | 222 |
| 17:58 | 222 |
| 18:1 | 288 |
| 18:3 | 288 |
| 18:11 | 199 |
| 18:12 | 25 |
| 18:20 | 288 |
| 18:25 | 224 |
| 18:28 | 25, 288 |
| 20:2 | 243 |
| 20:12–13 | 243 |
| 20:13 | 103, 104 |
| 20:13–17 | 105 |
| 20:17 | 288 |
| 20:21 | 108, 215 |
| 20:22 | 108 |
| 20:26 | 132, 199 |
| 20:27 | 304 |
| 20:30 | 304 |
| 20:38 | 142 |
| 21:3 | 238 |
| 22:1–4 | 24 |
| 22:3–4 | 20 |
| 22:5 | 85, 132 |
| 22:7–9 | 304 |
| 22:8 | 243 |
| 22:17 | 100, 243 |
| 24 | 25 |
| 24:1–4 | 202 |
| 24:2 | 84 |
| 24:3[4] | 192 |
| 24:20[19] | 156 |
| 24:22[21] | 249, 266 |
| 25:5 | 239 |
| 25:6 | 138 |
| 25:7 | 163 |
| 25:14 | 134 |
| 25:18 | 162 |
| 25:22 | 103 |
| 25:24 | 204 |
| 25:24–31 | 25, 160 |
| 25:27 | 158 |

# INDEX OF SCRIPTURE AND OTHER ANCIENT TEXTS

| | | | | | |
|---|---|---|---|---|---|
| 25:32 | 278 | 5:24 | 95 | 14:10 | 148 |
| 25:32−33 | 208 | 6:6 | 189, 217 | 14:15 | 124, 158 |
| 25:32−34 | 25 | 6:10 | 295 | 14:16 | 83 |
| 25:36 | 202 | 6:12 | 295 | 14:22 | 130, 149, 159 |
| 25:39 | 278 | 6:20 | 191, 193 | 15:7 | 124 |
| 25:41 | 159 | 6:20−22 | 204 | 15:19 | 150 |
| 25:42 | 25, 139, 208, 281 | 7:1−17 | 307 | 15:19−20 | 106 |
| 25:43 | 295 | 7:5 | 295 | 15:19−23 | 27 |
| 26:7 | 191 | 7:8 | 295 | 15:20 | 27 |
| 26:11 | 191 | 7:8−16 | 304−5 | 15:21 | 27, 106, 213 |
| 26:12 | 191 | 7:11 | 16 | 15:22 | 107 |
| 26:16 | 191 | 7:12 | 274 | 16:1 | 139 |
| 27:1 | 169 | 7:15 | 27 | 16:2 | 139 |
| 27:5 | 130 | 7:18 | 159 | 16:4 | 130, 159 |
| 28:5 | 203 | 7:27 | 243, 271 | 17:8 | 126 |
| 28:13 | 83 | 8:2 | 20 | 17:15 | 239 |
| 28:22 | 161 | 9−20 | 10 | 17:28 | 162 |
| 29:8 | 158 | 9:8 | 159 | 18:3 | 169 |
| 30:13 | 140 | 9:11 | 195 | 18:15 | 239 |
| 30:16 | 85 | 10:2 | 159 | 18:18 | 304 |
| | | 11−12 | 192 | 18:23 | 125 |
| **2 Samuel** | | 11:3 | 53, 275 | 18:28 | 138, 278 |
| 1:1 | 65 | 11:4 | 279 | 19:13−14[12−13] | 97 |
| 1:23 | 104 | 11:5 | 283 | 19:14[13] | 103 |
| 1:26 | 288 | 11:11 | 192, 193 | 19:40[39] | 96 |
| 2:5 | 174 | 11:15 | 199 | 19:43[42] | 124 |
| 2:5−6 | 88 | 11:27 | 281 | 20:1 | 304 |
| 2:26 | 84, 112 | 12:3 | 161, 193, 290 | 20:2 | 96 |
| 2:30 | 84 | 12:8 | 290 | 20:3 | 239 |
| 3:9 | 103, 104 | 12:20 | 190 | 20:9 | 217 |
| 3:10 | 251 | 12:24 | 282 | 21:1 | 75 |
| 3:12 | 139 | 13:1−22 | 192 | 21:20 | 292 |
| 3:18 | 295 | 13:16 | 94 | 22:44 | 154 |
| 3:35 | 103 | 13:25 | 94 | 22:51 | 27 |
| 3:37 | 169 | 13:28 | 139, 202 | 23:1 | 304 |
| 3:39 | 156 | 13:28−29 | 147 | 23:10 | 96 |
| 4:3 | 71 | 13:33 | 213 | 23:11 | 125 |
| 4:4 | 290 | 13:36 | 90 | 23:16 | 149 |
| 5:1 | 97 | 13:38 | 71 | 23:34 | 275 |
| 5:4−5 | 304 | 14:1−7 | 126, 249 | 23:39 | 275 |
| 5:13−8:18 | 24 | 14:2 | 190 | 24 | 189 |
| 5:20−25 | 304 | 14:4−19 | 160 | 24:16 | 189 |

333

## INDEX OF SCRIPTURE AND OTHER ANCIENT TEXTS

| | | | | | |
|---|---|---|---|---|---|
| 24:21 | 251 | 11:19 | 130 | **2 Kings** | |
| 24:22–23 | 242 | 11:28 | 126 | 2:2 | 100 |
| 24:24 | 243, 244 | 11:32 | 295 | 2:4 | 100 |
| | | 11:33 | 88, 98, 157 | 2:11 | 84 |
| **1 Kings** | | 11:38 | 271 | 2:17 | 125 |
| 1–2 | 24, 52, 306 | 12:8 | 74 | 3:7 | 104 |
| 1:11–31 | 117 | 12:10 | 74 | 3:9 | 204 |
| 1:42 | 126 | 12:14 | 74 | 3:13 | 94 |
| 1:45 | 110 | 12:15 | 136 | 4:3 | 278 |
| 1:48 | 278 | 12:16 | 304 | 4:7 | 156 |
| 1:51 | 217 | 12:18 | 106 | 4:16 | 94 |
| 1:52 | 126 | 12:33–13:1 | 138 | 4:17 | 283 |
| 2:1 | 201 | 14:8 | 295, 305 | 4:19 | 139 |
| 2:5 | 136 | 14:10 | 116 | 4:25 | 132 |
| 2:11 | 304 | 15:3 | 305 | 4:29 | 134, 138 |
| 2:23 | 80, 103, 104 | 15:4 | 251 | 4:37 | 149 |
| 2:33 | 136 | 15:17 | 108 | 4:42 | 162 |
| 3:1 | 280 | 15:29 | 108 | 4:43–44 | 162 |
| 3:6 | 27, 305 | 16:24 | 243, 244 | 5:1–14 | 272 |
| 3:7 | 159 | 17:1–6 | 78 | 5:18 | 213 |
| 3:20 | 202, 290 | 17:7–11 | 77 | 6:6 | 171 |
| 4:7 | 287 | 17:11 | 161 | 6:8 | 238 |
| 5:1 | 284 | 17:19 | 290 | 6:16 | 210 |
| 5:17[3] | 258 | 17:20 | 117 | 6:24–25 | 66 |
| 5:21[7] | 278 | 18:3 | 70 | 6:27 | 189 |
| 6:1 | 300 | 18:7 | 110 | 6:31 | 103 |
| 6:13 | 100 | 18:13 | 136 | 7:12 | 124 |
| 7:21 | 128 | 18:17 | 110 | 8:14 | 132 |
| 8:15 | 278 | 18:21 | 208 | 9:25–26 | 125 |
| 8:35–40 | 75 | 19:2 | 103, 104 | 10:1 | 239, 290 |
| 8:41–43 | 151 | 19:6 | 191 | 10:5 | 195, 239 |
| 8:56 | 89, 227, 278 | 19:20 | 90, 96 | 10:10 | 227 |
| 8:66 | 202 | 20:7–8 | 239 | 10:11 | 124 |
| 9:4 | 201, 305 | 20:10 | 103, 204 | 10:15 | 134, 138 |
| 9:21 | 171 | 20:12 | 143 | 13:5 | 136 |
| 10:9 | 172, 278 | 20:16 | 143 | 15:20 | 126 |
| 11:1 | 150, 281 | 21:8–12 | 239 | 18:3 | 305 |
| 11:1–8 | 48 | 21:17–19 | 130 | 18:6 | 96 |
| 11:2 | 96, 97, 281 | 21:29 | 116 | 18:27 | 192 |
| 11:4 | 305 | 22:1–36 | 14 | 19:25 | 145 |
| 11:7 | 88, 99 | 22:4 | 104 | 19:34 | 295 |
| 11:8 | 150 | 22:10 | 189 | 20:21 | 102 |

334

## INDEX OF SCRIPTURE AND OTHER ANCIENT TEXTS

| | |
|---|---|
| 21:1 | 70 |
| 21:8 | 201 |
| 22:2 | 305 |
| 22:20 | 102 |
| 23:5 | 285 |
| 23:11 | 285 |
| 23:13 | 88, 99 |
| 23:22 | 16 |
| 23:24 | 85 |
| 24 | 305 |
| 24:16 | 126 |
| 25:1–3 | 66 |
| 25:22 | 85 |

### 1 Chronicles

| | |
|---|---|
| 1:5 | 300 |
| 1:6 | 300 |
| 1:19 | 72, 292 |
| 1:34 | 271 |
| 2 | 302 |
| 2:1 | 271, 300 |
| 2:3–4 | 303 |
| 2:3–6 | 273 |
| 2:3–15 | 13 |
| 2:5 | 301 |
| 2:5–16 | 300 |
| 2:9 | 299, 302 |
| 2:9–10 | 299 |
| 2:9–33 | 302 |
| 2:10 | 302 |
| 2:10–12 | 300 |
| 2:11 | 299, 302 |
| 2:11–12 | 128, 302 |
| 2:12 | 295, 304 |
| 2:12–13 | 302, 304 |
| 2:13–15 | 304 |
| 2:13–16 | 304 |
| 2:15 | 295, 304 |
| 2:37–38 | 295 |
| 2:50–51 | 71 |
| 2:51 | 299 |
| 2:54 | 299 |

| | |
|---|---|
| 3:1 | 300 |
| 3:4 | 304 |
| 4:1 | 273, 301 |
| 4:4 | 71 |
| 4:9 | 70 |
| 4:10 | 70 |
| 4:17 | 283 |
| 5:1 | 271 |
| 5:3 | 271 |
| 5:15 | 70 |
| 6:7[22] | 302 |
| 6:23[38] | 271 |
| 7:23 | 283 |
| 7:29 | 271 |
| 9:13 | 126 |
| 9:20 | 257 |
| 10:14 | 304 |
| 11:13 | 125 |
| 11:17 | 149 |
| 11:26 | 295 |
| 11:46 | 70 |
| 11:47 | 295 |
| 12:40[39] | 71 |
| 13:9 | 217 |
| 15:10 | 302 |
| 17:4 | 295 |
| 17:6 | 16 |
| 17:7 | 295 |
| 17:10 | 16 |
| 17:25 | 271 |
| 21:1–22:1 | 189 |
| 21:18–22:1 | 305 |
| 21:24 | 244 |
| 22:5 | 124 |
| 24:31 | 227 |
| 25:8 | 227 |
| 26:6 | 126, 295 |
| 26:7 | 295 |
| 26:13 | 227 |
| 26:31 | 126 |
| 27:18 | 304 |
| 29:26 | 304 |

### 2 Chronicles

| | |
|---|---|
| 1:8 | 27 |
| 2:11[12] | 278 |
| 3:1 | 189, 305 |
| 3:17 | 128 |
| 6:4 | 278 |
| 6:32–33 | 151 |
| 7:17 | 201 |
| 9:8 | 172, 278 |
| 10:8 | 74 |
| 10:10 | 74 |
| 10:14 | 74 |
| 10:18 | 106 |
| 11:21 | 63, 281 |
| 13:3 | 126 |
| 13:7 | 106 |
| 13:21 | 63 |
| 18:3 | 104 |
| 20:9 | 66 |
| 23:1 | 295 |
| 24:3 | 63 |
| 28:15 | 190 |
| 29:6 | 73 |
| 30:8 | 73 |
| 31:10 | 162 |
| 33:15 | 151 |
| 36:17–21 | 305 |

### Ezra

| | |
|---|---|
| 2 | 120 |
| 6:19–21 | 120 |
| 7:6 | 95 |
| 7:9 | 95 |
| 7:27 | 278 |
| 9–10 | 22 |
| 9:1 | 48, 67 |
| 9:2 | 63, 72 |
| 9:12 | 63, 72 |
| 10 | 19 |
| 10:1 | 74 |
| 10:2 | 150, 226 |
| 10:10 | 48, 150, 226 |

## Index of Scripture and Other Ancient Texts

| | | | | | |
|---|---|---|---|---|---|
| 10:14 | 226 | 3:7 | 227 | 12:9–10 | 95 |
| 10:17 | 226 | 4:1 | 112 | 13:3 | 113 |
| 10:44 | 63, 72 | 4:4 | 139 | 15:6 | 116 |
| 20:9 | 66 | 5:2 | 130 | 15:31 | 257 |
| | | 5:3–4 | 90 | 17:2 | 101 |
| **Nehemiah** | | 5:6–8 | 90 | 19:14 | 124 |
| 2:8 | 95 | 5:8 | 130 | 19:15 | 150 |
| 2:13 | 82 | 5:11 | 289 | 19:25 | 46, 176, 293 |
| 2:15 | 82 | 6:10 | 227 | 20:18 | 257, 286 |
| 2:18 | 95 | 7:2–4 | 90 | 21:15 | 100 |
| 5:8 | 251 | 7:3 | 130 | 21:25 | 112 |
| 6:5 | 139 | 7:4 | 160 | 22:3 | 114 |
| 9:16 | 73 | 8:17 | 272 | 22:9 | 75, 224 |
| 9:17 | 73 | 9:1 | 82 | 22:17 | 114 |
| 9:25 | 162 | 9:10 | 289 | 22:23 | 114 |
| 10:29–30[Eng. 28–29] | | 9:12–14 | 289 | 22:25–26 | 114 |
| | 120 | 9:22 | 89 | 23:16 | 113, 114 |
| 10:32[31] | 240 | 9:24 | 227 | 24:1 | 113, 114 |
| 10:35[34] | 227 | 9:27 | 272 | 24:3 | 75 |
| 11:1 | 227 | | | 24:3–4 | 75 |
| 13 | 22 | **Job** | | 24:8 | 157 |
| 13:1 | 47, 67 | 1–2 | 10 | 24:10 | 141 |
| 13:4 | 124 | 1:1 | 62 | 26:13 | 95 |
| 13:5    257 | | 1:2 | 289 | 27:2 | 113, 114 |
| 13:15 | 240 | 1:15 | 139 | 27:10–11 | 114 |
| 13:19 | 139 | 2:9–10 | 117 | 27:13 | 114 |
| 13:20 | 240 | 2:10 | 37 | 27:14–23 | 113 |
| 13:23 | 47, 226 | 2:12 | 90 | 27:18 | 143 |
| 13:23–27 | 48 | 2:14 | 90 | 28:17 | 257 |
| 13:23–31 | 19 | 3:9 | 93 | 29:5 | 114 |
| 13:25 | 63, 72 | 3:20 | 112 | 29:10 | 96 |
| 13:26 | 150 | 5:17 | 113 | 30:27 | 92 |
| 13:27 | 226 | 5:17–27 | 78 | 31:2 | 114 |
| | | 6:4 | 113 | 31:7–10 | 104 |
| **Esther** | | 6:18 | 203 | 31:16 | 75 |
| 1:1 | 65 | 7:2 | 93 | 31:16–22 | 104 |
| 1:10 | 202 | 7:11 | 112 | 31:17 | 161 |
| 1:19 | 73 | 7:18 | 63, 78 | 31:35 | 113, 114 |
| 2:7 | 290 | 8:3 | 113 | 32:8 | 114 |
| 2:9 | 139 | 8:5 | 113 | 33:4 | 114 |
| 2:10 | 201 | 10:1 | 112 | 34:10 | 114 |
| 2:17 | 281 | 11:7 | 113 | 34:11 | 156 |
| 2:20 | 201 | 12:4–9 | 95 | 34:12 | 114 |

# INDEX OF SCRIPTURE AND OTHER ANCIENT TEXTS

| | | | | | |
|---|---|---|---|---|---|
| 34:20 | 202 | 34 | 157 | 100:5 | 31 |
| 35:13 | 114 | 36:4[3] | 84 | 102:26[25] | 257 |
| 37:23 | 114 | 36:8[7] | 31, 157 | 104:27 | 82 |
| 39:12 | 189 | 37 | 157 | 106:28 | 67 |
| 40:2 | 115 | 37:19 | 78 | 108:13[12] | 199 |
| 42:7–17 | 10 | 39:11[10] | 95 | 113:9 | 249 |
| 42:10 | 114 | 42:3 | 98 | 116:3 | 89 |
| 42:13 | 289, 293 | 45 | 91 | 116:7 | 89 |
| | | 55:14[13] | 124 | 116:16 | 159 |
| **Psalms** | | 56:13[12] | 156 | 118:1–4 | 31 |
| 1 | 30 | 57:2[1] | 31, 157 | 118:8–9 | 157 |
| 2 | 30 | 57:4[3] | 157 | 119:116 | 82 |
| 2:12 | 31, 157 | 57:11[10] | 157 | 119:154 | 46, 176 |
| 5:12[Eng. 11] | 31 | 59:6[5] | 63, 78 | 119:166 | 82 |
| 7:2[1] | 157 | 60:10[8] | 259 | 121:2 | 136 |
| 8:7[6] | 95, 258 | 60:13[11] | 199 | 126:1–2 | 78 |
| 15 | 157 | 61:5[4] | 31, 157 | 127:2 | 112 |
| 16:1 | 157 | 61:8[7] | 157 | 127:3 | 283 |
| 17:3 | 63, 78 | 63:4[3] | 157 | 128:5 | 139 |
| 17:7 | 31 | 63:8[7] | 31, 157 | 130:7–8 | 58 |
| 17:7–8 | 157 | 65:10 | 63, 78 | 136 | 31, 43, 87 |
| 17:8 | 31, 157 | 66:20 | 278 | 136:12 | 95 |
| 18:31[30] | 31 | 68:8[7] | 95 | 139:13–16 | 283 |
| 18:51[50] | 31 | 68:14[13] | 157 | 142:5–6[4–5] | 31, 157 |
| 19:8[7] | 286 | 68:15[14] | 113 | 145:15 | 82 |
| 21:8[7] | 31 | 69:9[8] | 150 | 146:3 | 157 |
| 22:26[25] | 156 | 69:22[21] | 161 | 146:5 | 82 |
| 22:27[26] | 162 | 71:21 | 159 | | |
| 23:2 | 89 | 72:20 | 304 | **Proverbs** | |
| 23:4 | 76, 159, 177 | 73:20 | 169 | 1:21 | 110 |
| 23:5 | 161 | 74:2 | 252 | 2:16 | 151 |
| 23:6 | 76 | 78:29 | 162 | 2:17 | 100 |
| 24 | 157 | 81:10[9] | 151 | 4:7 | 244 |
| 25:13 | 101 | 86:9 | 54 | 4:25 | 146 |
| 25:15 | 146 | 86:17 | 159 | 5:4 | 112 |
| 25:20 | 157 | 88:9[8] | 124 | 5:18 | 172 |
| 27:10 | 100 | 88:14 | 291 | 5:20 | 151 |
| 27:14 | 229 | 88:19[18] | 124 | 6:24 | 151 |
| 28:4 | 156 | 90:10 | 287 | 6:29 | 148 |
| 31:12[11] | 124 | 91 | 157 | 7:4 | 124 |
| 31:20[19] | 31 | 91:4 | 31, 157 | 7:22 | 208 |
| 32:4 | 95 | 94:6 | 75 | 9:17 | 193 |
| 33:18–19 | 78 | 95:11 | 89 | 10:26 | 161 |

337

## INDEX OF SCRIPTURE AND OTHER ANCIENT TEXTS

| | | | | | |
|---|---|---|---|---|---|
| 12:4 | 211 | 7:13–14 | 132 | 10:3 | 171 |
| 15:15 | 202 | 7:19 | 289 | 11:1 | 304 |
| 16:23 | 89 | 8:16–9:1 | 132 | 11:10 | 304 |
| 16:33 | 132, 227, 290 | 9:2–3 | 132 | 11:11 | 252 |
| 17:13 | 286 | 9:7 | 202 | 12:1 | 159 |
| 18:13 | 286 | 9:7–8 | 190 | 13:6 | 113 |
| 18:18 | 84 | 11:5 | 132 | 14:16 | 111 |
| 18:24 | 97 | | | 14:20 | 273 |
| 19:23 | 101 | **Song of Songs** | | 14:22 | 266 |
| 19:27 | 84 | 1:4 | 208 | 16:11 | 92 |
| 22:6 | 177 | 1:7 | 288 | 17:5 | 124 |
| 22:28 | 130 | 3:1 | 288 | 19:17 | 112 |
| 23:8 | 161 | 3:2 | 124, 288 | 20:2 | 258 |
| 23:10 | 130 | 3:3 | 288 | 20:4 | 193 |
| 23:11 | 46, 176 | 3:4 | 26, 32, 87, 126, 288 | 22:3 | 110 |
| 24:12 | 156 | 3:6–5:1 | 32 | 23:17 | 63, 78 |
| 24:26 | 286 | 5:4 | 92 | 25:4 | 157 |
| 24:29 | 156 | 5:7 | 32, 195, 214 | 26:21 | 95 |
| 25:13 | 286 | 8:2 | 26, 32, 87, 126 | 28:21 | 150 |
| 25:18 | 116 | | | 28:27 | 165 |
| 26:16 | 289 | **Isaiah** | | 28:28 | 165, 189 |
| 27:9 | 190 | 1:8 | 143 | 28:29 | 136 |
| 27:10 | 278 | 1:15 | 177 | 29:21 | 237 |
| 28:21 | 161 | 1:17 | 228 | 30:2 | 157 |
| 30:17 | 7 | 1:21 | 101 | 30:17 | 178 |
| 31 | 31, 32 | 2:2–3 | 54 | 31:5 | 157 |
| 31:10 | 126, 211 | 3:7 | 185 | 32:11 | 203 |
| 31:10–31 | 27, 31, 52, 211 | 3:22 | 217 | 33:24 | 278 |
| 31:15 | 31, 139 | 4:1 | 75 | 36:12 | 192 |
| 31:16 | 211, 241 | 4:6 | 143, 157 | 37:26 | 145 |
| 31:21 | 31 | 5:1 | 124 | 37:35 | 295 |
| 31:23 | 31, 211, 241 | 5:2 | 93 | 38:8 | 286 |
| 31:24 | 240 | 5:4 | 93 | 38:17 | 112 |
| 31:26 | 211 | 5:27 | 258 | 38:18 | 82 |
| 31:27 | 31 | 7:1 | 65 | 40:1–2 | 159 |
| 31:30 | 31 | 7:11 | 136 | 40:11 | 290 |
| 31:31 | 31, 211 | 8:3 | 283 | 40:31 | 229 |
| | | 8:3–4 | 279 | 41:13–14 | 210 |
| **Ecclesiastes** | | 8:18 | 136 | 42:1–4 | 295 |
| 2:14 | 125 | 8:19 | 83 | 42:13 | 95 |
| 2:14–15 | 132 | 9:5[6] | 292 | 43:9–10 | 263 |
| 3:1–15 | 132 | 9:7[8] | 227 | 43:12 | 263 |
| 3:19 | 132 | 10:2 | 75 | 43:24 | 244 |

## INDEX OF SCRIPTURE AND OTHER ANCIENT TEXTS

| | | | | | |
|---|---|---|---|---|---|
| 44:8 | 263 | 7:16 | 100 | 40:4 | 242 |
| 44:25 | 286 | 7:26 | 73 | 42:5 | 195 |
| 45:1–8 | 132 | 9:1[2] | 100 | 44:18 | 84 |
| 45:12 | 95 | 9:15[16] | 154 | 44:19 | 287 |
| 47:2–3 | 193 | 14:12 | 66 | 44:28 | 222 |
| 47:10 | 199 | 15:15 | 63, 78 | 46:16 | 153 |
| 47:11 | 116 | 20:14 | 172 | 48:7 | 99 |
| 48:13 | 95 | 20:15 | 292 | 48:13 | 99 |
| 48:19 | 266 | 22:3 | 228 | 48:46 | 99 |
| 49:1–6 | 295 | 22:10 | 153 | 50:21 | 201 |
| 49:6 | 251, 272 | 24:5 | 150 | 50:29 | 156 |
| 49:23 | 290 | 25:14 | 156 | 50:34 | 46, 176 |
| 50:4–9 | 295 | 26:17 | 239 | 51:3 | 213 |
| 50:10 | 120 | 27:18 | 100 | 51:30 | 84 |
| 52:13–53:12 | 58, 295 | 28:3–4 | 286 | | |
| 54:3 | 275 | 31:20 | 92 | **Lamentations** | |
| 54:4 | 75 | 31:23 | 134, 139 | 1:16 | 286 |
| 54:4–5 | 47, 176 | 31:33 | 104 | 1:20 | 92 |
| 54:5 | 59 | 32 | 243 | 2:11 | 92 |
| 55:6–7 | 120 | 32:1–15 | 242, 251 | 2:12 | 290 |
| 56:3 | 151 | 32:7 | 234, 261 | 2:15 | 111 |
| 56:3–7 | 272 | 32:8 | 234, 261 | 3:8 | 177 |
| 56:4–5 | 304 | 32:9 | 244 | 3:12 | 112 |
| 56:5 | 249 | 32:9–15 | 263 | 3:37–38 | 132 |
| 56:6 | 151 | 32:11 | 243 | 4:9 | 68 |
| 58:11 | 73 | 32:12 | 243 | | |
| 62:1 | 227 | 32:14 | 243 | **Ezekiel** | |
| 62:4 | 70 | 32:25 | 244, 261 | 1:1 | 65 |
| 63:16 | 58 | 32:33 | 73 | 1:24 | 113 |
| | | 32:38 | 104 | 3:6 | 77 |
| **Jeremiah** | | 32:44 | 244 | 3:12 | 77 |
| 1:3 | 65 | 34:14 | 241 | 3:26 | 96 |
| 2:2 | 208 | 34:18–20 | 104 | 6:10 | 116 |
| 2:21 | 150 | 35:6 | 201 | 6:11 | 66 |
| 2:27 | 73 | 35:8 | 201 | 6:12 | 72 |
| 2:33 | 185 | 35:10 | 201 | 9:11 | 286 |
| 3:1 | 82 | 36:8 | 201 | 10:5 | 113 |
| 4:19 | 92 | 38:7 | 295 | 11:15 | 240 |
| 5:19 | 151 | 38:8 | 295 | 14:1 | 239 |
| 6:5 | 252 | 38:10 | 295 | 14:6 | 120 |
| 6:15 | 63, 78 | 38:11 | 295 | 16:8 | 205 |
| 6:21 | 278 | 38:16 | 213 | 16:8–12 | 190 |
| 7:6 | 228 | 39:12 | 213 | 16:18 | 185 |

# Index of Scripture and Other Ancient Texts

| | |
|---|---|
| 16:25 | 192 |
| 16:42 | 227 |
| 18:30–31 | 120 |
| 20:1 | 239 |
| 22:10 | 191 |
| 23:15 | 153 |
| 27:30 | 112 |
| 28:18 | 169 |
| 34:23–24 | 295 |
| 36:20 | 68 |
| 36:30 | 68 |
| 37:24 | 295 |
| 45:11 | 166 |
| 48:16 | 213 |

**Daniel**

| | |
|---|---|
| 2:6 | 82 |
| 2:9 | 82 |
| 4:24 | 82 |
| 10:3 | 190 |
| 10:6 | 191 |
| 11:39 | 151 |

**Hosea**

| | |
|---|---|
| 1:3 | 279, 280, 281, 283 |
| 1:6 | 283 |
| 1:8 | 283 |
| 2:7[5] | 208 |
| 2:16[14] | 159 |
| 3:2 | 252 |
| 3:3 | 82 |
| 5:10 | 130 |
| 6:2 | 169 |
| 7:2 | 199 |
| 8:10 | 177 |
| 9:1 | 53, 189, 194, 214 |
| 9:10 | 67 |
| 9:16 | 177 |
| 10:5 | 278 |
| 11:1 | 283 |
| 13:3 | 189 |
| 14:3[2] | 156 |

**Joel**

| | |
|---|---|
| 1:4 | 66 |
| 1:15 | 113 |
| 2:14 | 72 |
| 2:22 | 80 |
| 2:26 | 162 |
| 4:3 | 74 |

**Amos**

| | |
|---|---|
| 2:6 | 259 |
| 2:12b | 147 |
| 3:6 | 132 |
| 4:1 | 80 |
| 4:6–11 | 120 |
| 4:7–8 | 120 |
| 5:15 | 237 |
| 7:17 | 71 |
| 8:5 | 165 |
| 8:6 | 259 |

**Obadiah**

| | |
|---|---|
| 3 | 199 |

**Jonah**

| | |
|---|---|
| 1:1 | 65 |
| 2:9[8] | 174 |
| 4:5 | 143 |

**Micah**

| | |
|---|---|
| 1:3 | 95 |
| 1:11 | 193 |
| 2:1–5 | 130 |
| 4:13 | 189 |
| 5:1–4[2–5] | 71, 295 |
| 5:2 | 272 |
| 6:3 | 116 |
| 6:10 | 166 |
| 6:15 | 190 |

**Nahum**

| | |
|---|---|
| 3:5–6 | 193 |

**Habakkuk**

| | |
|---|---|
| 3:13 | 95 |

**Zephaniah**

| | |
|---|---|
| 1:4 | 266 |

**Zechariah**

| | |
|---|---|
| 5:4 | 101 |
| 5:6–10 | 166 |
| 5:11 | 136 |
| 6:10 | 247 |
| 7:10 | 75, 228 |
| 7:14 | 154 |
| 8:5 | 74 |
| 8:22–23 | 54 |
| 8:23 | 272 |
| 11:1 | 124 |
| 14:3 | 95 |
| 14:16 | 54 |

**Malachi**

| | |
|---|---|
| 1:5 | 78 |
| 1:11 | 78 |
| 2:11 | 151 |
| 3:2 | 287 |
| 3:5 | 75 |

**DEUTERO-CANONICAL BOOKS**

| | |
|---|---|
| Judith | 6 |

**DEAD SEA SCROLLS**

| | |
|---|---|
| 2QRuth[a] | 34, 169, 185, 191 |
| 2QRuth[b] | 34, 198, 199, 220 |
| 4QRuth[a] | 34, 62, 63, 80, 81 |
| 4QRuth[b] | 34, 63, 82, 83 |

# INDEX OF SCRIPTURE AND OTHER ANCIENT TEXTS

## ANCIENT JEWISH WRITERS

### Josephus

*Against Apion*

| | |
|---|---|
| 1.7–8 | 32 |

*Jewish Antiquities*

| | |
|---|---|
| 3.8.3 §197 | 166 |
| 5.332 | 254 |
| 5.335 | 260 |
| 5.9.1–4 | 29 |

## NEW TESTAMENT

### Matthew

| | |
|---|---|
| 1:1 | 52, 305 |
| 1:1–6 | 52, 53, 275 |
| 1:1–16 | 291 |
| 1:1–17 | 11, 53 |
| 1:3 | 299, 302 |
| 1:3–4 | 299 |
| 1:4 | 299, 302 |
| 1:5 | 29, 128, 268, 299, 302, 303, 304 |
| 1:16 | 72, 303 |
| 1:17 | 300 |
| 1:19 | 53 |
| 2:6 | 296 |
| 2:13–15 | 182 |
| 5:14–16 | 56 |
| 5:17 | 56 |
| 5:33–37 | 267 |
| 6:9 | 118 |
| 6:11 | 78 |
| 9:27 | 305 |
| 10:37 | 107 |
| 11:28 | 229 |
| 11:28–29 | 120 |
| 12:23 | 305 |
| 12:33–34 | 89 |
| 15:18–19 | 89 |

| | |
|---|---|
| 15:21–28 | 183 |
| 15:22 | 305 |
| 19:5 | 153 |
| 20:30–31 | 305 |
| 21:9 | 305 |
| 21:15 | 305 |
| 22:1–14 | 161 |
| 22:37–40 | 56 |
| 23:37 | 157 |
| 25:1–13 | 202 |
| 25:35 | 183 |
| 25:40 | 183 |
| 27:34 | 161 |
| 27:48 | 161 |
| 28:18–20 | 56, 272 |

### Mark

| | |
|---|---|
| 7:24–30 | 183 |
| 10:7 | 153 |
| 10:47–48 | 305 |
| 12:29–31 | 56 |
| 12:35 | 305 |
| 15:36 | 161 |

### Luke

| | |
|---|---|
| 1:31–33 | 305 |
| 1:57–63 | 294 |
| 3:23 | 303 |
| 3:31 | 305 |
| 3:31–34 | 52 |
| 3:32 | 29, 128, 303, 304 |
| 3:33 | 299, 302 |
| 10:1–10 | 161 |
| 10:25–37 | 181, 229 |
| 10:37 | 229 |
| 11:3 | 78 |
| 13:1–5 | 76 |
| 13:34 | 157 |
| 14:26 | 107 |
| 15:1–32 | 161 |
| 18:38–39 | 305 |

| | |
|---|---|
| 20:41 | 305 |
| 23:36 | 161 |

### John

| | |
|---|---|
| 1:14 | 59 |
| 4:3–42 | 183 |
| 7:42 | 296 |
| 16:24 | 41 |
| 19:29–30 | 161 |

### Acts

| | |
|---|---|
| 1:8 | 182, 272 |
| 7:6 | 300 |
| 8:1 | 182 |
| 10:34–48 | 53 |
| 11:19 | 182 |
| 13:22 | 304 |
| 16:25–26 | 202 |
| 27:27 | 202 |

### Romans

| | |
|---|---|
| 1:16 | 53 |
| 3:23 | 58 |
| 3:24–25 | 58 |
| 5:12 | 58 |
| 6:16–20 | 58 |
| 6:23 | 58 |
| 8:3 | 59 |
| 8:15–17 | 59 |
| 8:28–29 | 118 |
| 8:28–30 | 76 |
| 8:29 | 59 |
| 10:11 | 58 |
| 13:8–10 | 56 |
| 15:12 | 304 |

### 2 Corinthians

| | |
|---|---|
| 1:3–4 | 76 |
| 8:1–15 | 167 |
| 8:9 | 225 |
| 9:6–15 | 225 |
| 9:7 | 167 |

## Index of Scripture and Other Ancient Texts

**Galatians**

| | |
|---|---|
| 2:11–14 | 161 |
| 3:17 | 300 |
| 3:28 | 53 |
| 4:3–7 | 59 |
| 5:14 | 56 |
| 5:22 | 57 |
| 6:10 | 56, 59, 167, 181 |

**Ephesians**

| | |
|---|---|
| 1:7 | 58 |
| 2:4–9 | 57 |
| 2:5 | 58 |
| 2:7 | 230 |
| 2:11–18 | 56 |
| 2:11–22 | 272 |
| 5:31 | 153 |
| 6:1–4 | 107 |

**Philippians**

| | |
|---|---|
| 2:7 | 59 |
| 3:20 | 182 |

**Colossians**

| | |
|---|---|
| 2:13 | 58 |
| 3:12 | 57 |

**1 Timothy**

| | |
|---|---|
| 6:17–19 | 225 |

**Titus**

| | |
|---|---|
| 3:4 | 57 |
| 3:4–7 | 230 |

**Hebrews**

| | |
|---|---|
| 2:10–17 | 59 |
| 2:11–13 | 59 |

| | |
|---|---|
| 4:1–11 | 121 |
| 4:1–13 | 183 |
| 9:12 | 269 |
| 11:13–16 | 182 |

**James**

| | |
|---|---|
| 1:1 | 121 |
| 1:27 | 56, 197 |
| 4:2 | 41 |

**1 Peter**

| | |
|---|---|
| 1:1 | 121 |
| 1:18–19 | 58, 269 |
| 2:6–7 | 58 |
| 2:9 | 56 |
| 2:9–12 | 56 |
| 2:11 | 182 |

**Revelation**

| | |
|---|---|
| 1:6 | 56 |
| 6:8 | 66 |
| 19–22 | 59 |

## Rabbinic Works

**Babylonian Talmud**

Bava Batra

| | |
|---|---|
| 14b | 30 |
| 91a | 240 |

Bava Metzi'a

| | |
|---|---|
| 79a–b | 241 |

Megillah

| | |
|---|---|
| 7a | 29 |

**Midrash**

Ruth Rabbah

| | |
|---|---|
| 2:10 | 47, 106 |
| 2:14 | 21 |
| 3:3 | 32 |
| 3:6 | 110 |
| 3:7 | 219 |
| 5:13 | 219 |
| 5:15 | 219 |
| 6:2 | 209 |
| 6:3 | 198 |
| 7:1 | 199 |
| 7:4 | 222 |
| 7:5 | 225 |
| 7:7 | 253 |
| 7:10 | 253 |
| 7:12 | 261 |

Ruth Zuta

| | |
|---|---|
| 4:13 | 302 |
| 55 | 210 |

## Ancient Near Eastern Texts

Arad

| | |
|---|---|
| 16:2–3 | 138 |
| 21:3–4 | 138 |

| | |
|---|---|
| Deir 'Alla Plaster Inscriptions | 114 |
| Gezer Calendar | 121, 191 |
| Mesha Inscription | 68, 99 |
| *line 12* | 73 |
| Siloam Inscription | 83 |

342